PRINCIPLES

OF

COPYRIGHT LAW

By

Roger E. Schechter
Professor of Law
George Washington University

John R. Thomas
Professor of Law
Georgetown University

CONCISE HORNBOOK SERIES®

WEST®

A Thomson Reuters business

Mat #40159783

Hornbook Series and Westlaw are trademarks registered in the U.S. Patent and Trademark Office.

© 2010 Thomson Reuters

610 Opperman Drive
St. Paul, MN 55123
1–800–313–9378

Printed in the United States of America

ISBN: 978–0–314–14750–9

For Justin and Katherine, with love and admiration

— R.E.S.

To the memory of Chief Judge Helen Wilson Nies

—J.R.T.

Summary of Contents

Table of Contents

PRINCIPLES
OF
COPYRIGHT LAW

Chapter 1

INTRODUCTION TO THE LAW OF COPYRIGHT

Table of Sections

Once an obscure specialty, copyright has become one of the more popular electives in the law school curriculum. For good reason: whether your background lies in the liberal arts or engineering, your reading preferences run towards speculative fiction or statutory compilations, or your practice focuses on personal liberties or international commerce, copyright has become a significant topic for every lawyer. Copyright is the law of text and of the arts,

1

and also of computer software, digital technology, and the Internet. Copyright is of extraordinary economic importance to U.S. information industries, including Hollywood, Silicon Valley, and Big Media; but it also fundamentally impacts our personal expression, our right to read, and our ability to remain informed citizens within the public discourse.

At some earlier time, a legal commentator could claim that although copyright was conceptually difficult, its governing legislation was relatively straightforward. At present the conceptual difficulties remain, but have been augmented by increasingly complex statutory provisions. The sophistication and economic importance of those U.S. industries for which copyright is a principal concern have caused the Copyright Act to become more intricate, more regulatory in character, and at times an extremely perplexing read. Understanding the "metaphysics of the law" presents many challenges.[1] Yet it offers considerable rewards. Copyright necessarily is the study of the creative works it encompasses, ranging from humanity's greatest artistic achievements to its most humble entertainments and petty imitations. Individual judicial opinions leave the reader sometimes elevated, sometimes amused or saddened, but ultimately immersion in this most humanist of disciplines is an exceptionally rewarding experience.

§ 1.1   Brief Overview of the Copyright Law

Copyright today is an exclusively federal, statutory subject. The governing law is the Copyright Act of 1976, effective for works created on or after January 1, 1978.[2] Works created before this date may be governed in part by the predecessor statute—the Copyright Act of 1909[3]—in part by the common law of the various states, and in part by selected provisions of the 1976 law.

Under the 1976 Act, copyright may extend to any work of authorship.[4] Among the works of authorship amenable to copyright protection are literary, musical, dramatic, choreographic, graphic, audiovisual, and architectural works, as well as sound recordings.[5] Such works are eligible for copyright protection as soon as they are memorialized in a sufficiently stable form, or, in the words of the copyright law, "fixed in any tangible medium of expression."[6] No formalities are necessary to secure protection. However, authors who register their works with the Copyright Office,[7] and who place

---

1. Folsom v. Marsh, 9 F.Cas. 342, 344 (C.C.D.Mass.1841) (No. 4,901).

2. Pub.L. 94–553, 90 Stat. 2541 (1976). This statute is codified in Title 17 of the U.S. Code.

3. Copyright Act of 1909, Ch. 320, 35 Stat. 1075.

4. 17 U.S.C. § 102(a).

5. *Id.*

6. *Id.*

7. 17 U.S.C. §§ 408–412.

a notice of copyright on copies of their works,[8] are provided certain advantages when enforcing their copyrights.

A work must be original to be protected under the copyright law.[9] The originality requirement is a lenient one, requiring that the work was created by that author and was not copied from another, and that there be a minimal amount of creative authorship. Importantly, copyright protection extends only to the expression of an idea, not the idea itself.[10] For example, no author can obtain copyright protection on the abstract idea of a human changing into an insect. But the expression of that idea in a particular work of authorship with its own characters, plot, mood, and setting—be it Franz Kafka's *The Metamorphosis* or the horror movie *The Fly*—may be accorded copyright protection.

Copyright confers a number of exclusive rights on the author or, in some circumstances, on the employer of the author under the "works made for hire" principle.[11] The copyright proprietor has the exclusive right to make copies of the protected work and to distribute it to the public. The 1976 Act also awards copyright owners the right to control derivative works, such as translations or screenplay adaptations, that are based upon the protected work. The proprietor further enjoys the exclusive right, with respect to most kinds of works, to display and perform the protected work publicly.[12] As we shall see, certain specific categories of works are also granted a variety of narrow or more specific rights.

The exclusive rights of copyright owners are limited by a number of exceptions and defenses, the most important of which is the fair use privilege. The fair use privilege allows the unauthorized use of copyrighted works in such contexts as educational activities, literary and social criticism, parody, and news reporting under certain circumstances.[13]

Each copyright ordinarily enjoys a term of the life of the author plus 70 years.[14] The copyright proprietor may file a suit in federal court in order to enjoin infringers and obtain monetary remedies.[15] Criminal penalties may also apply to copyright infringers.[16] A copyright, or any of the exclusive rights under a copyright, may be assigned or licensed to others.[17] Individual authors possess the right to terminate such transfers after 35 years, although the transferee

8. 17 U.S.C. §§ 401–406.
9. 17 U.S.C. § 102(a).
10. 17 U.S.C. § 102(b).
11. 17 U.S.C. § 201.
12. 17 U.S.C. § 106.
13. 17 U.S.C. § 107.

14. 17 U.S.C. § 302(a).
15. 17 U.S.C. §§ 501–505.
16. 17 U.S.C. § 506.
17. 17 U.S.C. § 201(d).

may continue to exploit derivative works produced under the transfer prior to its termination.[18]

§ 1.2   Historical Development

1.2.1   Early Origins

In many legal texts, a brief historical overview of the field is provided almost as a pro forma part of the introduction. In the field of copyright, however, familiarity with some basic history is more than mere background. Rather it is a valuable tool which can aid in the understanding of many of the ambiguities and controversies that confront copyright law to this day.

Copyright has evolved largely in response to the development of new and more efficient means of recording and reproducing the products of human expression. No copyright law existed in medieval Europe prior to the invention of the printing press, when few persons other than the clergy were literate and when manuscripts had to be copied out by hand. The invention of the printing press and the possibility of mass production of the books led to a desire to regulate in this area.

In the English-speaking world, the earliest versions of what we now know as copyright emerged in the 1500s.[19] In England, only a few skilled craftsmen had the know-how and resources to print books. These printers were organized in a guild known as the Stationers' Company. The members of the company agreed among themselves that whenever one of them printed a particular book, all the others would refrain from printing any copies of that book. They devised a system of recordkeeping to keep track of which member was entitled to print which books. Once a given printer's rights were memorialized in the records of the Stationers' Company, that printer had the "copyright" in the book. Obviously, this system did not reflect any effort to promote the larger good of society. Rather it was a self-interested arrangement that today would almost surely fall afoul of the antitrust laws if nothing else.

Of course there was a problem with the Stationers' Company system. Any non-member of the guild could buy a printing press and begin printing any books he or she wished, including those for which a Stationer member had purportedly exclusive rights. So, much like the lobbyist of our own era, the Stationers appealed to the government—in this case the crown. In 1534, a royal decree issued stating that it would be unlawful to engage in publishing activity without a government license. A system of censorship was

---

18. 17 U.S.C. § 203.

19. *See generally* L. RAY PATTERSON, COPYRIGHT IN HISTORICAL PERSPECTIVE (1968).

also implemented as part of this decree. Within a few decades—in 1557, to be precise—the King granted monopoly publishing rights to the Stationers' Company. This grant, combined with the Stationers' own practices, now meant that only the publisher with the Stationers' "copyright" could publish a given book. Once again, however, none of this had the least bit to do with the public interest. Rather the situation reflected the combination of the economic self-interest of the Stationers with the political self-interest of the crown in suppressing dissent.

1.2.2 The Statute of Anne

Experience with the Stationers' Company was mixed. When monopoly publishing rights expired in 1694, they were not renewed. Independent printers soon commenced publication and left the Stationers vulnerable to competition. Following a concerted lobbying effort—during which the publishers shifted tactics to stress the plight of authors, rather than themselves—Parliament in 1710 enacted the renowned Statute of Anne.[20] The Statute of Anne marked a paradigm shift from its predecessor licensing statutes. Rather than offering rights to the publishers of new works, it protected the authors that created them. As such, the enactment of the Statute of Anne is broadly recognized as a foundational event for copyright in the common law world.

The Statute of Anne granted a term of 14 years of exclusivity for authors and their assigns, starting with the date of first publication. Authors enjoyed a second term of 14 years if they survived until its commencement. Infringement occurred when an individual printed, reprinted, or imported a book without authorization. To enjoy these rights, the copyright proprietor had to register the title of the book at the Stationers' Hall and deposit nine copies of the book at official libraries.

1.2.3 Colonial Copyright and the Constitution

The Statute of Anne inspired twelve of the individual colonies to enact copyright statutes following the American Revolution.[21] Subsequently, the Framers of the Constitution recognized the need for a uniform federal law for both copyrights and patents. The result was Article 1, Section 8, Clause 8, which provides:

> The Congress Shall have Power ... To Promote the Progress of Science and useful Arts, by securing for limited Times to Authors and Inventors the exclusive Right to their respective Writings and Discoveries.[22]

20. 8 Anne, ch. 19 (1710).

21. *See generally* Francine Crawford, *Pre–Constitutional Copyright Statutes*, 23 BULL. COPYRIGHT SOC'Y 11 (1975).

22. U.S. Const. art. 1, § 8, Cl. 8.

This constitutional provision reveals a number of interesting features about the U.S. copyright law. First, the clause refers to "Authors" and their "Writings." While Congress might protect persons other than Authors or material other than constitutional Writings under other provisions of the Constitution, such as the Commerce Clause, the subject matter of copyright appears to be limited to the writings of authors. Indeed, the copyright law of 1909 defined the subject matter of copyright as "all the writings of an author."[23] The full implications of this constitutional limitation are best considered in the context of the present statutory language, and are taken up in the sections that follow. It is useful to note however, that from an early point, Congress and the courts have interpreted "writings" to include much material other than words written or printed on a page. Even the earliest copyright statutes provided protection for maps and prints.[24] More recent enactments have included materials ranging from photographs to computer programs.[25] When confronted with the question, the courts have found materials of this sort to be within the scope of the constitutional term "writings" and thus appropriate subject matter for copyright law.[26]

A second feature of the constitutional language worthy of note is that it contains not only a grant of power, but a statement of purpose as well. The clause indicates that the justification for copyright is the promotion of the "progress of science and useful arts." This raises the question of whether copyright must be further limited to those works that have cultural significance or are adjudged to be a significant addition to the national artistic heritage. Here again, the prevailing interpretation has been broad rather than narrow. Thus, in an early case, the Supreme Court held that posters prepared as advertisements for a circus were copyrightable subject matter, and that their protection was consistent with the constitutional language.[27] Indeed, the notion that copyright should be content-neutral has even lead courts to uphold the copyrightability of obscene material.[28]

23. 17 U.S.C. § 4 (1909 Act).

24. Copyright Act of 1790, Ch. 15, 1 Stat. 124. ("An Act for the encouragement of learning, by securing the copies of maps, charts, and books, to the authors and proprietors of such copies during the times therein mentioned.")

25. 17 U.S.C. § 101 (1988); 17 U.S.C. § 5(j) (1909 Act).

26. Burrow–Giles Lithographic Co. v. Sarony, 111 U.S. 53, 4 S.Ct. 279, 28 L.Ed. 349 (1884) (holding a photograph of Oscar Wilde copyrightable).

27. Bleistein v. Donaldson Lithographing Co., 188 U.S. 239, 23 S.Ct. 298, 47 L.Ed. 460 (1903).

28. See Jartech, Inc. v. Clancy, 666 F.2d 403, *cert. denied*, 459 U.S. 879, 103 S.Ct. 175, 74 L.Ed.2d 143 (1982); Mitchell Bros. Film Group v. Cinema Adult Theater, 604 F.2d 852 (5th Cir. 1979), *cert. denied*, 445 U.S. 917, 100 S.Ct. 1277, 63 L.Ed.2d 601 (1980).

Congress quickly took advantage of its constitutional authority by passing the Act of 1790. Reminiscent of the Statute of Anne, the 1790 Act also featured an initial 14–year term with the possibility of a 14–year renewal if the author survived. The 1790 Act offered protection to any "map, chart or book," but only if the copyright proprietor complied with certain formalities, including registering title with a district court and depositing a copy with the Secretary of State. General statutory revisions in 1831 and 1870, along with additional amendments in other years, continued the development of U.S. copyright law.

1.2.4 The 1909 Act

Animated by a sense that the copyright laws required modernization, Congress enacted the Copyright Act of 1909.[29] The 1909 Act remained in place until the current copyright statute, the 1976 Act, took effect on January 1, 1978. The 1909 Act is of considerable contemporary importance because a large number of economically and culturally important works created before 1978 are still under copyright and are governed to a large degree by the provisions of the 1909 Act. Familiarity with both the current and the former copyright statutes is thus often necessary to understand the nature of copyright protection in the United States.

Among the principal features of the U.S. copyright regime under the 1909 Act were: (1) state common law copyright of perpetual duration for unpublished works; (2) commencement of federal copyright protection at the time of publication, rather than at the time of registration as had previously been the case; (3) first and renewal terms of 28 years each, allowing a maximum possible copyright term of 56 years; and (4) formalities that were necessary to preserve copyright protection, including the placement of notice on all copies of published works and registration at the Copyright Office.

1.2.5 The 1976 Act

The 1909 Act began to show its age as new means of presenting works of authorship, including the phonograph, motion picture, radio, and television, altered the copyright landscape. Congress also grew increasingly concerned over the ability of U.S. authors to protect their works abroad. Serious law reform efforts began as early as 1955 and eventually resulted in the passage of the Copyright Act of 1976. Among the core features of the 1976 Act are:

(1) All works of authorship are protected under the federal copyright law from the moment they are fixed in a tangible

---

29. Copyright Act of 1909, Ch. 320, 35 Stat. 1075.

medium of expression.[30] State common law protection is expressly preempted.[31]

(2) A single term of copyright protection. At the time the 1976 Act was enacted, the term ordinarily consisted of the life of the author plus 50 years. (Congress subsequently increased this copyright term by an additional twenty years.[32])

(3) Individual authors generally possess the inalienable option of terminating transfers after 35 years, although the transferee may continue to exploit derivative works produced under the transfer prior to its termination.[33]

(4) The fair use privilege was for the first time expressly recognized in the statute.[34]

(5) Ownership of copyright is divisible, in that a copyright owner can separately license or enforce the different exclusive rights associated with the copyright.[35]

(6) A number of compulsory licenses allow individuals access to copyrighted works, provided that they comply with certain payment schemes and formalities. An entity known as the Copyright Royalty Tribunal was established to review or establish rates under such licenses, as well as to distribute royalty payments. (The Copyright Royalty Tribunal was subsequently abolished in favor of ad hoc arbitration panels formed by the Librarian of Congress.[36])

(7) The 1976 Act continued to require formalities, including notice, recordation, deposit, and registration, as a condition of copyright protection or enforcement. Congress did provide for more lenient curative provisions for notice deficiencies.[37] Subsequent amendments have relaxed or abolished many of the previously required formalities.

1.2.6 Subsequent Legislative Developments

Congress has frequently amended the 1976 Act since its enactment. Most notable among these amendments was the Berne Convention Implementation Act, which in 1988 brought U.S. law into compliance with the leading international copyright agreement.[38] The most significant of these changes involved a relaxation of the copyright formalities of notice, recordation, deposit, and registration.

30. 17 U.S.C. § 102(a).
31. 17 U.S.C. § 301.
32. 17 U.S.C. § 302.
33. 17 U.S.C. § 203.
34. 17 U.S.C. § 107.
35. 17 U.S.C. § 201(d)(1).

36. 17 U.S.C. §§ 801–803.
37. 17 U.S.C. §§ 401–412.
38. Pub. L. No. 100–569, 102 Stat. 2853 (1988).

Two major statutory developments occurred in 1998. The Sonny Bono Copyright Term Extension Act extended the usual term of copyright to life plus 70 years.[39] The term of anonymous and pseudonymous works, as well as works made for hire, increased to 95 years from publication or 120 years from creation, whichever is less. Congress also enacted the Digital Millennium Copyright Act, which, in part, made it illegal to circumvent technological measures controlling access to various works and which also prohibited altering or deleting certain identifying information that the statute refers to as "copyright management information."[40]

§ 1.3 Copyright Concepts

Copyright is an analytically complex field that is governed by an increasingly intricate statute. From the outset, grasp of a few fundamental themes of the field may assist understanding of more detailed concepts.

1.3.1 Intangible Property

Copyright law does not address the tangible, material object in which the creation of the mind has been embodied. It instead creates more abstract proprietary interests in the intangible.[41] For example, suppose a reader sends a letter to the co-authors of this text, offering a critique of our efforts. We are entitled to retain the document sent through the mails—the tangible pieces of paper on which the correspondence was physically written. However, the words of the letter constitute a work of authorship. Reproduction of that letter without the author's permission may implicate the copyright laws.

Ironically, although copyright law concerns abstract works of authorship, it does insist that the work of authorship be embodied in tangible form at least once.[42] This principle is intended to ensure that abstract ideas remain free from intellectual property rights. Intellectual property rights are instead allowed for the embodiment of that idea in a particular work of authorship. Put differently, intellectual property laws concern downstream products, not upstream ideas.

39. Pub. L. No. 105–298, 112 Stat. 2827 (1998).

40. Pub. L. No. 105–304, 112 Stat. 2860 (1998).

41. *See* White–Smith Music Pub. Co. v. Apollo Co., 209 U.S. 1, 19, 28 S.Ct. 319, 52 L.Ed. 655 (1908) (Holmes, J., concurring) ("But in copyright property has reached a more abstract expression. The right to exclude is not directed to an object in possession or owned, but is *in vacuo*, so to speak.").

42. 17 U.S.C. § 102(a).

1.3.2   The Right to Exclude

Copyright confers the right to exclude others from exploiting the protected intangible subject matter.[43] It does not affirmatively provide a marketing right that allows an author to place a particular work of authorship before the public. Rather, the sale, display, or other exploitation of a copyrighted work is subject to other laws. Libel and obscenity laws, among others, may prevent a copyright owner from distributing his work.

1.3.3   Exhaustion of Rights

Works subject to copyright are ordinarily subject to the concept of exhaustion.[44] Once copyright holders sell a physical product to which that copyright pertains, they cannot prohibit the subsequent resale of that product. Any copyright in that specific physical product is said to have been "exhausted" by this first sale. The exhaustion doctrine allows, among others, law students to purchase used casebooks at the campus bookstore without further compensation to the book's authors. It also allows goods to move through the stream of commerce unhindered by multiple claims to intellectual property rights.

1.3.4   The Public Domain

In addition to creating proprietary interests, copyright also accounts for the rights of consumers and other members of the user community. Out of recognition that one person's incentive can form another's limitation, various intellectual property doctrines strive to maintain a flourishing public domain. Chief among them is that copyright lasts for a set term—the life of the author plus 70 years[45] —after which the work of authorship becomes free for others to use. Works in the public domain support further creative expression, promote effective communication, and ultimately allow each of us to experience our culture.[46]

1.3.5   Territoriality

The nations of the earth have yet to agree upon a unified legal regime governing intellectual property rights. There is no global copyright. Innovators must secure and enforce these rights within the particular jurisdiction where they desire protection. Further, the reach of a particular intellectual property right extends only so far as the nation or region recognizing the right.

The intellectual property laws of the United States and its trading partners are nonetheless linked through a modest number of international agreements that, together, comprise the interna-

---

43. 17 U.S.C. § 106.
44. 17 U.S.C. § 109(a).
45. 35 U.S.C. § 154(a)(2).

46. *See, e.g.,* Jessica Litman, *The Public Domain,* 39 EMORY L.J. 965 (1990).

tional copyright regime. The foundational treaty, the Berne Convention,[47] established the basic principle of national treatment: the requirement that signatories treat nationals of other signatory states no worse than their own citizens in intellectual property matters. More recently, the World Trade Organization Agreement on Trade–Related Aspects of Intellectual Property Rights,[48] the so-called TRIPS Agreement, required its signatories to provide minimum substantive standards of copyright protection and enforcement. These international agreements have eased the ability of innovators to enjoy intellectual property protection in foreign countries.

§ 1.4   Rationales for Copyright Law

Copyright law has been with us for many years. Yet debate over the propriety of granting protection in intangible works of authorship has never been more vigorous. Two principal justifications for copyright have emerged from these exchanges: instrumental rationales, which view copyright in terms of its benefits to society as a whole, and natural rights, which stresses the inherent authority of authors to control works they have created. Intellectual property law has also attracted a range of dissenting views that are introduced below.

1.4.1 Instrumental Rationales

Like other sorts of goods, works of authorship may be analyzed in terms of two economic characteristics.[49] The first is whether the benefits of the work are excludable. The owner of a bottle of wine may prevent others from drinking, but the producer of radio signals broadcasts for all to hear. The second trait is whether consumption of the good is rivalrous. If one person's use of the good necessarily diminishes the benefits of another's use, then it is said to be a rival good. For nonrival goods such as pleasing parkway scenery, all may profit from the good without diminishing the benefits of others.

Goods differ in their degrees of excludability and rivalrousness. Those that are fully nonexcludable and nonrival are termed public goods. The production of public goods is subject to market failure, for their nonexcludable and nonrival traits suggest that they will be underproduced relative to social need. This follows because potential producers of public goods are uncertain whether they will

47. Convention concerning the creation of an International Union for the Protection of Literary and Artistic Works (Sept. 9, 1886, revised in 1896, 1908, 1928, 1948, 1967, 1971).

48. Agreement on Trade–Related Aspects of Intellectual Property Rights,

Apr. 15, 1994, Annex 1C, 33 I.L.M. 1197 (1994).

49. *See generally* Horace E. Anderson, Jr., *"Criminal Minded?": Mixtape DJs, The Piracy Paradox, and Lessons for the Recording Industry*, 76 Tenn. L. Rev. 111, 145 (2008).

benefit from the good sufficiently to justify their labors. To put the matter bluntly, they might conclude that there is no point in producing something if they have no assurance of being paid for their effort. Individuals will therefore tend to produce goods with greater excludability and rivalrousness and to underproduce public goods.

The production of desirable public goods is thus said to present a problem of collective action. Society as a whole favors the development of certain public goods, ranging from military defense to flood control projects. Private citizens may lack sufficient incentives to produce them, however, leading to suboptimal social outcomes. Government is uniquely suited towards solving collective action problems by modifying individual incentives to engage in desirable behavior.

Copyright laws are good examples of this sort of market intervention. Works of authorship exhibit the characteristics of public goods. They are nonexcludable, for whether the work consists of a new song, a sculpture, or a software program, others may easily become imitators. The cost of developing a new motion picture may run in the millions of dollars, but the work may be copied extremely cheaply. Information goods are also nonrival, for competitive uses do not impact an author's personal ability to exploit the invention. Individuals can sing a song repeatedly, for example, without exhausting the song or depriving another of its use. These externalities are said to discourage innovation. As a result, absent legal intervention, few authors would write and few artists would paint. In such a world consumers would have access to few new creative works.

The Copyright Act ameliorates this market failure by allowing individuals to obtain proprietary rights in their works of authorship. This property rule entitlement creates excludability, allowing innovators to prevent free riders from benefitting from their efforts. By diminishing the public goods aspects of works of authorship, copyright encourages individuals to increase their investment in creative activities. This rationale for the intellectual property system is sometimes termed the "incentive theory."

Under this view, the proprietary rights afforded through copyright are needed to prevent free riders from undermining the market for works of authorship. In addition, the copyright system is said to facilitate market mechanisms by creating discrete, well-defined property interests that decrease transaction costs and encourage commercial exchanges. Copyright is also believed to encourage individual expression on matters of interest to civil society, encouraging the discourse that is essential to democratic values.[50]

---

50. *See* Neil Weinstock Netanel, Copyright's Paradox (Oxford University Press 2008).

The Supreme Court has often invoked the incentive theory and declared it to be the basic animating purpose behind copyright law. For instance in *Twentieth Century Music Corp. v. Aiken*[51] the Court said "the immediate effect of our copyright law is to secure a fair return for an author's creative labor. But the ultimate aim is, by this incentive, to stimulate artistic creativity for the general public good." The Court reiterated the same themes in *Feist Publications, Inc. v. Rural Telephone Service Co.*,[52] when it observed that "the primary objective of copyright is not to reward the labor of authors, but 'to promote the Progress of Science and useful arts.' To this end, copyright assures authors the right to their original expression, but encourages others to build freely upon the ideas and information conveyed by a work."

1.4.2 Natural Rights

In contrast to the incentive theory, where author's rights are but a necessary means to an end, the "natural rights" school places the author front and center. The most celebrated proponent of natural rights, John Locke, posited that persons have a natural right of property in their bodies.[53] Reasoning further, Locke asserted that individuals enjoyed a property entitlement on the products of their labors. Lockean theory suggests that authors too should be entitled to enjoy the fruits of their labors, in terms of an exclusive rights in their works.[54]

Under this approach, the relationship between authors and their works of authorship is viewed as much more personal and intimate than the ordinary associations between individuals and objects. Creative works are seen as virtual extensions of the author herself, allowing others to view her consciousness and emotional, intellectual, or spiritual being. As such, authors possess the fundamental right to control, and should be compensated for, uses of their works.[55]

The most noteworthy manifestation of natural rights theories within the copyright law is the doctrine of moral rights. Moral rights laws generally include three principal components. The integrity right allows authors to prevent objectionable distortions, mutilations, or other modifications of their works. The attribution or paternity right allows authors to claim authorship of their

51. 422 U.S. 151, 156, 95 S.Ct. 2040, 45 L.Ed.2d 84 (1975).

52. 499 U.S. 340, 349–50, 111 S.Ct. 1282, 113 L.Ed.2d 358 (1991).

53. JOHN LOCKE, TWO TREATISES OF GOVERNMENT (Peter Laslett, ed., 2d ed. 1967).

54. *See* Wendy J. Gordon, *A Property Right in Self Expression: Equality and Individualism in the Natural Law of Intellectual Property*, 102 YALE L.J. 1533 (1993).

55. *See generally* Alfred C. Yen, *Restoring the Natural Law: Copyright as Labor and Possession*, 51 OHIO ST. L.J. 517 (1990).

works. Finally, the right of disclosure allows authors to decide when and in what form a work will be distributed to the public. Moral rights theories play a central role in many foreign copyright laws and have been recognized to a more limited degree in the United States.[56]

1.4.3   Criticism of the Copyright Law

Copyright has been subject to increasingly vitriolic criticism during this era of the Internet. Some commentators assert that strenuous enforcement of copyright can result in the elimination of parody and satire, the curtailment of free speech, and the suppression of creativity. Copyright law can indeed still voices, darken stages, and shut down presses; and as more individuals gain access to means for creating and disseminating sophisticated creative materials, the grasp of the copyright law seems to strengthen. Observers further note that Congress has recently augmented the scope of copyright in terms of such factors as the works subject to protection, the term of protection, and the scope of exclusive rights, leading to perceived imbalances between the rights and responsibilities of content providers and consumers.[57] Still others suggest that however noble the theoretical justifications for intellectual property, copyright law has in practice been corrupted by publishers, record companies, and media enterprises that exploit individual authors and have little regard for the interests of the user community.[58] Apparent from the vigor of this debate is that copyright has become an increasingly important discipline in the Information Age.

§ 1.5   International Copyright

There is no global copyright system. Property rights in works of authorship must be recognized and enforced in each jurisdiction where protection is sought. A number of international agreements nonetheless establish international copyright relations, allowing nonresident authors to enjoy intellectual property overseas. Although the international copyright landscape receives deeper coverage later in Chapter 12 of this volume, two of the more significant copyright treaties, the Berne Convention and TRIPS Agreement, are worthy of note at this early juncture.

1.5.1   The Berne Convention

The International Union for the Protection of Literary and Artistic Works, known as the Berne Union or Berne Convention,

---

56. 17 U.S.C. § 106A.

57. John Tehranian, *Infringement Nation: Copyright Reform and the Law/ Norm Gap*, 2007 Utah L. Rev. 537.

58. Johan Söderberg, *Copyright: A Marxist Critique*, First Monday (Feb. 26, 2002).

remains the foundational multilateral copyright agreement. The Berne Convention requires that signatory states observe the principle of national treatment and provide minimum standards of substantive protection, including specified exclusive rights and a copyright term consisting of the life of the author plus 50 years. The Berne Convention also rejects formalities, such as registration of the work of authorship with the government, as conditions of copyright protection. Works first published in the United States or other Berne signatory states—or first published in a non-Berne country, followed by publication within 30 days in a Berne member state—are eligible for protection in all Berne member states.

1.5.2   The TRIPS Agreement

The Agreement on Trade–Related Aspects of Intellectual Property Rights, or TRIPS Agreement, forms one component of the international agreement establishing the World Trade Organization (WTO). Joined by an impressive number of signatory countries, the TRIPS Agreement affirms and extends the Berne Convention. The TRIPS Agreement requires that WTO member states comply with much of the Berne Convention, recognize computer programs as subject to copyright, and provide certain protections for data compilations and cinematographic works. Disagreements between signatories over TRIPS Agreement compliance are subject to dispute resolution before the WTO.

§ 1.6   Other Forms of Intellectual Property

Several other legal regimes are akin to the copyright system in that they also give rise to proprietary interests in creations of the mind. Along with copyright, the so-called "intellectual property laws" include patents and trademarks. A comprehensive treatment of these areas can be found elsewhere.[59]

1.6.1   Patents and Related Rights

Patents provide exclusive rights to inventors of new, useful, and nonobvious inventions.[60] The patent law concerns hard technologies, including chemical, electrical, and mechanical products and processes, as well as other pragmatic innovations in fields ranging from biotechnology to business methods.[61] An inventor may obtain a patent by filing a patent application with the United States Patent and Trademark Office ("PTO"). Such an application must completely describe and precisely claim the invention.[62] Issued

---

59. *See* ROGER E. SCHECHTER & JOHN R. THOMAS, INTELLECTUAL PROPERTY: THE LAW OF COPYRIGHTS, PATENTS AND TRADE-MARKS (2003).

60. 35 U.S.C. §§ 101, 102, 103.

61. 35 U.S.C. § 101.

62. 35 U.S.C. § 112.

patents confer the right to exclude others from making, using, selling, offering to sell, or importing into the United States the patented invention.[63] The term of a patent is 20 years from the date the application was filed.[64]

In addition to the usual sort of patent, technically known as a "utility patent," the intellectual property laws also provide for other sorts of patents and patent-like rights. Design patents are available for new, original, and ornamental designs.[65] A plant patent may be issued for a distinct and new variety of plant that has been asexually reproduced, through grafting, budding, or similar techniques.[66] Plant variety protection certificates are available for sexually reproduced plants, including most seed-bearing plants, provided they are stable and clearly distinguishable from known varieties.[67]

The principal intellectual property alternative to patents is trade secret law.[68] Valuable information that is not publicly known and that is subject to measures to preserve its secrecy may be granted trade secret rights under state statutory or common law. Unlike patents, no formalities are required to maintain trade secret protection. Trade secret protection is more limited than that offered by the patent law, however. Trade secret law does not prevent reverse engineering or independent discovery of the protected information, for example, while patent rights would. Trade secret rights endure for as long as the protected information is not known to the public.

1.6.2 Trademarks and Related Rights

Trademarks consist of any word or symbol used by a merchant to identify its goods or services, and to distinguish them from those of others.[69] To be subject to protection under the trademark laws, a mark must successfully distinguish the origins of its associated goods, and not be confusingly similar to marks used by others or merely describe the characteristics of those goods.[70] Trademark rights arise under state law as soon as the mark is used on goods in commerce.[71] However, trademarks may be registered with the PTO, a step that affords significant substantive and procedural advantages.[72] Trademark law also protects the appearance of product packaging and, in some cases, the actual physical configuration of the goods, if these serve as brand identifiers. A trademark owner

---

63. 35 U.S.C. § 271.

64. 35 U.S.C. § 154(a)(2).

65. 35 U.S.C. § 171.

66. 35 U.S.C. § 161.

67. 7 U.S.C. § 2321 *et seq.*

68. *See* RESTATEMENT (THIRD) OF UNFAIR COMPETITION §§ 39–45.

69. *Id.* at § 9.

70. *Id.*

71. *Id.* at § 18.

72. 17 U.S.C. § 1051.

may prevent others from using any mark that creates a likelihood of confusion as to the source or sponsorship of the associated goods or services.[73] Trademark rights persist so long as the mark continues to be used and retains its distinctiveness.[74]

Trademarks form one arm of the common law of unfair competition, a collection of principles that encourage the maintenance of honest practices in commercial affairs. A number of other doctrines are grouped under this heading, including passing off, reverse passing off, dilution, and false advertising.[75]

---

73. *See* RESTATEMENT (THIRD) OF UN-
FAIR COMPETITION § 20.

74. *Id.* at § 30.

75. *See generally* RESTATEMENT (THIRD) OF UNFAIR COMPETITION.

Chapter 2

THE SUBJECT MATTER OF COPYRIGHT—BASIC REQUIREMENTS

Table of Sections

The boundaries of the subject matter that can be protected under federal copyright law are set out in the Intellectual Property Clause of the U.S. Constitution, located in Article 1, Section 8, Clause 8. It provides "To Promote the Progress of Science and useful Arts, by securing for limited Times to Authors and Inventors the exclusive Right to their respective Writings and Discoveries."[1] Although this clause suggests some vague outlines about the kinds of material that may be protected by copyright, it assigns to Congress the power to define those limits with greater specificity. Congress exercised that power most recently when it adopted the 1976 Copyright Act, which remains effect today. That statute provides a general definition of the subject matter of copyright in section 102.

Because section 102 is so fundamental to understanding the structure of the Copyright Act, its full text is worth a close look at the very outset. Its first sentence provides:

> Copyright protection subsists ... in original works of authorship, fixed in any tangible medium of expression, now known or later developed, from which they can be

---

1.   U.S. Const. art. 1, § 8, Cl. 8.

18

perceived reproduced or otherwise communicated, either directly or with the aid of a machine or device.[2]

The second sentence of the section goes on to itemize eight particular categories of work that are encompassed by the term "works of authorship." That list includes literary, musical, dramatic, choreographic, pictorial graphic, sculptural, audiovisual, and architectural works, as well as sound recordings.[3] These categories are, however, merely illustrative—they do not set the outer boundaries of copyrightable material.[4] While the vast bulk of copyrightable material falls into these itemized categories, a work can be protected even if it does not, because actual contours of copyright are strictly a function of the more general language in the indented quote immediately above.

There are some general observations that we can make about this language before getting into the nooks and crannies. Note first that the definition is technologically open-ended. It refers to works fixed in media that are now know or *later developed*. This reflects a congressional desire to cover works embodied only in those types of objects that were known in the mid–1970s, when Congress wrote the law, but also an intention to cover works embodied in new types of artifacts that can capture the products of human creativity as they are developed.[5] As we shall see, this Congress commanded this flexibility in response to the confusion and hesitance of some courts who refused copyright protection when they encountered novel types of media for the first time. It has also proven wise. In the decades since the 1976 Act became law we have seen the advent of a plethora of objects ranging from DVDs to MP3 players to USB drives that all can capture and store works of authorship.

Second, a close look at the language of section 102 reveals two separate requirements that an intellectual creation must satisfy before becoming protectable under the statute. Specifically, the work must be (1) an original a work of authorship that is (2) fixed in a tangible medium of expression. Each of these requirements is

---

2. 17 U.S.C. § 102.

3. *Id.*

4. As we shall see further on, the eight named categories in section 102 become important elsewhere in the statute, because certain provisions in copyright law only apply to certain named categories of works, such as "sound recordings" or "pictorial, graphic and sculptural works."

5. "Authors are continually finding new ways of expressing themselves, but it is impossible to foresee the forms that these new expressive methods will take. The bill does not intend either to freeze the scope of copyrightable subject matter at the present stage of technology or to allow unlimited expansion into areas completely outside the present congressional intent." H.R. Rep. No. 94–1416, 94th Cong., 2d Sess., p. 51 (1976). *See also* Lotus Dev. Corp. v. Paperback Software Int'l, 740 F.Supp. 37 (D. Mass. 1990) ("[T]he designation 'works of authorship' is not meant to be limited to traditional works of authorship such as novels or plays. Rather, Congress used this phrase to extend copyright to new methods of expression as they evolve....").

more elaborate than you might think at first glance. The former has been construed to be a dual requirement, implicating ideas both of independent effort and of intellectual creativity. The latter has required courts to grapple with the constantly changing ways that works can be memorialized in a permanent fashion. Let us, then, consider each of these fundamental pillars of the copyright scheme in turn.

§ 2.1　Originality

In order to be protected by copyright, a work must be "original."[6] Interestingly, however, Congress did not define this crucial term in the 1976 Act. While you might think that this is a pretty serious oversight, Congress claims that the omission was intentional. The legislative history declares that the absence of a definition of this crucial term was meant to incorporate the case law definition of originality that had evolved during the preceding seven decades of litigation under the 1909 Act.[7] Under that case law courts had determined that "originality" implicates two distinct but interrelated concepts. A work must satisfy both before it will achieve copyright protection.

First, the work in question must be the product of independent intellectual effort of the author. In this sense "original" is used as the opposite of something that is merely transcribed from a pre-existing source. Secondly, the work in question must have at least a modicum of creativity. In this sense "original" is used as the opposite of "mundane" or "routine" or "entirely banal." As the Supreme Court summed up this dualistic definition in its landmark *Feist* opinion, "[o]riginal, as the term is used in copyright, means ... that the work was independently created by the author (as opposed to copied from other works), and that it possesses at least some minimal degree of creativity."[8] Both of these requirements warrant considerable further exploration.

2.1.1　Independent Creation

A work is only considered original if the author created it "from scratch"—that is, without copying it from a pre-existing source. This makes sense as a matter of simple semantics and it is also good policy. A copycat is not engaged in original creation. Moreover, any other rule would reward those who contributed zero

---

6. Section 102 of the 1976 Act defines the subject matter of copyright as "*original* works of authorship ..." 17 U.S.C. § 102 (2000).

7. H.R. Rep. No. 94–1474, 94th Cong. 2d Sess. 51 (1976) ("the phrase 'original works of authorship," which is purposely left undefined is intended to incorporate without change the standard of originality established by the courts under the present copyright statute.").

8. Feist Publications, Inc. v. Rural Telephone Service, 499 U.S. 340, 111 S.Ct. 1282, 113 L.Ed.2d 358 (1991).

to our cultural inventory and could even permit them to withdraw works from the public domain merely by copying them. For instance, if someone copied Shakespeare's *Hamlet* by writing it out in longhand onto a legal pad, it would be absurd to permit that individual to claim copyright in the resulting text. Not only has this person contributed nothing new to our society's body of literary work, but he might then try to exact a payment from every school teacher who sought to hand out copies of the text of Hamlet to his or her students. A requirement of independent creation helps avoid this sort of silly result.

In the Hamlet example, of course, the copied work is in the "public domain." That is the umbrella phrase that designates all works of authorship not protected by copyright. Our point about originality is even more obvious, however, if the copied work is still protected by copyright. Someone who transcribes a novel by John Grisham or J.K. Rowling certainly should not be able to claim copyright in the transcribed text. That person is not an author in any meaningful sense. Not only do we deny such an individual a new copyright in his transcription but, as your intuition might suggest, we will hold him liable for copyright infringement.

Academic types and courts have concluded that this independent creation requirement is constitutionally required. Remember that the Constitution only empowers Congress to the protect the writings of *authors*. To "author" something means to be the originator or progenitor of it. One who merely copies pre-existing work is the very antithesis of an author. It follows that rote copying should be constitutionally ineligible for protection under the copyright law. This is exactly what the Supreme Court concluded. As Justice O'Conner, speaking for the unanimous Court in *Feist*, summed up, "[t]he *sine qua non* of copyright is originality.... Originality is a constitutional requirement."[9]

There is an interesting theoretical consequence to this focus on independent creation. If two authors each were to conceive of, and fix, the same work without knowledge of the other's work, each would be entitled to an independent copyright on the resulting work.[10] Such a hypothetical scenario is sometimes called "parallel independent creation," since each party creates his work independent of the other, but the works are identical or parallel. Learned Hand, in one of his many celebrated copyright decisions, put it this way:

9. Feist Publications, Inc. v. Rural Telephone Service Co., 499 U.S. 340, 346, 111 S.Ct. 1282, 113 L.Ed.2d 358 (1991).

10. *See e.g.,* Arnstein v. Edward B. Marks Music Corp., 82 F.2d 275 (2d Cir. 1936); Alfred Bell & Co. v. Catalda Fine Arts, Inc., 191 F.2d 99 (2d Cir. 1951).

Borrowed the work must indeed not be, for a plagiarist is not himself pro tanto an "author"; but if by some magic a man who had never know it were to compose anew Keats's *Ode on a Grecian Urn*, he would be an "author" and if he copyrighted it, others might not copy that poem, though they might of course, copy Keats's.[11]

Of course, the more elaborate the works in question, the more difficult it will be to believe that the second party actually created the work "from scratch" without referring to the first party's efforts. Hand, in the quote, says that it would require "magic" to coincidentally duplicate Keats's famous poem. As an evidentiary matter, the strong similarity between the two works may be powerful circumstantial evidence that the second of the two was copied from the first.[12] For those of you who are not fans of nineteenth century British poetry, we can take a more contemporary example. The claim by someone that they had authored a verbatim copy of *Harry Potter and the Sorcerer's Stone* without ever having seen J.K. Rowling's work by that name would be preposterous. Just when courts will make an inference of copying in the absence of direct evidence is a topic we will defer, however, until we come to the subject of copyright infringement much further on.

For present purposes, the importance of this doctrinal point is its illumination of one of the major distinctions between the scope of patent law and that of copyright. A patent will not issue unless the applicant for it can show "novelty"—in other words that the precise invention in question has never before been made by anyone else.[13] Copyright is not nearly so demanding. The work need not be novel. That something identical or virtually identical to it already was created by another is simply irrelevant so long as the second party did not copy from the first. Originality, as a legal term of art, is not synonymous with novelty.

There are at least two good reasons for this approach. First, in many areas of pop culture, works inevitably will resemble each other because of the limits of the genre and other conventions. A comic book about a superhero will resemble many previous works of the same sort because all superheroes have super powers, many such heroes come from other planets, most wear costumes and have secret identities, many fight costumed and eccentric villains, and

---

11. Sheldon v. Metro–Goldwyn Pictures Corp., 81 F.2d 49, 54 (2d Cir. 1936). Other courts have made the same point. *See, e.g.* Selle v. Gibb, 741 F.2d 896, 901 (7th Cir. 1984) ("As noted, two works may be identical in every detail, but, if the alleged infringer created the accused work independently ... then there is no infringement"); Ulloa v. Universal Music and Video Distribution Corp., 2004 WL 840279 (S.D.N.Y. 2004) ("a work may be original even though it closely resembles other works so long as the similarity is fortuitous, not the result of copying").

12. *See infra* § 9.1.

13. 35 U.S.C. § 102.

many have a particular weakness.[14] If the law required genuine novelty before granting copyright protection, new superhero comics might be denied copyright because other authors had previously created similar heroes. This would give the earlier authors too much of a monopoly and deny future authors of the ability to create variations on the theme. Our apologies for constantly deferring topics, but we will return to this notion again, when we consider something called "the idea-expression dichotomy" in section 2.3 of this chapter.

Second, a novelty test can only work if there is some formal way to compare newly created material with the body of previously existing work so that we can determine if it is genuinely novel. In the patent field, the conventions of scientific literature make it plausible to determine if anyone has previously invented an insomnia drug with a given chemical formula, or an umbrella with a particular wind-resistant configuration of ribs. You can look up previously issued patents in a database, and search the scientific and technical literature. In the world of copyright, it would be considerably more difficult to determine if anyone had previously written a novel about a wizard-in-training that tracks the plot features of the Harry Potter books before J.K. Rowling came along. The absence of a well-defined and searchable body of prior art makes a novelty test for copyright entirely unworkable as a matter of practical administration.

There are, of course, many intermediate possibilities between exactly copying a pre-existing work and creating a new work entirely from scratch. Many authors might start with a pre-existing public domain work and then modify it to a greater or lesser extent. For instance, someone might copy the first four acts of *Hamlet* verbatim, but write an entirely new Act Five in which Hamlet overcomes his indecisiveness and self-loathing and moves to the South of France; or might do a painting that looks exactly like Whistler's Mother but do it in bright neon colors instead of the blacks and grays of the original. These works, which are neither wholly original nor wholly copied, are usually called "derivative" works. There are a number of interesting issues concerning derivative works, but again we will keep you in suspense with the promise that we will take them up in the following chapter.[15]

For now, however, it is profitable to consider whether such works satisfy the requirement of "independent creation." The answer is that they do, to the extent—and only to the extent—that new material has been added. Thus the author of our hypothetical

---

14. *See generally*, 10 Obscure Superheroes Who Deserve Their Own Movies, http://blog.wired.com/geekdad/2008/ 08/10–obscure-supe.html (Discussing, inter alia, The Creeper and Squirrel Girl).

15. *See infra* § 3.9.

revised version of *Hamlet* can use the copyright laws to prevent others from duplicating the text of his new Act Five, or of the entire play including his new Act Five, but obviously could not prevent anyone from copying Shakespeare's original Acts One through Four. This is because he created Act Five from scratch, thus satisfying the requirement of independent creation. Same for the painter of the neon–colored–Whistler's Mother.

The problem of independent creation and derivative works has occasionally been litigated in connection with reproductions of two and three dimensional public domain artistic works. By definition, such reproductions are not the products of completely independent creation. More importantly, the success of an art reproduction is often measured by how faithfully it reproduces the original. The "best" reproduction is the one with the fewest variations from the underlying work being reproduced. Consequently, the courts have struggled to determine when, if ever, there is sufficient independent creation to justify copyright protection.

In one celebrated copyright case, *Alfred Bell & Co. v. Catalda Fine Arts, Inc.*,[16] the plaintiff had created mezzotint reproductions of famous "old master" oil paintings that were in the public domain. Mezzotints are prints made through the use of a roughened metal plate. Because of the nature of the process a mezzotint reproduction will not be a perfect duplicate of the original painting—differences in color and texture will necessary be introduced. In any event, the defendant copied the plaintiff's mezzotints by making lithographs[17] of them. When plaintiff sued, defendant argued that the mezzotints lacked originality because they were mere copies of the underlying paintings, and thus were not protected by copyright. The Second Circuit disagreed. The court found that the mezzotints contained more than trivial variations from the original oil paintings, and that those distinctions or variations were enough to make them separately copyrightable. They were not slavish copies—some new material, created from scratch, had been introduced by the plaintiffs.

This result seems a bit of a stretch. Within the limits of the mezzzotint process the plaintiff was striving to create an image that resembled the oil paintings in question as closely as possible. Original features would have been contrary to the objective. More recent cases have called the result in *Alfred Bell* into some doubt. Note that in any event, however, the protection afforded to the mezzotints would not prohibit others from making their own copies of the original oil paintings, which remained in the public domain.

16. 191 F.2d 99 (2d Cir. 1951).

17. We debated defining lithography and concluded that most readers would not be terribly curious about it.

A case taking the opposite view of the matter is *Bridgeman Art Library v. Corel.*[18] In this litigation the court had to determine whether exact photographic reproductions of public domain art works qualified for copyright. The court recognized that "[t]here is little doubt that many photographs, probably the overwhelming majority, reflect at least the modest amount of originality required for copyright protection. 'Elements of originality ... may include posing the subjects, lighting, angle, selection of film and camera, evoking the desired expression, and almost any other variant involved.'"[19] It went on to note, however that "'slavish copying,' although doubtless requiring technical skill and effort, does not qualify.... [T]here was no spark of originality—indeed, the point of the exercise was to reproduce the underlying works with absolute fidelity. Copyright is not available in these circumstances."[20]

More recently a federal appeals court came to the same result in a context that did not involve art reproductions or photography but rather the use of a new form of computer assisted design. In *Meshwerks, Inc. v. Toyota Motor Sales, U.S.A., Inc.*[21] Toyota needed two-dimensional digital frame models of its vehicles to use for advertising on television and on its website. Once created these models can be manipulated in various ways not possible with conventional photographs. For instance, a user viewing the vehicle on the website can change the color of the car with a simple mouse click or simulate the effect of seeing the car rotate 360° and a TV producer can place the car on top of a mountain or on a palm fringed beach without actually having to take a photograph of the car on location. A company called Meshwerks agreed to prepare the necessary digital images, which it did "by covering each car ... with a grid of tape and running an articulated arm tethered to a computer over the vehicle to measure all points of intersection in the grid. Based on these measurements, modeling software then generated a digital image resembling a wire-frame model." It added additional details to the image by hand to incorporate features of the cars that could not be accurately measured.

Meshwerks claimed that it had only granted contractual permission for Toyota and its advertising agency to use the digital models for a single television commercial. When the agency reused the models in other media Meshwerks sued for copyright infringe-

18. 36 F.Supp.2d 191 (S.D.N.Y. 1999)

19. *Id.*, quoting Rogers v. Koons, 960 F.2d 301, 307 (2d Cir.), *cert. denied*, 506 U.S. 934, 113 S.Ct. 365, 121 L.Ed.2d 278 (1992).

20. *See also* Mary Campbell Wojcik, *The Antithesis of Originality: Bridge-* *man, Image Licensors, and the Public Domain*, 30 HASTINGS COMM. & ENT. L.J. 257, 267 ("one possesses no copyright interest in reproductions of public domain works when these reproductions do nothing more than accurately convey the underlying image.").

21. 528 F.3d 1258 (10th Cir. 2008).

ment. The defendants argued that the digital models were insufficiently original to sustain copyright and the Tenth Circuit agreed. It noted that "Meshwerks' digital wire-frame computer models depict Toyota's vehicles without any individualizing features ... Meshwerks' models depict nothing more than unadorned Toyota vehicles ... the appearances of which do not owe their origins to Meshwerks." The court also noted that Meshwerks' very goal in making the digital models was to make a precise copy, an intent which bolstered the court's willingness to find a lack of originality. The court was careful to note that it was not laying down a general rule to the effect that all digital modelling was unoriginal, noting that "[j]ust as photographs *can be*, but are not *per se*, copyrightable, the same holds true for digital models." However because Meshwerks' computerized images were essentially slavish copies of the underlying cars, the court refused to protect them under the copyright law.

2.1.2 Minimal Creativity but Not Novelty

The fact that a work was created "from scratch" will not, by itself, suffice for copyright protection. The work in question must also evidence a minimal degree of creativity.[22] This is a fundamental aspect of the bargain between the author and the public. In return for a grant of exclusive rights to economically exploit a work, we demand that the author contributes something that contains at least a little trace or flicker of imagination. As one famous copyright commentator put it, "to make the copyright turnstile revolve, the author should have to deposit more than a penny in the box...."[23] Moreover, without this requirement we might run the risk of effectively removing large quantities of material from the public domain or constantly engaging in unnecessary litigation over the originality of pedestrian creations.

For instance, assume that I were to take out a blank piece of paper and, without looking at any source material, write the words "the dog barked at midnight" on the paper. I have not, literally, copied those words from anyone else. Rather it would appear that I have authored them "from scratch." The phrase, however, is totally banal and lacks even a molecule of anything we might be inclined to label "creativity." Granting me copyright in this phrase would be most unwise. First, my contribution to the stock of intellectual or aesthetic material in the world is virtually zero. Consequently, there seems little need to hold out the promise of decades of exclusive rights to someone like me as an incentive to get me to pen this unremarkable five–word phrase. Of course, one might argue

---

22. Feist Publications, Inc. v. Rural Telephone Service, 499 U.S. 340, 362, 111 S.Ct. 1282, 113 L.Ed.2d 358 (1991).

23. Benjamin Kaplan, An Unhurried View of Copyright 46 (1967).

that the social or cultural value of many longer works is also zero
or even negative—consider for instance a pamphlet whipping up
racial hatred and arguing in favor of genocide—and yet such a work
might be indubitably "creative" because of the various hateful
arguments that it propounds and how it phrases them. But while
not all creative works are valuable, there is strong reason to believe
that a such a high percentage of non-creative works lack value that
it makes sense to deny them copyright.

A second justification for a creativity requirement is that
without it, an author of uncreative material might attempt to
prevent others from using the same material, which could hinder
the production of truly creative work by those others. Of course,
those being sued could argue that the first author must have seen
those uncreative words elsewhere and subconsciously copied them
rather than created them from scratch, meaning that he should not
be entitled to copyright protection for them. Or those being sued
could argue alternatively that they derived the uncreative material
on their own via "parallel independent creation" rather than by
copying from the first party. But we would have to engage in a
lengthy litigation to sort out such claims and in many cases the
court would have no effective way to determine the truth of the
matter. To put the same point differently, giving me copyright in
uncreative material virtually invites frivolous and harassing litigation and acts as a deterrent to other others who might forego
creative work out of a fear of getting sued. Thus the requirement of
creativity seems amply justified based on both pragmatic and policy
considerations.

The amount of creativity required, however, is not particularly
great. As the Supreme Court has stated in its landmark declaration
on the subject, "[t]o be sure, the requisite level of creativity is
extremely low; even a slight amount will suffice. The vast majority
of works make the grade quite easily, as they possess some creative
spark 'no matter how crude, humble or obvious' it may be."[24] For
example, a picture of a cake on the label of a box of cake mix was
held copyrightable, the court remarking that "[t]he pictures of the
cakes used by plaintiff on its labels although possibly not achieving
the quality of a Leonardo 'Still Life' nevertheless have sufficient
commercial artistry to entitle them to protection ...".[25]

On the other hand, some works fail even this minimal test. As
one treatise writer wryly put it, the creative spark "need not

---

24. Feist, *supra* note 22, at 345. See
also Atari Games v. Oman, 979 F.2d 242
(D.C. Cir. 1992); West Publishing Co. v.
Mead Data Central, 799 F.2d 1219, 1223
(8th Cir. 1986).

25. Kitchens of Sara Lee, Inc. v.
Nifty Foods Corp., 266 F.2d 541, 545 (2d
Cir. 1959). The court's use of the word
"possibly" here suggests a certain lack
of appreciate for DaVinci.

provide a shock, but it must at least be perceptible to the touch."[26] Thus, titles and short slogans have traditionally been denied copyright protection, largely on the grounds that they are incapable of reflecting the necessary creativity. For instance one court found an advertising slogan for Pepsi–Cola reading "You got the right one, uh-huh" not copyrightable.[27] A district court in Pennsylvania found an envelope with a horizontal black stripe on the middle, pre-printed with the words "Priority Message: Contents Require Immediate Attention" insufficiently creative to warrant copyright protection,[28] and the Eighth Circuit came to the same conclusion when confronted with a professional sports team logo consisting of four lines forming an arrow, with the word "arrows" in script below.[29] Yet another trial court failed to see the literary merit in a four–page booklet containing use and care instructions for a pizza cooking stone.[30]

Thus far the courts have not articulated a general rule than can be used to determine with precision whether a work meets the creativity test. The decisions have an *ad hoc* quality to them. It would seem that the best that can be said is that the creativity requirement should be applied with an eye towards its purposes. If a phrase or image is so pedestrian that it is highly likely that others will independently and routinely come up with something quite similar, copyright protection of that particular image or phrase would likely create a risk that innocent authors could be subjected to harassing claims of infringement and a chilling effect that would hinder future authors in their own creative work. Moreover, if the material is so pedestrian that no incentive, in the form of copyright protection, is required to call forth its creation, that also militates in favor of a denial of copyright.

Regardless of how the creativity requirement is interpreted, the Supreme Court informed us over a century ago that the decision is not supposed to involve the courts in an assessment of the artistic merits of the work in question. In other words, the work has to be moderately creative, but it does not have to be

26. WILLIAM F. PATRY, PATRY ON COPYRIGHT § 3:27 (2007).

27. Takeall v. Pepsico, Inc., 14 F.3d 596, 29 U.S.P.Q.2d 1913 (4th Cir. 1993); *See also, Pelt v. CBS, Inc.*, 30 U.S.P.Q.2d 1639 (C.D. Cal. 1993) (slogan "Listen Up, It's More Than Talk, It's Feeling" not copyrightable); *Alberto–Culver Co. v. Andrea Dumon, Inc.*, 466 F.2d 705 (2d Cir. 1972) (slogan "most personal sort of deodorant" not copyrightable). Regulations promulgated by the Copyright Office which govern the registration of claims of copyright specifically provide that "[w]ords and short

phrases such as names, titles and slogans ..." are not subject to copyright. 37 C.F.R. § 202.1(a).

28. Magic Marketing v. Mailing Services of Pittsburgh, 634 F.Supp. 769 (W.D. Pa. 1986).

29. John Muller & Co., Inc. v. New York Arrows Soccer Team, Inc., 802 F.2d 989 (8th Cir. 1986).

30. Sassafras Enterprises Inc. v. Roshco Inc., 889 F.Supp. 343, 50 BNA PTCJ 371, 36 U.S.P.Q.2d 1194 (N.D. Ill. 1995).

particularly good. The case most associated with this proposition is *Bleistein v. Donaldson Lithographing Co.*,[31] where the court had to decide whether an advertising poster depicting circus performers was eligible for copyright. Justice Holmes rejected a claim that the work was insufficiently "artistic" to deserve copyright by observing that:

> It would be a dangerous undertaking for persons trained only to the law to constitute themselves final judges of the worth of pictorial illustrations, outside of the narrowest and most obvious limits. At one extreme some works of genius would be sure to miss appreciation. Their very novelty would make them repulsive until the public had learned the new language in which their author spoke. It may be more than doubted, for instance, whether the etchings of Goya or the paintings of Manet would have been sure of protection when seen for the first time. At the other end, copyright would be denied to pictures which appealed to a public less educated than the judge.... [T]he taste of any public is not to be treated with contempt.[32]

This is sometimes referred to as the principle of aesthetic or artistic non-discrimination. Pulp fiction is just as entitled to copyright as serious literature; amateur videos get the same protection as deeply moving feature films; and comic books get the same statutory exclusivity as magnificent oil paintings. The copyright laws are not a license for judges to act as art critics.

One last word of caution. The "modest creativity" requirement for copyright protection has led to some terminological confusion among courts and commentators. Some courts treat this requirement as a component of the statutorily required "originality,"[33] and do not distinguish between the "from scratch" and "creativity" themes when they discuss originality unless the context requires them to do so. Others, however, refer to a separate "creativity" requirement, and reserve the term "originality" to mean only "from scratch" or "not-copied."[34] Still others use the rubric of "authorship" to designate the requirement of a modicum of creativity.[35] The difference is purely semantic. There appears to be little substantive disagreement between these courts over the fact that there is a creativity requirement. It does mean, however, that you must read copyright opinions that grapple with the issue of "origi-

31. 188 U.S. 239, 23 S.Ct. 298, 47 L.Ed. 460 (1903).

32. 188 U.S. at 251–52

33. Feist, 499 U.S. at 346.

34. *See e.g.*, Folio Impressions, Inc. v. Byer California, 937 F.2d 759 (2d Cir. 1991); John Muller & Co. v. N.Y. Arrows Soccer Team, 802 F.2d 989, 990 (8th Cir. 1986).

35. Atari Games v. Oman, 888 F.2d 878 (D.C. Cir. 1989), *appeal after remand*, 979 F.2d 242 (D.C. Cir. 1992).

nality" with some care to be sure you understand just how the court is using the terms that it employs. To avoid that very confusion on the part of our readers, you should be aware that for the remainder of this book we will follow the practice of using the single term originality in the dual sense of both "not-copied" *and* "minimally creative" unless the context requires us to disentangle those two threads.

§ 2.2   Fixation

2.2.1   Basic Principles

The current copyright statute also requires that a work be "fixed" in order to receive copyright protection.[36] The statute defines fixation as the embodiment of the work in a tangible means of expression that is sufficiently permanent or stable to permit it to be perceived, reproduced, or otherwise communicated, for a period of more than transitory duration.[37] In other words, the work has to be written down, taped, filmed, or otherwise captured in some way in a physical artifact or object before federal copyright protection can attach. Once an original work is fixed, however, copyright protection attaches immediately. There are no formalities required of an author—no application to an administrative agency, no act of publication, no need to climb to the roof of your home and shout three times "I have a copyright!"—nothing other than the mere fixation and zap, like magic, you have a federal statutory copyright.

The fixation doctrine can be put the other way around—there is no federal copyright protection for unfixed creative works such as an extemporaneous speech, a brand new poem that the poet recites from memory but has never written down, or a jazz improvisation performed spontaneously at a night club. These "unfixed" works might, however, be eligible for protection under state law, either under the misappropriation doctrine, or some other principle,[38] and in the case of music, may also be protected by a federal anti-bootlegging law that we will come to shortly. This means that under the present copyright statute the moment of fixation of a work is the dividing line between potential common law protection under state law and federal statutory protection.[39]

---

36.   17 U.S.C. § 102 (2000).

37.   17 U.S.C. § 101 (2000).

38.   *See e.g.* Metropolitan Opera Ass'n, Inc. v. Wagner–Nichols Recorder Corp., 199 Misc. 786, 101 N.Y.S.2d 483 (1950) (common law remedy available for unauthorized recording of live opera performances); Hemingway v. Random House, Inc., 23 N.Y.2d 341, 296 N.Y.S.2d 771, 244 N.E.2d 250 (1968) (Court as-sumed, without deciding, that in a proper case common law protection in certain limited kinds of spoken dialogue might be recognized if the speaker indicated that he intended to mark off the utterance in question from the ordinary stream of speech and to exercise control over its publication). California has codified protection for unfixed works. *See* Cal. Civ. Code § 980(a) (West 1982).

Because the statutory definition of fixation requires permanence or stability, a variety of temporary or short-term fixations probably fail to satisfy the statutory test. To invoke some traditional, if silly, examples, a sculptural work fixed in a block of ice might not qualify as a copyrightable work because of the transitory duration of the icy work product. Ditto a sand castle built below the high water mark on a beach. Of course the creators of these ephemeral sculptures can secure protection by snapping a photograph or making a videotape to capture the appearance of the item before it melts or is washed into the sea.

While a work must, therefore, be fixed to be entitled to federal protection, there is an important distinction between the work itself and the object or objects in which it is fixed or embodied. Works can be embodied in two types of objects, which the statute labels "copies" and "phonorecords" respectively. Phonorecords are material objects in which sounds are fixed and thus would include objects such as compact discs and audio cassette tapes. All other material objects in which a work might be fixed are classified as "copies." Thus computer flash drives, old fashioned bound books, photographic negatives, bronze statuettes, sheet music, and architectural drawings would all be examples of copies. A given work might be embodied in only a single copy—as would be true of a handwritten letter or a one-of-a-kind oil painting,[40] or in multiple copies as would be true of a best selling novel or a movie released on DVD. In either case, these physical objects can be transferred or destroyed without affecting the existence or the ownership of the copyright in the work.[41] Indeed, copyright in a work will endure even after all physical copies of that work have been destroyed.[42]

---

39. See H.R. Rep. No. 94–1476, 94th Cong. 2d Sess. 53.

40. The statute provides that the "term 'copies' includes the material object, other than a phonorecord, in which the work is first fixed." 17 U.S.C. § 101 (2000). Thus, what we might call "the original" in common everyday speech is considered a "copy" under the Copyright Act, and when a work is embodied in only a single unique physical object, such as a one-of-a-kind art work, the physical object is similarly considered a "copy" in the terminology of the statute.

41. "Ownership of the material object or any of the exclusive rights under a copyright is distinct from ownership of any material object in which the work is embodied. Transfer of ownership of any material object ... does not in itself convey rights in the copyrighted work

embodied in the object." 17 U.S.C. § 202 (2000).

42. For instance, in *Pacific & Southern Co. v. Duncan*, 744 F.2d 1490, 1494 (11th Cir. 1984), a television station routinely erased videotapes of previous broadcasts after seven days. In infringement litigation against another firm that had sold unauthorized videotapes of the same broadcasts, the plaintiff prevailed despite the fact that all of its copies of the work had been destroyed. As the leading treatise puts it "once a work is fixed for a period of more than transitory duration, it does not lose its copyright protection because thereafter all authorized copies are destroyed." NIMMER, COPYRIGHT § 2.03[B] (2002). See also H.R. Rep. No. 94–1476, 94th Cong. 2d Sess. 52 ("It is possible to have an 'original work of authorship'

Although the requirement of fixation was not explicit in federal copyright law prior to the 1976 Act, it was a necessary component of the scheme established by all prior laws. Under those statutes, federal protection did not attach until the work was either published with notice or registered with the Copyright Office.[43] Both publication and registration necessarily presuppose that the work has been fixed in some fashion. Indeed, most observers believe that the Constitution requires fixation since it gives Congress power to protect only the *writings* of an author.[44]

On the other hand, the modes of fixation that courts considered adequate under earlier copyright statutes were significantly narrower than they are today. In *White–Smith Music Publishing Co. v. Apollo Co.*,[45] the plaintiff held federal copyrights in songs that it had published in the form of sheet music. At this time, player pianos were all the rage. Essentially a primitive form of CD player, they were self-playing pianos containing a pneumatic mechanism which could play songs through the use of perforated rolls of paper. The defendant in the case, without obtaining the permission of the plaintiff, made piano rolls of plaintiff's musical compositions and began selling them to the public. Plaintiff, not happy that it had been denied payment for this new potential use of its music, sued for infringement. The case is thus not about copyrightability in the first instance. There was no question that the plaintiffs songs were "fixed"—they had been published in sheet music, a fixation of musical symbols in ink on paper. But the defendant could only be liable for infringement if it had made a "copy" of the song. So the case turned on the question of whether a piano roll was a copy within the meaning the statute then on the books.

The Court held that it was not! It reasoned that because a piano roll was not capable of being read and deciphered by the unaided human eye, it was not a copy of the song. To this court, the new and exotic form of "fixing" a work by perforating paper was simply not the right kind of fixation. Presumably, if the original

---

without having a 'copy' or 'phonorecord' embodying it.").

43. Copyright Act of 1909, §§ 10, 11. The House Report to the 1976 Copyright Act states that "[a]s a basic condition of copyright protection the bill *perpetuates the existing requirement* that a work be fixed in a 'tangible medium of expression,'...." H.R. Rep. No. 94–1476, 94th Cong. 2d Sess. 52 (1976), further illustrating the long-standing pedigree of the "fixation" requirement. *See also Letter Edged in Black v. Public Building Com'n of Chicago*, 320 F.Supp. 1303, 1310 (N.D. Ill. 1970) ("It is settled

that a copyright can exist only in a perceptible, tangible work.").

44. *See Goldstein v. California*, 412 U.S. 546, 561, 93 S.Ct. 2303, 37 L.Ed.2d 163 (1973) ("By Art. I § 8, cl. 8, of the Constitution, the States granted to Congress the power to protect the 'Writings' of 'Authors'.... [A]lthough the word 'writings' might be limited to script or printed material, it may be interpreted to include any *physical* rendering of the fruits of creative intellectual or aesthetic labor.").

45. 209 U.S. 1, 28 S.Ct. 319, 52 L.Ed. 655 (1908).

composer had never prepared sheet music, but had instead embodied the melody in his mind only in piano rolls, the same logic would have required denying him copyright, because he would never have prepared and published "copies" of the song, as the then-governing statute required. In other words, back then, you not only had to fix your work, but not every fixation was acceptable. It had to result in a visually perceptible copy that others could interpret without the aid of a machine.

White–Smith is often cited as an example of judicial reluctance to extend the scope of copyright protection to works embodied in new technologies, or at least of judicial confusion in the face of new technologies. If the *White–Smith* ideology prevailed today, copyright protection might be denied to computer programs recorded on flash drives, motion pictures recorded on DVDs, and music recorded on CDs on the grounds of inadequate fixation because none of these items can be "read" by the naked eye. Congress sought to put a stake through the heart of this philosophy by providing in the 1976 Act that any fixation of the work would be acceptable so long as it permitted the work to be "perceived, reproduced, or otherwise communicated, either directly or with the aid of a machine or device," and regardless of whether the medium of expression chosen is "now known or later developed."[46]

2.2.2   Fixation and New Technologies

You may have noticed that the player piano has long since ceased to be state-of-the art entertainment technology. Nonetheless, the march of technology has continued to raise interpretative problems vis-a-vis the fixation requirement. Consider, for instance, video games. As we noted above, the current copyright statute tells us that a work is fixed only when its "embodiment in a copy or phonorecord ... is sufficiently permanent or stable to permit it to be perceived ... for a period of more than a transitory duration" in order to satisfy the statutory fixation requirement.[47] In computer video games the game's images are, momentarily, visually perceptible and could thus be said to be "fixed" on the screen, but they are constantly changing as the player operates the controls. Because some of the earliest of these games—specifically coin-operated arcade style games from the 1980s—proved enormously popular and lucrative, unauthorized parties began writing software to duplicate them. This lead to several cases in the early eighties concerning the copyrightability of the displays generated by such games.

There is no dispute that the underlying programs that operate these games were themselves "fixed," usually in silicon on a chip that was contained in the game console—at least after the death of

---

46. 17 U.S.C. § 102 (2000).   **47.** 17 U.S.C. § 101 (2000).

the *White–Smith* doctrine that had required visually perceptible copies . However, unauthorized third parties did not copy those programs—they simply wrote new ones that generated the same video and audio effects as plaintiffs' popular games. Consequently the games' authors also sought to protect the screen displays from copying by claiming a separate copyright in those displays as "audiovisual works." Those claims raised the question of whether the displays were sufficiently fixed—specifically whether they endured for more than a transitory duration.

In *Midway Mfg. Co. v. Artic Int'l, Inc.*,[48] the plaintiff held the copyrights for the venerable and much beloved PAC–MAN[49] and GALAXIAN video games. The defendant had prepared circuit boards that did not copy plaintiff's software, but produced images and sounds for a game that looked and sounded virtually identical to plaintiff's. Determining if those images and sounds were protected by copyright was the central issue in the case. The Seventh Circuit summarized the difficulty with that issue in this way:

> Strictly speaking, the particular sequence of images that appears on the screen of a video game machine when the game is played is not the same work as the set of images stored the machine's circuit boards. The person playing the game can vary the order in which the stored images appear on the screen by moving the machine's control lever. That makes playing a video game a little like arranging words in a dictionary into sentences or paints on a palette into a painting. The question is whether the creative effort in playing a video game is enough like writing or painting to make each performance of a video game the work of the player and not the game's inventor.

Despite these conceptual difficulties, the *Midway* court found that the screen displays were sufficiently "fixed" to qualify for protection under the statute, commenting that

> Playing a video game is more like changing channels on a television than it is like writing a novel or painting a picture. The player of a video game does not have control over the sequence of images that appears on the video game screen. He cannot create any sequence he wants out of the images stored on the game's circuit boards. The most he can do is choose one of the limited number of sequences the game allows him to choose. He is unlike a

---

48. 704 F.2d 1009, 1011 (7th Cir.), *cert. denied*, 464 U.S. 823, 104 S.Ct. 90, 78 L.Ed.2d 98 (1983).

49. If you are too young to remember Pac–Man, you can find a description of it in Atari, Inc. v. North American

Philips Consumer Electronics Corp., 672 F.2d 607, 610–611 (7th Cir. 1982). It is pretty primitive by the standards of, say World of Warcraft, but it was strangely addictive in its own way.

> writer or a painter because the video game in effect writes
> the sentences and paints the painting for him; he merely
> choose one of the sentences stored in its memory, one of
> the paintings stored in its collection.[50]

The court's metaphor here may not be entirely persuasive. While it
is true that the game player cannot create ANY sequence of images
he would like, because some would violate the rules or flow of the
game, the player surely does choose a specific sequence of images as
he or she moves the joystick around. To beat the metaphor to
death, then, it would seem that while some arrangements of the
"sentences" are forbidden because they violate the "grammar" of
the game, there were a large number of other arrangements that
the player could create. Nonetheless, the equities of the case
certainly favored the copyright claimant over the defendants, and
that may have induced the court to put its judicial thumb on the
scales. Indeed, other courts that considered that precise issue came
to the same conclusion.[51]

A similar problem, but one with considerably greater implications for the twenty-first century copyright lawyer, is whether to
treat the movement of information into the random or transient
memory of a computer (or RAM) as a fixation and, hence, as a copy.
This issue usually becomes significant not on the front end of a
copyright inquiry—where we ask whether there is a copyrightable
work in the first place[52]—but on the back end, when we ask
whether a third party has made an impermissible "copy." However,
as we noted in our discussion of the *White–Smith* piano roll case,
the conceptual issue is the same in both situations. If information
that resides in computer memory is not fixed, than it is not fixed
for either purpose—such material is ineligible for copyright *ab
initio* and the transfer of someone else's material into the memory
of your computer is not an infringement because it does not make a
copy.

At the time the 1976 Act was adopted, one might have predicted that the answer to the "RAM copy" question would have been

---

50.   704 F.2d at 1012.

51.   *See, e.g.*, Williams Elec. Inc. v.
Artic Int'l Inc., 685 F.2d 870, 874 (3d
Cir. 1982) ("Although there is player
interaction with the machine during the
play mode which causes the audiovisual
presentation to change in some respects
from one game to the next ... there is
always a repetitive sequence of a substantial portion of the sights and sounds
of the game, and many aspects of the
display remain constant from game to
game regardless of how the player operates the controls.").

52.   For instance, assume that you
type a poem on your computer keyboard
and just as you finish there is a power
surge that turns your computer off. Assume also that you had not saved the
poem to your hard drive nor had it been
saved automatically by the backup feature of your software—at the moment of
the surge, its words resided only in the
"random access memory" of the computer. If the presence of the words in
memory constitutes sufficient "fixation"
than you have federal statutory copyright in the poem. If not, then you don't.

negative. Not least of that, that would have been because language in the legislative history of the fixation provision said: "the definition of 'fixation' would exclude from the concept pure evanescent or transient reproductions such as those ... captured momentarily in the 'memory' of a computer."[53] Around that same time, however, Congress appointed a body called the Commission on New Techological Uses or CONTU to consider various unresolved issues concerning the treatment of computer technology under the new statute and to report back to Congress. Two years later, in 1978, CONTU filed a Final Report, which stated, in part "the introduction of a work into a computer memory would, consistent with the new law, be a reproduction of the work."[54] This observation seems flatly to contradict the legislative history of what was then a statute merely two years old. In the years that followed, however, courts began to embrace the CONTU position that the temporary retention of material in the random access memory (or RAM) of a computer did, indeed constitute making a copy.

One of the first cases to reach this result was *MAI Systems Corp v. Peak Computer Inc.*[55] MAI manufactured both computers and the software to run them. It also offered post-sale service of those systems to clients who hired it for that purpose. Peak was a competing computer maintenance company that provided routine service and emergency repairs for more than one hundred different clients who owned MAI computer systems. In the course of its work Peak's employees would often operate their clients' computers, which necessarily caused the MAI operating system program to be loaded into the computer's RAM. MAI, unhappy with the loss of some of its service business, sued Peak alleging that Peak violated its copyrights every time it turned on the clients' computers. To prevail on this argument MAI needed to establish that loading a program into RAM constituted making a "copy" of the program. The Ninth Circuit concluded exactly that. It felt that there was sufficient fixation by Peak because "by showing that Peak loads the software into the RAM and is then able to view the system error log and diagnose the problem with the computer, MAI has adequately shown that the representation created in the RAM is 'sufficiently permanent or stable to permit it to be perceived, reproduced, or otherwise communicated for a period of more than transitory duration.' "[56]

In 1998 Congress legislatively overruled the specific result in *MAI Systems* by adding a new section 117(c) to the copyright

53. H.R. Rep. No. 94–1476, 94th Cong. 2d Sess. at 53 (1976).

54. NATIONAL COMM'N ON NEW TECHNOLOGICAL USES OF COPYRIGHTED WORKS, FINAL REPORT (July 31, 1978).

55. 991 F.2d 511 (9th cir. 1993).

56. 919 F.2d at 518.

statute.[57] That provision provides that it is not infringement for the owner of a machine to make or to authorize the making of a copy of a computer program if the copy is made solely by virtue of activation of that machine containing a lawful copy of the program and done for the purposes of maintenance or repair of the machine. Under this provision, Peak's activities would have been lawful because it was authorized to engage in machine maintenance by the computer owners who were its clients. However, by enacting this statute Congress seems to have accepted the underlying and more general premise of *MAI Systems*, namely that the loading of a program into RAM constitutes the making of a copy.

Since *MAI Systems* a number of other courts have followed its lead. For instance, the DC Circuit declared that "if someone loads validly copyrighted software onto his or her own computer without the owner's permission, and then uses the software for the principal purposes for which it was designed, there can be no real doubt that the protected elements of the software have been copied and the copyright infringed."[58] The Copyright Office also seems to concur. In 2001 it issued a congressionally mandated report on a piece of legislation known as the Digital Milennium Copyright Act or DMCA. In that report, it analyzed this precise question and concluded that "[b]ased on the definitional language in the Copyright Act, RAM reproductions are generally 'fixed' and thus constitute 'copies' that are within the scope of the copyright owner's reproduction right."[59] However, that report went on to note:

> The definition of "fixed" leaves open the possibility, however, that certain RAM reproductions that exist for only a "period of ... transitory duration" are not copies. The statute does not define "transitory duration" directly. Since permanence is not required for fixation, "transitory" must denote something shorter than "temporary." ... Courts have not attempted to formulate a general rule defining how long a reproduction must endure to be

57. Called the "Computer Maintenance Competition Assurance Act" the legislation was actually Title III of the Digital Millenium Copyright Act. *See,* § 302(3) P.L. 105–304 (1998).

58. Stenograph L.L.C. v. Bossard Asso. Inc., 144 F.3d 96, 100 (D.C. Cir. 1998). This case was cited with approval by three concurring justices in Microsoft Corp. v. AT & T Corp., 550 U.S. 437, 127 S.Ct. 1746, 1760, 167 L.Ed.2d 737 (2007) (Justice Alito, concurring). *See also,* Triad Sys. Corp. v. Southeastern Express Co., 64 F.3d 1330, 1335 (9th Cir. 1995); Marobie–FL., Inc. v. Nat'l

Ass'n of Fire Equip. Distrib., 983 F.Supp. 1167, 1177–78 (N.D.Ill.1997) (downloading of file from website constitutes "copying" by host computer, where portions of file pass through RAM before being immediately transmitted over Internet). *See generally,* Ira L. Brandriss, *Writing in Frost on a Window Pane: E-mail and Chatting on Ram and Copyright Fixation,* 43 J. COPYRIGHT SOC'Y U.S.A. 237 (1996).

59. DMCA Section 104 Report at 110 (August, 2001), available on-line at http://www.copyright.gov/reports/studies/dmca/sec–104–report–vol–1.pdf.

"fixed," deciding instead on a case-by-case basis whether the particular reproduction at issue sufficed. Nonetheless, a general rule can be drawn from the language of the statute. In establishing the dividing line between those reproductions that are subject to the reproduction right and those that are not, we believe that Congress intended the copyright owner's exclusive right to extend to all reproductions from which economic value can be derived. The economic value derived from a reproduction lies in the ability to copy, perceive or communicate it. Unless a reproduction manifests itself so fleetingly that it cannot be copied, perceived or communicated, the making of that copy should fall within the scope of the copyright owner's exclusive rights.

The issue of just how long material must reside in computer memory in order to constitute a "copy" was at the center of the recent case of *Cartoon Network LP v. CSC Holdings, Inc.*[60] The defendant there was Cablevision, a major provider of cable television services. It wanted to offer its subscribers a feature known as a Remote Storage Video Recorder system or RS–DVR. As most tech savvy readers are aware, a DVR is a machine, like the well-known TiVo brand device, that permits a user to store programs for subsequent playback. It differs from a video tape recorder because it stores the programs digitally on an internal hard drive in the device, rather than in analog format on a cassette tape. The remote system devised by Cablevision allowed customers who did not own a stand-alone DVR to record programs on central hard drives maintained by Cablevision at a remote location. They would then be able to play back those programs whenever they wished, using their remote control and their cable box, which had been equipped with the RS–DVR software.

In order to facilitate the storage of programs, all signals received by Cablevision were run through a "buffer," which recorded the program in fragments of one-tenth of a second and, "as each new fragment [is] received, every tenth of a second, the data residing on this buffer are automatically erased and replaced.... The information is buffered before any customer requests a recording, and would be buffered even if no such request were made."[61] If no subscriber requested that a particular program be recorded—as might be the case with a Brady Bunch reunion special—nothing further was done with the buffered material—it just vanished as it was erased. On the other hand, if even one subscriber indicated

60.   536 F.3d 121 (2d Cir. 2008).

61.   *Id.* If any subscribers had requested that the program be stored for later playback, these fragments were sent to another area of the hardware which recorded them in their entirety.

that he wanted the program saved for future viewing, the material was sent from the buffer to more permanent storage for playback upon the subsequent request of the customer.

There was no question that the more permanent storage involved the making of a copy. Cablevision argued, however, that it was not liable for making this particular copy, because it did so passively on the request of the end-user (namely the home cable subscriber). We will consider that issue much further on when we get to the question of secondary liability for copyright infringement. Our concern at the moment is with the initial buffering done by Cablevision. That was indisputably done at its own initiative since it was done whether or not any subscriber wanted the program preserved. However it involved only fleeting reproductions, consisting of a succession of 1/10 of a second fragments of the programs. The court found that this did not constitute the making of a copy, saying

> We do not read *MAI Systems* as holding that, as a matter of law, loading a program into a form of RAM always results in copying. Such a holding would read the "transitory duration" language out of the definition, and we do not believe our sister circuit would dismiss this statutory language without even discussing it.... [U]nlike the data in cases like MAI Systems, which remained embodied in the computer's RAM memory until the user turned the computer off, each bit of data here is rapidly and automatically overwritten as soon as it is processed.... [T]hese facts strongly suggest that the works in this case are embodied in the buffer for only a "transitory" period ... and are therefore not "fixed" in the buffers.

This result seems sensible not just as a matter of statutory construction, but as a matter of technology as well. The architecture of the Internet often means that material is moved from computer to computer where it is fleetingly reproduced before being sent further on its way. To hold that every computer in this chain made a "copy" could have broad and ultimately troubling implications by imposing licensing requirements on numerous parties who have no practical way of securing those licenses. Sound construction of the statute as well as a pragmatic approach to the underlying policy question should lead other circuits to follow *Cartoon Network*.

Let us be sure, however that you have not lost the thread of our story. In this chapter we are interested in the requirements necessary to obtain federal statutory copyright in the first instance, not the question of when a second party infringes someone else's copyright. Fixation is one of those requirements. For present purposes, therefore, *Cartoon Network* seems to stand for the idea that if a party creates a work—a poem, perhaps—that resides in computer memory only for a brief few seconds, before disappearing due to some kind of electronic glitch, that work has *not* been fixed because it was not embodied for more than a transitory duration. If you have ever lost revisions to a document because of a power surge or software problem before you had a chance to save them, you probably find this result consistent with your intuition.

Moving away from the computer world, there is another potential problem posed by the fixation requirement, but one which was fully anticipated by Congress in the 1976 Act. We refer here to the the copyright status of a broadcast of a live event. When a television network broadcasts a football game, the game itself is not protected by copyright since it is a live event and not a work "fixed" in a tangible medium. Moreover, the broadcast itself does not satisfy the fixation requirement because it is merely an ephemeral transmission of the images on the TV screen and lacks the "permanent embodiment" required by the statute. Thus, it would seem that one who captures the broadcast images and either retransmits them or records them could not be charged with copyright infringement. That, however, would create serious economic problems for professional sports leagues, which rely on the ability to sell *exclusive* broadcast rights to a given network for much of their revenue.

To deal with this problem, Congress added an additional sentence to the definition of "fixed" in the current copyright statute. It provides that a "work consisting of sounds, images, or both, that are being transmitted, is 'fixed' for purposes of this title if a fixation of the work is being made simultaneously with its transmission."[62] In other words, if a television network broadcasts a live telecast of an NFL football game, and at the same time also makes a videotape of that broadcast, the network will have satisfied the fixation requirement and will have copyright protection with regard to the broadcast. Retransmission or commercial recordation thus become an infringement.[63]

Finally, it is important to note that the fixation which the statute speaks of is one made "by or under the authority of the author."[64] Thus, if a comedian were to launch in a series of ad libbed jokes during a performance, and an audience member taped the routine without the comedian's knowledge, that would not constitute a fixation under the 1976 Copyright Act. This means

---

62. 17 U.S.C. § 101 (2000).

63. Non-commercial recording of such a broadcast is non-infringing under the fair use doctrine, as interpreted by the Supreme Court. *See Sony v. Univer-*

sal, 464 U.S. 417, 104 S.Ct. 774, 78 L.Ed.2d 574 (1984).

64. 17 U.S.C. § 101 (2000).

that the comedian would have no copyrightable work and could not rely on copyright law to prevent the audience member from duplicating and selling the tapes. In some cases, the comedian would not be entirely without a remedy, as he might have a cause of action under state common law, but that is a far less sturdy bit of legal protection than a copyright claim.

This example suggests that so-called "bootleg" recordings could present a significant practical and economic problem for live performers. All a bootlegger needs to do is attend a live performance, covertly record it, generate a master tape, and begin selling copies. Such tapes are easy and cheap to make, but can result in substantial profits. However, because bootleg recordings are often of lower quality than legitimately produced recordings, their market presence can harm the reputation of the performer in addition to undercutting sales. Yet the fixation requirement of the copyright law has traditionally barred a federal copyright remedy against bootleggers.

In recognition of this problem, along with a desire to comply with U.S. obligations under the World Trade Organization agreements, Congress in 1994 enacted a special anti-bootlegging law.[65] Under this statute, one who makes unauthorized sound recordings and music videos of a live musical performance may be subject to both civil and criminal causes of action. Trafficking in—that is to say, transporting, transferring, or otherwise disposing of—the unauthorized sound recordings and music videos is also illegal. The protection appears to be perpetual, because the statute does not provide any duration limits on the rights that it provides.

This anti-bootlegging statute is lodged in 17 U.S.C. § 1101, near the Copyright Act but not formally a part of it. This choice of codification suggests the distinctions between this *sui generis* right and the traditional copyright law. Some have argued that the extent of these differences makes the anti-bootlegging law constitutionally suspect. The Intellectual Property Clause of the Constitution grants Congress the power only to protect "writings," a term which connotes some sort of embodiment in a material form. The Constitution also calls for protection to endure only for "limited times." In violation of these principles, the anti-bootlegging statute protected unfixed musical performances for an unlimited time. Nonetheless, the few courts that have considered the question have upheld the statute in the face of constitutional challenge, relying upon the Commerce Clause rather than the Intellectual Property Clause.[66]

---

65. Pub. L. No. 103–465, 108 Stat. 4809 (1994).

66. *United States v. Moghadam,* 175 F.3d 1269 (11th Cir. 1999); *United States v. Martignon,* 492 F.3d 140 (2d

§ 2.3   No Protection for Ideas

Copyright in a work does not protect the underlying ideas expressed in that work. This simple concept is a fundamental tenet of copyright law. It is embodied in the very structure of section 102 of the current copyright act. While the first subsection of that provision affirmatively sets out the prerequisites for protection—fixation and originality—section 102(b) negatively provides that:

> In no case does copyright protection for an original work of authorship extend to any idea, procedure, process, system, method of operation, concept, principle, or discovery, regardless of the form in which it is described, explained, illustrated, or embodied in such work.[67]

This means that copyright protects only the *expression* contained within a work and not the underlying plot, or theme, or insight of the work. In other words, if an author writes a book explaining how to repair automobiles in an efficient way, he or she may not prevent others from describing the technique in their own words in another book. Similarly, if an author writes a novel based on the notion of a highly placed CIA agent who is actually a spy for a foreign power, he or she may not prevent others from using that concept as the basis for their own, separate novel.

There are several justifications for this limitation on the scope of copyright. First, copyright is, according to the Constitution itself, supposed to promote the progress of science and the useful arts. Progress requires that subsequent authors remain free to build on the works of their predecessors. If the first person to articulate a theory, divulge a principle, or tap into a literary theme could prevent all others from using it, progress would be stymied rather than promoted.[68] Ideas are fundamental building blocks, and they are in relatively short supply. It would undermine public policy to allow them to be locked up under a system of exclusive rights.

Second, there already exists a legal regime to reward innovation in the development of principles and procedures—namely patent law. Unlike the easily satisfied criteria necessary for copyright protection, patent law has fairly rigorous prerequisites. The would-be patentee must show that his or her invention is both "novel" and "nonobvious".[69] If copyright protection extended to ideas, concepts, and the like, it would provide an alternative to patent law that would undermine the many significant policy

Cir. 2007); *KISS Catalog v. Passport Int'l Prods.*, 405 F.Supp.2d 1169 (C.D.Cal. 2005).

67. 17 U.S.C. § 102(b) (2000).

68. For development of this argument and, more generally, for a justification of the idea/expression dichotomy

from an economic point of view see William M. Landes & Richard A. Posner, *An Economic Analysis of Copyright Law*, 18 J. LEGAL STUD. 325, 347–53 (1989).

69. *See* 35 U.S.C. §§ 102, 103.

objectives of that distinct intellectual property regime. Why would an inventor of a new process obtain a patent if merely writing up the process conferred a copyright that included the right of prevent others from using that process?

Third, extending copyright protection to the ideas contained in works might poses serious problems under the First Amendment. Others might be effectively forbidden from discussing the material contained in the work of an earlier author. As Justice Douglas put it:

> The arena of public debate would be quiet, indeed, if a politician could copyright his speeches or a philosopher his treatises and thus obtain a monopoly on the ideas contained. We should not construe the copyright laws to conflict so patently with the values that the First Amendment was designed to protect.[70]

The idea-expression dividing line for protection is often traced back to the Supreme Court's decision in *Baker v. Selden*,[71] a somewhat opaque and controversial opinion even today, over 130 years after it was decided. Selden devised a new method of financial accounting for business. His new scheme made it possible to record the entire operations of the business for a given period of time on either a single page or on two facing pages. He published a short book explaining his new system, along with accompanying forms. Baker subsequently prepared forms that were not identical to Selden's, but resembled them to a considerable degree and were tailored for use with the Selden system.[72] Selden sued Baker arguing infringement.

Since Baker's forms were not identical, one way to interpret Selden's claim is as an argument that Baker had impermissibly copied the underlying idea or methodology of Selden's accounting system. Of course, Selden could only win on that theory if his copyright in his book and his forms extended to the underlying idea as well. The Court concluded that it did not, declaring that Selden's

---

70. *Lee v. Runge*, 404 U.S. 887, 893, 92 S.Ct. 197, 30 L.Ed.2d 169 (1971) (Douglas, J., dissenting). *See also* JAMIE BOYLE, THE PUBLIC DOMAIN, 94–95 (2008) (Noting that because of the idea-expression principle "the speaker's freedom of expression is never truly restrained. The only thing I am barred from is using your words, your exact plot, your photograph, your music—not your facts, your ideas, your genre, the events you describe." But also cautioning that "[s]ometimes ... the speaker cannot paraphrase around the restraints posed by copyright. He needs to use the partic-

ular text or image in question to convey his message.").

71. 101 U.S. 99, 25 L.Ed. 841 (1879). Some scholars trace the idea-expression distinction further back than *Baker. See, e.g.*, Pamela Samuelson, *Why Copyright Law Excludes Systems and Processes from the Scope of its Protection*, 85 TEX. L. REV. 1921, 1925–26 (2007).

72. "The defendant uses a similar plan so far as results are concerned; but makes a different arrangement of the columns, and uses different headings." *Baker*, 101 U.S. at 100.

copyright did not give him an exclusive right in the system of accounting he had developed and revealed to the world. The Court illustrated its result with an example:

> Take the case of medicines. Certain mixtures are found to be of great value in the healing art. If the discoverer writes and publishes a book on the subject (as regular physicians generally do), he gains no exclusive right to the manufacture and sale of the medicine; he gives that to the public. If he desires to acquire such exclusive right, he must obtain a patent for the mixture as a new art, manufacture or composition of matter. He may copyright his book, if he pleases; but that only secures to him the exclusive right of printing and publishing his book. So of all other inventions or discoveries.[73]

If *Baker* said no more than this, it would be a straightforward declaration of the rule that copyright does not extend to the underlying ideas of a work. As the Court put it more generally elsewhere in the opinion, "the truths of a science or the methods of an art are the common property of the whole world, an author has the right to express the one, or explain and use the other, in his own way."[74] Other portions of the opinion, however, seem to imply a different basis for decision.

At various points in the opinion, the Court seems to assume that Baker took not merely the idea of the accounting system, but its expression as well. Recall the facts of the case. As we noted, Baker's forms were not identical to Selden's. They were, however, similar, and copyright infringement does not require verbatim reproduction—as you would predict you cannot escape liability for infringing an author's copyright in a novel by merely changing a few sentences here and there. Thus, the *Baker v. Selden* Court might have felt that such differences as did exist between the two parties' forms were relatively minor, and Baker's forms could be considered a substantial copy of Selden's. Under that view, one might think that Baker would be held liable for copyright infringement, because he took expression, not just the idea of the new accounting system.

The Court, however, noted, that it was impossible to use the ideas of Selden's system without also borrowing the expression contained in the accounting forms. That being so, it suggested that the forms were dedicated to the public.[75] This goes beyond the basic

---

73. *Baker*, 101 U.S. at 102–03.

74. *Baker*, 101 U.S. at 100–01.

75. "The very object of publishing a book on science or the useful arts is to communicate to the world the useful knowledge which it contains. But this object would be frustrated if the knowledge could not be used without incurring the guilt of piracy of the book. And where the art it teaches cannot be used

idea-expression distinction to say that not only may one copy the ideas of a work without incurring infringement liability, but that one may also copy the expression of the work *if doing so is necessary in order to use the ideas.* This will generally be true of any system that is implemented through the use of blank forms of various sorts. Thus, *Baker* is also considered to be the genesis for the prevailing rule today that blank forms are not copyrightable subject matter.[76] Professor Nimmer, among others, has criticized this aspect of the *Baker* holding, pointing out that many blank forms can contain much creative expression.[77]

Baker is a difficult case because of the close interconnection between the ideas of Selden's system and the expression that is incorporated into his accounting forms. Another, somewhat different, situation where the ideas and expressions of a work are closely intertwined occurs when a given idea can only be communicated in one, or a limited number of expressions. For example, the idea of a "meatloaf" involves the combination of specific ingredients and a particular method of preparation. There are a relatively few numbers of ways to set out those ingredients and instructions. If the first author to publish a meatloaf recipe could prevent other authors from publishing recipes expressed in similar words, that would give him a monopoly not only over the original expression, but over the very idea of a meatloaf itself. In cases such as this, the courts generally say that the idea and the expression in question have "merged" and they deny copyright protection.

One of the better-know "merger" case is *Morrissey v. Procter & Gamble Co.,*[78] which held that a set of rules for a sweepstakes based on entrants' social security numbers was not copyrightable because there were only a limited number of ways to express the underlying idea of the sweepstakes instructions. Another example is *Herbert Rosenthal Jewelry Corp. v. Kalpakian,*[79] where the court

without employing the methods and diagrams used to illustrate the book, or such as are similar to them, such methods and diagrams are to be considered as necessary incidents to the art, and given therewith to the public; not given for the purpose of publication in other works explanatory of the art, but for the purpose of practical application." *Baker,* 101 U.S. at 103.

76. According to the regulations for registration of claims to copyright, "[b]lank forms, such as time cards, graph paper, account books, diaries, bank checks, scorecards, address books, report forms, mail order forms and the like, which are designed for recording information and not in themselves con-

vey information ..." are not subject to copyright. 37 C.F.R. § 202.1(c) (1994). *See e.g.,* Brown Instrument Co. v. Warner, 161 F.2d 910 (D.C. Cir. 1947); Bibbero Systems, Inc. v. Colwell Systems, Inc., 893 F.2d 1104 (9th Cir. 1990) (medical billing form not copyrightable); Sheplers Catalog Sales Inc. v. Old West Dry Goods Corp., d/b/a Old West Outfitters, 830 F.Supp. 566, 28 U.S.P.Q.2d 1555 (D. Kan. 1993) (order form in mail order catalog not copyrightable).

77. Nimmer, Copyright § 2.18[C] (2002).

78. 379 F.2d 675 (1st Cir. 1967).

79. 446 F.2d 738 (9th Cir. 1971).

permitted copying of a jewelry pin in the shape of a bee on the ground that the idea of a bee merged with the expression of that idea. The court there observed that "When the 'idea' and its 'expression' are thus inseparable, copying the 'expression' will not be barred, since protecting the 'expression' in such circumstance would confer a monopoly of the 'idea' upon the copyright owner free of the conditions and limitations imposed by the patent law."[80] We might make the same point by paraphrasing Gertrude Stein and observing that "a bee is a bee is a bee."[81]

None of the forgoing addresses the practical problem of how to distinguish the "idea" of a work from its "expression." This problem of classification is invariably controversial, because in many infringement cases involving non-literal copying, the defendant will claim that he or she took only the unprotected ideas of the plaintiff's work, rather than any of the protected expression. Moreover, the distinction between ideas and expression is not really a sharp dichotomy. Rather, it is a continuum. The general idea of a work can be phrased more and more specifically until, eventually, a line is crossed and we are dealing with expression instead. Learned Hand said it best in a case involving alleged copyright infringement of a play:

> Upon any work, and especially upon a play, a great number of patterns of increasing generality will fit equally well, as more and more of the incident is left out. That last may perhaps be no more than the most general statement of what the play is about, and at times might consist only of its title; but there is a point in this series of abstractions where they are no longer protected, since otherwise the playwright could prevent the use of his "ideas" to which, apart from their expression, his property is never extended.[82]

In other words, a given work does not have merely one "idea" behind it, but a multitude of ideas. That, unfortunately, does not make the task of separating protectable expression for unprotectable ideas any easier. As Judge Hand noted with some frustration in a different case, "no principle can be stated as to when an imitator

---

80. *Id.*, 446 F.2d at 742. *See also* Kern River Gas Transmission Co. v. Coastal Corp., 899 F.2d 1458 (5th Cir. 1990) (map of route of natural gas pipeline not copyrightable because maps express idea of the location of the pipeline in the only effective way); Hart v. Dan Chase Taxidermy Supply Co., Inc., 152 F.3d 918 (2d Cir. 1998) (taxidermy mannequins of fish are not copyrightable because they consist of minimal expression which merges with the idea of depicting the appearance of the fish in question).

81. For those not familiar with Gertrude Stein, the allusion is to a line in the poem *Sacred Emily* that "Rose is a rose is a rose is a rose." *See* Selected Writings of Gertrude Stein (Vintage Books, 1990).

82. Nichols v. Universal Pictures Corp., 45 F.2d 119, 121 (2d Cir. 1930).

has gone beyond copying the 'idea,' and has borrowed its 'expression,'.... Decisions must therefore inevitably be ad hoc."[83] In making these ad hoc decisions, however, it is important to remember the underlying purpose the distinction seeks to achieve. As the Ninth Circuit put it, "The guiding consideration ... is the preservation of the balance between competition and protection reflected in the ... copyright laws."[84]

This problem of distinguishing protectable expression from unprotectable ideas recurs with virtually every type of copyrightable subject matter. Cases involving alleged appropriation of the plot of novels and plays turn on the distinction, as do cases involving alleged appropriation of the structure of computer software. In the following chapter, as various types of copyrightable subject matter are taken up, we will repeatedly return to the principle that copyright does not afford protection for ideas and such kindred material as methods, processes, and systems.

§ 2.4 Procedural Considerations

Issues of fixation and originality arise both in copyright litigation and at the Copyright Office in connection with an author's request to register the copyright.[85] Section 701(d) of the 1976 Act makes registration decisions reviewable as "agency actions" under the Administrative Procedure Act.[86] Courts will usually afford considerable weight to the determination of the Register of Copyrights on these issues, and the prevailing rule is that the determinations of the Register will be reviewed under an abuse of discretion standard.[87]

In litigation, infringement defendants frequently will put into issue the question of whether a work has been adequately fixed, whether it is original, and whether the appropriated material constitutes unprotected ideas rather than protectable expression. For this reason procedural concerns such as who bears the burden of proof are significant. Generally speaking, the plaintiff in an infringement action bears the burden of proof on all elements of the prima facie case. Thus, plaintiff will bear the burden on the issues

83. Peter Pan Fabrics, Inc. v. Martin Weiner Corp., 274 F.2d 487, 489 (2d Cir. 1960).

84. Herbert Rosenthal Jewelry Corp. v. Kalpakian, 446 F.2d 738, 742 (9th Cir. 1971).

85. Indeed, because registration is a prerequisite for an infringement suit for most domestic authors, the Copyright Office will almost always have passed on the questions of fixation and originality

before the court has an opportunity to do so. See 17 U.S.C. § 411 (2000).

86. 5 U.S.C. § 101 et seq. (2000).

87. See John Muller & Co. v. New York Arrows Soccer Team, Inc., 802 F.2d 989, 990 (8th Cir. 1986); Norris Industries, Inc. v. International Tel. & Tel. Corp., 696 F.2d 918, 922 (11th Cir.), cert. denied, 464 U.S. 818, 104 S.Ct. 78, 78 L.Ed.2d 89 (1983).

of fixation, originality, and protectable expression.[88] This burden is made considerably lighter than might otherwise be the case by the current requirement that copyright registration is a prerequisite for filing an infringement suit for most copyright plaintiffs.[89] With the registration certificate in hand the plaintiff is entitled to the benefits of section 410(c) of the 1976 Act. That provision provides:

> In any judicial proceedings the certificate of a registration made before or within five years after first publication of the work shall constitute prima facie evidence of the validity of the copyright and of the facts stated in the certificate. The evidentiary weight to be accorded the certificate of a registration made thereafter shall be within the discretion of the court.

Since fixation, originality, and protectable expression are all requirements for a valid copyright, possession of a registration certificate gives the plaintiff a rebuttable presumption of validity of the work, provided the plaintiff registered within five years of publication.[90] Furthermore, even in cases where registration follows publication by more than five years, the certificate of registration will likely be afforded considerable weight within the judge's discretion. Thus, in the typical case, it falls to the defendant to produce evidence challenging the validity of the plaintiff's copyright if the defendant wishes to put that subject in issue.

For works created under the 1909 Act, infringement plaintiffs face a slightly different situation. The provision in that act which roughly corresponds to section 410 of the 1976 Act provides that the certificate "shall be admitted as prima facie evidence of the facts stated therein."[91] Unlike the 1976 Act provision, this section does not create a general presumption of validity. Instead, it speaks only of the specific facts recited in the certificate. Thus, the plaintiff's benefit from the certificate might be somewhat more narrow for a pre–1978 work.

---

88. NIMMER, COPYRIGHT § 12.11 (2002).

89. The requirement is found in 17 U.S.C. § 411 (2000). An exception is made for "Berne convention works whose country of origin is not the United States."

90. See Flick–Reedy Corp. v. Hydro–Line Mfg. Co., 351 F.2d 546, 549 (7th Cir. 1965), cert. denied, 383 U.S. 958, 86 S.Ct. 1222, 16 L.Ed.2d 301 (1966).

91. 1909 Act, § 209.

Chapter 3

THE SUBJECT MATTER OF COPY-RIGHT—SPECIFIC CATEGORIES OF PROTECTABLE WORKS

Table of Sections

After setting out the general requirements for copyrightability, section 102 of the current statute itemizes eight specific "works of authorship" that are potential subject matter of copyright. These are (1) literary works; (2) musical works; (3) dramatic works; (4) pantomimes and choreographic works; (5) pictorial, graphic, and sculptural works; (6) audiovisual works; (7) sound recordings; and (8) architectural works. In addition, section 103 of the statute indicates that "derivative works" and "compilations" are also within the subject matter of copyright.

The previous statute, the Act of 1909, provided that copyright would be extended to "all the writings of an author."[1] Because this language so closely echoes that of the Copyright Clause of the Constitution, it was assumed by some to reach to the full extent of congressional authority. Congress changed the wording to "works of authorship" in 1976 in part to clarify that it was not legislating to the outer limit of its constitutional powers.

The list of subject matter in section 102(a) of the current law is not meant to be exclusive. That statute says that the subject matter of copyright "includes" the listed materials, plainly indicating that other forms of original authorship fixed in a tangible medium of expression will qualify for copyright as well.[2] Moreover, the categories of section 102 are not mutually exclusive. There are numerous possible overlaps. For instance, a play is both a literary work and a dramatic work. In addition, the section 103 categories—derivative works and compilations—will always overlap with one of the section 102 categories. For instance, a French translation of an English novel is a derivative work, but it is also a literary work.

As you might expect, the vast majority of copyrighted works fall into the specific categories mentioned in the statute. Each of these types of copyrightable material has its own peculiarities and can pose its own problems. Some have been copyrightable subject matter since the founding of the republic, while others were added only recently.

Moreover, the category in which a work falls is not a mere formality. This classification can significantly influence the rights belonging to the owner of the copyright in that work since not all statutory rights are afforded to every type of copyrightable work.[3] For example, the proprietor of a copyright in a sound recording is not awarded the performance right,[4] and libraries enjoy greater privileges to copy literary and dramatic works than other sorts of works of authorship.[5] The Copyright Office has promulgated regulations specifying administrative classes for registration purposes, and makes determinations concerning classification for works submitted for registration.[6] In the final analysis, however, any dispute over the proper categorization of a work would be for the courts to decide.

---

1. 1909 Act, § 4.

2. The legislative history makes the point explicit: "The use of the word 'include' ... makes clear that the listing is 'illustrative and not limitative,' and that the ... categories do not necessary exhaust the scope of 'original works of authorship' that the bill is intended to protect." H.R. Rep. No. 94–1474 (94th Cong. 2d Sess.) at 53, 1976 U.S.Code Cong. & Ad. News 5659, 5666.

3. *See infra* Chapter 7.

4. 17 U.S.C. § 114.

5. 17 U.S.C. § 108.

6. *See* 37 C.F.R. § 202.3(b).

§ 3.1 Literary Works

Most people probably first think of "literary works" when they think of the subject matter of copyright. The 1976 Act defines literary works as:

> works, other than audiovisual works, expressed in words, numbers, or other verbal or numerical symbols or indicia, regardless of the nature of the material objects, such as books, periodicals, manuscripts, phonorecords, film, tapes, disks or cards, in which they are embodied.[7]

As the words of that definition indicate, the current copyright statute does not protect "books" or "magazines." Items of that sort are merely types of material objects in which a literary work can be embodied—in other words, those things are types of "copies." The literary work itself is the combination of words and numbers conceived of and fixed by the author, regardless of the form in which they may be fixed. Literary works can include works of both fact and fiction and works in both prose and poetic form.

3.1.1 Fictional Works

Fictional literary works are, of course, protected by copyright. A work of fiction is considered original, and therefore protectable, if it is expressed in an original way, even if the basic plot or theme of the work is a familiar one. Thus one is free to write a story about swashbucklers who protect their king against treachery notwithstanding that this story line is the basis for *Robin Hood*, *The Three Musketeers*, and numerous other famous works of fiction.

The reverse is also true. If an author conceives of a wholly new idea for a work of fiction, that underlying idea will not be protected against appropriation by a later author who wishes to use it. Copyright only protects the expressive elements of a work. Expression includes not merely the literal words, however, but also the detailed structure of the plot. Discerning just where the general idea of the work leaves off and the specific expression of the author begins is, as has been previously noted,[8] one of the most vexing aspects in all of copyright law.

As a general rule, the issue need only be confronted in the context of infringement litigation, where the defendant will assert that any similarities between the works relate only to unprotected ideas. This means that the court does not have to identify some precise point at which ideas shade over into expression. Instead, it only has to decide if the particular elements appropriated by the defendant fall on one side of the line or the other. That, nonetheless, can still be a daunting task. Our discussion of just how the

---

7. 17 U.S.C. § 101.   **8.** *See supra* Chapter 2.

courts have attempted to meet that challenge appears in the chapter on copyright infringement.

One recurring issue involving copyright in fictional work is the protection to be extended to the characters who appear in such works. This is merely a specific incarnation of the general idea/expression problem. Many novelists will populate a work with a large number of "generic" characters—the suave secret agent, the rumpled detective, the kindly old lady, and the like. These characters are common literary property, free for all to use. They are nothing more than mere ideas. However, if a character is sufficiently delineated, courts have been willing to extend protection to them.[9] The principle was summed up by Judge Learned Hand when he noted:

> If Twelfth Night were copyrighted, it is quite possible that a second comer might so closely imitate Sir Toby Belch or Malvolio as to infringe, but it would not be enough that for one of his characters he cast a riotous knight who kept wassail to the discomfort of the household, or a vain and foppish steward who became amorous of his mistress. These would be no more than Shakespeare's "ideas" in the play,.... It follows that the less developed the characters, the less they can be copyrighted; that is the penalty an author must bear for marking them too indistinctly.[10]

Ever since, courts have struggled to define the point at which a character becomes sufficiently delineated to warrant independent protection. In *Warner Bros. Pictures v. Columbia Broadcasting System*,[11] often referred to as the Sam Spade case, the court had to determine whether a grant to Warner Brothers of exclusive rights to make a movie version of the story *The Maltese Falcon* precluded Dashiel Hammett, the original author, from writing additional stories featuring the Sam Spade character. While the case turned, in large measure, on interpretation of the contract between the parties, the court took the opportunity to indicate when, in its opinion, a fictional character could be protected by copyright. According to the Ninth Circuit, a character would only be protected if "the character really constitutes the story being told, but if the character is only the chessman in the game of telling the story he is not within the area of the protection afforded by the copyright."[12]

---

9. *See generally* DOROTHY J. HOWELL, INTELLECTUAL PROPERTIES AND THE PROTECTION OF FICTIONAL CHARACTERS (1990); Leslie A. Kurtz, *The Independent Legal Lives of Fictional Characters*, 1986 WIS. L. REV. 429.

10. Nichols v. Universal Pictures Corp., 45 F.2d 119, 121 (2d Cir. 1930),

cert. denied, 282 U.S. 902, 51 S.Ct. 216, 75 L.Ed. 795 (1931). If the reference eludes you, *Twelfth Night* is a play by William Shakespeare.

11. 216 F.2d 945 (9th Cir.1954).

12. *Warner*, 216 F.2d at 950.

The approach of the Sam Spade case has been criticized as overly restrictive, and apparently rejected by other circuit courts of appeal.[13] For example, in *Burroughs v. MGM*,[14] the court considered whether copyright existed in the well-known character Tarzan. In reaching an affirmative result, the court stated: "Tarzan is the ape-man. He is an individual closely in tune with his jungle environment, able to communicate with animals yet able to experience human emotion. He is athletic, innocent, youthful, gentle, and strong. He is Tarzan." This analysis plainly concerns the delineation of Tarzan, rather than whether Tarzan was himself the story. This broader notion of the protection of fictional characters apart from the stories in which they appear seems the more appropriate course. Living in an era of prequels, sequels, and movie adoptions, modern readers can appreciate that fictional characters ranging from Sherlock Holmes to Superman exist beyond the reach of any individual work.

Bear in mind that the issue of protection for fictional characters can arise even though the alleged infringer does not use the same name for the character as the original author. For instance, imagine an writer who crafts an entirely original story, about a suave British secret agent, whom he calls Thomas Rogers. Rogers is also frequently referred to in the book by his code name X16. Agent X16 is cool under pressure; he uses high-tech gadgets supplied by his spy agency; he fancies martinis and fast sports cars; beautiful women are drawn to him and much of the novel digresses into his sexual exploits; and his mission is to thwart a super-villain bent on world domination. If the holders of the copyrights in the various books detailing the exploits of James Bond (also known as Agent 007) were to assert a claim of copyright infringement, the issue would be whether the attributes listed are those of a generic spy, or whether they have crossed the line and replicated a fully delineated character.

Where a fictional character has a visual appearance—as in the case of comic book characters like Mickey Mouse or Spider-Man—courts have had much less difficulty conferring protection. Unlike literary characters, where the "idea" of a cool-under-pressure spy shades into the expression of the fictional personage of James Bond, it is much easier to simply look at two drawings and decide if they resemble each other.

A dispute between two giants of the graphic novel trade, *Gaiman v. McFarlane*,[15] resulted in detailed judicial treatment of

13. *See e.g.*, Columbia Broadcasting Syst., Inc. v. DeCosta, 377 F.2d 315, 320 (1st Cir.), *cert. denied*, 389 U.S. 1007, 88 S.Ct. 565, 19 L.Ed.2d 603 (1967).

14. *Burroughs v. Metro–Goldwyn–Mayer, Inc.*, 519 F.Supp. 388 (S.D.N.Y. 1981), *aff'd*, 683 F.2d 610 (2d Cir.1982).

15. 360 F.3d 644 (7th Cir. 2004).

copyright for comic book characters. The litigation concerned Gaiman's request for a declaration that he was a co-owner of copyright in three characters appearing in the comic book series *Spawn*: "Count Nicholas Cogliostro," "Medieval Spawn," and "Angela." The first of these, Cogliostro, was as an elderly derelict who nonetheless possessed uncanny knowledge concerning Hellspawn's background and abilities. McFarlane countered by asserting that Gaiman had merely provided abstract concepts about the three characters that were ineligible for copyright protection. McFarlene further asserted that he had turned those ideas into original characters, via his distinctive illustrations and depiction in subsequent issues of *Spawn*, that were subject to a copyright that he solely owned.

The Seventh Circuit concluded that the characters were eligible for copyright and owned jointly by Gaiman and McFarlane. With respect to Cogliostro, Judge Posner explained that no copyright could be claimed for a character merely described as an unexpectedly knowledgeable old wino. But once Cogliostro was drawn, named, and give speech, the character became sufficiently distinctive so as to support copyright. The Court of Appeals stated that his "age, obviously phony title ('Count'), what he knows and says, his name, and his faintly Mosaic facial features combine to create a distinctive character. No more is required for a character copyright."

The holding in *Gaiman v. McFarlane* should be assessed within an era where fictional figures quickly transfer from one medium to another. It is now commonplace for a character who is described in a novel, using words alone, subsequently to be portrayed by an actor in a motion picture; to be the subject of a computer-based role-playing game; and to be depicted in a toy distributed with children's meals at fast food restaurants. In the absence of any contractual provisions to the contrary, the author of the novel would also own the copyright in the character in each of these "tie-ins." Given the relative ease in which the Seventh Circuit was willing to recognize the existence of a character copyright, legal issues regarding such copyrights are likely to grow more significant in the future.

3.1.2 Non–Fiction Works

The category of "literary works" includes works of non-fiction of all sorts, ranging from cookbooks to instruction manuals to catalogs to comprehensive and scholarly histories and biographies. Some of these types of non-fiction works, such as catalogs and directories, are actually forms of compilations, special types of works which are discussed further on in this chapter.[16]

---

16. *See infra* § 3.10.

Among the most common non-fiction literary works are prose works of history or biography. Such works are plainly copyrightable to the extent that they meet the requirements of fixation and originality. The copyright in such works does not, however, include protection for the facts or research revealed in the work. This is true, moreover, even if the discovery of those facts required a great deal of labor or ingenuity. Thus, if a biographer of Lincoln were to discover, after years of research in a dusty library in Springfield, Illinois, that Lincoln had held a heretofore unknown series of secret meetings with Robert E. Lee in an effort to end the Civil War, and had made disclosure of those facts the central aspect of his book about Lincoln, those facts could nonetheless be used in subsequent works without infringing any rights of the first author.[17] The justification for this approach is that the facts in question do not "originate" with the author. They are the products of research, not creative authorship. Professor Nimmer has also suggested that First Amendment concerns would be implicated if the first party to discover and publish a fact could prevent others from doing so.[18]

In a sense, of course, there are no such things as "facts." All attempts to reconstruct the past involve interpretation as well as research. Many of the most important non-fiction works go beyond merely setting out dates and figures and attempt to weave a body of factual information together into a coherent theory. In a number of cases, courts have denied copyright protection to these historical theories along with the underlying basic facts. For instance, in *Hoehling v. Universal City Studios, Inc.,*[19] Hoehling published a book entitled *Who Destroyed the Hindenburg?* in which he developed the thesis that the famous airship was destroyed by the sabotage of a member of the crew named Spehl. Sometime later, another author prepared a book about the destruction of the Hindenburg that Universal Studios eventually made into a movie. The second book and the movie both used Hoehling's theory that Spehl had been a saboteur. Nonetheless the court concluded that there was no copyright infringement because "an historical inter-

---

17. *See, e.g.,* Miller v. Universal City Studios, Inc., 650 F.2d 1365, 1369 (5th Cir.1981) ("since facts do not owe their origin to any individual, they may not be copyrighted and are part of the public domain available to every person."); Narell v. Freeman, 872 F.2d 907, 910–11 (9th Cir.1989) ("Historical facts and theories may be copied, as long as the defendant does not 'bodily appropriate' the expression of the plaintiff."). Certain earlier cases had held to the contrary, *see, e.g.,* Toksvig v. Bruce Publishing Co., 181 F.2d 664 (7th Cir.1950);

Huie v. National Broadcasting Co., 184 F.Supp. 198 (S.D.N.Y.1960). Those cases have since been repudiated.

18. NIMMER, COPYRIGHT § 2.11[E] ("Would anyone seriously suggest that the *Washington Post* was entitled to a copyright on the facts of the Watergate incident because its reporters, Woodward and Bernstein, through considerable labor, expense and ingenuity, discovered such facts?").

19. 618 F.2d 972 (2d Cir.1980).

pretation . . . is not protected by . . . copyright and can be freely used by subsequent authors."[20]

Of course, subsequent authors may not take the precise expression used by the first author and any fictional details added to a basically factual work will also be protectable.[21] On the other hand, if a non-fiction work contains quotations from historical personages or other celebrities, those are not protected by the copyright and can be reproduced by others, since the author of the work is not the originator or author of the particular quote in question. Of course, in some cases, the quoted material may still be under a copyright held by the original celebrity or other notable. In that case, the second author would need permission from that party unless he could invoke the fair use defense to excuse the copying.

Some might argue that denying protection to facts, research, and historical theory seriously undercuts incentives for authors to undertake such projects. On the other hand, readers of history and biography know that the expressive elements—the words chosen to recreate the past—are often the most memorable and distinguishing aspect of these works. Moreover, the Supreme Court has observed that leaving factual information unprotected by copyright is "neither unfair nor unfortunate. It is the means by which copyright advances the progress of science and art."[22] Consequently, limiting protection to the actual words and structure of a non-fiction work and leaving the facts and theories available for free copying by others may strike a reasonable balance between incentives to creativity and public access.

3.1.3 Computer Programs

From their very first appearance, computer programs proved to be a controversial and troublesome subject area in the law of copyright. Some of the issues that bedeviled the courts and Congress have been resolved, but others continue to percolate. In order to understand both the historic and the current controversies, it is necessary to know just a bit about computer programs.

Programs are sets of instructions for a computer. The 1976 Act defines a computer program as "a set of statements or instructions

---

20. *Hoehling*, 618 F.2d at 979. *See also* Rosemont Enterprises, Inc. v. Random House, Inc., 366 F.2d 303, 310 (2d Cir.1966), *cert. denied* 385 U.S. 1009, 87 S.Ct. 714, 17 L.Ed.2d 546 ("We . . . cannot subscribe to the view that an author is absolutely precluded from saving time and effort by referring to and relying upon prior published material. . . . It is just such wasted effort that the proscription against the copyright of ideas and facts . . . are designed to prevent.").

21. *See* De Acosta v. Brown, 146 F.2d 408 (2d Cir.1944) (Fictionalized aspects in generally factual screenplay about the life of Clara Barton held protectable and infringed).

22. Feist Publications, Inc. v. Rural Telephone Service Co., 499 U.S. 340, 350, 111 S.Ct. 1282, 113 L.Ed.2d 358 (1991).

to be used directly or indirectly in a computer to bring about a certain result."[23] Typically, programs are first written in one of any number of "high-level" programming languages, like "C" or "Javascript" or "HTML." In this form the program will consist of several cryptic but intelligible phrases, like "SET X=Y+Z" or "IF X > Y THAN GO TO LINE 250." Programs of this sort are said to be written in "source code." Computers cannot directly use source code instructions since computers cannot read English, even the garbled English of these phrases.

Computers really only understand pulses of electricity and their entire vocabulary is limited to the concepts of "on" and "off." This means that, in order to be usable, the program must be converted to a binary form consisting of strings of ones and zeros with the ones symbolizing "on" and the zeros symbolizing "off." Programs in this form are said to be written in machine language, or "object code." The process of converting source code into object code is known as "compilation." Compilation is usually accomplished by running the source code version of a program through a computer using software known, not surprisingly, as a "compiler."

Computer programs can be fixed in a wide variety of media. Either source code or object code versions can be written out in long hand or printed out on paper. The object code can also be stored on CDs, tape, flash drives, or other magnetic or digital media. In addition, programs can also be embedded in the silicon of computer chips. When you buy a computer, some software is typically sold as an integral part of the machine since it is included on the chips inside the computer.[24] Other software that you wish to use must be purchased separately and is typically distributed on disks.

It is also important to note that there are two broad categories of computer programs. First are the application programs. These are the programs that allow you directly to use your computer. They include things like word processors and spreadsheets, personal and business accounting programs, and a huge variety of games. Rather distinct from these application programs are the "operating systems." These are the programs that control the internal operations of a computer and enable it to interact with particular application programs. The Windows program developed by the Microsoft Company is, of course, one such operating system.

Starting in the mid-sixties, long prior to the adoption of the 1976 Act, the Copyright Office began accepting computer programs

---

23. 17 U.S.C. § 101.

24. Indeed, when you buy almost any durable consumer product these days it will include some software-on-a-chip, whether the product is an automobile, a clothes drier, or a garage door opener.

for registration as copyrightable works, but doing so under circumstances that left the significance of the action unclear. With the adoption of the 1976 Act, the ambiguity seemed to be eliminated. Computer programs, after all, fall within the literal language defining "literary works" in the 1976 Act since they plainly are "expressed in words, numbers or other verbal or numerical symbols or indicia...."[25] Moreover, Congress noted in the legislative history accompanying the 1976 statute that "literary works ... includes computer data bases and computer programs to the extent that they incorporate authorship in the programmer's expression of original ideas, as distinguished from the ideas themselves."[26]

Notwithstanding these legislative developments, Congress continued to harbor some uncertainties as to the workability of using copyright law to protect software. Consequently, Congress established the National Commission on New Technological Uses of Copyrighted Works, or CONTU, in 1974 to consider the appropriate scope of any copyright protection for software along with a variety of other issues.[27] CONTU submitted its final report in 1978, concluding that copyright law was indeed the appropriate legal mechanism to be used for software protection.

In response to the CONTU conclusions Congress ultimately adopted the Computer Software Copyright Act of 1980.[28] That statute added a definition of computer programs to the copyright statute,[29] and also revised section 117 of the statute to provide limited exceptions to the exclusive right of a software copyright owner to make copies of the program.[30] The legislative history of this 1980 statute along with these two provisions reflected Congress's final conclusion to leave programs under the ambit of copyright rather than to devise some alternative, *sui generis* form of protection for them.

This brief history might suggest that the post–1980 copyright status of software has been non-controversial, but nothing could be further from the truth. Controversy soon emerged over a variety of issues. Among the first problems to confront the courts were claims that Congress intended only to protect programs in their source code form, and/or that Congress only intended to protect application programs, not operating systems. Litigants, and some commentators, advanced several arguments in favor of these distinctions. First, they noted that object code versions of software, unlike most

---

25. 17 U.S.C. § 101.

26. H.R. Rep. No. 94–1476, 94th Cong. 2d Sess. 54 (1973).

27. Pub. L. 93–573, 88 Stat. 1873 (Title II).

28. Pub. L. 96–517 § 10, 94 Stat. 3015 (1980).

29. "A 'computer program' is a set of statements or instructions to be used directly or indirectly in a computer in order to bring about a certain result." 17 U.S.C. § 101.

30. *See infra* Chapter 6.

copyrighted works, are not intelligible to human users. In addition, unlike all other forms of copyrighted subject matter, the author's expression in object code is not meant ever to be communicated to human users. Even music on a compact disc, which is not immediately perceptible by you when you buy the disc, will communicate the very work that was composed and recorded by the musicians involved when you eventually play it on your CD player. When you buy software, you will never encounter the program as written by the programmers. You may play a video game or use a word-processor *generated* by that program, but that, it was argued, is not the same as experiencing the actual work as a series of commands or a series of ones and zeros.

These arguments were rejected in a number of cases decided in the early 1980s, shortly after adoption of the Software Copyright Act. One of the most notable of these is *Apple Computer Inc. v. Franklin Computer Corp.*[31] Franklin, the defendant in this case, wanted to manufacture computers that would run software originally written for Apple computers. In other words, it wanted to build an Apple-compatible clone. In order to do so, it copied the object code version of Apple's operating system software from computer chips contained within Apple computers. Without the Apple operating system, the Franklin machine would not be able to run software that was designed for Apple computers and thus would not be marketable.

Given the fairly clear copying in this case, Franklin had to argue that the Apple operating system was not copyrightable. To do so, it argued that programs in object code and operating systems ought not to be copyrightable. In addition, it argued that no copyright could exist in a program embedded on a computer chip because the chips were "machine parts." The court rejected all three contentions. The fact that object code is unintelligible to human readers did not affect copyrightability since the 1976 statute specifically applies to works fixed in a form that can be perceived "with the aid of a machine...." In this regard, *Franklin* was merely following earlier decisions that had held to the same effect.[32] The court also held with little discussion that a computer chip was a perfectly adequate medium in which to fix a computer program.

The most novel aspect of the case was the argument over copyrightability for an operating system. Franklin claimed that the operating system for a type of computer was a "process," "system," or "method of operation," and thus not eligible for copyright under the express terms of section 102(b) of the 1976 Act. The Third

31. 714 F.2d 1240 (3d Cir.1983).
32. *See e.g.*, Williams Elec., Inc. v. Artic Int'l, Inc., 685 F.2d 870 (3d Cir.
1982); Stern Elec., Inc. v. Kaufman, 669 F.2d 852 (2d Cir.1982).

Circuit rejected the argument, relying in part on policy and in part on statutory language. It noted that the statutory definition of computer programs was all-inclusive, making no distinction between application programs and operating systems. Moreover, it stressed that Apple "does not seek to copyright the method which instructs the computer to perform its operating functions but only the instructions themselves. The method would be protected, if at all, by the patent law ..."[33]

Nor was the court impressed by the related argument that protection of the operating system would be equivalent to granting copyright in an "idea." Since Franklin had taken not merely the idea of Apple-compatibility, but the actual expression contained within Apple's program, this argument effectively invoked the merger doctrine discussed in the previous chapter.[34] The court recognized that this would only be true if Apple's operating system program was the only way to "express" the idea of Apple compatibility. "If other programs can be written or created which perform the same function as an Apple's operating system program, then that program is an expression of the idea and hence copyrightable."[35] Thus the court rejected the argument that operating systems were per se uncopyrightable. It did, however, remand for further findings on that question.

The *Apple* case involved questions concerning copyright protection for the literal code of a computer program, and it clearly established that literal program code was copyrightable regardless of the form in which it was written, the function it was to perform, or the medium in which it was fixed. It did not consider, however, the degree of protection to be afforded to the non-literal elements of computer programs. Just as a novelist may claim protection not only for his or her words, but for the details of plot structure, a software author may seek to protect various aspects of a program beyond the actual code.

Courts have given considerable attention to two types of non-literal software attributes. The first of these is the "structure, sequence and organization" of a program, sometimes referred to as the "SSO." For example, complex programs often have sub-components called modules, that are designed to interact with each other in specified ways. The organizations of these inter-modular relationships would be one aspect of SSO. In the 1986 case of *Whelan Assocs. Inc. v. Jaslow Dental Laboratory*,[36] the Third Circuit held that copyright protection for software extended beyond the literal code of a program to embrace the SSO. In reaching that result,

33. *Apple*, 714 F.2d at 1251.

34. *See supra* § 2.3.

35. *Apple*, 714 F.2d at 1253.

36. 797 F.2d 1222 (3d Cir.1986).

however, the court suggested that the sole idea of a computer program is the purpose the program seeks to achieve. In *Whelan* that was "to aid the business operations of a dental laboratory." According to the Third Circuit, anything more specific in the program would be considered protectable expression. This approach is quite sweeping in the amount of protection it grants to non-literal elements of computer programs, and the case has been criticized by various academic commentators for providing over-broad protection to software.[37]

More recent cases have attempted to articulate a more precise boundary line between protected SSO and the unprotected ideas of a program. In *Computer Associates Int'l, Inc. v. Altai, Inc.*,[38] the court faulted the *Whelan* opinion for an insufficiently sophisticated understanding of software, and articulated a test to distinguish between protectable and unprotectable components of a computer program, which it labeled the "abstraction-filtration" test. Citing *Baker v. Selden*,[39] the court pointed out that not only are the underlying ideas of the work not part of the owner's copyright, but that aspects of a work which must necessarily be used as an incident to employing those ideas are also unprotected. To give full scope to that doctrine the court set out the following approach:

> [A] court would first break down the allegedly infringed program into its constituent structural parts. Then, by examining each of these parts for such things as incorpo-rated ideas, expression that is necessarily incidental to those ideas, and elements that are taken from the public domain, a court would then be able to sift out all non-protectable material. Left with a kernel, or possible ker-nels, of creative expression after following this process of elimination, the court's last step would be to compare this material with the structure of an allegedly infringing pro-gram.[40]

The first portion of the process described by this language—the breaking down into structural parts—is the "abstraction." The examination referred to in the second sentence is the "filtration." Only the "kernel" or "golden nugget"[41] of material left after this

---

37. The Nimmer treatise notes that the "crucial flaw in this reasoning is that it assumes that only one 'idea,' in copyright law terms, underlies any computer program, and that once a separa-ble idea can be identified, everything else must be expression.... [T]he broad purpose that the program serves ... is *an* idea. Other elements of the pro-gram's structure and design, however, may also constitute ideas for copyright

purposes." Nimmer, Copyright § 13.03[F] (2002).

38. 982 F.2d 693 (2d Cir.1992).

39. 101 U.S. 99, 25 L.Ed. 841 (1879). *See supra* § 3.3.

40. *Computer Associates*, 982 F.2d at 706.

41. Elsewhere in the opinion the *Computer Associates* court notes "[o]nce a court has sifted out all elements of the

process is protected by copyright. While some commentators have criticized this test, not least of all for being vague, other federal circuits have endorsed it.[42]

The second, and related, issue concerning protection of non-literal elements of software that has received judicial attention is the problem of protection for the "user interface" of computer programs. A program's user interface is essentially its "look and feel," in particular such elements as menu structures, layouts, text prompts, and the use of particular key combinations or mouse clicks to accomplish particular tasks. Thus, the fact that a word processing program will indicate in the lower right hand corner of the screen the number of inches the cursor sits from the left margin is a part of the user interface of that word processor, as is the fact that pressing the F6 key will permit you to mark text in **boldface** type.

In *Lotus Development Corp. v. Borland International, Inc.*,[43] the Court of Appeals for the First Circuit considered whether a software user interface was subject to copyright protection. The court specifically considered the command menu hierarchy of the then hugely popular Lotus 1–2–3 spreadsheet program. Accused infringer Borland had copied the Lotus menu tree so that former Lotus users could readily transition to Borland's competing Quattro software. The district court had held that the Lotus designers had made expressive choices in choosing and arranging the program's command terms and concluded that the command hierarchy was consequently a copyrightable aspect of the program.

On appeal, the First Circuit disagreed, concluding that the Lotus commands were a "method of operation" within the meaning of § 102(b), and therefore not copyrightable subject matter.[44] Analogizing the Lotus menu command hierarchy to the buttons on a VCR machine, the Court of Appeals concluded that just because the functions of the Lotus program were arranged and labeled did not make them copyrightable expression. At best the menu command hierarchy was structured so that individuals could quickly learn and efficiently use the Lotus program—matters outside the scope of

allegedly infringed program that are 'ideas' or are dictated by efficiency or external factors, or taken from the public domain, there may remain a core of protectable expression. In terms of a work's copyright value, this is the golden nugget." 982 F.2d at 710.

42. See e.g., Sega Enterprises Ltd. v. Accolade, Inc., 977 F.2d 1510, 1525 (9th Cir.1992) ("the Second Circuit's approach is an appropriate one"); Atari Games Corp. v. Nintendo of America,

Inc., 975 F.2d 832, 839 (Fed.Cir.1992); Gates Rubber Co. v. Bando Chemical Ind., Ltd., 9 F.3d 823 (10th Cir.1993). The Nimmer treatise on copyright law also endorses the same approach under the name "successive filtering." See NIMMER, COPYRIGHT § 13.03[F] (2002).

43. 49 F.3d 807 (1st Cir.1995), *aff'd by an equally divided Court*, 516 U.S. 233, 116 S.Ct. 804, 133 L.Ed.2d 610 (1996).

44. *See supra* § 2.3.

protection of the copyright laws, at least since the Supreme Court decision in *Baker v. Selden.*[45]

Judge Boudin's concurring opinion in *Lotus v. Borland* suggested additional policy issues at stake in the decision. Computer users had invested considerable time and effort, Judge Boudin recognized, in order to obtain the expertise needed to use Lotus 1–2–3. If that investment could not be transferred, then users would be discouraged from switching even to superior spreadsheet software. The effect of providing robust copyright protection for user interfaces that control the operation of a program would be to lock consumers into potentially inferior products—an aim wholly antithetical to the goals of the copyright system.

This legal and policy discussion of *Lotus v. Borland* does suggest that where elements of the user interface are not necessary to operate a program, copyright protection may be appropriate. The content of help screens, for example, or an animated figure offering suggestions during the operation of the program, such as an incredibly annoying paper clip that raps on the screen whenever it wants to get your attention, would not seem to bring the concerns of the *Lotus v. Borland* court into play and therefore ought to be subject to the copyright laws.

Yet another potential controversy concerning the copyrightability of computer software is the question of who owns the copyright in a "computer-generated work." For instance, software can be imagined which would permit a computer to generate elaborate works of music without any human input. The difficulty in such cases is whether the work itself qualifies as a "work of authorship" if it was not created through direct human involvement, and if so, who should be considered the author. While there is little law thus far on these problems, the CONTU Report suggested that such works should be protected and that the copyright owner should be the person using the program, rather than the author of the underlying program which generates the contested output. That is also the solution that has been adopted under British law.[46]

As the foregoing review illustrates, computer programs have proven to be controversial subjects under the copyright law because

---

45. 101 U.S. 99, 25 L.Ed. 841 (1879).

46. *See* Copyright, Designs and Patents Act, 1988, ch.48 § 9(3) (United Kingdom) ("In the case of a literary, dramatic, musical or other artistic work which is computer-generated, the author shall be taken to be the person by whom the arrangements necessary for the creation for the work are undertaken.").

For a thorough discussion of the issues involved in the copyrightability of computer-generated works, *see* Arthur R. Miller, *Copyright Protection for Computer Programs, Databases and Computer–Generated Works: Is Anything New Since CONTU?*, 106 HARV. L. REV. 977, 1042–72 (1993). *See also,* Pamela Samuelson, *Allocating Ownership Rights in Computer–Generated Works*, 47 U. PITT. L. REV. 1185, 1187 (1986).

they have utilitarian features uncommon for most other works. They don't just instruct users in how to perform tasks, they actually perform those tasks by themselves. Nonetheless, they are creative products of human intellect and it would appear that the courts are succeeding in applying existing doctrines such as the idea/expression distinction and the merger rule to strike a proper balance between protection and productive borrowing.

Another notable development concerning computer-related works was the advent of the Semiconductor Chip Protection Act (SCPA).[47] This legislation is housed in Chapter 9 of Title 17 of the U.S. Code, next to the 1976 Copyright Act but not formally part of it.[48] You will find a full discussion of this *sui generis* scheme of protection in section 7.6 of this volume. A few summary comments are in order here, however, to round out our discussion of copyright protection for software.

Congress enacted SCPA in response to the concerns of manufacturers of semiconductor chip products.[49] These products consist of thousands of miniaturized electrical circuits housed on small pieces of semiconductor material, such as silicon. In combination, these circuits are engineered to function as microprocessors, memories, and other devices. Once limited to computers and other expensive machinery, chips are now employed in automobiles, cameras, and all manner of common household appliances. The integrated circuit layouts on which chips are based are expensive to design but, thanks to a process known as photolithography, quite easy to copy.

Existing forms of intellectual property did not present a good fit with integrated circuit layouts. Because integrated circuit layouts are functional, utilitarian products, the copyright law was not a suitable form of protection. In addition, functional inventions must exceed the abilities of skilled artisans in order to be patented.[50] Although integrated circuit layouts are sophisticated products that are difficult to design, they nonetheless may be considered obvious variations of known circuit layouts.[51]

With neither the copyright law nor the patent law applicable, Congress came up with a unique and stand-alone scheme of protection. The SCPA creates a 10–year term for protection of integrated circuit layouts, provides exclusive rights to proprietors to reproduce

---

47. Pub. L. No. 98–260, 98 Stat. 3335 (1984).

48. 17 U.S.C. §§ 901–914.

49. *See* Leon Radomsky, *Sixteen Years After the Passage of the U.S. Semiconductor Chip Protection Act: Is International Protection Working?*, 15 BERKELEY TECH. L.J. 1049 (2000).

50. *See* ROGER E. SCHECHTER & JOHN R. THOMAS, PRINCIPLES OF PATENT LAW (2004), specifically Chapter 5.

51. *See, e.g.,* Carl A. Kukkonen, III, *The Need to Abolish Registration for Integrated Circuit Topographies Under TRIPS*, 38 IDEA 105, 107 (1997).

these layouts and manufacture chips embodying them, and allows others to reverse engineer the layouts to analyze or evaluate them. In order to obtain protection, chip designers must register the work with the Copyright Office, deposit four chips embodying the mask work, and submit drawings or plots of each layer of the mask work.

§ 3.2 Musical Works

The second category of work of authorship specifically itemized in section 102 are "musical works, including any accompanying words." Although there is no statutory definition of "musical works" in the act, the Copyright Office has defined music as "a succession of pitches or rhythms, or both, usually in some definite pattern."[52] Musical works typically consist of combinations of melodies, harmonies, and rhythms. Courts rarely find sufficient originality in the rhythm of a work to warrant protection because, as one court explained, it "is simply the tempo in which the composition is written. It is the background for the melody. There is only a limited amount of tempos; these appear to have been long since exhausted; originality of rhythm is a rarity, if not an impossibility."[53] The requisite originality of a musical work is therefore most often found in the melody.[54] Because of the constraints involved in writing music, courts find that musical works lack the requisite originality somewhat more frequently than is true for other categories of works.

Of course, musical works must be "fixed" in order to be protected. In *White–Smith Music Pub. Co. v. Apollo Co.*[55] the Supreme Court considered the alleged infringement of musical compositions based on defendant's reproduction of those works in player piano rolls. The songs at issue were protected by copyright, and had unauthorized copying of the sheet music occurred there would have been no question of infringement. In the case of the musical compositions encoded on a piano roll, however, the Court was troubled by the fact that one could not readily deduce the tune from visual examination of the piano roll itself. The Court therefore required "a written or printed record in intelligible notation," before it would find that defendant had made a "copy" of the plaintiff's protected songs. Because piano rolls could not be read by the naked eye, the Court denied relief.

52. COMPENDIUM II OF COPYRIGHT OFFICE PRACTICES § 402 (1984).

53. Northern Music Corp. v. King Record Distrib. Co., 105 F.Supp. 393, 400 (S.D.N.Y.1952).

54. *Id.* ("It is in the melody of the composition—or the arrangement of notes or tones that originality must be found. It is the arrangement or succession of musical notes, which are the finger prints of the composition and establish its identity.").

55. 209 U.S. 1, 28 S.Ct. 319, 52 L.Ed. 655 (1908).

This rule effectively meant that a musical composition could not be protected until it was reduced to the form of sheet music, and that was the rule that prevailed under the 1909 Act. Congress, however, wisely overruled the *White–Smith* doctrine when it enacted the 1976 Act. It is now clear that fixation on tape or compact discs is perfectly sufficient under the law, despite the fact that one cannot visibly interpret the music by looking at the tape or disc.

The copyright in a musical work includes both the music and the lyrics, if any. Use of either the words alone or the music alone are just as much forbidden as would be use of the words and music together.[56] While much important music is in the public domain—such as the vast body of works by composers such as Beethoven and Mozart—it is worth noting that an original "arrangement" of a musical work[57] will be separately copyrightable as a derivative work. Thus there may be a number of versions of Beethoven's Fifth Symphony in existence, each of which is independently copyrightable as a separate arrangement of that symphony.

§ 3.3 Dramatic Works

Dramatic works, including any accompanying music, are protectable works under the 1976 Act.[58] The statute does not define "dramatic works" because the Congress felt that the concept was well settled under previous law.[59] Indeed, the 1909 Act did not contain a definition of dramatic works either. The Copyright Office has promulgated its own definition of dramatic works to guide it in making registration decisions. It provides that:

> A dramatic composition is one that portrays a story by means of dialog or acting and is intended to be performed. It represents all or a substantial portion of the action as actually occurring, rather than merely being narrated or described. . . . If the narrator is to devise or improvise his or her own action, the dramatic content is not fixed and thus the work is not a drama.[60]

---

56. *See, e.g., Mills Music, Inc. v. Arizona,* 187 USPQ 22 (D.Ariz.1975).

57. The Copyright Office defines an arrangement as "a work that results from the addition of new harmony to a preexisting work." *Compendium II of Copyright Office Practices* § 408.1 (1984). Harmony, in turn, is defined as "the combination, simultaneous, or nearly so, of different pitches. These tones are spaced at certain prescribed distances from one another in related progressions." *Id.* at § 403.1.

58. See, e.g., Mills Music, Inc. v. Arizona, 187 USPQ 22 (D.Ariz.1975).

59. H.R. Rep. No. 94–1476, 94th Cong. 2d Sess. 53 (1973).

60. COMPENDIUM II OF COPYRIGHT OFFICE PRACTICES § 431 (1984). The compendium goes on to itemize various features that are characteristic of drama, namely plot, characters, dialog, and directions for action. *Id.* § 432.

In resolving whether a primitive film version of *Ben Hur* was a "dramatization" of the book of the same name, Justice Holmes gave us another, more pithy definition of drama. "The essence of the matter ... is ... that we see the event or story lived."[61] Professor Goldstein has suggested that these definitions may be unduly narrow in their insistence upon a story. He notes that non-narrative forms of drama are widely recognized as part of the dramatic arts by contemporary audiences and thus he advocates a definition including any work "in which performed actions, speech, or incident, or all three, convey theme, thoughts or character to an audience."[62]

Thus stage plays, screenplays, and teleplays are all examples of typical dramatic works, as are opera and operettas, along with their accompanying music. Of course all of these works also fall within the definition of literary works, as they are expressed, at least partially, in words.[63] There can be similar overlap with the "musical works" category for those dramatic works that contain musical portions such as a Broadway musical, and with the "audio-visual works" category for dramatic works captured on film. For clarity's sake, therefore, other sections of the statute occasionally refer to "nondramatic literary works" and "nondramatic musical works" when drama is meant to be excluded.[64]

The categorization of a work as "dramatic" or not is significant in determining the applicability of certain statutory limitations on the exclusive rights of a copyright owner. For example, certain limitations upon the performance right apply only to *non*-dramatic literary or musical works.[65] The 1976 Act also establishes a compulsory license that only applies to *non*-dramatic musical works.[66] This so-called "mechanical license" allows licensees to create copies of a recorded song in which they do not hold a copyright. As well, performing rights societies such as ASCAP and BMI confine the scope of the licenses they grant to nondramatic performances of works.

Although original dramatic works as a whole are protected by copyright, individual stock scenes, jokes, and gags are not by themselves copyrightable subject matter. Under a rule usually called the "scenes a faire" doctrine "sequences of events which normally follow from a common theme,"[67] are not protectable

---

61. Kalem Co. v. Harper Bros., 222 U.S. 55, 61, 32 S.Ct. 20, 56 L.Ed. 92 (1911).

62. 1 PAUL GOLDSTEIN, COPYRIGHT § 2.9.1 at p. 140 (1989).

63. *See supra* § 3.1.

64. For instance certain sections providing exceptions to the right to per-

form a work are limited to nondramatic literary and musical works. *See* 17 U.S.C. § 110(2),(3),(4) and (8).

65. *See, e.g.,* 17 U.S.C. § 110(3).

66. 17 U.S.C. § 115.

67. Reyher v. Children's Television Workshop, 533 F.2d 87, 91 (2d Cir.), *cert. denied* 429 U.S. 980, 97 S.Ct. 492,

elements of a dramatic work. Thus, in *Walker v. Time Life Films, Inc.*,[68] the court considered whether the movie *Fort Apache: The Bronx* infringed the copyright in a book entitled *Fort Apache*. Both the book and the movie concerned the trials and tribulations of New York City police officers working in the 41st precinct of the South Bronx. In refusing to find infringement, the court remarked, "[e]lements such as drunks, prostitutes, vermin and derelict cars would appear in any realistic work about the work of policemen in the south Bronx. These similarities therefore are unprotectable as 'scenes a faire,' that is, scenes that necessarily result from the choice of a setting or situation."[69] While not a glowing endorsement of life in the South Bronx, this analysis is both widely accepted and, in our view, sound. It would surely hinder subsequent authors if they could only portray the South Bronx as populated by the sober, the law abiding, and the chaste.[70]

General plot outlines of dramatic works may also be denied copyright protection through application of the idea/expression principle. While the actual details of a dramatic work like *West Side Story* may not be appropriated without permission, the general idea of the work—young lovers who belong to opposing groups and come to grief because of the group conflict—is freely available for others to use. As we have noted repeatedly elsewhere in this volume, deciding just where the line falls between general plot outline and expressive detail is, of course, a vexing and uncertain process. Nonetheless, it is well established as an abstract proposition that the copyright in a dramatic work only covers the expressive elements of that work.

§ 3.4   Pantomimes and Choreographic Works

Although the current copyright statute explicitly mentions pantomimes and choreographic works as a category of protectable subject matter,[71] it does not define those terms. According to the legislative history, the omission was deliberate because the terms have settled, generally accepted meanings.[72] The Copyright Office has, however, defined each of these terms for its own purposes in handling applications for copyright registration. It defines a pantomime as:

50 L.Ed.2d 588 (1976). *See generally* Leslie A. Kurtz, *Copyright: The Scenes A Faire Doctrine*, 41 FLA. L. REV. 79 (1989).

68. 784 F.2d 44 (2d Cir.1986).

69. *Walker*, 784 F.2d at 50.

70. We are, perhaps, being too harsh. There is some evidence that the South Bronx has improved markedly since the time of the *Fort Apache* era. *See, e.g.*, JILL JONNES, SOUTH BRONX RISING: THE RISE, FALL AND RESURRECTION OF AN AMERICAN CITY (Fordham University Press, 2002).

71. 17 U.S.C.A. § 102(a)(4).

72. H.R. Rep. No. 94–1476, 94th Cong. 2d Sess. 53 (1973).

[T]he art of imitating or acting out situations, characters or some other events with gestures and body movement. Mime is included under this category. Pantomimes need not tell a story or be presented before an audience to be protected by copyright.[73]

Choreography is defined quite similarly, as:

[T]he composition and arrangement of dance movements and patterns, and is usually intended to be accompanied by music. Dance is static and kinetic successions of bodily movement in certain rhythmic and spacial relationships. Choreographic works need not tell a story in order to be protected by copyright.[74]

Prior to the Copyright Act of 1976, U.S. copyright statutes made no explicit reference to either pantomime or choreography. Nonetheless, since a very large number of works of this sort are dramatic in nature, there is considerable overlap with the "dramatic works" category and protection for works of this type that could be labeled "dramatic" was available under earlier statutes.[75] On the other hand, protection for abstract dance would be problematic at best under the 1909 law. Professor Nimmer observes in his treatise that the inclusion of the separate category of pantomime and choreographic works in the current statute implies that non-dramatic renditions of this sort are now also eligible for protection,[76] and that view is reflected in the administrative definitions quoted above which note that the works "need not tell a story." Case law dealing with works of choreography and pantomime is meager.

Of course pantomime and choreography, like all other works of authorship, are only protected when they are original. Thus, while non-dramatic dance steps generally qualify for copyright protection, the legislative history makes it clear that " 'choreographic works' do not include social dance steps and simple routines."[77] Thus one could not claim copyright for the waltz or the tango. One can, however, combine social dance steps in an original fashion and the resulting work would be copyrightable.

Pantomimes and choreographic works must also be "fixed in a tangible medium of expression" in order to qualify for copyright protection. Fixation might be in the form of a motion picture of the

73. COMPENDIUM II OF COPYRIGHT OF-FICE PRACTICES § 460.01 (1984).

74. *Id.* at § 450.01

75. *See, e.g.* 37 C.F.R. § 202 (1959), which provided that "choreographic works of a dramatic character" would be eligible for copyright registration. *See also* Kalem Co. v. Harper Bros., 222 U.S. 55, 61, 32 S.Ct. 20, 56 L.Ed. 92 (1911),

where Justice Holmes noted that "[i]t would be impossible to deny the title of drama to pantomime as played by masters of the art."

76. NIMMER, COPYRIGHT § 2.07[B] (2002).

77. H.R. Rep. No. 94–1476, at 54 (1976).

dance or pantomime, in the form of a detailed verbal description, or in the form of special choreographic notation which can be used to record the movements of a dance. Any other fixation acceptable under the statute would suffice for these works as well. The form of fixation need not rigidly specify every single movement of the dance. The Copyright Office takes the position that "registration will not be refused simply because there is room for improvisation, or because some improvisation is intended."[78]

§ 3.5   Pictorial, Graphic, and Sculptural Works

The current copyright statute defines pictorial, graphic, and sculptural works as "two-dimensional and three-dimensional works of fine, graphic and applied art, photographs, prints and art reproductions, maps, globes, charts, diagrams, models, and technical drawings, including architectural plans."[79] The range of works covered by this statutory category is quite broad, reaching from the most sophisticated works of fine art to such things as the labels used on various types of consumer goods. Regardless of the type of work at issue, artistic merit is not a requirement for protection. Under the long-standing principle of artistic non-discrimination, neither the courts nor the Copyright Office will deny protection to a work merely because they believe it to be "ugly" or "commercial" or "simplistic."[80] Several types of works in this category deserve special comment.

Maps are one of the many types of works subsumed under the heading of pictorial and graphic works. They have been included as a category of copyrightable subject matter since the very first American copyright law was adopted in 1790, evidencing their importance to the exploration and settlement of the then undeveloped regions of the United States. Much of the content of the typical map is not, however, protected by the copyright. For instance, the place names indicated cannot be monopolized by the first cartographer to prepare a map, and subsequent authors have the right to use those names without any fear of infringement. The key to originality in a map, and hence the key to copyrightability, tends to be the selection of the materials to be included. While there are some cases holding that a map cannot be sufficiently original for copyright purposes unless the author has made direct observation of the geographic features depicted,[81] that view is now widely regarded as unduly restrictive. A cartographer who inspects

---

78. COMPENDIUM II OF COPYRIGHT OFFICE PRACTICES § 450.07 (1984).

79. 17 U.S.C. § 101.

80. Bleistein v. Donaldson Lithographing Co., 188 U.S. 239, 23 S.Ct. 298, 47 L.Ed. 460 (1903).

81. See Amsterdam v. Triangle Publications, Inc., 189 F.2d 104 (3d Cir. 1951).

a variety of textual sources and then selects and arranges the data obtained from them in order to prepare a wholly new map has plainly created an original work of authorship notwithstanding the absence of direct observation of the terrain.[82]

Another type of work falling within the scope of "pictorial" is photographs. Because photographs are produced with the aid of a machine, and because they typically capture some existing reality, like scenery or the image of a group of people, one might doubt whether there is sufficient originality in photographs to justify copyrightability. In *Burrow–Giles Lithographic Co. v. Sarony*,[83] the Supreme Court confronted the issue of whether a photographic portrait could qualify as copyright-protected material. The statute then in effect expressly listed photographs as copyrightable subject matter, but the defendant argued that this provision exceeded the constitutional power of Congress because photographs could not be considered "writings" of "authors" as required by the relevant constitutional clause. The Court rejected that argument and found sufficient authorship in the photographer's posing of the subject, selection of costume and accessories, and arrangement of lighting.

The more recent opinion of the District Court for the Southern District of New York in *Mannion v. Coors Brewing Co.* provides a thoughtful discussion of copyright in photographs.[84] Judge Kaplan identified three paths for a photograph to be considered original within the meaning of the copyright law: rendition, timing, and creation of the subject. Originality in rendition derives from the features of the photograph that result from the photographer's decision concerning film, camera, lens, light, filters, developing techniques, and other options. Most photographs are eligible for copyright in this respect. But not all: Judge Kaplan's earlier opinion in *The Bridgeman Art Library, Ltd. v. Corel Corp.* provides one such example. At issue there were photographs that, through technical skill and effort, were "slavish copies" of public domain works of art. Because these photographs were akin to a photocopy, they failed to meet the modest standard of originality and were ineligible for copyright.

With respect to timing, originality derived from the photographer being in the right place at the right time. One of the more notable cases is this respect is *Time, Inc. v. Bernard Geis Associates*,[85] a district court opinion which held the famous Zapruder film

---

82. Cases rejecting or questioning the direct observation rule include United States v. Hamilton, 583 F.2d 448 (9th Cir.1978); Andrien v. Southern Ocean County Chamber of Commerce, 927 F.2d 132 (3d Cir.1991). *See generally* the discussion on compilations in § 3.10 below.

83. 111 U.S. 53, 4 S.Ct. 279, 28 L.Ed. 349 (1884).

84. 377 F.Supp.2d 444 (S.D.N.Y. 2005).

85. 293 F.Supp. 130 (S.D.N.Y. 1968).

of the the Kennedy assassination to be protected by copyright. Finally, a photograph may be original to the extent the photographer created the scene or subject to be photographed. The photograph of the 27–year–old Oscar Wilde, held to be eligible for copyright by the Supreme Court in the *Burrow–Giles Lithographic Co. v. Sarony* case discussed above, falls into this category. It was also on the ground of "creation of the subject" that the court in *Mannion v. Coors* held that a photograph of basketball player Kevin Garnett, posing with a cocked head, dressed in athletic clothing, and wearing flashy jewelry, was protected by copyright.

Considerably more complex issues of copyrightability are raised by works of "applied art." This subcategory encompasses "all original pictorial, graphic, and sculptural works that are intended to be or have been embodied in useful articles, regardless of factors such as mass production, commercial exploitation, and the potential availability of design patent protection."[86] In other words, these are works that have an artistic or attractive appearance, but that also have a practical purpose. Examples might include such items as candlesticks, salt and pepper shakers, lamps, ash trays, stylized kitchen appliances, and the like. The reason these items pose difficulties is that copyright protection does not extend to the utilitarian features of a work.

The policy justification for denying protection to utilitarian works flows from the very nature of copyright. Copyright protection attaches automatically. Under the present statute, protection arises as soon as the work is fixed in a tangible medium of expression. Under the 1909 Act the protection generally arose upon publication with notice. There is no requirement of government examination of the "worth" of the creation before copyright protection becomes available. This is exactly opposite of the approach used in patent law, where no government protection is available until a patent examiner has determined if the proposed invention meets the statutory standards. If useful objects could be protected by copyright, technology might be withdrawn from the public domain, hindering the commercial activities of others without affording the public the benefit—such as disclosure—that the patent statute seeks to secure.

For instance, assume that a manufacturer developed a toaster with extra wide slots, to accommodate bagels, thick slices of bread, and the like. If a patent were sought on such a toaster it might well be denied on grounds of obviousness.[87] If the appearance of the toaster could be protected by copyright, however, there would be no inquiry into the question of obviousness. There would be no deter-

86. H.R. Rep. No. 94–1476, 94th   **87.** 35 U.S.C. § 103(a).
Cong. 2d Sess. at 54.

mination of "how good" a technical advance is represented by this wide-slotted toaster. Protection would be automatic. The result is that others would be hindered in their ability to make wide slot toasters.[88]

The evolution of the rule that utilitarian objects cannot be protected by copyright is a bit convoluted. Prior to 1870, the subject matter of American copyright law was sufficiently limited so that the issue did not come up. Even after 1870, when protection was extended for the first time to "statuary" and other three dimensional works, the statute spoke exclusively of the "fine arts."[89] That limitation effectively ruled out any possible controversy over protection for works of applied art. It was only with the elimination of references to "fine arts" in the 1909 Act that individuals began attempting to secure copyright on utilitarian objects.[90]

On its face the 1909 statute did not disqualify an otherwise eligible work from copyright merely because it had "utility." Copyright Office regulations interpreting the 1909 Act, however, contained language suggesting that productions of "industrial arts, utilitarian in purpose and character" would not be accepted for registration.[91] Over time the relevant regulations evolved and by the late 1940s they provided that registration would be permitted for "works of artistic craftsmanship, insofar as their form, but not their mechanical or utilitarian aspects are concerned."[92] By the middle decades of the twentieth century, the Copyright Office routinely accepted numerous utilitarian objects for registration because of their artistic "form."

The story continues in 1954, when the Supreme Court handed down its opinion in *Mazer v. Stein*.[93] The plaintiff in that case had obtained copyright protection for certain statuettes depicting male and female dancing figures. These figures were then used as bases for table lamps. The defendants in the case made copies of the figures to use in their own, competing lamps. In the resulting infringement suit, the defendants argued that where a work of art or artistic craftsmanship is ultimately incorporated into a useful

---

88. Others could make wide slot toasters independently without violating any copyright interests, since parallel independent creation is not forbidden under copyright law. But if the first manufacturer's toasters were widely distributed, there would be an inference that a second firm had access to them and thus had copied the design. The risk of litigation would be considerable and there would be a strong deterrent to use of the technology.

89. Act of July 8, 1870, ch. 230 § 86 16 Stat. 198.

90. For a more detailed exposition of this history, *see* Robert C. Denicola, *Applied Art and Industrial Design: A suggested Approach to Copyright in Useful Articles*, 67 MINN. L. REV. 707, 709–11 (1983).

91. Rules and Regulations for the Registration of Claims to Copyright, Bulletin No. 15 (1910), as quoted in *Mazer v. Stein*, 347 U.S. at 212 n.23.

92. 37 C.F.R. § 202.8(a) (1949).

93. 347 U.S. 201, 74 S.Ct. 460, 98 L.Ed. 630 (1954).

object, the work should not be copyrightable because the exclusive form of protection should be a design patent. The Court rejected the argument, concluding "[w]e find nothing in the copyright statute to support the argument that the intended use or use in industry of an article eligible for copyright bars or invalidates its registration."[94] In other words, the fact that an author intends to, and ultimately does, make a utilitarian use of a work of art does not deprive that work of copyright, assuming that it qualifies as a work of art in the first place. In reaching this conclusion, the Court approved the approach of the Copyright Office regulations mentioned above. It also declared that the presence or absence of a design patent should have no effect on the availability of copyright protection.

In the years immediately following *Mazer* a huge variety of useful articles were presented to the Copyright Office for registration. In response, the Copyright Office yet again modified its regulations. Under the version that came into effect in the mid–1950s:

> If the sole intrinsic function of an article is its utility, the fact that it is unique and attractively shaped will not qualify it as a work of art. However, if the shape of a utilitarian article incorporates features, such as artistic sculpture, carving or pictorial representation, which can be identified separately and are capable of existing independently as a work of art, such features will be eligible for registration.[95]

As tends to be the case in stories of this sort, this solution merely led to further problems. Determining whether the "sole intrinsic" function of an object is utilitarian, or instead whether there were artistic features that could be "identified separately," remained a puzzling challenge. Representative of these difficulties was the decision in *Esquire v. Ringer*,[96] which considered the copyright registrability of a nontraditional, decorative, outdoor lighting fixture.

In that case, the Copyright Office held that the sole purpose of the fixture was utilitarian and denied registration. Esquire, the designer of the lamp, sued to compel registration. The district court granted the requested relief, reasoning that the useful aspects of the fixture were not its *sole* function, since it also served the function of enhancing the decor of the parking lots where it was mounted. On appeal, the D.C. Circuit reversed, concluding that the regulation barred registration because "the overall design or config-

---

94. *Studio*, 347 U.S. at 218.

95. 37 C.F.R. § 202.10(c) (1959).

96. 591 F.2d 796 (D.C.Cir.1978), *cert. denied*, 440 U.S. 908, 99 S.Ct. 1217, 59 L.Ed.2d 456 (1979).

uration of a utilitarian object, even if it is determined by aesthetic as well as functional considerations, is not eligible for copyright."[97] Essentially, the *Esquire* court held that the overall design of a utilitarian object could never be protected by copyright as a sculptural work.

Although the *Esquire* case arose under the 1909 Act, that court opted to consult the text and legislative history of the newly adopted 1976 law for guidance. The drafters of the 1976 Act had attempted to confront directly the question of how to protect the aesthetic elements of pictorial, graphical, and sculptural works without protecting utilitarian objects. The 1976 Act ultimately provided:

> the design of a useful article ... shall be considered a pictorial, graphic, or sculptural work only if, and only to the extent that, such design incorporates pictorial, graphic, or sculptural features that can be identified separately from, and are capable of existing independently of, the utilitarian aspects of the article.

The legislative history of the 1976 Act elaborated on the theme of artistic elements that exist "independently" of utilitarian aspects.[98] It specified that a showing that artistic elements were *either* physically *or* conceptually separable from the utilitarian features of the object would suffice for copyrightability.

At least one part of this test is straightforward. The notion of physical separability is fairly easy to apply in practice. The classic example is the hood ornament of a car. While a car is a "useful article," the hood ornament in the shape, perhaps, of a jaguar, has sculptural features that can be identified separately and can exist independently of the utility of the car—using a hacksaw or blowtorch you could remove the ornament, which would now have no utility other than to sit there and look pretty. The problem arises with the notion of "conceptual" separability.

At the outset, it is important to remember that the issue only arises if we are dealing with a "useful article." These are defined in the statute as articles "having an intrinsic utilitarian function that is not merely to portray the appearance of the article or to convey

97. *Esquire*, 591 F.2d at 804.

98. The relevant passage of the House Report states "although the shape of an industrial product may be aesthetically satisfying and valuable, the Committee's intention is not to offer it copyright protection under the bill. Unless the shape of an automobile, airplane, ladies' dress, food processor, television set or any other industrial product contains some element that, *physically or conceptually*, can be identified as separable from the utilitarian aspects of that article, the design would not be copyrighted under the bill." H.R. Rep. No. 94–1476, 94th Cong. 2d Sess. 55 (1973) (emphasis supplied).

information.''[99] Thus, a sculpture in the shape of a toaster that does not function to actually toast bread has no function except to portray the appearance of a toaster. Hence it is not a useful article, and there is no need for further analysis—it is non-utilitarian and fully copyrightable. On the other hand, if the object serves a utilitarian purpose, even in part, *only* the conceptually separate artistic elements—if any—will be protected.

In the years since the adoption of the 1976 Act courts and commentators have struggled to define this notion of conceptual separability and it is our sad duty to report that the law is in disarray. Professor Nimmer has suggested that "conceptual separability exists where there is any substantial likelihood that even if the article had no utilitarian use it would still be marketable to some significant segment of the community simply because of its aesthetic qualities."[100] In other words, imagine an esoteric looking, but entirely functional toaster. To determine if there are aesthetically separable features, Nimmer asks if anyone would buy it if it was suddenly rendered incapable of making toast and could only function as a true "sculpture." Nimmer's test has been criticized however, because certain works may incorporate unpopular, but nonetheless legitimate aesthetic elements. The public might not buy the (hypothetical non-functioning) object, even though they recognized it as "sculpture" because it was "ugly" or violated contemporary norms. It would thus fail Nimmer's "marketability" test, despite meeting the criteria for copyright, which is, of course available just as much to ugly works as to beautiful ones.

In the courts, divergent tests of conceptual separability have been articulated, particularly by the Second Circuit. In *Kieselstein–Cord v. Accessories by Pearl, Inc.*,[101] the court sustained the copyrightability of certain ornate belt buckles made of precious metals. The *Kieselstein* court was influenced by the fact that some owners of the belt buckles actually used them not to keep their pants up, but as jewelry. The court concluded that the artistic aspects of the buckles, though not physically separable from the utilitarian aspects, were conceptually separable, because the artistic aspects of the object were "primary" and the utility was only "secondary." On the facts, this seems intuitively correct. Given the price of the buckles at issue and their elaborate decoration, it is likely that the aesthetic aspects dominated over the functional, but the test seems nothing more than an invitation for judges to indulge in subjective conclusions.

---

99. 17 U.S.C. § 101.

100. NIMMER, COPYRIGHT § 2.08[B] (2002).

101. 632 F.2d 989 (2d Cir.1980).

Later, in *Carol Barnhart Inc. v. Economy Cover Corp.*,[102] the Second Circuit confronted the question of whether to allow copyright protection for various male and female human torso forms with hollowed backs, designed to permit them to be used to display clothing. The court concluded that there was no conceptually separable aesthetic elements to these mannequins. The majority opinion noted that the aesthetic features of the disputed mannequins were "inextricably intertwined" with their utilitarian features, and thus seems to suggest that the aesthetic elements must be wholly unnecessary to the utilitarian function of the object before they can be protected. Judge Newman, in dissent, proposed an alternative test which lead him to the opposite result. In his view "[f]or the design features to be 'conceptually separate' from the utilitarian aspects of the useful article that embodies the design, the article must stimulate in the mind of the beholder a concept that is separate from the concept evoked by its utilitarian function."[103]

Just two years later, a different panel of the judges on the Second Circuit took another stab at this thorny area in *Brandir International, Inc. v. Cascade Pacific Lumber Co.*[104] *Brandir* involved the copyrightability of a curvilinear bicycle rack fashioned from bent tubing. The test in this case seems to focus on the creative process, and the subjective thought processes of the *artist* rather than the *observer*. As the court put it, "where design elements can be identified as reflecting the designer's artistic judgement exercised independently of functional influences, conceptual separability exists."[105] Of course, by the time of any litigation, the artist or artisan who designed the disputed object will have more than a little incentive to claim he was influenced by artistic judgment even if that is not the unvarnished truth. This may be a fatal shortcoming of the *Brandir* test

Although the leading opinions on conceptual separability issued over two decades ago, they continue to control more recent thinking on the subject. For example, in *Pivot Point International, Inc. v. Charlene Products, Inc.*,[106] the work at issue was a mannequin that had rather affectionately been named "Mara." Aspiring hair stylists and makeup artists could use Mara as a subject during the course of their studies. The Seventh Circuit held that Mara was eligible for copyright based upon the approach articulated in *Brandir*, reasoning that her facial features had resulted from a "creative process unfettered by functional concerns" with the goal of achiev-

---

102. 773 F.2d 411 (2d Cir.1985).

103. *Carol Barnhart*, 773 F.2d at 422.

104. 834 F.2d 1142 (2d Cir.1987). This opinion was written by Judge

Oakes, who had also authored the opinion in the *Kieselstein–Cord* belt buckle case.

105. 834 F.2d at 1145.

106. 372 F.3d 913 (7th Cir. 2004).

ing the "hungry look" of high-fashion runway models. A compelling dissenting opinion observed that Mara had been developed from the outset for the functional purpose of training hair stylists and makeup artists, and that absent the facial features that the majority had just declared eligible for copyright, that functionality would be greatly diminished or eliminated.

It should be apparent from these loose standards that conceptual separability analysis remains rather muddled, and that much room for good lawyering exists when arguing such cases. It would seem that many of the close cases can and should be resolved by asking whether granting copyright protection would subvert core values of patent law. If there is any risk of such an outcome, we would think the better course would be to deny the sought-after copyright. Indeed one of your humble authors would scrap the entire conceptual separability test and simply revert to the rule that unless the aesthetic features are *physically* separable, there should be no copyright.

§ 3.6   Motion Pictures and Other Audiovisual Works

Audiovisual works are specifically defined in the 1976 Act. They are "works that consist of a series of related images which are intrinsically intended to be shown by the use of machines or devices such as projectors, viewers or electronic equipment, together with accompanying sounds, if any, regardless of the nature of the material objects, such as films or tapes, in which the works are embodied."[107] All forms of audiovisual works are itemized as copyrightable subject matter under the current statute.

Although an audiovisual work must consist of multiple images that are "related" there is no implication in the statutory language that those images must be shown in a specific sequence. Several courts reached exactly this conclusion in determining that a video game is an audiovisual work. Because of player involvement, each time the game is played, the precise series of images appearing on the screen will differ. There is no set sequence. Nonetheless, all of the images are related, as they depict the same characters or background and integrate with each other to produce the effect of the game. Given this circumstance, they qualify as audiovisual works.[108] The same would be true, of course, for a series of still photographic images arranged to be shown together, as in the case of the usual "slide show." Note that in such a case, each individual image might be separately copyrightable as a pictorial work, while

---

107. 17 U.S.C. § 101.

108. *See e.g.,* Midway Mfg. Co. v. Artic Int'l, Inc., 704 F.2d 1009, 1011

(7th Cir.), *cert. denied,* 464 U.S. 823, 104 S.Ct. 90, 78 L.Ed.2d 98 (1983).

the assemblage of all the slides would qualify for a distinct copyright as an audiovisual work.

The second requirement for an audiovisual work is that it must be "intended to be shown by the use of machines...." Thus, a series of related photographs, mounted in a museum to form a coherent and unified exhibition does not constitute an "audiovisual work" because no machine or device is necessary to show the images.

Motion pictures are a subtype of audiovisual work, defined in the statute as "works consisting of a series of related images which, when shown in succession, impart an impression of motion, together with accompanying sounds, if any."[109] Since an "impression of motion" is required, certain audiovisual works, like the slide show mentioned in the previous paragraph, do not qualify as motion pictures.

The references to "accompanying sounds" in both of these definitions are important. Combined with language in the definition of sound recordings excluding "the sounds accompanying a motion picture or other audiovisual work" from that category, they make it clear that motion picture soundtracks are parts of audiovisual works. This means that several of the limitations on the rights granted to sound recordings do not apply to motion picture sound tracks. For example, the copyright owner will have a performance right in a motion picture soundtrack, where he or she would not have one in a sound recording.[110] Several other important distinctions between these two categories of works are discussed in the chapter dealing with the exclusive rights of copyright owners.

Like all other copyrightable material, audiovisual works must be fixed in a tangible medium of expression. As the statutory language reveals, there is no restriction on the type of objects in which the work may be fixed. Not only are photographic film and videotape adequate, but so are computer chips and other objects that may be developed for this purpose in the future. A pair of controversial cases went so far as to hold that a mechanical teddy bear with its accompanying cassettes that enabled the bear to "move" and "talk" was an audiovisual work, though that result has been criticized by Professor Nimmer.[111]

The creativity requirement for audiovisual works is often satisfied by the underlying material being captured on the film or videotape. The lines spoken by the actors and their inflection and bodily movement are surely creative in a copyright sense. On the

---

109. 17 U.S.C. § 101.

110. See § 7.4.1, infra.

111. Worlds of Wonder, Inc. v. Vector Intercontinental, Inc., 653 F.Supp.

135 (N.D.Ohio 1986); Worlds of Wonder, Inc. v. Veritel Learning Sys., Inc., 658 F.Supp. 351 (N.D.Tex.1986).

other hand, copyright is available for audiovisual works even when the underlying material is not at all creative. For instance, a film of traffic passing by a busy intersection or of wild buffalo stampeding through the prairie would also qualify for copyright, even though the buffalo cannot be said to be performing a choreographic routine. The creativity in works of this sort lies in decisions made about what types of cameras, and films to use, where to place those cameras, and a host of other related decisions. It is largely on this basis that the famous Zapruder film of the assassination of President Kennedy was found to constitute a copyrightable audiovisual work.

§ 3.7 Sound Recordings

Copyright protection for sound recordings is a relatively new feature of the American copyright law. Over time, protection for sound recordings became essential because of the ease with which record pirates could make cheap unauthorized duplicates of legitimate recordings. Pirates, of course, can undersell legitimate producers because they need not incur expenses for recording studios or for payments to performers. As the problems of piracy became more severe, Congress was moved to act in the early 1970s in advance of the general revision that led to the Copyright Act of 1976. Under the legislation adopted at that time, only those sound recordings first fixed on or after February 15, 1972, are protected by copyright.[112] Recordings fixed prior to that date may be protected under state law, but are not covered by federal copyright.[113] This continues to be true under the current statute.

The current copyright law defines sound recordings as "works that result from the fixation of a series of musical, spoken, or other sounds, but not including the sounds accompanying a motion picture or other audiovisual work, regardless of the nature of the material objects such as disks, tapes, or other phonorecords in which they are embodied,"[114] and provides for their protection by copyright. Sound recordings can include such items as instructional materials in foreign languages, recordings of bird songs, or the

---

112. Sound Recording Amendment, P.L. 92–140, 85 Stat. 391 (1971).

113. The 1976 Act provides that "[w]ith respect to sound recording fixed before February 15, 1972, any rights or remedies under the common law or statute of any State shall not be annulled or limited by this title until February 15, 2047. The preemptive provisions of [section 301(a)] shall apply to any such rights and remedies pertaining to any cause of action arising from undertakings commenced on and after February

15, 2047. . . . [N]o sound recording fixed before February 15, 1972, shall be subject to copyright under this title before, on, or after February 15, 2047." Under this provision, pre–1972 sound recordings continue to receive whatever state protections may be available until the middle of the next century. Thereafter those state protections are pre-empted and the recording are effectively injected into the public domain.

114. 17 U.S.C. § 101.

comedy routine of a popular stand-up comic. Most of the time, however, they consist of captured performances of musical works. By statutory definition, sound recordings can only be fixed in material objects called "phonorecords."[115] Phonorecords include such objects as vinyl records, compact discs, cassette, or reel-to-reel tapes, and any other material object that can be used to capture sounds.

The copyright interest in a sound recording is distinct from both the ownership of the physical objects in which it is embodied, and from the separate copyright that might exist in any underlying musical work captured in that sound recording. For instance, assume that Smith writes a musical composition called the Copyright Ballad. Thereafter, Acme Recording hires The Jones Band to make a recording of the Copyright Ballad, after obtaining permission to do so from Smith, the composer. Acme ultimately produces compact discs containing The Jones Band version of the song and sells them to the public. Green buys one of these CDs for her collection. Smith owns the copyright in the musical composition called the Copyright Ballad. Acme owns the copyright in a sound recording consisting of The Jones Band's aural version of that song.[116] Green owns the individual disc, which is a type of "phonorecord" in copyright parlance. If Green were to start making "bootleg" copies of the CD and selling them to her friends, she would infringe two separate copyright interests—that of Smith in the musical work and that of Acme in the sound recording.

Like all categories of protected works, sound recordings only qualify for protection when they are original. Indeed, the legislative history points out that no protection will be available when "sounds are fixed by some purely mechanical means without originality of any kind...."[117] Originality can flow from either the contributions of performers, whose performance is captured in the sound recording, or from contributions of the party who sets up the recording session and makes the decision about how to capture the sounds, and then compiles and edits them into a final work. While two singers may sing the same song note for note, each will bring to it their own vocal stylings and thus each would possess "originality" in the copyright sense. The same point applies to sound recordings of works other than musical compositions.

---

115. Phonorecords are defined in the statute as "material objects in which sounds, other than those accompanying a motion picture or other audiovisual work, are fixed by any method now known or later developed and from which the sounds can be perceived, reproduced or otherwise communicated, either directly or with the aid of a machine or device." 17 U.S.C. § 101.

116. Depending on the contractual relationship between Acme and The Jones Band, The Jones Band might be considered a co-author of the sound recording, and thus a co-owner of the resulting copyright.

117. H.R. Rep. No. 92–487, 92d Cong., 1st Sess. 6 (1971).

For instance, consider "books on tape." Two different actors—say Joe Pesci and Sir Ian McKellen—both record versions of a novel. Because of differences in accent, inflection, and dramatic intonation, each version would be original and both would qualify for a sound recording copyright even though the words spoken would be identical. Similarly, while two sound engineers or recording companies may decide to record the same song, the placement of microphones, the choice of acoustical setting, and decisions about how to capture and edit the results will yield two different, and original, sound recordings, each entitled to copyright protection.

As is developed elsewhere in this text, sound recordings receive more limited protections under copyright law than do most other types of works.[118] Most notably, the owner of a copyright in a sound recording does not have the right to prevent others from publicly performing the work.[119] This feature of the law is controversial, however, and the law is otherwise in most other nations of the world. There is a not insubstantial chance that Congress will eventually extend a performance right to sound recordings. Another significant limitation upon copyright in sound recordings is that these works are protected only against duplication of the work through mechanical means, such as a tape recorder. No matter how closely one band tracks a protected sound recording by imitating the earlier rendition, an independently fixed second version does not infringe the copyright in the first sound recording.[120]

§ 3.8 Architectural Works

An architectural work is defined in the current version of the copyright act as "the design of a building as embodied in any tangible medium of expression, including a building, architectural plans, or drawings."[121] This definition did not appear in the original text of the 1976 Act, nor were architectural works among the listed types of protectable works of authorship when Congress adopted the current law. Congress added the definition and the category "architectural works" to the list of protected subject matter in 1990, in partial response to the decision of the United States to ratify the international copyright treaty known as the Berne Convention.[122]

---

118. *See supra* § 6.4.

119. Recent amendments to the 1976 Act have granted the owners of copyrights in sound recordings a limited exclusive right to publicly perform the work by digital transmission. *See* 17 U.S.C. §§ 106(6), 114. You can find an extensive discussion of this right in section 7.3 of this book.

120. 17 U.S.C. § 114.

121. 17 U.S.C. § 101.

122. The Architectural Works Copyright Protection Act is Title VII of the Judicial Improvements Act of 1990, P.L. 101–650, 104 Stat. 5089, and it became effective on December 1, 1990.

Prior to the 1990 amendments, there was a crucial distinction between architectural plans and models on the one hand, and actual structures on the other. Plans, such as blueprints, were considered "pictorial" works, and thus fully eligible for copyright protection.[123] The same was true for three-dimensional scale models of buildings and other architectural works. Actual buildings, however, were considered "utilitarian" because they functioned to shelter humans, animals, or equipment.[124] Thus, it was not considered an infringement of the copyright in architectural plans to erect a building corresponding to those plans, so long as no copies of the plans themselves were made. Similarly, it was not infringement to inspect an already existing building, take measurements, and then duplicate it by building an identical building elsewhere.

During this pre–1990 period, courts did grant copyright protection to full-size, three-dimensional works of architecture that served purely decorative or aesthetic purposes, such as monuments or funeral markers, precisely because they did not have any "utility" other than their aesthetic purposes.[125] It was also true, prior to 1990, that individual decorative elements on a building could be protected, as they were effectively nothing more than sculptural works. The classic example is a gargoyle, placed on a building for purely ornamental effect. Nonetheless, the bottom line remained that no protection would be afforded for the overall appearance of a building, no matter how striking or aesthetically pleasing.

Effective in 1989, the United States decided, at long last, to adhere to the Berne Convention, an international copyright scheme that had been in existence since 1886. Article 2 of that Convention requires the participating member states to afford protection to, among other things, architectural works.[126] Though certain changes in U.S. law were made in 1988 in anticipation of U.S. adherence to Berne, no action was taken concerning architectural works at that time, pending the results of a review of the subject by the Copyright Office. That review was completed in mid–1989, and shortly thereafter Congress adopted the Architectural Works Protection Act of 1990 (AWCPA). As noted, this legislation extended copyright

123. *See e.g.*, Imperial Homes Corp. v. Lamont, 458 F.2d 895, 899 (5th Cir. 1972); Herman Frankel Org. v. Tegman, 367 F.Supp. 1051 (E.D.Mich.1973); Aitken, Hazen, Hoffman, Miller P.C. v. Empire Constr. Co., 542 F.Supp. 252 (D.Neb.1982); Demetriades v. Kaufmann, 680 F.Supp. 658 (S.D.N.Y.1988). *See also* H.R. Rep. No. 94–1476, 94th Cong. 2d Sess. 53 (1976).

124. For discussion of the reasons for, and the history of, denial of protection to utilitarian works, *see supra* § 3.5.

125. *See e.g.*, Jones Bros. v. Underkoffler, 16 F.Supp. 729 (M.D.Pa.1936).

126. More specifically, Article 2(6) provides that "works mentioned in this Article shall enjoy protection in all countries of the Union," and Article 2(1) provides that "the expression 'literary and artistic works' shall include ... illustrations, maps, plans, sketches and three-dimensional works relative to geography, topography, architecture or science."

protection to completed buildings and provided a new, comprehensive definition of architectural works. Under that definition, "[t]he work includes the overall form as well as the arrangement and composition of spaces and elements in the design, but does not include individual standard features."

The district court applied this standard in *Shine v. Childs*,[127] a case involving several spectacular designs of skyscrapers intended for construction in New York City. The accused work in that litigation was the proposed Freedom Tower at the World Trade Center site. Shine asserted that the Freedom Tower design was based on two of his designs. The first, called Shine '99, comprised a "tower that tapers as it rises, with two straight, parallel, roughly triangular sides, connected by two twisting facades, resulting in a tower whose top [is] in the shape of a parallelogram." The second, titled the "Olympic Tower," consisted of a "twisting tower with a symmetrical diagonal column grid, expressed on the exterior of the building, that follows the twisting surface created by the floor plates' geometry."

Shine subsequently brought an infringement suit, claiming that the Freedom Tower design was substantially similar in form to Shine '99, and also incorporated a grid and facade design identical to that of the Olympic Tower. In his defense, Childs asserted that neither of Shine's designs qualified for copyright protection. According to Childs, Shine's works were preliminary and conceptual, and hence incapable of allowing for construction of a building directly from them. As a result, neither work qualified as a "design for a building" within the Copyright Act's definition of "architectural work."[128] The court disagreed, observing that both Shine '99 and the Olympic Tower were sufficiently detailed and complete to constitute a specific expression capable of supporting copyright.

Childs also asserted that neither of Shine's designs met the standard of originality. The court again disagreed. Recognizing that each of the elements of Shine's skyscrapers—including those with twisting shapes and diamond facades—had been built before, the court nonetheless concluded that they incorporated a "particular combination of design elements" that were the result of "at least the mere dash of originality required for copyrightability." As suggested by the legislative history of the AWCPA, copyright in architectural works will often be in the nature of a compilation of preexisting structural elements into original works.

The legislative history further clarifies a number of points about this new category of works. First, it states explicitly that the separability test, which has caused so much difficulty in defining

127.   382 F.Supp.2d 602 (S.D.N.Y. 2005).

128.   17 U.S.C. § 101.

the limits of copyright for most works of applied art,[129] is inapplicable to architectural works, and that "the aesthetically pleasing overall shape of an architectural work could be protected...."[130] The legislative history also makes it clear that buildings include not only habitable structures, but also "structures that are used, but not inhabited by human beings, such as churches, pergolas, gazebos, and garden pavilions." On the other hand, structures such as bridges, dams, cloverleafs, overpasses, and the like are not meant to be included within the ambit of protectible subject matter.[131]

The court in *The Yankee Candle Co. v. New England Candle Co.*[132] relied in part on this legislative history when it considered whether a retail candle store within a shopping mall qualified as a "building" within the meaning of the AWCPA. The court concluded that it did not, reasoning that although an entire shopping mall would qualify as a building, an individual room within the mall did not. This reasoning is not immune from criticism. Although the fact that the store was not a free-standing structure was significant to the court, a shopping mall candle store is arguably more similar to the sorts of works Congress intended to protect (e.g., gazebos and pavilions) than those it did not (e.g., bridges and overpasses).

The expanded protection for works of architecture conferred by AWCPA applies to any works first created after December 1, 1990, and to any works that were unconstructed on that date and embodied in unpublished plans or drawings. In the latter case, however, protection expired on December 31, 2002, unless the work had been constructed by that date.[133]

The scope of copyright protection in architectural works is subject to three particular limitations spelled out in the Copyright Act. First, copyright in a constructed architectural work does not include the right to prevent others from making, distributing, or displaying pictures, paintings, photographs, or other pictorial representations of the work, provided that the constructed work is located in, or visible from, a public place.[134] As a result, tourists may pose in front of buildings, snap some photographs, and post them on social networking Internet sites without fear of infringing a copyright in an architectural work.

Second, the owner of a building embodying an architectural work may alter or destroy the building without the consent of the

129.　*See supra* § 3.5.

130.　H.R. Rep. 101–735, 101st Cong., 2d Sess. 20–21 (1990).

131.　H.R. Rep. No. 101–735, 101st Cong. 2d Sess. at 19–20.

132.　14 F.Supp.2d 154 (D. Mass. 1998), *vacated by settlement,* 29 F.Supp.2d 44 (1998).

133.　§ 706, Pub. Law 101–650, 104 Stat. 5089 (1990).

134.　17 U.S.C. § 120(a).

copyright owner.[135] This provision precludes both the copyright proprietor's usual right to prepare derivative works as well as recognition of the author's moral right, if any, in the building. This limitation balances the intellectual property interests of the copyright owner with the real property rights of the building owner and allows, for example, the owner of a home with a leaky roof to modify the structure without having to obtain the permission of the architect.

Finally, the Copyright Act provides that it does not preempt the common law or statutes of any state pertaining to "[s]tate and local landmarks, historic preservation, zoning, or building codes, relating to architectural works...."[136] For example, many state laws provide for the preservation of buildings of historic worth. Deeming this matter one of local, rather than federal, concern, Congress declined to allow the Copyright Act to preempt such legislation.

§ 3.9 Derivative Works

The Copyright Act explicitly lists "derivative works" as within the subject matter eligible for copyright protection. A derivative work is defined in the statute as "a work based upon one or more preexisting works, such as a translation, musical arrangement, dramatization, fictionalization, motion picture version, sound recording, art reproduction, abridgment, condensation, or any other form in which a work may be recast, transformed, or adapted. A work consisting of editorial revisions annotations, elaborations or other modifications which, as a whole represent an original work of authorship is a derivative work."[137] This means that the Copyright Act permits a work that is based in substantial part upon a preexisting work to obtain independent copyright protection, provided that the derivative work fulfills the requirement of originality. However, for a valid copyright in a derivative work to exist, the derivative work author must either base his work on an underlying work that is in the public domain source, or obtain permission from the owner of the copyright of the underlying work—"protection for a work employing pre-existing material in which copyright subsists does not extend to any part of the work in which such material has been used unlawfully."[138]

In some sense, of course, almost every work borrows to some degree from the cultural traditions in which the work originated.[139] Not all works of authorship are derivative works within the meaning of the Copyright Act, however. Use of the term "derivative

---

135. 17 U.S.C. § 120(b).

136. 17 U.S.C. § 301(b)(4).

137. 17 U.S.C. § 101.

138. 17 U.S.C. § 103(a).

139. *See* Emerson v. Davies, 8 F.Cas. 615 (C.C.D.Mass.1845).

work" implies a substantial copying of *expressive material* (not just ideas) from a particular prior work. As explained by Professor Nimmer, a work is considered a derivative work only if it would be judged to infringe the original work on which it was based if that first work were not in the public domain and there was no permission to use it.[140] What allows the derivative work to obtain its own copyright protection is that the pre-existing expressive material is combined with new, original expression.

Moreover, the scope of protection in a derivative work copyright extends only to the additional materials created by the creator of the derivative work.[141] The derivative work copyright implies no exclusive right in the pre-existing material employed in the work.[142] Nor does the derivative work copyright "affect or enlarge the scope, duration, ownership, or subsistence of, any copyright protection in the pre-existing material."[143]

Consider, for example, the novel *Alice in Wonderland*, first published by Reverend Charles Lutwidge Dodgson under the pseudonym Lewis Carroll. As *Alice in Wonderland* was first published in 1865, its copyright expired long ago. Any movie studio can produce a feature film based upon Dodgson's novel without running afoul of the copyright laws. Such a film would be considered a derivative work of the public domain novel because it would closely track the plot details of the book and maybe even use exact language from the book as part of the film's dialogue. While a distinct copyright would exist in this movie, Dodgson's novel retains its public domain status. Another studio would be free to consult the public domain source in order to produce its own independently copyrighted movie, but could not copy the original elements in the first movie, such as original dialogue.

As with other sorts of protected works of authorship, derivative works must fulfill the standard of originality in order to quality for copyright protection. In the context of derivative works, originality will be assessed in terms of the contribution the additional material makes to the pre-existing work. The additional material must recast, transform, or adapt the pre-existing work.[144] If the additional material makes only a trivial contribution to the pre-existing work, then no separate derivative copyright will be established.

A number of judicial opinions have considered the originality standard with respect to derivative works. The work at issue in *L. Batlin & Son, Inc. v. Snyder*[145] was a plastic reproduction of a cast-iron, mechanical "Uncle Sam" toy bank. The original, cast-iron

---

140. Nimmer, Copyright § 3.01 (2002).
141. 17 U.S.C. § 103(b).
142. 17 U.S.C. § 103(b).

143. 17 U.S.C. § 103(b).
144. 17 U.S.C. § 101.
145. 536 F.2d 486 (2d Cir. 1976).

bank had been publicly available for many years, and hence its design had passed into the public domain. The plastic bank—apparently produced just in time for the U.S. bicentennial celebration—differed from the original in only minor respects that were due to the translation of the original work into a different medium. The Second Circuit denied copyright protection for the plastic bank, explaining that some "substantial variation" must exist between the original and derivative work for the latter to enjoy copyright. Under the holding in *Batlin*, the mere reproduction of a work into a different medium cannot support copyright.

The Seventh Circuit opinion in *Gracen v. Bradford Exchange* was to similar effect, refusing to award copyright protection to Gracen's painting of the character Dorothy, as portrayed by Judy Garland in the movie "The Wizard of Oz."[146] The Court of Appeals explained that no substantial variation existed between the painting and the movie stills on which it was based—indeed, Gracen had made a concerted effort to depict Dorothy as she appeared in "The Wizard of Oz." In so holding, Judge Posner explained that the concept of originality in copyright law served to prevent overlapping claims of copyright infringement. If Gracen was allowed to copyright her work, it might be unclear whether subsequent artists who depicted Dorothy had based their efforts on the movie or the painting. Ensuring that a derivative work enjoys copyright only when it is "substantially different from the underlying work" serves to protect future artists from copyright litigation.

In *Lee v. A.R.T. Company*,[147] the plaintiff had created certain works of visual art that were embodied in notecards and small lithographs. A.R.T. Company purchased Lee's works, mounted them on ceramic tiles, and resold them. Lee contended that the ceramic tiles were derivative works within the meaning of the Copyright Act. Because the Copyright Act provides the copyright owner with the exclusive right to make derivative works—the so-called adaptation right of § 106(2)—then A.R.T. Company would have been an infringer.

The Seventh Circuit rejected Lee's contention. Judge Easterbrook reasoned that merely mounting copyrighted notecards and lithographs did not recast, transform, or adapt them. Although the art was bonded to a ceramic slab, it depicted the same image without alteration. To accept Lee's position would seemingly lead to the result that anyone who wrote on one of the notecards, or placed a frame on a lithograph, would require Lee's permission and, even more curiously, would have a separate copyright in the item if they had acted with Lee's permission. Judge Easterbrook acknowledged

146.   698 F.2d 300 (7th Cir.1983).   **147.**   125 F.3d 580 (7th Cir.1997).

that a prior decision of the Ninth Circuit, *Mirage Editions, Inc. v. Albuquerque A.R.T. Co.*,[148] had reached a contrary result on similar facts. The Seventh Circuit nonetheless refused to extend the concept of derivative works to allow authors to block physical modifications to purchased copies of work or to methods of displaying those copies.

If tile mounting does not yield a separate copyright as a derivative work, what steps would? An original arrangement of a traditional song has been held to be subject to copyright protection as a derivative work.[149] So has "panning and scanning" of a public domain film, a technique that alters the rectangular, widescreen version of a cinema film so that it was more readily viewed on a square TV display.[150] Some courts have spoken of the standard of originality for derivative works as one of "distinguishable variation" from the underlying work. Under this standard, a trivial variation will not fulfill the originality standard, but a difference that renders the derivative work distinguishable from the original in any meaningful manner suffices.[151]

§ 3.10 Compilations

A compilation is a "work formed by the collection and assembling of preexisting materials or of data that are selected, coordinated, or arranged in such a way that the resulting work as a whole constitutes and original work of authorship."[152] Compilations are specifically listed as copyrightable subject matter under the 1976 statute.[153] The pre-existing materials that are gathered together to form the compilation can consist of either items that are independently copyrightable as well—such as poems, for instance—or of material that is not within the subject matter of copyright—such as population data for every city in the world with over 10,000 inhabitants. In other words, one might think of compilations as encompassing works such as anthologies, almanacs, and even computerized databases.

Compilations of the anthology type are also known as "collective works," a term separately defined in the statute as a "work, such as a periodical issue, anthology or encyclopedia, in which a number of contributions, constituting separate and independent works in themselves are assembled into a collective whole."[154] Thus

148. 856 F.2d 1341 (9th Cir.1988).

149. Plymouth Music Co. v. Magnus Organ Corp., 456 F.Supp. 676 (S.D.N.Y.1978).

150. Maljack Prods. v. UAV Corp., 964 F.Supp. 1416, 1426–28 (C.D.Cal. 1997), *aff'd on other grounds*, 160 F.3d 1223 (9th Cir.1998).

151. Alfred Bell & Co. v. Catalda Fine Arts, 191 F.2d 99 (2d Cir.1951).

152. 17 U.S.C. § 101.

153. 17 U.S.C. § 103.

154. 17 U.S.C. § 101.

the typical issue of a law review and the typical law school casebook are "collective works."

Naturally, if one wishes to prepare a compilation consisting of copyrighted works, it is necessary to obtain permission to use each of those works first. Thus if one put together a volume of newspaper stories concerning the terror attacks of September 11, 2001, without obtaining permission from the copyright holder of each story, copyright in the compilation would be unavailable and the compiler would also be liable for infringement. The statute makes this plain by providing: "The subject matter of copyright ... includes compilations ... but protection for a work employing preexisting material in which copyright subsists does not extend to any part of the work in which such material has been used unlawfully."[155] If only small portions of pre-existing works are included in the compilation, however, the use of those small portions might not be "unlawful" because of the availability of the fair use doctrine, and thus the validity of the compilation copyright would remain unaffected.

It follows from the foregoing that the copyright interest in a compilation is separate from any copyrights that might exist in the individual works that comprise it. However, in order for the compilation to qualify for this separate copyright protection, it, like all other works, must satisfy the statutory requirement of originality. The historical difficulty with works of this sort has been determining what is original about a work that consists entirely of either pre-existing materials or of non-copyrightable facts.

For a number of years, some courts found the requisite originality for compilations in the fact that the author had invested effort in putting the compilation together. This was frequently referred to as the "sweat of the brow" or "industrious collection" test. In older cases this was the basis upon which copyright in directories, particularly phone directories, had been sustained.[156] Indeed, those cases often extended copyright to forbid not only the reproduction of the compilation as a whole, but also the use of component pieces of data in the protected compilation despite rearrangement of that data into a new format. The courts apparently felt that the only way to preserve incentives for parties to invest effort in creating such works was to force others to return to original sources rather than "piggy-back" on the work previously done by the first author.[157]

---

155. 17 U.S.C. § 103.

156. *See e.g.*, Leon v. Pacific Telephone & Telegraph Co., 91 F.2d 484 (9th Cir.1937); Jeweler's Circular Publishing Co. v. Keystone Publishing Co., 281 F.

83, *cert. denied*, 259 U.S. 581, 42 S.Ct. 464, 66 L.Ed. 1074 (1922).

157. *See e.g.*, Illinois Bell Tel. Co. v. Haines and Co., Inc., 683 F.Supp. 1204 (N.D.Ill.1988) ("a compiler commits

It was only in 1991 that the Supreme Court addressed the nature of the originality requirement for compilations in *Feist Publications, Inc. v. Rural Telephone Service Co.*[158] Rural, the original plaintiff in that case, was a local telephone company that had published a white pages telephone directory, as it was required to do under Kansas law. Rural was able to obtain the name, address, and phone number information for its directory from its own customer listings. Feist was a publisher of "wide-area" telephone directories that aggregated into a single volume the telephone listings for consumers in a large number of separate service areas. When it sought to produce a directory that included Rural's service area, Rural refused to grant Feist permission to use its listings. Feist then went ahead and used Rural's information anyway. A total of 1300 listings were copied verbatim, four of which were actually fictitious listings that had been inserted by Rural to detect copying.

The Court ultimately held that Rural's directory lacked sufficient originality to be copyrightable. The Court noted that the individual facts in the directory could not, in and of themselves, be protected by copyright. According to the Court any originality in a factual compilation must be found in the selection, coordination, and arrangement of the facts in that compilation, and protection extends only to those elements and not the underlying facts themselves. The Court specifically repudiated the "sweat of the brow" test, holding that the work invested in compiling the data could not, by itself, warrant copyright protection.

Regarding Rural's directory, the Court found the "selection" unoriginal because Rural simply included every single name within the designated service area. The "arrangement" was similarly unoriginal because, as the Court put it, "there is nothing remotely creative about arranging names alphabetically in a white pages directory. It is an age-old practice, firmly rooted in tradition and so commonplace that it has come to be expected as a matter of course."[159] Hence, the Court concluded that Rural's directory was "a garden-variety white pages directory, devoid of even the slightest trace of creativity,"[160] and was not eligible for copyright.

Feist, of course, does not mean that all or even most factual compilations are not copyrightable. As subsequent judicial opinions have revealed, many such works should be able to demonstrate the requisite creativity. What *Feist* does is to eliminate any remaining confusion over the status of the ill-founded sweat of the brow

copyright infringement if he copies the original compiler's information without conducting an independent canvass"), *aff'd*, 905 F.2d 1081 (7th Cir.1990).

158. 499 U.S. 340, 111 S.Ct. 1282, 113 L.Ed.2d 358 (1991).

159. 499 U.S. at 363.

160. 499 U.S. at 362.

doctrine, and ground compilation copyright analysis in the same concepts of originality as govern all other types of work.

Following *Feist*, courts have reviewed several compilations to determine whether the "selection or arrangement" utilized by the compiler rises to the statutorily required level of originality. As one might expect, application of the *Feist* standard has at times led to subtle distinctions and different outcomes. For example, if traditional white pages telephone directories cannot be protected via copyright, what about the yellow pages? The Second Circuit opinion in *Key Publications, Inc. v. Chinatown Today Publishing Enterprises, Inc.*[161] faced this issue when the owner of Key's directory asserted that the competing "Galore" directory infringed its copyright. The creator of the Key directory, Ms. Wang, collected business cards from enterprises that she believed were of particular interest to the Chinese–American community in New York City, sorted the information by the type of business, placed the listings in an appropriate category, and included the Chinese and English names of the enterprises in the directory.

The Second Circuit concluded that the Key directory was original because it fulfilled either element of the "selection or arrangement" standard. Because Wang had excluded from publication certain enterprises that she thought would soon close, she had achieved an original act of selection. And because Wang employed certain headings supposedly of particular interest to the Chinese–American community and not commonly seen in most yellow pages—for example, "BEAN CURD & BEAN SPROUT SHOP"—she had also accomplished an original arrangement. Although the Second Circuit held that the Key directory was amendable to copyright protection, it also concluded that no infringement had occurred. The accused Galore directory featured an arrangement that was not "even remotely similar" to the Key directory and the number of duplicate listings in the two directories was small.

However, in *BellSouth Advertising & Publishing Corp. v. Donnelley Information Publishing, Inc.*[162] the Eleventh Circuit reached a contrary result on the originality question in a case involving another, more conventional, yellow pages classified phone directory, In that case the accused infringer, Donnelley, obtained information about prospective customers for its proposed yellow pages directory by looking at another such directory, the one published by Bell-South Advertising & Publishing Corporation (BAPCO). Donnelley marked each line of the BAPCO directory with codes that indicated that enterprise's type of business, as well as the size and type of its advertisement. Donnelley then contacted those enterprises in order

161.   945 F.2d 509 (2d Cir.1991).   **162.**   999 F.2d 1436 (11th Cir. 1993) (en banc).

to encourage them to purchase a listing in its own, competitive directory. Publication of the Donnelley directory led to charges of copyright infringement by BAPCO.

The Eleventh Circuit structured its infringement determination by analyzing whether Donnelley copied original expression—if any—within the BAPCO directory. The Court of Appeals reasoned that BAPCO had not performed original acts of selection when it determined the geographic scope of its directory, identified prospective customers, and offered a number of free listings. Such acts were said to be merely "techniques for discovering facts" rather than the original selection of facts to be reported. The court also found the arrangement of headings in the BAPCO yellow pages— much like the arrangement of Rural's white pages in *Feist*—to be "entirely typical," dictated by functional considerations and common industry practice, and therefore unoriginal. As a result, because Donnelley had not copied any original expression, it was held not to have infringed.

So in the first case we have an original compilation but no infringement because the defendant used different methods of selection and arrangement and did not copy. In the second, we have an unoriginal compilation and hence no infringement despite close copying. The originality analysis of the two cases is not, of course, irreconcilable. The directory in *BellSouth* was entirely conventional, using well-know categories for the listed businesses and making no effort to select a subset of the available universe. The directory in *Key Publications* was clearly more innovative. The compiler made subjective decisions about which businesses would be of interest to a particular ethnic constituency, and organized the listings in her own innovative system. Taken together they suggest that the author of a directory is only likely to prevail in a copyright suit if the directory is both reasonably innovative and then is closely duplicated.

The often metaphysical question of what subject matter qualifies as a "fact," mentioned above,[163] becomes of great practical importance in compilation copyright cases. For example, in *CDN Inc. v. Kapes*,[164] accused infringer Kapes developed "The Fair Market Coin Pricer" that listed on his web page the retail price of many coins. The retail prices listed on the Kapes site were based in part upon the wholesale prices provided by CDN in its Coin Dealer Newsletter. When CDN brought charges of copyright infringement, Kapes asserted that both the listing, selection, and inclusion of particular prices was unoriginal; and that the prices themselves were unoriginal.

---

163. *See supra* § 3.1.2.   **164.** 197 F.3d 1256 (9th Cir.1999).

The Ninth Circuit disagreed. The Court of Appeals observed that CDN reviewed major coin publications in order to discern price information, taking into account whether a professional service had ascertained the coin's quality, the impact of public auctions and private sales, and the effect of the economy and foreign policies. Rather than discover a preexisting historical fact, CDN had exercised its own judgment and expertise to arrive at estimates of present value. This process imbued the coin prices with sufficient originality to make them subject to copyright.

Similarly, in *CCC Information Services, Inc. v. Maclean Hunter Market Reports, Inc.*,[165] the Second Circuit concluded that a directory of used car prices was eligible for copyright protection. The editors of the directory did not assess these values upon historical market prices or average sales prices. Rather, they used their expertise and professional judgments, based upon a variety of sources of information, to determine expected values for average vehicles within a region of the United States. As a result, the selection and arrangement of data displayed sufficient originality to be eligible for copyright protection.

Although the coin and used car pricing directories were considered eligible for copyright protection, the risk remains that those who develop a work with a great deal of practical use may discover that the courts will treat the sum of their efforts as an unoriginal factual compilation. Consequently, some scholars and industry representatives assert that the United States should adopt a *sui generis* database protection regime similar to the one found in the European Union.[166] Under the EU Database Directive, adopted in 1996, databases that result from "qualitatively and/or quantitatively a substantial investment in either the obtaining, verification or presentation of the contents" obtain a *sui generis* right, regardless of whether the database would qualify for copyright protection or not. The *sui generis* right prevents others from "extraction and/or re-utilization of the whole or of a substantial part, evaluated qualitatively or quantitatively, of the contents of that database."[167]

The EU approach, however, has proved controversial in Europe and some argue that it has actually hurt the database industry there because it is over protective. As one commentator summarized: "In addition to posing a threat to the public domain, an analysis of the E.U. database industry after the Database Directive issued suggests that data protection fails to encourage database creation."[168] Although the U.S. Congress has considered bills that

---

165. 44 F.3d 61 (2d Cir. 1994).

166. Directive 96/6/EC of the European Parliament and of the Council of March 11, 1996 on the Legal Protection of Databases, 1996 O.J. (L 77) 20.

167. *Id.* at Art. 7.

168. Dana Howells, *Log Me In to the Old Ballgame: C.B.C. Distribution & Marketing., Inc. v. Major League Baseball Advanced Media, LP*, 22 Berkeley

would establish a similar scheme in the United States, none has yet been enacted, and the issue seems to have receded somewhat on the congressional priority list.

§ 3.11   Non–Copyrightable Subject Matter

3.11.1   Works Prepared by the U.S. Government

Copyright protection is not available for any work of the U.S. government. As specified in § 105, the U.S. government cannot claim copyright in works prepared by government employees in the course of duties of their employment. Statutes, judicial opinions, regulations, reports, manuals, and similar works prepared by federal government employees within the scope of their official duties will therefore fall within the public domain. Section 105 does, however, allow the U.S. government to receive and hold copyrights transferred to it by assignment, bequest, or otherwise.

By its own terms, section 105 does not apply to state and local governments. On the theory that what is not denied is permissible, some state and local government entities have sometimes asserted that works created by their officials are subject to copyright.[169] The courts have often been hostile to such claims, however, reasoning that citizens must have access to the laws governing them.[170] Moreover, works prepared by state and local government employees acting in the scope of their employment would be work made for hire, and thus any copyright would belong to the state or locality as an entity. In a democratic society, these entities both represent and serve the people. It thus strikes your authors as entirely appropriate that citizens should be free to reproduce such governmental works without having to pay an economic toll to do so.

A more complicated issue arises when a state or local government "incorporates by reference" a model code drafted by private individuals. In *Veeck v. Southern Building Code Congress Interna-*

Tech. L.J. 477, 497 (2007). *See also,* Miriam Bitton, *Exploring European Union Copyright Policy Through the Lens of the Database Directive,* 23 Berkeley Tech. L.J. 1411, 1449 (2008) ("Evaluation of the empirical evidence to date suggests that no market failure existed in the database sector. In fact, the evidence suggests that the additional protections did not result in any increase in database production in the years following the implementation of the Directive in the Member States."); Robert Clark, *Database Protection in Europe—Recent Developments and Modest Proposal,* 6 Data Science J. OD12 (2007).

169. See Va. Code Ann. § 9–77.8 (A) (1998) (providing that "[a]ll parts of any code published or authorized to be published ... including statute text, regulation text, catchlines, historical citations, numbers of sections, articles, chapters and titles, frontal analyses and revisor's notes, shall become and remain the exclusive property of the Commonwealth. . . ."). See generally, Irina Y. Dmitrieva, State Ownership of Copyrights in Primary Law Materials, 23 Hastings Comm. & Ent. L.J. 81 (2000).

170. *See* Veeck v. Southern Building Code Congress Int'l, 293 F.3d 791 (5th Cir.2002).

tional, Inc.,[171] the *en banc* Fifth Circuit held that a model building code that had been drafted by a private entity could not be protected by copyright as a matter of law. Reasoning that citizens had the right to know the law, the Court of Appeals concluded that the code had entered the public domain upon its adoption as governing law by two small Texas towns. The Court of Appeals also concluded that the merger doctrine denied copyright protection as well, for the building code could only be expressed in one authoritative way. Stated differently, the law (the building codes) constitutes a fact for purposes of copyright's merger doctrine.[172]

Although the notion that citizens require free access to the laws that govern them is quite resonant, equally compelling is the assertion that experts may require the copyright incentive in order to produce model codes. Building and other codes are typically lengthy and complex documents that require considerable technical expertise to develop. The *Veeck* court was content to make the armchair judgment that trade organizations, builders, engineers, and designers already possessed sufficient incentives to develop model codes. More compelling circumstances may require future courts to make the difficult assessment of determining whether copyright is needed to encourage labors that lead to works of authorship, or whether free access to the fruits of those labors is the dominant value.[173]

3.11.2   Fonts and Typefaces

A House Committee Report accompanying the 1976 Act addressed typeface designs as follows:

> The committee has considered, but chosen to defer, the possibility of protecting the design of typefaces. A "typeface" can be defined as a set of letters, numbers, or other symbolic characters, whose forms are related by repeating design elements consistently applied in a notational system and are intended to be embodied in articles whose intrinsic utilitarian function is for use in composing text or other cognizable combinations of characters. The committee does not regard the design of a typeface, as thus defined, to be a copyrightable "pictorial, graphic, or sculptural work" within the meaning of this bill and the application of the dividing line in section 101.[174]

---

171. 293 F.3d 791 (5th Cir. 2002).

172. *See supra* § 2.3.

173. *See* County of Suffolk v. First American Real Estate Solutions, Inc., 261 F.3d 179 (2d Cir. 2001); Practice Management Info. Corp. v. American Medical Ass'n, 121 F.3d 516 (9th Cir. 1997).

174. H.R. Rep. No. 94–1476, 94th Cong., 2d. Sess. 56 (1976).

Copyright Office regulations are in accord with this statement, expressly disallowing registration of typeface as well as "mere variations of typographical ornamentation, lettering or coloring."[175] The Court of Appeals for the Fourth Circuit upheld these regulations in *Eltra Corp. v. Ringer*.[176] The court squarely held that "typeface had never been considered entitled to copyright" and refused to issue a writ of mandamus compelling the Register of Copyrights to register the plaintiff's copyright claim.[177]

Although this *per se* rule seems clear enough, commentators have cast doubt upon it.[178] The proposition that a typeface design may constitute a work of art seems beyond reasonable dispute. Any user of a modern word processing program also knows that a choice of typeface is often based upon aesthetic considerations. Although Congress and the Copyright Office may be motivated by concerns that typeface is utilitarian, the statutory definition of the phrase "useful article" is "an article having an intrinsic utilitarian function that is not merely to portray the appearance of the article or to convey information."[179] Typefaces would seem to fall directly within this latter exception. Despite this logic, the rule denying typefaces a place within the copyright system is long standing and will likely be retained for the foreseeable future. Moreover it does not seem to have greatly impeded creativity in the development of new and appealing font designs. Indeed, in the digital age, copyright protection for the underlying software that generates the fonts may discourage many from trying to copy the fonts because they would have to write entirely new software code in order to do so.

3.11.3 Titles and Short Phrases

It is a traditional rule that copyright may not be claimed in words and short phrases, including names, titles, and slogans.[180] Given that words such as "Supercalifragilisticexpialidocious"[181] and titles such as "Chew Toy of the Gnat Gods: Reflections on the Wildlife of the Southeast Coast"[182] appear to be original writings within the meaning of the Constitution, this result may appear surprising. Still, the courts and the Copyright Office have apparently reasoned that such writings are too minimal to constitute works of authorship.[183] Protection for titles and short phrases may, however, be available under the "passing off" theory of the unfair

---

175. 37 C.F.R. § 202.1.

176. 579 F.2d 294 (4th Cir.1978).

177. *Id.* at 298.

178. NIMMER, COPYRIGHT § 2.15 (2002).

179. 17 U.S.C. § 101.

180. 37 C.F.R. § 202.1(a).

181. RICHARD M. SHERMAN & ROBERT B. SHERMAN, SUPERCALIFRAGILISTICEXPIALIDOCIOUS.

182. BRUCE LOMBARDO, CHEW TOY OF THE GNAT GODS: REFLECTIONS ON THE WILDLIFE OF THE SOUTHEAST COAST (1997).

183. *See* Russ VerSteeg, *Rethinking Originality*, 34 WILLIAM & MARY L. REV. 801, 881 (1993).

competition law. In addition, short phrases that qualify as trademark slogans may be registered under the Lanham Act or protected under the common law of trademarks.

3.11.4   Blank Forms

Both the regulations of the U.S. Copyright Office and various judicial decisions indicate that blank forms are not copyrightable subject matter. Thus, the Copyright Office will not register claims for "blank forms, such as time cards, graph paper, account books, diaries, bank checks, scorecards, address books, report forms, order forms and the like, which are designed for recording information and do not in themselves convey information."[184]

The basis for this view is rooted in the celebrated case of *Baker v. Selden*,[185] discussed in section 2.3 of the previous chapter in connection with the rule that copyright does not protect ideas. The defendant in that case was making use of certain accounting forms similar to those that were included in plaintiff's book about a new accounting system. The *Baker* Court reasoned that while the text of the book was clearly protected by copyright, the forms themselves were not, because without the forms no one could use the accounting system disclosed by the book. As the Court put it, "[t]he description of the art in a book, though entitled to the benefit of copyright, lays no foundation for an exclusive claim to the art itself. The object of the one is explanation; the object of the other is use."[186]

Cases down to the present have continued this approach. For instance, in *Bibbero Systems, Inc. v. Colwell Systems, Inc.*[187] the plaintiff claimed copyright infringement of a type of medical insurance claim form called a "superbill." The bulk of the forms consisted of lengthy lists of medical diagnoses and treatments, corresponding to categories specified by the American Medical Association, along with accompanying code numbers. There were about two dozen different forms corresponding to different areas of medical specialization. Although the plaintiff had been granted a copyright registration on the forms by the Copyright Office, the Ninth Circuit held that these forms were not copyrightable, noting that "[t]he purpose of Bibbero's superbill is to record information. Until the superbill is filled out, it conveys no information about the patient, the patient's diagnosis, or the patient's treatment. . . . The superbill is simply a blank form which gives doctors a convenient method for

---

184.   37 C.F.R. § 202.1(c).

185.   101 U.S. 99, 25 L.Ed. 841 (1879).

186.   101 U.S. at 105.

187.   893 F.2d 1104 (9th Cir.1990).

recording services performed. The fact that there is a great deal of printing on the face of the form—because there are many possible diagnoses and treatments—does not make the form any less blank."[188]

188.   893 F.2d at 1107–08.

Chapter 4

PUBLICATION AND FORMALITIES

Table of Sections

§ 4.1 Publication

Once upon a time, the issue of publication stood at the very heart of copyright law. Under the 1909 Act, with a few exceptions that need not detain us at this point, no work could obtain federal copyright protection until it was published. Moreover, not any publication would do—to trigger federal rights the publication had to conform to the rules spelled out in the statute and embellished by the case law, the most important of which was the inclusion of a copyright notice on every publicly distributed copy of the work. In this system, *prior to publication* works were protected under state law via the so-called "common law copyright," which was perpetual in duration. If an author published the work without observing the specified federal statutory formalities, the common law copyright was lost and no federal statutory protection attached. In other words, such a publication terminated all protection, and injected the work into the public domain. Publication was thus both the crucial dividing line between state and federal law, and potentially perilous for careless authors and publishers.

Under the present copyright statute—the 1976 Act—none of this continues to be true. While the status of a work as either published or unpublished continues to have numerous consequences, publication no longer determines the key question of whether a work is federally protected. Federal statutory copyright now attaches the moment a work is *fixed* in a tangible medium of expression. Moreover, the current statute explicitly preempts state common law copyright except for works that have not yet been fixed.[1] Just as important, since 1989 publication without formalities no longer puts federal copyright protection at risk, because amendments adopted in that year made the use of a copyright notice optional on published works.

This revolutionary change in the significance of publication does not mean that the contemporary copyright lawyer can ignore the subject or view it merely as a bit of obscure legal history. Given the general non-retroactivity of copyright law and the large number of valuable works first produced and disseminated prior to 1978, issues can and do arise in twenty-first century lawsuits about whether a work was first published without the required notice 40, 50, or more years ago. That's annoying. It means that modern practitioners are obliged to become comfortable with the concept of publication, both as it was defined in the pre–1978 case law, and as it has been codified in the current statute.

The historic importance of publication is not surprising. The American view of copyright has always been largely about money. As we saw much earlier in this text, copyright law gives authors an exclusive right to exploit their works, which allows them to capture any economic returns if the work proves popular. It does this in order to induce (or perhaps we could say, bribe) them to invest effort in creative activities instead of pursuing less economically risky careers such as accountant or law professor. For most of American history, the principal way to obtain that financial reward in connection with a work of authorship was to physically reproduce the work and to then sell the resulting copies to the public—in other words, to publish it. Unpublished works such as private diaries or letters, or draft manuscripts and preliminary sketches that had not been finalized, generally were not material from which authors expected to obtain an economic benefit. In addition, published works may pose a more compelling case for legal protection because they are likely to be more vulnerable to copying as they are, by definition, more widely available. So into the time machine we must go, for a look at publication under the old statute.

---

1. 17 U.S.C. § 301.

4.1.1 Publication Under the 1909 Act

Under the Copyright Act of 1909, publication formed the crucial dividing line between protection under state common law and protection under the federal statute. Before publication, an author whose work was reproduced without his or her permission could maintain a cause of action for infringement of "common law copyright" under the law of his or her home state.[2] There was no time limit on this right. In other words, the "common law copyright" was perpetual—it endured as long as the author kept the work unpublished. This approach, which can be traced back to a venerable nineteenth century decision titled *Wheaton v. Peters*,[3] was premised on the notion that authors had a privacy interest in their manuscripts and other private papers. So long as they kept their work confidential—which is to say, so long as they did not publish it—they could maintain a cause of action against anyone who violated their privacy by duplicating their work. Under this regime, federal law simply did not apply to most unpublished works. Indeed, in 1954, the Supreme Court indicated that authors' rights prior to publication were not technically copyrights at all, but rather a "property right" in the "unpublished manuscript."[4]

Under this system, once an author published the work ***with proper copyright notice*** federal protection of the work replaced the common law remedy. (Such a publication was often characterized as an "investitive" publication because it invested the work with federal statutory rights.) It is for this reason that common law copyright under the regime of the 1909 (and previous) copyright acts was sometimes also referred to as a "right of first publication."[5] As or more important, however, that same act of publication, if done ***without*** notice, would be considered "divestitive." It still terminated the common law protection, but it also rendered the work ineligible for federal statutory copyright and immediately injected the work into the public domain.[6] The rationale for this doctrine was that once an author foregoes the privacy of the work in favor of commercial exploitation, that author should be forced to

---

2. Although referred to as common law copyright, in some states, the protection for unpublished works of authorship was actually a matter of statutory law. *See* West's Ann. Cal. Civ. Code § 980.

3. 33 U.S. 591, 8 L.Ed. 1055 (1834).

4. Mazer v. Stein, 347 U.S. 201, 215, 74 S.Ct. 460, 98 L.Ed. 630 (1954).

5. *See e.g., Stanley v. C.B.S.*, 35 Cal.2d 653, 221 P.2d 73 (1950).

6. In the U.S. law, this rule was first laid down in the landmark opinion

of *Wheaton v. Peters*, 33 U.S. (8 Peters) 591, 8 L.Ed. 1055 (1834). For a more recent example of divestitive publication see *Bell v. Combined Registry Co.*, 397 F.Supp. 1241 (N.D. Ill. 1975) (distribution of copies of poem *Desiderata* to members of U.S. military held to work a forfeiture where copies lacked notice). *See generally* Howard B. Abrams, *The Historic Foundations of American Copyright Law: Exploding the Myth of Common Law Copyright*, 29 WAYNE L. R. 1119 (1983).

enter into the tradeoff of federal copyright law—comprehensive statutory protection, but only for a limited term and only if statutory requirements are observed—rather than continue to enjoy the indefinite protection of common law copyright.[7] As Professor Nimmer put it in his treatise, "upon an author receiving the rewards that flow from the exploitation of his work he must make his treaty with the public by subjecting his work to the limited monopoly of statutory copyright."

Many have characterized the rule concerning divestitive publication as a "trap for the unwary." Perhaps it was. A simple omission of a one line notice on the title page of a book could result in the loss of control over a novel that took years of toil to prepare. On the other hand, during most of the twentieth century, most works were published by professional publishers who were repeat players in the copyright world and had the advice of counsel; relatively few works were self-published by naive authors, likely to be clueless in the intricacies of copyright law. Moreover, many areas of the law attach significant consequences to relatively small failures—for instance, a meritorious claims for millions of dollars can be lost if the compliant is filed one day after the expiration of the statute of limitations. Whether or not the rule was a "trap" however, the existence of such a rule suggests that a precise definition of the concept of publication would be crucial for coherent administration of the statute.

But you might guess where the story is headed—despite its central importance to the scheme created by the 1909 Act, that statute itself did not contain such a definition, leaving it to the courts to work out the notion on a case by case basis. The eventual result was a rather intricate set of rules. The most important of these was the judicially created distinction between a limited publication on the one hand, and a general publication on the other.

4.1.1.1   Limited and General Publication

According to the case law that developed under the 1909 Act, a limited publication is one "which communicates the contents of a manuscript to a definitely selected group and for a limited purpose, without the right of diffusion, reproduction, distribution or sale."[8] For example, if a law professor drafted a law review article on some arcane and tedious topic, such as the law of publication under the 1909 Copyright Act, and then circulated that manuscript to 10 colleagues at other schools for their comments, with the understanding that they could not pass the manuscript on to others, that

7. NIMMER, COPYRIGHT § 4.07 at 4–39 (2002).

8. Intown Enters., Inc. v. Barnes, 721 F.Supp. 1263, 1265 (N.D. Ga. 1989).

See also White v. Kimmell, 193 F.2d 744 (9th Cir.), *cert. denied*, 343 U.S. 957, 72 S.Ct. 1052, 96 L.Ed. 1357 (1952).

would fall within the definition of a limited publication. In a bit of linguistic gymnastics that only a lawyer could love, a limited publication was not considered a publication at all for purposes of divesting common law protection. That is a bit bizarre, so let us say it again. A limited publication is not a publication! Consequently, even under the strict rules of the 1909 Act, circulation of that law review article manuscript in the fashion described above would *not* cause a forfeiture of common law copyright even if the copies in question did not bear a copyright notice.

By contrast, a general publication occurs when, as Professor Nimmer summarized in an oft-quoted[9] formulation, "by consent of the copyright owner, the original or tangible copies of a work are sold, leased, loaned, given away, or otherwise made available to the general public, or when an authorized offer is made to dispose of the work in any such manner even if a sale or other such disposition does not in fact occur."[10] Under the 1909 law, only a publication of this sort—a "general" publication—would divest common law rights and, if done properly, could trigger federal statutory copyright.

In all likelihood, the courts conjured the distinction between general and limited publication to provide a bit of a safety zone for careless authors, who might make preliminary distribution of copies of their work lacking the statutorily required notice. It ameliorated the harsh consequences of the law in cases where an author had not yet really abandoned all privacy interests in his manuscript and had not yet manifested an unequivocal desire to resort to the economic rewards of the marketplace. In many cases, a work circulated via limited publication was still a "work-in-progress," like our hypothetical law review article mentioned above.

The key aspects of the limited publication doctrine were the requirements that distribution be limited to a "selected group" and that it be for a "limited purpose." As one court put it, for publication to be limited the distribution must be "restricted both as to persons and purpose."[11] A good illustration of the doctrine in action is *Academy of Motion Picture Arts and Sciences v. Creative House Promotions, Inc.*[12] The Motion Picture Academy, as all movie lovers know, holds an annual awards event at which it honors the best films and performers of the year. Winners receive praise, glory, the ridicule of hosts like Jon Stewart or Chris Rock and, of course, the

9. *See e.g.* Bartok v. Boosey & Hawkes, Inc., 523 F.2d 941, 945 (2d Cir. 1975); Shoptalk, Ltd. v. Concorde–New Horizons Corp., 168 F.3d 586 (2d Cir. 1999); Brown v. Tabb, 714 F.2d 1088 (11th Cir. 1983).

10. NIMMER, COPYRIGHT, § 4.04 at 4–14 (2002).

11. White v. Kimmell, 193 F.2d 744 (9th Cir.), *cert. denied*, 343 U.S. 957, 72 S.Ct. 1052, 96 L.Ed. 1357 (1952).

12. 944 F.2d 1446 (9th Cir. 1991).

Oscar statuette. From 1929 through 1941, however, those statuettes did not bear any notice of copyright. During that same period,
the Academy did not place any express restriction on how recipients
could use or dispose of their Oscars. In 1941 the Academy belatedly
registered the Oscar with the Copyright office as an unpublished
work, and from that date on included a copyright notice on all the
statuettes.

In 1976, Creative House, a manufacturer of awards and tro-
phies, designed an award that strongly resembled the Oscar statuette, and offered it for sale to corporations who were in the market
for something tangible (other than a raise) that they might give as
a reward to outstanding employees. Eventually, the Academy demanded that Creative House either change the appearance of its
trophy or stop distribution, and when Creative House refused, the
Academy filed suit. Creative House defended by arguing that the
distribution of Oscars without copyright notice over the 12 year
period prior to 1941 constituted a "divestitive" publication that had
injected the work into the public domain. Of course, if the statuette
was in the public domain anyone—including Creative House—
would be free to copy it without incurring liability under the
copyright laws.

After a bench trial, the district court ruled in favor of Creative
House. On appeal the Ninth Circuit reversed. The appellate court
first noted that the 1941 registration of the work created a presumption that it has not been published prior to that date. It then
considered whether the distribution of Oscars during the crucial
12–year period had been limited to a selected group. It had no
trouble finding that it had been, endorsing a district court finding
to that effect and making the indisputable observation that "the
majority of performers in the industry will never receive an Oscar."
It then considered the somewhat trickier question of whether the
Oscars had been distributed for a limited purpose. As the court
explained, to satisfy that element of the limited publication doctrine, the Academy would have to show both "that the purpose of
distributing the Oscar was limited" and "that Oscar recipients had
no right of sale or further distribution."

On the first point, the lower court had found that the Academy's purpose had not been sufficiently limited because its goal in
distributing the Oscar was not just to honor the recipients but also
to promote the film industry. The Ninth Circuit, however, concluded any such promotional objective did not conflict with the "limited
purpose" requirement because the purpose of advancing the motion
picture arts and sciences was itself also a limited purpose.

Regarding the right of further distribution, the appellate court
found that although there had been no express limitation of further

distribution, such a limited distribution has been implied. Effectively, the court reasoned backwards from the fact that no living Oscar recipient ever offered to transfer an Oscar to the general public;[13] the fact that the Oscars were each personalized with the name of the recipient; and the fact that the Academy had done nothing to suggest that recipients were free to either make copies of the Oscar or to sell or distribute them.

In terms of the formal doctrine of limited publication, the analysis of the *Creative House* court does not seem entirely persuasive. The conclusion that the Academy had in some way limited the rights of the Oscar recipients to further distribute their statuettes is surprising given that Academy had made no effort to ever communicate such a limit to recipients, and had no sanctions to use against any recipient who might have attempted to sell or give away his Oscar. Moreover the Academy was using the image of the Oscar to promote the movie industry, and had thus opted to seek economic benefits in the marketplace flowing from this particular work of authorship. To characterize this as a "limited purpose" seems a bit like saying that selling copies of a novel to the public is done for the limited purpose of making money.

On the other hand, it would have been quite harsh to find that the distribution of a hundred or so statuettes in the 1930s destroyed all possibility of copyright decades later when the Oscar had become a world famous icon of enormous commercial value. Perhaps, therefore, the case is most illuminating not only for what it says about the formal rules of the limited publication doctrine, but as a striking example of how courts have sometimes used doctrine creatively to avoid finding a forfeiture of copyright.

Not every litigant can count on being so lucky, however. In *Penguin Books U.S.A., Inc. v. New Christian Church of Full Endeavor, Ltd.,*[14] the plaintiff was a foundation that claimed copyright in materials called *A Course in Miracles*. Although the work had been published with a copyright notice in 1975, the original authors had distributed copies of the work prior to that date. The crucial issue at trial became whether the pre–1975 distribution amounted to a general publication. The evidence revealed that work was initially created over a seven year period from 1965 through 1972 by a psychology professor named Helen Schucman, who testified that she was actually transcribing the words of a divine voice. Between 1973 and 1975 she shared copies of the manuscript with a

---

13. The estate of one recipient had offered an Oscar for sale at auction but a representative of the Academy attended the auction was the high bidder and repurchased the statuette. Thus no Oscar had even been sold to a non-winner.

14. 288 F.Supp.2d 544 (S.D.N.Y. 2003). *See also* Milton H. Greene Archives, Inc. v. BPI Communications, Inc., 378 F.Supp.2d 1189 (C.D. Cal. 2005).

number of individuals interested in religions, psychology, and new age spirituality. Some copies not bearing a copyright notice were distributed at meetings and there was speculation that the recipients likely passed their copies on to others or perhaps made further copies.

The court first considered if distribution had been limited to a "select group." Noting that a "select group cannot be created by an author's subjective test of cordiality" the court concluded that this prong of the definition had not been satisfied. It pointed out that the recipients of the manuscript in this case were persons originally unknown to the author—"congenial strangers" it called them—united only by common interest in the subject matter of the work. Regarding the question of "limited purpose" the court began by noting that there was no evidence of a written limitation on use, and no evidence of any kind of such a limitation regarding at least some of the recipients. It also observed that "an author's lack of personal knowledge or friendship with persons that receive the work is indicative that a distribution was not limited as to the group or the purpose." It concluded that all the interested parties intended to make the book "as available as possible without limitation." As a result, it found that there had been a general, rather than limited publication which operated as a forfeiture of all federal rights. The result is that the book is in the public domain, as is evidenced by the fact that you can now find the full text on the World Wide Web.[15]

As *Penguin Books* illustrates, general publication under the 1909 Act did not require particularly widespread distribution of the work, nor did it require that copies be sold—lending, leasing, or even giving copies away all could suffice.[16] Indeed, there are occasional statements in the case law under the 1909 Act that general publication could be effected by the sale of even a single copy[17] or by a mere offer to sell. However defined, a doctrine that came close to ensnaring a party as presumably sophisticated about copyright as the Motion Picture Academy certainly took on considerable significance in the administration of the 1909 statute.

---

15. http://courseinmiracles.com/ ACIM_Urtext_of_A_Course_In_Miracles _Ready_to_Print_Book.pdf

16. See, e.g., American Vitagraph, Inc. v. Levy, 659 F.2d 1023, 1027 (9th Cir.1981) ("publication occurs when by consent of the copyright owner, the original or tangible copies of a work are sold, leased, loaned, given away, or otherwise made available to the general public . . .") (quoting Nimmer treatise).

17. Grandma Moses v. This Week Magazine, 117 F.Supp. 348 (S.D.N.Y. 1953) (sale of single copy of work of art lacking copyright notice held to inject work into public domain).

4.1.1.2 Performance or Display as Possible Publication

Not all works are shared with the public through the distribution of tangible copies. Some works, such as plays or operas, are primarily destined to be publicly performed. Others, such as paintings or sculptures, are meant to be displayed. The cases under the 1909 Act thus had to determine whether a public performance or display should be treated as a general publication, with all the implications that would follow. Because those cases treated the two topics slightly differently, it is probably best to consider them separately. Regarding performances, the pre–1976 case law consistently held that a public performance was *not* a publication that forfeits copyright and dedicates the work to the public domain.[18] This result obtained even if the public in attendance had paid for their tickets, was permitted to make notes on the performance, and was true even if there were numerous performances or if the audience was extremely large.

What is curious about this doctrine is that it seems at odds with the underlying rationale of the publication rule in the first place. As noted above, courts treated publication as a significant event because it represented an act of economic exploitation of the work. They reasoned that, by choosing to make a profit from the work, the author should only receive federal protection if he observed the statutorily defined pre-requisites, and that the resulting protection should only be on the statutory terms, for only a limited time. Surely, the performance of a dramatic or musical work is a form of economic exploitation—indeed, in the case of drama it is perhaps the chief form.

Nonetheless, the rule grew up that a performance would not be treated as a publication for largely practical reasons. Under section 12 of the 1909 Act, the only way to obtain federal statutory copyright in work "of which copies are not reproduced for sale" was to deposit a complete copy of the work with the Copyright Office. In the case of works like a play written for live performance, changes are often made to the script right up until the moment of performance, making it practically impossible to deposit the statutorily required "complete copy" prior to the time the performance takes place. In this system, if the subsequent performance were considered a "publication" it would have then divested all further opportunity to secure federal copyright. In effect the work would have become ineligible for federal copyright. Another practical problem

---

18. *See e.g.*, Ferris v. Frohman, 223 U.S. 424, 435, 32 S.Ct. 263, 56 L.Ed. 492 (1912) ("The public representation of a dramatic composition, not printed and published, does not deprive the owner of his common-law right, save by operation of statute. At common law, the public performance of the play is not an abandonment of it to the public use"); Nutt v. National Inst., 31 F.2d 236 (2d Cir. 1929); Heim v. Universal Pictures Co., 154 F.2d 480 (2d Cir. 1946); King v. Mister Maestro, Inc., 224 F.Supp. 101 (S.D.N.Y. 1963); Estate of Martin Luther King, Jr., Inc. v. CBS, Inc. 194 F.3d 1211 (11th Cir. 1999).

would have been determining just where and how to provide a formal copyright notice in the case of a work that was being performed. Without physical copies, there seems to be nothing on which to place the notice.

A vivid—indeed perhaps the iconic—illustration of the principle that a performance does not constitute a publication concerns the copyright to Dr. Martin Luther King's famous "I Have A Dream" speech given at the Lincoln Memorial during the 1963 March on Washington. The copyright status of the speech has been litigated twice, first in *King v. Mister Maestro, Inc.*,[19] and more recently in *Estate of Martin Luther King, Jr., Inc. v. CBS, Inc.*[20] Although there were over 200,000 persons present on the national mall to hear the speech live, and although the speech was also made available to a nationwide television audience, both cases concluded that the delivery of the speech was not a divestitive publication, meaning that Dr. King retained copyright. As the Eleventh Circuit put it in the more recent case, "the huge audience and the Speech's significance in terms of newsworthiness and history are features that, according to the case law, are not significant . . .".

The King cases also involved the problem discussed in the previous sub-section concerning the distinction between limited and general publication because, prior to delivering the speech, Dr. King had delivered a copy of it to the press liaison personnel for the March on Washington. The speech was duplicated and put into a "press kit" which was distributed to reporters covering the march. These copies did not bear a copyright notice. Dr. King testified that this distribution was without his knowledge or consent, but there was nothing to indicate that he had expressly forbidden such reproduction. Both cases nonetheless held that this distribution was only to a limited group—the press—for a limited purpose—namely to enable them to better cover a public event. It seems more than a little odd to treat the sharing of the text with the media so that they can, in turn, publicize the text in newspapers and magazines as a limited purpose, so the case may be yet another example of judicial manipulation of the limited publication doctrine, in this case to avoid unwitting copyright forfeiture by an author of extraordinary historical stature.

The law regarding whether a display of a work such as a painting should constitute a general publication under the 1909 Act is a bit more nuanced. Where the work was put on display for the purpose of offering it for sale to the public, the artist is plainly forgoing the privacy in favor of a hoped-for economic reward. The logical basis of the pre–1976 Act approach to publication suggests,

19. 224 F.Supp. 101 (S.D.N.Y. 1963).

20. 194 F.3d 1211 (11th Cir. 1999).

therefore, that this type of display should be considered a general publication even before the work is actually sold, and there is some sparse authority to that effect.[21] On the other hand, if the display was for purposes of exhibition of the work to the public, with no intention to transfer control of the physical object—as would be true of display in a museum—the same underlying logic suggests that no publication should be found. In that case, the artist has not really relinquished control of the work, nor has he or she taken steps toward exploiting the work economically. However, the Supreme Court endorsed only a modified version of this second proposition, when it considered the issue in 1907. In *American Tobacco Co. v. Werckmeister*,[22] the Court held that public exhibition did not constitute publication *provided that there was an express or implied condition imposed on the public not to copy the work.*

Applying this proposition several decades later, the district court in *Letter Edged in Black Press, Inc. v. Public Bldg. Comm'n of Chicago*[23] found a general publication based on the public display of a scale model of a proposed monumental statute by the artist Pablo Picasso because "there were no restrictions on copying [of the publicly displayed sculpture] and no guards preventing copying" and "every citizen was free to copy the [sculpture] for his own pleasure and camera permits were available to members of the public."[24] Where it is unclear if public copying was permitted or prohibited there is some language in the cases saying that a prohibition will be implied. This default rule, like the doctrine of limited publication itself, tends to err on the side of protecting authors against inadvertent loss of potential federal protection.

4.1.1.3 Distribution of Sound Recordings as Publication of Musical Work

Another difficult question that arose under the pre–1978 publication jurisprudence was whether the public distribution of phonograph records constituted a publication of the underlying musical

---

21. *See generally* NIMMER, COPYRIGHT § 4.01[C][1] at n.35.19. *But see* 122 Cong. Rec. 31980 (Sept. 22, 1976) ("in the case of a work of art, such as a painting or statute, that exists in only one copy . . . it is not the Committee's intention that such a work should be regarded as 'published when the single existing copy is sold or offered for sale in the traditional way . . .' ") (Remarks of Congressman Kastenmeir, discussing the bill that became the 1976 copyright act).

22. American Tobacco Co. v. Werckmeister, 207 U.S. 284, 300, 28

S.Ct. 72, 52 L.Ed. 208 (1907) ("We do not mean to say that the public exhibition of a painting or statue, where all might see and freely copy it, might not amount to publication within the statute, regardless of the artist's purpose or notice of reservation of rights which he takes no measure to protect."). *See also* Patterson v. Century Productions, 93 F.2d 489 (2d Cir. 1937).

23. 320 F.Supp. 1303, 1311 (N.D.Ill. 1970).

24. *See also*, Scherr v. Universal Match Corp., 297 F.Supp. 107 (S.D.N.Y. 1967).

composition (or other material) recorded on those records.[25] If it was, that would inject those musical works into the public domain in any case where the records did not bear a notice of copyright. Given that industry practice during much of the early and mid–twentieth century had not been to mark vinyl records with a copyright notice, treating the dissemination of the records as publication of the underlying musical works would have put a vast library of music into the public domain.

A handful of lower court decisions during the 1950s and 1960s found that the sale of records did constitute a publication of the musical works involved. A notable exception arose in 1976, however, when the Second Circuit ruled in *Rosette v. Rainbo Record Mfg. Corp.*,[26] that the sale of notice-less phonorecords did not inject the musical works recorded on those records into the public domain. *Rosette* relied on the doctrine of the early twentieth century case of *White–Smith Music Co. v. Apollo Co.*[27] That case involved the reproduction of songs onto perforated player piano rolls without the permission of the copyright owner of the songs. The Supreme Court held in *White–Smith* that the piano rolls in question were not copies of the songs because they were not "visually perceptible"—in other words, you could not deduce the melody by looking at the rolls. Since the defendant did not "make copies" the Court refused to find any infringement. On the logic of *White–Smith*, vinyl records were not "copies" of the songs they contained because on could not look at them as "see the notes." The Second Circuit therefore reasoned in *Rosette* that, the parties who sold records had not sold "copies" of the underlying songs, and thus they did not "publish" those songs, and thus no notice was requires. Voila.

Twenty years later, however, the Court of Appeals for the Ninth Circuit explicitly took issue with *Rosette* in *La Cienega Music Co. v. ZZ Top*.[28] That opinion, which accurately characterized *Rosette* as the minority rule, reasoned that treating the sale of records as a publication of the musical works they contained was "in accord with the underlying rationale of the publication doctrine. That is, an author in permitting records of his work to be publicly marketed is certainly engaging in a form of exploitation of his work and should therefore be required to seek protection, if at all, only under the limited monopoly concept of the federal Copy-

---

25. We use the term "records" in this sub-section because in the pre–1978 era vinyl records were virtually the only type of publicly distributed phonorecords and more modern media—such as CDs—did not exist. For younger readers who do not know what a vinyl record is, *see e.g.*, http://en.wikipedia.org/wiki/Gramophone_record.

26. 546 F.2d 461, 462 (2d Cir.1976).

27. 209 U.S. 1, 28 S.Ct. 319, 52 L.Ed. 655 (1908).

28. *See La Cienega Music Co. v. ZZ Top*, 53 F.3d 950 (9th Cir.), *cert. denied*, 516 U.S. 927, 116 S.Ct. 331, 133 L.Ed.2d 231 (1995).

right Act." Not only did the *LaCienega* case create a division of authority in the federal courts, but it threw the music industry into turmoil. If the *LaCienega* view prevailed, a significant amount of mid-twentieth century music stood to lose copyright protection.

In the face of that threat, the industry appealed to Congress for clarification, and two years later Congress responded by legislatively overruling *La Cienega*. Newly added § 303(b) of the 1976 Copyright Act provides that the "distribution before January 1, 1978, of a phonorecord shall not for any purpose constitute a publication of a musical work embodied therein." While some might question whether after-the-fact changes to the 1976 Act can legitimately alter judicial interpretations of the 1909 Act, the courts that have considered the question have found no problem with the 1997 amendments, concluding that the statute applies to all cases pending at the time of its enactment.[29]

4.1.1.4 Publication of Motion Pictures

One final set of specialized publication issues that arose under the 1909 Act concerned the motion picture industry. Given the rule that the performance of a work did not constitute the publication of the work, the mere projection of a motion picture in a movie theater was never thought to be a publication. Of course, the producer of a motion picture makes multiple copies of the movie, so that it can be simultaneously displayed in many theaters. However, it has long been the custom in the motion picture industry for companies to lease, rather than to sell, prints of their films to distributors for exhibition to the public. Since this practice does not involve the transfer of ownership of copies to members of the general public, one might think that it too would not amount to publication.

However, the case law interpreting the 1909 Act held that once a distributor placed a movie into general commercial distribution, there has been a general publication, with all the attendant consequences.[30] Thus it was necessary under the 1909 Act for prints of the movie to bear a proper copyright notice to avoid having the movie fall into the public domain. Of course, if the movie has been placed on videocassettes (or more recently DVDs) and those videocassettes or discs are sold directly to members of the public, a general publication occurs under the conventional analysis.

29. *See* Mayhew v. Allsup, 166 F.3d 821 (6th Cir. 1999); ABKCO Music, Inc. v. LaVere, 217 F.3d 684 (9th Cir. 2000).

30. American Vitagraph, Inc. v. Levy, 659 F.2d 1023 (9th Cir. 1981).

4.1.2 Publication Under the Current Statute

In 1976, the authors of the new copyright statute decided to drain publication of much of its importance by moving the dividing line between common law and federal statutory protection backwards, from the moment of publication to the moment of fixation of the work. Under the current statute, once a work is written down or otherwise fixed, federal protection attaches regardless of whether the work is published or not. State common law copyright for *fixed* works is explicitly preempted.[31] This had the effect of eliminating the common-law copyright, at least for any works that were written down, taped, or otherwise embodied in a tangible artifact. As we shall see below, in our discussion of copyright notice, during the first decade after passage of the 1976 Act, publication without notice still could result in loss of copyright protection unless the author took prompt corrective steps. Since 1989, however, the omission of a copyright from copies of a published work has no effect on federal copyright protection at all.

This is not to say that the fact of publication has become entirely irrelevant for post–1978 works. Professor Nimmer itemizes in his treatise over a dozen features of the current, post–1989, American copyright regime where publication remains important.[32] For example, the obligation to deposit copies of a work with the Library of Congress arises only upon publication;[33] registration of the work within 5 years after publication is necessary in order for the registration to operate as *prima facie* evidence of the validity of the copyright;[34] the duration of copyright in works made for hire, anonymous works, or pseudonymous works are all measured from the date of publication;[35] and the scope of fair use may be broader in cases involving published works than is cases where the work is unpublished.[36] Publication also retains considerable importance in the international context. Under the major international copyright treaty, the Berne Convention, it is *publication* of a work in one participating state that triggers the obligations of other states to afford the work the same copyright protection as it would to works published in its own territory.[37]

---

31. 17 U.S.C. § 30. States can continue to protect unfixed works (such as impromptu speeches or musical improvisations) through their common law. See the discussion of fixation at § 3.2 *supra*.

32. NIMMER, COPYRIGHT § 4.01[A] at 4–4 and 4–5 (2002). Among the situations in the statute where publication remains important are the measuring periods for terminating certain transfers, the durational period for works made for hire and certain other works, limitations on performance rights in certain dramatic works, and rules concern-ing the availability of statutory damages for infringement of unregistered works. These various publication-dependant rules are developed elsewhere in this text, in the sections that cover the relevant topics.

33. 17 U.S.C. § 407(a).

34. 17 U.S.C. § 410(c).

35. 17 U.S.C.§ 302(c).

36. 17 U.S.C. § 107.

37. *See* Berne Convention, Art. 5(1).

Given the residual legal relevance of publication, and to eliminate some of the ambiguities that prevailed under the 1909 law, Congress decided to include an explicit definition of publication in the new statute. Its goal in doing so was substantially to codify the approach that had emerged in the earlier cases while simultaneously clarifying some of the more ambiguous aspects of that case law. The current statute provides that a publication is:

> the distribution of copies or phonorecords of a work to the public by sale or other transfer of ownership, or by rental, lease or lending. The offering to distribute copies or phonorecords to a group of persons for purposes of further distribution, public performance, or public display, constitutes publication. A public performance or display of a work does not of itself constitute publication.[38]

Note that the language referring to distribution to a group for purposes of public performance codifies the rule under the 1909 Act that treats general distribution of a motion picture as a publication. Note also that the statutory definition eliminates any ambiguity over whether to treat a display as a publication, by making it quite plain that a display does not constitute a publication under any circumstances, and regardless of whether the author has forbidden viewers to make copies.

Over the last 15 years or so, technological evolution has raised a new definitional problem in the area of publication. Today authors may choose to disseminate their works digitally, by posting them on a Web Site or otherwise making them available on the Internet. This can be done with no expectation of profit, as is the case on most blogs, where individuals might post lengthy prose essays analyzing the events of the day or short rants merely to unburden themselves or for reasons of ego. On the other hand, resort to the Internet can be done with the goal of making money, because the author may limit electronic access to only those who have paid a fee. For all the purposes for which publication is still relevant under the copyright laws, then, posting on-line might logically be considered to be a form of publication. It makes the work widely available and it represents a classic resort to the marketplace for economic gain.

This appears to be the consensus of several district courts that have considered either this question or the closely related issue of whether uploading someone else's works to the Internet violates the owner's distribution rights.[39] As one district court noted:

38. 17 U.S.C. § 101.

39. *See, e.g.*, Playboy Enterprises, Inc. v. Frena, 839 F.Supp. 1552 (M.D.Fla.1993); Playboy Enterprises, Inc. v. Chuckleberry Pub., Inc., 939 F.Supp. 1032 (S.D.N.Y. 1996). *See also* Kristy Wiehe, *Dollars, Downloads and Digital Distribution: Is "Making Avail-*

> [M]erely by accessing a webpage, an Internet user acquires the ability to make a copy of that webpage, a copy that is, in fact, indistinguishable in every part from the original. Consequently, when a website goes live, the creator loses the ability to control either duplication or further distribution of his or her work. A webpage in this respect is indistinguishable from photographs, music files, or software posted on the web—all can be freely copied. Thus, when a webpage goes live on the Internet, it is distributed and "published" in the same way the music files in Napster or the photographs in the various Playboy decisions were distributed and "published."[40]

While these decisions make sense in terms of the commercial and technical realities of the Internet, they seem to stretch the statutory language. The current act defines publication as a distribution of "copies or phonorecords" to the public, and defines copies and phonorecords in ways that make it clear that we are referring to specific tangible objects. Posting a poem or photograph on a website arguably does not result in giving members of the public a "copy" of that work. Rather, it essentially exhibits the work and invites members of the public to make their own copy, which is what they do when they visit the relevant web site and load the text or image into the memory of their own computer. This, of course, sounds like an unrestricted "display" which, we have noted earlier, is specifically excluded from the definition of publication.[41] The result is a judicial interpretation that, in an effort to treat a new technology sensibly, has done some violence to the actual statutory text—an increasingly common state of affairs in copyright law.

As we leave the subject of publication, bear in mind that a work first published prior to 1978 without the legally required notice does not regain any protection under the new act.[42] Having been injected into the public domain by a divestitive publication, it cannot be withdrawn from the public domain. Consequently, controversies can continue to arise today concerning the copyright

---

able" a Copyrighted Work a Violation of the Author's Distribution Right?, 15 UCLA Ent. L. Rev. 117 (2008).

40. Getaped.com Inc v. Cangemi, 188 F.Supp.2d 398 (S.D.N.Y. 2002).

41. On this point, *see generally,* R. Anthony Reese, *The Public Display Right: The Copyright Act's Neglected Solution to the Controversy over RAM "Copies,"* 2001 U. Ill. L. Rev. 83.

42. There is an exception to this principle for works that were first pub- lished abroad without notice. Courts disagreed whether such foreign publication was divestitive under the 1909 Act. Effective in 1996, however, Congress provided for the restoration of copyrights in such foreign-published works if they were still protected in their country of origin. 17 U.S.C. § 104A. A full discussion of the history and mechanics of this provision can be found in the chapter on Copyright Duration elsewhere in this volume.

status of older works, which turn on whether those were "published" without notice.

§ 4.2 Notice

As we have seen, under the 1909 Act general publication of a work without proper notice had grave consequences for an author attempting to claim copyright—it divested common law copyright, precluded federal copyright, and injected the work into the public domain. As we have also seen, Congress relaxed that draconian approach in two stages—first allowing parties who omitted notice to cure the deficiency by taking prescribed steps and then, ultimately, dispensing with the notice requirement entirely. This meant that there are three separate eras in American copyright law insofar as notice is concerned—the pre–1978 period; the period from January 1, 1978 through February 28, 1989; and the post-March 1, 1989 period. The state of the law in each of these eras is discussed in the subsections that follow.

Before addressing the doctrinal particulars, it is worth pausing to consider briefly some of the competing views on the value of the notice requirement. Proponents of the view that copyright owners should be obligated to include a notice on copies of their works point to several benefits of that practice. They note that a copyright notice informs the public that the work is protected and serves as a warning against unauthorized use, while the absence of a notice allows parties to use the work confident that it lies in the public domain. Moreover, the notice also aids in identifying the owner, permitting those acting in good faith to attempt to contact that owner for a license if they want to use the work. The notice also provides the date of publication, which can be a valuable piece of information in calculating the term of the copyright in some cases, and thus sometimes assisting users to determine if the work has fallen into the public domain. Finally, advocates of the traditional notice requirement point out that it has the beneficial effect of instantly injecting into the public domain works that the author did not wish to copyright.[43]

On the other hand, opponents of a copyright notice requirement have long argued that it is a trap for the unwary. They stress that the technicalities of the notice requirement undoubtedly deprived some worthy but inattentive authors of the benefits of copyright protection over the years. The requirement of notice also prevented the United States from acceding to the Berne Convention for many decades after that important treaty first appeared on the scene, and generally stands in opposition to the world-wide consensus against conditioning copyright on the observance of formalities.

---

43. H.R. Rep. No. 94–1476, 94th Cong., 2d Sess. 143 (1976).

The permissive notice regime of the present U.S. copyright law can be seen as a compromise between these two positions. It builds in incentives for parties to use a copyright notice. To the extent that they do so, the public will realize some of the benefits of the notice itemized above. However, by eliminating sanctions for omitting notice and making its use optional the statute attempts to eliminate the most serious downsides that opponents have identified over the years, particularly the inadvertent forfeiture of rights.

4.2.1 Prior to 1978

The 1909 copyright statute required a valid copyright notice on all copies of a published work, on pain of loss of rights. That statute set out the details of the notice requirements in sections 19 through 21. Section 19 generally provides that the notice consist either of the word "Copyright," the abbreviation "Copr.", or the symbol ©, along with the name of the copyright proprietor. If the work was a printed literary, musical, or dramatic work, the notice also had to include the year of the work's first publication. The elements of the notice had to appear in sufficient proximity to each other to make it obvious that they were all part of the single notice required by law. If they were "dispersed" the notice requirement would not be met, even if all elements could be found somewhere on a single title page.[44]

The 1909 Act also set out the mandatory location for the notice in section 20. For example, for a book or printed publication, notice had to be given on the title page or the page immediately thereafter. In a concession to artistic integrity, section 19 of the 1909 Act allowed for a "short form" notice that may be placed on pictorial, graphical, and sculptural works. For such works, the initials or mark of the copyright proprietor, along with the symbol ©, would suffice, provided that the proprietor's full name also appeared on the margin, base, pedestal or other accessible portion of the work.

Section 21 of the 1909 Act sets forth certain circumstances where the omission of notice would be excused. Section 21 is narrowly worded and has been construed strictly by the courts. As a result, most would-be copyright proprietors found this provision did little to ameliorate the harsh consequences of publishing without notice. In particular, section 21 operates only where an omission occurred by "accident or mistake." Mechanical difficulties encountered by the printer, such as a damaged printing plate, were the prototypical incident within the meaning of this provision.[45] In

44. *See, e.g.*, Moger v. WHDH, Inc., 194 F.Supp. 605 (D.Mass. 1961) (prominent display of author's name under title of work not adequate notice where copyright symbol not accompanied by author's name).

45. Leon B. Rosenblatt Textiles, Ltd. v. M. Lowenstein & Sons, Inc., 321 F.Supp. 186 (S.D.N.Y. 1970).

contrast, courts reasoned that negligence did not amount to the type of accident or mistake contemplated by the 1909 Act.[46] As well, section 21 states that notice must have been omitted only on "a particular copy or copies." Consequently, judicial opinions suggest that the omission of notice must have occurred in only a limited number of copies for section 21 to apply.[47]

4.2.2 Between 1978 and 1989

Special rules apply to works published in the ten-year period between 1978—when the 1976 Act came into effect—and 1989, when Congress enacted the Berne Convention Implementation Act. Professor Nimmer termed such works "decennial works" because of the relevant period is almost exactly one full decade.[48] As initially enacted, section 401(a) of the 1976 Act provided:

> Whenever a work protected under this title is published in the United States or elsewhere by authority of the copyright owner, a notice of copyright as provided by this section shall be placed on all publicly distributed copies from which the work can be visually perceived, either directly or with the aid of machine or device.

Note the word "shall." It makes it absolutely plain that copyright notice was mandatory under the original version of the 1976 Act, just as it had been under the 1909 law.

The 1976 Act slightly modified the components of a proper copyright notice from the rules set out in the 1909 Act. It specified that a proper notice of copyright must consist of three elements: (1) the familiar symbol ©,[49] the word "Copyright," or the abbreviation "Copr."; (2) the year of first publication; and (3) the name of the copyright proprietor.[50] The statute does not specify the relative locations of these elements, suggesting that any order creates effective notice. Unlike the 1909 Act, the 1976 Act also does not specify the precise position where notice should be put on particular sorts of works, but rather instructs the Register of Copyrights to issue regulations governing that issue.[51] If the copyright notice

---

46. Puddu v. Buonamici Statuary, Inc., 450 F.2d 401 (2d Cir. 1971).

47. Wabash Pub. Co. v. Flanagan, 14 USPQ2d 2037 (N.D. Ill. 1990).

48. Nimmer, § 7.02[C][2].

49. For phonorecords, copyright owners must use the symbol ℗ instead. 17 U.S.C. § 402(b).

50. Many publishers also included the words "All Rights Reserved" in the copyright notice. This phrase was re-quired by a copyright treaty known among Western Hemisphere nations known as the Buenos Aires Convention. By 2000, all parties to that treaty had ratified the Berne convention making its provisions as to notice moot. The words "All Rights Reserved" are therefore entirely superfluous in modern practice, but continue to be used as a matter of habit or in the belief that they serve as a deterrent to copying.

51. *See* 37 C.F.R. § 201.20.

contains no name or no date, the work is considered to lack copyright notice.[52]

But there was a significant liberalization embodied in the 1976 Act. In contrast to works published under the 1909 Act, the absence of notice upon copies of works published during the "decennial" was not invariably fatal. First, copyright was not affected if the notice was removed without the authorization of the copyright owner.[53] Similarly, the owner retained his copyright if a distributor failed to comply with an express written agreement that the distributor observe the notice requirement.[54] Third, an omitted notice was wholly excused if the omission occurred in "no more than a relatively small number of copies of phonorecords distributed to the public."[55] In interpreting the phrase "no more than a relatively small number," courts have tended towards a percentage test, rather than looking at the absolute number of copies on which notice was not given. For example, in *Ford Motor Co. v. Summit Motor Products, Inc.*, the U.S. Court of Appeals for the Third Circuit excused the omission of copyright notice on four million out of 100 million works, concluding that under these facts four million constituted "a relatively small number."[56]

Even if the author could not claim one of these three exceptions, the 1976 Act provided an additional curative mechanism for those who published without notice which could enable them to avoid forfeiture of copyright. Under the original version of section § 405(a)(2) an omission of notice would be excused if "registration for the work has been made before or is made within five years after the publication without notice, and a reasonable effort is made to add notice to all copies or phonorecords that are distributed to the public in the United States after the omission has been discovered...."[57]

Before we untangle these requirements, let us consider if this provision still has any relevance to the modern copyright practitioner. The latest works governed by "notice-is-mandatory-but-you-can-cure-an-omission" system would have been published in early 1989. As we shall see shortly, after that point, notice became optional. Cure required registration no later than 5 years after the relevant notice-less publication. Thus, one would have had to register no later than 1994 in order to comply with the cure requirement. A party trying to invoke this provision today either did or did not register the work in time. If not, it is too late now—running to the Copyright Office in 2010 to register the copyright will not help.

---

52. 17 U.S.C. § 406(c).

53. 17 U.S.C. § 405(c).

54. 17 U.S.C. § 405(a)(3).

55. 17 U.S.C. § 405(a)(1).

56. 930 F.2d 277 (3d Cir. 1991).

57. A similar provision governs errors in the name or the date provided in the notice. *See* 17 U.S.C. § 406.

However, it is possible that we might have a scenario involving a work published in, say 1987, without notice, and then registered in 1990, whose status is only first called into question in litigation taking place in 2010 or 2015. To determine the status of that work we would have to consider compliance with original section 405.

That determination can be thorny because of two difficulties in the provision. First, the few courts to have considered the section disagreed over what constituted "reasonable effort" to add notice to subsequently distributed copies; and second they had trouble defining the moment at which an omission would be deemed "discovered." Let us consider reasonable effort first.

Under the cure provision of the original 1976 Act, once a copyright owner learned of a notice problem, he had to use "reasonable effort" to put a notice on all copies subsequently distributed to the public. If there were undistributed copies still in the hands of the copyright owner, there was little ambiguity—plainly the copyright owner was obligated to affix notice to those copies before sending them on their way to consumers. And of course, any newly manufactured copies would also have to bear notice now that the omission was discovered. For instance, assume a book publisher printed 1000 copies of a book in 1988, all lacking notice, and shipped 300 to bookstores that year. It became aware of the lack of notice in January, 1989. Clearly it had a duty to go to its warehouse and add a notice to the remaining 700 copies sitting there (probably by affixing an adhesive sticker to them) as well as a duty to include notice on any subsequently printed copies.

There was also little ambiguity with respect to copies that had reached end users. Let us assume that of the 300 copies that had gone to bookstores, 100 had been sold to consumers prior to the publisher's discovery of the missing notice. Those copies would already have been distributed to the public *before* rather than *after* the date of discovery, so there is no duty at all to try to add notice to them. That certainly seems logical because no one would have any records of who those purchasers were or what they did with the copies.

The difficulty arose with respect to copies that had moved partway down the channel of distribution before the notice problem was discovered. Notice-less copies in the hands of wholesalers, retailers, and other distributors are not yet "distributed to the public" and thus the statute seemed to require that some effort be made to add notice to these as well. In our hypothetical, that would be the 200 copies that were still on the shelves at Borders or Barnes & Noble or other booksellers. But what kind of effort? Obviously, the question requires a case by case determination, but, as one court noted, "[i]mplicit in the concept of a 'reasonable effort' under § 405(a)(2) is the expectation that an expenditure of time and money over and above that required in the normal course of business will be made."[58]

The decision of the Court of Appeals for the First Circuit in *Charles Garnier, Paris v. Andin International, Inc.* took a strict position on this question.[59] Garnier claimed copyright in a "swirled hoop" earring. Unfortunately for the company, it began distributing copies of that work without notice in 1988, before the notice requirement was relaxed. Eventually, Garnier discovered the problem, and attempted to cure the absence of notice, in part, by supplying retailers with "story cards"—written statements explaining that each earring embodied "a copyrighted design." Garnier instructed its retailers to include a story card with each purchased earring. Garnier also contended that its curative efforts need only relate to earrings distributed prior to March 1, 1989, the effective date of the Berne Convention Implementation Act (BCIA). Because most, if not all of these earrings had already made their way into the hands (and ears) of consumers, Garnier's view would have significantly limited its responsibilities.

The First Circuit disagreed with Garnier, however, on both points. First, it held that § 405(a)(2) imposed a cure requirement for *all copies* of a work that was first published prior to the effective date of the BCIA, regardless of when the individual copies were distributed. Thus if Garnier shipped only a few copies of the earrings lacking notice to retailers in 1988, then shipped extensive quantities (also lacking notice) throughout late 1989 and 1990, finally discovering the problem in 1991, its obligation would be to add notice to all the copies still in retail hands at that point, not just those that were shipped before the notice rules were relaxed.

The result seems dubious as a matter of policy. The requirement to add notice in the original version of the 1976 Act was presumably based on the beneficial effects of such notice in giving consumers valuable information about the copyright status of the work. It is unlikely that Congress included the "add notice" requirements to the cure merely to punish the careless copyright holder or to make its life difficult. With the 1989 amendments reflecting a new Congressional assessment devaluing the notice requirement, there seems little reason to force a party in Garnier's position to add notice to those copies distributed after 1989.

On the second point, the *Charles Garnier* court went on to hold that the jeweler's efforts were insufficient to constitute reasonable efforts under § 405(a)(2), noting in particular that its "story cards"

---

58. Videotronics, Inc. v. Bend Electronics, 586 F.Supp. 478, 483 (D.Nev. 1984).

59. 36 F.3d 1214 (1st Cir. 1994).

were not physically attached to the earrings. Presumably, the court envisioned that a proper effort in these circumstances required providing retailers and wholesalers with a label or other means that could be permanently affixed to each copy of the work in their possession. Perhaps the copyright owner would also have to send out personnel to check that the retailers actually did affix the labels, rather than simply throw them in the trash, although the court did not offer any guidance on that point. Although the determination of whether a copyright plaintiff made a reasonable effort or not is determined on a case-by-case basis as a question of fact,[60] *Charles Garnier* suggests that courts will apply this standard strictly.

The statutory reference to "discovery" of an omission of notice in the original cure provision of the 1976 Act has also led to some puzzlement. Determining the moment at which the absence of notice was discovered presents no special complexities in cases of accidental omissions. Cases of deliberate omissions of notice present more difficulties. One possibility is that § 405(a)(2) does not apply to such cases. Under this view, a deliberate omission cannot be "discovered" in the sense of the statute because it was never hidden. Both the case law[61] and the legislative history of the 1976 Act[62] reject this position, the latter expressly stating that even deliberate omissions can be excused if the statutory conditions are met.

A second position, with some support from the judicial decisions,[63] is that deliberate omissions are discovered only when the author or publishers learns that the existence of a copyright has become an issue. A third, even more lenient view is that the moment of discovery occurs when the copyright proprietor learns of the legal significance of the failure to provide notice.[64] A difficulty with these extremely tolerant stances is that it eliminates incentives for copyright owners to place notice on copies of their works. Professor Marshall Leaffer has promoted a sensible fourth position: that the discovery of deliberate omissions occurs automatically when the work is first published.[65] The point remains unresolved, and given that there are likely to be very few additional cases involving decennial works, it may fall into the category of such questions as how many angels can dance on the head of a pin.

---

60. *See Princess Fabrics, Inc. v. CHF, Inc.*, 922 F.2d 99, 103 (2d Cir. 1990).

61. *See Hasbro Bradley, Inc. v. Sparkle Toys, Inc.*, 780 F.2d 189 (2d Cir. 1985).

62. H.R. Rep. No. 94–1476, 94th Cong., 2d Sess. 147 (1976).

63. *See O'Neill Devs., Inc. v. Galen Kilburn, Inc.*, 524 F.Supp. 710, 714 (N.D. Ga. 1981).

64. *See Charles Garnier, Paris v. Andin Int'l, Inc.*, 36 F.3d 1009, 1113 (7th Cir. 1983).

65. MARSHALL LEAFFER, UNDERSTANDING COPYRIGHT LAW § 4.11[D] (5th ed. 2010).

Given all this, you might wonder about the rights of a party who encountered a copy of a decennial work that lacked notice. Such a party might have justifiably thought that the work had fallen into the public domain due to the lack of notice, and have gone ahead and made copies of the work, only to learn that the author subsequently cured the lack of notice and was now suing him for infringement. Section 405(b) provides that in such a case, if the alleged infringer demonstrates that he was misled about the copyright status of a work because the copy that he consulted lacked a notice, he is immune from actual or statutory damages, until he received actual notice that the work had been registered.

4.2.3   After 1989

The Berne Convention Implementation Act (BCIA) of 1988 abolished the notice requirement for works distributed on or after March 1, 1989. Amended section 401(a) now merely states that notice "may be placed" on publicly distributed copies of works of authorship, as compared to its earlier mandate that such notice "shall be placed" on published works. The one word change means that notice is optional, and lack of notice no longer puts the validity of a copyright at risk.

This step was considered necessary to bring U.S. copyright law into compliance with the Berne Convention, which bars notice and other formalities from serving as conditions of copyright protection.[66] Bear in mind, however, that the BCIA acts only prospectively. Thus works published prior to the BCIA must be judged as to the notice requirements prevailing at the time they were published.

Although Congress eliminated notice as a requirement, it retained a statutory incentive to induce publishers to continue to include a notice. Under section 401(d), if the copy of a work that an alleged infringer consulted had a copyright notice, "no weight" will be given to that person's claim of innocent infringement in mitigation of damages.[67] Whether because of this inducement, or simply out of habit, the vast majority of American publishers continue to include a copyright notice on all published works.

---

66. Berne Convention, Art. 5(2).

67. Section 504 provide minimum "statutory damages" of $750 for infringement of each copyrighted work. However, § 504(c)(2) provides, in part, that "in a case where the infringer sustains the burden of proving, and the court finds, that such infringer was not aware and had no reason to believe that his or her acts constituted an infringement of copyright, the court in its discretion may reduce the award of statutory damages to a sum of not less than $200." Section 401(d) precludes this reduction of statutory damages in cases where the owner of the work used the optional notice.

4.2.4 Copyright Notice on Collective Works

Original section 404 of the 1976 Act also dealt with the notice requirements for collective works. A collective work, you will recall, is one consisting of a number of contributions, each of which is a separate copyrightable work, which has been assembled into a collective whole, such as a magazine or an anthology of stories written by different authors.[68] The compiler of the collective work is entitled to a copyright for the collective work as a whole because there is original authorship in the selection and arrangement of the materials.[69] Under section 404, a single "blanket" notice covering the entire collective work in the name of the compiler was deemed to satisfy the notice requirement for not only the collective work, but for each of its constituent elements as well.[70] Put the other way around, under the original 1976 Act a separate notice of copyright for each individual component part of a collective work was not required so long as the collective work contained a blanket notice.

However that rule came with a downside. The statute declares that any "person who innocently [began] an undertaking that infringes the copyright has a complete defense to any action for such infringement if such person proves that he or she was misled by the notice and began the undertaking in good faith under a purported transfer or license from the person named therein...."[71] Thus, if a third party obtained, in good faith, permission to use a single contribution to the collective work from the copyright owner of the collective work, that third party would be immune from suit by the copyright owner of the individual contribution. This would be true even if the copyright owner of the collective work did not have the authority to license the use of the individual contribution. On the other hand, this rule would not apply if, before the third party began his activities, the author of the individual contribution had filed a copyright registration or if there were any other documents on file at the Copyright Office revealing the true ownership of the individual work.[72]

Let us see if we can put all that more concretely. Assume that Connie Compiler put together a collection of American poetry of the 1980s titled *Decennial Ditties* by obtaining copyright licenses to publish 50 previously unpublished poems from 50 different poets and then organizing them, with accompanying commentary in a single volume. Let us assume that *Decennial Ditties* was published in 1986 bearing only a single copyright notice at the front of the

---

68. 17 U.S.C. § 101 (definition of "collective work").

69. 17 U.S.C. § 103. See Section 3.10 *supra* for a discussion of the copyrightability of compilations and collective works.

70. This rule did not, however apply to any advertising contained in the collective work. They required a separate notice to avoid being injected into the public domain.

71. 17 U.S.C. § 406(a).

72. 17 U.S.C. §§ 404(b), 406(a). Note that this creates an incentive for parties to register claims of copyright.

volume that read "Copyright, 1986, Connie Compiler." No notice appeared alongside each poem in the name of its respective author. This single notice would be sufficient to avoid injecting any of the individual poems into the public domain, even though they each did not bear a separate notice in the name of the particular poet in question.

Now let us further assume that in the following year, Ned Novelist wants to reproduce, at the beginning of a chapter of a novel he is working on, one of the poems appearing in *Decennial Ditties* which had been penned by Robert Frigid and titled *Stopping By Lakes on A Sunny Morning*. Checking the title page of *Decennial Ditties*, Ned discovers the notice naming Connie and contacts her. She tells him that he may reproduce the poem for free "as a courtesy," and so Ned goes ahead and does that. Frigid, the poet, subsequently learns of this and sues Ned for copyright infringement. Ned would have a complete defense to that infringement suit because he relied in good faith on the license from Connie, unless Frigid had registered his claim of copyright in the poem before Novelist reproduced it.

Post–1989, of course, none of this matters. That is because copyright notice is entirely optional for works published after the Berne Convention Implementation Act. Moreover, the statute now provides that "a single notice applicable to the collective work as a whole is sufficient to invoke the provisions of section 401(d) . . . as applicable with respect to the separate contributions it contains . . . regardless of the ownership of copyright in the contributions. . . ." To refresh your memory, section 401(d) is the provision that forecloses the mitigation of damages argument for innocent infringers in cases where an optional copyright notice appears. Thus the reproduction of a single contribution in a collective work cannot be argued to be an "innocent infringement" if the collective work as a whole contained a notice of copyright.

§ 4.3　Registration

While copyright ownership arises immediately upon the creation of a work, without the necessity of any governmental examination or approval, copyright owners have the option of registering their claim of ownership in the Copyright Office of the United States. This process is analogous to the registration of an automobile with the state Department of Motor Vehicles. You own your car as soon as you pay for it and receive the title from the seller. Thereafter, you can—and in most states you must—register that claim of ownership by filing some paperwork at the Department of Motor Vehicles. Of course, whether you register or not, you are still the owner of the car.

The difference between auto registration and copyright registration, however, is that copyright registration under the present law is not mandatory.[73] That observation may itself be misleading, though, because there are numerous incentives in the current statute designed to encourage prompt registration of copyright claims, and registration remains a prerequisite to the filing of an infringement suit for many copyright owners.

Registration was not always optional under American copyright law. Under the earliest copyright statute in the United States, the law required the filing of the title page of a work with the clerk of the U.S. district court in the district where the claimant resided as a formal condition of copyright protection.[74] Without the filing, copyright protection under federal law would be lost. By the time of the 1909 Act, however, registration was to be made with the Copyright Office rather than with the district courts, and was no longer an essential condition of copyright protection.[75] Registration of the claim of ownership was, however, a prerequisite to the filing of any infringement suit.

The current statute largely continues that pattern. Under the original version of the 1976 Act, registration continued to be permissive, but, as under the former statute, no infringement suit could be filed until registration was made. This rule changed somewhat in 1989. As you know, the United States signed the Berne Convention in that year, and that treaty forbids conditioning copyright protection on the observance of formalities such as registration. Consequently, Congress amended the rule requiring registration as a pre-requisite to infringement suits in 1989 so that it now applies only to "United States works."[76] In most cases, a United States work is one first published in the United States, or an unpublished work authored by U.S. nationals.[77] Thus, if an author (of any nationality) first publishes a book in Australia, and then subsequently distributes that book in the United States, the author need not register the claim of copyright before commencing an infringement suit because the work would not be a U.S. work.

---

73. 17 U.S.C. § 408(a). This subsection is entitled "Registration Permissive." The last sentence of the subsection reads "... registration is not a condition of copyright protection."

74. Act of May 31, 1790, 1 Stat. 124 (1790). *See* WILLIAM F. PATRY, COPYRIGHT LAW AND PRACTICE 408 (1994).

75. *See* 1909 Copyright Act, §§ 11, 13. *See also Washingtonian Pub. Co. v. Pearson*, 306 U.S. 30, 40, 59 S.Ct. 397, 83 L.Ed. 470 (1939).

76. 17 U.S.C. § 411(a) ("no action for infringement of the copyright in any

United States work shall be instituted until ... registration of the copyright claim has been made ..."). This requirement has been characterized as a jurisdictional prerequisite to an infringement suit. *See, e.g.,* La Resolana Architects, PA v. Clay Realtors Angel Fire, 416 F.3d 1195, 1200 (10th Cir.2005), Xoom, Inc. v. Imageline, Inc., 323 F.3d 279 (4th Cir. 2003).

77. 17 U.S.C. § 101 (definition of "United States work").

Some observers have labeled this a "minimalist" approach to Berne compliance because it dispenses with the pre-suit registration requirement in only those cases where the treaty absolutely required the United States to do so. It does result in the anomaly of a U.S. statute making things more difficult for U.S. copyright owners than they are for owners from other nations.

Moreover, one aspect of the pre-suit registration rule might seem particularly problematic. While most applications for copyright registration are approved by the Copyright Office, a nontrivial number are denied. With registration a prerequisite to infringement litigation for U.S. works, that might leave a copyright owner in the position of being unable to even gain access to the courts to press a claim of infringement. The statute deals with that contingency by providing that:

> In any case, however, where the deposit, application and fee required for registration have been delivered to the Copyright Office in proper form and registration has been refused, the applicant is entitled to institute an action for infringement if notice thereof, with a copy of the complaint, is served on the Register of Copyrights.[78]

Thus, one must at least attempt to register before filing an infringement suit (unless we are dealing with a non-U.S. work), but if the effort to register is unsuccessful, the copyright owner will still be allowed to go forward. In such a case, the Register of Copyrights "may, at his or her option, become a party to the action with respect to the issue of registrability of the copyright claim by entering an appearance within sixty days after such service, but the Register's failure to become a party shall not deprive the court of jurisdiction to determine that issue."[79]

Under this scheme, one might think that the best course would be for a copyright owner of a U.S. work to dispense with registration—thus saving expense and inconvenience—until he or she learned of infringing activity. At that point, the author could register the work, and then go ahead and file an infringement complaint. While such a course of action is certainly permissible under the statute, it would be rather inadvisable. This is because the statute contains a number of incentives for prompt registration and, effectively, a number of penalties for a tardy registration that is deferred until the eve of an infringement suit.

Before considering these statutory incentives in detail, it is worth pausing to consider why Congress adopted this type of scheme—optional registration with incentives. One might wonder on the one hand why, if registration is not important enough to be

---

78. 17 U.S.C. § 411(a)   **79.** *Id.*

mandatory, it shouldn't simply be abolished. After all, most other countries of the world do not have such an elaborate system.[80] On the other hand if registration is important enough to encourage with incentives, why not go all the way and make it a mandatory pre-condition of copyright protection, at least for U.S. works? Registration is beneficial, of course, because it establishes a system of public records that aids would-be users of copyrighted material in locating the owners of the material so that they can secure the necessary permissions. As the economically minded might put it, a registration system reduces transaction costs.

On the other hand, for certain authors, the registration process might prove unduly burdensome or expensive. Unlike large publishing houses or record companies that can hire personnel whose entire function is the prosecution of copyright registration applications, the local garage band, the independent commercial photographer, and the fledgling film maker may not have the resources to devote to compliance with a registration system, yet it seems unfair in the extreme to declare the copyright in these works forfeited merely because the authors find it difficult to comply. Thus, the statute can be seen to represent a compromise—encouraging registration to the maximum extent possible, in order to secure the benefits of reasonably comprehensive registration records, without imposing draconian consequences on those who fail to register by taking away their copyrights.

So what, then, are the legal benefits of registration to copyright proprietors? The first benefit of prompt registration is found in section 410(c), which makes a registration prima facie evidence of the validity of the copyright and of all the other facts stated in the registration certificate, but only does so if the registration is made before or within five years after the first publication of the work.[81] If the registration is made after the prescribed time limit "the evidentiary weight to be accorded the certificate of a registration ... shall be within the discretion of the court." In the event of litigation, this evidentiary significance of the registration certificate can be a significant advantage to the copyright owner, thus making registration desirable.

The second compelling incentive for registration is that prompt registration is a prerequisite for some of the more important remedies under the current law. Under section 412:

80. *See* Ralph Oman, *The United States and the Berne Union: An Extended Courtship*, 3 J. L. & TECH. 71 (1988).

81. 17 U.S.C. § 410(c). Congress also included comparable benefits for prompt registration of claims to renewal interests for works first published after 1964 when it made renewal of copyright in those works automatic in 1992. *See supra* § 8.3.

> no award of statutory damages or of attorney's fees …
> shall be made for (1) any infringement of copyright in an
> unpublished work commenced before the effective date of
> its registration; or (2) any infringement of copyright com-
> menced after first publication of the work and before the
> effective date of its registration, unless such registration is
> made within three months after the first publication of the
> work.[82]

Thus, in order to insure that the powerful remedial tools of attorneys fees and statutory damages are available, a copyright owner is
well advised to register as soon as possible. Moreover, this provision
applies both to U.S. and non-U.S. works alike. Consequently, although registration is not literally a prerequisite to suit for non-
U.S. works, the owners of copyrights in such works still have strong
reason to register their works promptly.[83]

Note that for published works there is a three-month "grace
period." That means that if a work is published on June 1st, an
infringer makes unlawful copies on June 20th, and the owner does
not register until August 10th, the owner will still be able to claim
statutory damages and attorney's fees because even though he did
not register until after the infringements began, he did register
within three months of publication. On the other hand, if an
unpublished work, having been created on June 1st, is infringed on
June 20th before any registration is made, the owner of copyright
cannot claim the enhanced remedies.

There are a few other positive consequences of registration
scattered throughout the 1976 Act. For instance, the recordation of
a transfer of ownership in a copyright will give constructive notice
of the facts surrounding that transfer only if registration has also
been made for the work in question.[84] Also, as discussed above, for
decennial works published without notice, filing a registration
within a five-year period was one step in effecting a "cure" so as to
avoid loss of rights.[85] These are a bit less important than the prima
facie effect of the certificate and the enhanced remedies for infringement that were discussed above, but they reinforce the gener-

---

82. 17 U.S.C. § 412. The "statutory
damages" referred to are those provided
for by section 504(c). That provision permits an infringement plaintiff to waive a
claim of actual damages and instead to
claim "a sum of not less that $500 or
more than $20,000 as the court consid-
ers just."

83. Some have questioned whether
conditioning certain remedies on prompt
registration is consistent with U.S. treaty obligations under the Berne Conven-

tion. Berne forbids making copyright
protection dependent on the observance
of "formalities" and a registration requirement is plainly a formality. For a
discussion of this issue see Shira Perl-
mutter, *Freeing Copyright From Formalities*, 13 CARDOZO ART & ENT. L.J. 565,
575 (1995).

84. *See supra* § 5.5.

85. 17 U.S.C. § 405(a)(2). *See infra*
§ 5.1.

al statutory approach of encouraging as many claimants as possible to make registration.

Assuming a copyright owner, in the face of these incentives, wishes to register a work—or, in the case of a U.S. work is required to do so in order to commence an infringement suit—how is registration accomplished? The actual registration process is not particularly complex. Registration may be made at any time during the life of the copyright by any party holding any exclusive right in the copyright. (In other words, not only may the owner of copyright in a novel register the claim of copyright to the novel, but the holder of the exclusive movie rights to that novel may do so as well.) The applicant for registration must submit three items to the Copyright Office. First is an application. Section 409 specifies some of the categories of data that such an application must include[86] and the Register of Copyrights has promulgated further requirements by regulation.[87] Under these provisions, parties seeking registration for a derivative work must identify the preexisting works upon which it is based. In actual practice, the Copyright Office has developed different forms for different categories of works, such as Form TX for non-dramatic literary works and Form VA for works of the visual arts. This permits the office to solicit information that is specific to particular categories of works. All of the forms are available and can be submitted online.

The second item required for registration is the registration fee. Section 708 of the statute instructs the Registrar of Copyrights to fix the fee and at this writing, the fee is $45 for a basic copyright registration application. The statute provides that the Register of Copyrights may increase fees to keep pace with the Consumer Price Index.[88] While $45 is not an exorbitant sum, the registration process can become oppressively expensive for creators who generate large numbers of works in a short period of time, such as commercial photographers or the publishers of daily newsletters. Thus, the relevant regulations also provide for group registration of multiple works under certain specified conditions.[89]

The third requirement for a proper copyright registration application is a "deposit." The subject of registration deposits is dealt with in sections 408(b) and (c) of the present act, and the requirements differ depending on whether the work in question is published or unpublished. In the case of unpublished works, the application for registration must be accompanied by one complete

---

86. Among those listed are the name and address of the copyright claimant; a statement that the work was made for hire if that is the case; the title of the work; the year in which the work was completed; and the date and nation of first publication. For the full list, see 17 U.S.C. § 409.

87. 37 C.F.R. § 202.3.

88. 17 U.S.C. § 708(b).

89. 37 C.F.R. § 202.3(a)(5).

copy or phonorecord of the work. If the work has been published, then two complete copies or phonorecords of the "best edition" of the work are required, unless the work was first published outside of the United States, in which one copy will suffice.[90]

The "best edition" of a work is statutorily defined as that edition that the "Library of Congress determines to be most suitable for its purposes."[91] The Copyright Office has issued detailed regulations specifying the attributes of a best edition.[92] For example, for printed textual matter, a best edition features a hard cover rather than a soft cover, library binding rather than commercial binding, and a trade edition rather than a book club edition. Those regulations also contain extensive clarifications and embellishments of the deposit requirements and provide that in certain cases—such as where the work is very large, like a sculpture—"identifying material" may be submitted in lieu of a deposit copy of the actual work. Still other regulations modify the deposit rules in cases where the work is confidential and its value would be destroyed by making it publicly available, such as in the case of certain secure tests and computer programs.

Once these materials have been submitted they will be examined by the Copyright Office, which must grant the registration if "the material deposited constitutes copyrightable subject matter and ... the other legal and formal requirements ... have been met."[93] Of course, if the examiner determines that the material is not copyrightable, registration will be denied, and such findings are often, but not always subsequently upheld by the courts.[94] Where registration is initially denied, the registration applicant can pursue an internal appeal within the copyright office to the Board of Appeals, and thereafter can seek judicial review.

§ 4.4 Pre–Registration

In recent years, infringers have sometimes been able to obtain unauthorized copies of certain types of works before publication and then to reproduce and distribute them, often via the Internet. For instance, this has been a problem in the motion picture industry where pre-release copies of films are often obtained and disseminated via various file sharing sites before the movie has

---

90. 17 U.S.C. § 408(b).

91. 17 U.S.C. § 101.

92. 37 C.F.R. §§ 202,20(b)(1), 202.19(b)(iii).

93. 17 U.S.C. § 410(a).

94. *Compare Norris Indus., Inc. v. International Tel. & Tel. Corp.*, 696 F.2d 918 (11th Cir.) *cert. denied*, 464 U.S. 818, 104 S.Ct. 78, 78 L.Ed.2d 89 (1983) (upholding Copyright Office determination that wire-spoked wheel covers were utilitarian objects not eligible for copyright protection) *with Atari v. Oman*, 979 F.2d 242 (D.C. Cir. 1992) (reversing Copyright Office determination that video game was not eligible for copyright because of lack of originality).

opened in legitimate theaters. Perhaps even more famously, the last book in the *Harry Potter* series was available on-line before it had even been shipped to bookstores. From the perspective of the copyright holder, the most important first step in such a situation is to secure a prompt injunction against the further distribution of the work—usually through a request for a temporary restraining order. That, of course, requires filing an infringement complaint. And that infringement suit requires registration of work (unless it is a non-U.S. work).

The problem, however, is that minor changes are often being made to the work up until the last minute. Thus it is neither practical nor customary to register the work until the moment of its release. This historically hindered copyright owners in situations like the ones described in the previous paragraph. Moreover, in cases of pre-release/pre-publication infringement, because the infringing acts pre-dated the registration, the copyright owner would not be able to secure statutory damages or attorney's fees in any eventual infringement suit.[95] Consequently, in 2005, Congress passed new legislation that created a pre-registration mechanism for copyright owners in this situation.

To be eligible for pre-registration, a work must be unpublished, and it must be in the process of being prepared for commercial distribution either via physical copies or through digital means. Some creation and fixation must already have taken place—you cannot pre-register if all you have is a tune in your head. In addition, the work must be a type of work that the Register of Copyrights has determined to have a history of pre-release infringement. In her initial determination the Register declared that the following classes of works met that test: motion pictures, sound recordings, musical compositions, literary works being prepared for publication in book form, computer programs (including video games), and advertising or marketing photographs.[96]

The pre-registration process is quite simple—the Copyright Office characterizes it as "streamlined." It requires only an on-line application and a non-refundable fee. The application requires such basic information as when creation of the work began and the anticipated completion and publication dates. There is no need to deposit a copy of the work with the application. Instead, the relevant regulation requires a "detailed description" of "approximately 330 words" which should be "based on information available at the time of the application sufficient to reasonably identify

95. 17 U.S.C. § 412 ("In any action under this title.... No award of statutory damages or of attorneys fees ... shall be made for (1) any infringement of copyright in an unpublished work com-menced before the effective date of its registration.").

96. 37 C.F.R. § 202.16(b)(1).

the work.''[97] These regulations go on to provide examples of the kind of information that should be included in the description of various kinds of works. The pre-registration application is not substantively examined to determine if the work is eligible for copyright.

Preregistration is not a substitute for registration. Rather, it permits an infringement action to be commenced prior to publication and registration of a work and, if the copyright owner subsequently does register, the statute provides that he or she will be able to receive statutory damages and attorneys' fees in an eventual infringement suit. However, in order to preserve those remedies, registration must occur either within three months after publication or within one month after learning of an act of infringement, which ever comes first. Note also that successful pre-registration is no guarantee that the work will be registered when a registration application is eventually submitted.

§ 4.5 Deposit

As noted in our discussion of copyright registration, if an author chooses to register a claim of copyright, he or she will have to submit copies or phonorecords of the work as part of the registration process. This "registration deposit" enables the Copyright Office to determine if the work in question meets the standards of copyrightability. There is, however, a second and entirely separate deposit requirement in the statute. This requirement applies to all works published in the United States regardless of whether the copyright owner chooses to file for copyright registration. The requirement appears in section 407 of the 1976 Act, which provides:

> the owner of copyright ... in a work published in the United States shall deposit, within three months after the date of such publication—(1) two complete copies of the best edition; or (2) if the work is a sound recording, two complete phonorecords of the best edition, together with any printed or other visually perceptible material published with such phonorecords.[98]

This deposit of materials called for by this section is sometimes referred to as "archival deposit" because its chief purpose is to ensure that the collections of the Library of Congress are both comprehensive, and maintainable without undue cost to the government. As is the case for the "registration deposit," the archival deposit must be of the "best edition" of the work in question. The

97. 37 C.F.R. § 202.16(c)(6). **98.** 17 U.S.C. § 407(a).

Register of Copyrights can exempt certain types of works from the archival deposit requirement and has done so.[99]

Failure to make the archival deposit called for by section 407 does not affect the validity of the underlying copyright. The statute specifically declares that the section 407 deposit is not a condition of copyright protection. Rather, failure to make the deposit will subject the party involved to liability for fines. No liability will be incurred until the Register of Copyrights first makes a written demand for the materials in question. Thereafter, failure to deposit incurs a $250 fine for each work plus the cost of acquiring the copies of the work on the open market. The fine escalates to $2500 if the failure to deposit is either willful or repeated.[100]

If a copyright owner of a work opts to make voluntary registration, the copies submitted as part of that registration application will also be deemed to satisfy the archival deposit requirement under section 407.[101] In effect, this functions as another incentive for registration. After all, if authors must deposit two copies shortly after publication anyway—on pain of a fine—they might as well fill out the short registration form, pay a small fee, and obtain the benefits of registration at the same time.

The mandatory archival deposit requirement has been challenged on constitutional grounds, as a taking of property without any compensation. And we have to admit that it is a pretty good deal for the Library of Congress, which gets to build the most comprehensive collection of bibliographic materials in the country without having to spend any money buying books. The Ninth Circuit, however rejected the challenge in *Ladd v. Law and Tech. Press.*,[102] reasoning that "conditioning copyrights on a contribution to the Library of Congress furthers" the purpose of promoting the progress of arts and sciences. To say the least, this language is curious because copyright is *not* conditioned on the archival deposit requirement—you are forced to donate copies of your work on pain of a fine, but your copyright is never in jeopardy if you don't comply. Even if *Ladd* is not the most compellingly reasoned judicial analysis, there have been no further efforts to set aside the section 407 deposit requirement.

---

99. *See* 37 C.F.R. § 202.19(c).

100. 17 U.S.C. § 407(d).

101. Section 408, dealing with registration, provides that "[c]opies or phonorecords deposited for the Library of Congress under section 407 may be used to satisfy the deposit provisions of this section if they are accompanied by the prescribed application and fee...." 17 U.S.C. § 408(b).

102. 762 F.2d 809, 814 (9th Cir. 1985).

Chapter 5

OWNERSHIP AND TRANSFER OF COPYRIGHT INTERESTS

Table of Sections

§ 5.1   Initial Ownership

One might reasonably assume that the initial ownership of any copyrightable work would belong to the person who created the work—its author—and this is indeed the law. As the current statute, the Copyright Act of 1976, puts it, "copyright in a work protected under this title vests initially in the author or authors of the work."[1] Interestingly, the term "author" is itself left undefined in the statute, but is commonly understood to refer to the actual

---

1.   17 U.S.C. § 201.

individual person or persons who created the work. As the Supreme Court explained, "the author is the party who actually creates the work, that is, the person who translates an idea into a fixed, tangible expression entitled to copyright protection."[2]

In a great many situations the author is the one who both conceives of the work and then performs the physical fixation of the work. He or she, in other words, is the person holding the pen, the paintbrush, or the movie camera as the case may be. But this need not be the case. Some authors may, because of the nature of the work, or because of their own physical circumstances, ask someone else to do the fixation for them. In such a case, the party who conceives of the expression and directs the fixation is the author, not the one who mechanically records the work. Thus the celebrated theoretical physicist, Stephen Hawking, is unequivocally the author of his many books and articles on astronomy and cosmology even though he suffers from a paralytic disease and likely must dictate his books to an assistant who does the actual typing.[3]

While this straightforward rule resolves the issue of copyright ownership in many cases, certain situations require special consideration. For instance, a work may be created by an employee on the job, raising the question of whether the employer of the creator should be deemed the legal owner of the resulting copyright instead of the creator himself. In other cases, multiple parties might collaborate to create a work, leading to ambiguity over which of them owns the copyright interest. Finally, an original owner of copyright might want to transfer the copyright to someone else, but such transfers may require the observance of certain formalities. These problems, which have required a fair amount of judicial attention, are the subject of the balance of this chapter.

§ 5.2　Works Made for Hire

For over 100 years, U.S. copyright law has treated the copyright in works prepared by employees not as the property of the individual creator but rather as that of the creator's employer. The principle—known as the work-made-for-hire doctrine—can be traced back to Justice Holmes' 1903 opinion in *Bleistein v. Donald-*

---

2. Community for Creative Non-Violence v. Reid, 490 U.S. 730, 737, 109 S.Ct. 2166, 104 L.Ed.2d 811 (1989).

3. *See, e.g.,* Robinson v. Buy–Rite Costume Jewelry, Inc., 2004 WL 1878781 (S.D.N.Y. 2004) ("a person need not hold the camera or push a button to be considered the author of a visual work, since one can exercise control over the content of a work without holding the camera"); Gillespie v. AST Sportswear, Inc., 2001 WL 180147 (S.D.N.Y.2001); Lindsay v. Wrecked & Abandoned Vessel R.M.S. Titanic, 52 U.S.P.Q.2d 1609, 1999 WL 816163 (S.D.N.Y. 1999) ("the fact that Lindsay did not literally perform the filming, i.e. by diving to the wreck and operating the camera, will not defeat his claims of having 'authored" the illuminated footage.").

son Lithographic Co.[4] Congress subsequently codified it in the 1909 Act[5] and, with substantial changes, carried it forward into the 1976 statute as well. The current law provides:

> In the case of a work made for hire, the employer or other person for whom the work was prepared is considered the author for purposes of this title, and unless the parties have expressly agreed otherwise in a written instrument signed by them, owns all of the rights comprised in the copyright.[6]

A number of significant consequences follow from classifying a work as a work made for hire, over and above the obvious consequences of deeming the employer the owner of the copyright, and therefore the party able to profit from any exploitation of the work. First, the duration of copyright in works made for hire is not defined as the life of the author plus 70 years, but instead as either 95 years from publication or 120 years from creation, whichever comes first.[7] Second, while transfers of copyright interests initially owned by individual authors can sometimes be "terminated," permitting the original author to recapture copyright ownership, no such termination rights are available in the case of works made for hire.[8] Third, although individual creators of "works of visual art" have certain protections against the mutilation or destruction of their work, such protections are not available for works made for hire.[9] Consequently, determining whether a work is a work made for hire is quite important for a host of both economic and technical legal reasons.

You might wonder at the outset, however, whether the work made for hire doctrine is consistent with the congressional power under the copyright clause of the Constitution. That clause gives congress the power to secure exclusive rights in writings to "authors." It is not self-evident that a corporate employer with dozens or even hundreds of employees whose jobs entail preparing copyrightable works such as computer programs or greeting cards or wallpaper designs can legitimately be considered a constitutional "author."

Of course the Constitution itself is silent on this point. However, it does not strain the idea of authorship terribly much to designate the party who takes the necessary steps to bring an

---

4. 188 U.S. 239, 248, 23 S.Ct. 298, 47 L.Ed. 460 (1903) (because works were "produced by persons employed and paid by the plaintiffs in their establishment to make those very things," copyright belonged to plaintiff-employer).

5. 1909 Act, § 26.

6. 17 U.S.C. § 201(b).

7. 17 U.S.C. § 302.

8. 17 U.S.C. §§ 203(a), 304(c). *See supra* § 8.5.

9. 17 U.S.C. § 101 (defining "work of visual art"). *See supra* § 7.1.2.

expressive work into being as its "author." In many cases, if an employer did not raise the funds to pay the salary of its creative employees, the work in question would never be created. Moreover, such employees get paid whether the works they create succeed or fail in the marketplace—it is the employer who bears the financial risk associated with the creative activity. At least in that sense, works created on the job "owe their origin" to the employer, and it thus seems justified that the employer could be considered a constitutional "author."

Whether or not you find this compelling, the courts have shown no particular willingness to question the constitutionality of the work made for hire doctrine, although their analysis of the issues has been terse at best.[10] Against this background, the constitutional status of the doctrine at this point seems fairly secure.

In addition to the constitutional question, there is also the issue of the policy justification for the works made for hire doctrine. It might be constitutionally permissible to treat employers as the copyright owners of works created by employees, but is it a good idea to do so? The usual justification for the work made for hire rule is that it places the legal incentive where it will likely do the most good—in other words where it will be most effective in inducing the creation of intellectual works. If employers know that they will control the copyright to works created on the job, they have the motivation to hire the right people and give them the right resources to engage in the creative endeavor, in ways that will prove successful in the marketplace. Without the incentive of copyright, those works might never be created. In addition, the employer may also be in the best position to disseminate the work once it is actually created. Thus, there seems to be considerable plausible policy support for the work made for hire doctrine.[11]

While these preliminary theoretical issues are worthy of consideration, the courts have more often concerned themselves with a more mechanical question—given both the constitutionality and wisdom of the doctrine, which works should be considered as works made for hire? Those created by employees, of course, but that hardly moves the inquiry very far. It simply re-frames the question—who, exactly do we mean, by the term "employees"?

The question is difficult because there is no clear dividing line between employees and their legal opposites—independent contrac-

---

10. As the Second Circuit put it, without further elaboration, "Though the United States is perhaps the only country that confers 'authorship' status on the employer of the creator of a work made for hire ... its decision to do so is not constitutionally suspect." Childress v. Taylor, 945 F.2d 500, 506 n.5 (2d Cir. 1991).

11. For an article developing some of these themes see I. Trotter Hardy, *An Economic Understanding of Copyright Law's Work–Made–For–Hire Doctrine*, 12 COLUM.-VLA J. L. & ARTS 181 (1988).

tors. For instance, one might hire a portrait artist to do an oil painting of the family dog, or a corporation might retain a sculptor to prepare an abstract work for the plaza in front of a corporate headquarters building. In such a situation, the hiring party is providing the economic impetus for the creative activity, and the creator gets paid a lump sum whether the work is good or bad. In addition, the hiring party is likely to have significant input about how the work should actually look. On the other hand, such individuals are not, in the usual sense, employees. They work only on a single project for a short period of time without the close oversight customary for conventional employees. Determining whether the resulting painting or sculpture is a work made for hire is therefore a somewhat ambiguous task.

5.2.1 Works Made for Hire Under the 1909 Act

Under the 1909 Act, Congress dealt with the issue in a rather unilluminating fashion. Section 26 of that act provided that "the word 'author' shall include an employer in the case of works made for hire." Nowhere, however, did the 1909 Act define "work made for hire" which left the problem to the courts. The result was a line of cases under the former statute holding that *both* works created by conventional full-time employees and commissioned works prepared by independent contractors were presumptively works made for hire, unless there was an agreement providing to the contrary.[12]

For instance, in *Murray v. Gelderman*,[13] Joy Gelderman approached Carol Murray about the possibility of producing a book containing the menus of famous New Orleans restaurants. While Murray was initially uninterested in the project she eventually agreed to undertake the editorial and artistic work, provided she was given full creative control. Gelderman agreed to that condition and formed a corporation called New Orleans A La Carte to handle the project. Thereafter Murray set to work on the actual task of putting the book together. Unfortunately, after the book was published the parties could not agree over ownership of the copyright. Murray claimed ownership as the actual author, but Gelderman claimed that the book was a work-made-for hire, meaning that the corporation would hold the copyright.

In resolving the question under the 1909 Act, the court identified the crucial questions as (1) "whether the work was created at the employer's insistence and expense, or, in other words, whether the motivating factor in producing the work was the employer who

---

12. *See, e.g.,* Scherr v. Universal Match Corp., 417 F.2d 497, 500 (2d Cir. 1969), *cert. denied,* 397 U.S. 936, 90 S.Ct. 945, 25 L.Ed.2d 116 (1970); Brattleboro Publishing Co. v. Winmill Publishing Corp., 369 F.2d 565, 568 (2d Cir. 1966).

13. 566 F.2d 1307 (5th Cir. 1978).

induced its creation" and (2) "whether the employer had the right to direct and supervise the manner in which the work was being performed," regardless of whether that right was actually exercised. Applying these criteria to the facts of the case, the court concluded: "It is abundantly clear that Murray was not working for herself, but rather for the corporation. We hold that, on these facts, an employment relationship existed." Murray protested that the way she was compensated revealed that she was not an employee but rather an independent contractor, but the court was unpersuaded, noting in a footnote that "the nature of the employment relationship is not dispositive; for example, the works for hire doctrine is applicable when the parties are employer and independent contractor."[14]

The result in *Murray* and cases like it tips very heavily in favor of hiring parties. Even in situations very far removed from the typical employer-employee case, the *Murray* test was often satisfied because the hiring party was the one who was the "motivating factor" for the project and who had at least a theoretical "right to supervise" the work. As a result, under the 1909 Act most artists working on special commission could not expect to retain copyrights in their works unless they explicitly reserved them in advance.

While this approach no longer governs for works created after January 1, 1978, bear in mind that this pro-employer case law continues to be relevant today because the 1976 Act is not retroactive. Thus, the work made for hire status of older works is determined under the standards of the 1909 Act.[15]

5.2.2 Works Made for Hire Under the 1976 Act

Mindful of this history, Congress left less discretion to the courts in the 1976 Act by dealing more explicitly with the problem of works-made-for hire. In that definition, it tried to recalibrate the balance between hiring parties and creators and to embrace a somewhat more pro-creator position. Under the current statute a work made for hire is defined as follows:

---

14. 566 F.2d at 1311, n.7. *See also,* Lin–Brook Builders Hardware v. Gertler, 352 F.2d 298 (9th Cir. 1965) ("when one person engages another, whether as employee or as an independent contractor, to produce a work of an artistic nature, that in the absence of an express contractual reservation of the copyright in the artist, the presumption arises that the mutual intent of the parties is that the title to the copyright shall be in the person at whose instance and expense the work is done.").

15. Roth v. Pritikin, 710 F.2d 934 (2d Cir.), *cert. denied,* 464 U.S. 961, 104 S.Ct. 394, 78 L.Ed.2d 337 (1983), reasoned that a retroactive application of the 1976 Act provisions might run afoul of the constitutional provisions concerning the taking of property without compensation, because commissioning parties prior to the adoption of the new law would have had an expectation that they would own the copyrights in the resulting works.

(1) a work prepared by an employee within the scope of his or her employment; or

(2) a work specially ordered or commissioned for use as a contribution to a collective work, as a part of a motion picture or other audiovisual work, as a translation, as a supplementary work, as a compilation, as an instructional text, as a test, as answer material for a test, or as an atlas, if the parties expressly agree in a written instrument signed by them that the work shall be considered a work made for hire.[16]

It would appear from the structure of this statutory definition that Congress meant to address the situation of the full-time or conventional employee in the first provision, and the situation of the independent contractor in the second. In the former case, works prepared on the job would clearly be works for hire, and the employer would be the owner of the copyright. Alas, Congress still did not define what it meant by an "employee." Nonetheless, the two-part structure of the statute makes it quite clear that "independent contractors" are *not* employees. This language thus overturns the result in *Murray v. Gelderman* and kindred cases.

Note further that in the independent contractor situation, the new definition seems to strongly favor the creator. First only certain itemized types of works can ever be treated as works made for hire when prepared by a non-employee—namely the curious set of nine itemized in the statutory text (contributions to collective works, parts of motion pictures, translations, supplementary works, compilations, instructional texts, tests, answer material for test, or atlases).[17] Where the work is not one of the "named nine," as would be the case with a commissioned oil portrait or a computer program prepared by an outside consultant, work-made-for-hire status will be impossible. Moreover, even with these nine types of works the parties must clearly specify their agreement on work made for hire

16. 17 U.S.C. § 101. The provision goes on to define a "supplementary work" as "a work prepared for publication as a secondary adjunct to a work by another author for the purpose of introducing, concluding, illustrating, explaining, revising, commenting upon, or assisting in the use of the other work, such as forewords, afterwords, pictorial illustrations, maps, charts, tables, editorial notes, musical arrangements, answer material for tests, bibliographies, appendixes, and indexes ..." It also specified that an "instruction text" is "a literary, pictorial, or graphic work prepared for publication and with the purpose of use in systematic instructional activities."

17. This listing of nine appears to be the result of a legislative compromise. Various industry representatives were able to persuade Congress that in cases involving the nine itemized categories, the works were typically prepared only at the instigation of the hiring party and that the availability of work for hire status was something of a commercial necessity. *See* Marci Hamilton, Comment, 135 U. Pa. L. Rev. 1281 (1987).

status in writing. The default rule, in the absence of an agreement, is that the creator owns the copyright.

5.2.2.1 Who Is an Employee?

Notwithstanding the seeming congressional desire to shift to a more "creator-friendly" version of the work made for hire doctrine, in the years immediately following the adoption of the 1976 Act, some courts began to interpret the word "employee" in the first prong of the definition more and more broadly so as to encompass a number of situations beyond the stereotypical full-time salaried nine-to-five employee. That, of course, had the effect of broadening the range of works within the work made for hire definition, and depriving certain creators of copyright in favor of the commissioning parties.

For instance in *Aldon Accessories, Ltd. v. Spiegel*,[18] the court held that an independent contractor could be considered an "employee" under the first prong of the statutory definition where the commissioning party directed and supervised the work of that independent contractor.[19] That case involved the copyright ownership of a unicorn statuette. An Aldon executive named Ginsberg worked closely with a model maker in Japan on the development of the statuette, but there was no plausible argument that the model maker was a full-time or conventional employee of Aldon. Nonetheless, the Second Circuit found it significant that "[w]hile [Ginsberg] did not physically wield the sketching pen and sculpting tools, he stood over the artists and artisans at critical stages of the process, telling them exactly what to do." Some courts went even further than *Aldon* and held that the creator was an "employee" within the first prong of the definition if there hiring party merely retained the right to control the work, regardless of whether that control was actually exercised.[20]

Of course, these approaches had the effect of blurring the distinction between employees and independent contractors, since they permitted those who hired individuals such as painters or sculptors for single projects to argue that those painters or sculptors were nonetheless "employees" under the particular circumstances in question. If a court agreed, that would give the hiring party ownership of the copyright under the first prong of the work

---

18. 738 F.2d 548 (2d Cir.), *cert. denied*, 469 U.S. 982, 105 S.Ct. 387, 83 L.Ed.2d 321 (1984).

19. Other courts refused to follow this approach, and interpreted the term "employee" in the first prong of the work for hire definition narrowly, as covering only those who would be employees under the law of agency. *See,*

e.g., Easter Seal Society for Crippled Children and Adults of Louisiana, Inc. v. Playboy Enterprises, 815 F.2d 323 (5th Cir. 1987).

20. *See e.g., Peregrine v. Lauren Corp.*, 601 F.Supp. 828, 829 (D. Colo. 1985); *Clarkstown v. Reeder*, 566 F.Supp. 137 (S.D.N.Y. 1983).

made for hire definition in case that by its very terms it could not have qualified under the second prong.

Ultimately, the Supreme Court stepped in to clarify the meaning of "employee" in *Community for Creative Non-Violence v. Reid.*[21] In that case, Reid, a sculptor in Baltimore, was asked by the Community for Creative Non-Violence or CCNV, a Washington-based charitable organization, to prepare a sculpture that would depict a "modern day nativity scene" of a homeless family on a steam grate. There were numerous consultations between the parties as the work progressed, CCNV supplied plans and sketches to Mr. Reid and also supplied the base or pedestal upon which the statue was to be mounted. Eventually, Reid and the CCNV had a falling out when CCNV wanted to take the statue on a fund-raising tour, and Reid objected. Litigation ensued over the ownership of the copyright in the statue.

The CCNV argued that Reid was an employee, and that the work was thus a work made for hire because they had the right to control his work, and because they had actually exercised such control as the work progressed. The Supreme Court disagreed. It criticized the actual control test by noting that since "it turns on whether the hiring party has closely monitored the production process, the parties would not know until late in the process, if not until the work is completed," whether the work was a work made for hire. It held that employee status should be determined instead by application of the law of agency. The Court was influenced by the structure of the definitional provision of the statute which seems to draw a sharp distinction between "employees" and "independent contractors."

To assist the lower courts in applying its test, the Court identified several factors relevant under agency law in classifying a party as an employee. In a key passage, the Court instructed lower courts to consider:

> the hiring party's right to control the manner and means by which the product is accomplished; or, [including such factors as] the skill required; the source of the instrumentalities and tools; the location of the work; the duration of the relationship between the parties; whether the hiring party has the right to assign additional projects; the hired party's discretion over when and how long to work: the method of payment; the hired party's role in hiring and paying assistants; whether the work is part of the regular business of the hiring party; whether the hiring party is in

21. 490 U.S. 730, 109 S.Ct. 2166, 104 L.Ed.2d 811 (1989).

business; the provision of employee benefits; and the tax treatment of the hired party.[22]

In propounding this list, the Court looked to the Restatement (Second) of Agency. The American Law Institute has since issued a new version of that documents (with the predictable title Restatement (Third) of Agency) which declares in the relevant section that "For purposes of this section, (a) an employee is an agent whose principal controls or has the right to control the manner and means of the agent's performance of work . . . ." As noted above, this "right of control test" was explicitly rejected as the definition of an employee by the *Reid* Court. However, any seeming contradiction between the new Restatement and the logic of *Reid* is largely eliminated by a comment to the section that includes a list of factors quite similar to those in the opinion.[23]

Applying its newly announced test to the facts of the case before it, the Court found that Reid had not been an "employee" of CCNV. That meant that the sculpture could only qualify as a work made for hire if it fell under the second prong of the statutory definition. Because no written agreement stipulated that the work would be a work made for hire, and because works of sculpture do not appear on the "named nine" list in that prong, the Court found that the second prong of the statute was also unsatisfied. The end result was that the work was not a work made for hire and that Reid, as the individual author, owned the copyright.[24]

Of course, the use of agency law factors by the *Reid* Court does not mean that future decisions in this area will be easy or mechanical. As the Second Circuit put it in a post–*Reid* opinion:

> *Reid* established that no one factor was dispositive, but gave no direction concerning how the factors were to be weighed. It does not necessarily follow that because no one

22. 490 U.S. at 751.

23. *See* Restatement (Third) of Agency, § 7.07, comment f ("Numerous factual indicia are relevant to whether an agent is an employee. These include: the extent of control that the agent and the principal have agreed the principal may exercise over details of the work; whether the agent is engaged in a distinct occupation or business; whether the type of work done by the agent is customarily done under a principal's direction or without supervision; the skill required in the agent's occupation; whether the agent or the principal supplies the tools and other instrumentalities required for the work and the place in which to perform it; the length of time during which the agent is engaged by a principal; whether the agent is paid by the job or by the time worked; whether the agent's work is part of the principal's regular business; whether the principal and the agent believe that they are creating an employment relationship; and whether the principal is or is not in business.").

24. Actually, there was a further issue in the case. CCNV argued that it was also a "joint author" of the work with Reid. This issue was not addressed by the Supreme Court, and was left for consideration on remand. The parties settled before the joint authorship issue could be judicially resolved. For a discussion of joint authorship see § 5.3 infra.

factor is dispositive all factors are equally important, or indeed that all factors will have relevance in every case. The factors should not merely be tallied but should be weighed according to their significance in the case.[25]

Indeed, because the *Reid* test is so fact-specific some commentators have criticized *Reid* as perpetuating all the uncertainty that existed under the former law.[26]

Regardless of ease of application, however, the thrust of the CCNV test is to more sharply distinguish between the classic full-time employee situation, where work made for hire status is the rule, and independent contractor situations, where work made for hire status will be available only in limited circumstances, and only if the parties have explicitly contracted for it.

5.2.2.2　When Is Work Done in the Scope of Employment?

Just because a person is an employee under the law of agency, and thus within the meaning of the copyright statute as interpreted in the *Reid* case, it does not follow that every bit of copyrightable work he creates should be considered a work-made-for hire. The full-time programmer at Microsoft who paints watercolor landscapes on the weekends would surely be surprised if told that the company owned the copyright to his paintings. It does not, of course. These watercolors are clearly not works made for hire. This sensible result is implemented by the language in the first prong of the work-made-for hire definition that requires the work to be prepared not merely by an "employee" but by an employee acting within the "scope of employment" in order for work-made-for-hire status to attach.

The "scope of employment" concept is a basic concept in the law of agency, and familiar from the law of torts, where it sets the boundaries of an employer's vicarious liability for the torts of employees. In the works-made-for-hire context, scope of employment issues have been more frequently litigated in recent years. Unlike former times, when employees traveled to a physical location maintained by the employer (known quaintly as "the office" or "the plant") and remained there during specified hours (until a time known quaintly as "quitting time"), many employees now work from home, carry a battery of electronic communications devices, and are considered to be "on duty" at all hours of the day and night.

25. *Aymes v. Bonelli,* 980 F.2d 857, 861 (2d Cir. 1992).

26. *See* Assaf Jacob, *Tort Made for Hire—Reconsidering the* CCNV *Case,* 11 YALE J. L. & TECH. 96 (2008–09).

The computer programmer who writes code in a home office and shares it with colleagues over a private network, the journalist who emails stories composed on a laptop out in a war zone, and the young attorney answering frantic email messages from a neurotic partner on a hand-held device at 11:00 PM are all probably acting "within the scope of their employment" even though they are not within the conventional time and space parameters of a traditional job. The problem is that the same computer programmer may also write computer games in his home office on that same computer supplied by his employer; the journalist may be working on a memoir during lulls in the battle when he is not filing stories; and the associate may use his Blackberry® device to send a draft of a will to a former college roommate. If their employers claim rights to these latter materials, ownership will turn on how courts interpret "scope of employment."

Most courts confronting this issue use a three-prong test borrowed from the Restatement of Agency. In determining whether work was done within the scope of employment it instructs courts to consider (1) whether the work in question was work of the kind of work the employee was employed to perform; (2) whether work occurred substantially within authorized work hours; and (3) whether the work was actuated, at least in part, by a purpose to serve the employer.[27]

One illustration of the application this test to a concrete set of facts is *City of Newark v. Beasley.*[28] In that case, defendant Michael Beasley worked for the Newark Police Department. He had prepared a student workbook and a police officer's training manual for use in connection with a program designed to deter juvenile car theft called People Against Car Theft, or P.A.C.T. Beasley testified that he did not use any police department resources to complete the materials, that he worked on them at home during his off-duty hours, and that he did not create the P.A.C.T. materials specifically to benefit the Newark Police Department. He did show portions of them to the Director of Police, who was impressed by them, and who promoted Beasley to the rank of detective so that he could begin to implement the program. Newark city regulations provided that "Police Officers shall devote their entire time to the service of the Department."

On these facts, the court found that the materials had *not* been prepared within the scope of Beasley's employment and that therefore Beasley owned the copyright. It reasoned that because the City of Newark had no control over Beasley's creation of the P.A.C.T. materials and because he did not derive the necessary knowledge to

---

27. Restatement (Second) of Agency § 228.

28. 883 F.Supp. 3 (D.N.J.1995).

write the materials from his work as a police office, his work on the materials was not the kind of work he was hired to perform. His testimony that he drafted the materials at home during off-hours and did not use City facilities to create the materials led the court to conclude that he did not create the materials within his authorized work hours. Finally, the court observed that "Beasley testified that he was not motivated to create the P.A.C.T. materials to benefit his employer, but rather hoped that the P.A.C.T. materials would be used by a number of different cities. Therefore, the Court holds that Beasley was not motivated by a desire to serve his employer when he created the Student Workbook and the Police Officer's Training Manual."[29]

It would not have been preposterous for the *Beasley* court to have found that materials on policing prepared by a police officer, and then shared with his superior, which resulted in his promotion to a post where he could implement a program relying on those materials, were materials that had been prepared within the scope of his employment. Beasley's own testimony that he was not motivated to benefit the Newark Police Department would seem, in the context of the eventual copyright dispute, to be at least a bit self-serving. On the other hand, his superiors did not ask him to prepare the materials and there is a good chance that his normal duties consisted of running after bad guys, stopping wayward motorists, and eating donuts, not writing workbooks, making the outcome of the case more than defensible.

By way of contrast, let us consider *Shaul v. Cherry Valley–Springfield Cent. School Dist.*,[30] which came to the opposite result. The factual context here is a bit out of the ordinary for a copyright dispute. Plaintiff William Shaul was a high school math teacher who worked for the defendant school district. Apparently he was fond of extracurricular activities. In 1990, he was found guilty of having an inappropriate relationship with a female student. Eight years later, he was accused of sexually harassing another female student, and a few months after that he was arrested for stalking the first student, now out of school, with whom he had subsequently become romantically involved. After that arrest he was suspended, given an opportunity to remove his belongings from his classroom, and required to surrender his keys. Thereafter, the school seized various items that he had left in the classroom, including certain teaching materials he had prepared such as tests, quizzes, and homework problems. Shaul sued, claiming that the school district's failure to return these materials was an illegal seizure in

---

29. *See also* Avtec Systems Inc. v. Peiffer, 67 F.3d 293 (4th Cir. 1995) (computer program prepared by an employee working at home over a period of three year held not to have been prepared within the scope of employment).

30. 363 F.3d 177 (2d Cir. 2004).

violation of his Fourth Amendment rights. The District responded by arguing that he did not have a possessory interest in those materials as they constituted works-made-for-hire because they were prepared by an employee within the scope of his employment.

The Second Circuit used the same three-prong test as *Beasley*, but came to the opposite result, even though Shaul had prepared many of the materials at home and after school hours. The way the court saw the situation:

> It is clear that preparing materials for class was the kind of work that [Shaul] was employed to perform as a teacher (satisfying the first prong) and that Shaul was motivated to spend the time to prepare materials for class in order to fulfill his duties as a teacher (satisfying the third prong), regardless of his purported desire to publish the materials. With respect to the second prong, the instant case is distinguishable from *Beasley*, in which a police officer deliberately worked on an educational program at home for the express purpose of retaining ownership of the materials. Here, the very nature of a teacher's duties involves a substantial amount of time outside of class devoted to preparing lessons, problem sets, and quizzes and tests—which is clearly within the scope of his employment.[31]

In trying to avoid this result Shaul had also invoked the so-called "academic" or "teacher" exception to the work-made-for-hire doctrine. A tiny handful of cases decided under the 1909 statute had held that academic writings by faculty members should not be considered to be works made for hire.[32] Such an exception could be justified on a number of bases. First, professors' primary motive in publishing books and articles is usually not to serve the immediate purposes of their universities, but rather some combination of their desire to advance the frontiers of knowledge and to enhance their own reputations. Also, you will recall that the 1909 case law focused very much on the degree of control the hiring party or employer had over the work. Since the tradition of academic freedom guarantees faculty members a great deal of independence in their writing, a work made for hire doctrine that focused on the employer's oversight of the employee seemed a poor fit with the reality of academic writing.

31. 363 F.3d at 186.

32. *See, e.g.,* Williams v. Weisser, 273 Cal.App.2d 726, 78 Cal.Rptr. 542 (1969) (university professors' lectures are not works made for hire); Sherrill v. Grieves, 57 Wash. L. Rep. 286 (D.C. 1929) (book prepared by instructor teaching topographic skills to army officers held not to be a work made for hire).

In any event, as discussed above, the 1976 Act added a new definition of works made for hire in an effort to clarify the topic. Some commentators have interpreted the new language as abolishing any previously existing teacher exception. As Professor Rochelle Cooper Dreyfuss put it:

> Scholars have indeed concluded that the 1976 Act abolishes the teacher exception to the work for hire doctrine. They reason that since the 1976 Act suggests that courts should limit their inquiry to the existence of an employment relationship, employees under long-term contracts—such as academics—may no longer argue that the factors surrounding their employment rebut the presumption of employer ownership. Accordingly, the circumstances under which the work was created and the expectations of the parties have now become largely irrelevant. The dispositive issue is whether production of scholarly material is "within the scope of employment," that is, a part of the job. Since scholarship clearly is a factor in decisions regarding tenure, promotion, salary increases, sabbatical leaves, and reduced teaching loads, scholarly works should now belong to universities rather than to faculty members.[33]

Other commentators have disagreed however,[34] and two judges on the Seventh Circuit—both of whom came to the bench after long and distinguished careers as law professors—have suggested that the academic exception may have continued vitality despite the language of the new act.[35]

It is certainly the case that settled practice in the academic world presupposes some kind of a teacher exception. When two professors collaborate on, say, a Concise Hornbook® on the law of copyright, they are the ones who assign copyright in the book to their good friends at West Publishing. West might be rather too startled to learn that it had obtained invalid assignments on all the books it publishes because the true owners of the copyright to the

33. Rochelle Cooper Dreyfuss, *The Creative Employee and the Copyright Act of 1976*, 54 U. Chi. L. Rev. 590, 598–99 (1987). Professor Dreyfuss cites two earlier articles in support of her statement—Todd F. Simon, *Faculty Writings: Are They "Works Made for Hire" Under the 1976 Copyright Act?* 9 J. Coll. & Univ. L. 485 (1982–83) and Leonard D. DuBoff, *An Academic's Copyright: Publish and Perish*, 32 J. Copyright Soc'y 17 (1984). *See also*, Patry on Copyright § 5:71 (arguing that there is not general teacher exception, but that universities and faculty members can contract con-

cerning what materials are within the scope of employment and what materials are not).

34. Laura G. Lape, *Ownership of Copyrightable Works of University Professors: The Interplay Between the Copyright Act and University Copyright Policies*, 37 Vill. L. Rev. 223 (1992).

35. See Hays v. Sony Corp. of America, 847 F.2d 412, 426 (7th Cir. 1988) (per Posner J.) Weinstein v. University of Illinois, 811 F.2d 1091 (7th Cir. 1987) (per Easterbrook, J.); see generally   Nimmer,   Copyright § 5.03[B][1][b][I].

works in question were the universities where the authors were employed. Moreover, most universities have promulgated copyright policies that specify that except in limited cases, individual faculty members hold the copyrights to their academic writings. One could debate whether the existence of such policies proves that the works would *otherwise* be works made for hire if no policy had been issued, but the practical effect is that university professors currently have an undisputed claim of copyright ownership to most of their academic writings at most institutions of higher learning.

The *Shaul* court dodged the issue of the academic exception somewhat, by distinguishing between a high school teacher and a university professor. It noted that the school district did not have a copyright policy guaranteeing faculty members the right to retain copyright ownership in works of authorship prepared as part of their jobs. It also observed that "the 'academic tradition' granting authors ownership of their own scholarly work is not pertinent to teaching materials that were never explicitly prepared for publication by Shaul, as opposed to published articles by university professors."[36]

The Nimmer treatise criticizes the *Shaul* opinion—justifiably in our view—for delving into the work-made-for-hire issue at all.[37] The search-and-seizure problem it confronted involved the ownership of the actual physical copies of the tests and homework problems prepared by the teacher, not the ownership of the underlying copyrights. If Shaul had written and published a book, and had kept in his classroom a copy of his own book that had been bought with school funds, the school would, of course, have had the right to seize that book and retain it when he was suspended, even though he owned the copyright!

With regard to scope of employment issues, perhaps the most that can be said is that the inquiry is necessarily fact specific. Although courts invoke the three-part test discussed in this section, at the end of the day they are likely influenced as much by intuition and common sense, which is not a terrible place for the law to settle.

5.2.2.3 Works Made for Hire by Independent Contractors

It is customary to refer to works that fall into the second prong of the 1976 Act's work-made-for hire definition as "specially commissioned" works. As noted earlier, no specially commissioned

---

36. At least one of the cases invoking the academic exception under the 1909 Act dealt with lecture notes rather than with materials prepared for publication, making this statement somewhat inaccurate as a summary of the scope of the purported exception.

37. NIMMER, COPYRIGHT § 5.03[B][1][b][I] at n. 95.1

work can be deemed a work made for hire unless it is one of those on the nine-item list that appears in the statute. Some of the listed items are not the kinds of works that would normally be produced by individuals on their own initiative; rather they are the kinds of works that are almost always solicited by others for incorporation in a larger final product. For instance, two of the listed items are fragmentary by their very nature—contributions to collective works and parts of motion pictures. Contemplated here would be things such as a short article on armadillos for inclusion in an encyclopedia, or two minutes of special effects footage showing the birth of an alien baby for inclusion in a science fiction move. Few authors would undertake such projects on their own initiative and these works would have no market standing alone. It thus makes some sense to allow the commissioning party to secure the copyright in the fragment by contract at the very outset.

A third itemized category, "supplementary works," is defined as a "secondary adjunct to work by another author" such as a chart, table, foreword, or index. Again, an author would rarely create such works unless asked, and centralizing copyright ownership in the hands of the party that created the primary work makes economic and practical sense.

Other items on the list, however, do not seem to share these attributes. For instance instructional texts and atlases are also named, and it is quite plausible that two people might write, oh, perhaps a book about the basics of copyright law, on their own initiative just for the hell of it. There might even be a market for such a book. On the other hand, if those same two brilliant scholars were solicited by a major law book publisher to write the book at its behest, it does not seem terribly odd to place the copyright in the hands of the publisher rather than the authors. While the search for thematic coherence among the "named nine" types of works is not a wholly pointless enterprise, it is thus probably more efficient, and certainly more candid to note that the list is something of a hodgepodge and reflects the results of the ebb and flow of lobbying at the time the statute was drafted, more than fidelity to any grand principle.[38]

38. The Register of Copyrights has explained the items in the statutory list as follows: "With respect to specially ordered or commissioned works, each category was proposed by a particular copyright industry and each proposed category was fully debated. The question considered was why should a particular type of work be treated as a 'work made for hire.' Works included in these categories tend to be works done by freelance authors at the instance, direction, and risk of a publisher or producer where it was argued that it would be unfair to allow such authors to terminate assignments of rights. Other exceptions (contributions to collective works, parts of motion pictures), were based on the fact that the resulting work involved numerous authors and that permitting terminations of grants of rights to such works would cause chaos." Statement of Marybeth Peters. Register of Copyrights, before the Subcommittee on

Before moving on, however, there is one particular category of work about which another few words are in order, namely sound recordings. Sound recordings do not appear in the statutory itemization. This means that if a record company contracts with a performer to make a recording, the resulting recording can only be classified as a work made for hire if the performer is deemed an employee of the record company. Absent an employment relationship there is no way to characterize a "specially commissioned" sound recording as a work made for hire, meaning that the performer will own the copyright in the recording.

At first blush, this might seem like a technicality or perhaps more accurately a nuisance. If the record company wants to insure that it owns the copyright and the recording is not a work made for hire, merely means that the record company must be sure to secure an assignment of the copyright from the performer as part of the recording contract. There is, however, one huge difference between owning a copyright in a work made for hire and owning it as a result of an assignment. In the latter case, the assignor can terminate the assignment 35 years after the contract is executed and reclaim the copyright.

For many decades, the typical industry practice in the music world has been for the recording contract to declare that the work is a work made for hire—presumably on the theory that the performer is in fact an employee or an independent contractor who was commissioned to make a contribution to a collective work (namely a record album)—with a back-up clause providing that if a court thereafter should find the work *not* to be a work made for hire that the performer assigns all his rights to the record company. This employee characterization might, at one time, have been plausible, because in earlier days record companies often hired the back-up singers and musicians, provided the studio and sound engineer, and saw to all the details of production associated with a recording session. In recent decades, however, changes in the industry have undermined any claim of employer-employee relationship. As the Register of Copyrights has summarized "[b]y hiring or acting as producers, by retaining back-up singers, musicians and engineers, and by recording in their own studios or at independent studios, featured artists have increasingly come to control the creative elements of a sound recording, making it considerably more difficult now for record companies to characterize artists as employees producing works within the scope of their employment."[39] Moreover, after *Reid*, it seems unlikely that most

Courts and Intellectual Property, Committee on the Judiciary, U.S. H. Rep., 106th Congress, 2nd Session (May 25, 2000) available on-line at http://www.copyright.gov/docs/regstat52500.html.

39. *Id*. The Register also noted in this testimony that some record companies relied on the theory that even if the performers were not employees and the sound recordings were thus "specially

courts would find the relationship between a record company and a performer to satisfy the "law of agency" test.

Alas, during the first two decades the 1976 Act was on the books no court definitively resolved the question of whether, and under what circumstances, sound recordings should be considered works made for hire. Meanwhile, the time when performers might begin serving potential notices of termination of purported assignments of copyrights was getting closer and closer. Consequently, in 1999, at the behest of the recording industry, and without conducting any hearings, Congress added sound recordings to the list of works referenced in the section 101 definition of works made for hire.[40]

Although Congress characterized the change as a "technical amendment" the provision proved controversial almost immediately—indeed the Nimmer treatise characterizes the resulting outcry as "a firestorm of criticism."[41] The protests were so great that Congress relented to the pressure, and in a complete about-face repealed the change the very next year.[42] That second piece of legislation also added the following language to the works-made-for-hire definition in the statute:

> In determining whether any work is eligible to be considered a work made for hire under paragraph (2), neither the amendment contained in section 1011(d) of the Intellectual Property and Communications Omnibus Reform Act of 1999, as enacted by section 1000(a)(9) of Public Law 106–113, nor the deletion of the words added by that amendment—
>
> (A) shall be considered or otherwise given any legal significance, or
>
> (B) shall be interpreted to indicate congressional approval or disapproval of, or acquiescence in, any judicial determination, by the courts or the Copyright Office.
>
> Paragraph (2) shall be interpreted as if both section 2(a)(1) of the Work Made For Hire and Copyright Corrections Act of 2000 and section 1011(d) of the Intellectual Property

commissioned works," they would still be works-made-for-hire because they were contributions to a compilation or collective work—namely an album consisting of multiple songs. She went on to note, however, that this theory was called into doubt by consumers' movement away from purchasing CDs containing a collection of songs in favor of downloading individual songs.

40. *See* section 1011, Satellite Home Viewer Improvement Act of 1999, enacted as part of Pub. L. No. 106–113, 113 Stat. 1501, 1501A–544 (1999).

41. NIMMER, COPYRIGHT, § 5.03[B][2][a] at n. 121.12a.

42. Work Made for Hire and Copyright Corrections Act of 2000, Pub. L. 106–379, 114 Stat. 1444 (October 27, 2000).

and Communications Omnibus Reform Act of 1999, as enacted by section 1000(a)(9) of Public Law 106–113, were never enacted, and without regard to any inaction or awareness by the Congress at any time of any judicial determinations.

In other words, Congress, with its tail between its legs, did as much as it possibly could to restore the law to its pre–1999 status. As noted, however, that status was one of uncertainty, with the record industry and featured performers taking diametrically opposite views of whether sound recordings should be treated as works made for hire.

What all this means is that at least some performers will undoubtedly go forward with attempts to terminate assignments in the years to come, and the record companies will likely argue in response that termination is not possible because the works are works made for hire. It will then be up to the courts to resolve the issue. As the Nimmer treatise concludes, "even after the millennial flip-flop, the controversy over potential termination of transfers in sound recordings remains live."[43]

Returning to the main thread of the story, there is yet another issue worth considering with regard to specially commissioned works. The statute requires a "written instrument" specifying that the work is a work-made-for-hire in order for that status to attach. What exactly qualifies as a written instrument, and when must it be executed? First, the statutory text says that the instrument must be signed "by them" and the courts have interpreted this to mean that *both* the hiring party and the commissioned artist must sign the document in order for it to effectively create a work made for hire.[44]

In addition, the agreement must be fairly explicit in referring to the work-made-for-hire concept. Thus, in one case the commissioning party sought to rely on a check endorsement that stated "[b]y endorsement of this check, payee acknowledges payment in full for the assignment to Playboy Enterprises, Inc. of all right, title and interest in and to the following items." The Second Circuit found this inadequate, stating "[t]his agreement does not mention a work-for-hire relationship. It only mentions an 'assignment.' It does not, therefore, satisfy the writing requirement of § 101(2)."[45] This does not mean that the parties must use the specific phrase "work-made-for-hire" in order to satisfy the statute. As the Ninth

43. Nimmer, Copyright, § 5.03[B][2][a] at n. 121.64.

44. *See*, Schiller v. Schmidt, Inc. v. Nordisco Corp., 969 F.2d 410 (7th Cir. 1992); Rubloff Inc. v. Donahue, 1994 WL 161098 (N.D.Ill.1994).

45. Playboy Enterprises, Inc. v. Dumas, 53 F.3d 549 (2d Cir. 1995), *cert. denied,* 516 U.S. 1010, 116 S.Ct. 567, 133 L.Ed.2d 491 (1995).

Circuit put it, there is no need for "talismanic words."[46] However, given the desire to protect creators in the commissioned-works context, a fairly high degree of clarity on the point is usually demanded.

The question of timing of the agreement has proven to be a bit more vexing. Clearly an agreement executed before the creator begins the product will suffice. The harder question is whether an agreement signed after the work is finished can also be adequate. Judge Posner, speaking for the Seventh Circuit, sees the written agreement requirement as one designed to eliminate uncertainty about copyright ownership. Consequently he held that only a pre-creation agreement would suffice, "in order to serve its purpose of identifying the ... owner unequivocally."[47] The Second Circuit, however, disagreed. In its view, the statute can be satisfied "by a writing executed after the work is created, if the writing confirms a prior agreement, either explicit or implicit, made before the creation of the work."[48] The Ninth Circuit casts its lot with Posner, finding the issue so mundane that it disposed of it in an unpublished opinion with the observations that "[t]he plain language of the statute indicates that a work-for-hire agreement cannot apply to works that are already in existence. Works 'specially ordered or commissioned' can only be made after the execution of an express agreement between the parties."[49] At least one lower court in the Fifth Circuit has endorsed the Second Circuit view. In other words, we have a good old-fashioned circuit split on this question.

Since a post-creation *assignment* (as distinguished from a work-made-for-hire agreement) is clearly effective, the real question here is—as it was with the controversy over sound recording—about the ultimate right to terminate the transfer of ownership. The Posner rule puts the burden on the commissioning party to obtain the writing before the work begins or face the risk that an assignment executed after the fact could be terminated 35 years down the road. Given that the drafters of the 1976 Act meant to tilt the work-made-for hire rules somewhat more in favor of creators, this does not seem a harsh or unfair result. This is also the position of another leading copyright treatise.[50] Hopefully Congress or the Supreme Court will opt to clarify the point sooner rather than later.

46. Warren v. Fox Family Worldwide, Inc. 328 F.3d 1136, 1141 (9th Cir. 2003).

47. Schiller & Schmidt, Inc. v. Nordisco Corp., 969 F.2d 410, 413 (7th Cir. 1992).

48. Playboy Enterprises, Inc. v. Dumas, 53 F.3d 549, 559 (2d Cir. 1995),

cert. denied, 516 U.S. 1010, 116 S.Ct. 567, 133 L.Ed.2d 491 (1995).

49. Gladwell Government Services, Inc. v. County of Marin, 265 Fed.Appx. 624, 626 (9th Cir. 2008).

50. Patry on Copyright § 5:49.

§ 5.3　Joint Works

It is not uncommon for multiple parties to collaborate with each other to produce copyrightable works. Typical examples include the efforts of a composer and lyricist, who work together to develop one or more songs or the efforts of a screenwriter and a cinematographer who cooperate to produce a motion picture. These collaborative efforts raise a number of questions under the copyright laws concerning ownership of the copyright in the resulting work.

5.3.1　Determining Whether a Work Is a Joint Work

Under the current copyright statute the products of most of these collaborations are considered "joint works." More specifically, the 1976 Act defines a joint work as one "prepared by two or more authors with the intention that their contributions be merged into inseparable or interdependent parts of a unitary whole."[51] Elsewhere, the statute tells us who the owners of such "joint works" will be, and the answer is predictable—when multiple parties work together to create a "joint work," they are treated as co-owners of the copyright in that work.[52] More specifically each owns an undivided equal fractional interest in the final product.

Authors need not contribute equally to the creative process in order to be considered co-owners of a joint work. If two playwrights work on a play together, and one crafts 80 percent of the lines while the other authors the remaining 20 percent, the two will nonetheless own the copyright in the resulting play equally. (Some courts, however, have found that if one party has contributed to the work in only a minimal fashion there is at least a presumption against joint authorship.[53]) It also does not matter which of the collaborators does the "fixation" of the work. Even if only one of

---

51. 17 U.S.C. § 101. Joint creation is not the only situation that can lead to joint ownership of a copyright interest. For instance, a copyright could be assigned jointly to two or more individuals or multiple parties might inherent undivided interests in a single copyright. Nonetheless, the situation of joint ownership resulting from collaborative creation is the situation raising the most intriguing legal questions.

52. The statute provides that "the authors of a joint work are co-owners of copyright in the work." 17 U.S.C. § 201(a). Collaboration is not the only way that multiple parties could be joint owners of copyright in a work. The original author might assign the copyright to

multiple assignees who would become joint owners, or multiple parties might inherit the work after the death of the author. The material in this section of the text is confined to the situation where there has been alleged collaborative authorship.

53. See e.g. Eckert v. Hurley Chicago Co., Inc., 638 F.Supp. 699, 704 (N.D. Ill. 1986) ("While a co-author's contribution need not equal the other author's, at least when the authors are not immediately and obviously collaborating, the co-author's contribution must be 'significant' both in quality and quantity in order to permit an inference that the parties intended a joint work").

them has done the writing or typing, they are both co-owners of the eventual copyright.

It is not even necessary for either co-author to know the identity of the other, so long as each intended and anticipated that their material would be combined with someone else's contribution to create the finished product. Thus, in *Edward B. Marks Music Corp. v. Jerry Vogel Music Co.*,[54] a man named Edward Marks composed lyrics for a song entitled *December and May*. He was not, at the time, working with any particular musical composer as his collaborator. Marks then transferred the copyright in the lyrics to someone named Harding, who in turn retained someone named Loraine to write the music. After Loraine did so, Harding then secured copyright in the music and lyrics as a completed song. Marks, the lyricist, and Loraine, the composer, only met each other several years later. Decades thereafter a dispute arose over the renewal of the copyright.[55] In holding that Marks was entitled to renew the copyright, Learned Hand declared that the song was a joint work. Hand observed that "it makes no difference whether the authors work in concert, or even whether they know each other; it is enough that they mean their contributions to be complementary in the sense that they are to be embodied in a single work to be performed as such." Although the *Marks* case was decided under the 1909 statute, the rule is the same under the current law.

On the other hand, if an author creates a work that he envisions as standing alone at the time of his creation, and some time later he (or an assignee) then recruits a second author to add new material, the resulting work would not be a joint work. Let's make that a bit more concrete. If a composer creates an instrumental piano work with no notion that it will have any accompanying words, and then three years later asks someone to write words for that song, the resulting song-plus-lyrics is not, under the current law, a joint work.[56] Rather it is a derivative work. The composer would own a separate copyright in the music, and the lyricist would

---

54.   140 F.2d 266 (2d Cir. 1944).

55.   We discuss the various rules governing copyright renewals under the 1909 statute in the chapter of this book dealing with questions of copyright duration.

56.   At least one court came out the other way under the 1909 statute. In Shapiro, Bernstein & Co. v. Jerry Vogel Music Co., 221 F.2d 569 (2d Cir. 1955), a case commonly called the Twelfth Street Rag case, a composer wrote an instrumental tune and then assigned away the copyright. Four years later the assignee of the copyright commissioned a lyricist to write words for the song. The Second Circuit held that the resulting song was a joint work even though it assumed that the composer had no intention of creating a joint work at the time he wrote the music. The Second Circuit retreated from the position in *Twelfth Street Rag* even before the enactment of the 1976 Copyright Act, and the position of that case seems to be clearly rejected by both the text and legislative history of the current statute.

own one in the derivative work—the song plus lyrics—but that derivative work copyright would extend only to the new material contributed by the second party, namely the lyrics and thus would not allow the second party to use the music alone, unaccompanied by the words.[57] The crucial issue for a joint work analysis, then, is that each contributor intended to be one of multiple collaborators at the time of creation, even if the other collaborators are, to use the sports expression, merely "players to be named later."

Perhaps the most contentious—or at least the most discussed—issue involving joint works is whether each collaborator must contribute copyrightable expression to the final product in order to qualify as a joint author. The Nimmers argue forcefully in their famous treatise that there should be no such requirement.[58] Most of the cases, however, take the opposite view and insist that each collaborator contribute materials that would itself qualify for copyright in order to achieve the status of a joint author. Under this predominant view, if one party develops only the general idea for the plot of a novel or a play, and reveals it to another party who then executes the idea by crafting the actual prose—the protectable expression—there is no joint work. The wordsmith is the sole author and the idea contributor is out of luck. The same would be true if one party supplied merely non-copyrightable facts or research.

This situation is illustrated by *Childress v. Taylor*,[59] where Taylor, an actress, conceived of the idea for a play about the renowned black comedienne Moms Mabley. She did considerable research about Mabley's life, including interviews with Mabley's friends and family, and then turned over her materials to Childress, an accomplished playwright, who was to write the actual play. As Childress worked, Taylor periodically discussed with her the "inclusion of certain general scenes and characters in the play."[60] Unfortunately, the two artists ultimately could not agree over the ownership of the copyright interest in the resulting play.

In the ensuing litigation, the Second Circuit held that Taylor was not a joint author because she did not contribute copyrightable material.[61] In reaching the conclusion that a copyrightable contribu-

---

57. *See*, Batiste v. Island Records Inc., 179 F.3d 217, 222 n.7 (5th Cir. 1999). The rule was to the contrary under the 1909 statute, under a doctrine under the so-called *Twelfth Street Rag* doctrine set out in Shapiro, Bernstein & Co. v. Jerry Vogel Music Co., 221 F.2d 569, modified on reh'g, 223 F.2d 252 (2d Cir.1955).

58. Nimmer, § 6.07[A][3][a] ("given the requisite preconcerted intent, there

should be no further requirement that A and B each independently contribute copyrightable expression."). The Patry copyright treatise appears to also endorse this view. Patry on Copyright § 5:16.

59. 945 F.2d 500 (1991).

60. 945 F.2d at 502.

61. *See also S.O.S., Inc. v. Payday, Inc.*, 886 F.2d 1081 (9th Cir. 1989).

tion was required to achieve the status of joint author, the court commented:

> [T]he person with non-copyrightable material who proposed to join forces with a skilled writer to produce a copyrightable work is free to make a contract to disclose his or her material in return for assignment of part ownership of the resulting copyright ... It seems more consistent with the spirit of copyright law to oblige all joint authors to make copyrightable contributions, leaving those with non-copyrightable contributions to protect their rights through contract.[62]

The Seventh Circuit has, however, intimated that in at least some cases, the requirement that each co-author must contribute copyrightable material should be relaxed. In *Gaiman v. McFarlane*,[63] Judge Posner had to determine the ownership of three new characters introduced in a charmingly entitled comic book called *Hellspawn*. The basic character traits of this new trio, along with their names, were developed by an outside writer named Gaiman. The characters were drawn and inked by McFarlane, the originator of the *Hellspawn* series. McFarlane argued that Gaiman could not be a joint author of the new characters because his literary descriptions of them were too simplistic to constitute copyrightable works—as he put it they were mere stock characters.

Judge Posner disagreed. His opinion in *Gaiman* permitted the party who only contributed an uncopyrightable idea to be designated a co-author. Unfortunately, the scope of his decision is a bit unclear. Some of his language suggests that he would only relax the requirement of copyrightable contributions when *all of the contributions* are non-copyrightable, but the resulting mix crosses the line for protection, to avoid the anomaly that there would be no co-authors at all of the resulting work. He suggested that this "whole is greater than the sum of the parts" situation would obtain particularly for "mixed media" works, such as comic books, where the literary attributes of characters and their simple cartoonish appearance might both lack sufficient creativity to be copyrightable, but where the combination deserved protection.

Elsewhere in his opinion, however, while discoursing on the issue, Judge Posner gave the example of one "professor [who] has brilliant ideas but can't write; another is an excellent writer but his

---

62. 945 F.2d at 507. To the same effect is *Erickson v. Trinity Theatre, Inc.*, 13 F.3d 1061 (7th Cir. 1994), where the Seventh Circuit quoted the following passage from Professor Goldstein's treatise with approval: "[A] collaborative contribution will not produce a joint work, and a contributor will not obtain a co-ownership interest, unless the contribution represents original expression that could stand on its own as the subject matter of copyright." 13 F.3d at 1070.

63. 360 F.3d 644 (7th Cir. 2004).

ideas are commonplace. So they collaborate on an academic article, one contributing the ideas, which are not copyrightable and the other the prose envelope, and ... they sign as co-authors. Their intent to be the joint owners of the copyright in the article would be plain, and that should be enough to constitute them joint authors...."[64] Regrettably most academic articles are not "mixed media" works like comic books; some cartoonish illustration would likely improve most of them. More to the point, however, the quoted hypothetical seems squarely contrary to the majority view exemplified by the *Childress* case from the Second Circuit, and thus creates a circuit split on the question of whether a copyrightable contribution is required from each of several purported co-authors.

Although the Posner–Nimmer position appears to be the minority view, your present authors find it to be the more persuasive. All copyrightable works represent the union of an underlying idea and a concrete expression. While ideas by themselves cannot be withdrawn from the public domain because of the burden that would place on future authors, the quality of the ideas that underlie a work are at least as crucial to its economic and cultural importance as its expression. If two parties have an intent to collaborate, with one supplying ideas and the other giving those ideas concrete form, it seems to accord with both the intent of the parties and simple common sense to treat the two as co-owners of the resulting work. A rule requiring the idea-supplier to secure an assignment of a half interest of copyright in the result working before disclosing the idea in order for him to become a co-owner seems both cumbersome and a trap for the unwary.

Nonetheless, assuming the Second Circuit's approach to be controlling for the moment, note that under its view parties who commission independent contractors and ask them to create copyrightable works cannot claim the status of joint authors merely because they provided the idea for the work or general instructions about how it was to be accomplished.[65] In other words, the patron of the arts who hires a painter and instructs him or her to paint "a still life consisting of two apples, a peach and a white rose" will not be able to claim joint ownership of the resulting painting. Similarly,

---

64. *Id.* At 659. The result in *Gaiman* seems to have emboldened other judges to align themselves with the Nimmer–Posner position. *See* Brown v. Flowers, 196 Fed.Appx. 178, 189 (4th Cir. 2006) (Gregory, J., *concurring in part and dissenting in part*) ("I would recognize that an individual who, in collaboration with another, provides a substantial original contribution to a copyrightable work satisfies the authorship requirement, regardless of whether his contribution, standing alone, would be individually copyrightable"); Gordon v. Lee, 2007 WL 1450403 (N.D.Ga. 2007) ("A joint author is not required to establish that his or her contribution to a work was independently copyrightable").

65. For a general discussion of this situation, *see,* Robert Penchina, *The Creative Commissioner: Commissioned Works Under the Copyright Act of 1976,* 62 N.Y.U. L. Rev. 373 (1987).

one who hires an architect and provides instructions concerning the number and sizes of rooms to be included is not a co-author of the resulting building, as numerous cases have held.[66]

Since the intent of the various creators is crucial in determining if their work product should be treated as a joint work, we must now return to that subject and say a few more words on the subject of intent. While the statute speaks of an intention "that their contributions be merged into an inseparable or interdependent parts of a unitary whole," the courts have refined that requirement. The cases further require that both parties intend to be *joint authors* as well. As the *Childress* court explained, if the statutory definition were taken literally it

> would extend joint author status to many persons who are not likely to have been within the contemplation of Congress. For example, a writer frequently works with an editor who makes numerous useful revisions to the first draft, some of which will consist of additions of copyrightable expression. Both intend their contributions to be merged into inseparable parts of a unitary whole, yet very few editors and even fewer writers would expect the editor to be accorded the status of joint author, enjoying an undivided half interest in the copyright in the published work. Similarly, research assistants may on occasion contribute to an author some protectable expression or merely a sufficiently original selection of factual material as would be entitled to a copyright, yet not be entitled to be regarded as a joint author of the work in which the contributed material appears. What distinguishes the writer-editor relationship and the writer-researcher relationship from the true joint author relationship is the lack of intent of both participants in the venture to regard themselves as joint authors.[67]

How can we know if the parties intended their collaboration to result in the status of joint authors? Courts often rely on a variety of circumstances surrounding the publication of the work to ascertain the intent of the collaborators. For instance it is at least some evidence that the crucial intent was lacking when one party has promulgated copies of the work listing only himself or herself as the author.[68] Similarly a court would probably find the requisite intent

66. *See e.g.* M.G.B. Homes, Inc. v. Ameron Homes, Inc., 903 F.2d 1486, 1496 (11th Cir. 1990); Aitken, Hazen, Hoffman, Miller, P.C. v. Empire Const. Co., 542 F.Supp. 252, 259 (D. Neb. 1982).

67. 945 F.2d at 507.

68. *See* Childress, 945 F.2d at 508 ("[t]hough 'billing' or 'credit' is not decisive in all cases and joint authorship can exist without any explicit discussion of this topic by the parties, consideration of the topic helpfully serves to focus the fact-finder's attention on how the par-

lacking when one of the litigants has registered a claim of copyright in the work naming only himself as the sole author. As the *Childress* excerpts suggests, in certain recurring cases, industry practice or settled custom can tell us that the requisite intent to be co-authors is missing, as in the research assistant example. Given that the parties have strong temptations to adjust their memories of their earlier intent to their own self-interest at the time of trial, the issue requires considerable judicial wisdom and skepticism.

5.3.2 Consequences of Joint Work Status

Assuming the requirement of a joint work are met, the several authors are, as we have noted, tenants in common of the copyright in question.[69] As is true with the similar relationship in the world of real property, this means that each owns an undivided and equal fractional interest in the copyright. On the death of one co-author, his copyright interests in the work passes to his heirs, as specified in his will or under the relevant intestacy laws, and not the other co-author (as would be the case with joint tenancy). As tenants in common, all co-authors of copyright are also free to exercise any of the rights of a copyright owner without the permission of the other joint owners, and to grant non-exclusive licenses others to exercise those rights as well.[70] Note, however, that a co-author acting alone cannot grant *exclusive* licenses. Such a license is a promise that no one else will be granted the same rights, and one author cannot guarantee his licensee that his co-author will not want to issue similar licenses to others.[71]

If one co-author either directly exploits the work, or grants a license, he will have a duty to account to the other co-owners for any profits realized from that direct use or licensing.[72] Thus, if a

ties implicitly regarded their undertaking."). *See also* Thomson v. Larson, 147 F.3d 195 (2d Cir. 1998), which placed considerable weight on how the authorship of the play *Rent* was listed in copies in deciding the intent of the dominant author.

69. *See* H.R. Rep. No. 94–1474, 94th Cong. 2d Sess. 121 (1976). The use of the "tenant-in-common" analogy has led courts to look to cases dealing with real estate to resolve issues concerning the ownership rights to jointly authored works.

70. This is not the rule outside of the United States. Most foreign nations will not treat a license to use a jointly authored work to be valid unless all of the co-authors have joined in the license. Thus, if a licensee is planning to exploit a work outside of the United States,

such as a book publisher who wants to sell copies of a co-authored novel in Canada, it will be necessary to get all co-authors to sign the license. *See generally* Nimmer, § 6.10[D] at n.14.

71. *See e.g.,* Davis v. Blige, 505 F.3d 90, 101 (2d Cir. 2007) ("a co-owner cannot unilaterally grant an exclusive license"); Siegel v. Warner Bros. Entertainment Inc., 542 F.Supp.2d 1098, 1143 (C.D.Cal. 2008) ("in order for an exclusive license in the entirety of the interest in a joint work itself ... to be effective, the consent of both joint owners in the copyrighted work is required.")

72. *See e.g.* Oddo v. Ries, 743 F.2d 630 (9th Cir. 1984); Shapiro, Bernstein & Co. v. Jerry Vogel Music Co., 221 F.2d 569 (2d Cir. 1955), *modified* 223 F.2d 252 (2d Cir. 1955).

composer and lyricist collaborate on a song, the composer may enter into a (non-exclusive) license with a record company to record the song, allowing them to reproduce that recording on compact discs and to sell the resulting CDs to the public without consulting with or getting the permission of the lyricist. The composer would, however, have to split the royalties earned from the license with the lyricist. By way of contrast, if a co-owner of copyright in a joint work fully conveys his interest in the work, he is entitled to keep the full proceeds of that sale, and the new owner will become a co-owner of the copyright will all the rights and obligations associated with that status. Thus, if the composer assigns his rights in the song to a music publisher, that music publisher steps into the composer's shoes and becomes a co-owner of the copyright with the lyricist.

You might also wonder if a co-owner of a joint work can assign his interest to an alleged infringer "retroactively" after the date of the alleged infringement, so as to cut off an infringement claim by other co-authors. That was the issue in *Davis v. Blige*.[73] There, plaintiff Sharice Davis claimed that she and Bruce Chambliss had co-authored two songs that were infringed by some songs collectively written by celebrated soul diva Mary J. Blige and her brother Bruce Miller, along with others. Davis sued for infringement in 2003, but in June 2004, her co-author Chambliss transferred his share of the rights in the Davis–Chambliss songs to Miller (who, just to make things more interesting, was his son).[74] That transfer of rights specified that it was retroactive to the date of the creation of the songs. Miller then defended the lawsuit by claiming that because of the assignment, he had stepped into the shoes of Chambliss and was thus a co-owner of the complaining works. As such, he argued he was entitled to exploit those work as he wished, and license others (such as Blige) to do so as well.

The Second Circuit did not buy it, declaring that "such retroactive transfers violate basic principles of tort and contract law and undermine the policies embodied by the Copyright Act." Expanding on the theme, the court declared that it had "no doubt that Chambliss can release his own accrued claims of copyright infringement against Miller and his fellow defendants.... But we know of no authority to sanction his attempt to release any rights Davis has against Miller, for they are not Chambliss's to release." The court's bottom line was that a copyright assignment by one co-author can only be prospective in order to avoid prejudice to other co-author. That result has been criticized in the secondary literature,[75] howev-

73. 505 F.3d 90 (2d Cir. 2007).

74. Blige, by the way, is Chambliss's step-daughter. 505 F.3d at 94.

75. *See e.g.*, Patry on Copyright § 5:103; Katie Idzik, Note: *No More Drama? The Past, Present, and Potential Future of Retroactive Transfers of Copy-*

er, and it remains to be seen if other circuits agree or if the Second Circuit itself rethinks its position.

Co-authors can also prepare derivative works based on a prior joint work, and if only one co-author adds new material in order to produce the derivative work, that co-author will become the sole owner of copyright in that derivative work. Let's see if we can put that in English. Assume Alice and Bob jointly author a travel guide to New England in 2010, with numerous listings of charming country inns and fine restaurants. By 2012, their book has become somewhat out of date. Some inns have closed, new ones will have opened, some restaurants will have new chefs, and the prices of all will no doubt have bubbled upwards. Consequently, Alice, acting on her own, prepares a new edition. She adds numerous entries, she deletes others, and rewords the descriptions of some that are retained. On the other hand, a good portion of the text is carried forward from the earlier joint work verbatim.

Is the new edition a joint work in which Bob, the non-participating party, can claim a joint interest? The Second Circuit confronted this problem in *Weissmann v. Freeman*.[76] In that case two doctors, Leonard Freeman and Heidi Weissman, co-authored materials for a review course in nuclear medicine. Over the next five years they periodically revised and updated the document. Eventually, however, Dr. Weissman prepared a further update on her own. That document contained new materials, but also included much text taken verbatim from the earlier versions. When Dr. Freeman subsequently attempted to use this new version in a review course he was offering, Dr. Weissman sued him for infringement. Of course, Dr. Freeman could not be an infringer if he was a co-author of the disputed version, so that became the key issue in the case. The court concluded that Dr. Weissman—the author of the derivative work—was the sole owner of copyright in that work. The court reasoned that any other rule

> would convert all derivative works based upon jointly authored works into joint works, regardless of whether there had been any joint labor on the subsequent version. If such were the law, it would eviscerate the independent copyright protection that attaches to a derivative work

---

right Ownership, 18 DePaul J. Art, Tech. & Intell. Prop. L. 127 (2007). *But see,* Hunter Rodriguez, Note: *"No More Drama": In Davis v. Blige, the Second Circuit Invalidates Retroactive Transfers, but What about Other Unilateral Acts by a Copyright Co-owner?*, 38 Sw. L. Rev. 307 (2008) (defending opinion.)

76. 868 F.2d 1313 (2d Cir. 1989). The case did not involve travel guides, but rather study guides prepared for medical students studying for licensing exams in radiology.

that is wholly independent of the protection afforded the preexisting work.[77]

This means that in our hypothetical case Bob cannot exploit the derivative version of the New England travel guide without Alice's permission and if he does so, he is guilty of infringement.

Weissman did not address, however, the question of whether the preparer of the derivative work owes any financial recompense to the other joint author of the underlying work if the derivative work is exploited for profit. In other words, in the preceding hypothetical, does Alice have to share profits from the second edition of the guidebook (the one she prepared all by herself, and for which she owns the sole copyright) with Bob? After all, there is still some material from the joint work carried forward in that new edition, and Bob might have been able to license someone else— Cathy if we continue the tedious alphabetization—to prepare a derivative work in return for a royalty payment.

There is no question that making a derivative work is just as much a form of "exploitation" of a copyrighted work as is reproducing and selling copies, or licensing third parties to perform the work. Since there is a duty of an accounting in those cases, it follows that there ought to be a similar duty in this case as well. The exact amount of compensation owed under these circumstances might be difficult to calculate, however. A court could attempt to estimate the amount of new material and the amount of material carried forward from the previous version and calculate a payment accordingly. In other words, in the guidebook case, if the new material added by Alice to the most recent edition totals 20 percent of the material in that edition, a court could decide that Alice should retain 20 percent of the profits of the new edition "off the top" and then be obligated to split the rest with Bob, her co-author from the earlier editions. Thus if the new edition made $10,000, Alice would owe Bob $4,000 as an accounting for her use of the previously prepared jointwork. Of course, in many cases, calculating a percentage of "new" versus old material will be impossible. If the underlying work were, for instance, a novel, and the derivative work were a motion picture or stage play, it might be purely speculative to assign percentages. In such a case, an alternative approach would be for the court to estimate the amount an independent licensee would have paid as a royalty in an arms length transaction for the right to prepare the type of derivative work in question.

§ 5.4   Ownership of Copyright in Compilations and the *Tasini* Case

Compilations, as you will recall from an earlier chapter, are works formed from the collection and assembly of preexisting

---

77. 868 F.2d at 1317.

materials or of data. Where the selection and arrangement of the underlying materials displays originality, the compiler is entitled to a separate copyright in the compilation which is distinct from any copyrights in the individual items she has chosen to include. For instance, an English professor might put together an anthology of twentieth century American short stories by selecting 20 such stories and sequencing them in a way that she thought would be effective for a student in a literature course. This English professor would naturally need to obtain permission to include each of the stories in the ultimate anthology, unless they had fallen into the public domain,[78] because to include copyrighted stories without permission is infringement. Note, however, that the English professor now owns an entirely new and distinct copyright in the anthology as single work.

The new copyright granted to the author of the compilation or anthology does not in any way extinguish the copyrights in the individual contributions—in our example the individuals who authored each story retain their own copyrights in those works. The 1976 Act is explicit on this point, declaring:

> Copyright in each separate contribution to a collective work is distinct from copyright in the collective work as a whole and vests initially in the author of the contribution. In the absence of an express transfer of the copyright or of any rights under it, the owner of copyright in the collective work is presumed to have acquired only the privilege of reproducing and distributing the contribution as part of that particular collective work, any revision of that collective work, and any later collective work in that same series.[79]

One interesting context involving compilation copyrights is that of newspapers, periodicals, and journals. Some material appearing in your daily newspaper is written by reporters who are full-time employees of the paper. The copyright in those stories plainly belongs to the newspaper under the work made for hire doctrine. Other stories, however, are written by freelance reporters, and then submitted to the newspaper for potential publication. You may recall from earlier in this chapter that "contributions to a collective work" are one of the "named nine" categories of works

---

78. Such works could have fallen into the public domain if they were published without notice at a time when notice was required; if the owner of the copyright had failed to renew the copyright when a renewal was required; or if all copyright protection had expired, as would be the case for works first published before 1923.

79. 17 U.S.C. § 201(c).

that can be treated as works made for hire when specially commissioned, provided the parties execute a contract to that effect. If there is no such agreement, however, and if the freelancer does not assign the copyright in the work, the newspaper would publish it under a license. That would mean that the newspaper would own a copyright in the newspaper as a whole, but the freelancer would retain the copyright in his individual story as a "stand-alone" work.

This situation set the stage for a dispute that ultimately found its way to the Supreme Court in the case of *New York Times Co. v. Tasini*.[80] That controversy began in the early 1990s when six different freelance authors contributed a number of stories to three well-known periodicals—the New York Times, Newsday, and Sports Illustrated. The parties agreed that the authors had retained copyright ownership in their individual works and that the periodicals held a copyright in their respective materials as collective works. The problem arose when the periodicals made the stories available to various electronic databases, such as LEXIS/NEXIS®. The freelance authors claimed that this use of their stories was unauthorized and thus filed suit for copyright infringement against both the original print publishers and the electronic databases as well. In effect, the freelancers asserted that the sums they had been originally paid by the periodicals did not contemplate (and did not compensate for) this additional use of their work product.

By way of a defense, the periodicals pointed to the very last clause of section 201(c), which grants the owner of a compilation copyright "the privilege of reproducing and distributing the contribution as part of that particular collective work, any revision of that collective work, and any later collective work in that same series." The crucial question was whether the on-line materials could be considered either a "revision" or "later work . . . in the same series" as the original print newspapers and magazines. The Supreme Court held that it did not.

Writing for a 7–2 majority, Justice Ginsburg began by pointing to language in the legislative history of the Copyright Act that offered an example of what the statutory drafters had in mind. According to the relevant House Report explicating § 203(c) a "publishing company could reprint a contribution from one issue in a later issue of its magazine, and could reprint an article from a 1980 edition of an encyclopedia in a 1990 revision of it; the publisher could not revise the contribution itself or include it in a new anthology or an entirely different magazine or other collective work."[81] This suggested, according to the court, that the essential

---

80. 533 U.S. 483, 121 S.Ct. 2381, 150 L.Ed.2d 500 (2001).

81. 533 U.S. at 496–67, quoting H.R. Rep. 122–123, U.S. Code Cong. & Admin. News 1976, pp. 5659, 5738.

requirement under the section was that the various multiple works making up the collective product could not be disaggregated if the periodical was to remain within the statutory privilege. As Justice Ginsburg put it, the electronic databases

> present articles to users clear of the context provided either by the original periodical editions, or by any revision of those editions.... When the user conducts a search, each article appears as a separate item within the search result ... without the graphics, formatting, or other articles with which the article was initially published ... we cannot see how the Database perceptibly reproduces and distributes the article "as part of" either the original edition or a "revision" of that edition.... The Databases' reproduction and distribution of individual Articles—simply as individual Articles—would invade the core of the Authors' exclusive rights under § 106.

Further illumination of the meaning of *Tasini* came a few years later in *Faulkner v. National Geographic Enterprises, Inc.*[82] In that case, the National Geographic reproduced all of its back issues in a digital CD–ROM collection which it called *The Complete National Geographic (or CNG)*. Freelance photographers alleged that the inclusion of their works in this new product was infringing. The Second Circuit disagreed. The key was that in this case:

> The CNG was produced through digital scanning. Each issue of the magazine was scanned two pages at a time into a computer system. As a result, the CNG user sees exactly what he or she would see if viewing an open page of the paper version, including the fold of the magazine.... [T]here are no changes in the content, format, or appearance of the issues ... The pages appear as they do in the print version, including all text, photographs, graphics, advertising, credits and attributions. Issues of the Magazine appear chronologically with the first issue published appearing at the beginning of the first disk and the last appearing at the end of the last disk. The individual images and texts are therefore viewed in a context almost identical—but for the use of a computer screen and the power to move from one issue to another and find various items quickly—to that in which they were originally published.

Because the full context of the materials was preserved and the collective work was reproduced in a way that retained the creative

---

82. 409 F.3d 26 (2d Cir. 2005), *cert. denied,* 546 U.S. 1076, 126 S.Ct. 833, 163 L.Ed.2d 707 (2005).

selection and coordination of the National Geographic's editors, this situation came within the boundaries of the section 203(c) privilege.

On its face *Tasini* might seem like a win for freelancers. If so, however, it has proven to be something of a pyrrhic victory. Even before the case was decided, periodicals began routinely demanding that freelance authors include electronic republication rights to the materials they supply for inclusion in print editions. There is no evidence to indicate that when they did so, they increased their payments to the freelancers, and given the respective bargaining power of the parties, that seems unlikely. Since § 203 merely provides a default rule, these express agreements trump the limitation in the statutory privilege and allow the periodicals to send the articles to the databases without risk of infringement.

Nonetheless, you might think that the freelancers will at least benefit by receiving past-due royalties for the electronic use of their works prior to the widespread adoption of these new contracts. That has not yet proven to be the case either. In the wake of *Tasini* several class actions were certified and the parties came close to creating a multi-million dollar fund in settlement of these claims. In 2007, however, the Second Circuit ruled that the plaintiff class could not include any authors who had not registered their copyrights,[83] thus throwing a monkey wrench into the pending settlement. At this writing the case is still pending and the freelance authors have yet to receive any compensation for those now decades-old articles reproduced in electronic formats.

§ 5.5   Transfer of Copyright

Copyrights are freely transferable, just like all other types of personal property. They can be transferred outright, in a transaction usually denominated as an assignment, or the owner can merely give another party the right to exercise certain rights of copyright ownership by granting either an exclusive or non-exclusive license. These transfers can be for compensation or can take the form of a gift. Moreover, copyrights will be treated as part of the owner's legal estate upon his or her death, and thus can be transferred by provisions in a will, or under the relevant provisions of state intestacy laws.

Because of the intangible nature of the copyright interest, however, a number of issues concerning transferability of ownership call for clarification.

83. In re Literary Works in Electronic Databases Copyright Litigation,   509 F.3d 116 (2d Cir. 2007).

5.5.1 Copyright Ownership Independent of Ownership of Copy

Under the Copyright Act of 1909, there was some ambiguity about copyright ownership in situations where the creator of a one-of-a-kind work of authorship, such as a painting, sculpture, manuscript, or master tape recording sold or otherwise disposed of the sole copy of the work. Where the work was protected by a federal statutory copyright, section 27 of that now-defunct statute specifically declared that the sale, conveyance, or gift of the material object "shall not of itself constitute a transfer of the copyright, nor shall the assignment of the copyright constitute a transfer of the title to the material object." The situation was more murky, however, where the work was unpublished and protected only by a common law copyright. At least some cases held that in that situation a sale also constituted a transfer of the underlying copyright interest, unless the seller specifically reserved his rights.

Perhaps the leading case reaching this holding was *Pushman v. New York Graphic Society, Inc.*[84] In that case a well-known artist of the day named Hovsep Pushman sold a painting called *When Autumn Is Here* to the University of Illinois. Thereafter, the University purported to sell reproduction rights in the painting to the New York Graphic Society. Such a transaction would only have been valid if the University had acquired the reproduction rights when it purchased the physical painting. Pushman filed suit, asserting that he had not transferred the reproduction rights when he sold the canvas, and thus that any reproductions of the work by the Graphic Society would be infringements of his retained rights. The New York Court of Appeals disagreed, and held that because the sale was unconditional, Pushman had parted with the reproduction rights as well as with the painting. As the court put it, "an artist must, if he wishes to retain or protect the reproduction right, make some reservation of that right when he sells the painting." This meant that the artist, having sold the work, could no longer control subsequent exploitation of the work in further copies or other media—for instance, he couldn't prevent the purchaser from making posters or postcards, nor could he make such reproductions himself, without running the risk of a charge of copyright infringement.

The scope of the *Pushman* doctrine was murky. Because it dealt with common law copyright, it was only binding authority in New York; some states followed its lead, but many never had occasion to address the issue. New York itself eventually adopted legislation partially overruling it, though it was unclear if that

---

84. 287 N.Y. 302, 39 N.E.2d 249 (1942).

legislation was retroactive.[85] Some courts noted that *Pushman* merely established a presumption, and that the ultimate question would turn on the intent of the parties.[86] The doctrine apparently did not apply to letters, even though they are clearly one-of-a-kind works of authorship which are usually transferred to the recipient without a reservation of the right of reproduction. Nonetheless, the doctrine continues to have some importance, because in limited cases it may control the copyright status of a work where there was a pre–1978 transfer of the sole physical copy of that work.

The authors of the 1976 Act sought to prevent this result and eliminate any ambiguities in situations such as the one described above. To some extent, they accomplished that result by abolishing common law copyright. Just to be crystal clear, however, the present statute explicitly declares that the sale or other disposition of a tangible copy of a work by the author does not in anyway affect or diminish that author's continued ownership of the copyright interest in the work. In other words, the ownership of any particular copy of a work and the ownership of the copyright are entirely independent.[87] The relevant provision is section 202 of the current act, which provides:

> Ownership of a copyright, or of any of the exclusive rights under a copyright, is distinct from ownership of any material object in which the work is embodied. Transfer of ownership of any material object, including the copy or phonorecord in which the work is first fixed, does not of itself convey any rights in the copyright work embodied in the object; nor, in the absence of an agreement, does transfer of ownership of a copyright or of any exclusive rights under a copyright convey property rights in any material object.[88]

Of course, as a practical matter, an artist who sells the only copy of a painting will have trouble exercising the rights of a copyright owner, such as reproduction, unless he can secure access to the painting. It may be that the artist can replicate the work from memory, and thus produce copies in the form of posters,

---

85. N.Y. Laws 1966 ch. 668, providing that whenever a work of fine art is transferred, the right of reproduction is reserved to the grantor unless specifically transferred in writing. Presumably this left the *Pushman* rule in place for other types of materials protected by common law copyright that did not fall within the category of fine art, such as a manuscript.

86. *See, e.g.,* Forward v. Thorogood, 985 F.2d 604, 607 (1st Cir. 1993); Community for Creative Non–Violence v. Reid, 846 F.2d 1485, 1495 n.12 (D.C. Cir. 1988), *aff'd,* 490 U.S. 730, 109 S.Ct. 2166, 104 L.Ed.2d 811 (1989) (characterizing the *Pushman* doctrine as a presumption).

87. The House Report concerning the 1976 Act cited *Pushman* by name and indicated that the new statute would reverse the rule of the case. H.R. Rep. No. 94–1476 at 124 (1976).

88. 17 U.S.C. § 202.

silkscreens, or notecards, but in most instances, a mechanical reproduction would be preferable, and that would require some opportunity to borrow the original. The prudent artist will therefore retain a copy for his own purposes or negotiate a right of access before parting with a one-of-a-kind original.

5.5.2   Divisibility of Copyright Interests

The best economic exploitation of copyrighted material often will motivate a copyright owner to deal with a variety of different intermediaries. The author of a novel, for instance, might wish to grant one publisher hardcover publication rights, another publisher paperback rights, a movie studio the right to make a derivative work in the form of a motion picture, and a record company the right to produce and market recording of the book on CDs or as digital downloads. Such a strategy is only possible if the copyright interest in the novel is "divisible"—permitting the copyright owner to transfer or license each right separately. The current copyright law provides for such divisibility in section 201, which states:

> Any of the exclusive rights comprised in a copyright, including any subdivision of any of the rights specified by Section 106, may be transferred . . . and owned separately.[89]

As a consequence, the assignee or exclusive licensee of any right owns a slice of the copyright in question and has standing to sue for infringement where that transferee's rights are being violated.[90] For instance if a playwright were to grant an exclusive license to a theater company to perform a particular play in New York City, during the month of September 2011, that theater company could sue anyone else who attempted to perform the play in New York during the month in question. It could not, of course, sue someone for performing the play in Los Angeles that month or one who performed the play in New York in October, 2011, nor would it have a claim against a production company that turned the play into a motion picture, because it had not licensed the right to do any of those things itself.

By way of contrast, however, a non-exclusive licensee does not have standing to sue for infringement.[91] For instance, if a movie theater receives a non-exclusive license to exhibit (that is, "to perform") a particular motion picture, that license contemplates that others may be showing the same movie in the same town at the same time. Even if some of those other exhibitors are infringing

---

89. 17 U.S.C. § 201(d)(2).

90. 17 U.S.C. §§ 201(d), 501(b).

91. *See* Nimmer, § 10.02[B][1] ("a nonexclusive licensee has no standing to sue in his own name even for infringement of the rights as to which he is a licensee.").

by showing the movie illegally, the copyright owner could have licensed them, and thus the non-exclusive licensee is no worse off than it bargained for. In such a case, the copyright owner can sue the unauthorized theater, but the non-exclusive licensee may not.

The "divisibility" approach of the current statute represents a shift from the rule that purportedly prevailed under the 1909 statute. Under the 1909 Act, a copyright was said to be an indivisible interest. That did not preclude licensing under the old law, but it lead to complexity. For instance, if a party obtained a license to publish a previously unpublished work in a limited format—such as in a periodical—and did so with a copyright notice in its own name, the copyright notice would be defective. That is because the author was still considered the owner of the single and indivisible copyright, and it was the copyright owner's name that had to appear in the notice. The result was that the work would be injected into the public domain because of a defective notice![92] In addition, licensees also lacked standing to sue for infringement, since a licensee did not "own" the copyright—there could only be one owner and that was the licensor.[93] Over time, courts came up with several doctrines to make it possible for licensees to enforce their rights, so that the "indivisibility" standard of the old law was something of a legal fiction by the time Congress adopted the 1976 Act. Nonetheless the older provision proved troublesome, and its replacement with the principle of infinite divisibility is a major improvement in the state of the law.

5.5.3   Requirements for Valid Transfers

The divisibility of copyright discussed above has the potential to lead to considerable confusion. Multiple parties might claim a variety of rights to the same work, and sorting out those claims, particularly if they overlap, could prove quite complex. To reduce some of this potential confusion the 1976 Act requires certain formalities to be observed in connection with copyright transfers. These are in the nature of a statute of frauds requirement, as well as a variety of provisions relating to the recordation of transfers.

5.5.3.1   Writing Required

A "transfer" of copyright must be in writing. According to the statute:

A transfer of copyright ownership ... is not valid unless an instrument of conveyance, or a note or memorandum of

92. This harsh rule was eventually rejected in Goodis v. United Artists Television, Inc., 425 F.2d 397 (2nd Cir. 1970).

93. *See e.g.,* Field v. True Comics, Inc., 89 F.Supp. 611 (S.D.N.Y. 1950); Local Trademarks, Inc. v. Powers, 56 F.Supp. 751 (E.D. Pa. 1944).

the transfer is in writing and signed by the owner of the rights conveyed or such owner's duly authorized agent.[94]

This provision, of course, is akin to the Statute of Frauds, familiar from contract law. In interpreting it, however, one must bear in mind that the term "transfer" is specifically defined in the current copyright law and that definition is not entirely intuitive. That's why we put it in quotes. According to the statute:

> A "transfer of copyright ownership" is an assignment, mortgage, exclusive license, or any other conveyance, alienation or hypothecation of a copyright or of any of the exclusive rights comprised in a copyright, whether or not it is limited in time or place of effect, but not including a nonexclusive license.[95]

As you can see, under this definition the grant of a non-exclusive licenses is not a "transfer." This means that, unlike an assignment or exclusive license, a *non-exclusive* license need not be in writing in order to be valid.[96] Although this distinction may seem curious at first glance, it is actually quite logical. After all, in a system where a copyright interest in infinitely divisible it would become very difficult, without a writing requirement, to determine the precise boundaries of the rights of various exclusive licensees. On the other hand, where the purported license is non-exclusive, the only real effect of the license is to immunize the licensee from suit by the copyright owner. The non-exclusive licensee has no rights to sue others and thus the precise boundaries of the rights licensed become less important.

Also not included within the definition of transfer are transfers by will or bequest. Consequently these are also not covered by the federal statutory writing requirement. For transfers of this sort, state law will control. Since the vast majority of states require that a valid will be in writing in all but the most unusual circumstances, the practical importance of this observation is small, but if a state did permit an individual to pass property via an oral will, and if such a testator owned copyright interests, the will would be valid and the legatee of the copyright would become the owner despite the absence of a written document.[97]

94. 17 U.S.C. § 204(a).

95. 17 U.S.C. § 101.

96. Effects Associates, Inc. v. Cohen, 908 F.2d 555 (9th Cir. 1990), *cert. denied,* 498 U.S. 1103, 111 S.Ct. 1003, 112 L.Ed.2d 1086 (1991). Some states may have laws that require even non-exclusive licenses to be in writing. That raises the question whether such requirements are pre-empted by the provision in the federal statute. Courts that have considered the issue have held that there is no federal preemption and have refused to enforce the oral licenses under state law. *See e.g.,* Freedman v. Select Information Sys., Inc., 221 U.S.P.Q. 848 (N.D. Cal. 1983).

97. An oral will, also known as a nuncupative will, is permitted in certain states if made during the testator's "last sickness" in front of a specified number

Where a writing is required, the courts have been fairly liberal in finding the requirement satisfied. For instance, if the assignment or exclusive license is first granted by an oral promise and then subsequently confirmed in a document, the grant is considered effective as of the date of the oral promise.[98] Courts have also been willing to find the necessary memorandum in the contract for sale of a business that did not even mention copyright explicitly[99] and in the endorsement on the back of a check.[100]

A modern classic applying the writing requirement in copyright law is Judge Kozinski's opinion in *Effects Associates v. Cohen*.[101] Larry Cohen was a movie producer engaged in the development of what he surely expected to be a cinematic classic. Called *The Stuff*, the movie detailed the invasion of earth by an alien life form that both looked and tasted like frozen yogurt. Per the script, it would take over the mind of anyone who ate it.[102] In the climatic scene, the hero alerts the public and blows up the yogurt factory which, in Judge Kozinski's works makes "the world safe once again for lovers of frozen confections." Cohen hired Effects Associates to create the footage of the exploding factory for the movie, but he was unsatisfied with the results. Although he incorporated the footage into the film, he only paid Effects half of the specified price. Instead of suing for breach of contract, Effects brought suit for copyright infringement.

Effects argued that as the author of the disputed footage, it owned the copyright in that material and that Cohen had violated its exclusive rights to reproduce the work by incorporating it into the film. Cohen responded by claiming that Effects had transferred the copyright interest to him when they turned over the footage, even though there was no written agreement so providing. Kozinski wryly summarized this argument as "moviemakers do lunch not contracts," and quickly rejected it. He observed that "section 204's writing requirement is not unduly burdensome; it necessitates

---

of witnesses. *See, e.g.,* N.C. Stat. § 31–3.5.

98. *See e.g.,* Arthur Rutenberg Homes, Inc. v. Drew Homes, Inc., 29 F.3d 1529, 1532 (11th Cir.1994), Eden Toys, Inc. v. Florelee Undergarment Co., 697 F.2d 27, 36 (2d Cir. 1982). ("The 'note or memorandum of the transfer' need not be made at the time when the license is initiated; the requirement is satisfied by the copyright owner's later execution of a writing which confirms the agreement.").

99. Schiller & Schmidt, Inc. v. Nordisco Corp., 969 F.2d 410, 413 (7th Cir. 1992).

100. Franklin Mint Corp. v. National Wildlife Art Exch., Inc., 575 F.2d 62 (3d Cir.), *cert. denied,* 439 U.S. 880, 99 S.Ct. 217, 58 L.Ed.2d 193 (1978). Cf. Playboy Enterprises, Inc. v. Dumas, 53 F.3d 549 (2d Cir. 1995) (finding endorsement on check insufficient to meet writing requirement of § 204(a) because it was ambiguous).

101. 908 F.2d 555 (9th Cir. 1990), *cert. denied,* 498 U.S. 1103, 111 S.Ct. 1003, 112 L.Ed.2d 1086 (1991).

102. You really have to take a study break, go to YouTube, and watch the trailer for this movie, which is available here: http://www.youtube.com/watch?v=uE6Z1nBqLwo.

neither protracted negotiations nor substantial expense. The rule is really quite simple: If the copyright holder agrees to transfer ownership to another party, that party must get the copyright holder to sign a piece of paper saying so. It doesn't have to be the Magna Charta; a lone-line pro forma statement will do."

That was not the end of the matter, however. The court went on to consider whether or not Cohen had a *non-exclusive* license to use the footage. As noted above, licenses of this sort need not be in writing. Although there was no evidence of an express oral license of copyright on the facts of the case before it, the court noted that such a license can be implied from conduct. It found just such an implied license in the transaction involving *The Stuff*, noting that "Effects created a work at defendant's request and handed it over, intending that defendant copy and distribute it. To hold that Effects did not at the same time convey a license to use the footage in *The Stuff* would mean that plaintiff's contribution to the film was 'of minimal value,' a conclusion that can't be squared with the fact that Cohn paid Effects almost $56,000 for the footage." Judge Kozinski concluded his opinion by noting that Effects still could sue for the balance due on the contract and, perhaps more importantly, still owned the copyright in the footage and could license it to others.

One final historical observation before we move on. The writing requirement under the 1909 Act differed from the current statutory scheme in two interesting respects. First, that law did not require a writing for a license of any sort. Thus an oral exclusive license granted prior to January 1, 1978, is valid and enforceable, if it can be proved. That approach is not entirely surprising, given the assumption of non-divisibility of copyright interests that prevailed under the older law. Second, where a writing was required, only a formal instrument of transfer would suffice—a "note or memorandum" would not be adequate.[103] These differences can still be important today where a claimant traces his or her rights back to events occurring before 1978.

5.5.4 Rights of Licensees

An exclusive licensee is the owner of the licensed rights under the copyright, and as such, has all rights of a copyright owner. This means that an exclusive licensee can sue others for infringement in his own name without the participation of the copyright owner. Congress implemented this system by abolishing the "indivisibility" concept of the 1909 Act when it adopted the current statute. If,

103. The relevant provision is section 28 of the 1909 Act, which reads "copyright secured under this title or previous copyright laws of the United States may be assigned, granted, or mortgaged by an instrument in writing signed by the proprietor of the copyright, or may be bequeathed by will."

however, a party claims the status of exclusive licensee based on a license received from only one of several co-authors of a work, that party will not have standing to sue, because, as you will recall, one co-author lacks the authority to grant an exclusive license. The result is that such a licensee merely holds a non-exclusive license and cannot sue others for infringement.[104]

Although exclusive licensees have the rights of a copyright owner, at least one court has held that an exclusive licensee may not sublicense others, or transfer the licensed rights to another party, without the consent of the copyright owner. In *Gardner v. Nike, Inc.*[105] Nike held the copyright to a cartoon character called MC Teach. It granted Sony an exclusive perpetual, worldwide license to use the character in connection with musical recordings and related advertising and promotional activities, in return for royalties. Some time thereafter, Sony purported to assign all of its rights under this license to Gardner. Apparently Nike did not approve of this transaction and threatened to sue Gardner. Gardner acted first and brought a declaratory judgment action, but the court ruled that he did not have standing because the assignment from Sony was not valid.

The court reached this result by reading section 201 of the 1976 Act narrowly. That section gives an exclusive licensee the "right to all of the protection and remedies accorded to the copyright owner by this title." The Ninth Circuit found that the words "protection and remedies" was not equivalent to all the rights of a copyright owner, and thus did not include the right to further transfer the license to another party. The court found support for this result in the policy that a copyright owner should have the right to evaluate licensees to determine if they are appropriate—a policy that would be defeated if original licensees could transfer the rights to others without the permission of the copyright owner.

Gardner has been criticized by at least one lower court decision, as well as by treatise writers and academic commentators.[106] Those criticisms strike us as well founded. *Gardner* relies on an odd interpretation of the language of the 1976 Act, taking the words "protection and remedies" out of context and assigning them a curious meaning. Perhaps more importantly, the opinion undermines the concept of divisibility that was a key innovation of the 1976 statute. After the 1976 Act an exclusive licensee is, effectively,

104. Sybersound Records, Inc. v. UAV Corp., 517 F.3d 1137 (9th Cir. 2008).

105. 279 F.3d 774 (9th Cir. 2002).

106. *See, e.g.,* Traicoff v. Digital Media, Inc., 439 F.Supp.2d 872, 877–78 (S.D. Ind. 2006), and sources cited there-in. *See also,* PATRY ON COPYRIGHT § 5:103 ("The Ninth Circuit decision in *Gardner v. Nike, Inc.* may be one of the most baffling copyright opinions ever.... Even a cursory examination of the statutory language demonstrates *Gardener* is incorrect.").

the owner of the slice of the copyright he has licensed. As an owner, the statute indicates that he is free to do whatever he would like with his copyright interest including sell it to someone else. To forbid such transactions is to reintroduce the arcane business of divisibility into the law 30 years after Congress tried to put a stake through its heart. Alas, as of this writing, no other circuit court of appeals has weighed in on the question and *Gardner* remains the sole court of appeals decision on point.

A somewhat different problem concerning licensee rights is the recurring one of interpreting the scope of the license. Many copyright licenses are granted for the full term of the copyright. During that period, technology continues to march forward often producing new ways to exploit the work that no one contemplated at the time the license was drafted. Several cases have confronted the question as to whether these new economic opportunities should be considered within the rights granted to the licensee or whether they should be deemed reserved by the copyright owner. Some have labeled this the "new media" or "new use" or "scope of the grant" problem. It is, at root, not an issue of copyright law as such, but rather a matter of contract interpretation.

Ideally, the parties might anticipate the problem even without being able to foretell the future by including language in the agreement such as "this license covers all uses now known or subsequently invented or developed," or, alternatively, language "reserving to the copyright owner all rights and uses except those specifically granted herein." For instance, *Cohen v. Paramount Pictures*,[107] Paramount had licensed a song for use in connection with a movie, in the late–1960s. With the advent of home videotape players, it subsequently wanted to release the movie on videocassettes (a primitive precursor of DVDs). There was language in the license that allow Paramount to perform the musical work in connection with exhibition of the movie "by means of television." The agreement also contained a reservation of rights provision in favor of the grantor. The court sided with the copyright owner (grantor) in this case, reading the language alluding to television narrowly and stating that "the holder of the license should not now 'reap the entire windfall' associated with the new medium."

Some courts have articulated a rule of license construction that would resolve doubts in favor of the copyright owner.[108] Others have endorsed the use of "neutral principles of contract interpretation

---

107.   845 F.2d 851 (9th Cir. 1988).

108.   *See, e.g.,* Warner Bros. Pictures v. Columbia Broadcasting Sys., 216 F.2d 945, 949 (1954) ("The clearest language is necessary to divest the author of the fruits of his labor."); Leisure Time Entertainment, Inc. v. Cal Vista 79 F.3d 1153 (9th Cir. 1996) ("Generally, if the transferee prepared the contract, the owner of the copyrighted work reserves those rights not expressly granted").

rather than solicitude for either party."[109] As one treatise writer notes, where the agreement is truly ambiguous and there is no other evidence of the intent of the parties, "courts will—consciously or not—avail themselves of either a policy preference or—what may be the same thing—a canon of contract construction that places the burden on one of the parties."[110]

5.5.4.1　Recordation of Transfers

In addition to the writing requirement specified in the preceding subsection, the current law also has detailed provisions providing for the recordation of transfers of copyright interests, as well as for other documents "pertaining to a copyright."[111] These provisions operate on rough analogy to those governing the recording of deeds and other instruments relating to land. Unlike the system controlling land transfers, however, the recordation system established by the copyright statute is, at the present time, entirely optional. That is to say, an unrecorded assignment or exclusive license will be enforceable *as between the parties* regardless of whether it has been recorded. For transfers prior to 1989, however, recordation was a prerequisite to the filing of an infringement suit. For more than 20 years, however, this has no longer been the case, because this requirement was dropped from the statute when the U.S. joined the international copyright treaty known as the Berne Convention.[112]

Although it is optional there are, as you would expect, numerous advantages that flow from recording. The recording of a document relating to a transfer of copyright or otherwise pertaining to copyright gives constructive notice to all other persons of the facts stated in the document, provided that the document specifically identifies the work in question and that registration has also been made for the work.[113] The constructive notice principle also means that, as a practical matter, anyone intending to secure an assignment of license of a copyright interest would be well advised to search the records of the copyright office before entering into such a transaction to discover if there are any prior recorded transfers lurking out there that could receive priority.

Perhaps a more important feature of the recordation system established by the copyright act is its specification of rules govern-

---

109. Boosey & Hawkes Music Publishers v. Walt Disney Co., 145 F.3d 481 (2d Cir. 1998).

110. PATRY ON COPYRIGHT, § 5:115.

111. Bear in mind that a non-exclusive license in not a "transfer" of copyright. Nonetheless, a document granting such a license in a work would be recordable under this provision, since it "pertains" to copyright.

112. Berne Convention Implementation Act of 1988, § 5, Pub. L. No. 100–568, 102 Stat. 2853 (1988).

113. 17 U.S.C. § 205(c).

ing which of several inconsistent grants will prevail in the event of a dispute. Under those rules:

> As between two conflicting transfers, the one executed first prevails if it is recorded ... within one month after its execution in the United States or within two months after its execution outside the United States, or at any time before recordation ... of the later transfer. Otherwise the later transfer prevails if recorded first ... and if taken in good faith, for valuable consideration or on the basis of a binding promise to pay royalties, and without notice of the earlier transfer.[114]

This is what your property teacher would have called a "race-notice" type of recordation system. To understand the operation of this provision imagine that Olivia, a copyright owner, assigns the entire copyright in her novel to Alan on March 1, and then, on March 15th purports to assign the same copyright to Betty. This means that Olivia either has a very bad memory or is more than a little bit unethical. If Betty knows of the earlier transaction with Alan, then Betty will have no rights and Alan will prevail—a result that certainly seems both fair and intuitive. After all, if Betty is buying a copyright interest from Olivia that she knows Olivia has already sold to someone else, Betty deserves what the statute gives here, which is nothing. Note also that if Betty received the copyright as a "gift"—that is, she did not pay Olivia any consideration for it—once again Alan will prevail even if Betty was unaware of the earlier transaction. As between a party who paid and one who did not, the law favors the former.

Assuming, however, that Betty took the assignment for valuable consideration and with no notice of Olivia's prior dealings with Alan, the statute sets up a race to record.[115] The first of the two parties to record will prevail, with the qualification that Alan, as the first transferee, has a grace period of either one or two months, depending on whether the transfer was executed domestically or abroad. Thus, if Betty records on March 16th (the day after the transfer to her) and Alan does not get around to recording until March 20th, Alan will still prevail, since he recorded within the one month grace period. But if Alan waits until May 3rd to record, Betty will prevail. The grace period creates a hazard for assignees, since they might exercise full due diligence and search the records at the Copyright Office, find nothing, pay for an assignment, and then be startled to lean that they have no rights because the earlier transferee records a few days later. In terms of our simple hypo,

---

114. 17 U.S.C. § 205(d) (2000).

115. This approach is often called a "race-notice" statute in the real estate context.

anyone who does business with Oliva between March 1st and March 31st might not find a record of Alan's earlier purchase, but could be defeated if Alan filed by that latter date.

The system just described applies to inconsistent or conflicting "transfers," which as noted includes assignments, exclusive licenses, and a variety of other itemized events. Slightly different rules in the statute govern conflicts between a transfer and a non-exclusive license. Under those provisions a *written* non-exclusive license prevails over a subsequent transfer, even if the license itself was not recorded. It will also prevail over a prior transfer, if the license was granted without knowledge of the prior transfer and before that prior transfer was recorded.[116] Of course a non-exclusive license need not be in writing, but if an oral license is granted, it will effectively terminate when the underlying copyright interest is transferred.

Some examples will make this provision a bit more concrete. Assume Paul is a playwright who owns the copyright to a play. In our first case, assume that on April 1st he grants Lucille a non-exclusive license to perform the play in Chicago during the month of September, and further assume that this license is in writing. If, on May 1st, Paul then assigns the copyright in the play to the Shubert organization, that transfer will not affect Lucille's right under the license. She may go ahead and perform the play as agreed. Her written license has priority over the subsequent transfer.

Now, let us change the situation to assume that on March 1st, Paul assigned the rights to Shubert, but then granted the non-exclusive license to Lucille on April 1st. In this case, Paul is obviously giving away rights that he no longer owns. If Lucille knows that—if she has notice of the transfer to Shubert—she has no rights. Even if Lucille doesn't actually know about the transfer to Shubert, if that transfer to Shubert was recorded, Lucille would have constructive notice and her purported license would also be no good. On the other hand, if Lucille had no notice of the prior transfer, and if the prior transfer was not recorded until after April 1st, then the law will protect Lucille by forcing the transferee to honor the license according to its terms.

Prior to 1989, the recordation of a transfer of copyright was also required before the transferee could institute suit for copyright infringement. Congress deleted that provision from the statute as part of U.S. adherence to the Berne Convention, because that treaty forbids the imposition of formalities as a condition of copyright protection.[117]

---

116. 17 U.S.C. § 205(e).   **117.** Berne Convention, Art. 5(2).

Although different in a number of particulars, the recordation scheme under the 1909 copyright law generally resembled the one described above. Just as is true today, subsequent transferees would prevail under the older law if they had no notice, actual or constructive, or a prior transfer, if they paid value, and if they promptly recorded.[118] Unlike the 1976 Act section, however, the 1909 Act provision did not deal with all copyright "transfers" but rather was limited to "assignments"—which was a function of the "indivisibility" philosophy that permeated that older law.

5.5.5   Involuntary Transfers

Just like tangible property, copyright interests can be seized involuntarily. An interesting provision of the 1976 Copyright Act, section 201(e), deals with that situation. It provides that:

> When an individual author's ownership of a copyright . . . has not previously been transferred voluntarily by that individual author, no action by any governmental body or other official or organization purporting to seize, expropriate, transfer, or exercise rights of ownership with respect to the copyright . . . shall be given effect under this title except as provided under Title 11 [Bankruptcy].[119]

This provision was added to the statute out of a Cold War era concern that the then Soviet Union might attempt to suppress the writings of dissidents by expropriating the copyrights to those works under Soviet law and then—asserting its purported status as a lawful copyright owner—suing disseminators of those works in the United States for infringement. By its terms, the provision only applies to expropriation from the original individual author. That means that works made for hire are not within the scope of this section. It also means that once an author has parted with title to the work by assignment, the work can be seized from the assignee without violating this provision.

Despite its broad language, section 201(e) will not insulate a copyright holder from a variety of events that might, at first blush look "involuntary." Thus, loss of the copyright through foreclosure on a mortgage or execution of a lien, are entirely permissible. In these cases, the copyright owner is said to have voluntarily entered into the underlying transaction, making the section inapplicable. Moreover, at least one court construed this provision "as dealing

---

118. Act of 1909, § 30 ("Every assignment of copyright shall be recorded in the copyright office within three calendar months after its execution in the United States or within six calendar months after its execution without the limits of the United States, in default of which it shall be void as against any subsequent purchaser or mortgagee for a valuable consideration, without notice, whose assignment has been duly recorded.").

119. 17 U.S.C. § 201(e).

with actions initiated by governmental bodies, not with those where, as in the case of a judgment lienholder, the instruments of government are merely acting in furtherance of private objectives."[120]

While one commentator has suggested that the division or transfer of a copyright interest upon the termination of a marriage under state domestic relations might violate section 201(e),[121] Professor Goldstein, in his treatise, suggests that the provision should be considered inapplicable for several reasons, including the fact that entry into the marriage in question is just as voluntary as entering into a mortgage or other loan.[122]

---

120. *National Peregrine, Inc. v. Capitol Fed. Sav. & Loan Assn. of Denver,* 116 B.R. 194, 205–06, n.16 (C.D. Cal. 1990).

121. Francis M. Nevins, *When an Author's Marriage Dies: The Copyright–*

Divorce Connection, 37 J. COPYRIGHT SOC'Y 382 (1990).

122. GOLDSTEIN, COPYRIGHT, 1994 Supplement 92.

Chapter 6

THE TRADITIONAL EXCLUSIVE RIGHTS OF A COPYRIGHT HOLDER

Table of Sections

———————

The government grants copyrights so that authors can make money. As we have noted earlier, this arguably provides them with the incentive to devote time and effort to the creative process. The precise mechanism by which copyright does this is to grant certain rights to the holder of a copyright and, most importantly to make those rights exclusive. Since all others are forbidden from using the work in certain ways without permission, the copyright owner can force them to pay for the privilege and thereby reap an economic reward. A full understanding of copyright requires an understanding of the nature and scope of these exclusive rights.

When it originally enacted the Copyright Act of 1976, Congress conferred five rights on the owner of a copyright. In the years since, Congress has made several significant changes to the statute, granting additional and, in some cases, considerably more exotic rights as well. In this chapter, we will confine ourselves to the quintet of rights that Congress included in the initial version of the statute. We refer to these as the "traditional" rights of a copyright owner. In the next chapter we will turn our attention to the more specialized rights that have been added to the law over the last few decades.

The five traditional rights of a copyright owner are all found in section 106 of the statute, which explicitly declares that the various itemized rights are "exclusive" to the copyright owner.[1] In other words, only the copyright owner may engage in conduct that constitutes an exercise of any one of these rights or authorize others to do so. It follows, therefore, that it is infringement for anyone else to engage in the listed acts without the permission of the owner. This might lead you to believe that once you have understood the rights conferred by the statute, there is not much more to the topic of infringement. Alas, you would be mistaken. Most infringement cases involve non-literal duplications of copyrighted works and it is rare that a copyright owner can produce eyewitnesses to acts of infringement. As a result, an enormous body of case law has grown up on the topic of infringement—most of which concerns the type of evidence that must be offered to prove it

---

1. The introductory language in 17 U.S.C. § 106 declares that "the owner of copyright under this title has the exclu-sive rights to do and to authorize any of" the listed acts.

and the manner in which courts should evaluate that evidence. That material is not the subject of the present discussion; we will come to it a bit further on.[2] To put this point somewhat differently, an understanding of the scope and limitations of a copyright owner's rights is necessary to understanding infringement, but not by itself sufficient.

Each of the exclusive rights is independent from the others. An unauthorized party need only violate one right to be subject to liability for copyright infringement. As we shall see, however, the exclusive rights are related, and often one infringing act implicates multiple exclusive rights granted by the copyright law.[3]

Lest we keep you in suspense any longer, the specific statutory rights that we will be considering in this chapter are: (1) the right to make physical objects (copies or phonorecords) embodying the copyrighted work, usually called the "reproduction right"; (2) the right to sell, rent, or give away those physical artifacts, usually called the "distribution right"; (3) the right to use the work as the basis for the preparation of new, derivative works, usually called the "adaptation right"; (4) the right to publicly perform the work; and (5) the right to publicly display the work. Not all types of works are granted each of these five rights. In some cases that is a matter of simple logic. You cannot "perform" a painting, and there would be little point to displaying a CD, so the statute does not grant performance rights to pictorial and sculptural works and it does not grant the display right to sound recordings. However, in at least one case, namely that of sound recordings, certain rights are denied for historical and policy reasons, rather than as a matter of pure logic.

The Copyright Act also subjects each exclusive right to a number of limitations. These limitations are set out in sections 107 through 122 of the statute. A review of these provisions reveals that many of them are not light reading. The limitations they create are often quite detailed and intricate. Many of them are the product of extensive negotiations between representative of various interested industries. The most notable among them is the fair use privilege of § 107. The fair use privilege operates as a limit on all five of the traditional rights of a copyright owner by allowing third parties to make limited and reasonable uses of protected works without the consent of the copyright owner. Because of the centrality of the fair use privilege to the entire scheme of copyright law, and the amount of material touching on that subject, it is the one limitation on the

---

2. In Chapter 9 to be precise.

3. If, for example, a publisher prepared a foreign-language translation of a protected novel without authorization from the copyright holder, both the reproduction and adaptation rights would be violated.

traditional rights that you will not find here. We have, instead, granted it the honor of a chapter unto itself.[4]

Most of the remaining limits on the exclusive rights contained in the 16 numbered sections that follow section 106 allow certain categories of persons to engage in certain very specific uses of copyrighted works under certain highly defined conditions without incurring liability for infringement. For instance, as we shall see shortly, one provision allows non-profit libraries to make a small number of copies of copyrighted literary works for various specific purposes such as preservation. Thus the facially broad rights of section 106 actually resemble pieces of Swiss cheese, with each limiting provision carving out an area where the copyright owner is powerless to prevent a use or charge a fee.

Note, however, that some of the limiting provisions in the statute take a different approach and provide for what are known as compulsory licenses. Unlike a complete limitation on a right, which allows certain users to engage in certain acts without permission or payment, a compulsory license allows use but requires the payment of a royalty, set by a government agency. Thus, where a compulsory license is available, the copyright owner cannot "veto" another parties' use, but the copyright owner does receive some compensation for the use. We will consider some of the more important compulsory licensing provisions in the statute in the detailed discussion that follows.

§ 6.1　The Reproduction Right

6.1.1　Basic Principles

The fundamental privilege provided by the copyright laws is the exclusive right to reproduce a copyrighted work in copies or phonorecords. Indeed, this is the right that gives the field of law its very name—the exclusive right to make copies is the heart of copyright. To refresh your memory, section 101 of the Copyright Act defines the term "phonorecords" as "material objects in which sounds, other than those accompanying a motion picture or audiovisual work, are fixed by any method now known or later developed. . . ." "Copies" are defined as "material objects, other than phonorecords, in which a work is fixed by any method now known or later developed. . . ." These definitions clarify that in order to violate the reproduction right, an infringer must tangibly reproduce the protected work in a material object. As one commentator concisely put it, "the right of reproduction is really the right to produce new fixations of the copyrighted work."[5]

---

4. That would be Chapter 10.

5. Tyler T. Ochoa, *Copyright, Derivative Works and Fixation: Is Galoob a Mirage, or does the Form(gen) of the* *Alleged Derivative Work Matter?*, 20 SANTA CLARA COMPUTER & HIGH TECH. L.J. 991, 996 (2004).

For example, suppose that the actor Gerald Garrick lawfully purchases a copy of the play *King John: A One–Man Show*. Without permission from the copyright owner, Garrick memorizes the script of *King John* and performs before paying audiences. Although Garrick has likely infringed the public performance right, he has not violated the reproduction right. Garrick's mere performance or oral recitation of *King John* does not result in the creation of a material object embodying the protected work. He did not make a copy. Thus he did not violate the reproduction right.

On the other hand, if the beauty of the lines of the play so struck Garrick that he decided to copy them out in longhand into a notebook, he would violate the reproduction right. That is so even if he never sold that notebook, or, for that matter, even showed it to anyone. Unless fair use or another limitation upon the reproduction right is applicable, even a wholly private, undistributed reproduction is a *prima facie* violation of the reproduction right and counts as a copyright infringement. The reproduction right is also implicated when a work is copied into a different medium—for instance when an oil painting is photographed. It is also triggered even though only a portion of the protected work is copied—meaning that it violates the reproduction right to copy out one chapter of a novel or one act of a five act play.

As a practical matter, of course, few copyright owners would bother to litigate a claim involving wholly private copying even if they became aware of it, which is unlikely (at least in the analog world). To a large degree that is because Garrick's decision to make a private copy will not likely have much impact on the playwright's ability to make money from the play. But it could. After all, Garrick might want to leave his purchased copy of the play at home and keep the transcribed copy at work so that he can contemplate the beauty of the words in either venue. His handwritten transcription allows him to avoid incurring the expense of purchasing a second copy and thus deprives the copyright owner of a second sale. So a feisty copyright owner might just decide to sue. If he did, the key point for present purposes is to appreciate that Garrick would lose unless he could invoke a defense.

This same result follows even if the unauthorized copy is merely being made as an intermediate step to creating a new work. For instance, in *Walt Disney Productions v. Filmation Assoc.*,[6] Filmation wanted to make its own animated film versions of various public domain works such as *Pinocchio* and *Alice in Wonderland*. Copyright law permits them to do that, of course, without

---

6. 628 F.Supp. 871 (C.D. Cal. 1986).

asking permission of anyone. In the course of its work it prepared "storyboards" which included sketches of various scenes from the Disney movie versions of these same works. Those Disney movies were (and still are) protected by copyright. Filmation did not plan to use those images in the final film, and argued that they were only "transitory steps en route to a fixed product, and that until its film is completed and ready for distribution, there exists no article that could be said to infringe any of Disney's copyrights." The court disagreed, declaring that "the fact that the articles may never be published or, indeed, may be prepared only for the use of Filmation's animators, does not obviate the possibility of infringement."[7]

One of the most significant developments in copyright law over the past few decades has been the acceptance by Congress and the courts of the idea that a "copy" includes the loading of the content of a work into the memory of a computer provided it resides there for more than a fleeting period of time. We explored this development at length earlier in this volume, in section 2.2.2 entitled *Fixation and New Technologies.* Consider, however, the implications of what we learned there in light of the reproduction right.

Every time you visit a page on the World Wide Web, your computer loads the contents of that page—words and images—into its memory. Every time you open an email, the same thing happens. As Professor James Boyle of Duke has artfully put it:

> If you are a person who routinely uses computers, the Internet, or other digital media, imagine a day when you do not create—intentionally and unintentionally—hundreds of temporary, evanescent copies.... In a networked society copying is not only easy, it is necessary part of transmission, storage, caching, and, some would claim, even reading.... Intellectual property is now in and on the desktop and is implicated in routine creative communicative, and just plain consumptive acts that each of us performs every day. Suddenly, the triggers of copyright—reproduction, distribution—can be activated by individual footsteps.[8]

There are many reasons why these activities may not be infringing in particular cases—permission to make a reproduction for the purposes of viewing the material on a computer might be implied from the facts and circumstances, as would be the case with

---

7. *Id.* at 876. *See also* Sega Enterprises Ltd. v. Accolade, Inc., 977 F.2d 1510, 1518 (9th Cir. 1992) For an expanding discussion of "intermediate copying," *see* Gregory C. Padgett, *Intermediate Copying in the Digital Age*, 30 COLUM. J.L. & ARTS 655, 657–62 (2007).

8. JAMES BOYLE, THE PUBLIC DOMAIN: ENCLOSING THE COMMONS OF THE MIND 51–52 (2008).

the publicly available website; your conduct might be covered by a specific limitation to the reproduction right; or the conduct might constitute fair use.

Moreover, in some unusual cases, the material might be retained in the computer's memory for such a fleetingly brief time that it might not satisfy the statutory definition of a "copy." This was the conclusion of the court in *Cartoon Network LP v. CSC Holdings, Inc.*[9] There, Cablevision, a major cable television services provider, made available a service to its subscribers which it characterized as a "remote storage digital video recorder" (or RS–DVR) system. Unlike a stand alone DVR system, such as TiVo, which utilizes a set-top box with its own hard drive for recording stored programs, the RS–DVR system allowed users to record shows for later view on a central hard drive housed and maintained by Cablevision. Using their remote control, the subscriber could then retrieve and playback the stored program at any time of their choosing. The system necessitated making both transient "buffer" copies of fragments of the shows as they were recorded and, of course, copies of the programs as a whole.

Various copyright owners sued for copyright infringement pointing to both the buffer and full copies as violations of their reproduction rights. With regard to the full copies, the court found that these were not being "made" by Cablevision, but rather by the subscribers who selected which shows would be recorded for them.[10] More relevant to our present discussion is the finding that the buffering of the works did result in the making of impermissible copies. As the court pointed out, "no bit of data remains in any buffer for more than a fleeting 1.2 seconds... [and] each bit of data ... is rapidly and automatically overwritten as soon as it is processed.... [T]hese facts strongly suggest that the works in this case are embodied in the buffer for only a 'transitory' period, thus failing the duration requirement.... Accordingly, the acts of buffering in the operation of the RS–DVR do not create copies, as the Copyright Act defines that term."

The *Cartoon Network* court did not, however, disagree that copies in general computer random access memory, which are retained until the computer is switched off, do satisfy the definition of a copy. The resulting extensive exposure to potential infringement liability by everyone who uses a personal computer suggests— at least to us—that copyright law needs a wholesale rethinking to make it coherent with twenty-first century reality. A system of law

---

9. 536 F.3d 121 (2d Cir. 2008), *cert. denied sub nom* Cable News network, Inc. v. CSC Holdings, Inc., 557 U.S. ___ (2009).

10. The court did not reach the question of whether the cable company could be secondarily liable for facilitating the direct copying of the home subscribers.

that makes virtually everyone in society an infringer dozens of times each day does not serve any rational purpose and is unenforceable to boot. Pursuing that line of thought is not the purpose of this book, but much has been written about it[11] and it ought to be central to the thinking of any student or practitioner of copyright law.

We must return to more mundane matters. Given the expansive nature and broad sweep of the reproduction right, it follows that the law would be stifling without some exceptions and limitations. Most of those we find in the statute were the product of special appeals by affected constituencies—record companies, librarians, broadcasters, and computer software developers. In the next several sections we will explore several of these limitations.

6.1.2 Limitations on the Reproduction Right

The 1976 Act includes a number of provisions that limit the reproduction right. Many of these exemptions are highly technical, complex statutes that reflect hard-fought debates between content providers and the community of users, or between interested constituencies with divergent interests. On their face these provisions may seem tedious, bristling with multi-part tests to be memorized or ignored depending on your agenda. Each of them, however, reflects the result of passionate political horse-trading, and behind their dry language often lies significant choices about how we are allowed to use and experience cultural material. Space limitations in this book will not permit us to explore every nook and cranny of each of these provisions—there are multi-volume treatises for that—but we hope to give you a rough idea of the macro structure and key details in the subsections that follow.

6.1.2.1 Reproduction by Libraries and Archives

Whether and when a library can make a copy of a copyrighted book or other item without paying for the privilege may seem like something that would only be of interest to librarians and perhaps those from whom they get their budgets. However libraries usually wish to make copies in order to insure that materials are available to their patrons—namely you and me. Moreover, libraries have burst out of their bricks-and-mortar locations and are now as much "virtual" entities as they are physical places. In other words, the rules governing library copying may determine what you can access

---

11. Two outstanding—and eminently readable—volumes that deal with this issue, are JESSICA LITMAN, DIGITAL COPYRIGHT (2001), and JAMES BOYLE, THE PUBLIC DOMAIN: ENCLOSING THE COMMONS OF THE MIND (2008). See also Mark A. Lemley, *Dealing with Overlapping Copyrights on the Internet*, 22 U. DAYTON L. REV. 547, 555 (1997); Jessica Litman, *The Exclusive Right to Read*, 13 CARDOZO ARTS & ENT. L.J. 29, 40 (1994).

over the Internet at your desktop, and whether that access will be free, modestly priced, or expensive.

The provision dealing with library reproduction is section 108 of the statute.[12] Congress has amended this section a number of times since first adopting it. Even so, there has been increasing concern that the provision is no longer responsive to the needs of libraries, patrons, or copyright owners in the digital age. Consequently, in 2004, the Copyright Office put together a study group to consider whether further changes to this provision would be necessary. That group issued its report in March of 2008, recommending several further amendments to section 108.[13] While Congress has not yet shown any interest in acting on the recommendations in the report,[14] it reminds us that the doctrinal details that follow are in flux, and resort to a current version of the statute is, as always, the only way to be sure what the law is.

Most of the subsections of section 108 deal with specific scenarios where a library might want to copy materials protected by copyright. Subsection (a) begins, however, with three general prerequisites that must be met before a library or archive[15] can take advantage of the privileges that are set out in any of the remaining parts of the statute. If an institution cannot satisfy these requirements, section 108 simply does not apply and it must look elsewhere for legal protection if it seeks to copy without obtaining a license.

The first general requirement is that all reproductions must be made without purpose of "direct or indirect commercial advantage." The legislative history notes that a commercial advantage that renders a facility ineligible for the protection of section 108 "must attach to the immediate commercial motivation behind the reproduction or distribution itself, rather than to the ultimate profit making motivation behind the enterprise in which the library is located."[16] Thus libraries within profit-making enterprises such as law firms or pharmaceutical companies are not automatically precluded from relying on this section, provided that they do not

---

12. 17 U.S.C. § 108.

13. The full 212 page report, and an Executive Summary, can be found on-line at http://www.section108.gov/. For a somewhat more manageable discussion of the issue that the Study Group considered, see Laura N. Gasaway, *Amending the Copyright Act for Libraries and Society: The Section 108 Study Group,* 70 ALB. L. REV. 1331 (2007).

14. *See* PATRY ON COPYRIGHT, § 11:8:50.

15. Because this introductory provision refers only to libraries and archives, it follows that other cultural organizations, such as museums, cannot take advantage of this provision. They are left to rely on the general fair use doctrine if they find it necessary to make copies of protected materials. The Section 108 Study Group recommended expanding the provision to include museums but as noted, Congress has not shown any enthusiasm for acting on its suggestions.

16. H. Rep. 94–1476 at 75.

copy works with the goal of selling the copies or otherwise profiting from the copying activity itself, even though the copies may ultimately assist them in their larger profit-making activities.

The second prerequisite condition requires that the library or archive collections be open to the public or at least open to researchers who are not affiliated with the institution that runs the library or archive in question. Thus a law firm that maintains an in-house library of treatises, case reports, and law reviews can only use section 108 if it allows others besides its own employees to use its library. Finally, any copies made under the provisions of the statute must either reproduce any notice of copyright that appears on the item being reproduced or must contain a legend saying that the work may be protected by copyright. This last provision is mildly interesting because it suggests that copyright notice performs a useful function in educating the public and deterring unlawful copying—a view that the Congress arguably repudiated when it did away with mandatory copyright notice in 1989.[17] Hardly the most shocking example of Congressional inconsistency, but intriguing nonetheless.

The next two subsections of the statute deal with situations where the library wishes to make additional copies of materials already in its own collection for its own purposes, or to give to another library. Subsection (b) deals with *unpublished* works. An example would be doctoral dissertations that may be held in the collections of a university library. This subsection allows the library to make up to three copies for purposes "of preservation and security or for deposit for research use in another library." Thus our hypothetical university library can make a few photocopies of the doctoral dissertation to guard against the contingency that the original may be damaged by fire or water or stolen by an unscrupulous patron, or so that they can send one to another university that has requested it.

Of course the most logical method of copying for preservation and security today would be to make a digital copy (by scanning the original) and to keep that digital version either on a physical medium such as a compact disc, or a server accessible over an intranet,[18] or on the Internet. Section 108(b) permits the making of digital copies provided that such a copy is not distributed in that format and is not made available to the public in that format off the premises of the library. Thus, the library could store a "pdf" version of our supposed doctoral dissertation on its own computers, but it could not allow library users to access that digital copy from

---

17. *See supra* § 4.2.

18. An intranet is a computer network contained within a single enterprise, usually accessible only by persons affiliated with that enterprise.

home. Rather the document can only be available on terminals located in the library's building.

As the Section 108 Study Group noted, this provision ignores the "RAM copy" issue entirely. Every time a staff member at the library accesses the "pdf" file, another "copy" of the doctoral dissertation is made. Since the statute only allows the making of three copies, the library will very quickly find itself outside the scope of the section 108(b) privilege. While such "copying" would almost certainly be held to be fair use, it seems that a clarification to section 108 might be in order to remove any doubt.

Subsection (c) deals with replacement copies of *published* works already held in a library's collections. Here again, the library can make up to three copies, but the requirements are more onerous. First, the copy in its collection must be "damaged, deteriorating, lost or stolen" or it must be in a format that has become obsolete. This would cover copies of decades-old books with yellowing and crumbling pages, and it could cover as well materials that might be stored on varieties of microfilm for which no one is making film-readers any longer. Presumably, the library is allowed to borrow a copy of a lost or stolen item that was formerly in its collection in order to make the permissible 108(c) replacement copy—otherwise the statute would be a cruel hoax, permitting the library to copy a book that it no longer physically possessed. In addition, before proceeding under subsection (c), the library must also determine, after making a reasonable effort, that an unused replacement cannot be obtained at a fair price. The statute does not define "fair price" but the obvious intent here is to require the library to purchase a replacement on the open market if it can do so easily and cheaply, and to only permit free and unauthorized copying when doing that would be impossible or prohibitively expensive.[19]

The next pair of subsections deals with the making of copies for the use of library patrons. Here, the distinction is not between published and unpublished materials, but between copies of fragments of a work, and copies of an entire work. These two provisions do not require that work be in the collection of the library that the user patronizes. In other words, the provisions contemplate the practice of "inter-library loan" which allows a given library to request the material from another library that is also open to the public or to non-affiliated researchers. Subsection (d) deals with the scenario where a patron would like a copy of a "small part" or a work, or a single article or essay from a periodical issue or compilation. In this case, a library is permitted to make a single copy (for

---

19. Professor Gasaway has suggested that librarians are reluctant to rely on section 108(c) because of the difficult of demonstrating compliance with this requirement. *See* Gasaway, *supra* note 13.

its own patron, or for the patron of another library with whom it cooperates) provided that the copy become the property of the user and the library has no notice that the copy will be used for "any purpose other than private study, scholarship or research." The library is also required to post "a warning of copyright" at order desks and on order forms.[20]

The closely related subsection (e) deals with the case where the user requests a copy of an entire work or a "substantial part of it." As you might expect, the statute imposes somewhat stricter requirements here. First, the library must determine that a copy of the work cannot be obtained at a fair price. Such a copy could be either new or used, which is a different standard than we noted in subsection (c), which involves copies for the libraries' own collections. Obviously, the statutory drafters did not want library patrons to be able to make an end run around the market by securing a low cost copy of a work from a library instead of going out and buying a copy. The remaining requirements in subsection (e) are identical to those in subsection (d)—the copy must become the property of the library patron, the library must have no notice that it will be used for purposes other than private study and the like, and the library must display the relevant warning of copyright.

Subsection (f) deals with user-operated reproduction equipment on library premises, such as the ubiquitous coin-operated (or swipe card operated) photocopy machines one sees in most university libraries. It immunizes the library for any secondary library flowing from copying done by the users of such equipment, provided that the equipment displays a notice that copying may be subject to the copyright laws—thus explaining those sternly worded signs titled "Warning Concerning Copyright Restrictions" posted in libraries across the United States.[21] This same portion of the statute also explicitly declares that nothing in section 108 immunizes the individual user of unsupervised reproduction equipment from copyright infringement liability if he or she exceeds the bounds of fair use. Finally, subsection (f)(4) provides that nothing in section 108 affects the rights of fair use or supercedes any contractual obligations of the library in connection with particular material it has obtained. Thus, if a library purchases a work on CD–ROM pursuant to a license under which it agrees to make no copies whatsoever, that contractual promise trumps the rules of section 108 that allow limited copying for specified purposes.

Subsection (g) clarifies that the various exemptions for library copying only cover "isolated and unrelated reproduction" and do

---

20. The exact form of this warning is prescribed by regulations. *See* 37 C.F.R. § 2.14 (Warnings of Copyright for Use by Certain Libraries and Archives).

21. 37 C.F.R. § 201.14(b).

not extend to the related or concerted reproduction of multiple copies of the same material or programs of systematic reproduction.

Congress added subsection (h) when it adopted the Copyright Term Extension Act in 1998. It relaxes the rules for library copying during the last 20 years of the life of the copyright in any published work.[22] It allows unlimited reproductions, distributions, performances, and displays for purposes of preservation, scholarship, or research so long as the following is true: (1) the work cannot be subject to "normal commercial exploitation"—meaning presumably that it is out of print, not being commercially performed, or otherwise not being used by the copyright owner to generate revenues; (2) a copy of the work cannot be obtained at a reasonable price; and (3) the copyright owner has not filed a notice with the Copyright Office declaring that the work is being commercially exploited or that copies can be obtained on the open market at a reasonable price. This is, in effect, an "orphan works" provision designed to allow exploitation of works where it would be very difficult to even know whom to ask for a license and where the economic consequences of the exploitation are likely to be minimal.[23]

The final subsection indicates that the privileges of section 108(d) and (e), regarding copies made for users, do not apply to musical works, pictorial, graphic or sculptural works, or audiovisual works (other than those dealing with news). Thus a library cannot rely on section 108 to make a copy of a music CD or a movie on a DVD and give the resulting copy away to a requesting user. Clearly this provision is meant to prevent libraries from becoming competitors of the retail outlets that sell copies or phonorecords of these types of works.

The ornate provisions of section 108 are supposed to serve as safe harbors. So long as a library stays within the technical requirements of the provision it is absolutely immune from liability for violating the reproduction right. As subsection (f) makes clear as crystal, it can go beyond the limits of section 108 provided it can show that its behavior constitutes fair use. In other words, the provision is meant to set out a floor—an amount of copying which will never constitute infringement. Alas, in the real world, detailed provisions like this tend to set a ceiling. Librarians are understandably reluctant to go beyond the limits of section 108 because the fair use defense is uncertain and one can never know in advance

---

22. This, of course, is a period during which the work would have been in the public domain, but for the 20–year term extension implemented by the Term Extension Act.

23. *See generally* Olive Huang, *U.S. Copyright Office Orphan Works Inquiry: Finding Homes for the Orphans*, 21 BERKELEY TECH. L.J. 265, 276–77 (2006).

whether the conduct is permissible. Copyright owners tend to send threatening letters when copying exceeds the bright line tests set out in a provision like section 108. This reality, along with the changing nature of librarianship and the use of archived materials in the digital age, suggest that the current version of section 108 may not be the optimum way to deal with the problem it purports to address.

6.1.2.2 Emphemeral Recordings

Radio and television broadcasters are in the business of "performing" works, the vast majority of which are protected by copyright. They routinely obtain the necessary licenses to do this, either from entities known as "performing rights societies" (discussed further on in this chapter) or on an individually negotiated basis, depending on the nature of the work(s) and their own business model. In the course of making those performances, however, they sometimes find it necessary to make a copy of the material in question.

For instance, consider a nationwide network of radio stations that has licensed the right to broadcast Rush Limbaugh's syndicated talk show. The show may be transmitted live via satellite by the producer at a particular hour of the day—let us say 9:00 AM. While the network could just receive and instantaneously retransmit the show, that might not make sense because its various stations are located in different times zones. Moreover, they might want to offer different programming at morning "drive time" and save Rush for later in the day after listeners have had some coffee.

Consequently, the radio network may simply tape the initial transmission, and then play the tape one or more times that afternoon to share Limbaugh's profound insights[24] with those of its stations located in different parts of the country. Now it is easy enough for the radio network to negotiate with the producers of Limbaugh's show for the right to make this copy. After all, they have to negotiate with them anyway for the right to "perform" the show by broadcasting (which is how the producer makes money), and the chances are that the right to make this transient copy for broadcast later in day will simply be "bundled" into that license. The problem is that Limbaugh may play some copyrighted music during his show. The radio network already has a license covering its right to perform that music obtained from ASCAP or BMI.[25] It does not, however, have a license permitting it to make a copy of that music and it does not normally have occasion to deal directly with the owner of the copyright in that music.

---

24. You may read this as serious or sarcastic depending on your political ideology and view of Mr. Limbaugh.

25. *See supra* § 6.4.3.

One could imagine the copyright statute requiring a radio network in this position to license the right to reproduce the music. That would be onerous and expensive. In any event, the industry practice prior to the 1976 Act had been to treat these recordings as ancillary to the ASCAP or BMI licensed performance, especially because the recordings were usually not retained for any significant period of time.[26] Copyright holders did not charge a separate royalty for the privilege of making the recordings, and did not claim infringement when they were made. In drafting the 1976 Act, Congress codified this approach in section 112. It refers to these reproductions of this type as "ephemeral recordings."[27]

The general exemption for ephemeral copying is set out in the first subsection of section 112. It first specifies that the exemption only applies to "transmitting organizations"[28] that have a legal right to transmit the program in question by virtue of a negotiated license, statutory license, or under some other provision of the copyright statute. In other words the *performing* of the material must be lawful before the *reproduction* of it will be allowed under section 112. If that is the case, the organization is allowed to make one copy of the material, provided it adheres to three limitations: first, it must retain the copy solely for its own use and not make any additional copies from the copy; second, it must use the copy only for transmitting the program or for archival purposes[29]; and third, it must destroy the copy within six months unless it is "preserved exclusively for archival purposes."

Interestingly, subsection (a) also specifies that section 112 does not apply to motion pictures or other audiovisual works. So if a television network like NBC beams a movie to its affiliates around the country for prime time broadcast, those affiliates are not allowed to tape the movie and show it at a subsequent time. They must air it when they receive it unless they have separately licensed the right to make a copy.

You might wonder whether copyright owners could thwart the section 112 privilege to make ephemeral copies by encrypting their works with copy-control technologies. The statute deals with that contingency by requiring the copyright owner to "make available to the transmitting organization the necessary means for permitting the making" of the legally allowed copy, so long as it can do so in an economically reasonable and technologically feasible way. If it

---

26. *See* PATRY ON COPYRIGHT, § 11:9.

27. 17 U.S.C. § 112.

28. This term is not defined in the statute, but clearly includes radio and television networks, individual radio and television stations, and cable and satel-

lite transmitters as well. *See* NIMMER, § 8.06[A], at n.3.

29. Obviously, a copy retained for "archival purposes" will be kept indefinitely, making the label "ephemeral" a "misnomer" according to the Nimmer treatise. *See* NIMMER, § 8.06[A][4].

fails to do so, the transmitting organization is allowed to circumvent the copy-control technology and is given immunity from the relevant anti-circumvention provisions of the Digital Millennium Act[30] in order to do so.[31]

Most of the remaining subsections of section 112 provide more liberal exemptions for educational broadcasters, governmental bodies engaged in public broadcasting, broadcasters of religious works, and entities that broadcast to those with visual or auditory disabilities. These broadcasters often need to retain copies of a program in order to retransmit it in subsequent semesters or to different groups of students at different times of the year. Speaking very generally, the relevant provisions allow the making of multiple copies, provide for longer retention periods, and permit the sharing of copies between different non-profit transmitting enterprises,

Finally, subsection (e) of the statute also provides for a compulsory licensing mechanism which allows digital transmitters such as webcasters and satellite radio stations (such as XM), to make ephemeral recordings upon the payment of a governmentally set royalty.[32] The details of this provision are quite arcane and beyond the scope of our present enterprise. If you have need for the particulars, we refer you to more detailed works, and of course to the statutory text.[33]

6.1.2.3 Pictures of Pictorial, Graphic, and Sculptural Works

Section 113 of the statute contains a very narrow exception to the exclusive reproduction right involving copyrighted works that have been reproduced in "useful articles." Let us consider an example drawn from the facts of the celebrated decision in *Mazer v. Stein*.[34] A table lamp is a utilitarian object, since it serves the purpose of providing illumination. There are many ways to design a table lamp, and most of them will not be protected by copyright unless they have "conceptually separable" aesthetic features, a

---

30. *See infra* § 7.2.

31. 17. U.S.C. § 112(a)(2).

32. In 2008, the Copyright Royalty Judges (CRJ) undertook a royalty rate proceeding to determine royalties for digital audio transmissions of sound recordings by satellite radio stations such as XM. As part of that proceeding it also had to set the royalty for the making of ephemeral copies of those sound recordings under section 112(e). After setting a total royalty rate, the CRJ decided not to attribute any portion of the royalties to the ephemeral copies, finding such copies to be of little value. On review,

the Librarian of Congress conceded that the CRJ erred in this regard. As a result the D.C. Circuit remanded the matter back to the CRJ to allow them to determine what percentage of the overall royalty should be allocated to the section 112(e) ephemeral copying. *See* Sound Exchange v. Librarian of Congress, 571 F.3d 1220 (D.C. Cir. 2009).

33. *See   generally   NIMMER,* §§ 8.06[B]–[F]; PATRY ON COPYRIGHT, § 11:9.

34. 347 U.S. 201, 74 S.Ct. 460, 98 L.Ed. 630 (1954).

point explored at length earlier in this book.[35] However, one might start with a work of art such as a statue, mass produce it, and use those reproductions as the base of the lamp (in *Mazer*, the statue in question depicted a dancer from the Indonesian island of Bali). The statute is not utilitarian and is entirely subject to copyright. Moreover, *Mazer* holds that a copyrighted work, such as the statues in our hypothetical, do not lose their protected status by being incorporated into the utilitarian lamps. This rule is now codified in the 1976 Act.[36]

However, despite the continued copyright in the statues, section 113(c) declares that it is not an infringement of the reproduction rights of the copyright owner of those statues for others to make and distribute pictures or photographs of the lamp connection with advertisements or commentaries related to the distribution or display of such articles, or in connection with news reports, "so long as the lamp has been offered for sale or distributed to the public."[37] Consequently it is lawful for a furniture store to feature a picture of the lamp in a newspaper advertising circular or catalog, even though that would involve making a two-dimensional photographic reproduction of the statue which might otherwise violate the reproduction (and adaptation) rights of the copyright owner. Similarly, it would be acceptable for a newspaper printing a story about the theft of a shipment of these lamps to run a picture of one of them to accompany the story.

This all presupposes that the copyright work manufacturer of the utilitarian article "lawfully reproduced" the copyrighted work. If the maker of the lamps never secured permission to use the statues as the base for them, and simply reproduced them without permission, section 113(c) does not allow others to make pictures or photographs of those lamps. Just how an advertiser, much less a newspaper, is supposed to ascertain if the material was lawfully or unlawfully reproduced in the first place is not revealed by the statute.

Of course, it is also not a violation of the reproduction right to construct a utilitarian object that is depicted in a copyrighted work. For instance, a painter might make a very detailed painting of a rocking chair. It might be a painting of an existing chair, or it might be a painting of a chair whose appearance is conceived by the artist for the very first time as he composes the painting. Either way, others are free to build a rocking chair that looks identical to the one in the painting.[38] This is not really a "limitation" on the

---

35. *See supra* § 3.5.

36. 17 U.S.C. § 113(a).

37. 17 U.S.C. § 113(c).

38. *See, e.g.,* Niemi v. American Axle Mfg. & Holding Inc., 2006 WL 2077590 (E.D. Mich. 2006) (no infringement where defendant used drawings of

reproduction right. Copyright does not confer an exclusive right to exploit utilitarian works—that is the domain of patent law. The point is dealt with in section 113(b) of that statute, but the provision dodges the heart of the issue somewhat, saying only that the right to physically manufacture the utilitarian article depicted in the copyrighted work is "no greater or lesser" than it was on December 31, 1977. In other words, the precise contours of this rule are left to be determined by consulting the case law under the 1909 Act.

6.1.2.4 Imitative Sound Recordings

Sound recordings were taken into the family of protected works late in the history of copyright,[39] and are still treated as disfavored stepchildren in several respects. As we will see later in this chapter, they are denied a general public performance right. More relevant to the present discussion, they also received a diminished form of the reproduction right.

Under § 114(b), the reproduction right for sound recordings is limited to recapturing the actual sounds fixed in that recording. Thus, it clearly violates the reproduction right to take a phonorecord (for instance a CD) and to *mechanically duplicate it* in order to produce one or more new additional CDs, (unless, of course, the party engaged in this activity has secured a license or can point to a defense). Indeed, when carried out on a large scale this kind of reproduction of sound recordings is often called record piracy, and there is no question that the copyright statute forbids it. This also means that file sharing over peer-to-peer networks clearly contravenes the reproduction right afforded to sound recordings because it involves a mechanical duplication or the original sounds on the hard drive of the computer of the downloading user.

However, section 114(b) goes on to provide that the reproduction right in sound recordings does "not extend to the making or duplication of another sound recording that consists entirely of an independent fixation of other sounds, even though such sound imitate or simulate those in the copyrighted sound recording."[40] This means that it is *not* a violation of the reproduction right in a sound recording to make your own new recording of the material contained within it, even if you slavishly mimic the precise tones,

stabilizer benders, welders, and other automotive manufacturing machinery to construct those items without the permission of the copyright owner of the drawings).

39. Congress extended copyright protection to sound recordings in the Sound Recording Act of 1971, Pub. L. No. 92–140, 92d Cong., 1st Sess., 85 Stat. 391. That law became effective on February 15, 1972. Sound recordings created prior to that date are protected, if at all, under state law.

40. 17 U.S.C. § 114(b). *See also* H. Rep. No. 94–1476, p. 106 (Sept. 3, 1976).

pitches, and sonic effects of the original recording.[41] Normally, such imitative activity is included within the reproduction right. You violate the reproduction right of the copyright owner in a painting by painting a look-alike version just as surely as you do if you take a photograph of the painting. Not so with sound recordings.

Note that a person preparing an imitation of a prior sound recording would also be making a reproduction of the underlying musical composition contained in that sound recording. If that musical composition was not in the public domain, the author of the new version would be an infringer of the copyright in the musical composition unless he obtained a license or had a defense. As we shall see shortly, those who prepare new versions of sound recordings—often called "cover recordings" or "covers"—usually can take advantage of a statutory license with regard to the musical works contained within them. The key point for present purposes, however, is that absent such a license or some other grant of permission, the imitative recording would violate the rights of the original composer of the musical composition.

Consider, for instance, a recording of the song Single Ladies (Put A Ring on It), composed by Kuk Harrell (and others), performed by Beyonce Knowles, and released in CD format on the Columbia record label.[42] This CD contains two works—(1) Harrell's music and lyrics, and (2) the particular sounds of the musicians and singers that are captured on the CD. Let us assume that some time after this CD is released that the recording artist Rihanna decides that she wants to make a recording of this same song and wishes to mimic Beyonce's exact style of performance. Section 114(b) tell us that she is free to do that without violating Columbia's copyright in the sound recording.[43] However, she would need a license—either a negotiated license or a statutory license—from Harrell and the other composers (or more likely, their music publisher)—in order to avoid infringing the copyright in the musical composition. On the other hand, if the underlying song had been, say Beyonce's recording of *When Irish Eyes Are Smiling*, which is in the public domain, Rihanna would need no license at all.

Section 114(b) also provides that the reproduction right in sound recordings is entirely inapplicable to sound recordings "included in educational television and radio programs ... distributed

---

41. *See, e.g.,* Griffin v. J–Records, 398 F.Supp.2d 1137, 1142 n. 14 (E.D.Wash.2005) ("A performing group that makes a recording that attempts to imitate the style of another performing group's recording does not violate any rights in a sound recording copyright.").

42. If you are not familiar with this recording you are spending too much time in the law library. You may remedy your unfamiliarity by visiting here: http://www.youtube.com/watch?v=8mVEGfH 4s5g.

43. To be precise, Columbia is just a "label" used by Sony Music Entertainment, which is the actual copyright owner of this particular sound recording.

or transmitted by or through public broadcasting entities. . . ." This provision is not limited to imitative recordings, and permits the mechanical duplication of a protected sound recording as well. However, this exception only applies if copies or phonorecords of the educational programs in question are not distributed to the public. Thus, the producer of an educational broadcast may incorporate others' sound recordings as part of a program without seeking permission or paying a fee, but cannot then sell DVDs or videotapes of that program to the public. Moreover, it bears repeating that this only immunizes the preparer of that education program from liability vis-a-vis the holder of copyright *in the sound recording*. It would still be necessary to license the underlying music composition or point to some other provision of law that permits it to be used without permission.[44]

6.1.2.5 Compulsory Licensing of Musical Compositions for Cover Recordings

At the dawn of the twentieth century, when Congress debated what became the Copyright Act of 1909, it feared that control over music copyrights would be concentrated in the hands of a few dominant players.[45] This anxiety over a potential monopoly led the drafters of that statute to include a compulsory licensing provision in that statute to insure that those seeking to exploit music would be free to do so upon payment of a royalty to be fixed by the government. Congress carried over this compulsory licensing provision to the Copyright Act of 1976, where we now find it in section 115. It is a significant limitation on the reproduction rights of music copyright owners, and a major feature of the modern recording industry.

Before we explore the details of the section 115 license, it is useful to stress that while section 114(b), considered immediately above, relates to *sound recordings*, section 115 relates to *musical compositions*. The privileges of each of these sections must be considered separately, and neither will immunize misuse of a work that it does not address. A terminological note is also in order. The provision now under discussion is often referred to as the "mechanical license"—an allusion to the fact that it permits the production of physical objects (in days of yore, piano rolls; today, CDs) that are created by a mechanical process. The terms "mechanical reproduction" and "phonorecord" are synonymous, as both refer to physical

---

44. In many cases, the ephemeral recording limit on the reproduction right, codified in section 112, may permit the educational broadcaster to make copies of the underlying musical composition, assuming that it has the relevant permission to perform the work. Moreover, section 110 may confer permission to perform without the need for securing a license.

45. *See* H.R. Rep. No. 2222, 60th Cong., 2nd Sess. 6 (1909).

objects that embody sounds. Finally, bear in mind that section 115 deals only with *nondramatic* musical works, meaning that works such as operas and musicals are not affected by this provision.

The section 115 licensing provision is triggered only when the owner of copyright in a non-dramatic musical work has authorized the distribution of phonorecords of the work to the public in the United States. This pre-condition means that the holder of copyright in a song gets to decide who will first record it—some random singer, band, or production company cannot swoop in and secure a compulsory license and make their own version of the song until after an initial recording authorized by the composer is released. This guarantees the composer some control over how the public will first hear the work, which quite properly vindicates both economic and artistic concerns. Note also that if someone has made unauthorized recordings of the song, that does not set the provisions of section 115 in motion—there is no reason why the copyright owner of the song, having been victimized by an infringer, should then be subject to compulsory licensing by others.

Once that first, authorized sound recording has been distributed, others become free to invoke the statutory license. This allows them to make their own phonorecords of the musical composition or, in the parlance of the music business, to "cover" the song. They may only do so, however if their purpose is to distribute the resulting phonorecords to the public for private use.[46] Moreover, the section 115 license only permits the making of phonorecords. It does not permit the making of "copies." Consulting the definitional section of the statute, we see that the current copyright statute excludes the sound track of an audiovisual work from the definition of a phonorecord. Consequently, the section 115 license is unavailable to a party who wants to record a copyrighted song for use as part of a movie, music video, television show, TV commercial, or any other audiovisual work. Such a party must license the rights to use the song directly from the relevant composer or music publisher. In the music and movie industries, this type of license is known as a "synch" license.[47]

This distinction between "copies" and "phonorecords" became dispositive in *Leadsinger, Inc. v. BMG Music Pub.*[48] In that case, Leadsinger wanted to make a device which it described as " 'an all-in-one microphone player' that has recorded songs imbedded in a microchip in the microphone. When the microphone is plugged into a television, the lyrics of the song appear on the television screen in

---

46. 17 U.S.C. § 115(a)(1).

47. *See generally*, M. WILLIAM KRASI-LOVSKY & SYDNEY SHEMEL, THIS BUSINESS OF MUSIC 226–234 (9th ed. 2003); Maljack

Prods., Inc. v. GoodTimes Home Video Corp., 81 F.3d 881, 884–85 (9th Cir. 1996).

48. 512 F.3d 522 (9th Cir. 2008).

real time as the song is playing, enabling the consumer to sing along with the lyrics." In other words, it was essentially an at-home karaoke machine.[49] BMG, the holder of copyrights in songs that Leadsinger wanted to use in this device, demanded that Leadsinger pay it for a "synch" license and a license to reproduce the lyrics. Leadsinger insisted that it needed only the section 115 mechanical license, and it filed a declaratory judgment action to secure a ruling to that effect.

The Ninth Circuit noted that the definition of phonorecords excluded audiovisual works. It then focused on the definition of "audiovisual works" as a series of related images that are intrinsically intended to be shown by the use of machines.[50] It observed that "the visual representation of successive portions of song lyrics that Leadsinger's device projects onto a television screen constitutes 'a series of related images.'" This followed because Leadsinger's device presented the lyrics in sequence and paced them to correspond to the music. As the court put it, "[a]n essential function of Leadsinger's device is its ability to indicate to the consumer exactly when to sing each lyric. Leadsinger's device is able to do so only because it utilizes a machine to project the song lyrics 'in real time' with the accompanying music." This distinguished the situation from one where a distributor of phonorecords also includes "liner notes" setting out the lyrics of the songs. Consequently, the court found in favor of BMG.[51]

In addition to the precondition discussed above, and the limitation of the compulsory license to phonorecords, the prospective licensee must also observe a notice requirement.[52] "Before, or within thirty days after making, and before distributing any phonorecords of the work, [he must] serve notice of intention to do so on the copyright owner."[53] The notice is to be served on the copyright owner, but if the identity of that party cannot be ascertained from the records of the Copyright Office, it can be filed with the Office instead. The statute is crystal clear on the consequences of the failure to observe this notice requirement: "Failure to serve or file the notice required ... forecloses the possibility of a compulsory license and, in the absence of a negotiated license, renders the making and distribution of phonorecords actionable as acts of infringement."[54]

49. Karaoke is Japanese for singing loudly and poorly in public while under the influence of alcohol.

50. 17 U.S.C. § 101 (definition of "audiovisual work").

51. For another case holding that karaoke recordings are outside the scope of the section 115 compulsory license,

see, ABKCO Music, Inc. v. Stellar Records, Inc., 96 F.3d 60 (2d Cir. 1996).

52. The precise form of the notice is prescribed by regulation. See 37 C.F.R. § 201.18.

53. 17 U.S.C. § 115(b)(1).

54. 17 U.S.C. § 115(b)(2).

Assuming the notice is timely filed, the relevant party is now free to begin making and distributing his own phonorecords. The royalty rate to be paid is periodically adjusted by an administrative panel within the Library of Congress staffed by the Copyright Royalty Judges.[55] The statute includes a provision permitting the copyright owner to terminate the license if the licensee fails to make the payments required by the law.[56] As of this writing the royalty rate is 9.1 cents per phonorecord, or 1.75 cents per minute of playing time or fraction thereof, whichever is greater for each phonorecord that is actually distributed. Since the typical CD contains about 10 songs, the producer of a CD can expect to pay about 91 cents per CD for the rights to use those songs.

While some cover artists may try to emulate the vocal stylings of the original recording, others want to make their own musical interpretation of the song. Section 115 permits them to do so, within reason. It provides the statutory licensee with "the privilege of making a musical arrangement of the work to the extent necessary to conform it to the style or manner of interpretation involved...."[57] To comply with the mechanical license, however the licensee's version must not "change the basic melody or fundamental character of the work."[58] Moreover, the licensee is not entitled to a new copyright in the arrangement as a derivative work.

To cement our understanding, let us take an example. Suppose that composer Bart Backrub composes a song entitled *What's New Puppydog* and licenses Galaxy Records to produce a recording. After procuring the services of a famed singer John Tones and relevant back-up musicians, Galaxy produces and distributes a sound recording of the song. Some time later singer Benny Tonnett decides that he would like to record the song as well. He is entitled to invoke the mechanical license of § 115 to make a cover recording. Tonnett must serve notice on Galaxy (or the Copyright Office if Galaxy's address cannot be determined), within thirty days after making his recording, and before beginning distribution of it to the public. Tonnett is free to sing the song in a different key than the original recording, sing it at a different tempo, use a different orchestration, or otherwise accommodate the tune to his personal singing style, so long as he does not change the "fundamental character" of the work.[59]

---

55. *See* 17 U.S.C. § 804(b)(4) providing for a royalty adjustment in 2006 and every five years thereafter.

56. 17 U.S.C. § 115(c)(6).

57. 17 U.S.C. § 115(a)(2).

58. *Ibid.* The House Report on the 1976 Act explains that the adaptation of the song must not allow "the music to be perverted, distorted, or travestied." H.R. Rep. 94–1476 p. 109 (94th Cong. 2d Sess.).

59. *Ibid.*

What if Mr. Tonnett is not a singer, but instead owns a record company and wants to make mechanical copies of the original Galaxy recording of the Backrub song as performed by John Tones? In this case, Tonnett would be copying *both* the musical composition (copyright by Backrub or his music publisher) and the sound recording (copyright by Galaxy) As to the former work, he would be covered by the statutory compulsory license we have been discussing provided he observed the statutory conditions. Regarding the sound recording, however, section 115 provides no protection to Tonnett whatsoever. He would need to secure rights from Galaxy, otherwise he would be an infringer of their copyright despite having obtained a section 115 license. To put the point more bluntly, the statutory license of section 115 will not insulate a record pirate.[60]

You might be surprised to learn that in the real world, few record companies or performers use the compulsory licensing mechanism of section 115. The procedures under that provision—particular the requirement of payments to the Copyright Office, with subsequent distribution to the copyright owner, make it cumbersome. Consequently, those requiring license deal directly with the relevant copyright holder, usually though a designated intermediary who is empowered to enter into such transactions. The largest such agent is the Harry Fox Agency. Founded in 1927, it represents the vast majority of music copyright owners with regard to mechanical licensing rights.[61] This does not make section 115 irrelevant because the statutory royalty rate fixed pursuant to that provision will be the prevailing rate in private transactions with Harry Fox or others. After all, no licensee would be willing to pay more, and the copyright owner would be foolish to settle for less.

All this talk about mechanical licenses may strike some readers as a bit dated. The distribution of music in the form of tangible objects such as CDs may be headed the way of the rotary telephone, the typewriter, and the buggy whip as more and more people buy their music on-line though services such as Apple's iTunes and store that music on the hard drive of a computer or on a portable device such as an MP3 player.[62] In 1995, as part of the Digital Performance Right in Sound Recordings Act, Congress added provisions to section 115 to deal with this new method of delivering music to consumers.

Brief reflection will reveal that every time an entity like iTunes allows you to download a song you are making a copy of that song.

---

60. *See*   *generally*   NIMMER, § 8.04[E][2].

61. For more on the Harry Fox Agency, consult its web site at http://www.nmpa.org/hfa.html.

62. *See*   *generally*   NIMMER, § 8.23[A][1].

You are also making a copy of the particular sound recording as well, just as we hypothesized that Mr. Tonnett might want to do in the *What's New Puppydog* hypothetical discussed just a few paragraphs above. Companies in this line of business effectively are in the business of making mechanical reproductions of the song (and sound recording) "on demand." It is as if you went into a CD factory, or retail record store, with no inventory and requested a particular recording, at which point they physically produced it for you on the spot. This means that such parties need the relevant licenses from the copyright owners of the musical work and the sound recording.

Under section 115, the practice of selling music files on-line is referred to as a "digital phonorecord delivery" (hereafter DPD for short).[63] The statute provides that representatives of music copyright owners and of prospective licensees may negotiate royalties and agree on how the resulting royalties shall be divided, and grants them immunity from the antitrust laws in order to do so.[64] If the relevant parties are unable to come to an agreement, the royalty rate is fixed by the Copyright Royalty Judges, under proceedings similar to those applicable to the conventional mechanical license that permits the production of a physical phonorecord. Indeed, the current governmentally determined royalty for DPDs is identical to the rate for physical recordings. Thus, for every song you download from iTunes for $1.29, just over 9 cents goes to the composer or his music publisher as a royalty for the use of the song.

As a practical matter it would be very time consuming for firms in the DPD business to obtain a separate license for each song they deliver digitally even with the efficiencies provided by the Harry Fox Agency. Fortunately, the statute facilitates the DPD business model by allowing the record companies—which themselves need to license the song in order to make their initial sound recordings—to sublicense those who want to make downloads.[65] Thus, iTunes and others of their ilk need only enter into contracts with the major record companies in order to license all the rights they need to both

---

63. 17 U.S.C. § 115(d) states that a "digital phonorecord delivery is each individual delivery of a phonorecord by digital transmission of a sound recording which results in a specifically identifiable reproduction by or for any transmission recipient of a phonorecord of that sound recording . . ."

64. 17 U.S.C. § 115(c)(3)(B).

65. The legislative history explains: "The Committee intends that a compulsory license for digital phonorecord deliveries may be obtained, and the required mechanical royalties may be paid, either directly by a digital transmission service making a digital phonorecord delivery or by a record company authorizing a digital phonorecord delivery. Thus, the changes to section 115 are designed to minimize the burden on transmission services by placing record companies in a position to license not only their own rights, but also, if they choose to do so, the rights of writers and music publishers to authorize digital phonorecord deliveries . . ." S. Rep. 104–128, at 37 (1995).

sound recordings and musical works for purposes of making DPDs.[66]

Evolving technology in the music industry led to an even more esoteric controversy in 2006 over the sale of ringtones for cell phones. The holders of copyrights in musical works claimed that the transmission of ringtones should not be considered "digital phonorecord deliveries" and thus should not be subject to compulsory licencing. Presumably, they hoped that this would free them to demand higher royalty rates than those that might be fixed by the Copyright Royalty Judges. They argued that section 115 only applied to a reproduction of an entire musical work, not a mere portion of "snippet" of the work. They also argued that section 115 should be construed narrowly and that Congress did not mean for it to allow the reproduction of musical works for uses in conjunction with utilitarian items. The Register of Copyrights rejected those arguments.[67] As a result, the sale of ringtones is subject to compulsory licensing, unless the musical work is transformed or combined with other materials to such a degree as to constitute a derivative work. The current royalty rate for ringtones is 24 cents, which will be in effect through 2012.

6.1.2.6 Permissible Reproductions of Computer Programs

You will recall that the transfer of material into the memory of a computer constitutes a reproduction of that material, at least if the material resides in memory for more than a fleeting period of time. It follows, therefore, that it is impossible, as a practical matter, to use computer programs without "reproducing" them, since the minute you launch a program it is loaded into memory. In order to avoid the bizarre result of condemning all computer users as infringers, Congress carved out three situations where making copies of computer programs would not violate the reproduction right. These parameters of these limits on the reproduction right are spelled out in section 117.

Section 117(a)(1) allows owners of computer software to make or authorize the making of a copy (or adaptation) of that program if "such a new copy or adaptation is created as an essential step in the utilization of the computer program...." This provision covers the situation alluded to immediately above, where the program is

---

66. For specifics of iTunes licensing arrangements, see http://www.harryfox.com/docs/9–08Soundcheckfinal.pdf at page 4.

67. *See* Mechanical and Digital Phonorecord Delivery Rate Adjustment Proceeding, 71 Fed. Reg. 64303 (October 26, 2006). *See also* Daniel M. Simon,

Cell Phone Ringtones: A Case Study Exemplifying the Complexities of the § 115 Mechanical License of the Copyright Act of 1976, 57 DUKE L.J. 1865 (2008); Daniel H. Mark, *Wringing Songwriters Dry: Negative Consequences of Compulsory Licensing for Ringtones*, 10 VAND. J. ENT. & TECH. L. 533 (2008).

"reproduced" in memory every time the computer owner turns on the computer.[68] It also presumably covers copying a program or CD onto a hard drive, in order to make using the program less cumbersome and to allow the program to run more efficiently.

While this second example is not arguably "essential" to the utilization of the program, since the user could run the program off the CD every time she wanted to use it, it is indispensable to the use of the computer as a practical matter and should be considered with the provision. As the Nimmer treatise puts it, "[g]iven that efficiency lies at the heart of the rationale for computerization in the first place, to forbid such practices ... represents an impoverished view of users' rights under Section 117."[69] Moreover, because this provision also allows the adaptation of the program, the owner of the original copy can modify it to make it compatible with new generations of computer systems, to add new features, or to otherwise accommodate it to the user's hardware configuration.[70]

The second limitation on the reproduction right set out in section 117 allows the owner of a copy of a program to make one backup copy of a computer program for archival purposes.[71] This provision requires, however, that the archival copy must be destroyed "in the event that continued possession of the computer program should cease to be rightful." The statute also forbids the sale of copies made under section 117 unless the copy from which they were made is also transferred.[72] In plain English, that means you cannot sell the back-up copy of a program you purchased while retaining the original copy, thereby depriving the copyright owner of a sale.

Close reading reveals that these first two provisions in section 117 allude to the "owner of a copy" of the program. Most software today is sold pursuant to clickwrap or shrinkwrap licenses. There might be some tendency, therefore, to think that modern computer users cannot rely on section 117 because they are only a licensee, not owners. As the Patry copyright treatise makes clear, however, "the statutory phrase 'owner of a copy of a computer program' refers solely to the owner of title in the physical object and not to ownership of any intellectual property rights in the work of authorship."[73] Most opinions have recognized the distinction and recognized that while the user may be a licensee of the *program*, in most cases he *owns* a physical copy of that program, such as a CD,

---

68. Sony Computer Entertainment, Inc. v. Connectix Corp., 203 F.3d 596, 600 n.1 (9th Cir. 2000).

69. NIMMER, § 8.08[B][1].

70. *See, e.g.* Krause v. Titleserv, Inc., 402 F.3d 119 (2d Cir. 2005); Aymes v. Bonelli, 47 F.3d 23 (2d Cir.1995).

71. 17 U.S.C. § 117(a)(2).

72. 17 U.S.C. § 117(b).

73. PATRY ON COPYRIGHT, § 11:32.

entitling him to the benefits of section 117. Moreover, the Second Circuit has advocated a pragmatic approach to the issue of "ownership" declaring that:

> [F]ormal title in a program copy is not an absolute prerequisite to qualifying for § 117(a)'s affirmative defense. Instead courts should inquire into whether the party exercises sufficient incidents of ownership over a copy of the program to be sensibly considered the owner of the copy for purposes of § 117(a). The presence or absence of formal title may of course be a factor in this inquiry, but the absence of formal title may be outweighed by evidence that the possessor of the copy enjoys sufficiently broad rights over it to be sensibly considered its owner."[74]

The final substantive provision of § 117 allows the owner or lessee of a computer to make, or to authorize the making of, a copy of a computer program for purposes of maintenance or repair of that computer.[75] Congress added this provision in 1998 in order to protect independent computer maintenance enterprises from charges of copyright infringement.[76] Independent maintenance enterprises frequently turn on a client's computer in order to service it, resulting in the automatic loading of another party's software into the computer's memory (RAM). Prior to this amendment, in an attempt to prevent third party providers from engaging in the software maintenance business, copyright holders had successfully asserted that the act of loading the program into a computer's memory infringed the reproduction right.[77] Section 117(c) effectively exempted this practice from the scope of the copyright laws and prevents copyright owners in software programs from leveraging their copyrights into a monopoly over the computer repair business.

6.1.2.7   Pictures of Architectural Works

When Congress added architectural works to the list of copyrightable subject matter, they became entitled to all the rights set out in the statute. However, as the legislative history of that amendment noted: "Architecture is a public art form and is enjoyed as such. Millions of people visit our cities every year and take back home photographs, posters, and other pictorial representations of prominent works of architecture as a memory of their trip."[78]

---

74. Krause v. Titleserv, Inc., 402 F.3d 119, 124 (2d Cir. 2005). *See also,* UMG Recordings, Inc. v. Augusto, 558 F.Supp.2d 1055, 1060 (C.D.Cal. 2008.) ("In determining whether a transaction is a sale or a license, courts must analyze the 'economic realities' of the transaction.").

75. 17 U.S.C. § 117(c).

76. *See* Title III of the Digital Millennium Copyright Act, Pub. L. No. 105–304, 112 Stat. 2860 § 301 (1998).

77. See MAI Sys. Corp. v. Peak Computer, Inc., 991 F.2d 511 (9th Cir. 1993).

78. H.R. Rep. 101–735, 1990 U.S.C.C.A.N. 6935, 6953 (1990).

Congress concluded that it would serve no purpose to treat such activities as copyright infringements.

Congress accomplished this by adding a new section 120 to the statute. It provides that once an architectural work has been constructed such that it is "ordinarily visible from a public place," the copyright owner may not "prevent the making, distributing, or public display of pictures, paintings, photographs, or other pictorial representations of the work."[79] Note that this exception is limited to pictorial representations, and would not exempt the making of three-dimensional replicas of the building, for example.

6.1.2.8 Reproductions for Persons With Visual or Other Disabilities

Organizations devoted to providing education for blind and visually impaired persons have often sought permission to make reproductions of copyrighted works in formats that would be suitable for their students or other constituents. Unable to secure much cooperation from the publishers that held copyright in these works, they appealed to Congress in the early 1990s and it responded by adding section 121 to the statute.

This section allows "authorized entities" to make copies and phonorecords of previously published nondramatic literary works. Authorized entities are defined as non-profit organizations or governmental agencies with a primary mission of providing specialized training or educational services to those who are blind or who have other disabilities.[80] The copies or phonorecords made under this provision must be in "specialized formats," which are defined to include Braille versions as well as audio versions and material using digital text. The copies and phonorecords produced under section 121 must bear a notice that any further reproduction in a format other than a specialized format would be an infringement, and must also contain a notice identifying the copyright owner of the work in question.

§ 6.2 The Adaptation Right

6.2.1 Basic Principles

The second paragraph of § 106 invests the copyright holder with the exclusive right "to prepare derivative works based upon the copyrighted work." This entitlement is commonly known as the adaptation right. The adaptation right is violated when a third party makes an unauthorized derivative work that recasts, transforms, or adapts the protected work. Typical derivative works include dramatizations, translations, and musical arrangements.

---

79. 17 U.S.C. § 120(a).   **80.** 17 U.S.C. § 121(c)(1).

Thus, only the author and copyright owner of a novel is entitled to write (or license) a screenplay based on that novel. When one reads in the popular press that a studio has purchased the "movie rights" to a best seller, it is really a reference to a copyright license under which the studio has secured permission to prepare a derivative work.

Like all of the rights in the copyright statute, the adaptation right is mostly about money. It seeks to include within the copyright owner's economic reward all the profits that can be reaped when a work is sold in secondary markets. The greater potential reward arguably makes for a greater incentive to create in the first place. In other words, a novelist might not expect sales of the novels to return much in the way of royalties, but he might invest the time and effort in writing with the hope that the eventual sale of "movie rights" to the story could be lucrative indeed. The adaptation right can serve a second purpose as well—namely to protect an artist from unauthorized distortions of his or her work.

This idea that artists have a right to have their artistic vision presented to the public free from distortions is considered one of the author's "moral rights"—a loose and only partially accurate translation of the French phrase *droit morale*. American law has not traditionally provided strong protection of moral rights. The only express provisions dealing with the subject in the copyright statute are those added by the Visual Artists Rights Act, which we will take up in the next chapter. Nonetheless, the adaptation right does achieve some of the same purposes. If a film maker does not want his black-and-white movie colorized, so long as he holds the copyright he can prevent anyone else from doing that by invoking his adaptation right—since the colorized version would be a derivative work, only the copyright owner can prepare it or authorize another to do so. Similarly, if a poet does not want his poetry recast as a work of prose, the adaptation right will provide protection. Of course, like all rights in the statute, the adaptation right is limited by the fair use principle. Consequently some alterations of works may be permissible even though they mock or distort the work because they may be considered legitimate forms of commentary or parody.

A significant number of copyright infringement suits involve conduct by the defendant that simultaneously violates both the reproduction and the adaptation right. This follows because, as we will explore in some depth in the chapter on infringement, violation of the reproduction right only requires substantial similarity, not verbatim copying. For example, assume that film maker Steven Spielman decides to make a movie version of the best selling novel *Larry Cotter and The Goblet of Water* by author J.K. Howling, but does not secure the author's permission to do so. The movie is clearly a "dramatization" of the novel and thus a derivative work. Spielman has thus violated Howling's *adaptation* right. But the movie and the novel are also "substantially similar." The plot details and characters of each will be identical, and perhaps even some of the dialogue will be nearly identical as well. This means that the movie also violates Howling's *reproduction* rights.

As a practical matter, in cases like the *Larry Cotter* scenario, plaintiffs and courts do not distinguish between the two rights. The plaintiffs simply allege generic copyright infringement, and courts grant them relief upon proof of substantial similarity. In fact, an attempt to deal with the adaptation and reproduction rights separately in a case like this might even lead to illogical or incoherent analysis. In order to prove violation of the latter right, a plaintiff would attempt to show that the two works (his and the defendant's) were as similar as possible. But in order to prove an impermissible adaptation, the plaintiff would, at that same time have to show some non-trivial differences between the two works in order to label the defendant's creation a "derivative" work![81] It would be odd indeed to hear a copyright plaintiff stressing how *different* the works are.[82]

In one of his reports prepared during the years prior to the adoption of the current copyright act, the Register of Copyrights actually suggested that a separate adaptation right might be "unnecessary" but advocated including it to be on the safe side, saying "[i]t could be argued that, since the concept of 'reproduction' is broad enough to include adaptations and recast version of all kinds, there is no need to specify a separate right 'to prepare derivative works based upon the copyrighted work.' ... [H]owever this has long been looked upon as a separate exclusive right, and to omit any specific mention of it would be likely to cause uncertainty and misunderstanding."[83]

So when does the adaptation right take center stage in a copyright analysis? Often it is when a defendant manipulates plaintiff's work, but does not create a second physical object that could be considered a reproduction of plaintiff's work. In cases such as these, the plaintiff has no choice but to invoke the adaptation right. Such plaintiffs argue that the adaption right is the right to prepare derivative works, and point out that the statutory definition of derivative works does not require that derivative works be

---

81. *See infra* § 9.1.

82. Yet your humble authors have been crushed to see such arguments more than a few times in final exams in copyright courses.

83. Supplementary Report of the Register of Copyrights on the General

Revision of the U.S. Copyright Law: 1965 Revision Bill, 89th Cong. 1st Sess. at 17 (May, 1965), reprinted in NIMMER, Appendix 15 at page App. 15–41.

"fixed."[84] They also invoke the House Report on the current act, which declared at one point that "the preparation of a derivative work, such as a ballet, pantomime, or improvised performance, may be an infringement even though nothing is ever fixed in tangible form."[85]

Taken literally, however, this view of the adaptation right would lead to absurd results. As one academic commentator put it, "if fixation is not required, that means that the preparation of any unfixed derivative work, even only in one's own mind, would be a prima facie infringement of the copyright in the underlying work. If in your mind's eye (or ear) you imagine an original arrangement of a popular song, or you imagine an altered version of a copyrighted work of art ... you would be a copyright infringer."[86] It would also make it infringement to doodle on a photo in a magazine by darkening some of the teeth of the individual depicted or adding devil's horns to his head; it would make it infringement to fast forward through a scene on a DVD; it would make it infringement to underline or highlight passages in a textbook; and it would be infringement to watch or listen to materials while under the influence of drugs or alcohol because the listener in such a case might perceive the work to be slower, faster, louder, more colorful, or otherwise more "trippy" than the copyright owner intended.

If an impermissible adaptation does not require a reproduction, it must have some other limits to avoid leading us to absurd results. Alas, the cases that have tried to set out rational limits for the adaptation right have not had great success. Indeed, some are inconsistent with each other, and a few are even internally inconsistent. We can only assure the frustrated reader of these opinions that we share your pain.

One group of cases has involved owners of copies of work who physically alter them without producing new additional copies. For instance, in *Mirage Editions, Inc. v. Albuquerque A.R.T. Co.*,[87] the defendant purchased commemorative books celebrating the life and artistic works of Patrick Nagel. The defendant then cut photographs of Nagel's works from the books and mounted them on ceramic tiles, which he then offered for sale. When the copyright owner sued for infringement, the Court of Appeals for the Ninth

84. *See*, 17 U.S.C. § 101 (definition of "derivative work").

85. H.R. Rep. 94–1476, at 62, 1976 U.S.C.C.A.N. 5675. *See also,* Paul Goldstein, *Derivative Rights and Derivative Works in Copyright*, 30 J. COPYRIGHT SOC'Y 209, 231 n.75 (1983) ("while a derivative work, to be protected, must be 'fixed in a tangible medium of expression,' section 106(2) does not require

that the work be fixed in order to infringe.").

86. Tyler T. Ochoa, *"Copyright, Derivative Works and Fixation" Is Galoob a Mirage, or Does the Form(gen) of the Alleged Derivative Work Matter?*, 20 SANTA CLARA COMPUTER & HIGH TECH. L.J. 991, 1001–02 (2004).

87. 856 F.2d 1341 (9th Cir. 1988).

Circuit held that this practice resulted in unauthorized derivative works and infringed the adaptation right. According to the Ninth Circuit, the defendant both recast and transformed Nagel's images through its tile preparation process.[88]

Although the Ninth Circuit confirmed this holding in a subsequent opinion,[89] commentators have criticized its conclusion.[90] Moreover, under virtually identical facts, the Seventh Circuit, in *Lee v. A.R.T. Company*,[91] subsequently reached a contrary result. The defendant there purchased notecards and small lithographs that had been produced by artist Annie Lee. These works were then mounted on ceramic tiles. The plaintiff argued that even though the defendant did not create any reproductions of her work, no reproductions were required to violate the adaptation right. She also claimed that although defendants only minimally transformed the work, the first sentence of the definition of derivative works does not require "originality" and hence "a work may be derivative despite the mechanical nature of the transformation."

Judge Easterbrook, rejected these contentions. He concluded that the mounted notecards were not derivative works because in making them the defendant did not "recast," "adapt," or "transform" the underlying art work. Lee's works instead remained exactly as they were when they left her studio. The court in *Lee* declined to turn the humble picture framer into a copyright infringer, or to give artists such an extraordinary degree of control over even slight modifications to their works, and thus declined to find the adaptation right infringed.

As between the two decisions, *Lee* strikes us as the more soundly reasoned case.[92] To change the context in which a work is presented—by putting it in a gilt frame, hanging it upside down, mounting it on a ceramic tile, or putting it along side a poster that says "this is ugly" with an arrow pointing to the work, may change a viewer's artistic impression of the work, but it does not really involve any "adaption" or "transformation" of the work itself. Moreover, in all of these cases, it is important to bear in mind that the original copyright owner has already received an economic reward from the sale of the original copy that is subsequently

---

88. The court also rejected the defendant's reliance upon the first sale doctrine, concluding that the mere purchase of a book does not transfer the right to make derivative works to the buyer. We address the first sale doctrine in § 6.3.2, just a bit further on in this chapter.

89. See Munoz v. Albuquerque ART Co., 38 F.3d 1218 (9th Cir. 1994).

90. *See* Wendy J. Gordon, *On Owning Information: Intellectual Property and the Restitutionary Impulse*, 78 Va. L. Rev. 149, 255 n. 401 (1992).

91. 125 F.3d 580 (7th Cir. 1997).

92. Not just us; *see also* Patry on Copyright § 12:16 (criticizing *Mirage*); Peter Letterese & Asso., Inc. v. World Inst. of Scientology Enterprises, 533 F.3d 1287, 1299 (11th Cir. 2008) (same).

manipulated by the defendant. As Judge Easterbrook put it, "[a]n alternation that includes (or consumes) a complete copy of the original lacks economic significance." Finally, to treat matters of contextual presentation as infringing adaptations would also conflict with the spirit, if not the letter, of the first sale principle, which allows owners of copies to do with them as they wish.[93]

Another group of adaption-right cases have involved computer hardware and software products, particularly those that alter or enhance the experience of playing various video games. In *Lewis Galoob Toys, Inc. v. Nintendo of America, Inc.*[94] Galoob manufactured a device which it called the Game Genie. When used in conjunction with Nintendo's video game devices, it temporarily altered certain computer variables and thus allowed the user to alter the experience of the game.[95] For instance, one could give Super Mario an infinite number of lives rather than have him perish after a few ill-timed jumps over a cliff. The Game Genie did not copy (reproduce) any of Nintendo's copyrighted computer code and did not produce its own independent audiovisual displays. Nonetheless, Nintendo sued alleging infringement of its adaptation right. The Ninth Circuit ultimately found that resulting altered video displays were not derivative works, and that therefore Galoob had not violated the adaptation right.

At one point the court noted that "the definition of a derivative work does not require fixation."[96] On the very next page, however, it declared that "[a] derivative work must incorporate a protected work in some concrete or permanent form." Because it found that the Game Genie neither physically incorporated any portions of Nintendo's copyrighted work, nor did it supplant demand for it, it refused to find infringement. Professor Ochoa has concluded that this "conclusion is self-contradictory: the requirement of 'concrete or permanent' incorporation is nothing more than fixation by another name."[97] Perhaps the opinion's coherence can be saved by reading it to say that while the statutory language doesn't require fixation explicitly, nor does it clearly endorse the view that unfixed and transient variations should be treated as derivative works. With the statute silent one way or the other, the court felt free to articulate its "incorporate the protected work ... in some form" test.

---

93. See discussion in section § 6.3.2.1.

94. 964 F.2d 965 (9th Cir. 1992).

95. Devices of this sort have become known colloquially as "cheat cartridges" because they allow the users to evade the rules of the game by altering values—for instance they permit the user to give game characters an infinite amount of strength or to never run out of ammunition.

96. 964 F.2d at 968.

97. Ochoa, *supra*, at 1004.

Only a few years later, the Ninth Circuit found itself back in the video game world when it had to decided *Micro Star v. Formgen Inc.*[98] The work under copyright this time was Duke Nukem 3D, a "first-person shooter" style computer game featuring "a beefy commando type named Duke who wanders around post-Apocalypse Los Angeles, shooting Pig Cops with a gun, lobbing hand grenades, searching for medkits and steroids, using a jetpack to leap over obstacles, blowing up gas tanks, [and] avoiding radioactive slime."[99] Duke Nukem 3D (D/N–3D) included 29 levels featuring different combinations of scenery, aliens, and other challenges. The computer game further included a "Build Editor," a utility that allowed users to create their own levels, but under the relevant software license users were not permitted to exploit those new levels for commercial purposes. The accused infringer, Micro Star, gathered 300 user-created levels and sold them on a CD titled "Nuke It" or N/I.

When accused of copyright infringement, Micro Star in part asserted that its "Nuke It" CD did not use any protected expression from the Duke Nukem 3D software. It seems that the Duke Nukem 3D software consisted of three distinct components: (1) a game engine, the program that ran the game using the computer's hardware capabilities and software resources; (2) the source art library, which contained images of scenery, objects, and other encounters within the game; and (3) the so-called MAP files, which instructed the game engine about the arrangement of particular levels. The "Nuke It" levels were expressed as MAP files, which the Duke Nukem 3D game engine would consult in order to make the computer hardware to run the game. Micro Star argued that although "Nuke It" levels referenced the source art library, they did not actually contain any art files themselves. As a result it claimed it could not have violated the adaptation right.

The *Micro Star* court did not disturb the holding of *Galoob* that an infringing derivative work must exist in a concrete and permanent form and that it must "embody" protected material from the pre-existing work. It found the two cases factually distinguishable however. As Judge Kozinski explained:

> [W]hereas the audiovisual displays created by Game Genie were never recorded in any permanent form, the audiovisual display generated by D/N–3D from the N/I MAP files are in the MAP files themselves. In *Galoob*, the audiovisual display was defined by the original game cartridge, not by the Game Genie; no one could possibly say

---

98.   154 F.3d 1107 (9th Cir. 1998).   **99.** This eloquent description is quoted from Judge Kozinski's statement of the facts in the case.

that the data values inserted by the Game Genie described the audiovisual display. In the present case the audiovisual display that appears on the computer monitor when a N/I level is play is described—in exact detail—by a N/I MAP file.

This raises the interesting question whether an exact, down to the last detail, description of an audiovisual display (and—by definition—we know that MAP files do describe audiovisual displays down to the last detail) counts as a permanent or concrete form for purposes of Galoob. We see no reason it shouldn't. What, after all, does sheet music do but describe in precise detail the way a copyrighted melody sounds?[100]

Judge Kozinski also noted that the N/I disk was specific to the D/N–3D game—unlike the Game Genie, it was not a generic game enhancer that could be used with multiple games. He found this significant because he determined the adaptation right included the right to create sequels, and that the "Nuke It" levels constituted new, if somewhat repetitive stories of the protagonist's post-Holocaust travails.

Thus far, the other federal circuits have not weighed in on whether they will follow the Ninth Circuit and require a defendant to produce something that exists in a concrete and permanent form and that substantially incorporates protected material from the pre-existing work before finding a violation of the adaptation right. While this approach may give short shrift to the more plausible reading of the statutory language and ignores some inconvenient legislative history, it does function to keep the adaption right descending into absurdity by reaching conduct that either has no economic consequences for the copyright owner or that represents legitimate uses of purchased copies of work, as in the tile-mounted art cases.

6.2.2 Limitations on the Adaptation Right

Given the significant overlap between the adaptation right and the reproduction right, some of the limitations on the former right also limit the latter. For instance, when one photographs a utilitarian object that incorporates a sculpture, the resulting photo is obviously not a precise "reproduction" of the three dimensional sculpture. Moreover the photo may be in black-and-white while the sculpture may be painted in vibrant colors. In other words, the photo is really a derivative work based upon the sculpture. As we saw in the discussion of the limitations on the reproduction right, it is not an infringement to take such a photo under section 113 of

---

100.   154 F.3d at 1111–12.

the statute. It is thus fair to say that section 113 limits the adaptation right. Another example would be the privilege granted to non-profit organizations to prepare braille editions of certain works for blind persons. These works are obviously not verbatim copies of the works as they were rendered in English. The conversion to braille involves a "translation" of sorts and the braille edition might be considered a derivative work. Thus the section 121 provision limits the adaptation right (the exclusive right to translate) just as much as it limits the reproduction right.

There are, however, a few provisions in the statute that speak somewhat more specifically to adaptations. Let us first consider section 110(11), which Congress added to the copyright act when it adopted the Family Movie Act of 2005.[101] By 2005 a few companies had developed technologies that enabled individual watching audio-visual works at home to filter out objectionable material such as coarse language or sexually explicit materials.[102] Some of these technologies could be used with movies being transmitted to the home, as on a cable channel such as HBO, and others could be used with movies being watched on DVD or similar media placed in a set top box. The users of these technologies would thus experience an altered version of the movie—one with substantially the same plot, dialogue, and scenes, but absent the occasional stray bosom or vulgar epithet. If, however, those altered versions were deemed to be derivative works, the home users of these technologies would have infringed the adaptation right of the copyright owner, and, perhaps more importantly, the maker of the technology would be exposed to liability as a contributory infringer.[103]

As we have discussed above, it is unclear whether infringement of the adaptation work requires a *fixed* version of a derivative work to be made. The "sanitized" version of the movie seen by the user of the censoring technology we described above is not designed to make a recording of the edited version. The home user merely watches it "on the fly" and it vanishes into the ether as soon as it

---

101. Pub. L. 109–9, 119 Stat. 218 (2005).

102. The leading vendor of this technology is a company called Clear-Play, which holds patents on the relevant technology. At least one reviewer has panned the technology. David Pogue, *State of the Art; Add "Cut" and "Bleep" to a DVD's Options,* N.Y. TIMES, May 27, 2004, at G1 ("To filter out violence, sex and 'disturbing images,' ... the player simply skips ahead. A quarter-second video freeze, a discontinuity in the music and, sometimes, bizarre holes in plot or staging make you quite aware when ClearPlay's magic scissors are at work. (Among its most ham-handed edits: In *The Matrix Reloaded,* Neo and Trinity kiss longingly, and then—blink!—instantly appear, sweaty and tousled, chatting in bed. ClearPlay just sent three and a half minutes to the cutting-room floor).... ClearPlay is not objectionable just because it butchers the moviemakers' vision. The much bigger problem is that it does not fulfill its mission: to make otherwise offensive movies appropriate for the whole family.").

103. For a discussion of contributory infringement, see § 9.4.2.

is visually perceived. When Congress began considering legislation to address these technologies, the Register of Copyrights took the position that in order to infringe the adaptation right there must either be a *public* performance of the derivative work, or the derivative work must be fixed. Since neither of those conditions obtained with the use of the movie censoring devices, she felt that legislation was unnecessary. As she put it in her testimony on the bill:

> Because a plain reading of the statute leads to the conclusion that in order to have an infringement of the derivative work right, the derivative work must be fixed, I find it difficult to conclude that there is an infringement of the derivative work right when software instructs a DVD player to mute certain sounds or skip past certain images in a motion picture being played on the DVD. The putative derivative work is never fixed. Moreover, if, as I understand to be the case, the software itself consists of instructions to mute the soundtrack at a point a certain number of minutes and seconds into the performance of the movie, or to skip past the part of the movie that begins at a point a certain number of minutes and seconds into the performance of the movie and ends certain number of seconds later, I find it difficult to characterize that software as a derivative work, since none of the underlying work is actually incorporated into the software.[104]

Perhaps out of an abundance of caution, or perhaps because Congress concluded that an infringing adaptation did *not* need to be fixed, it decided to adopt legislation anyway. The resulting provision declares that it is not an infringement of copyright to "make imperceptible" limited portions of the audio or video content of a motion picture, provided the performance was being made from a lawful copy, and provided that no fixed copy of the altered version is created. The statute immunizes both the home user of the technology and the manufacturer of any device from infringement liability. It does not, however, shield those who manufacture edited versions of movies and reproduce them on DVDs, cassettes, or other media for sale to the public. That conduct remains an unequivocal violation of the reproduction and adaptation rights of the copyright owners of the original movie.[105]

Turning to the music industry, two provisions we touched on earlier specifically limit the adaptation right. The first is contained

---

104. *Family Movie Act of 2004: Hearing Before the Subcommittee on Courts, the Internet and Intellectual Property of the H. Comm. On the Judiciary*, 108th Cong. 13 (June 17, 2004) (statement of Marybeth Peters, Register of Copyrights).

105. *See* Clean Flicks of Colorado, LLC v. Soderbergh, 433 F.Supp.2d 1236 (D.Colo. 2006).

in section 114. You will recall that this section limits the reproduction right in sound recordings to the recapture of the actual sounds fixed in the recording. Section 114 similarly restricts the adaptation right, limiting the scope of exclusivity to "the right to prepare a derivative work in which the actual sounds fixed in the sound recording are rearranged, remixed, or otherwise altered in sequence or quality."[106] Thus, just as it is not infringing to produce an imitative recording that mimics the plaintiff's earlier sound recording down to the most minute detail, it is not an infringing adaptation to use the a similar orchestration and general musical style, but to change certain aspects of the earlier recording, such as the tempo or the musical key in which it is recorded.

The second limitation on adaptation rights is found in section 115, the section that permits interested parties to obtain a compulsory license to make phonorecords of a music work. As we noted during our discussion of that provision above, it explicitly grants the compulsory licensee "the privilege of making a musical arrangement of the work to the extent necessary to conform it to the style or manner of interpretation involved change the basic melody or fundamental character of the work."[107] Thus a cover artist is not obligated to try to sound like the original singer or musicians. He or she can use his own style without risk of being accused of making an impermissible derivative work. A good thing, we suppose, when Brittany Spears opts to cover *My Prerogative* (originally performed by Bobby Brown) or when William Shatner tries his hand at *Lucy in the Sky With Diamonds*.

In the world of computer programs, the section 117 limitation on exclusive rights explicitly allows adaptations as well as reproductions. Thus, if the owner of a copy of a program must modify the program as an "essential step" in using it with his particular computer he may do so without any copyright liability. This privilege is particularly useful for the corporate owner of a copy of a complex, custom-designed computer program which may have cost many thousands of dollars. As new computers are purchased and as other aspects of the firm's information technology are upgraded, the program may no longer operate without revisions. Section 117 thus eliminates the need for the firm to buy an entirely new program.

Finally, when Congress added works of constructed architecture to the subject matter of copyright it adopted a provision—section 120(b)—that explicitly allows the owners of a building embodying an architectural work "without the consent of the author or copyright owner of the architectural work" to "make or

106. 17 U.S.C. § 114(b).   **107.** 17 U.S.C. § 115(a)(2).

authorize the making of alterations to such building, and destroy or authorize the destruction of such building.''[108] If one takes the view that the adaptation right is only triggered when one also creates a new physical copy of the work, then this provision is, of course, superfluous. Altering a building would be like ripping pages out of a book or painting the proverbial moustache on a painting. Destroying the building would be like throwing the book or painting into a roaring fireplace. Of course, if one believes that mounting a copy of a painting on a ceramic tile constitutes making a derivative work, then adding a balcony to the facade of a building would likely be as well. Section 120(b) eliminates the need to stress out over the question by unambiguously immunizing the conduct from infringement liability.

§ 6.3   The Distribution Right

6.3.1   Basic Principles

The distribution right is provided by § 106(3), which creates the exclusive right "to distribute copies or phonorecords of the copyrighted work to the public by the sale or other transfer of ownership, or by rental, lease, or lending." The distribution right has been described as the "right to vend,"[109] and is essentially synonymous with the right to publish the work, since publication consists of the distribution of copies of phonorecords to the public.[110] As the quoted language makes clear, the right covers not only sales of material objects, but any other "transfer of ownership" thus including, among other things, the right to give away copies for free. The distribution must, however, be "to the public" meaning that a limited circulation of tangible objects embodying a copyrighted work to a group of carefully chosen recipients does not violate the distribution right.[111]

Unlike most of the other § 106 rights, the distribution right is not founded upon the making of an unauthorized copy. The distribution right instead concerns the *transfer* of copies or phonorecords to members of the public. This means that an individual can infringe the distribution right without impinging upon the copyright owner's other exclusive rights. For example, a retailer could purchase pirated movies recorded on DVDs and sell them to members of the public. If the retailer did not itself make the illegal copies, then it has not violated the reproduction right. Yet the retailer could face liability for violation of the distribution right.

---

108. 17 U.S.C. § 120(b).

109. Nimmer, § 8.11[A].

110. *See* UMG Recordings, Inc. v. Hummer Winblad Venture Partners, 377 F.Supp.2d 796, 803 (N.D. Cal. 2005).

111. If this sounds vaguely familiar, it is because it tracks the concept of "limited publication" discussed earlier in this tome. *See supra* § 4.1.1.1.

This would be true even if the retailer did not know that the copies were unlawfully made, and bought them in complete good faith. In this way, the distribution right gives the copyright holder some protection even where the party making illegal reproductions cannot be found and subjected to a lawsuit.

Logic suggests that for a distribution to take place someone, somewhere must have first made a copy (or phonorecord) of the work, and then either that person or someone else must transfer that object to a member of the public. After all, you cannot distribute something you don't have in your possession in the first place. One needs to print the book, press the CD, or duplicate the software onto a disc—or obtain those objects from others—before one can then "distribute copies or phonorecords" to the public. In the digital age, however, this sequence of events is often reversed. The owner of a copy can beam electrons over the Internet to any number of recipients without parting with his own copy, and with a second "copy" only being made when the information reaches the receiving computer. Such a "sender" is engaged in a transmission that results in the production of a new copy, but does not actually "send" a physical embodiment of the work from point A to point B. That raises the question whether a digital transmission that results in the production of a new copy on the "back end" of the transaction should be considered a distribution of the work.

While the case law is not extensive, those decisions that squarely address the point treat a digital transmission as a "distribution." For instance, *London–Sire Records, Inc. v. Doe 1*[112] was a lawsuit filed by several record companies against unnamed parties for illicit peer-to-peer sharing of music files over the Internet. Some of the defendants had not downloaded any files, but only had transmitted files to others. The plaintiffs insisted that these parties had violated their distribution rights, and the court agreed concluding that:

> while the statute requires that distribution be of "material objects," there is no reason to limit "distribution" to processes in which a material object exists throughout the entire transaction—as opposed to a transaction in which a material object is created elsewhere at its finish.... Read contextually, it is clear that this right was intended to allow the author to control the rate and terms at which copies or phonorecords of the work become available to the public.... What matters in the marketplace is not whether a material object "changes hands," but whether, when the transaction is completed, the distributee has a material object. The Court therefore concludes that electronic file transfers fit within the definition of "distribution" of a phonorecord.

112.   542 F.Supp.2d 153 (D.Mass. 2008).

Congress appears to have come the same conclusion back in 1995, when it added detailed provisions addressing "digital phonorecord deliveries" to the statute.[113] Specifically, section 115(c)(3)(A) provides that "a compulsory license under this section includes the right of the compulsory licensee to distribute . . . a phonorecord . . . by means of a digital transmission which constitutes a digital phonorecord delivery." There would be no need to include a "right to distribute" in the compulsory license if Congress did not think that the process of digitally transmitting files was not a distribution in the first place.[114]

Interestingly, however, in that same year, a bill that would have explicitly amended the distribution right section of the copyright act to include the word "by transmission" failed to secure passage,[115] making it difficult, as usual, to be sure of congressional intent. Moreover, some academic commentators have argued that both the plain language of the copyright statute and its legislative history exclude transmissions from the scope of the distribution right.[116] As we have noted earlier in this volume,[117] this view strikes us as the more plausible way to read a statute that Congress drafted long before the advent of digital networks. The statute affords other mechanisms to make sure that this interpretation does not become a loophole for infringers. Nonetheless the trend in the law seems in favor of treating digital transmissions as violative of the distribution right.

But what if a party merely makes a work available to the public without physically handing it over or electronically transmitting it? This problem first arose in the analog context. In *Hotaling v. Church of Jesus Christ of Latter–Day Saints*[118] the Hotalings had created a copyrighted compilation of genealogical materials which they published on microfiche. The Mormon church purchased one copy of this work for its main library in Salt Lake City. It then made additional copies from that one copy which it sent out to its branch libraries nationwide.[119] When the Hotalings learned of this

---

113. *See supra* § 7.4.

114. *See also Intellectual Property and the National Information Infrastructure*, Report of the Working Group on Intellectual Property Rights of the Information Infrastructure Task Force, September 1995 at 214 ("the distribution right as set forth in Section 106(3) of the Copyright Act can be . . . interpreted to include transmissions which distribute copies of works to, for example, the memories of computers.") (This report is often referred to as the White Paper in IP circles. It is available on-line at http://www.uspto.gov/go/com/doc/ipnii/ipnii.pdf).

115. H.R. 2441, 104th Cong., 1st Sess. (Sept. 29, 1995).

116. R. Anthony Reese, *The Public Display Right: The Copyright Act's Neglected Solution to the Controversy over RAM "Copies,"* 2001 U. ILL. L. REV. 83, 125–38.

117. *See supra* § 4.1.2 ("Publication Under the Current Statute").

118. 118 F.3d 199 (4th Cir. 1997).

119. It was undisputed that the library's activities exceeded the privileges provided in section 108.

practice and complained, the Church recalled and destroyed many of the illicit copies that it had made, and ceased making additional copies. Unfortunately, the Church also inadvertently destroyed the one legitimate copy that it had purchased. Consequently, it retained one of the other copies at its main library.

The Hotalings eventually filed suit, but by the time they did so, their claims for violation of the reproduction right were barred by the three-year statute of limitations.[120] Similarly, their claims of impermissible distribution based on the original transfer of copies to the branch libraries were time-barred as well. Consequently they argued that the Church violated their exclusive right to distribute the work by continuing to make available to the public the remaining illicit copy contained in its main library in Utah. The Church responded "that holding a work in a library collection that is open to the public constitutes, at most, an offer to distribute the work. In order to establish distribution, the Church argues, the evidence would need to show that a member of the public accepted such an offer." Because the library did not keep records of public use of their microfiche materials, the plaintiffs could not prove that anyone had ever looked at the work.

The Fourth Circuit nonetheless found a violation of the distribution right, noting that:

> [w]hen a public library adds a work to its collection, lists the work in its index or catalog system, and makes the work available to the borrowing or browsing public, it has completed all the steps necessary for distribution to the public. At that point, members of the public can visit the library and use the work. Were this not to be considered distribution within the meaning of § 106(3), a copyright holder would be prejudiced by a library that does not keep records of public use, and the library would unjustly profit by its own omission.[121]

One member of the panel dissented from this conclusion, finding that it did not conform to the statutory language. As Judge Hall explained:

> The owner of a copyright does not possess an exclusive right to "distribute" the work in any conceivable manner; instead, it has the exclusive right "to distribute copies . . . of the copyrighted work to the public by sale or other transfer of ownership, or by rental, lease, or lending." The Church did not sell or give an infringing copy to anyone.

---

120. The statute of limitations is found in 17 U.S.C. § 507(b). The Hotalings did not sue until the summer of 1995, and all of the impermissible copying had taken place in 1991.

121. 118 F.3d at 203.

The Church did not "rent" or "lease" a copy; indeed, the public may use the Church's libraries and all of their contents for free.

"Lending" is the only remaining candidate. Because they are for research, the libraries do not permit materials to be checked out and used by a member of the public off-premises. Do the libraries nonetheless "lend" a work each time a patron consults it? I think not. The patron might report that he "used" or "looked at" the work, but he would not likely say that it had been "lent" to him. Moreover, in this case, the plaintiffs do not even have any evidence that anyone used or looked at an infringing copy during the limitations period.

Cases on facts like *Hotaling* are likely to be exceedingly rare—the court addressed the distribution right in detail only because claims for impermissible reproduction were barred by the limitations period. What is considerably more common, however, is making computer files available for others to access and download at their request. If *Hotaling* is correct, the mere availability of materials on your hard drive would constitute a distribution of those materials if you connect your computer to the Internet and allow others to access those materials at their option. A number of courts have considered this problem—sometimes referred to as the "making available" or "deemed distributed" question—with inconsistent results.

For instance, the court in *A&M Records, Inc. v. Napster, Inc.*[122] took the view that when users of the infamous Napster service uploaded file names to a search index so that other users could find and download those files, they had violated the distribution rights of the relevant copyright holders even though they didn't transmit those files themselves.[123] A few years earlier, a district court in Illinois held that putting files of copyrighted materials on a web server so that others could download them violated the distribution right.[124] These cases and others that follow their lead essentially apply *Hotaling's* logic to the digital world.

On the other hand, the same court that decided *Napster*—the Ninth Circuit—declared a few years later in *Perfect 10, Inc. v.*

122. 239 F.3d 1004 (9th Cir. 2001).

123. "Napster users who upload file names to the search index for others to copy violate plaintiffs' distribution rights." 239 F.3d at 1014.

124. Marobie–FL, Inc. v. National Ass'n of Fire Equip. Distribs., 983 F.Supp. 1167, 1173 (N.D. Ill. 1997). *See also,* Motown Record Co., LP v. DePie-

tro, No. 04–CV–2246, 2007 WL 576284, at *3 n. 38 (E.D.Pa. Feb.16, 2007) ("While neither the United States Supreme Court nor the Third Circuit Court of Appeals has confirmed a copyright holder's exclusive right to make the work available, the Court is convinced that 17 U.S.C. § 106 encompasses such a right. . . .").

Amazon.com, Inc.,[125] that "distribution requires an actual dissemination of a copy," although elsewhere in that same opinion the panel seems to back away from that conclusion in an effort to reconcile its opinion with *Napster*. Similarly, Judge Wake, writing for the district court in Arizona, observed that "[m]erely making an unauthorized copy of a copyrighted work available to the public does not violate a copyright holder's exclusive right of distribution,"[126] and described this view as being in accord with "the great weight of authority." Another decision, this one from the Southern District of New York, specifically criticized the analysis of the *Hotaling* majority, noting that "*Hotaling* did not cite any precedent in holding that making copyrighted works available to the public constitutes infringement," and that its "interpretation, even if sound public policy, is not grounded in the statute."[127] Still a third group of courts have remained agnostic on the question, pleading ignorance of the technologies involved to avoid deciding the issue.[128]

With the law in this state of confusion it is hard to proffer safe generalizations. The more recent and more carefully reasoned opinions are, in our view, the ones that conclude that mere "making available" on a computer or otherwise is *not* a form of distribution.[129] A vendor who stocks his shelves and gets no customers has not distributed any goods. The fact that some courts have labeled this theory the "deemed distributed" theory indicates that even they recognize that no distribution has actually occurred, and that they are invoking a legal fiction by "deeming" something a distribution when nothing has yet been distributed. Moreover, a making available theory will rarely be necessary to vindicate a copyright owner's rights—most parties who "make available" electronic files

---

125. 508 F.3d 1146, 1162 (9th Cir. 2007).

126. Atlantic Recording Corp. v. Howell, 554 F.Supp.2d 976, 983 (D. Ariz. 2008).

127. Elektra Entm't Group, Inc. v. Barker, 551 F.Supp.2d 234, 242–43 (S.D.N.Y.2008).

128. Interscope Records v. Duty, 2006 WL 988086, at *2 n.3, 79 U.S.P.Q.2d 1043 (D.Ariz. 2006) ("To be clear, we do not conclude that the mere presence of copyrighted sound recordings in Duty's share file constitutes copyright infringement. We have an incomplete understanding of the Kazaa technology at this stage."); Warner Bros. Records, Inc. v. Payne, 2006 WL 2844415 at *4 (W.D.Tex.) ("[T]he Court

is not prepared at this stage of the proceedings to rule out the Plaintiffs' 'making available' theory as a possible ground for imposing liability. A more detailed understanding of the Kazaa technology is necessary...").

129. Of course, as we have already noted, we are dubious that even a digital *transmission* of a work meets the statutory definition of a distribution, so it should hardly surprise the reader to learn that we view the mere making available of a work on a digital network to fall far short of what the statute requires. For a detailed analysis of all of the relevant cases through 2008, *see* John Horsfield–Bradbury, *"Making Available" as Distribution: File–Sharing and the Copyright Act*, 22 Harv. J.L. & Tech. 273 (2008).

for illicit downloads by others can be found liable as contributory infringers when and if the file is impermissibly reproduced.[130]

6.3.2   Limitations on the Distribution Right

Many of the provisions we considered as limitations on the reproduction right also contain language that limits the distribution right as well. For instance, we saw that the libraries were free under certain conditions to make copies of works for patrons. Such a privilege would be silly if they could not then hand over the resulting copy to the patron, so the statute includes an explicit limit on the distribution right. Similarly the right to make Braille copies under section 121 also includes the right to distribute those resulting copies, and the right to take photographs of architectural works under section 120 includes the right to distribute those photographs. While it would be perilous to rely on common sense alone in dealing with the copyright statute, these limits on the distribution right are, well, just common sense.

6.3.2.1   First Sale Doctrine

Even though the owner of copyright in a work has the exclusive right to distribute copies or phonorecords of that work, the law has long recognized an important exception to the right. Usually called the "first sale doctrine," this limitation provides that once the copyright owner has parted with ownership of a particular copy of the work, he or she could not restrict further distribution of that particular copy. The Supreme Court held as much over a century ago in *Bobbs–Merrill Co. v. Straus*[131] and the principle has been codified in the present copyright statute as section 109. That section provides generally that:

> [T]he owner of a particular copy or phonorecord lawfully made under this title, or any person authorized by such owner, is entitled without the authority of the copyright owner, to sell or otherwise dispose of the possession of that copy or phonorecord.[132]

As one court summarized this provision, "[t]he first sale doctrine prevents the copyright owner from controlling the future transfer of a particular copy once its material ownership has been transferred."[133] The justification for the doctrine is that by selling the

---

130. *See id.,* concluding, "[t]he 'making available" doctrine does not survive a careful analysis ... A file-share who makes his file available for copying should not be found primarily liable for the eventual infringement. Instead, secondary liability is appropriate, and then only when the plaintiff demon-strates that actual reproduction has taken place" 22 HARV. J.L. & TECH at 299.

131. 210 U.S. 339, 28 S.Ct. 722, 52 L.Ed. 1086 (1908).

132. 17 U.S.C. § 109.

133. Columbia Pictures Industries v. Redd Horne, Inc., 749 F.2d 154, 159 (3d Cir. 1984).

physical copy initially, the copyright owner has already received the economic reward to which he or she is entitled, and it accords with a centuries-old common law hostility to "restraints on alienation" that prevent the owner of a chattel from disposing of it.[134]

The first sale doctrine only applies to the owner of a particular copy, or a person authorized by the owner, and then only if the copy was "lawfully made." So, the person who buys a bootleg or pirated DVD of a movie, and then resells it will not be protected by section 109—he is an infringer, liable for violating the copyright owner's distribution right. On the other hand, if the copy was made under authorization of the copyright owner, or pursuant to a compulsory license, it is subject to the first sale or exhaustion doctrine. This means that once you purchase a lawfully made book, CD, DVD, or other physical object embodying copyrighted material, it is yours to do with as you please. You may sell it on craigslist or at a tag sale on your front lawn. You may give it to you niece for her birthday. You can even throw it in the fireplace for the sheer pleasure of watching it burn.[135]

This is not the entirety of the story, however. Looking back at the scope of the distribution right, you will see that it includes the right to engage in rental, lease, or lending of copies of protected works. That means that—because the first sale exception of section 109 limits the distribution right—it permits the owner of a copy to engage in lending, leasing, and renting along with selling or gifting away. This is confirmed by the language of section 109 itself which allows the owner of a copy to sell or "otherwise dispose of the possession" of that copy. Consequently public libraries do not violate the distribution work when they lend out books—since they have purchased and own the books in their collection. For certain easily copied works, however, a rental market could quickly become a thinly veiled invitation to infringement.

For instance, imagine a store that—in old days—offered vinyl records or pre-recorded audio cassette tapes of popular music for overnight rental. It would not take a particularly fertile imagination to realize that instead of buying a new album or cassette for $10 at a retail record store, one could just rent it for a dollar, buy a blank cassette for another dollar, and copy the former onto the

---

134. *See, e.g.,* Dr. Miles Medical Co. v. John D. Park & Sons Co., 220 U.S. 373, 404, 31 S.Ct. 376, 55 L.Ed. 502 (1911) ("the right of alienation is one of the essential incidents of a right of general property in movables...."). *See generally,* PATRY ON COPYRIGHT § 13:18 ("The exhaustion doctrine was initially a creature of the judiciary, which re-acted against attempts to impose restraints on the alienation of tangible property.").

135. Unless it is a work of visual art of "recognized stature, in which case the Visual Artist Rights Act prevents you from destroying it." *See supra* § 7.1.2.

latter.[136] Voila. An almost perfect copy of the music for an eight dollar savings. The same problem could occur with other types of works such as computer programs. Of course, this would significantly diminish the economic reward that the copyright owner of the music and sound recording embodied in that cassette would be able to secure. While the copyright owner would have a theoretical cause of action against the duplicator for violation of the reproduction right, he would have no ability to shut down the rental store—they are protected by the first sale principle.

Not long after the adoption of the current statute, Congress decided that the first sale doctrine had to be limited to prevent this sort of practice. To do that it amended section 109 twice—first in 1984 via the Record Rental Amendment,[137] and then again in 1990 with the Computer Software Rental Amendments.[138] Because these provisions limit the first sale doctrine, which itself limits the distribution right, we can think of them as "exceptions to the exception." They are codified in section 109(b).

This section prohibits the rental—or "any other act or practice in the nature of rental, lease, or lending"—for commercial advantage to the public of either (1) phonorecords that contain a protected sound recording or musical work, or (2) storage media, such as disks or CDs, on which computer software has been recorded. The "any other act or practice" language insures that the statute reaches those who might try to evade the law by superficially structuring a transaction as something other than a rental—such as a sale with a promise to buy back the item the next day for one dollar less than the sale price. Lending of phonorecords or software by non-profit libraries or educational institutions for non-profit purposes are expressly excluded from § 109(b), and thus remain permissible. Note also that this "exception to the exception" does not cover copies of audiovisual works. Thus it is lawful for the owner of a copy of such a work to rent it for profit. This explains the legal viability of Blockbuster and Netflix.

The ban on software rentals in section 109(b) had the potential to cause surprising mischief. Virtually all products of any complexi-

---

136. For those few customers lacking the requisite fertile imagination, some of the rental stores sold (or gave away) blank tapes, and advertised "Never, ever buy another record." *See* PATRY ON COPYRIGHT, § 13:26, *citing* Audio and Video First Sale Doctrine: Hearings on H.R. 1027, H.R. 1029 and S. 32, Before the Subcommittee on Courts, Civil Liberties and the Administration of Justice of the House Committee on the Judiciary, 98th Cong. 1st & 2nd Sess. at 30 (1983, 1984).

137. Pub. L. 98–450 (1984). This legislation was set to expire after 5 years, but Congress extended it for another 8 years in 1988 (Pub. L. 100–617 (1988)), and then made it a permanent feature of the statute in the 1993 legislation that ratified the North American Free Trade Agreement or NAFTA (Pub. L. 103–182 (1993)).

138. Title VIII of Pub. L. 101–950 (1990).

ty today include various computer chips which embody copyrighted software. Companies from Hertz to Xerox might find themselves accused of copyright infringement for renting cars or photocopy machines because by doing so, they were also renting "copies" of "computer programs!" To negate any such result, the statute does not cover the rental of a computer program "which is embodied in a machine or product and cannot be copied during the ordinary operation or use of the machine or product."[139]

Another problem could have arisen with respect to the rental of video games cartridges meant to played on devices like a Nintendo Wii or an Xbox. Just like the modern automobile or photocopy machine, these items embody not just audiovisual works, but computer programs as well. Thus their rental might be thought an illegal violation of the distribution rights of the copyright owner. Nonetheless, the shelves of your local video store likely bulge with such games, leading you to intuit that it is probably not forbidden to rent them. Your deductive powers in this regard are validated by a further bit of statutory language that allows the rental of "a computer program embodied in or used in conjunction with a limited purpose computer that is designed for playing video games...."[140] An exception to the exception to the exception, if you will.

In *Brilliance Audio, Inc. v. Haights Cross Communications, Inc.*[141] the court had to determine whether a party who owned phonorecords of books-on-tape could legally rent them under the general first sale exhaustion principle, or was barred from doing by the record rental "exception to the exception." Finding the statutory language ambiguous, the court resorted to a study of the legislative history and policy considerations. It concluded that:

> § 109(b)(1)(A) is best read as providing only a limited exception to the first-sale doctrine for sound recordings of musical works. When considered with the legislative history and the policy rationales underlying the Copyright Act, Congress's use of the phrase "and in the musical works embodied therein" limits the statute's application to only those sound recordings that contain musical works. The language of the statute does not unambiguously apply to audiobooks, and we have found no evidence that it should be so construed.

One member of the panel dissented, and the opinion has attracted some academic criticism.[142]

---

139. 17 U.S.C. § 109(b)(1)(B)(I).
140. 17 U.S.C. § 109(b)(1)(B)(ii).
141. 474 F.3d 365 (6th Cir. 2007).

142. *See* Sean N. Kass, *Misinterpreting the Record Rental Amendment: Brilliance Audio v. Haights Cross Com-*

Our take is that the statute is indeed ambiguous on this point, and we find the majority opinion in *Brilliance Audio* persuasive. In divining Congressional intent, we think it salient that there is no more reason to forbid the rental of audiobooks than there is to forbid the rental of videotapes or DVDs. As a general rule, people enjoy listening to the same song, and using the same computer programs, over and over again. Thus, the incentive to duplicate a rented copy is very strong, especially if it can be done more cheaply than buying an authorized copy. By contrast, once you have seen a movie or read (or listened to) a book, your interest in seeing or hearing it again is usually much reduced. It follows that you are less likely to make a copy. That justifies a scheme in which it remains lawful for libraries to loan books and for video stores to rent DVDs, but in which you cannot rent a CD containing your favorite tunes or a copy of your favorite word processing program. Since the provisions of 109(b) were meant to prevent the widespread copying of rented materials, resolving ambiguities to exclude materials like audiobooks—where such copying will be relatively rare—strikes us as sound.

Finally, there is another "exception to the exception" worth at least a passing mention. Although the first sale rule of section 109 gives the owner of a particular copy of a work control over the disposition of that copy, at least one state has enacted legislation that, in a sense, limits that control. Under California's Resale Royalties Act,[143] when a work of fine art is sold for more than $1000 by an owner other than the original artist, the artist is entitled a royalty equal to five percent of the gross sales price, to be paid by the seller. The goal of the legislation is to permit the artist to share in the economic appreciation of the value of his work. The right to this royalty lasts for 20 years after the artists' death. A number of western European countries recognize a similar right under the name *droit de suit*. Laws of this sort have been criticized as actually depressing the market for art and as benefitting only a handful or prominent artists with significant name recognition whose works actually appreciate in value over time.[144] The California Resale Royalties Act was challenged shortly after its adoption by a litigant who claimed it was preempted by section 301 of the Copyright Act, but the Ninth Circuit found no preemption and the law remains on the books.[145]

munications, 21 HARV. J.L. & TECH. 297 (2007).

143. Cal. Civil Code § 986 (West 1983).

144. *See, e.g.,* Jon D. Stanford, *Economic Analysis of the Droit de Suite— The Artist's Resale Royalty*, 42 AUSTRA-

LIAN ECONOMIC PAPERS, 386 (2003) (available online at http://papers.ssrn.com/sol3/papers.cfm?abstract_id=461803).

145. Morseburg v. Balyon, 621 F.2d 972 (9th Cir. 1980), *cert. denied* 449 U.S. 983, 101 S.Ct. 399, 66 L.Ed.2d 245 (1980).

Digital technology has significantly changed the relevance of the first sale doctrine as a limit on the rights of copyright owners. Recall that any digital transfer of a copy involves making a new copy on the recipients machine. Thus when you re-sell a lawfully purchased downloaded music file or book you are not just "distributing" that copy or sound recording, you are also engaging in an act that triggers the copyright owner's reproduction rights. The first sale privilege of section 109 does not limit the reproduction right, and thus you would be an infringer if you did not have permission or could not point to another statutory safe harbor. This seems fair enough if you retained your original copy on your own computer. In that case the situation is analogous to making a photocopy of a book you own to give to a friend while retaining your own copy in your library.

What if, however, you destroy your digital copy of the work when you transmit it to a friend or purchaser, or if such destruction happens automatically through the operation of a "forward and delete" technology? Now the situation resembles the first sale fact pattern much more closely. You have parted with your copy in order to give it to someone else. The making of a copy is merely an artifact of digital technology and does not seem substantively significant, but it clearly transmutes this type of resale from legal act into an infringing one.

Other aspects of copyright law may also make first sale doctrine irrelevant in digital contexts. Much digital content is acquired under click-through licenses which may purport to forbid alienation of the material even if the original buyer (ahem ... licensee) destroys his copy in the process. Increasingly, much digital content is also protected by various forms of "digital rights management" software making it impossible to transfer the material to another computer, and it can violate the Digital Millennium Copyright Act (DMCA) to circumvent that software in order to effectuate a transfer.[146]

As part of the DMCA legislation, Congress instructed the Register to assess whether that statute had a serious effect on the operation of section 109. The Register submitted her report to Congress in December 2001.[147] In that report, she noted that "the tangible nature of a copy is a defining element of the first sale doctrine and critical to its rationale. The digital transmission of a

---

146. For a general discussion, *see* Victor F. Calaba, *Quibbles 'N Bits: Making a Digital First Sale Doctrine Feasible*, 9 MICH. TELECOMMUNICATIONS & TECH. L. REV. 1 (2002).

147. Statement of Marybeth Peters, The Register of Copyrights before the Subcommittee on Courts, the Internet, and Intellectual Property, Committee on the Judiciary, United States House of Representatives 107th Congress, 1st Session, available online at http://www.copyright.gov/docs/regstat121201.html.

work does not implicate the alienability of a physical artifact." Consequently she concluded no legislative change in section 109 was needed at this time. She did indicate, however, that changes in the marketplace might alter that conclusion.

While the Register's points may be well taken, the increasing migration of content to digital formats may mean that the day will not be far off when we will no longer have the equivalent of a used book market. In that world, the copyright holder who distributes a work will retain total control over the subsequent use and disposition of copies of that work. Many have questioned whether that would be desirable and advocated some kind of digital first sale doctrine.[148] A few years ago, Representative Zoe Lofgren introduced legislation to incorporate a digital first sale doctrine into the copyright statute, but it went nowhere.[149] A survey text on copyright law is not the place to explore all the pros and cons of this issue, but we will use our very small soapbox here to note that copyright law should reflect underlying policies and not merely be a Procrustean exercise in applying old law mindlessly to new technology—the fact that a computer necessarily makes copies as part of their routine operation does not seem, by itself, a good enough reason to declare the first sale doctrine inapplicable regardless of the other aspects of the transaction.

6.3.2.2 Imported Materials and the First Sale Doctrine

An interesting interpretive problem involving the first sale doctrine occurs when an importer purchases copies of copyrighted works abroad and seeks to bring them into the United States. Under section 602 of the Copyright Act, any such importation without the authority of the copyright owner is declared a violation of the distribution right and an actionable infringement.[150] When

---

148. *See, e.g.,* Nakmuli Davis, *Re-selling Digital Music Is There a Digital First Sale Doctrine?*, 29 Loy. L.A. Ent. L. Rev. 363 (2009); Matthew J. Astle, *Will Congress Kill the Podcasting Star?*, 19 Harv. J.L. & Tech. 161, 208 (2005); David W. Opderbeck, *Peer-to-Peer Networks, Technological Evolution, and Intellectual Property Reverse Private Attorney General Litigation*, 20 Berkeley Tech. L.J. 1685 (2005); Ann Bartow, *Electrifying Copyright Norms and Making Cyberspace More like a Book*, 48 Vill. L. Rev. 13, 110 (2003); and R. Anthony Reese, *The First Sale Doctrine in the Era of Digital Networks*, 44 B.C. L. Rev. 577 (2003).

149. H.R. 4536, 109th Cong. 1st Sess. (2005) would have added a new subsection (f) to section 109 reading: "(f) The privileges prescribed by subsections (a) and (c) apply in a case in which the owner of a particular copy or phonorecord of a work in a digital or other nonanalog format, or any person authorized by such owner, sells or otherwise disposes of the work by means of a transmission to a single recipient, if the owner does not retain the copy or phonorecord in a retrievable form and the work is so sold or otherwise disposed of in its original format." It never made it out of Committee.

150. 17 U.S.C. § 602. The section provides: "Importation into the United

the copies involved were made without the permission of the U.S. copyright owner, the rule seems to make perfect sense and poses no conflict with the first sale doctrine. Such "piratical" copies were never "sold" by the copyright owner, nor did it realize any revenue from them. It seems quite logical that their sale in the United States should be deemed a violation of the distribution right, and in this particular situation, the statute even provides for seizure of the copies at the border by U.S. Customs and Border Protection.[151]

On the other hand, if the copies in question were originally made and sold abroad legally and under the authority of the U.S. copyright owner, a conflict between the logic of the first sale doctrine and the language of section 602 emerges. Assume, for instance, that John Grisham were to license a publisher in London to reproduce and sell copies of his novel *The Runaway Jury.* Perhaps the book does not sell well there, and hundreds of copies are sitting unsold in a warehouse. At this point, an entrepreneurial American—let us call him Jay Rogers—buys up all these copies for a pittance, and ships them to the United States where there continues to be strong demand for copies of that particular novel.

Rogers will argue that, as owner of these particular lawfully made copies, the first sale doctrine permits him to resell them to whomever he wishes at whatever price he thinks best. Grisham would respond that the language of section 602 should trump the first sale principle and allow him to forbid the imports or to treat any domestic sales by Rogers as an act of infringement. The statute does not provide a ready reconciliation of these two provisions. Moreover, there is a variant on the situation. It might be that Grisham never licensed an English publisher, but rather had the books printed here in the United States and then exported them to England, where they languished in the aforementioned warehouse until Rogers bought them up and re-imported them.

In *Quality King Distributors, Inc. v. L'Anza Research International, Inc.*[152] the Supreme Court had occasion to consider that latter scenario. There, L'Anza made hair care products bearing a copyrighted label and sold them to distributors in the United States. Some products that L'Anza had produced in the United

States, without the authority of the owner of copyright under this title, of copies or phonorecords of a work that have been acquired outside the Untied States is an infringement of the exclusive right to distribute copies or phonorecords under section 106, actionable under section 501." The section then goes on to list three limited exceptions to the prohibition—importations by federal, state, and local government, importations for scholarly or educational purposes, and importations of single copies for personal use by tourists returning from abroad.

151. 17 U.S.C. § 602(b).

152. 523 U.S. 135, 118 S.Ct. 1125, 140 L.Ed.2d 254 (1998).

States and then exported were re-imported back into the United
States. These products were sold in California by unauthorized
retailers who purchased them from Quality King. L'Anza sued
Quality King for copyright infringement, asserting that the importation and sale of products bearing copyrighted labels violated the
distribution right.

The Supreme Court held that where a copy of a work of
authorship is lawfully made and sold in the United States, the first
sale doctrine applies under § 109. (In her concurring opinion,
Justice Ginsburg characterized the case as involving a "round trip
journey" in which copies of the copyrighted work travel "from the
United States to places abroad, then back again.") The result of the
Court's holding is that even if a copyright owner designates copies
for export, those copies may be re-imported without violating the
distribution right. The Court rejected L'Anza's argument that
§ 602(a) compelled a different result. Section 602(a) states that:
"[i]mportation into the United States, without the authority of the
owner of copyright . . . of copies or phonorecords of a work that has
been acquired outside the United States is an infringement of the
exclusive right to distribute copies or phonorecords under Section
106. . . ." The Court reasoned that the express language of § 106
provides that the distribution right is "subject to sections 107
through 121"—which included the first sale doctrine of § 109.
Stated differently, the Court reasoned that the ban on importation
set out in § 602(a) was really a species of the distribution right of
§ 106, which in turn is subject to the first sale doctrine of § 109.

In a number of subsequent cases, however, various courts have
held that if the imported goods were physically manufactured
outside the United States, the result will differ. Thus, in *Omega
S.A. v. Costco Wholesale Corp.*[153] the defendant, a well-known low-
price warehouse style retailer, imported Swiss-made Omega
watches which were marked on their underside with copyrighted
designs. When it offered them for sale in its U.S. stores, Omega
sued. Noting that the first sale doctrine of section 109 only applies
to copies "lawfully made under this title," the Ninth Circuit
reasoned that goods made abroad—even legally and with the permission of a multi-national copyright owner—were not made "under" Title 17 of the U.S. Code because of the presumption that U.S.
law does not operate extraterritorially.

The result is that in our original John Grisham scenario,
Grisham could prevent Rogers from selling books made in London
in the United States, even though Grisham licensed the production
of those books in London and received a royalty for their sale. The
net effect is that copyright owners can use section 602 to prevent

---

153.   541 F.3d 982 (9th Cir. 2008).

the importation of so-called "gray market" goods. This enables them to price discriminate between different national markets without fear that their U.S. prices will be undercut by sales of cheap imports.

Whether the facilitation of this type of strategy promotes the progress of science and useful arts has been subject to vigorous debate. Further discussion of this issue will surely be fueled by the Supreme Court's grant of *certiorari* in *Costco v. Omega* on April 19, 2010. Shortly after this book goes to press, the Supreme Court may issue a significant opinion regarding the applicability of copyright's exhaustion doctrine to foreign sales—a doctrine conveniently known as "international exhaustion." Because our publishers have already demonstrated an almost inhuman level of forbearance in awaiting to receive the manuscript for this text, your authors chose not to wait for a possible decision in *Costco v. Omega* before authorizing it for publication. Readers interested in international exhaustion should nonetheless be certain to follow developments in that litigation as they arise.

§ 6.4   The Public Performance Right

6.4.1   Basic Principles

Section 106(4) of the Copyright Act provides proprietors with the exclusive right to perform certain copyrighted works publicly. Section 101 reveals that the term "perform" means "to recite, render, play, dance, or act [the work], either directly or by means of any device or process." Suppose that a troupe of actors purchases a copy of a play still under copyright and, without permission from the playwright, stages a public theatrical performance of the work. This public stage production would constitute a copyright infringement. Because the performance right is independent of the reproduction right, the troupe has violated the public performance right even if no unauthorized mechanical copies of the play were made.

6.4.1.1   Doctrine of Multiple Performances

With the advent of broadcasting technology in the early decades of the last century, the courts had to consider whether each retransmission or reception of a broadcast constituted a separate performance. While it is clear that when a radio station plays a record, it is "performing" the music composition involved, does the owner of a radio also perform the work when he or she turns on the radio and makes the work audible? In a series of decisions from the 1930s through the late 1960s the Supreme Court vacillated on this question. The drafters of the 1976 Act came down firmly on the side of treating each retransmission or reception as a separate performance—a rule sometimes denominated the "doctrine of multiple performances." This means that you do indeed "perform" works whenever you turn on your radio, television, or more currently, direct your web browser to receive and transmit audio or video materials. It also means that entities such as cable and satellite television systems that pick up broadcast signals and forward them onwards to their subscribers are also engaging in performances of the various works involved.

6.4.1.2 Works Granted the Performance Right

The public performance right does not apply to all sorts of works. Section 106(4) expressly covers literary, musical, dramatic, and choreographic works; pantomimes; and motion pictures and other audiovisual works. Consequently, the public performance right does not apply to pictorial, graphic, or sculptural works. Those works, by their very nature, are not recited, rendered, acted, or danced. As the final section of this chapter explains, these categories of copyrighted material are, instead, entitled to the public display right of § 106(5).

More significantly, sound recordings are not accorded a public performance right. Of course most sound recordings are renditions of an underlying musical compositions. Thus when a disc jockey plays a CD on the radio, the station is performing *both* the musical composition in question and the sound recording. The performance of the musical composition must be licensed (unless the work is in the public domain) otherwise the station will be liable for copyright infringement. By contrast the performance of the sound recording has no copyright implications—that station is free to do that without seeking any permission or paying any royalties.

Congress denied the performance right to sound recordings on the assumption that the relevant copyright owner primarily made money through the sale of phonorecords, and that the public performance of their works—particularly on the radio—acted as free publicity that tended to encourage such sales. Indeed, for much of the twentieth century, record companies made covert payments to radio stations to induce them to play their phonorecords—a practice known as "payola" or pay-for-play.[154] For sound recordings, in other words, money did not flow from the performer (e.g., radio station) to the copyright owner in the form of a royalty, but rather in the opposite direction.

---

154. For a brief history and discussion of the legal regulation of Payola, see Peter M. Thall, WHAT THEY'LL NEVER TELL YOU ABOUT THE MUSIC BUSINESS: THE MYTHS, THE SECRETS, THE LIES (& A FEW TRUTHS) 135–42. *See also Sony Agrees to Halt Gifts for Airtime*, N.Y. TIMES, July 25, 2005 ("Sony BMG Music Entertainment, one of the world's largest record companies, agreed today to stop providing lavish gifts, free trips and other giveaways in exchange for airtime for its artists on radio stations, under the terms of a settlement with the New York attorney general's office.").

The historic business model of the record industry began to unravel during the last decade of the twentieth century. It became increasingly easy for individuals to call up and listen to sound recordings that they enjoyed on the Internet without having to purchase a physical object such as a CD. Bricks and mortar record stores went out of business and the sale of phonorecords plummeted. The record labels appealed to Congress and it responded by granting them a limited right to perform their works by "digital audio transmission." We will consider this digital performance right in the next chapter. More recently, however, the record labels have launched a full court press in Congress to secure full performance rights comparable to those granted to other works such as musical compositions.[155] Consequently, readers should be aware that the situation regarding performance rights for sound recordings is fluid and the law may have changed by the time you find yourself reading these words.

6.4.1.3 Right Limited to Public Performances

One of the most important aspects of the exclusive performance right is that it is limited to *public* performances. As observed by Justice Stewart: "No license is required by the Copyright Act, for example, to sing a copyrighted lyric in the shower."[156] Such a performance would, except for those who have very large showers and are unusually outgoing, be a private one. Determining precisely when a performance is public requires resort to the definition of that term found in section 101 of the current copyright act. When we deconstruct the relevant language we see that there are five different situations that can constitute a "public" performance.

The first is if the performance occurs "at a place open to the public." We can call this a performance in a "public place" and it would include such performances at venues such as concert halls, stadiums, movie theaters, and various open air locales such as a beach, public park, or city sidewalk. Second, a performance is also considered public if it occurs "at any place where a substantial number of persons outside of a normal circle of family and its social acquaintances are gathered." This is sometimes denominated a "semi-public" place, and it might include a law school classroom or a catered banquet hall in a hotel. It does not include your home, even if you invite a dozen friends over to watch the Super Bowl. We will, however, have more to say on watching the Super Bowl in a few moments.

155. At this writing, a bill to accomplish that has been passed by the House Committee on the Judiciary and reported to the full House for action. *See* H.R. 848, 111th Cong. 1st Sess.

156. Twentieth Century Music Corp. v. Aiken, 422 U.S. 151, 155, 95 S.Ct. 2040, 45 L.Ed.2d 84 (1975).

The third situation creating a public performance occurs if one were to "transmit or otherwise communicate" a work to a public place, and the fourth is if one were to transmit it to a semi-public place. Fifth and finally, it is also a public performance to transmit or communicate the work "to the public . . . whether the members of the public capable of receiving the performance . . . receive it in the same place or in separate places and at the same time or at different times." This last definitional scenario brings radio and television broadcasts directed to home audiences sitting in the privacy of their own family rooms within the scope of what is "public," even though the audience does not gather at the same location or receive the broadcast at the same time.

Like most definitions in the law, the definition of "public" in the copyright statute is fuzzy around the edges, which has led, inevitably, to litigation concerning ambiguous situations. For instance, in *Columbia Pictures Industries, Inc. v. Aveco, Inc.*[157] Aveco—the eventual defendant—operated a video cassette rental business. It also had fitted out several rooms on its premises that included seating, a video cassette player, and a television monitor. Customers could rent a room and a video cassette from Aveco and view it right on the premises, or bring a video cassette from outside the facility in order to play in a rented room. Of course, they could also rent video cassettes and simply take them home to watch on their own equipment.

When sued by various motion picture producers for violation of the public performance right, Aveco asserted that it prohibited unrelated groups of customers to share a viewing room. According to Aveco, the only performance occurred in a private viewing room rather than a public setting. Aveco further asserted that because it had legitimately purchased its videocassettes, the first sale doctrine of § 109(a) immunized its business model from copyright liability.[158]

The Third Circuit disagreed and held that Aveco had infringed the public performance right. Analogizing Aveco's viewing rooms to telephone booths, taxi cabs, and pay toilets, the court reasoned that each was "open to the public" even though usually not crowded with people. The key concept was that the viewing rooms were open to any member of the public with the inclination and means to employ Aveco's services. The court therefore judged the performances at Aveco's facilities to be "public" performances. Nor did the first sale doctrine insulate Aveco—the court noted that section 109(a) only limits the public distribution right of § 106(3), not the public performance right of § 106(4).[159] As a result, the fact that Aveco's owned the (lawfully made) video cassettes in question did

---

157. 800 F.2d 59 (3d Cir. 1986).

158. 800 F.2d at 63.

159. 800 F.2d at 64.

not affect the movie producers' exclusive right to authorize public performances.

By way of contrast, consider *Cartoon Network LP v. CSC Holdings, Inc.*[160] We described the basic factual situation in this case—involving remote storage DVR systems—at the beginning of this chapter, in connection with our discussion of reproduction rights.[161] The copyright holders in the case also asserted violations of their performance rights. They claimed that when users of the RS–DVR system called up their stored programs for playback, the cable system "transmitted" those programs to "members of the public" thus satisfying the definition of a public performance. The court disagreed, finding no public performance on these facts.

It began its analysis by noting that "it is relevant, in determining whether a transmission is made to the public, to discern who is 'capable of receiving' the performance being transmitted." While it recognized that the same *program* might be transmitted to many different individuals (for instance if thousands of people taped an episode of *Grey's Anatomy* for later viewing), it emphasized that each specific transmission of a recorded program would be directed only to one specific subscriber. As they put it, "the universe of people capable of receiving an RS–DVR transmission is the single subscriber whose self-made copy is used to create that transmission." This led to the conclusion that the transmissions were not "to the public" generally, as the statutory definition requires.

One final, recent, controversy concerning public performances deserves a quick note. For some time, many churches have hosted Super Bowl parties, inviting parishioners to watch the climactic game of the NFL season as a group in a community hall on a wide screen television. In 2007, the NFL "sent a letter to Fall Creek Baptist Church in Indianapolis, warning the church not show the Super Bowl on a giant video screen. For years, the church had held a Super Bowl party in its auditorium, attracting about 400 people and showing the game on a big screen usually reserved for hymn lyrics."[162]

The NFL apparently took the position that showing the game on a screen larger than 55 inches made it possible for a large audience to gather, making the event an infringing "public performance" absent a license. Many churches cancelled their annual events in response to the threats. A few days later, Senator Arlen Specter introduced legislation that would have specifically immu-

---

160. 536 F.3d 121 (2d Cir. 2008), *cert. denied sub nom.* Cable News network, Inc. v. CSC Holdings, Inc., 557 U.S. __ (2009).

161. *See supra* § 6.1.1.

162. *NFL Pulls Plug On Big-Screen Church Parties For Super Bowl,* Wash. Post, Feb. 1, 2008, available online at http://www.washingtonpost.com/wp-dyn/content/article/2008/01/31/AR2008013103958.html.

nized such performances from copyright liability.[163] Apparently, the NFL got the message. A few weeks later, they reversed themselves. According to a league spokesman, "the change was made to clarify confusion about the matter. 'We were not going after churches, not investigating churches and we have never sued a church,' [the spokesman] said ... 'What we're doing now is simply eliminating the question and confusion about copyright law.' "[164]

While other exotic performance scenarios on the fuzzy border between public and private performances can be imagined, the truth is that most cases do not present difficult problems of categorization. Radio stations, Broadway theaters, bars and clubs, and cable television networks are indubitably engaged in public performance. Listening to radio or TV in the privacy of your home or office is private. Much more legislative and judicial attention has been devoted to the question of when an indubitably public performance should be exempted from potential infringement liability through an exception to the performance right.

6.4.2 Limitations on the Public Performance Right

The Copyright Act includes a number of detailed exceptions to the public performance right. The 1976 Act's specific provisions stand in contrast to the 1909 Act, which generally exempted all non-profit public performances.[165] Experience under the 1909 Act suggested not only considerable difficulties in distinguishing non-profit and for-profit public performances, but also that many non-profit organizations possessed the means to pay copyright royalties.[166] As a result, the 1976 Act rejected the 1909 Act's blanket exemption for non-profit public performances in favor of more particularized exemptions. The majority of these are codified in section 110 of the current statute. In the sections that follow we will look at some of these exemptions in detail, and then take up the remainder somewhat more tersely in a grab-bag discussion. For each exception in the section pay particular attention to the types of works that may be legitimately performed, because each provision has its own list of included and excluded materials.

6.4.2.1 Educational Public Performances

There are two subsections of section 110 that deal with performances for educational purposes. The first and more straightfor-

---

163. S.2561, 110th Cong. 2nd Sess.

164. Adelle M. Banks, *NFL OKs Big–Screen Church Super Bowl Events,* February 21, 2008, The Pew Forum on Religion and Public Life, Religion News, http://pewforum.org/news/display.php?NewsID=15014.

165. *See* 1909 Act, § 1(c).

166. *See* Julien H. Collins III, *When In Doubt, Do Without: Licensing Public Performances by Nonprofit Camping or Volunteer Service Organization Under Federal Copyright Law,* 75 Wash. Univ. L.Q. 1277 (1997).

ward involves face-to-face teaching activities in conventional class-rooms, while the second deals with "distance learning." Congress thoroughly overhauled the distance learning provision in 2002 when it adopted legislation known as the Technology, Education and Copyright Harmonization Act, the acronym for which is, amazingly enough, the TEACH Act!

The face-to-face teaching exception to the public performance right is found in section 110(1). This provision covers works of all types provided that the performance is done by either a teacher or a pupil in a classroom or similar place, in the course of teaching activities of a nonprofit educational institution. As a result a teacher may lawfully read a poem or newspaper story aloud to his or her students, play a CD for the class or show the class a movie by putting a DVD in a DVD player and projecting the images on a screen. Note, however, that in that last case, involving an audiovisual work, the exemption is lost if the copy of the work (the DVD) was not lawfully made and the person performing it knew of that fact. This section deals solely with the right to perform the work and does not include any language limiting the copyright owner's *reproduction* rights. Thus, if a teacher wants to duplicate an article and distribute copies to the students, he or she must find refuge in the fair use doctrine; section 110(1) will be of no help.

By its own terms, the section 110(1) exemption does not apply to "for-profit" schools. Thus a profit-making organization that conducts Continuing Legal Education courses or a proprietary school offering training to aspiring hair stylists or bartenders cannot take advantage of this section. An instructor in such an environment would need a license to read excerpts of a book to the class or to show them a video, unless the situation could be characterized as fair use.

Like any legal rule, one can envision disputes on the margin about the scope of section 110(1). For instance, is the showing of a movie as part of a co-curricular event—let us say the meeting of a law school student organization—part of the "teaching activities" of the university? Do guest lecturers count as "teachers"?[167] Is a school auditorium a place that is "similar" to a classroom? However one resolves these relatively minor quibbles, it is important to bear in mind that teachers and students remain entitled to the privileges of the fair use doctrine of section 107 even for activities not covered by section 110(1). In other words, section 110(1) does

---

167. The legislative history declares that guest lecturers are covered by the provision, but that the exemption does not extend to actors, singers, or musicians brought in to perform works for the students. H. R. Rep. 94–1476 (994th Cong. 2nd Sess.) at p. 82. The Nimmer treatise wryly observes that "this suggests that any outside performer can be brought within the exemption by the simple expedient of conferring the title 'guest lecturer.'" NIMMER, § 8.15[B][4].

not represent the outer boundary of permissible classroom performances, but rather sets out only a floor.

Not all education is conducted face-to-face. For instance, back in the late 1970s, when the current copyright statute came into force, various non-profit and governmental entities provided regular programs of instruction via radio and television broadcasts. Consequently, the drafters of the statute also included, in section 110(2), exceptions to the performance right applicable in such circumstances. By the early years of this century, "distance learning" had migrated to the Internet, with students in many contexts taking on-line courses and accessing a variety of digital course materials. The TEACH Act also revised section 110(2).

Revised section 110(2) applies to the performance (or display) of any non-dramatic literary or musical work and "reasonable portions" of all other works by or in the course of a transmission. A non-dramatic literary work would include a short story, a newspaper article, or a poem. Works of this sort can be performed in their entirety under conditions that we will set out momentarily. On the other hand instructors or students can only show excerpts of works such as plays or movies, if they wish to remain within the safe harbor of this section. Presumably, this distinction reflects the fact that there is a market for on-line distribution of movies and other similar works, and that allowing them to be fully performed as part of distance learning programs might unfairly impact that market and the copyright owner's ability to make a profit.

Moreover, the statute excludes two kinds of works from its coverage entirely. The first exclusion is for works "produced or marketed primarily for performance or display as part of mediated instructional activities transmitted via digital networks." Here again, the congressional concern with market effects is apparent. If an author creates teaching materials that are meant to be licensed for on-line performances in connection with distance learning courses, a rule that allowed teachers to perform those materials for free would preclude any possibility of profit. That, in turn, would destroy the incentive for parties to prepare such materials in the first instance. The other exclusion relates to a performance or display given from a copy that was not lawfully made, where the performing party is aware of that fact. This is identical to the comparable limitation in the face-to-face teaching exception.

Assuming the right kind of work is being performed, the statute imposes four conditions on those who seek the benefit of the exception. First the performance must be either by or at the direction of the instructor and it must be an "integral part of a class session offered as a regular part of the systematic mediated instructional activities of a governmental body or an accredited non-profit education institution." The statute goes on to define "mediated instructional activities" as those that use the work in question as an integral part of the class experience, and where there is direct involvement of an instructor analogous to what would take place in a classroom.[168]

Second, the performance or display must be directly related and of material assistance to the teaching content of the transmission. Thus, the statute would not exempt the performance of background music while slides containing bullet points appeared on the screen, as the music would be incidental to the pedagogic purpose at hand and merely for the entertainment of the students watching the transmission. On the other hand, the statute would cover such musical performances in an on-line course on the history of modern jazz, where the instructor used the performances to illustrate the evolution of musical technique.

The third requirement is that the transmission is made solely for enrolled students or relevant government employees, and can only be received by them, to the extent that it is technologically possible to limit the transmission in such a fashion. Thus, the performances cannot be conducted over a publicly available web site to which anyone might navigate because that would enlarge the audience that might be able to enjoy the performance for free, to the economic detriment of the copyright owner. A log-in or password requirement ought, in most cases, suffice to satisfy this prong of the statute.

Finally, the relevant school or other transmitting body must institute policies regarding copyright, such as informing students that materials used in the course may be protected by copyright and by giving students materials that "promote compliance with" the copyright laws. Presumably this does not obligate the school to undertake the role of general copyright educator, but rather only requires them to explain proper usage of materials that their instructors may display or perform. In this regard section 110(2) also requires the school to apply technological measures to prevent retention or further unauthorized dissemination of the privileged performance, and to avoid interfering with anti-retention or anti-dissemination technology that the copyright owner may have included in the work. The purpose of this requirement is to prevent the version used in connection with the class in question to substitute for a permanent copy of the work which the student might otherwise purchase.

168. This definition appears in the second, unnumbered paragraph of section 110, following subsection (11).

The TEACH Act also provides that no entity engaging in a performance or display permitted by section 110(2) will be liable for infringement because of "the transient or temporary storage of material carried out through the automatic technical process of a digital transmission." This limit on the reproduction rights of relevant copyright holders is necessary on the theory that the loading of material into computer memory makes a copy. It follows that every time a teacher transmits a performance of a work via a digital network, he or she is also copying the work as well. Without the quoted language, the teacher and school would be immunized from violating the performance rights, but could be exposed to liability for violating reproduction rights.[169] Curiously, the statute does not explicitly extend this immunity from reproduction right infringement to the students, who necessarily also make copies when they receive the transmission on their own computers. Surely, however, such reproductions would fall safely within the fair use concept, otherwise the entire scheme of section 110(2) would be rendered null and void.

Before leaving the subject of educational uses of copyrighted works, there is one more feature of the current copyright act worthy of note. That is the compulsory license provided for public broadcasters found in section 118 of the statute. Broadcasters eligible for this license include noncommercial educational stations that actually transmit programs, and nonprofit organizations that produce programming for such stations. Thus a municipal radio station that offers programming for home-bound students (as well as National Public Radio and PBS television) can take advantage of this license, as could an organization such as the Sierra Club that produced a film concerning endangered species designed to be shown on an educational television station.

The section 118 license only applies to musical and pictorial, graphic, and sculptural works; parties are left to consensually negotiate royalty rates for other types of material such as literary works or audiovisual works. Upon payment of the governmentally determined royalty rate, the licensees may duplicate and distribute works as necessary to achieve their respective educational purposes and, of course, the licensed stations may perform and display the relevant works as well.[170]

---

169. The legislative history declares that the paragraph immunizing parties from liability for making transient copies "is not intended to create any implication that such participants would be liable for copyright infringement in the absence of the paragraph." S. Rep. 107–31 (107th Cong. 1st Sess.) at p. 13.

170. Royalty rates can be found in 37 C.F.R. §§ 253.4–253.8. The rate schedule is mind-numbingly specific. For instance, for the performance of musical work as background or theme music in a PBS program, PBS must pay a royalty of $56.81; entities other than PBS must pay $22.80 to display a work of visual

6.4.2.2 Non–Profit Public Performances

The copyright law of 1909 limited the copyright owner's exclusive public performance right to performances for profit. That meant that all non-profit performances were non-infringing. Of course, it also meant that courts periodically had to determine whether a given performance fell on the profit or non-profit side of the line—a question that proved troublesome in a number of cases. When Congress crafted the 1976 Act it eliminated the "for profit" reference in defining the public performance right. Instead, it created a limit exception to the right for certain non-profit performances. That exception is found in section 110(4).

Under this subsection, it is not an infringement to perform a nondramatic literary or musical work if the performing party has no purpose of direct or indirect commercial advantage and if the performers and promoters are not paid. Generally speaking, commercial establishments that play recorded or live music to enhance the ambiance of their facilities are considered to be performing the work for a commercial advantage.[171] They cannot rely on section 110(4) and must either secure a license, come within some other statutory exemption, or be adjudged infringers.

This exemption is limited to performances made in front of a live audience—transmissions are expressly outside the scope of the § 110(4) exemption. Consequently, non-profit broadcasters must look elsewhere in the statute for protection. In addition, to stay within the metes and bounds of § 110(4) there must either be no admission fee charged to the members of the audience, or, if a fee is charged, the net proceeds must be used exclusively for "educational religious or charitable purposes and not for private financial gain."

The non-profit exception removes many casual and economically insignificant acts from the realm of potential infringement. For instance, although it is a public performance to turn on a radio receiver or play CDs on a boom box in a public place such as a park or beach, doing so will not, in most cases, constitute copyright infringement.[172] This follows because playing your boom box at the beach is not done for commercial advantage, you don't pay anyone to put on the performance, and you don't charge admission. Similarly, you can stand on a soap box on a street corner and read

art as background or in a montage; and so on!

171. *See, e.g.,* Herbert v. Shanley, 242 U.S. 591, 37 S.Ct. 232, 61 L.Ed. 511 (1917); Major Bob Music v. Stubbs, 851 F.Supp. 475, 480 (S.D.Ga.1994) ("a profit-making enterprise which publicly performs copyrighted musical compositions is deemed to do so for profit.").

172. The qualification "in most cases" is necessary because the radio station could be playing an opera which would be a *dramatic* musical work, and if that opera were still under copyright section 110(4) would not apply. It is likely, however, that the fair use doctrine would preclude liability on those facts.

excerpts from copyrighted books or magazines to your heart's content because doing so falls within the provisions of section 110(4). By way of contrast, the typical busker, who plays a musical instrument out on the street while hoping that passers-by will deposit some coins in his open guitar or trumpet case, is ineligible for the exemption because he seeks a direct commercial advantage from the performance.

Section 110(4) also includes a special "veto" provision available to copyright proprietors. If an admission will be charged for the public performance, § 110(4) allows the copyright proprietor to serve a notice of objection. If the copyright owner provides timely notice in the proper format, then he may assert all rights applicable under the Copyright Act without regard to § 110(4). This "veto" insures that copyright proprietors are not required to provide fund-raising support towards causes they find objectionable by "donating" rights to use their works against their wishes. Curiously, however, section 110(4) does not require the non-profit performer to actually give notice of intent to perform the work, so in many cases, the copyright owner will not know of the performance in time to exercise the "veto" rights.

6.4.2.3 The "Home–Style" Exception

In the early 1970s George Aiken, the owner of a fast-food restaurant in Pittsburgh called "George Aiken's Chicken," found himself in the middle of a copyright controversy. He had placed a radio in his establishment and installed four speakers in the ceiling so that customers could listen to music and other programs while they dined at the few tables or waited for carry-out orders to be prepared. Apparently it was not a place to linger over finely prepared poultry—the record revealed that most customers spent only 15 minutes or less in the store. In any event, George did not have a copyright license permitting him to perform musical works, and Twentieth Century Music, the owner of copyright in some of the songs that customers had heard over the radio, sued him for infringement. Whatever his merits as a chicken chef, Aiken proved a feisty litigator, and he fought the matter all the way to the U.S. Supreme Court. Relying on earlier precedents involving cable television systems, the Court held that Mr. Aiken did not "perform" the works by merely making them audible when he turned on his radio.[173]

When Congress adopted the 1976 Copyright Act, it repudiated this analysis. As we have already seen, under the definition of performances in the current law, and under the "doctrine of

---

173. Twentieth Century Music v. Aiken, 422 U.S. 151, 95 S.Ct. 2040, 45 L.Ed.2d 84 (1975).

multiple performances," making a radio or television broadcast audible by turning on the receiver is now clearly considered a performance. Moreover, as we have also seen, publicly performing works at a place of business would not come within the non-profit exception of section 110(4) because it is considered to be for indirect commercial gain. Nonetheless, Congress decided to preserve the result of *Aiken*—despite legislatively overruling its logic—by enacting a specific exception to the performance right. This exception, codified in section 110(5) of the statute came to be called the "homestyle exception" for reasons that will become apparent shortly. It has proven politically controversial, led to a surprising amount of litigation, and ultimately triggered an international trade dispute.

As originally crafted, § 110(5) immunized the "communication of a transmission embodying a performance or display of a work by the public reception of the transmission." In English, that means that it does not violate the copyright laws to turn on a "receiver" such as a radio or television set, so that members of the public could see or hear the programming, even though portions of that programming consist of copyrighted material such as musical or audiovisual works. The privilege is limited however to reception of the transmission on "a single receiving apparatus of a kind commonly used in private homes." Hence the moniker "homestyle" for this subsection of the statute. The provision further requires that, to retain the exemption, no charge can be made to customers to see or hear the transmission, and the transmission cannot be retransmitted.

Nothing in section 110(5) limits its operation to the non-profit context, and the legislative history makes it plain that Congress was thinking of the George Aikens of the world when it inserted the relevant language into the law. Thus a corner bar may play a ceiling-mounted television so that patrons can watch programs while having a beer without the need to fear infringement liability, and a retail store may keep a radio blaring away on the counter to amuse customers and employees without having to secure and pay for a copyright license. Note however, that because the section is limited to receiving transmissions, it does not immunize a person who plays pre-recorded music (such as by placing an MP3 player in a cradle, or by playing CDs) nor does it immunize the hiring of persons to perform music live, such as "cover band" or piano player at a bar. Business wishing to resort to these sources of music must procure the necessary licenses to avoid violating the law.

The original version of § 110(5) resulted in two principal difficulties. First, the wording of § 110(5) contributed to uncertainty in judicial application. In the decades since the law was adopted home audio and video equipment has continuously evolved, becoming ever more elaborate, while often declining in price. This creates uncertainty about what sorts of apparatus are "of a kind commonly used in private homes."[174] Multi-speaker home theaters with in-ceiling wiring and massive video screens are no longer rare or the province only of the super-rich. As a result, copyright owners and small businesses have often had to litigate arcane equipment-related questions such as whether the use of a certain number of speakers or the arrangement of those speakers in a particular configuration is or is not a "homestyle" stereo device.[175]

Second, section 110(5) also seemingly focuses upon the presence of "a single apparatus" at an establishment—a rule that allowed chains with hundreds of stores to claim the exemption so long as they used no more than one apparatus at each one.[176] Given that such stores seem to be able to pay for numerous amenities that add appeal to the shopping experience, such as stylish carpeting and warm lighting, copyright owners argued that they should also pay for the music they use. On the other hand, retailers and restauranteurs have long argued that the demand for payments in connection with radio and television broadcasts is a form of double dipping, because the copyright owners have already been paid by the broadcasters, who securing performing rights licenses. The case law seems the embrace the view that the exception should be interpreted on a store-by-store, rather than on a chain-wide, basis.[177]

Feeling harassed by litigious copyright owners, the small business lobby appealed to Congress for both a clarification and expansion of the protections in section 110(5). Congress responded in 1998 by passing the Fairness in Music Licensing Act. That legislation redesignated the original exemption as section 110(5)(A) and added a new, excruciatingly detailed 110(5)(B) to the statute. Unlike the original provision, which continues to apply to works of all kinds, the new provision only applies to the performance of *nondramatic musical works*. The new provision otherwise retains the basic requirement of the original—it only applies to the "communication of a transmission" (and thus does not cover the playing of

---

174. *See* John Wilk, *Seeing the Words and Hearing the Music: Contradictions in the Construction of 17 U.S.C. § 110(5)*, 45 Rutgers L. Rev. 783 (1993).

175. *See, e.g.* Springsteen v. Plaza Roller Dome, Inc., 602 F.Supp. 1113 (M.D.N.C. 1985) (finding use of six speakers within exception because speakers were "inferior" to many used in homes); International Korwin Corp. v. Kowalczyk, 665 F.Supp. 652 (N.D. Ill. 1987), *aff'd* 855 F.2d 375 (7th Cir. 1988)

(exception unavailable where eight speakers used).

176. See Broadcast Music, Inc. v. Claire's Boutiques, Inc., 949 F.2d 1482 (7th Cir. 1991).

177. *Id. See also* Edison Bros. Stores, Inc. v. Broadcast Music, Inc., 760 F.Supp. 767 (E.D. Mo. 1991), *aff'd*, 954 F.2d 1419 (8th Cir. 1992), *cert. denied*, 504 U.S. 930, 112 S.Ct. 1995, 118 L.Ed.2d 590 (1992).

live music or pre-recorded material); no admission charge can be levied and the material cannot be further transmitted.

The innovation of the newly added subsection is the creation of "safe harbors" for small businesses based alternatively on the size of the establishment or on the equipment used. Restaurants of less than 3,750 square feet and other commercial establishments of less than 2,000 square feet are exempted from copyright infringement liability regardless of the equipment used.[178] Enterprises of larger size may also enjoy an exemption so long as they have a limited number of speakers (not more than 6, with no more than 4 in one room) and video monitors (no more than 4, with a maximum diagonal screen size of 55 inches).[179] For situations that do not come within these provisions, the original section still remains available. Thus a 4000 square foot restaurant that installs seven speakers connected to a radio receiver is ineligible for either safe harbor (too big, too many speakers), but still could attempt to convince a court that this arrangement is a "homestyle" receiving apparatus.

The Fairness in Music Licensing Act did throw a bone to copyright owners. It added a provision to the section of the statute dealing with damages providing that if a business owner invoking section 110(5) as a defense in an infringement suit did not have "reasonable grounds to believe that its use of a copyrighted work was exempt under such section," the plaintiff can recover additional damages equal to twice the amount of the license fee that the business owner should have paid for the use of the work during a period of up to the preceding three years.[180] In the decade since Congress added this language to the statute there are no reported cases reflecting an award of enhanced damages under its provisions.

Most observers view the Fairness in Music Licensing Act as a victory for retailers and restaurant owners. The generous size and equipment specifications of § 110(5)(B) significantly exceed what many assumed to have been the outer limit of the original homestyle exception. However, the provisions of section 110(5) had, from

---

178. The statute contains details on how the size of an establishment should be calculated. For instance, patio seating areas are included, but parking areas are not.

179. The inclusion of video monitors may seem odd given that this subsection only deals with the performance of non-dramatic musical works, but many television broadcasts include a musical component. Thus if a copyright owner of a musical composition sued for infringement of the performance right

because his tune was made audible by a television set playing at a restaurant, the restaurant owner could rely on the size-of-premises or equipment provisions to escape liability. By way of contrast, if the owner of copyright in a poem that was read during a television broadcast brought suit for the unlicensed performance of the poem, section 110(5)(B) would be unavailable and the restaurant owner would have to rely on 110(5)(A) to escape liability.

180. 17 U.S.C. § 504(d).

the outset, been a sore point with U.S. treaty partners under the Berne Convention. That agreement expressly provides authors, in Article 11*bis*, with the exclusive right to authorize "the public communication by loudspeaker or any analogous instrument transmitting, by signs, sounds, or images, the broadcast of the work." Although international agreements allow certain narrow exceptions to this exclusive right, some observers believed that the original version of § 110(5) exceeded their permissible scope, especially after various judicial interpretations that seemed to broaden the scope of the exemption. Consequently, the 1998 amendments became something of a last straw on the proverbial camel's back, and precipitated an international challenge to U.S. law.

Specifically, member states of the European Community, after receiving complaints on behalf of the Irish Music Rights Organization, filed a formal complaint with the World Trade Organization (WTO), which ultimately rendered its judgment in 2000. The panel rendered something of a split decision. In favor of the United States, the WTO held that the original "homestyle exemption," now codified in § 110(5)(A), conformed with Berne Convention requirements. In favor of the European Community, however, the WTO found that the § 110(5)(B) exemption added by the Fairness in Music Licencing Act did not satisfy the Berne Convention because it constituted too great an imposition on the rights of copyright owners.[181]

Despite the adverse WTO holding, Congress has yet to amend § 110(5) to eliminate those provisions found violative of our treaty obligations. In the interim, the United States has assured our treaty partners that it is working with Congress to secure a legislative fix, although, as the Nimmer treatise notes, this "pronouncement about continued consultation with Congress seems like a fig leaf that is wearing thin."[182]

6.4.2.4   Other Section 110 Exceptions

Six other subsections of section 110 limit the public performance right in various ways. Most of these provisions are fairly narrow and have not given rise to any litigation. In some cases, they represent accommodations to special groups with special needs that appealed to Congress for a relaxation of the general copyright rules of the road.

---

181. The decision is captioned simply *United States–Section 110(5) of the U.S. Copyright Act,* and designated by the docket number WT/DS160/R. It is available on line at http://www.wto.org/english/news_e/news00_e/1234da.pdf.

182. NIMMER, § 18.09[D].

Section 110(3) deals with public performances that take place during religious services. It covers performances of nondramatic literary and musical works and/or dramtico-musical works of a religious nature as well as displays of works, provided they take place in course of services at a place of worship or other religious assembly. Thus a rabbi may quote from a newspaper article during a sermon in a synagogue and a church choir may sing a popular song during Sunday morning services.

Section 110(6) permits governmental bodies or nonprofit agricultural and horticultural organizations to perform nondramatic musical works at an annual agricultural or horticultural fair. The listed entities are not only exempted from liability for their own performances, but also excused from vicarious liability for illicit performances by parties such as concessionaires at the fair. Those parties themselves, however, remain liable if they perform without the necessary licenses. As your devoted authors both hail from highly urban parts of the country, we can offer little further insight about this importance of this exemption, except to note that it conjures up notions of overall-clad banjo players strumming a tune to amuse fairgoers en route to the tractor pull.

Section 110(7) immunizes the performance of nondramatic musical works by "vending establishments" where the purpose of the performance is to promote either the sale of copies or phonorecords of the work, or to promote the sale of equipment used to play the work. Thus Best Buy may play music in order to encourage customers to purchase a given CD player and a record store (if any still exist) may play music in order to encourage patrons to buy the CD to which they are listening. The exception is lost if the performance is transmitted beyond the immediate confines of the store. Because this section does not cover audiovisual works, it does not protect a DVD rental store such as Blockbuster if it chooses to play those DVDs on video monitors in the store. In most cases, however, such stores have secured the necessary permission from the distributor of the DVDs and thus are safe from infringement claims.

Sections 110(8) and 110(9) both deal with non-profit performances via transmissions that are specifically designed for and directed to visually or aurally handicapped persons, such as those who are blind or deaf. The former subsection deals with performances of non-dramatic literary works—in others words the reading of excerpts from works of prose or poetry—while the latter deals with performances of dramatic works. The scope of permissible performances of dramatic works are considerably narrower than that for other works, which explains the need for two separate subsections. A dramatic work can only be performed once, and no earlier than 10 years after its first publication.

Finally, section 110(10), added to the statute in 1982, immunizes performances of both non-dramatic literary works and musical works at social functions held by veterans' organizations or nonprofit fraternal organizations, provided the general public is not admitted to the event, and that the proceeds of the event are used for charitable purposes. Thus a chapter of the Kiwanis Club sponsoring a dinner to raise funds for a local hospital, may play (live or recorded) music at that dinner without the need to secure a copyright license.

6.4.3 Performing Rights Societies

The enormous number of musical performances that occur every day in the United States suggests the great potential value of the public performance right. Not only is music being constantly performed on terrestrial and satellite radio and conventional and cable television, but it is the background soundtrack for much of our lives. We hear music as we board an airplane, when we walk through a shopping mall, when we wait "on hold" on the phone, and when we attend an athletic event. However, the sheer number of times musical works are played, as well as the ephemeral nature of each performance, make it difficult for copyright owners to police their rights. And even a well-intentioned performer who wants to perform a relatively small number of musical works could find it time-consuming and burdensome to obtain licenses from multiple musical copyright holders. As an economist would summarize, the transaction costs associated with exploitation of the performance right are thus very high.

Composers and songwriters, along with their publishers, have attempted to reduce these transaction costs by designating entities called "performing rights societies" as their collective agent for licensing the performance rights to their musical works, and empowering them to enforce their rights by policing the market to discover and prevent unauthorized (which is to say uncompensated) public performances. As the copyright statute puts it, a "performing rights society" is "an association, corporation, or other entity that licenses the public performance of nondramatic musical works on behalf of copyright owners of such works, such as the American Society of Composers, Authors and Publishers (ASCAP), Broadcast Music, Inc. (BMI) and SESAC, Inc."[183] Performing rights societies essentially act as middlemen, streamlining the process through which copyright proprietors can offer, and performers can obtain, licenses under the public performance right.

A review of the operations of ASCAP provides a helpful example of the workings of a performing rights society. ASCAP is the

---

183.   17 U.S.C. § 101.

largest U.S. performing rights society, boasting hundreds of thousands of members and a repertory of several million songs. Composers, songwriters, and publishers who join ASCAP grant it a nonexclusive right to license nondramatic public performances of their works. Members also grant ASCAP the right to police the performance right and, if necessary, to bring copyright infringement suits in their names.

In turn, persons or enterprises that wish to perform works within this repertory—including radio broadcasters, restaurants, bars, shopping malls, concert halls, and sports arenas—may contract with ASCAP. ASCAP offers a "blanket license" that allows licensees to perform publicly any song within its repertory as frequently as the licensee desires during a specified period of time—usually a year. ASCAP license fees are calculated based upon the size and revenues of the licensee, and can range from a modest few hundred dollars a year for a corner bar that has a live garage band one night a week to many millions of dollars for a major television network. After deducting operating expenses ASCAP distributes these licensing fees to its members to compensate them for the performance of their works.

ASCAP employs sophisticated sampling methodologies and complex calculations to determine how often a work has been publicly performed as well as the value of each performance. To give you some sense of the scale of this enterprise, ASCAP reported revenues of $863 million in 2007 and after deducting approximately 12 percent for its own operating expenses it distributed $741 million to its members.[184] Because ASCAP is able to pay employees to visit establishments to determine if they are playing unlicensed music, and because it is empowered by its members to file infringement suits, music users have significant incentives to purchase a license rather than risk litigation. Some music users contend, however, that ASCAP uses overly aggressive methods and may even harm the interests of up-and-coming acts who would prefer greater exposure for their music to a nominal royalty fee.

Given the collective nature of ASCAP and the other performing rights societies and the power that it exerts in the music industry, various parties have asserted antitrust claims against them over the year. As a result of one of these lawsuits, ASCAP operates under the terms of a consent decree issued by the U.S. District Court for the Southern District of New York. That decree compels ASCAP to adhere to practices designed to preserve some degree of competition in the music field, including a requirement that ASCAP obtain only nonexclusive (rather than exclusive) authority from its members to grant licenses. This allows composers and

184. http://www.ascap.com/press/
2008/0208_financial.aspx.

music publishers to license performing rights directly and allows a music user who wants only to play a single song on a single occasion to deal directly with the copyright owner instead of with ASCAP.

ASCAP and the other performing rights societies do not license rights to make physical reproductions of musical works, whether on sheet music, on CDs, or via digital downloads. Those "mechanical" licensing rights are handled by the Harry Fox agency, mentioned earlier on in this chapter. Similarly, ASCAP and the others do not grant licenses to reproduce music as part of the sound track of motion pictures. Those rights are licensed directly by the relevant copyright owners. Nor do they grant the right to use music in connection with live theatrical productions. Those rights, known as dramatic or "grand" rights, remain for the copyright owner to license and enforce. (A performance is considered dramatic when it assists in the development of a larger plot, while nondramatic performances do not advance a separate story line.[185]) The rationale for this distinction is that dramatic performances occur less frequently than nondramatic ones and, given the usual publicity and attendance surrounding them, are easier to detect.[186]

Finally, note that performing rights societies do not license the right to perform sound recordings. In many cases, no license is needed to perform a sound recording because sound recordings are not granted a general performance right under the statute.[187] As we have seen earlier, however, the copyright owner in a sound recording (usually a record company) does have an exclusive right to perform that recording by digital transmission. Parties wishing to license that right—such as satellite radio stations, digital music channels on cable systems, or webcasters—must obtain the necessary license from the non-profit performing rights society Sound Exchange.

6.4.4   Secondary Transmissions

The practice of making additional, simultaneous transmissions of original broadcast transmissions is known, not surprisingly, as a "secondary transmission."[188] Secondary transmissions are considered public performances under the current copyright statute and thus implicate the exclusive rights of the copyright owners whose works are being retransmitted.[189] When a purely "passive carrier"

---

185. See Seltzer v. Sunbrock, 22 F.Supp. 621, 628–29 (S.D.Cal. 1938).

186. *See* I. Fred Koenigsberg, *Overview of Basic Principles of Copyright Law*, 238 PLI/PAT. 9, 44 (1987).

187. *See supra* § 6.4.1.2.

188. 17 U.S.C. § 111(f).

189. The Supreme Court had held just the opposite in Fortnightly Corp. v. United Artists Television, 393 U.S. 902, 89 S.Ct. 65, 21 L.Ed.2d 190 (1968) and Teleprompter Corp. v. Columbia Broadcasting Sys., 415 U.S. 394, 94 S.Ct. 1129, 39 L.Ed.2d 415 (1974), decided under the 1909 Act.

engages in a secondary transmission—not making any decisions about what to retransmit or about the content of the transmission but merely receiving the signal and then sending it further on its way—the copyright statute immunizes that party from infringement liability.[190]

Things get more complicated, however, when we consider secondary transmissions by parties other than passive carriers. The most common entities that fall in that category are cable and satellite television systems. Cable and satellite television systems engage in secondary transmissions, by definition, because they receive the signals of certain broadcast stations and retransmit them to their subscribers.[191] They are not passive carriers, however, because they make decisions about which primary broadcasts they will retransmit, and they also choose the recipients (limiting the transmission to their own paid subscribers). Congress therefore decided to create compulsory license systems that would insure that these entities would be legally allowed to retransmit, while simultaneously providing copyright owners appropriate compensation for the use of their material.

The Copyright Act currently contains three separate compulsory licenses. Section 111 deals with retransmission by cable television systems; section 119 deals with the retransmission by satellite systems of transmissions from distant markets; and section 122 deals with the retransmission of local signals by satellite systems. These provisions are quite complex. Understanding them requires at least some knowledge of the technology, the economics, and the larger regulatory context of the industries involved. Space limitations preclude delving into this material in great depth in this volume,[192] but a few key points can be grasped quite easily.

First, note that retransmitted broadcast signals can originate in the same local market where subscribers are located or can come from a distant market. For instance, if you live in suburban

---

190. 17 U.S.C. § 111(a)(3). A typical example of a "passive carrier" is a long distance telephone provider, which does not get to pick and choose whose conversations to transmit and does not control the content of the conversations. There are entities that essentially perform the same function for video communications, receiving signals from broadcast stations and then sending them on their way over their own wires, without making any choices about what to send or to whom to send it.

191. Of course most of the channels carried by cable and satellite systems are not retransmissions of broadcast channels. Rather they are the so-called "cable channels" such as ESPN, CNN, Comedy Central, the Food Network, Bravo, and so on. The cable and satellite systems contract directly with each of these entities and those contracts include relevant copyright license and payments sufficient to compensate the copyright owners in question.

192. Lest you think we are wimping out, the eight-volume Patry copyright treatise declares that the "many details of Section 111 [are] well beyond the scope of a general treatise on copyright." PATRY, § 14:50.

Washington, DC, and subscribe to either DISH TV (a satellite provider) or COMCAST cable TV, you will be able to tune into WRC, the local Washington NBC affiliate station, on your cable or satellite equipped television. You will also likely be able to receive some stations from distant markets such as WGN in Chicago or WOR in New York City.[193] When Congress considered the subject, it concluded that retransmission of local signals is less economically significant to copyright owners than retransmission of distant signals.

This follows because of the economics of the industry. Television stations earn revenue by selling advertising time. Advertisers do not pay cable or satellite systems, who are generally obligated to retransmit material "as is" with all the commercials intact. A local advertiser—let us say a car dealership in Chicago—pays Chicago station WGN based on the number of viewers who will see the advertisement, including local viewers who see the ad on cable rather than "over-the-air." That advertising car dealer, however, is unlikely to pay WGN any extra money because its advertisement is retransmitted by a cable system to viewers in distant markets like Atlanta or Seattle because those remote viewers are not going to patronize a car dealership in Chicago. Since WGN cannot charge any extra for the fact that programming is retransmitted, the royalties it pays for a program will not take those extra viewers into account. Consequently, if the copyright owner is to be compensated for the use of the material in Atlanta and Seattle, the compensation would have to come from a royalty paid by the retransmitting party (i.e., the cable system).

As a result, under section 111, cable systems are essentially allowed to retransmit local (and network) signals for free, but are obligated to pay significant sums for the privilege of retransmitting distant signals. This is also why Congress dealt with satellite retransmission of local and distant signals in two different provisions of the statute, and why—parallel to the approach for cable systems—the satellite local retransmission provision provides for a royalty-free compulsory license.[194]

Second, common sense tells us that the more subscribers a cable or satellite system has, the more viewers there are who can see a given retransmitted work. The statutory royalty rates for cable systems under retransmission of distant signals take this fact into account by classifying systems by size. Third, the Federal Communications Commission heavily regulated the cable television

---

193. These stations are sometimes referred to as "superstations."

194. 17 U.S.C. § 122(c) ("A satellite carrier whose secondary transmissions are subject to statutory licensing under subsection [122](a) shall have no royalty obligation for such secondary transmissions.").

industry when Congress drafted the 1976 Copyright Act. In 1980, the FCC deregulated the cable industry. As a result, the administratively set royalty rates for cable retransmissions now include a variety of complex computations designed to compensate copyright owners for lost revenues flowing from these changes.

The royalties due under the cable license are paid to the Copyright Office. The various copyright owners who claim entitlement to portions of this fund—such as movie producers (represented by the Motion Picture Association of America), sports leagues, and music copyright owners (represented by ASCAP and BMI)—can agree among themselves how the money should be split, and are granted immunity from antitrust laws to reach such an agreement. If they cannot do so, the allocation will be the subject of an administrative decision by the Copyright Royalty Judges with review by the courts.[195]

The section 119 license for satellite retransmission of distant signals is similar but not identical to the cable license. For instance, it contains differences in how royalties are calculated, and complicated provisions about just when satellite systems can retransmit network programming. The original 1976 Act did not include this provision, for the obvious reason that satellite TV systems did not exist at that time! By the late 1980s however, such systems had proliferated and had become economically important, so in 1988 Congress added the satellite licensing provision to the law. It did so, however, on an explicitly temporary basis, expecting that within five years the industry and copyright owners could negotiate royalties under voluntary licensing.

It didn't happen. Instead Congress reauthorized the section 119 license in 1994, and then in 1999 it passed the Satellite Home Viewer Improvement Act. That legislation created the special, royalty-free license for retransmission of local signals, which was codified in new section 122, extended the section 119 license for yet another five years, and reduced the royalty rates that had been previously set administratively. In 2004 Congress returned to the subject of satellite retransmissions for a fourth time, when it adopted the Satellite Home View Extension and Reauthorization Act of 2004, or SHVERA.[196] You may not be entirely surprised to hear that this bill extended the section 119 license for another five year, through December 31, 2009. At this writing, a bill entitled the Satellite Television Modernization Act of 2009[197] has been passed by

---

195. For one example of a dispute over the division of royalties from the section 111 license, *see* Program Suppliers v. Librarian of Congress, 409 F.3d 395 (D.C. Cir. 2005).

196. The legislation is actually a part of the Consolidated Appropriations Act of 2005, Pub. L. No. 108–447.

197. S.1670 (111th Cong. 1st Sess.).

the Senate Judiciary Committee and is working its way through the legislative process. Try not to be too astonished to learn that this bill would extend the section 119 license for five years, through the end of 2014.

§ 6.5   The Public Display Right

6.5.1   Basic Principles

Section 106(5) of the Copyright Act grants copyright owners the exclusive right to display the copyrighted work publicly. Under § 101, to display a work means to show a copy of it, either directly or indirectly, through the use of a film, slide, television image, or any other device or process. The public display right applies to literary, musical, dramatic, and choreographic works, pantomimes, and motion pictures, and other audiovisual works.[198] Thus, absent licensing or exemption, it is infringing to display a painting in a gallery, to hold up a page of a book before a live audience, or to broadcast images of sheet music during a television transmission. The display right is not extended to sound recordings, because such works do not have visual components and there is no economic value associated with the display of a compact disk or audio cassette. The display right is also not extended to works of architecture.

Like the performance right, the display right is only triggered if the display is public. Moreover, the same definition of "public" applies in this case as in the case of public performances.[199] Consequently, when an individual displays a work of visual art within the privacy of his home, no concerns over the public display right will arise.

The distinction between the public performance right and the public display right can sometimes be a fine one. If a theater uses a projector to show a copyrighted motion picture without authorization, would this act constitute a public performance or public display? The answer, it turns out, depends on whether the images of the motion picture are shown in sequence or not. If these images are shown in sequence, then the public performance right is implicated.[200] If the theater instead showed individual images nonsequentially—such as stills from the motion picture—then the public display right would be at stake.[201]

The display right had not been a subject of much controversy in copyright law until recently. The details of Internet technology, however, have spawned a few intriguing disputes, most notably the

---

198. 17 U.S.C. § 106(5).

199. *See supra* § 6.4.1.

200. 17 U.S.C. § 101.

201. 17 U.S.C. § 101.

one involved in *Perfect 10, Inc. v. Amazon.com Inc.*[202] The plaintiff in this litigation operated an adult-oriented web site that posted images of nude models and sold access to its site for a fee. Various individuals not involved in the lawsuit had copied those images and re-posted them on other sites where they were often accessible for free. Google, and the other defendants, operate search engines with image-search capability. Those search engines provide responses to a user query in the form of reduced-size low resolution images (so-called "thumbnails") depicting what is available on other parties' sites.

In the case of Google, when a user clicks on one of the thumbnails, a two-part screen appears with a smaller upper section containing the thumbnail and data about the image, and the larger lower section opening the actual web site where the full-sized image resides. The material in the upper frame, including the thumbnail, comes from Google's own computers; the material in the large lower frame is generated by the distant computer, although all the material appears on a single screen. (This juxtaposition of material from different sources is known as "in-line linking"). The end result is that web surfers using Google could find, and see, full-sized versions of copyrighted images owned by Perfect 10 without having to go to Perfect 10's web site, or pay for the privilege, because the search engine turned up various unauthorized copies lurking all over the Internet. Perfect 10 was not happy and sued Google and other search engines (at the time Amazon, named in the caption, operated a search engine known as A9). Perfect 10 alleged, among other claims, that Google's image search constituted an infringement of its display rights in the full-sized images.

The district court applied what it called a "server test" to resolve the claim. Under that test, if a party stores an image on its own computers and then delivers that image to a user on demand, it is engaged in a public display in violation of the copyright statute. On the other hand, if the image is not stored on that party's own computers, linking to the image would not constitute a display. Applying the test to the facts before it, the court exonerated Google and the other defendants because they did not store the full-sized images on their own computers. The Ninth Circuit accepted this analysis.

As that court put it, "instead of communicating a copy of the image, Google provides HTML instructions that direct a user's browser to a website publisher's computer that stores the full-size photographic image. Providing these HTML instructions is not equivalent to showing a copy." The court reaching this conclusion because the HTML computer code consisted of lines of text, not a

---

202. 508 F.3d 1146 (9th Cir. 2007).

photographic image, and because that HTML code does not itself cause the contested image to appear, but merely gives the computer user's browser the address of the website where the image resides. In other words, the "linked-to" website displayed the image, not Google. If you find this a bit murky, try a fanciful analogy. Imagine that your humble authors have compiled a massive index of all the paintings hanging in all the museums of the world, along with a pair of extremely powerful x-ray binoculars. When you ask us about a given painting, we immediately tell you where it is located, hand you a pair of our binoculars, and give you the coordinates of the museum. You are enabled, as a result, to see the painting, but that is not because we "displayed" it to you—rather it was displayed by the museum where it hangs.

Perfect 10 protested that this interpretation effectively requires a reproduction of the image in order to make out a violation of the display right, and it argued that this tended to merge two entirely different privileges of copyright ownership that should be kept separate. The court dismissed that complaint with the observation that "nothing in the Copyright Act prevents the various rights protected in section 106 from overlapping." Despite this response, the court's approach does come close to reading the display right out of the statute in the Internet context because it becomes impossible to violate the display right without simultaneously violating the reproduction right.

6.5.2 Limitations on the Public Display Right

The Copyright Act includes a significant limitation on the public display right. Under section 109(c) the owner of a lawfully made copy of a work, or any person authorized by that owner, is allowed to publicly display the work without authority of the copyright owner, either directly or by projecting no more than one image at a time to viewers located in the same place as the copy of the work.[203] This means that if a museum or art gallery makes a legitimate purchase of a work of visual art from an artist, then § 109(c) allows it to display that work to the public without needing to secure a license or pay a fee to the copyright owner in order to do so. Similarly, a museum can borrow a painting from the owner of the physical canvas and, with that owner's permission, display it without liability to the painter who may have retained the copyright.

In a sense § 109(c) acts similarly to the "first sale" doctrine associated with the public distribution right. You will recall that once members of the public have acquired ownership of a legitimate copy of a protected work, they may further distribute those copies

---

203. 17 U.S.C. § 109(c).

without regard to the copyright proprietor.[204] That rule conforms copyright law to our notions about the rights of an owner of personal property—if it's your book, or painting, or DVD, you should be able to resell it or give it away. Most of us would conclude that the owner of a given copy of a work also ought to have the right to display it to the public if he is so inclined—indeed, public display rather than private contemplation is often the point of the purchase in the first place. Section 109(c) implements this intuition.

The § 109(c) exception applies whether the copy is displayed directly or by means of projection. In the latter case, however, only one image may be projected at a time, and that image must be visible only to viewers present at the place where the copy is located.[205] If a San Francisco-based art dealer employed video-conferencing technology to display a page of calligraphy to a public audience in New York, then the public display right would be violated even though the broadcasting dealer owned a legitimate copy of the literary work.

Another source of limitations on the public display right is § 110. Recall that this statute creates numerous limitations on the public performance right. Section 110 also applies in part to the public display right. In particular, paragraphs 1, 2, and 3 of § 110, pertaining to classroom instruction, distance learning activities, and religious services, apply to the public display right.

204. *See supra* § 6.3.2.

205. 17 U.S.C. § 109(c).

Chapter 7

NEWER AND MORE SPECIALIZED RIGHTS OF A COPYRIGHT HOLDER

Table of Sections

In the decades since Congress enacted the 1976 Copyright Act, it has amended the statute several dozen times. Some of those amendments relaxed formalities. Some adjusted penalties. Some expanded the scope of material protected by copyright. And quite a few of the amendments granted new rights to either existing or new subject matter. In this chapter we will canvass several of the most important provisions in this last category. Some have attracted little attention and generated little litigation. Others have proven far more consequential. All, however, raise interesting questions about how sensible intellectual property law should be structured and what its boundaries should be.

We note, as a technical matter, that not all of the provisions we will discuss here are part of the "copyright laws" of the United States, though all are codified in Title 17 of the U.S. Code, which is where the "true" copyright laws are found. This distinction sometimes reflects congressional uncertainty about its authority to legislate regarding certain subject matter under the Patent and Copyright Clause of the Constitution, and sometimes reflects a desire to set up a remedial or durational scheme with different features than those used in traditional copyright situations. In most situations, there is little practical consequence to whether a provision is technically part of "the copyright laws." Bear in mind, however, that various other federal statutes sometimes refer to the "copyright laws of the United States" and, in such cases, it becomes relevant that some of the material that follows would not be part of any such statutory cross-reference.

§ 7.1 Moral Rights

7.1.1 Basic Principles

In the United States, copyright law traditionally has had a utilitarian focus. Protection of authors has not been seen as the ultimate purpose of copyright, but rather as a means to achieve the broader social goal of promoting expression.[1] One ramification of this focus is that the U.S. copyright statute provides rights that center upon the economic interest of authors, on the theory that giving authors an economic incentive encourages them to create work that would otherwise not be produced.

Many European and other non-U.S. copyright laws share this economic grounding, but additionally recognize a concept known as "moral rights."[2] The term is an imprecise or perhaps overly literal translation from the French term "droit morale" or its plural "droits moraux." It might be more subtly rendered as "inherent non-economic personal rights of an artist or author" or something to that effect. Alas, that is a bit clumsy. Because the phrase "moral rights" is both more concise and in common usage, we will confine ourselves to that label in the discussion that follows.

Moral rights resemble rights of personality or individual civil rights. They are premised on the notion that authored works have significance beyond the marketplace; that they are also cultural artifacts and symbols of human aspirations. The moral rights philosophy also considers these same works of authorship to be reflections or extensions of their creator's personality. On this view, alteration of a work of art is tantamount to a physical attack on the person of the artist. In the same vein, moral rights are said to recognize the dignity and worth of individuals by providing authors with certain controls over their creative processes and their completed works of authorship.

Although details vary in different jurisdictions overseas, moral rights generally call for three basic rights: integrity, attribution,

---

1. See supra § 2.4.1.

2. See Henry Hansmann & Marina Santilli, *Authors' and Artists' Moral* *Rights: A Comparative Legal and Economic Analysis*, 26 J. Legal Studies 95 (1997).

and disclosure. The integrity right allows authors to prevent objectionable distortions, mutilations or other modifications of their works. The attribution right (formerly and still sometimes called a right of "paternity" despite the gendered implications of that label) allows authors to claim authorship of their works. Finally, the right of disclosure allows authors to decide when and in what form a work will be distributed to the public.

A few foreign jurisdictions offer additional moral rights. For example, some countries recognize a withdrawal right. This right allows works to be removed from the public eye, if the author or artist determines that the work no longer reflects his or her artistic or political perspective. This right can be so broad as to even require current possessors of the works to return them to the author. Although the precise formulations of each of these moral rights differ in various states overseas, moral rights are ordinarily independent of the author's pecuniary interests and remain with the author even after any transfer of ownership of either the physical work of art, the legal copyright interest, or both.[3]

The United States paid little attention to moral rights prior to its decision to join the Berne Convention in 1989. Once the United States decided to go that route, it could not continue to ignore the issue, however, because article 6*bis* of the Berne Convention requires signatories to provide the rights of integrity and attribution.[4] Notwithstanding this language, Congress declined, at the time of our accession to Berne to establish a full-fledged moral rights regime. The United States instead took the position that a combination of various state common law causes of action, including the right of privacy, the right of publicity, and tort remedies for defamation and unfair competition, provided rights equivalent to the moral rights required in Article 6bis of the Berne Convention

Perhaps eager to see the United States at last join the world's copyright system, many other Berne signatories did not choose to make an issue of U.S. shortcomings in moral rights protection. Doubts nevertheless persisted over whether the United States had fully met its Berne Convention obligations. Congress responded one year after Berne accession by enacting the Visual Artists Rights Act of 1990 ("VARA").

7.1.2   The Visual Artists Rights Act of 1990

VARA is a fairly narrow statute. Its substantive protections only apply to "works of visual art," a new construct in copyright

---

3. *See* Adolf Dietz, *The Moral Right of the Author: Moral Rights and the Civil Law Countries*, 19 COLUMBIA-VLA J. L. & ARTS 199 (1995).

4. To quote chapter and verse, Article 6*bis*(1) provides: "Independently of the author's economic rights, and even after the transfer of the said rights, the author shall have the right to claim authorship of the work and to object to any distortion, mutilation or other modification of, or other derogatory action in relation to, the said work, which would be prejudicial to his honor or reputation."

law, which the statute explicitly defined in language added to § 101 of the statute. Under that definition, a work of visual art is a painting, drawing, print, or sculpture, existing in a single copy, or in a limited edition of 200 copies or fewer that are signed and consecutively numbered by the author. A still photographic image produced for exhibition purposes also qualifies, provided that it exists in a single copy signed by the author, or in a limited edition of 200 copies or fewer that are signed and consecutively numbered by the author. The reference to "exhibition purposes" in the case of photographs quite logically excludes your vacation snapshots from protection under the VARA scheme. Note also that motion pictures and other audio visual works are not mentioned in this definition, which means that they, too, are outside the scope of protection enacted by VARA.

The definition explicitly *excludes* works made for hire. It also specific *excludes* "any work not subject to copyright protection under this title." This presumably removes from VARA protection works that are so lacking in creativity as to fail the test for an "original work of authorship." Imagine, for instance, a work of "modern," non-representational art consisting of nothing more than a single blue paint stroke in the middle of a white canvas. The statute also explicitly excludes from the crucial definition any merchandising item or advertising or promotional materials, and a long list of other more utilitarian or commercial works such as posters, maps, globes, charts, or technical drawings.

The significance of the statutory definition as a threshold plaintiffs must surmount in order to assert a VARA claim is illustrated by *Pollara v. Seymour*.[5] There, Joanne Pollara, a professional artist working in upstate New York, prepared a banner for a non-profit group called the Gideon Coalition which provides legal services to indigent clients. The banner depicted a long line of figures waiting to get legal services from a man at a desk, along with text declaring "preserve the right to counsel—now more than ever" and "executive budget threatens the right to counsel." Gideon planned to use her 10–foot by 30–foot banner as a backdrop for a table that it was going to set up on the Empire State Plaza in Albany as part of its efforts to lobby the state legislature for more funding.

Unfortunately, Gideon had failed to secure the necessary permit to put up the banner or leave it there overnight, suggesting that the Gideon Coalition itself could have used some legal services. Consequently, state employees removed the banner and, in the

5.   344 F.3d 265 (2d Cir. 2003).

process—this being New York, a state not known for the delicacy of its inhabitants—managed to tear it into three pieces. They left it, crumpled and torn, in the corner of a manager's office where Polara found it the next morning. On discovering the affront to her work, Pollara filed claims under VARA.

The Second Circuit found she was not entitled to any remedy. It pulled no punches about the limited scope of VARA, declaring early in its opinion that "not every artist has rights under VARA and not everything called 'art' is protected by such rights." The court determined that Pollara's banner was outside the scope of the statute because it had been created to draw attention to an information desk and to promote a lobbying message, and was thus a form of promotion and advertising. It gave no weight to Pollara's claim that, because her message was a political and social one rather than one of crass commercial promotion, it should not be considered "advertising." As the court put it "there is a lot of public interest advertising, including advertising for museums and art. There is political advertising. And 'promotion' has an even broader exclusionary sweep.... the banner in this case was created for the purpose of promoting and advertising, and we hold that it was therefore not a 'work of visual art' subject to protection under VARA."

As a concurring member of the panel in *Pollara* pointed out, this seems quite an over-broad interpretation of the meaning of "advertising and promotion." In that concurrence, Judge Gleeson argued that the majority's interpretation means that "a sculpture commissioned to promote AIDS awareness could *never* receive protection under VARA."[6] Indeed, one could go further and note that much art is designed to "promote" a point a view—about the eternal truth of some religious belief, or about the cruelty of war perhaps, or about matters more pedestrian such as the point of view that "puppies are cute" and "flowers are pretty." Surely an artist's intention to advance such artistic points of view ought not to deprive her work of protection under VARA.[7]

Perhaps the *Pollara* court was influenced by the fact that the banner in question seemed to have been created for an essentially utilitarian purpose—to call attention to the lobbying table set up by the Gideon Coalition. In other words, perhaps Ms. Pollara's banner just didn't feel like "true art" to the court. Perhaps, also, they were also influenced by the fact that the banner was prepared at the behest of Gideon and not on Pollara's own initiative. This latter point reminds us that VARA does not reach a work-made-for-hire,

---

6. Emphasis in original.

7. For a more fully developed version of this argument, *see*, Brook Davidson, *A Thousand Words: Pollara v. Sey-* mour and the Trend to Under-value and Under-protect Political Art, 14 DePaul–LCA J. Art & Ent. L. 257 (2004).

even if it is indisputably otherwise a work of visual art. While the banner in *Pollara* was *not* a work made for hire,[8] the Second Circuit might have felt there was enough of an analogy to warrant stretching its interpretation of "advertising and promotion."

Assuming that we are dealing with an undisputed work of visual art, VARA grants several rights to the author of that work. Before we consider those in detail, however, it is important to stress that these rights belong to the *author* and not to the copyright owner nor to the owner of the physical art object.[9] Assume that Claude Monay prepares an oil painting depicting a bouquet of tulips. Some weeks later, Monay sells the canvas and assigns the copyright in the work to wealthy art collector Amanda Amasser. A year later, Amasser sells the canvas to the Urban Institute of Art, but retains the copyright. At this point, the Urban Institute owns the physical object, which it can resell, give away, or display as it wishes. Amasser retains the copyright, allowing her to make (or authorize others to make) reproductions and derivative works based on the painting. But Monay still holds the VARA rights.

What rights, then, does VARA grant to our fiction M. Monay? Review of the statute reveals five substantive protections for authors of works of visual art. These are codified in section 106A of the statute and include both attribution-type rights, integrity-type rights and one that might be considered a hybrid of both categories. The first guarantees an author the ability to "claim authorship" of the work while the second grants the author a privilege to prevent the use of his or her name as the author of any work which he or she did not create. These rights vindicate the author's ability to be associated with works that reflect his artistic vision, and only with those works. Thus, if a museum owns an oil painting by Paul Sayzane and displays it without a tag showing Sayzane's name, Sayzane can insist that he be identified as the artist. If they put his name next to a work by Pablo Peekasso, he can demand that his name be removed.

The third itemized right allows the author to prevent the use of his or her name as author of a work of visual art that has been distorted, mutilated, or modified in a way that would be "prejudicial to his or her honor or reputation." As one court noted, "This

---

8. Ms. Pollara was not an employee of the Gideon Coalition under the "law of agency" test used by the Supreme Court in CCNV v. Reid, 490 U.S. 730, 109 S.Ct. 2166, 104 L.Ed.2d 811 (1989), and the banner would not fall with any of the nine itemized types of independently commissioned works that can become works-made-for-hire through agreement. *See generally* § 5.2.2. For a case denied VARA protections to a sculptural work on the grounds that it was a work-made-for-hire, *see* Carter v. Helmsley–Spear, Inc., 71 F.3d 77 (2d Cir. 1995), *cert. denied* 517 U.S. 1208, 116 S.Ct. 1824, 134 L.Ed.2d 930 (1996).

9. See 17 U.S.C. § 106A(e)(2).

aspect of VARA protection would prevent a third party from taking Artist A's finished sculpture, for example, and chopping pieces off it, or painting it blue, and then exhibiting it as A's work."[10] This right can be seen as blending considerations of both attribution and integrity since it forbids the combination of alteration of a work juxtaposed with an inaccurate imputation that the altered work came from the original artist.

The fourth listed statutory protection allows the author to prevent distortions, mutilations, or modifications of his or her works, but again, only if they would be prejudicial to honor or reputation. Finally, the last itemized right allows the author to prevent the destruction of a work of visual art, but only if the work is one of "recognized stature." Alas, the statute does not provide any further guidance about the concept of "prejudice to honor" nor does it define when a work has achieved "recognized stature," leaving those concepts to case law development. In the two decades since Congress adopted the statute, however, there have been relatively few VARA cases, and thus not much law has developed on these questions. One of the few published opinions to consider the recognized stature issue was the Seventh Circuit opinion in *Martin v. City of Indianapolis*.[11]

Artist Jan Martin constructed a twenty-by-forty-foot outdoor metal sculpture titled "Symphony #1," which was placed on privately owned land after obtaining a necessary zoning variance from the city of Indianapolis. The city later purchased the property that was home to Symphony #1 as part of an urban renewal project. The property owner and Martin offered to donate Symphony #1 to the City provided that the City bear the costs of removal to a new site. Although the City told Martin that he would be contacted in the event Symphony #1 was to be removed, it neglected to do so prior to bulldozing and removing the sculpture. Martin then brought suit against the City for violating the VARA provision that forbids destruction of a work of recognized stature. As evidence of the "recognized stature" of his work of visual art, Martin provided the court with letters and newspaper articles extolling Symphony #1, as well as an art show program indicating that the sculpture had won "best of show" honors.

Acknowledging that its jurists "are not art critics, do not pretend to be and do not need to be to decide this case," the Seventh Circuit held that Martin had demonstrated his work was of recognized stature. The Court of Appeals agreed with the district court's finding that respected members of the art community

10. Massachusetts Museum of Contemporary Art Foundation, Inc. v. Büchel, 565 F.Supp.2d 245, 256–57 (D.Mass. 2008).

11. 192 F.3d 608 (7th Cir. 1999).

believed that Martin's work was socially valuable and possessed artistic merit. In addition, newspaper articles indicated the newsworthiness of Symphony #1 and Martin's work more generally. Taken together the court felt this was enough to establish "recognized stature."

Judge Manion's dissent instead urged that recognized stature should *not* be shown through old newspaper articles and unverified letters, some of which were not specifically directed towards Symphony #1. The dissent viewed the "recognized stature" requirement as an important gatekeeping mechanism, limiting protection to "only those works of art that art experts, the art community or society in general views as possessing stature."[12] Judge Manion expressed concerns that a broad interpretation of VARA could interfere with urban renewal endeavors and cautioned donees of art to obtain waivers of VARA rights before accepting the works, lest they become "the perpetual curator of a work of art that has lost (or perhaps never had) its luster."[13]

VARA's limitation of its anti-destruction provision to works of "recognized stature" can be seen as an effort to avoid silly or harassing claims. There would be no point letting the creator of elaborate doodles on a notepad left behind in a conference room assert a claim against a janitor who destroyed the page on which those doodles appeared. The provision might also be seen as a statutory effort to preserve important cultural artifacts. In other words, it operates as something of an art preservation law, but one vesting enforcement powers in the artist himself, rather than in some public agency. Under this latter view, one might attempt to assess "recognized stature" by asking if the work has lasting or significant cultural importance and if its destruction would represent a loss to the public inventory of valuable cultural artifacts. Such a test would not make specific determinations any more certain, but it might refocus the inquiry on at least one key Congressional objective.

The five VARA rights are not absolute. Section 106A sets out three specific exceptions to the integrity based rights. First, the statute provides that a work is not distorted, mutilated, or otherwise modified if the modification is the result of the passage of time or the inherent nature of the materials, unless the modification is caused by gross negligence.[14] Thus if the vibrant colors of a painting fade over the years, the continued exhibition of that painting will not trigger any VARA liability even though the painting could be said to be "distorted" and even though the changes might be

---

12. *Id.* at 616 quoting Carter v. Helmsley–Spear, Inc., 861 F.Supp. 303, 325 (S.D.N.Y.1994), *rev'd in part and aff'd. in part,* 71 F.3d 77 (2d Cir.1995).

13. *Id.* at 616.

14. 17 U.S.C. § 106A(c)(1).

prejudicial to the painter's honor. Secondly, modifications due to conservation or public presentation, such as placement or lighting, also do not violate the integrity right unless caused by gross negligence.[15] Thus, if a painting on a fragile material were treated by a museum curator with some kind of coating to preserve it, and if that resulted in the image looking less vivid, the painter would have no VARA claim.

Finally, the reproduction of a work in or on any of the items excluded from the definition of a work of visual art also does not violate VARA. Thus, if a newspaper were to publish a story about the opening of a new art gallery, and included with that story a photograph of a painting that was cropped or out of focus, that would not violate VARA, because a "newspaper" is explicitly excluded from the statutory definition of works of visual art and thus the "reproduction" of the painting "in" the newspaper is excluded from VARA condemnation.[16] This certainly squares with the art preservation rationale of VARA that we noted above, because any modifications to the image in the newspaper still leave the original work intact, and most members of the public realize that a picture of a painting or sculpture in a magazine or book is no substitute for seeing the original if they want to get a true sense of the painter's artistic vision.

The relationship between the VARA exception denying relief for harm to a work due to placement or manner of presentation and the merits of the integrity rights themselves came to the forefront in *Phillips v. Pembroke Real Estate.*[17] In 1999, Pembroke Real Estate commissioned a sculptor named David Phillips to create and install a number of abstract and realistic granite and bronze sculptural works in a Eastport Park, located in Boston. A few years later Pembroke decided to alter the park in a number of ways, and as part of its redesign, proposed to remove and relocate some of Phillips' sculptures. Phillips filed suit under VARA. His theory was that relocation of his sculptures was impermissible because they should be considered a work of "site specific" art. As the court explained, a site specific work of art is one where the physical setting of the work is claimed as a constituent element of work as a whole. By severing the connection of site specific art with its setting, Phillips claimed that the relocation of sculptures was an illegal mutilation or destruction. He further argued that the "public presentation" exception in the statute should be read as not applying to site specific art.

---

15. 17 U.S.C. § 106A(c)(2).

16. *See* Berrios Nogueras v. Home Depot, 330 F.Supp.2d 48 (D.P.R. 2004) (reproduction of plaintiff's work in advertising brochures without including artist's name not actionable as VARA violations).

17. 459 F.3d 128 (1st Cir. 2006).

The First Circuit disagreed with Phillips and sided with the defendants, holding that VARA does not apply to site specific art. It found the "public presentation" exception in the statute dispositive. Alluding to the language of the statutory exception, the court declared that it found "nothing remotely ambiguous about the word 'presentation,' which is modified by the word 'placement'. The word 'placement' inescapably means location." The court also noted that the implication of the plaintiff's argument was that once a work of site specific art was installed in a given locale it could never be moved without consent of the artist—a result which it said "could dramatically affect real property interests and laws."

While the court in *Phillips* declared that VARA "does not protect site-specific art," that may overstate the court's true holding. Surely the court did not mean that once a work was found to be site-specific, it falls wholly outside the VARA scheme, so that the property owner could legally start vandalizing it by chipping bits off of sculptural pieces or painting them with fluorescent polka dots. Rather, the court seems to have meant only that where a property owner proposes to relocate purportedly site-specific sculptures intact, such relocation is not a VARA violation.[18]

Where works of visual arts are incorporated into buildings the conflict between the building's owner desire to make subsequent modifications to the building and the moral rights of the artist can be particularly vexing. An example would be when an artist paints a mural on an interior wall in the lobby of an office building and the building owner thereafter wishes to tear down that wall to enlarge the lobby. Congress attempted to strike a balance between the competing interests in cases such as this by adding some special provisions to § 113 of the statute.

Under those provisions, if the work can be removed without being destroyed, distorted, or mutilated, the relevant VARA rights apply unless either of two conditions is satisfied. The first of those obtains if the building owner makes a diligent, good faith attempt to notify the author of his intended plans to remove the work, and that attempt is unsuccessful, presumably because the artist could not be located.[19] Alternatively, VARA rights will also not apply if

---

18. In Kelley v. Chicago Park Dist., 2008 WL 4449886 (N.D.Ill. 2008) the plaintiff had installed wildflower plantings in Grant Park in Chicago, and brought a VARA suit when the local park district destroyed them. The district court found that the paintings were not works of visual art because they were not copyrightable due to lack of originality. Thus they could not be protected under VARA. The court then noted that if the plantings were works of

visual art at all, that they were a site specific work, and it held relying on *Phillips*, that VARA was inapplicable to site specific works. Note however that here, unlike in *Phillips*, the defendants did not propose to move the material to a new site. It seems unlikely that the *Phillips* court would have allowed the defendants there to simply bulldoze the sculptures.

19. Authors of works of visual art that have been incorporated into build-the building owner gave a successful notice of this sort and the artist "failed, within 90 days after receiving such notice, either to remove the work or to pay for its removal."[20] Thus, the building owner cannot act impetuously in a way that will physically damage a salvageable work, but he will not be held hostage indefinitely if he cannot find the author, and once warned, it is up to the artist to come fetch the work if he does not want it damaged. If the artist cannot be found or does not remove it within 3 months, VARA rights do not apply, meaning that the building owner is free to do as he wishes.

If, on the other hand, the work has been incorporated into a building in such a way that attempting to remove it will result in its destruction or mutilation, there will be no VARA rights provided the author of the work consented to its installation in writing. This leaves one possibility unaddressed. What if a work is installed in a building in such a way that it cannot be removed without being destroyed, and the artist did *not* consent to that installation? In this situation, it would appear that full VARA rights continue to apply. Effectively this means that the building owner could not remove the work without facing legal liability until the VARA rights expire.

The rights granted by VARA cannot be transferred. Thus there is no secondary market in VARA rights. The rights can, however, be waived, provide the waiver is in the form of a written, signed instrument.[21] In 1996, not long after VARA became law, the Copyright Office conducted a study of the waiver provisions of VARA, which included a survey of visual artists.[22] It found that only 7 per cent of survey respondents reported that waiver clauses were "routinely" included in artists' contracts, but nearly 40 per cent said such clauses were included in contracts for commissioned works. Of course, many works of visual art are sold without the execution of any written contract at all, and in such cases, there can be no waiver of VARA rights.

VARA rights do not last in perpetuity. The statute, however, establishes a rather unusual durational scheme. For works created

---

ings may specially record their address and other contact information with the Copyright Office. 17 U.S.C. § 113(d)(3). Regulations governing this so-called "Visual Arts Registry" can be found at 37 C.F.R. § 202.25. The statute defines a diligent and good faith notification attempt to be communication by registered mail sent to the address that appears in such a record.

20. If the artist responds to the notice and removes the work at his own expense, the statute specifies that title to that physical object "shall be deemed to be in the author." 17 U.S.C. § 113(d)(2).

21. 17 U.S.C. § 106A(e)(1).

22. The study was undertaken pursuant to (uncodified) section 608 of Pub.L. 101–650, the original VARA legislation. The executive summary of the report can be found online at http://www.copyright.gov/reports/exsum.html. See also, Roberta Kwall, *How Fine Art Fares Post VARA*, 1 MARQ. INTELL. PROP. L. REV. 1 (1997).

after the effective date of VARA (June 1, 1991), the integrity rights endure for the life of the artist. For works created before June 1, 1991, the duration of VARA rights depends upon whether the artist transferred title to the qualifying work or not. If the artist has parted with title prior to June 1, 1991, no VARA rights exist at all. However, if the artist created the work before June 1, 1991, but did not transfer title to the work before that date, then the artist's VARA rights endure for a term of life plus 70 years.[23] As the Nimmer treatise notes, this is more than a little curious. They posit an author who died in the year 2000 and observe that a

> 1980 painting will ... enjoy integrity and attribution rights for most of the current century. By contrast, a 1992 painting by the same artist saw its artists' rights cease at the artist's death in 2000. Therefore, pre-existing works may paradoxically achieve a far longer term of artists' rights protection than works created during the pendency of the Visual Artists Rights Act of 1990. No explanation other than sloppy draftsmanship presents itself for this state of affairs.[24]

The rights granted by section 106A are specifically made subject to the fair use defense, discussed elsewhere in the volume.[25] It is hard to imagine many cases where fair use could be invoked in a scenario implicating VARA, but let us say that a university professor wanted to illustrate, as part of a course on the role of art and culture, the degree to which damaging a work of art can be subversive or shocking and, as part of the lesson, actually spilled paint all over an original, one-of-a-kind oil painting (to the gasps of the shocked students, no doubt). If the result was prejudicial to the reputation or honor of the artist—which seems likely—there would be a prima facie VARA violation. Presumably, however, the professor would be able to invoke the fair use defense by pointing to his educational purpose.

The Patry treatise notes that

> the most likely case of fair use ... was to permit traditional parody or satire of works of visual art to continue. For parody or satire to succeed, the original must be distorted or modified in a way that prejudices the original artist's honor or reputation. Authors of works of visual art who have deliberately sold a copy of their work should not be able to stifle criticism by resort to VARA.[26]

While in some cases one might parody a work by mutilating the actual original (for instance by painting a moustache on a figure in

23. 17 U.S.C. § 106A(d).   **25.** *See infra* Chapter 10.

24. Nimmer, § 8D.06[E].   **26.** Patry, § 16.35.

a painting or mural) we suspect that most parodists would be more likely to mass produce their altered, parodic versions, leaving the original painting or sculpture unmolested. In those situations, there would be no VARA violation in the first place and thus no need for fair use to defend against a VARA claim (as opposed to the underlying copyright infringement claim). Moreover, the fair use factors itemized in the copyright statute fit uneasily at best with VARA, and it is likely that any court forced to conduct a fair use analysis in a VARA case would find it an awkward judicial exercise.

Finally, the reader should bear in mind that several states have their own moral rights statutes.[27] Perhaps the most important of these are the California Art Preservation Act[28] and the New York Artists' Authorship Rights Act.[29] The details of these statutes differ from state to state, of course, and space considerations do not allow us to explore them all in detail. In many cases, however, these statutes are not likely to be particularly important because VARA included a preemption provision. Found in section 301(f) of the copyright statute, it provides that "all legal or equitable rights that are equivalent to any of the rights conferred by section 106A with respect to works of visual art ... are governed exclusively by section 106A and section 113(d) ... [N]o person is entitled to any such right or equivalent right in any work of visual art under the common law or statutes of any State."[30] To date, there has been virtually no case law construing this language.

While some features of these state laws may survive preemption, in many cases they confer rights closely similar to those in VARA and thus are pre empted. However, federal law does not preempt state moral rights protection that "extend[s] beyond the life of the author."[31] Consequently, to the extent that a given state confer post-mortem rights on artists (via their heirs) to prevent misattribution, mutilation, or destruction of works of visual arts, those rights remain intact and potentially significant.

§ 7.2 The Anti-Circumvention Provisions of the DMCA

7.2.1 Basic Principles

Most of us rely on two distinct strategies to protect our tangible property. First, we depend on the law. We know that criminal sanctions deter many would-be thieves, and that where deterrence has not worked, civil remedies will allow us to recover

---

27. *See, e.g.*, Conn. Gen. Stats. §§ 42–116s, 42–116t; La. Rev. Stat. § 2152;Mass Gen. L. § 85S; and Pa. Stat. Ann. § 2102.

28. Cal. Civ. Code § 987.

29. New York Arts & Cult. Aff. Law, Articles 11 through 14.

30. 17 U.S.C. § 301(f)(1).

31. 17 U.S.C. § 301(f)(2)(C).

back stolen property or an equivalent amount of money, assuming that we can find the thief, bring a suit, and collect a judgment. Few property owners are, however, content to rely on the law alone. Some thieves will not be deterred, some of those not deterred will not be caught, and many of those caught will be judgment-proof. So as a second strategy we resort to common sense self-protection measures. We put locks on our doors and engage them when we go out. We equip our homes with burglar alarms, or perhaps with stickers warning of a non-existent alarm system. We get guard dogs. We put Lojack® in our car. Some of us get guns. In other words, we use self-help measures.

Copyright owners are no different. They rely on the law to protect their intellectual property. They hope that the specter of copyright liability deters infringers, and that for those not deterred, civil suits for copyright infringement will compensate them for their losses. But especially in the digital era, copyright owners are not naive. They know that many will not be deterred by legal sanctions, that many infringements will go undetected, and that lawsuits are cumbersome, expensive and not always successful in securing a recovery. So they too resort to self-help, particularly in the digital environment. They make it impossible to see or hear their works without obtaining a password. They encrypt or scramble their works so that they can only be perceived by using authorized equipment. They incorporate various digital technologies to trace reproductions. This aggregate of these digital self-help measures are often called "technical" or "technological" protection measures, or TPM.[32] They are also often called "digital rights management technologies" or DRM.

Of course, any self-help measure can be defeated by someone with enough time, skill, and determination. In the bricks-and-mortar world, locks can be picked, dogs can be distracted or shot, and burglar alarms can be disabled. In the digital world, intrepid programmers can devise ways to defeat copy protection systems, to spoof legitimate passwords, and to decrypt encrypted content. In other words, TPM can be circumvented.

In 1996, the World Intellectual Property Organization promulgated a treaty called, with stunning lack of imagination, the WIPO Copyright Treaty, designed, in part, to address this situation. Article 11 of that Treaty provides: "Contracting Parties shall provide adequate legal protection and effective legal remedies against the circumvention of effective technological measures that are used by authors in connection with the exercise of their rights

---

32. The Nimmer treatise uses the label "copyright protection systems." *See generally* NIMMER, Chapter 12A.

under this Treaty or the Berne Convention and that restrict acts, in respect of their works, which are not authorized by the authors concerned or permitted by law."[33] The United States signed this treaty in 1997.[34] Prior to ratification, however, there was the minor matter of conforming domestic U.S. law to the new treaty obligation.

We thus arrive, in 1998, at the Digital Millennium Copyright Act or DMCA. This somewhat infamous statute contains several different and totally unrelated changes and additions to the copyright statute, including limitations on the secondary liability of Internet service providers, protection for the design of boat vessel hulls, and prohibitions against tampering with "copyright management information."[35] Among the most controversial of all the provisions in DMCA are those that make it impermissible to defeat or "circumvent" technological protection measures that protect copyrighted works.[36]

7.2.2   Anti–Circumvention Measures

It is important to understand at the outset that the prohibitions against circumventing TPM are independent of the rules forbidding copyright infringement. When DMCA applies, it violates the law to engage in circumvention even if that circumvention is not done as a first step in order to facilitate infringement. It is as if the law made it a felony to disable a burglar alarm *whether or not* the person in question planned to or actually did commit a burglary. Under this scheme, someone who merely walked down the street, idly aiming a laser beam at houses in order to switch off their alarm systems would be subject to sanction even if he never entered the homes in question or stole any property.

The key anti-circumvention provision of the statute is codified as § 1201 of Title 17. In proscribing anti-circumvention § 1201 divides TPM into two kinds—those that "control access" to a work, and those that "protect a right of a copyright owner." The distinction is important and requires a bit of elaboration. Let us first dissect the notion of "access." In the pre-digital age, one typically gained access to a work by obtaining a physical copy of the work. You gained access to the text of a novel or a biography by purchasing a copy of the work from a bookstore, borrowing a copy from the

---

33. Available online at http://www.wipo.int/treaties/en/ip/wct/trtdocs_wo033.html#P87_12240.

34. At this writing approximately 70 nations have signed the WIPO Copyright Treaty.

35. These various topics are taken up elsewhere in this book.

36. The anti-circumvention provisions refer to works "protected by this title," meaning copyrighted works. A work that is in the public domain is not protected by Title 17 and thus it is not impermissible to circumvent any technological measures that impede access to, or exploitation of, such a work.

library, or perhaps from a friend. For works that were performed, you might also have gained access by attending a performance, such as a concert or stage play. For works that were displayed, you went to a location where a copy of the work could be viewed such as a museum or a gallery.

To protect its economic interests a copyright owner would "control access" by insisting that you pay to buy a copy of the book, and by locking up the book store at night when it was closed so that you couldn't help yourself to a copy without paying for it. You could, of course, defeat this "access control" by breaking into the bookstore and stealing the book. This was usually not thought of as a copyright problem, however. It was theft pure and simple.

In the digital world, one typically gains access to a work by summoning it to a computer screen or other device in a way that makes it visible or audible.[37] The copyright owner could, of course allow you to do that free of charge, just as a copyright owner can distribute free copies of a literary work. Alternatively the copyright owner might restrict access to those who have paid for it, by requiring the use of a password or the use of a particular piece of equipment in order to see or hear the work. If, in this latter case, a computer user defeated the password protection features installed by the copyright owner so that she could summon the work to her screen, or if she altered an unauthorized piece of hardware so that it could receive the work and render it visible, she would have "circumvented" a technical measure that was designed to "control access" to the work. To complete the comparison with the pre-digital example, this conduct could be roughly analogized to breaking into the bookstore to steal the book.

A key difference between the physical and digital world, however, is that, with digital material, even after you have purchased and own a physical object that embodies the work—such as a music CD, a DVD, or a game cartridge—every time you make the images or sound visible or audible by putting it in a computer, DVD player, or game box, you are "accessing" the work anew. For instance, assume you have bought a music CD designed to play only a PC type computer running Windows® software. Assume that you have a PC computer at home, but an Apple® computer at your vacation cabin. If you bring the CD with you to the cabin, you will be unable to play it on the Apple computer you have there, unless you "circumvent" the features that control your access to music that it contains. This is different from the situation with analog (conventional) works—having bought a copy of a literary work in book

---

37. Of course, in the process of doing so, you also reproduce the work in the sense that it will load into your computer's memory. As noted previously, the prevailing view is that loading a work in the random access memory of a computer constitutes a reproduction of that work. *See* § 2.2., *supra.*

form once, we do not say that you "access" the work, each time you pick it up, glance at a page, and perceive the printed words, and you are of course free to bring the book with you to your cabin and read it there just as you could read it at home.

This has led critics of the DMCA anti-circumvention provisions to argue that the statute interferes with the ability of citizens to make fair use of copyrighted works. For instance, Professor Jamie Boyle at Duke analogizes access control measures to barbed wire, and circumvention to cutting that wire. As he sees it, copyright owners have not only fenced their own private land, but have fenced public roads as well and DMCA now makes it impermissible to cut the barbed wire in order to gain access to the public roads.[38]

Defenders of the legal ban on circumvention respond that the fair use doctrine never guaranteed a right of access to a work in the first place—only the right to exploit the work in various ways once a legal copy had been obtained. In other words, fair use does not allow you to break into someone's home to look at their diary so that you can quote it in a biography, nor does it allow you to slip into a theater without buying a ticket to see a play in order that you might then write a review of it. Moreover, they point that in the digital world, some protection against circumvention is necessary to encourage authors to create and disseminate works in the first place, otherwise they could never be sure of securing an economic reward.

Professors Gorman and Ginsberg frame the issue slightly differently. They observe in their copyright casebook that

> [i]n granting copyright owners a right to prevent circumvention of technological controls on "access," Congress may in effect have extended copyright to cover "use" of works of authorship.... But in theory, copyright does not reach "use"; it prohibits unauthorized reproduction, adaptation, distribution, and public performance or display ... Not all uses correspond to these acts. But because access is a prerequisite to "use," by controlling the former, the copyright owner may well end up preventing or conditioning the latter.... "Access" probably will become the most important right pertaining to digitally expressed works,

---

38. JAMES BOYLE, THE PUBLIC DOMAIN 83–88 (2008). In a true example of practicing what one preaches, Professor Boyle and his publishers at Yale University Press have made this eminently readable book available for free download as a pdf file. *See* http://thepublicdomain.org/thepublicdomain1.pdf. For another broad ranging critique of DMCA see Electronic Frontier Foundation, *Unintended Consequences: Ten Years Under the DMCA*, http://www.eff.org/wp/unintended-consequences-ten-years-under-dmca (2008). *See also* Gideon Parchomovsky & Kevin A Goldman, *Fair Use Harbors*, 93 VA. L. REV. 1483, 1522 (2007) (reviewing and agreeing with the criticisms of several other commentators).

and its recognition, whether by the detour of prohibitions on circumvention of access controls, or by express addition to the list of exclusive rights under copyright may be inevitable. . . .[39]

Dwell on this for a further minute. In the digital world, if copyright owners cannot control access to their works, they may lose the ability to reap any economic reward from them. That is because one need not make and distribute hundreds or thousands of physical copies for all interested viewers to see the work, as tends to be true in the analog world. Rather, if a work resides on a single computer hooked up to the Internet, everyone else on the Internet can read it, hear it, and enjoy it, unless access is somehow restricted, *and* unless the law forbids circumventing those restrictions. Moreover, once people have access to digital works they can make perfect copies effortlessly and often without any risk of being discovered and sued for the unauthorized reproduction.

On the other hand, consider how a regime of airtight access restrictions that cannot lawfully be circumvented could change how users would use and experience copyrighted works. In the analog world, after you finish reading a book that you lawfully purchased, you can give it to a friend, so that he can read it as well.[40] You could bring your vinyl records or audio cassette tapes to a party at someone's home and play them during a party. You could browse the books at the local bookstore, skimming excerpts to decide which ones you want to buy and take on your upcoming vacation. In the digital world, the copyright owner might use TPM to make all these things impossible. Your digital music collection might contain technology that makes it impossible to play the songs on any device that is not previously registered with the copyright owner—there goes your ability to use your playlist at your friend's party. Digital books for sale at a web site might not be viewable until you register and perhaps even pay a fee—there goes your ability to browse before purchase. Some digital works may be programmed to simply "evaporate" after a specified number of views, plays, or hours. Moreover, if you try to get around these restrictions, you will be breaking the law.

This tension is, to a large degree, why the anti-circumvention provisions of DMCA have proven so controversial. Copyright owners view them as a matter of economic life and death, while many in the end user community view them as radical new restrictions on how members of the public can experience and enjoy copyrighted works. Congress has, for the moment, resolved that dilemma in

---

39. ROBERT A. GORMAN & JANE C. GINSBURG, COPYRIGHT: CASES AND MATERIALS 948 (7th ed. 2006).

40. This activity is the essence of the "first sale" principle discussed at § 6.3.2.1, *supra*.

favor of the copyright owners, but not without attempting to build some breathing room into the scheme. Let us turn to the specifics and see precisely what they have done.

There are two separate provisions in section 1201 that deal with circumventing access controls. One can be consider a "conduct" regulation and one can be considered a "device" regulation. The conduct regulation is found in § 1201(a)(1)(A). It provides that: "No person shall circumvent a technological measure that effectively controls access to a work protected under this title." Elsewhere, the statute explains circumvention means "to descramble a scrambled work, to decrypt an encrypted work, or otherwise to avoid, bypass, remove, deactivate, or impair a technological measure without the authority of the copyright owner."[41] One violates this provision by engaging in acts of circumvention.

The device provision in § 1201(a)(2) declares that "No person shall manufacture, import, offer to the public, provide, or otherwise traffic in any technology, product, service, device, component or part thereof ..." that contravenes any one of three alternative tests. First, the product or technology is condemned if it "is primarily designed or produced for the purposes of circumventing...." Second, it is also forbidden if it "has only limited commercially significant purpose[s] or use[s] other than to circumvent...." Finally, the device is impermissible if it is "marketed by that person ... with that person's knowledge for use in circumventing...." Oversimplifying somewhat, the first test focus on the physical attributes of the product or technology, the second on its uses, and the third on the marketing strategy or exhortations of the distributor.

In addition to measures that control access to a work, a copyright owner can also use TPM to prevent certain uses of the work by those who already have access. The most obvious example would be to incorporate a copy-control feature into the work so that the end-user cannot duplicate it. The statute refers to measures of this sort as those that "effectively protect a right of a copyright owner." The reference to "right of a copyright owner" is meant to capture the various rights itemized in section 106 of the copyright statute, namely reproduction, adaptation, distribution, performance, and display. Having explored those concepts at length earlier in this text, we need not revisit them here. For convenience we can refer to these types of TPM as "copy control" features with the understanding that they may deal with matters other than "copying" in some cases.

If you are having trouble with this distinction, just think about YouTube. That site does not control your access to its content. You

---

41. 17 U.S.C. § 1201(a)(3)(A).

need not use any special equipment, enter any passwords, or pay any fee to call up a video that is stored there, even though many of those videos are copyrighted. However, YouTube does not permit you to "download" the video by making a copy on your hard drive.[42] The software is set up to prevent you from making a copy. There is technological "copy control" here, but no "access control."

Unlike the dual provisions dealing with circumvention of access control, the statute only has one provision dealing with circumventing copy control. That provision is § 1201(b). It is a device provision. Essentially parallel to the device provision dealing with circumventing access control, it forbids the same litany of activities— manufacturing, importing, trafficking—in products and technology that meet any of the three tests alluded to above—namely those that have physical design features designed to circumvent exploitation control measures; that have only limited purposes other than circumvent such features; or that are marketed for use in circumventing such features. Note that there is no conduct prohibition dealing with circumvention of measures that control exploitation of a work. Thus it is a DMCA violation to distribute software that permits people to download videos from YouTube, but it is not a DMCA violation to simply tinker with your own computer in order to accomplish that same result. Do note however, that when you download that YouTube video, all other provisions of the copyright laws still apply—you are making a reproduction, and can be found liable for plain old copyright infringement unless you have a valid defense, such as fair use.

The following chart recaps this material and may help you visualize the various anti-circumvention provisions of section 1201 at a glance.

		Type of Technological Measure	
		Controls Access to Work	*Controls Exploitation of Work*
Type of Circumvention Activity	*Conduct*	Forbidden by § 1201(a)(1) EXAMPLE: Altering your own PC so that it can play DVDs designed to be played only on authorized DVD players	Not forbidden NOTE: Although conduct of this sort does not violate § 1201, it may still constitute copyright infringement unless covered by fair use or another defense
	Making or Selling a Product or Device	Forbidden by § 1201(a)(2) EXAMPLE: Selling or giving away a software program that descrambles images to make them visible to users who have not paid to access the site where they are posted	Forbidden by § 1201(b) EXAMPLE: Selling or giving away a software program that allows computer users to make permanent copies of streaming audio or video files encrypted to be non-copiable

42. This is what is known as "streaming" video.

Violation of the anti-circumvention provisions is no trivial matter. The statute provides for both civil and criminal remedies. Available civil remedies include an injunction against further violations of the law, impounding and eventual destruction of any devices or products used to commit the violation, and monetary remedies such as damages, costs, and attorney's fees.[43] A plaintiff may elect to receive either his actual damages plus additional profits of the violator, or statutory damages. Statutory damages are "in the sum of not less than $200 or more than $2,500 per act of circumvention, device, product, component, or offer or performance of service as the court considers just."[44] Damages can be tripled if the defendant is a repeat violator of the statute. On the other hand, if the "violator was not aware and had no reason to believe that its acts constituted a violation," the court can reduce the damage award or deny damages entirely.[45] In addition, if a violation is willful, the violator can be prosecuted and is subject to up to 5 years imprisonment and a $500,000 fine for a first offense, and to double those sanctions for subsequent offenses.[46]

Most of the litigation spawned by the anti-circumvention provisions has revolved around the device provisions. Those provisions sweep broadly. For instance, as we shall see in the chapter on infringement, the Supreme Court held in *Sony Corp. v. Universal City Studios, Inc.*, that a party distributing a device "capable of substantial non-infringing uses" cannot be held liable as a secondary or contributory infringer of copyrights if end-users employ the device as a tool for copyright infringement. However the language in section 1201 proscribing devices with "limited commercial purposes" other than to circumvent means that even "dual purpose" devices that can be used to both circumvent technological controls and for other lawful purposes, and which thus might be legal under *Sony*, will nonetheless trigger liability under the DMCA.[47]

---

43. 17 U.S.C. § 1203(a).

44. 17 U.S.C. § 1203(c)(3).

45. 17 U.S.C. § 1203(c)(5). A special provision of this section protects nonprofit libraries, educational institutions, and public broadcasters by requiring the court to forego a damage award if such a defendant can show that it "was not aware and had no reason to believe that its acts constituted a violation."

46. 17 U.S.C. § 1204. Nonprofit libraries, educational institutions, and public broadcasters are not subject to the criminal sanctions.

47. As the Nimmer treatise explains, "[A] given piece of machinery might qualify as a staple item of commerce, with a substantial noninfringing use and hence be immune from attack under *Sony*'s construction of the Copyright Act—but nonetheless still be subject to suppression under section 1201." NIMMER, § 12A.19[B].

Thus, in one of the first cases to be litigated after the adoption of the statute, a firm distributed software that allowed users to install a virtual video player on their computer emulating a "secret handshake" protocol used by the makers of the REAL PLAYER device. This software allowed those users to play audiovisual content meant solely for the Real Player and also permitted users to make copies of the content, which the plaintiff's device was designed to prevent.[48] The defendant argued that their software was capable of non-infringing uses because it allowed users to make copies that would be permissible under the fair use doctrine. Nonetheless, a district court rejected that argument and found a violation of both device prohibitions.

Perhaps the most cited decision to date arising under the anti-circumvention provisions has been the case of *Universal City Studios, Inc. v. Reimerdes*,[49] which on appeal was captioned *Universal City Studios v. Corley*.[50] This litigation was brought by eight U.S. motion picture studios that distributed their copyrighted motion pictures for home use on DVDs. The studios protected the motion pictures from copying by using an encryption system called "Content Scramble System" or "CSS." CSS employs an algorithm configured by a set of "keys" to encrypt a DVDs contents. CSS-protected DVD movies may be viewed only on players and computer drives equipped with licensed technology that decrypts the films but prevents copying.

By late 1999, a 15–year–old Norwegian computer prodigy named Jon Johansen and two other individuals wrote their own software, called "DeCSS," that was able to circumvent the CSS protection system. DeCSS allowed CSS-protected motion pictures to be copied and played on devices lacking the licensed decryption technology. One of the defendants in the litigation, Corley, posted the code for the DeCSS program on his website along with an explanation of how to use the program. The movie studios sued under the anti-circumvention provisions of DMCA to prevent the defendants from posting DeCSS and posting links to other sites that housed DeCSS.

At trial, the defendants offered a number of arguments in response to the plaintiff's contentions. They first asserted that the DMCA did not apply to the present case because the CSS did not "effectively control access" to the plaintiffs' copyrighted movies within the meaning of § 1201(a). District Judge Kaplan disagreed,

48. Realnetworks, Inc. v. Streambox, Inc., 2000 WL 127311 (W.D. Wash. 2000).

49. 111 F.Supp.2d 294 (S.D.N.Y. 2000).

50. 273 F.3d 429 (2d Cir. 2001). When we say "most cited" we are not exaggerating. At this writing, Westlaw's KeyCite shows over 1400 citations to the district court opinion in the case law and secondary literature.

however, observing that users could not watch CSS-protected movies without the encryption keys, and as well that users could not obtain the keys without purchasing a DVD player or computer drive under the appropriate license.

The district court also held that DeCSS was developed primarily for the purpose of circumventing CSS. The evidence of record on this point was rather complex. Johansen, the Norwegian teenage programmer, testified that at the time DeCSS was written no Linux-compatible DVD players were available on the market.[51] Johansen further explained that he created DeCSS in order to make a DVD player that would operate on a computer running the Linux operating system. The seeming difficulty with Johansen's explanation was that DeCSS was a Windows compatible file that would operate only on computers running the Windows operating system. The reason the authors constructed a Windows program rather than a Linux program, Johansen stated, was that at the time DeCSS was written Linux also did not support the file system used on DVDs. As a result, DVDs would have to be first decrypted on a Windows computer before being employed on a Linux machine.

Judge Kaplan did not attach much significance to this sequence of events. The court instead stressed that Johansen and his colleagues created DeCSS with full knowledge that the software could be used on computers running Windows rather than Linux. The court further believed that the three programmers were well aware that the movie files, once decrypted, could be copied like any other computer files. The district court therefore concluded that the only purpose or use of DeCSS was to circumvent CSS and that the DMCA had been violated.

The defendants further argued that DeCSS was created for research purposes: namely to further interoperability between computers using the Linux system and DVDs. The court rejected this position by concluding that the defendants were not involved in good faith encryption research, but instead had simply posted the DeCSS software on their web sites.

Finally, the defendants sought to rely upon the fair use privilege. Now DMCA itself does not contain a "fair use" exception to its prohibitions, nor does it incorporate by reference the general fair use doctrine from copyright law.[52] Nonetheless, the defendants argued that the DMCA device prohibitions should be construed to accommodate fair use considerations, lest they make illegal the very tools necessary for people to engage in fair use. As Judge Kaplan summarized the defendant's argument,

51. Linux is an open source computer operating system that can be freely used and freely modified by anyone.

52. We discuss this doctrine in depth in Chapter 10 of this book.

certain uses that might qualify as "fair" for purposes of copyright infringement—for example, the preparation by a film studies professor of a single CD–ROM or tape containing two scenes from different movies in order to illustrate a point in a lecture on cinematography, as opposed to showing relevant parts of two different DVDs—would be difficult or impossible absent circumvention of the CSS encryption. Defendants therefore argue that the DMCA cannot properly be construed to make it difficult or impossible to make any fair use of plaintiffs' copyrighted works and that the statute therefore does not reach their activities, which are simply a means to enable users of DeCSS to make such fair uses.

Indeed, the defendants argued that if Congress meant to eliminate fair use considerations from the DMCA scheme, the statute would run afoul of the First Amendment and should declared unconstitutional.

Professor Boyle has offered up a useful analogy that helps put this First Amendment argument in focus. He says:

> Imagine that Congress had passed the following law instead of the DMCA: "Any copyright owner can make it illegal to make a fair use of a copyrighted work by putting a red dot on their books, records, and films before selling them. It shall be a crime to circumvent the red dot even if, but for the dot, the use would have been fair." That would be clearly unconstitutional. It gives copyright owners a new intellectual property right to "turn off fair use" in copyrighted works distributed to the mass market. Is the DMCA not the same thing?[53]

Apparently Judge Kaplan thought not. He conceded that "access control measures such as CSS do involve some risk of preventing lawful as well as unlawful uses of copyrighted material." He nonetheless rejected the defendants' claim, holding that Congress had considered this very issue and consciously decided to outlaw all access circumvention. He found support for this conclusion in various features of DMCA that retained privileges for users of copyrighted materials once they had lawfully gained access to it, and he cited the legislative history of the DMCA for the conclusion that the congressional "decision not to make fair use a defense to a claim under Section 1201(a) was quite deliberate." Consequently the court enjoined the defendants from further distribution of the DeCSS software.

53. JAMES BOYLE, THE PUBLIC DOMAIN 96 (2008).

On appeal, the Second Circuit affirmed. It devoted the bulk of its opinion to an analysis of the First Amendment issue. The Court of Appeals conceded that computer programs qualified as speech protected by the First Amendment and characterized the DMCA as a content-neutral restraint on speech. According to Judge Newman, however, DMCA passed constitutional muster because it furthered a substantial government interest unrelated to the suppression of free expression—namely the protection of digitally encoded works of authorship—and was narrowly tailored, not burdening substantially more speech than necessary to further that interest.[54]

The Court of Appeals also affirmed the district court's conclusion that, as a matter of statutory interpretation, the defendants could not successfully employ the fair use privilege. Declining to decide the question of whether the fair use privilege was constitutionally required, Judge Newman noted that nothing in the DMCA prevented viewers from quoting dialogue from movies or even pointing a video camera at a monitor as it displayed a DVD movie, since those acts did not involve the circumvention of a technological measure that controlled access to the work. Thus, in his view, DMCA did not foreclose all forms of fair use. He concluded that the fair use principle did not require that the viewer be allowed to access a copyright work via his preferred technique.

The *Reimerdes/Corley* decisions have been criticized by numerous commentators, chiefly for their failure to give sufficient weight to the fair use defense.[55] The courts' classification of CSS as an "access control" under § 1201(a)(2) rather than a "copying control" under § 1201(b)(1) might be disputed. After all, the movie studios principally intended CSS to prevent copying rather than unauthorized access. The court's classification held consequences for both its analysis of the plaintiff's prima facie case and the defendant's fair use claims, for as noted earlier in this section, § 1201(b) is the more narrowly worded provision of the two. One

---

54. The clash between DMCA and First Amendment values also was at the center of a controversy in 2001 involving a Princeton computer science professor named Edward Felten. Felten had written a paper explaining how a "watermarking" technique that had been developed by a consortium called the Secure Digital Music Initiative or SDMI, could be defeated. He planned to appear at a conference in Pittsburgh to discuss his paper, but was threatened with legal action by the Recording Industry Association of America. Felten then filed a lawsuit seeking a declaratory judgment that he could lawfully publish his research. By the time of the hearing on Felten's claim, SDMI and the RIAA disavowed any intention of filing suit, so the court dismissed the case on the grounds that there was no "case or controversy" and that it therefore lacked jurisdiction. For a full discussion see Tieffa Harper, *Much Ado About the First Amendment—Does the Digital Millennium Copyright Act Impede the Right to Scientific Expression?: Felten v. Recording Industry Association of America,* 12 DePaul-LCA J. Art & Ent. L. 3 (2002)

55. *See, e.g.,* Ryan Van Den Elzen, *Decrypting the DMCA: Fair Use as a Defense to the Distribution of DeCss,* 77 Notre Dame L. Rev. 673 (2002).

might also argue that neither *Reimerdes* nor *Corley* gives appropriate weight to § 1201(c)(1), which states that: "Nothing in this section shall affect rights, remedies, limitations, or defenses to copyright infringement, including fair use, under this title." That said, subsequent cases have followed the approach in these opinions, and change, if it is to come, will likely require legislative action.[56]

This is not to say that every DMCA plaintiff prevails, however. Where parties have used non-technological chicanery to obtain access to a work, courts have found DMCA inapplicable. For instance, in some cases, parties have obtained legitimate passwords to access copyrighted material without paying for them by, for instance, "borrowing" those passwords from authorized users. Courts have not found this practice to constitute "circumvention" of a technological measure controlling access, concluding that such a defendant "is not said to have avoided or bypassed [a] deployed technological measure in the measure's gatekeeping capacity.... [W]hat defendant avoided and bypassed was permission to engage and move through the technological measure from the measure's author ... Whatever the impropriety of defendant's conduct, the DMCA and the anti-circumvention provisions at issue do not target this sort of activity."[57]

In other cases, firms have tried to use DMCA as a tool to control the market for replacement parts or supplies for a mechanical device, arguing that their products are controlled by copyrighted software, and that the seller of the replacement part is evading some kind of "lockout" protocol embedded in that software. The courts have generally refused to go along with efforts to use DMCA in this fashion. Thus, in one such case, Lexmark, a seller of computer printers, installed computer chips in both its printers and its brand of toner cartridges that were designed to "interact" with each other.[58] When a Lexmark brand toner cartridge was installed, the two programs would perform an "authentication sequence" and the printer would only work if it verified it was dealing with a genuine Lexmark cartridge. Of course the purpose of this technology was to prevent cartridges that had been refilled by third parties from working in a Lexmark printer.

---

56. For proposals that would amend DMCA to provide for greater recognition of activities resembling fair use, *see, e.g.*, H.R. 4539, 109th Cong. 1st Sess; H.R. 1201, 110th Cong. 1st Sess. Neither of these bills was reported out of Committee.

57. I.M.S. Inquiry Management Sys., Ltd. v. Berkshire Information Sys.,

Inc., 307 F.Supp.2d 521 (S.D.N.Y 2004). *See also* Egilman v. Keller & Heckman, 401 F.Supp.2d 105 (D.D.C. 2005); R.C. Olmstead, Inc. v. CU Interface, LLC, 657 F.Supp.2d 878 (N.D.Ohio 2009).

58. Lexmark International v. Static Control Components, 387 F.3d 522 (6th Cir. 2004).

Static Controls, the eventual defendant in the case, made a chip that would "mimic" the Lexmark cartridge chip and fool the printer into working. It sold these chips to third parties who made refilled or re-manufactured toner cartridges for use with Lexmark printers. Lexmark sued Static Controls, claiming that their chips were devices that circumvented a technological measure that controlled access to a copyright work—namely the computer program in the printer (called the Printer Engine Program).

The court concluded that the verification protocols that operated between the toner cartridge chip and the printer chip were not devices that "controlled access" to a copyrighted work, and that emulating them was therefore not a violation of DMCA. The court noted that the programs were not in any way encrypted, pointing out that "each can be read (and copied) directly from its respective memory chip." The crucial issue thus became defining "access"—did it mean "making use of the program" or did it mean "getting to see the program" If the former definition controlled, Static's chips did circumvent a technology that was designed to block the use of the program. But the court did not think that this was the proper way to interpret the word "access" in DMCA. It observed:

> Just as one would not say that a lock on the back door of a house "controls access" to a house whose front door does not contain a lock and just as one would not say that a lock on any door of a house "controls access" to the house after its purchaser received the key to the lock, it does not make sense to say that this provision of the DMCA applies to otherwise-readily-accessible copyrighted works.... [I]t seems clear that this provision does not naturally extend to a technological measure that restricts one form of access but leaves another route wide open.

As another member of the *Lexmark* panel summarized in his separate opinion, "the Digital Millennium Copyright Act (DMCA) was not intended by Congress to be used to create a monopoly in the secondary markets for parts or components of products that consumers have already purchased."[59]

The *Lexmark* court distinguished cases involving circumvention software that controlled access to DVDs or video games by noting that in those cases, the "work" that had been accessed impermissibly was not just the "lockout" software, but the underlying audiovisual work as well (that is, the movie or the game), and pointed out that underlying works of this sort are themselves protected by copyright. "Unlike the code underlying video games or DVDs, 'using' or executing the printer Engine Program does not in

---

59. Feikens, J., *concurring in part and dissenting in part*, 387 F.3d at 553.

turn create any protected expression. Instead the program's output is purely functional . . . ."[60]

7.2.2.1 Administrative Exceptions to the Anti–Circumvention Provisions

Congress tried to build some flexibility into the DMCA anti-circumvention provisions by empowering the Librarian of Congress to identify classes of works where a prohibition on circumvention would be overly onerous.[61] The Librarian is to identify these classes of works in regulations to be published once every three years. At this writing, the most recent version of that regulation was promulgated in October 2009. It identifies 6 classes of works that are exempted from the ban on circumvention of access controls.[62] Most of the listed categories are fairly narrow, but it is interesting to look at each of them to see how the Librarian has construed the congressional mandate to carve out exceptions.

The first exemption is for movies held by college and university libraries where circumvention is done in order to create a compilation of excerpts from those movies for classroom use. This bears an uncanny resemblance to a scenario cited by Judge Kaplan in his *Remeirdes* decision, which we quoted above. The second category is computer programs or video games that were distributed in formats that are now obsolete where the method of access control was to require original media or hardware, where the access is made in order to enable subsequent reproduction for preservation purposes. This exception might apply if a primitive video game from the dark ages of the 1990s had been marketed so as to only work on a game console that is no longer available in the market place. The only way to preserve the game for posterity would be to "access" it in some manner that bypassed the need to have the original, and now extinct, game console.

The third regulatory exception deals with computer programs protected by obsolete dongles. While the reference to "dongles" may sound vaguely pornographic, a dongle is merely a piece of hardware that prevents you from activating a program. For instance, you might be required to insert what amounts to a physical "key" into a designated port of your computer before a program will load. If no one is making the dongle anymore and you have lost

---

60. 387 F.3d at 548. The Federal Circuit reached a similar conclusion—on slightly different reasoning—in a case involving replacement garage door openers. The Chamberlain Group, Inc. v. Skylink Techs. Inc., 381 F.3d 1178 (Fed. Cir. 2004).

61. "The Librarian of Congress . . . shall [determine] . . . whether persons who are users of a copyright work are,

or are likely to be in the succeeding 3–year period, adversely affected by the prohibition under subparagraph (A) in their ability to make noninfringing uses under this title of a particular class of copyrighted works." 17 U.S.C. § 1201(a)(1)(C).

62. *See* 37 C.F.R. § 201.40.

your dongle, you could legally use the program unless you are allowed to bypass this primitive form of access control. So the regulation lets you proceed sans dongle. The next exception in the regulation is equally narrow—it deals with literary works that were distributed in an ebook format, where all the ebook editions prevent the work from being accessed via a read-aloud function or other special format that would enable individual with disabilities to perceive the content.

Exception number five may be of some interest to the reader who covets a particular cell phone but does not want to do business with the cellular provider that is connected with that phone. It allows the circumvention of TPM controlling access "to computer programs in the form of firmware that enable wireless telephone handsets to connect to a wireless telephone communication network, when circumvention is accomplished for the sole purpose of lawfully connecting to a wireless telephone communication network." In other words, if it is not otherwise unlawful, it will not be a DMCA violation to hack a cell phone so that it can connect with a particular cellular service company—a practice that goes by the charming name of "jailbreaking."

Finally, the Librarian's regulation allows circumvention of access control features in CDs containing sound recordings that create security flaws or vulnerabilities in personal computers in order to engage in research or correct those security flaws.

7.2.2.2 Statutory Exceptions to the Anti–Circumvention Provisions

In addition to this administrative monitoring and tweaking of the anti-circumvention provisions, Congress itself included a number of exceptions and limitations directly in the statutory text. As with the Librarian's regulations, however, these are drawn rather narrowly. We will mention a few here in the text, and allude to the remainder in a footnote for the reader motivated, or required, to be familiar with all.

The statutory qualification that has probably received the most attention is the one provided for reverse engineering. It permits a person who has lawfully obtained the right to use a copy of a computer program—presumably by purchasing a physical object and entering into a licensing agreement to use the software—to circumvent, and to develop devices to circumvent, a technological measure "for the sole purpose of identifying and analyzing those elements of the program that are necessary to achieve interoperability of an independently created computer program with other programs . . . "[63] Interoperability refers to the ability of two comput-

---

63.   17 U.S.C. § 1201(f)(1).

er programs to function together. Software on a game cartridge must be "interoperable" with the game console in order for the game to play and an application program such as a word processor must be interoperable with the operating system on a given computer in order for it to run on that computer.

This exception thus permits the developer of a potential new game cartridge or word processor to circumvent technological measures designed to prevent it from having a look at the "guts" of another party's game console or operating system software. Having bypassed the technological measure, the developer can study the program in order to design his own software in a way that will be interoperable. The exception is only available "to the extent any such acts of identification and analysis do not constitute infringement." Generally, the courts have found any copying done as part of reverse engineering software to be fair use, and thus non-infringing.[64]

Another statutory exception provides latitude for nonprofit libraries, archives, and educational institutions. Such entities are permitted to circumvent access controls in order to make a good faith determination of whether they wish to acquire the work. This has been labeled a "shopping privilege."[65] The exception only applies if the work has been "commercially exploited," which essentially means it is a published work available on the open market. Moreover, the copy accessed via circumvention cannot be retained any longer than necessary to make the good faith determination whether to buy, and the exception is only available if a copy of the work is not reasonably available in another form. This defense only applies to the conduct provisions of the statute, not the device provisions. Thus, the protected entities may not sell or otherwise distribute devices or technologies designed for circumvention purposes.

Yet another exemption immunizes local, state, and federal law enforcement officers from DMCA liability for engaging in lawfully authorized investigative, protective, information security, or intelligence activities.[66] Thus an FBI agent can hack past technological measures designed to control access to material relevant to an investigation, secure in the knowledge that even if the material is protected by copyright, she cannot be held civilly or criminal liable for that act of circumvention.

These three examples give a flavor of the narrow nature of the exemptions, and of the many preconditions and limitations that are found within each of them. As promised, we refer the reader to the

---

64. *See* § 10.5, *infra.*

65. *See* Nimmer, § 12A.04[A][1].

66. 17 U.S.C. § 1201(e).

footnote for mention of the other limitations.[67] Suffice it to say that because of the way these exceptions have been drawn, they have not placated DMCA critics, who do not feel that, taken as a whole, they give sufficient weight to considerations of fair use and free speech.

§ 7.3   Protection of Copyright Management Information Under DMCA

The term "copyright management information" or CMI refers to information conveyed in connection with a digital work, including the name of the author, the name of the copyright owner, and terms and conditions for use of the work.[68] This information can be embedded in the work or, for works, available on the Internet, be placed only a hyperlink away. The ready availability of copyright management information may facilitate the licensing and dissemination of protected works in the digital environment. To achieve these ends, however, copyright management information must be accurate and reliable, and it must continue to accompany the work as it moves to different "virtual locations" in cyberspace.

One of the goals of the DMCA was therefore to protect copyright management information against falsification, removal, or alteration.[69] There are two substantive prohibitions in this portion of the law. Section 1202(a) prohibits individuals from knowingly providing false copyright management information with the intent to facilitate or conceal infringement. The following subsection,

67. Section 1201(g) permits circumvention for purposes of "encryption research." In other words, you can try to circumvent technological measures in order to determine whether a given encryption technology has flaws or vulnerabilities. In applying this exemption, the court must consider whether the person involved is employed and trained in encryption research, and whether he shares his findings with the copyright owner of the encrypted work. Section 1201(h) allows a court to consider whether a device that facilitates circumvention has the sole purpose of preventing access of minors to on-line material. Thus, if a device is marketed to parents to allow them to monitor their childrens' Internet surfing, that factor can excuse the vendor from liability. This exemption is not automatic, but rather committed to the discretion of the court. Section 1201(i) allows circumvention of software that collects identifying information in the course of on-line activities. Under this exception it is permissible to

access and disable software that places "cookies" on your computer. Section 1201(j) allows circumvention of access controls as a form of security testing. This provision is related to the encryption research exception, but covers testing of methods of access control that do not rely on data scrambling via mathematical algorithms, which is the definition of "encryption."

68. *See* Julie E. Cohen, *Some Reflections on Copyright Management Systems and Laws Designed to Protect Them*, 12 BERKELEY TECH. J. 161, 161–62 (1997).

69. As with the anti-circumvention provisions of DMCA, the provisions relating to Copyright Management Information were prompted in part by obligations the United States assumed as a party to the 1996 WIPO Copyright Treaty. *See generally*, Jane C. Ginsburg, *Copyright Legislation for the "Digital Millennium,"* 23 COLUMBIA-VLA J. L. & ARTS 137, 157 (1999).

1202(b), prohibits the intentional alteration or removal of copyright management information, knowing (or having reasonable grounds to know) that the alteration or removal will facilitate or conceal infringement. Note that these provisions incorporate a "scienter" requirement. Not every deletion of CMI will trigger liability—the defendant must be acting intentionally or negligently to aid and abet acts of infringement by others.[70]

As it did in the case of the anti-circumvention provisions, Congress included some exemptions from liability in the CMI provisions, though a smaller number in this case. Thus lawfully authorized investigative, protective, information security, or intelligence activities of local, state, and federal law enforcement and intelligence personnel are not prohibited by the CMI provisions of DMCA.[71] Analog broadcasters who do not intend to facilitate or conceal copyright infringement need not comply with § 1202 if doing so is not technically feasible or would create an undue financial hardship.[72] Finally, the DMCA encourages digital broadcasters to engage in a voluntary, consensus standard-setting process to place copyright management information in transmitted works. Until such a standard has been established, the DMCA exempts digital broadcasters if the transmission of copyright management information would degrade the digital signal or conflict with a government regulation or industry standard.[73]

Courts have disagreed over whether the definition of "copyright management information" in the statute should be taken at face value and thus held applicable outside the digital environment, or whether it should be construed to only encompass information of a digital nature. Thus in one case, defendants sold garments in a style similar to plaintiff's fabric designs, but did not include with those garments the copyright notice that appeared on the border of the plaintiff's rolls of fabric. The district court held that section 1202 was not "intended to apply to circumstances that have no relation to the Internet, electronic commerce, automated copyright protections or management systems, public registers, or other technological measures or processes as contemplated in the DMCA as a whole."[74] On the other hand, in a dispute between the Associated Press, and a service that rewrote AP news dispatches and sold the rewritten versions to web sites, the court declared "[t]he defendants have cited no textual support for limiting the DMCA's

---

70. *See, e.g.,* Gordon v. Nextel Communication et al., 345 F.3d 922 (6th Cir. 2003); Schiffer Publications, Ltd. v. Chronicle Books, LLC, 73 U.S.P.Q.2d 1090 (E.D. Pa. 2004).

71. 17 U.S.C. § 1202(d).

72. 17 U.S.C. § 1202(e)(1).

73. 17 U.S.C. § 1202(e)(2).

74. Textile Secrets International, Inc. v. Ya–Ya Brand Inc., 524 F.Supp.2d 1184, 1201 (C.D. Cal. 2007). *See also,* The IQ Group Ltd. v. Wiesner Publications, LLC, 409 F.Supp.2d 587 (D.N.J. 2006).

application to 'the technological measures of automated systems'— a phrase that appears nowhere in the statute.'"[75]

Some of the other cases dealing with the CMI provisions of DMCA have considered the question of whether CMI must actually be "on" the copyrighted work in question, as opposed to merely adjacent to it, in order to receive protection. For instance, in one early case, the defendant operated a search engine that retrieved images. The thumbnail versions of those images on the results page did not include any copyright management information, such as the copyright notices that had been adjacent to the images on the sites where those images came from. The court did not, however find a violation of the law, reasoning that the CMI had not been embedded in the images themselves.[76]

Yet another group of cases has addressed the intent issue. Many of these find that the defendant's deletion of CMI was not done with the purpose of promoting copyright infringement or with knowledge that it would have that effect. Thus, in the case just described involving the thumbnail images, the court concluded that the availability of a link to the original site hosting the image meant that the defendant did not have knowledge that the omission of any CMI would encourage infringement.[77] Any user who clicked on a thumbnail would see the relevant CMI when he arrived at the relevant web site. In another case, the defendant prepared a television commercial for its two-way messaging service and included in one of the shots, as background, some dental illustrations that had been prepared by plaintiff, with relevant CMI removed. Here again, the court found no intent to induce infringement, and thus no violation of section 1202.[78]

In some cases, copyright holders seem to assert violations of section 1202 as an "add-on claim" in a traditional suit for copyright infringement. In these cases, a plaintiff alleges that the defendant's work is a non-literal copy of its copyrighted material, but the defendant argues that it either produced the material independently, or there is insufficient resemblance to make his work infringing of the plaintiff's. Of course such defendants do not normally include plaintiff's copyright notices or other identifying materials on copies of their own works! Thus the plaintiff adds a claim for violation of section 1202 to the underlying copyright claim. Of course, if the defendant is not guilty of infringement, than it did not delete CMI

---

75. Associated Press v. All Headline News Corp., 608 F.Supp.2d 454, 462 (S.D.N.Y. 2009). *See also* Fox v. Hildebrand, 2009 WL 1977996 (C.D.Cal. 2009).

76. Kelly v. Arriba Soft Corp., 77 F.Supp.2d 1116 (C.D. Cal. 1999), *aff'd in*

part, *rev'd in part*, 336 F.3d 811 (9th Cir. 2003); *see also* Schiffer Publications, Ltd. v. Chronicle Books, LLC, 73 U.S.P.Q.2d 1090 (E.D. Pa. 2004).

77. Kelly, *supra* note 75.

78. Gordon v. Nextel Communications, 345 F.3d 922 (6th Cir. 2003).

from plaintiff's work, and the section 1202 claim fails with the underlying copyright infringement claim. On the other hand, if defendant is guilty of infringement, plaintiff will usually have adequate remedies regardless of the section 1202 claim.

Thus far, the copyright management provisions of DMCA have not proven to be of particularly great significance. As noted above, the provisions were drawn narrowly by Congress and have been given further limiting interpretations by a number of courts. Some commentators have also faulted them for compromising privacy rights and the right to read anonymously.[79] It may be that the continuing expansion of the digital realm will make the integrity of CMI even more important and thus spawn more claims under section 1202 in the years to come. To date, however, they do not seem to have achieved much of what Congress presumably intended.

§ 7.4 The Digital Performance Right in Sound Recordings

As we have noted elsewhere, for most of the twentieth century owners of rights in sound recording made money by selling physical objects such as vinyl records, pre-recorded cassette tapes, or CDs. Users who wanted to listen to specific songs at specific times effectively had no choice other than to buy such objects. They could listen to the radio, of course, but they had no control over the songs being played. Even at their favorite bar, the jukebox likely only had a minute fraction of all the music that they might want to listen to, and to hear it you had to get dressed (in most neighborhoods) and go out to the bar.

All that began to change with the arrival of the Internet. In a networked digital world it became theoretically possible to locate songs and, with a few clicks on a keyboard or a mouse, play them on demand, without needing to possess any physical object embodying the sound recording. Those who coin clever names called this phenomenon the "celestial jukebox" because it would be like having a giant jukebox in the sky which contained all music ever recorded.[80] Not only would the music be instantly available, but being in a digital format the sound quality would be flawless—none of the pops, hissing, or scratches that music lovers put up with when playing vinyl records, cassettes, or even CDs. It promised to be a glorious new age of music on demand.

79. *See* Julie E. Cohen, *A Right to Read Anonymously: A Closer Look at Copyright Management in Cyberspace,* 28 Conn. L. Rev. 981 (1996).

80. There is a website called www. thecelestialjukebox.org. Its tagline reads "whatever you want to hear, whenever you want to hear it, wherever you are . . . if the bastards ever let us."

The only problem with this utopia, at least from the perspective of the holders of copyrights in sound recordings (usually record companies or "labels"), is that no one would have any reason to buy CDs any more. Consequently, in such a world, the continued financial viability of the record companies turned on their ability to secure royalty payments for the on-line performance of their works, to make up for lost CD sales. You will recall, however, that the Copyright Act of 1976 does not confer a performance right on sound recordings.[81] As we noted earlier in this book, radio stations and others who perform pre-recorded music must pay performance right royalties to copyright owner of *musical works* (usually though performing rights societies such as ASCAP) but they do not have any obligation to pay anything to owners of the copyrights in the *sound recordings*.

The record labels pressed Congress to come to their aid. While Congress could have responded to the new realities of the digital age by granting sound recordings a general performance right, it opted for a narrower, and much more technical solution, passing the Digital Performance Right in Sound Recordings Act (DPRA) in 1995.[82] That statute added a new section 106(6) to the copyright statute, which confers the right "in the case of sound recordings to perform the copyrighted work publicly by means of a digital audio transmission." This new digital performance right was intended to allow copyright owners to license sound recordings to digital music subscription and interactive services,[83] and to receive performance royalties when these services thereafter transmitted their works to listeners in their homes.

Congress viewed DPRA as creating a "carefully crafted and narrow performance right, applicable only to certain digital transmissions of sound recordings."[84] Reflecting this intent, as well as the political tradeoffs that led to the DPRA, § 106(6) is subject to a bewilderingly complex set of limitations in § 114.[85] Those provisions, in turn, were significantly amended in 1998 by various sections of the Digital Millennium Copyright Act. Given space limitations, and our assumptions about the interests and needs of our readers, we have opted to omit some details from our descrip-

---

81. *See* § 6.4.1.2, *supra.*

82. Pub. L. No. 104–39, 109 Stat. 336.

83. *See* David M. Kroeger, *Applicability of the Digital Performance Right in Sound Recordings Act of 1995,* 6 UCLA ENT. L. REV. 73 (1998).

84. S. Rep. No. 104–128, at 13 (1995).

85. Some evidence of the complexity of the scheme is that no less a copy-right authority than David Nimmer, current custodian of the esteemed Nimmer on Copyright treatise, wrote an article a few years after the adoption of the DPRA entitled *On the Absurd Complexity of the Digital Audio Transmission Right,* 7 U.C.L.A ENT. L. REV. 189 (2000). If he finds it absurdly complex, that probably means it really is pretty darn complex.

tion of this baroque scheme and confine ourselves to a general overview in the paragraphs that follow.

The first point worthy of note is that the new digital performance right only covers public performances "by means of a digital audio transmission." This means that a performance of a sound recording that is digital, but *not transmitted*, does not implicate the right, and can be engaged in without the need to secure permission or pay royalties. For instance, assume that the sponsor of a speech by a prominent scientist held in a large auditorium opts to play some music as audience members are arriving and being seated. Assume that the music is played via the use of a digital audio tape player, and pre-recorded digital audio tapes. In this case, the sponsor is not engaging in a digital audio *transmission* of the sound recordings embodied on those tapes, even though it is engaged in a digital *performance* of those recordings. Thus it would not need to secure a license from the holder of copyright in the sound recordings being played.[86] Of course *private* performances, whether digitally transmitted or not, also do not implicate the statutory right created by DPRA because it only confers a right to perform "publicly."

Second, the statute defines a "digital audio transmission" as a "digital transmission ... that embodies the transmission of a sound recording. This term does not include the transmission of any audiovisual work."[87] The exclusion of audiovisual works is significant. It means that the § 106(6) digital performance right is not implicated by the digital transmission of movies or video clips. Assume that an adoring mom decides to film her toddler dancing to a pop tune, and then uploads the video to a service like YouTube. The mom has made a reproduction of the sound recording by incorporating it onto the audio track of her home video, and could be accused of copyright infringement for that act. Of course she might have a fair use defense, given that her activities are non-commercial and modestly transformative. YouTube itself also reproduces the sound recording when it stores a copy of the video on its servers, but it might be protected from liability for that act by the provisions of section 512 of the statute, taken up elsewhere in our discussion of infringement issues in the on-line context.[88] The key

86. The sponsor would, of course, need a license to perform the musical compositions in question. In the real world, it is likely that owner of the auditorium would have secured ASCAP and BMI licenses, which would confer the necessary rights to perform those compositions.

87. 17 U.S.C. § 114(j)(5). Section 101 tells us that a "digital transmission" is a "transmission in whole or in part in a digital or other non-analog format" and that to transmit a work, in turn, is "to communicate it by any device or process whereby images or sounds are received beyond the place from which they are sent." 17 U.S.C. § 101.

88. *See* § 9.3 *infra*.

point for present purposes, however, is that when web surfers access the video and YouTube "performs" it by digitally transmitting it to their computers, DPRA is not implicated because the transmission of an *audiovisual work* is not, definitionally speaking, a "digital audio transmission."

Assuming that we have an undisputed digital audio transmission of a sound recording, the transmitter still might not need a license. Section 114 essentially divides such transmitters into three groups. Those in the first group are entirely exempt from any obligation to obtain permission or pay royalties in order to digitally transmit the sound recording. In the second group are entities that are subject to the provision but entitled to a statutory license at a governmentally fixed royalty rate. The third group consists of entities fully subject to the new right embodied in section 106(6)—they must negotiate directly with the copyright owners and pay royalties at whatever rates they can negotiate, and the copyright owners can deny them permission to use the material.

Let us tackle these categories in the order mentioned above. First, section 114(d)(1) identifies six categories of exempt transmissions.[89] The first and most important are "nonsubscription broadcast transmissions." A broadcast transmission is one made by a terrestrial broadcast station licensed by the FCC.[90] Terrestrial means earth based. Congress worded the definition this way not to exclude radio stations run by little green men on Uranus, but rather to exclude satellite radio stations from the exemption. A "nonsubscription" transmission is one that is not limited to particular recipients and for which no fee is paid.[91] Translated to English, then, this first exempt category refers to conventional over-the-air radio and television broadcasters whose signals are capable of being received by all members of the public within a given area. While some radio stations still transmit analog signals and would thus not have been affected by the new right in section 106(6), many have switched to digital format, and all over-the-air television went digital in 2009.[92] This exemption means, therefore, that radio and TV stations need not pay performance royalties to the copyright owners of sound recordings when they perform those sound recordings, regardless of whether their signals are analog or digital.

The second exemption covers retransmissions of broadcasts that fall in the first category. Retransmitters include entities such as cable providers that receive and then retransmit network television programming, or a subscription radio service that receives and

---

89. One of these appears in section 114(d)(1)(A), one appears in section 114(d)(1)(B) and the remaining four appear in section 114(d)(1)(C).

90. *See* 17 U.S.C. § 114(j)(3).

91. *See,* 17 U.S.C. § 114(j)(9), (14).

92. *See* http://www.dtv.gov/whatis dtv.html for a description of some of the key aspects of digital TV.

retransmits radio signals. Retransmitters are exempt even if they charge a fee. However, if the retransmission is of a radio broadcast, the retransmitter must observe further restrictions, such as geographic limits on the area where the retransmission can be sent.[93]

The third exempt category is for "a prior or simultaneous transmission incidental to an exempt transmission, such as a feed received by and then retransmitted by an exempt trasmitter." This convoluted language essentially exempts a network that beams a digital signal (containing sound recordings) to a local affiliate station. For instance, assume that CBS sends a "feed" of its nightly news program to WLMN, its local station in Lansing, Michigan, and that audible in the news program are copyrighted sound recordings. This "feed" would not qualify under the first exception because it is not to the public generally—CBS only transmits it to a limited group, namely its own affiliate stations. But those stations themselves are exempt, and retransmit the program out to the public. Moreover they receive the feed prior to putting it on the air, or they broadcast it as it come in (that is, simultaneously). So CBS is exempt from the DPRA for this activity.

A fourth exemption is provided for a "transmission within a business establishment, confined to its premises or the immediately surrounding vicinity." Thus, if a merchant chooses to install a system to transmit digital music throughout its store, it would need to license the performance rights for the musical compositions involved, but would not need any license from those who own copyright in the sound recordings. Some merchants, of course, choose to subscribe to an outside commercial music service such as MUZAK® so the statute contains another exemption for transmissions "to a business establishment for use in the ordinary course of its business."

The last exception allows the simultaneous retransmission of a *licensed* transmission if that retransmission is authorized by person making the original transmission. Let us try to render that in actual English. Consider a premium entertainment channel like HBO®. Because it is not licensed by the FCC, it charges for its programming and it only makes the programming available to those who have paid—not to the general public—it would not be exempt from the 106(6) digital performing right as a broadcaster. It therefore needs a license to engage in digital audio transmissions of sound recordings, and we can safely assume that it has taken all steps to obtain the relevant licenses. Note, however, that HBO does not transmit directly to viewers. Rather it transmits to cable companies, such as Comcast, Cablevision, or Time Warner. They, in

---

93. The restrictions are found in 17 U.S.C. § 114(d)(1)(B). The statute lists four separate ways that a retransmitter of an original radio station digital transmission can secure exemption from DPRA.

turn, "retransmit" the HBO material to their subscribers. The final exemption simply means that the cable provider is not obligated to secure its own separate license to digitally transmit any sound recordings contained within the HBO programs—it is making an authorized, simultaneous retransmission of a licensed transmission.

This arrangement facilitates what is sometimes called "through to the listener" licensing, since HBO basically pays the full performance royalty to the copyright owner, adjusts its price to the cable systems accordingly, and they, in turn, pass the cost on to their subscribers. Effectively, then, a licensing fee for digital performance of sound recordings by non-broadcast entities like HBO is "built in" to your monthly cable charge.

We now move to the second category mentioned at the outset. If a transmitter is not exempt entirely exempt from the digital performance right, the next question is whether it qualifies for a statutory license. Speaking generally, any *non-interactive* service will be eligible. A non-interactive service is one where listeners or viewers cannot select content on demand, as you would with a jukebox or pay-per-view television station, but rather must listen or watch whatever is served up by the provider, as you would with conventional radio and television.

The statutory license is available both to "subscription based" non-interactive transmitters where users pay for the service—think XM® radio or the music channels included in your cable TV package—and to non-subscription based services as well—think Pandora® radio. A non-subscription service is only eligible for the license, however, if its primary purpose is to provide entertainment, and "not to sell, advertise, or promote particular products or services."[94]

To retain qualification for the statutory license such entities must observe a large number of further requirements. For instance: They must include in their transmissions any identifying information that the copyright owner has encoded in the sound recording. They cannot automatically and intentionally cause any device receiving the transmission to switch from one channel of programming to another. They cannot transmit more than specified amounts of material from a single phonorecord within a specified period of time.[95] They cannot publish a program guide with advance

---

94. 17 U.S.C. § 114(D)(2). *See also* 17 U.S.C. § 114(j) (6). As the Nimmer treatise explains, this means that "a seller of non-musical goods could not use music on its website in order to make surfing there a more enjoyable experience" and still qualify for the statutory license. NIMMER, § 8.22[D][1]. The stat-

ute also includes a "grandfather clause" declaring that certain satellite digital audio radio services that were already up and running at the time the statute was amended in 1998 are also eligible for the statutory license.

95. The calculation of this amount—called the "sound recording

notice of the songs they plan to transmit. They cannot replay the same series of songs over and over, unless the group of songs runs for at least a specified minimum amount of time. They cannot take steps that would encourage the recipients to make copies of the sound recordings. And on and on.[96] Most of these requirements are designed to reduce the tendency of the licensed transmissions to substitute for the purchase of CDs or other phonorecord.

The statute specifies that the royalty rates for the statutory license will be fixed by the Copyright Royalty Judges for periods of five years at a time, and that the rates should be those "that most clearly represent the rates and terms that would have been negotiated in the marketplace between a willing buyer and a willing seller."[97] However, the parties are encouraged to engage in voluntary negotiations over royalty rates and the statute provides that negotiated rates "shall be given effect in lieu of any decision by the Librarian of Congress or determination by the Copyright Royalty Judges."[98] To facilitate these negotiations, the law allows both copyright owners (essentially the various major and independent record labels) and performing entities (such as cable systems, webcasters and the like) to designate collective agents, and confers antitrust immunity on the parties in connection with these collective negotiations.[99] The distribution of the royalties collected is specified by statute: 50 percent of the royalties are payable to the copyright owner (usually the record label), 45 percent goes to the featured recording artist who made the recording, 2.5 percent goes to non-featured musicians (the band playing in the background) and 2.5 percent goes to non-featured vocalists (the back-up singers).[100]

If you have followed the story to this point—and we commend you if you have—you may be wondering specifically about the status of "webcasters." Let us first consider a webcaster whose only presence is in cyberspace—for instance sites such as So-

---

performance complement"—is insanely complex.

96. The full list of these requirements is found in 17 U,.S.C. §§ 114(d)(2)(A) and (d)(2)(c). They are explicated in depth in NIMMER, § 8.22[D][1][c].

97. 17 U.S.C. § 114(f)(2)(B).

98. 17 U.S.C. § 114(f)(3).

99. 17 U.S.C. § 114(e)(1). Copyright owners have designated an entity called Sound Exchange as their common agent for this purpose. Originally an unincorporated division of the record industry trade association—the Recording Industry Association of America—it be-

came an independent organization with its own board of directors in 2003. Information about Sound Exchange is available at http://www.soundexchange.com/. Sound Exchange has also been designated by the Copyright Office to receive and distribute statutory royalties to copyright owners. See 37 C.F.R. § 261.4(b). The performing entities are represented in royalty negotiations by the Digital Media Association or DiMA. Information about DiMA is available at www.digmedia.org. It would not be inaccurate to say that DiMA and Sound Exchange have an adversarial relationship.

100. 17 U.S.C. § 117(g)(2).

maFM.com, Smoothjazz.com, Radioparadise.com, and literally thousands of others.[101] When the DPRA was first enacted in 1995, such entities were entirely exempt from the new digital performance right, but that changed when the statute was amended in 1998. They are now subject to the digital performance right under section 106(6). We pause to let you review the discussion above and the current statutory language to see if you can deduce why this is so. Thinking concluded? Good. The reason is that webcasters are not "terrestrial broadcasters" licensed by the FCC.[102] They do not "broadcast" because their signals do not go out over the air, and they do not need a license from the FCC to operate. However, to the extent a webcaster runs a non-interactive service, it is eligible for compulsory licensing.

Would it make a difference if the webcaster in question was owned by a conventional, FCC licensed radio station, and if its on-line programming was a digital "stream" of the same music it broadcasts over the air?[103] The statutory language is not entirely clear. It refers to transmissions "made by" a terrestrial broadcast "station" licensed by the FCC. Does that mean that exemption applies if the *corporate entity* making the transmission is an FCC licensee? Or does it mean that the specific *transmitting facilities* under analysis must be licensed by the FCC, in which case the exemption would be unavailable, because the computer servers from which the webcasts emanate are not, of course, FCC licensed?

In *Bonneville Int'l Corp. v. Peters*,[104] the Third Circuit affirmed a decision of the Copyright Office embracing the latter interpretation. The court looked to the Federal Communications Act for guidance and based on its scrutiny of that statute concluded that "it is ... clear that a 'station' that is 'licensed' is something other than a 'licensee,' and, in fact, means a physical broadcasting facility." It also found this conclusion fortified by the structure of other provisions of the DPRA. The result is that *all* webcasters are treated the same, whether they are owned by a terrestrial broadcast

---

101. Readers who enjoy listening to music on-line may have noted that some webcasters or "Internet Radio Stations" have domain names that end in ".fm." You may be interested to learn that this is not a special on-line top level domain reserved for radio stations. Rather it is the country code for the Federated States of Micronesia. One need not be in Micronesia however, to secure a domain name from a registrar based in that country.

102. Before the 1998 DMCA amendments DPRA exempted all non-subscription, non-interactive services.

Thus the typical Webcaster—who did not charge a fee and did not allow listeners to select specific sound recordings— did not need any license at all. The most significant aspect of those 1998 amendments was narrowing the exemption to FCC licensed broadcasters.

103. For example, the classic hits station in Washington, DC is WBIG, available on the FM radio dial at 100.3. It is, of course, also available on line at <wbig.com>.

104. 347 F.3d 485 (3d Cir. 2003).

station or not. None are exempt, and all qualify for the statutory license, provided they are non-interactive.

The administration of the statutory licensing scheme as applied to webcasters, however, has proven to be something of a legal soap opera. In 2002 a royalty rate arbitration panel[105] charged with coming up with a royalty rate for webcasters set the rate at .07¢ per performance for commercial webcasters and .02¢ per performance for non-commercial webcasters.[106] Many webcasters—particularly smaller entities—argued that they simply could not afford to pay royalties at this level. They appealed to Congress and the result was the Small Webcaster Settlement Act of 2002.[107] It directed small webcasters and Sound Exchange to negotiate more appropriate rates, and gave them time to do so. The parties eventually reached a settlement, with rates based on a percentage of revenues earned by the webcasters, instead of on a per-performance basis.

When that arrangement expired in 2005, however, the parties could not reach agreement on a new royalty rate. History now essentially repeated itself. The parties went to the Copyright Royalty Judges to adjudicate their dispute. In 2007 the Judges released a decision reverting to a per-performance royalty, with rates escalating each year through 2010.[108] The webcasters reacted to this ruling with great distress, arguing that the required payments would essentially mark the end of free streaming music on the Internet.[109] For instance, in Congressional hearings, representatives of Pandora, one of the most popular internet radio sites, testified that they would have pay nearly 70 percent of their income in sound record-

---

105. Such *ad hoc* panels have now been replaced by the Copyright Royalty Judges. *See* 17 U.S.C. § 802.

106. *See Determination of Reasonable Rates and Terms for the Digital Performance of Sound Recordings and Ephemeral Recordings*, 67 Fed. Reg. 45240–01, 2002 WL 1446448

107. Pub. L. 107–321, 116 Stat. 2780 (codified in scattered sections of Title 17).

108. *See, Digital Performance Right in Sound Recordings and Ephemeral Recordings*, 72 Fed.Reg. 24,084 (May 1, 2007). This rate determination was affirmed on appeal in Intercollegiate Broadcast System, Inc. v. Copyright Royalty Board, 571 F.3d 69 (D.C. Cir. 2009).

109. *See, e.g.*, Kellen Myers, *The RIAA, the DMCA, and the Forgotten Few Webcasters: A Call for Change in Digital Copyright Royalties*, 61 Fed. Comm. L.J. 431 (2009) ("due to . . . the Copyright Royalty Board's (CRB) recent setting of royalty rates for webcasters, the mixtape genre of independent Internet radio may soon be gone."); Erich Carey, *We Interrupt this Broadcast: Will the Copyright Royalty Board's March 2007 Rate Determination Proceedings Pull the Plug on Internet Radio?*, 19 Fordham Intell. Prop. Media & Ent. L.J. 257 (2008). ("These rate increases have proven so dramatic that even the largest commercial webcasters have expressed an intention to cease webcasting operations if the rates remain in effect. Some webcasters have shut down and others fear they will soon be forced to follow suit. Indeed Time Warner Inc.'s AOL has even gone so far as to sell its webcasting business to CBS Broadcasting Inc., because it felt '[t]here's no way [it could] build an Internet radio business . . . with these kinds of royalties.' ").

ing performance royalties.[110] Congress once again stepped in with the Webcaster Settlement Act of 2008,[111] which once again forced the parties back to the bargaining table. When the parties could not agree by the deadline in that statute, Congress adopted the Webcaster Settlement Act of 2009![112] In mid–2009 the parties finally came to an agreement that will run through 2015.[113] If the parties find this arrangement livable over the next few years, perhaps the next round of negotiations will go more smoothly, but your humble authors would be disinclined to bet on that.

This leaves us to consider the last group of digital transmitters—those that are neither exempt nor eligible for the statutory license. These are the "interactive" services. The statute defines an interactive service as "one that enable a member of the public to receive a transmission of a program specially created for the recipient, or on request, a transmission of a particular sound recording, whether or not as part of a program, which is selected by or on behalf of the recipient." It is clear that a true "on-line jukebox" where users can search for specific songs and then, via a mouse click, hear those songs in their entirety, falls within this definition. An example of such a service is Rhapsody.com which charges users a monthly fee and permits them to select the precise songs they would like to have transmitted to them.

There are, however, other services, where users can customize a listening experience to some degree, but may not select specific songs, such as Pandora.com. On sites of this sort, you may enter the name of an artist or a song and the site will automatically select and play a variety of songs with a musical profile similar to that artist's recordings or that specified song. On other sites you might enter information about musical genres that you like or other similar data. Are these sites interactive? After all, it could be said that these sites are transmitting a program "specially created for the recipient."

That was precisely the question that confronted the Second Circuit in *Arista Records v. Launch Media.*[114] Launch Media operated a website called LAUNCHcast.com "which enables a user to create 'stations' that play songs that are within a particular genre

---

110. *Performance Rights Act: Hearing on H.R. 4789 Before the Subcomm. on Courts, the Internet, and Intellectual Property of the H. Comm. On the Judiciary,* 110th Cong. 2nd Sess. at p.160 (2008).

111. Pub. L. No. 110–435, 123 Stat. 4974.

112. Pub. L. No. 111–36, 123 Stat. 1926.

113. *See,* Edmund DeMarche, *Internet Radio Sites Ink Royalty Deal,* http://money.cnn.com/2009/07/07/technology/internet_radio_royalty_settlement.cnnw/index.htm. The full text of the highly complex agreements can be found in the Federal Register at 74 Fed. Reg. 40614 (August 12, 2009).

114. 578 F.3d 148 (2d Cir. 2009).

or similar to a particular artist or song the user selects."[115] Listeners could also rate songs to indicate which ones they liked the best. Several record labels sued Launch, arguing that any service that "reflects user input" is "specially created for and by the user and therefore qualifies as an interactive service." Since interactive services require negotiated licenses and since Launch did not have such licenses, the plaintiffs accused Launch of copyright infringement.

LAUNCHcast used several complicated algorithms to insure that a listener would not hear merely the songs which he had rated highly in the past, to insure that a listener would not hear too many songs by the same artist or from the same album, to insure that a non-trivial number of songs would be ones that the listener had not heard previously on that particular channel, and to make it impossible for a listener to predict which songs would be played in which order. As the court noted "[i]t is hard to think of a more complicated way to 'select songs,' but this is the nature of webcast music broadcasting in the digital age."

After reviewing the details of this system, the court identified the purpose of the DPRA as protecting "sound recording copyright holders—principally recording companies—from the diminution in record sales." It then observed that "part and parcel of the concern about a diminution in record sales is the concern that an interactive service provides a degree of predictability—based on choices made by the user—that approximates the predictability the music listener seeks when purchasing music." This led the court to conclude that "LAUNCHcast does not provide a specially created program within the meaning of [the DPRA] because the webcasting service does not provide sufficient control to users such that playlists are so predictable that users will choose to listen to the webcast in lieu of purchasing music, thereby—in the aggregate—diminishing record sales." In other words, a listener who created a "Lady Gaga" channel on LAUNCHcast in the hope of hearing *Poker Face* often enough on the website to make buying a CD or digital download of that song unnecessary would likely be sorely frustrated.

There is one final point to note regarding negotiated licenses under DPRA. The recording industry in the United States is a highly concentrated oligopoly. Four record labels (and their affiliates)—Universal, Sony/BMG, Warner, and EMI—control approximately 85 percent of the market.[116] That would mean that if a given

---

115. LAUNCHcast has since been acquired by Yahoo. *See*, http://docs.yahoo.com/docs/pr/release789.html.

116. *See Top Record Labels: Artists, Market Share*, USA Today, October 10,

2008, http://www.usatoday.com/tech/products/2008-10-10-367143278-x.htm.

interactive music service entered into an exclusive copyright license with one or more of these labels, it would be essentially impossible for other interactive music services to offer a viable service to the public. Those other services would, in other words, not be able legally to play the vast majority of recorded songs, and, finding themselves limited to a relatively small group of recordings on independent labels might not be able to attract sufficient traffic to make their business viable. To reduce the risk of such a situation, DPRA forbids exclusive licenses for a period in excess of 12 months and specifies that a grantee of an exclusive license cannot receive another such license for 13 months after expiration of a prior exclusive license.[117]

Criticizing the scheme just described would be like shooting fish in a barrel. It is insanely complicated. It was crafted by interested industry participants with little consideration of the public interest. Despite its intricacy it leaves enormously complicated issues—and disputes involving tens of millions of dollars—to the determination of the Copyright Office and the Copyright Royalty Judges. It has required repeated congressional intervention in the last dozen years in the form of the various Webcaster laws discussed above. Lengthy litigation will likely be required to resolve other unforeseen ambiguities in this byzantine statute. Moreover, the entire elaborate edifice, like much recent copyright legislation, is closely tethered to the technology and business models of a given moment in time. It is hard to believe, therefore, that events will not make the whole thing obsolete in a relatively few years time. Until then, alas, we are stuck with it.

§ 7.5 The Audio Home Recording Act

The Audio Home Recording Act (AHRA) is a another testament to the perils of trying to draft technology-specific legislation. The story here begins in the late 1980s. At that point a hot new technology emerged for recorded music, called digital audio tape. The sound quality of music recorded on digital tape and played in a digital audio tape deck was vastly superior to that of the analog tape that had dominated during the 1960s and 1970s. Even more interesting was the fact that successive recordings of the same material suffered no degradation in quality. In other words, a copy of a copy of a copy of a copy of an original digital tape would sound as good as the original. This was in stark contrast to analog, where each subsequent copy would have less clarity and more distortion

---

See also, Recording Industry Assoc. of Amer. v. Diamond Multimedia Sys. Inc., 180 F.3d 1072, 1074 (9th Cir. 1999) ("half-dozen major record companies . . . control approximately ninety percent of the distribution of recorded music in the United States.").

117. 17 U.S.C. § 114(d)(3)(A).

than the one before. The perfect replicability of digital tape, however led to something of an impasse between major players in the recorded music industry.

In a concern that now seems positively quaint in light of on-line music piracy in the Internet age, copyright owners felt that selling pre-recording digital tapes for use with the newly developed digital tape machines would be too risky. They feared that a single tape would "father" dozens or hundreds of perfect digital copies, thus displacing significant sales of pre-recorded music.[118] So they approached the manufacturers of the digital audio recorders— mostly big electronics companies like Phillips and Sony—and asked them build copy control technology into the machines. Those companies, however refused, perhaps recognizing that the ability to make perfect copies was one of the prime selling points of their machines in the first place. In response, the copyright owners informed the device makers that they would not release any of their copyrighted material in a digital audio tape format. In effect, they said to the electronics companies "OK, let's see how many machines you sell when there is no music to play in them."

Eventually the parties came to a compromise which was ratified in the form of a 1992 law called the Audio Home Recording Act.[119] There are essentially two key features to the law. First, it requires that all "digital audio recording devices" contain a copy control technology called Serial Copy Management System.[120] This technology permits the making of a copy of an *original* tape, but precludes making a copy *from a copy*. Thus if Alan bought a pre-recorded digital audio tape, he could make a copy of the tape for Betty. He could also make a copy for Claire. But neither Betty nor Claire could use their copies to generate further copies. So if Dan heard the tape at Betty's house and wanted a copy for himself, he would have to go buy one (unless he knew Alan).

Second, the statute imposes what is essentially a tax on digital tape machines and blank digital tapes designed to compensate the sound recording copyright owners for supposed lost sales due to casual copying by consumers. The royalty on the machines was set at 2 percent of the purchase price and the royalty on the tapes at 3 percent of the price.[121]

---

118. Digital tape recorders could also be designed to make digital tape copies of CDs. Obviously an enormous amount of music already existed in the CD format, and the copyright owners certainly feared that this material would be subject to promiscuous copying as well.

119. Pub. L. 102–563, 106 Stat. 4237, codified at 17 U.S.C. §§ 1001–1010.

120. 17 U.S.C. § 1002.

121. 17 U.S.C. § 1004. The statute further provided a minimum and maximum royalty for the recording devices of $1 and $8 (or $12 for a dual recorder) respectively.

These royalties are divided according to a detailed formula set out in the statute. Two-thirds of the collected sum goes into what is called a "sound recording fund." Of that amount, 2 5/8 percent is paid to non-featured musicians who participated in making copyrighted recordings, and 1 3/8 percent is paid to non-featured vocalists. Of the remaining 96 percent left in the sound recording fund after those payments, 40 percent of that amount goes to the copyright holders in the recordings (record labels) and 60 percent goes to the featured artists on the recording. The other one-third of the collected amounts goes into a fund to compensate those who created the underlying musical work, with half of that fund being paid to music publishers, and the other half to be paid to the actual composers and lyricists.[122] The writers and music publishers can designate the Harry Fox Agency[123] as their agent to collect and distribute these royalties. This function is performed for performers and record labels by an entity called The Alliance of Artists and Recording Companies, Inc. (AARC).[124]

Any interested copyright owner may bring a civil action for violation of the provisions of AHRA. Successful parties can recover actual damages or alternatively, statutory damages of up to $2,500 per device involved in the violation, as the court considers just. The court is also empowered to grant injunctive relief and to order that violative devices be impounded and either be modified to conform to the statute or be destroyed.[125]

The "pivot point" for the AHRA is the definition of a "digital audio recording device" (hereinafter DARD). According to the statute, this is "any machine or device of a type commonly distributed to individuals for use by individuals ... the digital recording function of which is designed or marketed for the primary purpose of, and that is capable of making a *digital audio copied recording* for private use."[126] A "digital audio copied recording" in turn is defined as "a reproduction in a digital recording format of a digital musical recording" and a digital musical recording is defined as "a material object (i) in which are fixed, in a digital recording format, *only* sounds and material, statements, or instructions incidental to those fixed sounds, if any and (ii) from which the sounds and material can be perceived, reproduced, or otherwise communicated, either directly or with the aid of a machine or device."[127] Only devices that fall within this definition must contain the Serial Copy Management System, and only such devices must pay the statutori-

---

122. 17 U.S.C. § 1006.

123. We have encountered the Harry Fox Agency previously. It is the organization that licenses "mechanical" rights in musical works. *See* § 6.1.2.5, *supra*.

124. *See*, http://www.aarcroyalties. com/2008/intro.html

125. 17 U.S.C. § 1009.

126. 17 U.S.C. § 1001. [emphasis supplied].

127. *Id.* [emphasis supplied].

ly imposed per-unit royalty. The leading case interpreting this definition is *Recording Industry Assoc. of America v. Diamond Multimedia Sys.*[128]

In that case, Diamond sold a device it called the Rio. This device was essentially a first generation MP3 player—an early precursor of the iPod®. After a user downloaded MP3 music files to a personal computer she could attached the Rio to the computer with a cable and transfer those files to the Rio, and thereafter listen to the music from the Rio with headphones. The court breathlessly reports in its opinion that the Rio could store a full hour of music! The Rio could not download or transmit those files in turn to any other device. Nonetheless, the RIAA felt that this device would cut into its members' sales of tangible phonorecords and make the unauthorized downloading of MP3 music files from pirate sites more attractive by making the illegally downloaded music portable. So it sued Diamond, claiming that the Rio was a "digital audio recording device" which, because it lacked the statutorily required copy control technology was illegal.

The court sided with Diamond and concluded that the Rio was not a DARD. Parsing the statutory definitions, the court determined that the computer hard drives from which the Rio obtained the MP3 files were not "digital musical recordings," because they did not contain *only* musical sounds plus incidental instructions. Rather, computer hard drives contain multiple programs and user generated data, along with any musical files. True "digital musical recordings" would be objects such as CDs or digital audio tapes, which contain only music. Therefore, the court concluded, "the Rio appears not to make copies from digital music recordings, and thus would not be a digital audio recording device under the Act's basic definition ..."[129] Since the Rio could not make copies of CDs or digital tapes, the statute did not oblige it to include the Serial Copy Management System. Moreover the court found that "the Rio's operation is entirely consistent with the Act's main purpose—the facilitation of personal use."

There is one other feature of AHRA that deserves note. Section 1008 provides that "no action may be brought under this title alleging infringement of copyright based on the manufacture, importation, or distribution of a digital audio recording device, a digital audio recording medium, an analog recording device, or an analog recording medium, or based on the noncommercial use by a consumer of such a device or medium for making digital musical recordings or analog musical recordings." Read that again. Got it?

128. 180 F.3d 1072 (9th Cir. 1999).

129. Indeed, the statute also specifically provides that a digital musical recording does not include a material object "in which one ore more computer programs are fixed...." 17 U.S.C. § 1001(5)(B).

It seems to say that the private copying of recorded music cannot be copyright infringement. That, in turn, seems to suggest that downloading and sharing music files does not violate the law. Lest you drop your book and head for your computer to begin downloading all the music you can grab, we are constrained to tell you that such an interpretation would be incorrect. The reason is, once again, the definitional provisions of AHRA.

As the *Diamond* court pointed out, "under the plain meaning of the Act's definition of digital audio recording devices, computers (and their hard drives) are not digital audio recording devices because their 'primary purpose' is not to make digital audio copied recordings."[130] Of course, a computer is also not an "analog" recording device, because it uses digital technology. What section 1008 means, therefore, is that it is permissible for you to use a digital tape recorder to copy a file on your computer, and it is permissible for you to use an ancient analog cassette tape deck to tape a song off the radio, but it is not permissible to use your computer to copy a file from another computer or elsewhere (unless you can come within some other defense provided elsewhere in the copyright laws). Sorry to be the bearers of bad tidings.

The AHRA has largely been consigned to the dustbin of history. The technology that prompted its adoption—digital audio tape—never caught on, so its minute regulation of machines that could play and copy digital audio tapes turns out to have been wasted effort. It is one of the most conspicuous examples of how difficult it is to legislate in an age of rapid technological change. The approach of the statute, however, remains intriguing, especially the idea of taxing hardware to provide royalties to copyright owners, and then allowing consumers some latitude to engage in copying without fear of legal liability. It remains to be seen if that approach can be pressed into service again to deal with issues in the twenty-first century.

§ 7.6   The Semiconductor Chip Protection Act

An enormous number of the mechanical devices we use in our daily lives are operated by little bits of silicon known as semiconductor chips.[131] These chips, usually smaller than the size of a fingernail, contain tens of thousands of tiny transistors or switches, connected to each other by even tinier filaments, stacked on top of each other in multiple layers like a club sandwich gone mad. Semiconductor chips are manufactured by etching the chip with a

---

130. 180 F.3d at 1078.

131. Actually, semiconductor chips can be made out of materials other than silicon, such as germanium or gallium arsenide. The key is that the material must have the capacity to partially conduct electricity—hence the name "semi" conductor.

prescribed pattern using a photographic stencil. This stencil, often taking the form of a glass disc, is known as a "mask." It is very expensive and time consuming to design and prepare these mask works. The process can take years and cost millions of dollars.[132] Once the chip has been designed, however, others can replicate the pattern for a fraction of the cost in a fraction of the time. This is a classic scenario calling for intellectual property protection in some form in order to preserve the first party's incentives to engage in creative activity.

In 1984 Congress adopted a form of sui generis protection for semiconductor chips and the associated mask works. Technically, this statute—the Semiconductor Chip Protection Act (or SCPA)—is not part of the copyright law. You can find it codified as Chapter 9 or Title 17 of the U.S. Code, immediately following provisions of the copyright law.[133] The threshold requirements for protection of a mask work track those found in the copyright laws. A mask work only gets protection when it has been fixed *in a semiconductor chip* product by or under the authority of the owner of the mask work.[134] Note that fixation in other forms—such as in a multi-colored composite drawing showing the layers of the chip design—does not suffice. In addition, protection is denied if the work is "not original,"[135] or if the design of the mask work is "staple, commonplace, or familiar in the semiconductor industry."[136]

Unlike copyright law, protection under the SCPA does not attach immediately upon the fixation of the work. Rather, it begins only when the work is "first commercially exploited anywhere in the world" or when it is registered—whichever occurs earlier.[137] This approach resembles the copyright scheme as it existed under the 1909 statute, under which protection was triggered by publication with notice or, in some limited cases, by registration. Although one need not register prior to beginning sales of the chip, protection will be lost if a registration application is not filed within two years after the first commercial exploitation.[138] Registration is also a statutory pre-requisite for an infringement lawsuit, just as it is in cases of conventional copyright infringement.

Substantively, the statute grants the owner of a protected mask work the exclusive right to reproduce the work by any means, and the exclusive right to import or distribute a semiconductor chip product in which that mask work is embodied. The Act does not, however, extend protection "to any idea, procedure, process, sys-

---

132. H.R. Rep. 98–781, (98 Cong., 2d Sess. 1984) at 2, 1984 U.S.C.C.A.N. 5750, 5751, 1984 WL 37536.

133. *See* 17 U.S.C. §§ 901–914.

134. 17 U.S.C. § 902(a)(1).

135. 17 U.S.C. § 902(b)(1).

136. 17 U.S.C. § 902(b)(2).

137. 17 U.S.C. § 904(a).

138. 17 U.S.C. § 908(a).

tem, method of operation, concept, principle, or discovery, regardless of the form in which it is described, explained, illustrated, or embodied in such work."[139] The analogies to copyright law are self-evident. Moreover, just as with conventional copyright law, an impermissible reproduction need not involve copying of the entire protected mask work. As one of the very few cases to construe the SCPA put it, " 'If the copied portion [of the mask work] is qualitatively important, the finder of fact may properly find substantial similarity under copyright law and under the Semiconductor Chip Protection Act,' even if other portions of the chip were not copied."[140]

These substantive protections last for a term of ten years. This relatively short time reflects the congressional judgment that the rate of technical progress in the semiconductor industry is quite rapid, and that a decade of exclusivity would be sufficient time to allow the developer to recoup its costs and make a significant profit from the chip design.

The SCPA provides an optional form of notice that an owner may use on protected mask works and chips embodying those works. The notice must include either the words "mask work" the capital letter M enclosed in a circle, or the capital letter M between two asterisks (i.e., *M*) accompanied by the name of the owner of the work. Omission of the notice does not affect protection under the statute, but when it is included it constitutes prima facie evidence that other parties are on notice of the claim of protection.

There is no general defense in the SCPA analogous to the fair use concept under traditional copyright law. However a specific provision allows for the reproduction of a mask work if that reproduction is done solely for the purpose of teaching or the purpose of analyzing the logic and techniques embodied in the work.[141] This provision thus permits duplication for the limited purpose of reverse engineering, in order to gain access to unprotected aspects of the mask work such as its abstract logic.[142] Moreover this same provision of the chip act goes on to allow the person doing the reverse engineering to incorporate elements of plaintiff's protected mask work into his own new mask work, provided that the new mask work is itself original.[143]

The statute also incorporates other defenses. One is essentially the first sale defense familiar from traditional copyright law. Under

---

139. 17 U.S.C. § 902(c).

140. Altera Corp. v. Clear Logic, Inc., 424 F.3d 1079, 1085 (9th Cir. 2005), quoting Brooktree Corp. v. Advanced Micro Devices, Inc., 977 F.2d 1555, 1564 (Fed.Cir.1992).

141. 17 U.S.C. § 906(a)(1).

142. *See* the discussion of *Sega v. Accolade,* 977 F.2d 1510 (9th Cir. 1992) in the discussion of the Fair Use defense in Chapter 10.

143. 17 U.S.C. § 906(a)(2).

that provision the owner of any particular semiconductor chip product may use, distribute, or dispose of that product without the permission of the owner of the underlying mask work.[144] Another is a fairly strong version of an innocent infringer defense, which exculpates a party who had no notice that particular products were infringing from any liability for importing or distributing those products. After receiving such notice such a party will only be liable for a reasonable per unit royalty.[145]

Because the SCPA is not technically part of the copyright laws, it has its own provisions governing procedures for infringement suits and for remedies. Monetary remedies under the statute include actual damages suffered by the plaintiff plus defendant's profits, to the extent those are not included in the damage calculation. Alternatively, a plaintiff may elect to receive "statutory damages" in whatever amount the court deems just, up to a maximum of $250,000 for any one work. Successful plaintiffs can also secure injunctions and request that infringing chip products be destroyed.

In the more than a quarter of a century since the SCPA has been part of the law, it appears to have generated only two reported judicial decisions. Perhaps this means that it has had a significant deterrent effect and that everyone in the semiconductor industry is respecting the intellectual property of their commercial rivals. More likely, it may mean that infringing activities may be very difficult to discover and that innovative firms may have resorted to other techniques—such as patent and trade secret law—to protect their work.

§ 7.7   The Vessel Hull Design Protection Act

Anyone vaguely acquainted with the American political process knows that state legislatures often pass laws that are designed to benefit or protect local industries. Whether the beneficiaries are salmon fishermen in Alaska or insurance executives in Connecticut, it is no surprise to find specialized legislation on the books that favors the home team. The state of Florida has many such industries, one of which is boat building. Boat builders compete with each other, in part, by coming up with hull designs that allegedly make their boats faster, safer, or simply more attractive. The problem is that these innovative designs can be easily copied in a process that is sometimes called "plug molding" or "hull splashing." So, in 1983 Florida passed a law making this process illegal.[146] Specifically, it declared that it was "unlawful for any person to use the direct molding process to duplicate for the purpose of sale any

---

144.   17 U.S.C. § 906(b).
145.   17 U.S.C. § 907.

146.   It was codified as Fla. Stat. § 559.94.

manufactured vessel hull or component part of a vessel made by another without the written permission of that other person."

In 1984 a company called Bonito sued a competitor called Thunder Craft Boats, alleging that Thunder Craft had violated this state statute by copying its hull designs via the impermissible molding process. The defendants responded with a claim that the state statute was pre-empted because it conflicted with the patent laws. They argued, in other words, that the Florida law prevented persons from copying material that was not protected by federal patent and that was thus arguably in the public domain. The case ultimately went to the U.S. Supreme Court and in *Bonito Boats, Inc. v. Thunder Craft Boats, Inc.*[147] the Court unanimously agreed with the defendants and struck down the Florida law as being pre-empted.

As is typical in stories of this sort, having lost in the courts, the boat makers appealed to Congress. The lobbying effort took nearly a decade, but in 1998, as part of the Digital Millennium Copyright Act, Congress included a title called the Vessel Hull Design Protection Act (VHDPA) that effectively reversed the result in *Bonito* and granted the boat makers the protection they sought.[148] The statute remains, to this day, the sole federal law protecting industrial designs apart from the provisions of the patent statute relating to design patents.[149]

The VHDPA provides a stand-alone scheme of protection for the original design of a vessel hull, a vessel deck, or a combination of hull and deck taken together.[150] Interestingly, this statutory protection is available for hull designs that make the boat more attractive or distinctive *even when* the hull design was dictated solely by utilitarian considerations (such as a desire to make the boat more stable or to allow it to operate at a higher speed).[151] The

147. 489 U.S. 141, 109 S.Ct. 971, 103 L.Ed.2d 118 (1989).

148. Title V, Pub. L. 105–304, 112 Stat. 2860, codified at 17 U.S.C. §§ 1301–1332. The legislation was originally scheduled to expire after two years, but by subsequent legislation Congress made it permanent. *See* Title V, Pub. L. 106–113, § 5005, 113 Stat. 1501, 1501A593.

149. At this writing, Congress is considering extending design protection to fashion designs, but the relevant bills have not advanced very far in the legislative process. *See* H.R. 2196 (111th Cong. 1st Sess.).

150. As originally enacted, the statute protected "the design of a vessel hull" and defined the hull as "the frame or body of a vessel, including the deck of

a vessel, exclusive of masts, sails, yards and rigging." *See* § 502 of Pub. L. 105–304, 112 Stat. 2860. After the decision in Maverick Boat Co. v. American Marine Holdings Inc., 418 F.3d 1186 (11th Cir. 2005), Congress became concerned that courts might refuse to find infringement where a defendant duplicated a hull but made significant variations to the deck design. Consequently it passed legislation denominated the Vessel Hull Design Protection Amendments of 2008, Pub. L. 110–434, 122 Stat. 4972, to clarify that the design of *either* the hull or the deck of a vessel could be separately protected. *See generally* NIMMER, § 8A.14[B].

151. This result is achieved by a curious turn of statutory drafting. Section 1302(4) of the statute specifies that no protection is available for a design

reader will recall that design elements of other utilitarian objects— cars, furniture, computers—dictated solely by utilitarian consideration are *ineligible* for traditional copyright protection.[152] Unoriginal or commonplace boat hull designs are ineligible for protection under VHDPA, but a "substantial" revision or adaptation of commonplace elements is protectable.

In a number of respects, the VHDPA is parallel to the Semiconductor Chip Protection Act, which we just considered in the preceding section. Protection under the vessel hull law begins either when the design is first made public, or when a registration of the design is published by the copyright office, which ever comes first.[153] As with semiconductor chips, the term of protection for vessel hull designs is 10 years.[154] Protection is lost, however, if an application to register the design is not made within two years after the designer or owner makes it public.[155] The statute specifies that a design is made public not only when products (boats) embodying that design are sold or offered for sale, but also when they are publicly exhibited. Thus, displaying a newly designed boat at a boat show will start the clock on the two-year period for registration even if actual boats of that type are not yet available for purchase.

Once a design is made public the VHDPA mandates that it bear a statutorily prescribed notice. This can consist of the letter "D" in a circle, or surrounded by asterisks (*D*), or alternatively the words "Protected Design" or the abbreviation "Prot'd Des." In addition the notice must include the year that statutory protection began and the name of the owner. Alternatively, it can include the registration number in lieu of date and name.[156] Omission of this notice precludes monetary recovery against anyone who "began an undertaking leading to infringement ... before receiving written notice of the design protection" and an injunction will only be available if the plaintiff reimburses the defendant for "any reasonable expenditure or contractual obligation in connection with such undertaking that was incurred before receiving written notice

that is "dictated solely by a utilitarian function of the article that embodies it...." However, section 1301(a)(2) declares that "the design of a vessel hull, deck, or combination of a hull and deck, including a plug or mold, is subject to protection under this chapter *notwithstanding section 1302(4)*." (emphasis supplied). Since the statute as a whole deals *only* with boat hull designs, 1301(a)(2) renders 1302(4) completely irrelevant.

152. *See supra* § 3.5.

153. 17 U.S.C. § 1304. General information about the registration process for boat hull designs can be found online at http://www.copyright.gov/vessels/.

154. 17 U.S.C. § 1305.

155. 17 U.S.C. § 1310(a). *Cf.* Maverick Boat Co. v. American Marine Holdings Inc., 418 F.3d 1186 (11th Cir. 2005). If a claimant has registered the design in a foreign country which extends reciprocal benefits to U.S. citizens within the required 2 year period, that party has 6 months from the date of the foreign application to file in the U.S. even if that would extend beyond the two year period. 17 U.S.C. § 1311.

156. 17 U.S.C. § 1306(a)(1).

..."[157] The consequences of omission of the notice are thus severe, and stand in stark contrast to the situation that obtains with respect to the more traditional copyright notice on conventional works of authorship.[158]

As is the case in conventional copyright practice, registration is a prerequisite to an infringement suit. That would be significant in the following scenario: A party might commence sales of a boat embodying an original design, properly marked with the prescribed notice, and plan on deferring registration until near the end of the statutory two-year period for business or strategic reasons. It might then learn of infringing copying by a competitor six months later. At that point, it would have to register before it could proceed to litigate.

An owner of a protected design is given the exclusive right to make, authorize others to make, or import any useful article (presumably that would be a boat) embodying the design, and to sell or otherwise distribute those useful articles.[159] These rights obviously track the reproduction and distribution rights well known in conventional copyright law. While the rights are "exclusive" it is not an infringement to make, distribute, or import protected items without knowledge that the product embodies a design that copied from one that is protected under the statute. This means that "innocent" infringement will preclude liability. There is also a statutory defense permitting the reproduction of protected designs for purposes of teaching or analysis. This allows competitors to make copies as part of a process of reverse engineering to deduce the hydrodynamic principles that make a design effective.[160]

Protection under the VHDPA and the design patent statute are effectively mutually exclusive. The issuance of a design patent terminates all protection under the vessel hull statute.[161] For boat makers who are able to secure the design patent, this is no hardship as the design patent protection is more robust and endures for a longer term.

Boat makers presumably view the protections of the VHDPA as at least somewhat valuable. The records of the Copyright Office reveal over 400 registered hull designs since the law took effect a little over a decade ago. On the other hand, there has been only one reported decision on the merits of the statute in all that time,

---

157. 17 U.S.C. § 1307(b). The omission of notice will not, however, prevent monetary recovery against a party who only begins infringing activities after receiving written notice of the fact of statutory protection. *See* 17 U.S.C. § 1307(a).

158. *See generally* § 4.2 *supra.*

159. 17 U.S.C. § 1308.

160. 17 U.S.C. § 1309(g).

161. 17 U.S.C. § 1329.

suggesting much the same conclusion we proffered in the context of the semiconductor chip act—either registration alone has a desired *in terrorem* effect, deterring would-be pirates (how apt) from copying boat hulls or, alternatively, such copying as does go on may simply be too difficult to discover and too expensive to pursue in court.

Chapter 8

DURATION OF COPYRIGHT INTERESTS AND TERMINATION OF TRANSFERS

Table of Sections

That it is necessary to devote an entire chapter in a copyright text to the issue of copyright duration is an extraordinary thing. One might have expected a simple sentence to do the trick—something like "a copyright lasts for 'x' years" ought to have been sufficient. After all, this is essentially how the matter is disposed of regarding patents and trademarks. Alas, the story of copyright duration is not so simple. Congress has frequently changed the term of protection, and has adopted an overlay of transitional rules to deal with pre-existing works. Different categories of works are protected for different periods of time. The now obsolete requirement of copyright renewal continues to haunt the law. New provisions providing copyright owners the opportunity to nullify decades-old transactions also complicate the picture. Calculating copyright duration can be, in other words, a fairly byzantine enterprise. We begin our effort to untangle the mess by turning to the rules under the now-defunct 1909 statute.

§ 8.1 Duration Under the 1909 Act

The impatient reader might think that the rules concerning copyright duration under the 1909 Act would be a matter of purely historical interest, as that statute was supplanted more than 30 years ago by the Copyright Act of 1976. However, many works first created and published prior to 1978 have a great deal of continuing commercial and popular importance today. Movies like *Gone With the Wind* and *The Wizard of Oz*, books like *The Old Man and the Sea*, and the songs of composers like Cole Porter and Irving Berlin—not to mention Elvis and the Beatles—are just a few of the literally thousands of examples that prove the point. Since the duration of the copyright in these older works cannot be calculated or even understood without reference to the provisions of the 1909 statute, there is considerable practical reason for studying the approach of the 1909 Act.

8.1.1 Basic Principles

In its basic outline, the durational scheme of the 1909 Act was reasonably simple. It provided for an initial term of copyright protection of 28 years, dating from the time copyright was "first secured." In most cases, copyright was secured when the work was first published with a valid copyright notice.[1] During the final year of this initial term of protection, the copyright could then be renewed for an additional 28 years, making for a total maximum duration of 56 years of legal exclusivity.[2] If the copyright was not renewed, the work fell into the public domain. In actual practice, the vast majority of copyrighted works were not renewed because they had only modest (if any) commercial appeal and their authors saw no point in bothering to extend protection beyond the initial 28 year term. In some cases, however, even though the work retained popularity in the marketplace, the author inadvertently failed to renew. The result was an unintentional forfeiture of valuable exclusive rights. This so-called "trap for the unwary" was a frequently criticized feature of the 1909 durational approach.

1. In the case of unpublished works, federal copyright could be secured under the 1909 Act by registration of the work prior to publication. *See* Copyright Act of 1909 § 12.

2. 1909 Act, § 24. While federal copyright protection for most works un-der the 1909 Act began upon publication with notice, some works that were typically never published, such as motion pictures, would receive federal protection upon registration. In cases of this sort, the initial 28 year term ran from the date of inception of federal protection.

Under the 1909 scheme, prior to publication, works of authorship were was protected by "common law copyright" under state law.[3] This meant that the author had a state law cause of action against anyone who used or duplicated the work without his or her permission. This common law right was *perpetual* in duration. This effectively gave the original author the exclusive right of "first publication," because even though the unpublished manuscript was not protected by federal law, it could not be published by anyone other than the author without violating state law. As discussed in the earlier chapter concerning publication, the act of publishing the work consequently marked the dividing line between the state and federal regimes of protection. It signified that the author had traded state law protection of perpetual duration in favor of the greater protection, but limited term of federal copyright.[4]

While we have characterized this scheme as "relatively simple" it leaves a number of questions for further scrutiny. The first of these questions is determining who owned the right to the renewal term in any given work. For four declared types of works, the 1909 Act declared that the renewal interest belonged *not* to the actual human author, but rather to the "proprietor" of the work. These statutorily itemized categories are (a) posthumous works;[5] (b) periodic, cyclopedic, or other composite works; (c) works copyrighted by corporate bodies; and (d) works made for hire.[6] Thus if an employee of a graphic arts company had prepared some illustrations for her employer within the scope of her employment back in 1939, and those works were first published in 1940, when the initial copyright term expired 28 years later in 1968, the graphic arts company—not the artist—owned the right to renew for the second 28-year term since it was the "proprietor" of a work for hire.

3. In many states, this right was actually statutory in nature, but it has become customary to use the label "common law copyright" to refer to this pre-publication state law protection. See, Nimmer, Chapter 1, Overview, fn. 20.

4. *See* § 4.1.1, *supra,* for a more detailed analysis.

5. The term "posthumous" was construed in Bartok v. Boosey & Hawkes, Inc., 523 F.2d 941 (2d Cir. 1975). In that case, the composer Bela Bartok wrote his *Concerto for Orchestra* in 1943, and it was performed publicly in 1944 and 1945. In this time frame, Bartok also assigned his rights to the work to a music publisher who was to prepare and publish printed sheet music for the work. Bartok died in late 1945, and the work was not published and copyrighted until March of 1946. Upon the expiration of the initial copyright term in 1974, both the music publisher and Bartok's son claimed the right to renew. Since the work was not published until after Bartok died, the publisher argued that the work was "posthumous" and that it owned the right to renew. The court disagreed and held that a posthumous work is one as to which no copyright assignment or other contract for exploitation occurred during an author's lifetime. Since there had been exploitations during Bartok's life (the public performances and the assignment), the work was not posthumous and the renewal rights belonged to the surviving son.

6. 1909 Act, § 24. *See also* 17 U.S.C. § 304(a)(1)(B), which carries this rule concerning ownership of renewal terms forward into the 1976 Act.

For all other works, the renewal right belongs to the author who created the work—*provided he or she lived to the end of the initial 28-year term.* This is a hugely important condition, because if the author died before the end of the initial term, the 1909 law granted the renewal right to "the widow, widower, or children of the author, if the author be not living, or if such author, widow, widower or children be not living, then the author's executors, or in the absence of a will, his next of kin ..."[7] Moreover, the statute did not allow the author to vary this scheme. In other words, under this system, the listed statutory heirs cannot be "disinherited."

Assume, for instance, that a novelist published a literary work in 1947, and then died 10 years later in 1957. Assume that his wife had pre-deceased him, but that at time of his death he had one surviving child. This hypothetical novelist, however, did not like his child, and consequently left a will providing that all of his assets "including all initial and renewal term interests in copyright" would go to the American Red Cross. The Red Cross would be able to exploit the copyright in the novel from 1957 through the end of the initial term of copyright in 1975. However, when it came time to renew the copyright, the renewal term would belong to the deceased author's estranged child, not to the American Red Cross.[8]

All this was at least apparent on the face of the 1909 statute. Curiously, however, the statute did not indicate how the renewal interest should be shared if the author had died and left both a surviving spouse and children. Did each person get an equal fractional share, or did the widow(er) take 50 percent with the children splitting the other half? Although the Nimmer treatise advocates the equal shares view,[9] the two federal circuits that have squarely addressed the question favored the 50/50 approach.[10]

More significantly, the statute was also ambiguous concerning whether copyright owners could convey away their interests in the renewal term in advance—during the original term of copyright—or only after the commencement of the renewal term. Those who argued that copyright owners should not have the power to convey

---

7. 1909 Act, § 24. The case law under the 1909 Act held that the residual category of "next of kin" would be determined as a matter of state law. See *Silverman v. Sunrise Pictures Corp.*, 273 F. 909 (2d Cir. 1921).

8. *See, e.g.*, *Saroyan v. William Saroyan Foundation*, 675 F.Supp. 843 (S.D.N.Y. 1987). The irony here is that the rules regarding renewal ownership were meant to bolster the incentive effects of the copyright system. The author, knowing that his children would secure an economic return if his works proved popular, was allegedly encouraged to devote time to the creative enterprise. The incentive rationale breaks down, however, when you hate your kids but have no way to legally disinherit them.

9. Nimmer, § 9.04[A][1].

10. *Broadcast Music, Inc. v. Roger Miller Music, Inc.*, 396 F.3d 762 (6th Cir.), *cert. denied*, 546 U.S. 871, 126 S.Ct. 374, 163 L.Ed.2d 162 (2005); *Venegas–Hernandez v. ACEMLA*, 424 F.3d 50, 55 (1st Cir. 2005).

the renewal interest during the initial term based their claims on the need to protect the author. They pointed out that the whole point of the two-term approach to copyright duration was to provide a "second bite at the apple"—allowing an author to reassess the value of the work on the basis of its reception in the marketplace. They feared that an author might be pressured to convey away a copyright interest in the both the original and renewal terms for a meager sum shortly after creating the work because he or she was unaware of the true value of the work or in dire need of funds. Thereafter, the work might prove to be fabulously popular. If the author had an inalienable right to the renewal interest, he or she would be able to capture the economic value of the work during the second 28 year period, regardless of any unremunerative bargain that he or she had previously entered into.

Despite this argument, when confronted with the issue the Supreme Court held in the *Fred Fisher* case that there was no legal prohibition against the conveyance of renewal interest of copyright during the initial term.[11] Writing for the majority, Justice Frankfurter observed that "[i]f an author cannot make an effective assignment of his renewal, it may be worthless to him when he is most in need. Nobody would pay an author for something he cannot sell. We cannot draw a principle of law from the familiar stories of garret-poverty of some men of literary genius. Even if we could do so, we cannot say that such men would regard with favor a rule of law preventing them from realizing on their assets when they are most in need of funds."

Of course no property owner can transfer to another more than he himself owns. This creates a very significant limitation on the rule that authors can assign away renewal term interests during the initial term of copyright, because during that initial term the author only owns a *contingent* interest in the renewal. Recall that the renewal only vests in the author if the author lives to the start of the renewal term. Thus, the grantee of a renewal term interest only will secure rights during the renewal term if the grantor survives to the start of that renewal term.[12] As the Supreme Court explained, the 1909 Act embodied "a consistent policy to treat renewal rights as expectancies until the renewal period arrives.... Until that time arrives, assignees of renewal rights take the risk that the rights acquired may never vest in their assignors. A purchaser of such an interest is deprived of nothing. Like all

11. Fred Fisher Music Co. v. M. Witmark & Sons, 318 U.S. 643, 63 S.Ct. 773, 87 L.Ed. 1055 (1943). The case concerned the copyright to the well-known song *When Irish Eyes Are Smiling.*

12. Miller Music v. Daniels, 362 U.S. 373, 80 S.Ct. 792, 4 L.Ed.2d 804 (1960).

purchasers of contingent interests, he takes subject to the possibility that the contingency may not occur."[13]

This approach treats the renewal interest much like a contingent remainder interest in real estate. It can be conveyed, but the conveyance would only ripen into actual ownership by the grantee if the relevant contingency came to pass—namely the author's survival through the full 28-year first term of copyright. To appreciate the practical consequences of this, assume an author conveys away both the original and renewal terms of copyright under the 1909 Act in a conveyance executed shortly after the work is published. Assume further that the author then dies only a few years later, before the commencement of the renewal term. Who now has the right to renew and who will own the renewal interest? It can't be the author, because he or she is, by hypothesis, dead. Nor will it be the original grantee even though the grant assigned the renewal term because that party's interest in the renewal term was only contingent and failed upon the death of the author. In this case the renewal interest will belong to the surviving spouse, children, executor, or next of kin of the original author, as the case may be.

Thus a grantee who took an assignment early in the first term of copyright could only be sure to enjoy the copyright during the renewal term if it also obtained assignments of the renewal term interest from all the listed statutory heirs. This follows because there is no way to know in advance which of those parties would be alive 28 years down the road, and thus which one would be considered a copyright owner. Moreover, even with assignments from all these parties, divorce, remarriage, and the birth of new children after the original copyright transaction could stymie the plans of even the most cautious grantee. The situation was, to put it mildly, complicated and unsatisfactory.

8.1.2   Renewal and Derivative Works Under the 1909 Scheme

In virtually every case, parties purchase copyright interests in order to exploit them economically. One way a grantee can exploit a copyright is to simply reproduce the work and sell the copies for a profit. Thus a publisher, having obtained assignment of copyright in a novel from an author, can then print copies of the novel and sell them. Another mode of exploitation, however, is for the grantee to prepare derivative works based on the copyrighted work. Thus the publisher could prepare a Spanish translation of the novel for reproduction and sale. Similarly, it could prepare a screenplay and then license a film company to produce a movie. Indeed, sometimes

---

13.   362 U.S. at 377–78.

a party will not purchase a copyright outright, but instead take a license permitting it to create and exploit derivative works.

As we have seen in the preceding section, under the 1909 Act no assignee or licensee could be absolutely certain that it would continue to own the copyright after the first 28–year term. An assignment of the renewal term from the author might not vest if the author died before the end of the first term. This situation created an interesting ambiguity in the case of the grantee or licensee who had prepared derivative works during the first term. Should such a grantee or licensee be able to continue to exploit the derivative work during the renewal term without regard to the survival of the grantor? Or, should such continued exploitation be contingent on the survival of the grantor as well?

The Supreme Court addressed this question in its well known *Stewart v. Abend* decision.[14] There, an author named Cornell Woolrich published a mystery story entitled *It Had to Be Murder*. Shortly thereafter, he assigned the movies rights in the story to a production company. The assignment covered both the initial and renewal term of copyright in the story. Through a series of additional transactions, famed actor Jimmy Stewart and legendary director Alfred Hitchcock acquired these rights and prepared a movie based on the story—the critically acclaimed *Rear Window*, starring Stewart and Grace Kelly. Unfortunately for Stewart and Hitchcock (and we suppose for Woolrich as well), Woolrich died before the start of the renewal term. He left no wife and no children. He did have a will, however. Consequently, at the appropriate time, the executor of Woolrich's estate, as the relevant statutory party entitled to the renewal term, renewed the copyright. The executor then assigned the renewal term to a man named Sheldon Abend.[15]

Abend then demanded royalties to allow continued exhibitions and broadcasts of *Rear Window* and when the holders of the rights in the movie refused, he sued, claiming that their continued use of the movie infringed his rights as the owner of the renewal term copyright in the underlying story. As Justice O'Connor put it, the case posed the question of "whether the owner of the derivative work infringed the rights of the successor owner of the pre-existing work by continued distribution and publication of the derivative work during the renewal term of the pre-existing work." That is

---

14. 495 U.S. 207, 110 S.Ct. 1750, 109 L.Ed.2d 184 (1990).

15. To say that the executor assigned the copyright is another way of saying that they sold it, to realize cash for the beneficiary of Woolrich's will— which happened to be Columbia University. The purchaser, Abend, who is sometimes referred to as a "speculator" in discussions of this litigation, was a movie producer and during his career had acted as the representative of the estates of many noted authors and playwrights.

quite a mouthful. Rephrasing, the controversy concerned whether a grantee who had invested its own creative effort in creating a derivative work could avoid the normal rule that rights in the renewal term did not vest where the grantor died before the start of the renewal term. The Court said no and sided with Abend.

The *Abend* Court reasoned that "[i]f the assignee of all of the renewal rights holds nothing upon the death of the assignor before arrival of the renewal period, then, a fortiori, the assignee of a portion of the renewal rights, e.g., the right to produce a derivative work, must also hold nothing." It could find no language in the 1909 Copyright Act limiting the basic principle that a licensee can exploit only as much copyrighted material as it was authorized to use. Because the assignment of the renewal term to the film rights in *It Had to Be Murder* was no more than a contingent interest, and because the predicate condition of the survival of Woolrich to the renewal term had not occurred. As a result, the Court concluded that continued distribution of *Rear Window* violated copyright in *It Had to Be Murder*. The Court also dismissed concerns that this might tend to suppress the further distribution of the derivative work, noting that the owner of the renewal rights was presumably interested in realizing a profit from the work, not in driving it off the market place. The result is that a party such as the owners of the rights to the movie must negotiate with and pay royalties to a party such as Abend in order to continue exploiting the movie during the renewal term.

The merits of the *Stewart v. Abend* holding have been roundly debated.[16] Critics of the decision observe that its holding offers a windfall to authors' heirs at the expense of the creators of derivative works. A comparison of the commercial success of the critically acclaimed "Rear Window" with that of the obscure "It Had to Be Murder" suggests that in many cases, the creators of the derivative work have added more value to the licensed work than the original author himself. And, to the extent that the renewal copyright holder cannot reach a deal with the author of the derivative work, valuable derivative works may actually be removed from the market. On the other hand, the derivative work theoretically would never have been created but for the underlying material. Moreover, while Mr. Abend may not have been the most sympathetic party to demand compensation for use of the underlying story, the same rule would guarantee payments to the impoverished widow and

---

16. *See, e.g.,* Daniel A. Saunders, *Copyright Law's Broken Rear Window: An Appraisal of Damage and Estimate of Repair,* 80 CAL. L. REV. 179 (1992); Barbara A. Allen and Susan R. Swift, *Shattering Copyright Law: Will James Stewart's Rear Window Become a Pane in the* *Glass?* 22 PAC. L.J. 1 (1990); Donald A. Hughes, Jr., *Jurisprudential Vertigo: the Supreme Court's View of "Rear Window" Is for the Birds,* 60 MISS. L.J. 239 (1990). The title of the movie is, sadly, an irresistible provocation to bad puns by legal commentators.

starving children of the author of the underlying work. As we shall see, the 1976 prospectively changes the result in this kind of situation in at least some cases. So let us shift our focus to the durational scheme under current law.

§ 8.2   Duration Under the 1976 Act

Works created after January 1, 1978, are not governed by the two-term approach of the 1909 statute. Instead, the current statute provides for a single unitary term of duration of copyright. As originally enacted, the 1976 Act specified that a copyright protection began as soon as the work was fixed in a tangible medium of expression, and would then last for the life of the author plus 50 years after the authors's death. In 1998, Congress enacted the Sonny Bono Copyright Term Extension Act (which we will hereafter sometime refer to as the CTEA and sometimes as the Bono Act).[17] The Bono Act lengthened the term of works still under copyright in 1998 by 20 years and extended the term of copyright by the same amount for newly created works. Consequently, the present term of copyright is now the life of the author plus 70 years.[18] In the case of jointly authored works, the copyright lasts for 70 years after the death of the last surviving author.[19] Under § 305, all copyright terms run to the end of the calendar year in which they would otherwise expire. Note that under this scheme, there is no longer any state "common law copyright." We will have more to say about that a bit further on.

Brief reflection reveals that under this system all the works of an author pass into the public domain at the same time. By contrast, under the scheme of the 1909 Act, the various works of an author who was productive over a stretch of years would each pass into the public domain on different dates as different 28– or 56– year periods expired.

A slightly different approach is taken for certain works where the identity of a specific human author is either unclear or irrelevant. Thus, works for hire, anonymous works, and pseudonymous works are all governed by a different duration rule. Originally the copyright in such works endured for either 75 years from publication or 100 years from creation, which ever term expired first. After the CTEA, they are now protected for 95 years from publication or 120 years from creation, which ever term expires first.[20] Thus if an employee of a fabric pattern company developed a new fabric design in 2015 and the company published that design any time within the

17. Pub. L. No. 105–298, 112 Stat. 2827 (1998).

18. 17 U.S.C. § 302(a).

19. 17 U.S.C. § 302(b).

20. 17 U.S.C. § 302(c). The statute goes on to provide that anyone having an interest in the copyright to an anonymous or pseudonymous work may file a statement with the Copyright Office identifying the author of the work, in which case the copyright term becomes the life of that identified author plus 50 years.

next 25 years, the copyright would expire 95 years from the publication date. But if they did not publish the design until 2040 or later, the copyright would expire in the year 2135 (2015 + 120).[21]

Under the 1909 Act it was quite easy to determine if a work was still protected by copyright—you simply checked the copyright notice and did a little math. (If you couldn't find a copyright notice, the work was in the public domain.) Under the current law, things are not so easy. First, copyright notice is now optional. More important, under the current scheme you cannot determine the copyright status of work unless you know whether the author of a given work is still living, or if not, when exactly he or she died.

The 1976 Act handles this problem by setting up a procedure for registering deaths at the Copyright Office. Under section 302(d) anyone with an interest in a copyright may record at any time a statement either indicating the date of the author's death or the fact that the author is still living. This permits those who want to learn the status of the copyright of a work to check the records at the copyright office to see if the "life plus 70" term has expired. Of course, in many cases, no one will have bothered to file a section 302(d) document. In these cases, the statute goes on to provide that a presumption that the author has been dead for 70 years will arise if, after 95 years from the publication of a work, or 120 years from its creation (which ever comes first) the Copyright Office certifies that nothing in its records indicates that the author is living or died less than 70 years earlier.[22] Thus, for older works, users have a sure-fire way of ascertaining if the work is still protected by copyright.

§ 8.3 Works Created Under the 1909 Act and Still Protected Under the 1976 Act

When the 1976 Copyright Act became effective on January 1, 1978, there was, of course, a large body of already existing material still protected by copyright. The drafters of the new law included specific provisions adjusting the copyright duration of these older works. The goal of these transitional provisions was to provide some degree of comparability in the durational period applicable to these already existing works and new works that would be governed by the new life-plus-fifty rule, while at the same time avoiding an approach that would overly upset settled expectations such as existing copyright licenses.

---

21. If they had published in 2039, that year plus 95 would be 2134, which is before the creation date of 2015 plus 120, namely 2135.

22. 17 U.S.C. § 302(e).

The transitional rules deal with three categories of works separately. First were works that were in their renewal term of copyright on January 1, 1978. Second are those that were in their original term of copyright on that same date—and as we shall see, works in this group are actually divided into two sub-categories by subsequent legislation. Finally there are works that had not been published by the effective date of the new law and were thus still protected under state common law copyright.

8.3.1   Works Published Before 1950

Simple arithmetic indicates that any work first published[23] before 1950 would have exhausted its first 28-year term of copyright under the 1909 Act before the January 1, 1978 effective date of the current law. If the copyright in such a work was not renewed at the relevant time, that work would have fallen into the public domain and there is nothing in the 1976 Act that changes that result so as to restore the copyright in such a work. For example, the initial term of copyright for a work first published in 1945 would have expired in 1973, and if no renewal application was filed at that time, the work would thereafter be free for others to use, with no restoration of rights under the 1976 Act.

On the other hand, if a work in this category was renewed on the relevant date its renewal copyright term would, under the 1909 Act, have lasted for another 28 years. Thus in the preceding example, if the work had been renewed in 1973, the renewal term would have been scheduled to expire in 2001. This durational situation was changed by provisions in the 1976 Act. As originally enacted, if the renewal term of copyright was subsisting during 1977, the year immediately preceding the effective date of the current law, the statute provided that the total term of copyright shall be calculated as 75 years from the date of first publication.[24] Congress selected this total 75–year term because they felt this term approximated the average length of the life-plus-fifty durational rule that would apply to works first created after January 1, 1978.[25] As a result, this system provided an extra 19 years of

---

23. For simplicity, the text refers to works "published" on a certain date, since that is the time when most works obtained federal copyright protection under the 1909 Act. It should be noted, however, that for certain unpublished works, federal copyright protection could be obtained by registration. In those cases, all of the durational time periods referred to in the text would be measured from the date that federal protection was originally secured.

24. 17 U.S.C. § 304(b).

25. In other words, the drafters of the 1976 Act assumed that most creators will die about 25 years after they create the bulk of their works, making a term of 50 years after death equivalent to about 75 total years. Among the arguments in favor of extending copyright term via the Bono Act was that lifespans are increasing. Note also that for a long-lived child prodigy, the actual duration of the current life-plus-seventy-year term can be much more than 95 years. For instance, if a 10–year–old child

protection to copyright owners in comparison to the scheme under the 1909 Act (since 75 is 19 more than 56) and did so by expanding the length of the renewal term from 28 to 47 years.

With the passage of the Bono Act in 1998, the copyright term of works in this category was extended by another 20 years. In other words, the renewal term, already lengthened from 28 years to 47 years, was increased again to a total of 67 years. To put the same math in a different way, the copyright in such works would now expire 95 years after the date of publication. To continue the hypothetical from the preceding paragraph, if a work was first published in 1945, its copyright would thus expire in 2040, if it had been renewed in 1973. Importantly, the Bono Act did not restore copyright in any works that had fallen into the public domain before its date of adoption in 1998. The 20–year term extension only affected works that were still under copyright.

A further bit of arithmetic reveals that under this scheme any work first published in 1922 or earlier now lies within the public domain. Assuming effective renewal registration, the copyright on a work published in 1922 expired $28 + 47 = 75$ years thereafter, or in 1997. As a result, such a work could not take advantage of the Bono Act, which was not adopted until 1998—it was already in the public domain and would remain there. On the other hand, the copyright of a work published in 1923—again assuming effective renewal registration—will not expire until 2018.

The astute reader will realize that this means that the CTEA effectively "froze the public domain" for a 20–year period. In other words, prior to the CTEA, each new year saw copyright expire on works from the year 75 years earlier—in 1995, all work published in 1920 fell into the public domain ($1920 + 75 = 1995$); in 1996 the public became free to use everything published in 1921; and in 1997 the material from 1922 became available. Starting in 1998, however, no new material will enter the public domain until 2018.

One further complication should be mentioned here. The discussions that led to the ultimate passage of the 1976 Copyright Act actually started in the early 1960s. In anticipation of an ultimate elongation of copyright terms as part of the new law, Congress periodically extended the terms of copyrights that were already in their renewal periods on an interim basis.[26] Thus, any works that were in their renewal terms on September 19, 1962, or later, had those renewal terms extended bit-by-bit until the new act was to

---

writes a symphony, and then lives to age 90, the total term of copyright would actually be 150 years—80 remaining years of the composer's life, plus 70 years after death.

26. The statutes in questions are Public Laws 87–668, 89–142, 90–141, 90–416, 91–147, 91–055, 92–170, 92–566, and 93–573.

become effective, and thereafter were subject to the new term provided by the 1976 Act.

An example will show how this system works. Assume that a work was first published in 1910, and then the copyright was duly renewed in 1938 at the expiration of the initial 28–year term. Ordinarily, the renewal term would have expired in 1966, 28 years after the 1938 renewal. Because of the legislation described above, however, the renewal term of the work was extended until the 1976 Act became law, whereupon the work became entitled to the full "75–years–from–publication" term of copyright described in the previous paragraphs. Thus, copyright in this work did not expire until 1985. Because the work had already entered the public domain at the time the Bono Act was passed in 1998, the work was not eligible for the additional twenty years of copyright protection granted by that statute.

8.3.2 Works Published Between 1950 and 1963

Any work published in 1950 or later would have been in its first term of copyright when the 1976 Act became effective. That is because 1950 plus the 28 years of the original term of copyright under the 1909 law takes you past the magic date of January 1, 1978. As part of the original 1976 Act Congress decided to retain the requirement of mandatory renewal. It thus provided that works in this category would continue to enjoy a 28–year initial term of protection and then could be renewed for an additional term of 47 years.[27] This would provide a total of 75 years of protection, which as we previously noted is the period Congress used to approximate the life-plus–50 term that applied to works first created after 1978. With the advent of Bono Act in 1998, the renewal term was increased again, from 47 to 67 years, resulting in a maximum of 95 years of possible legal exclusivity. *Failure to renew, however, would result in a forfeiture of all further protection.* Thus a work first published in 1960 would have been under its first term of copyright protection until 1988, whereupon it would have been eligible for a renewal term that would have conferred further protection through the year 2035 (1988 +47 = 2035), which, in turn, would now automatically be extended to 2055 under the Bono Act. On the other hand, if no steps were taken to secure the renewal, the work would have fallen into the public domain in 1988.

This scheme, of course, retains one of the central defects of the 1909 law—the "trap for the unwary" quality of the renewal requirement. As a result, Congress decided in 1992 make renewal automatic.[28] However, that provision was written to operate pro-

---

27. 17 U.S.C. § 304.

28. Pub. L. No. 102–307, 106 Stat. 264 (1992).

spectively only. This means that only works first published between 1964 and 1977 secured the benefit of automatic renewal—1964 being 28 years before 1992, and 1977 being the last year that the "old" renewal system was still in effect. Works published between 1950 and 1963, and thus due to be renewed before 1992,[29] could not take advantage of an "automatic renewal." If the copyright owner failed to renew such a work by taking the affirmative step of filing at the Copyright Office, his copyright protection terminated and the work fell into the public domain.

8.3.3 Works Published Between 1964 and 1977

After 1992, works whose first 28–year term under the 1909 statute expire are granted an automatic renewal term of 67 years. Thus a work first published in 1970 would reach the end of its first term in 1998 and thereupon be granted protection through 2065 by operation of law—no filing required. Although the renewal term is conferred automatically when the first term ends, without the need to register, the statute retained an optional renewal filing mechanism, and included incentives to encourage parties to make these optional renewals.

Note that the most recent works in this group—those published in 1977—would have reached the end of their first 28–year term of protection is 2005, at which point they would have received the automatic renewal term. The year 2005 is therefore also the last year that any optional renewal applications could have been filed. For the contemporary copyright lawyer, then, there will never be either the need or the possibility to file any renewal applications. It is useful to know, however, what extra benefits were secured by those authors in this group who opted to file for the optional renewals.

First, if an optional renewal registration was not pursued, then the renewal term vested in the person who was the copyright proprietor as of the last day of the original term.[30] However, if a permissive registration was made, then the right to the renewal term would have been determined as of the (earlier) date of that permissive renewal application. Thus, permissive registration allowed the contingent holder of the renewal copyright term to lock in his rights before the end of the 28th year of the original term.

Suppose, for example, that Malfoy secures copyright in the novel "The Rowling Writ" on March 1, 1975 by publishing the novel with proper notice on that date. Assume further that Malfoy then assigned the original and renewal copyright terms in the work

29. This category consists of works published in 1963 or before, as 1963 + 28 is 1991.

30. 17 U.S.C. § 204(a)(2).

to Potter on January 19, 1978. Finally, add the sad detail that Malfoy passes away on November 1, 2003, part-way through the 28th and final year of the original copyright term.

Because this work was published after 1964 the renewal copyright term automatically commenced on January 1, 2004 and endures for 67 more years, until 2071. However, there is a question as to who owns that renewal—Malfoy's grantee (Potter) or Malfoy's statutory heirs (lets say his executor Crabbe). The answer to that question depends upon whether a permissive renewal registration was filed. If Potter had filed such a registration prior to Malfoy's death—but no earlier than January 1, 2003, the earliest possible date under the statute—then Potter would be entitled to the renewal term. Otherwise, vesting of the renewal term would be judged as of December 31, 2003, the last day of the initial term of copyright. Because Malfoy was already dead by this date, Potter, the grantee would not own the renewal term, and it would belong instead to Malfoy's executor Crabbe, for the benefit of the heirs named in Malfoy's will.

A second incentive to file the optional renewal registration concerned derivative works legitimately created under license from the copyright proprietor during the original term. If a permissive renewal registration was timely filed, then the rule of *Stewart v. Abend* applies to any derivative works created by licensees and they could not be exploited during the renewal term without permission of the owner of the renewal copyright.[31] However, if no renewal had been filed, then a derivative work prepared during the original term may continue to be used under the term of the grant. However, no new derivative work may be made during the renewal term even in the absence of a registration.[32]

Finally, permissive renewal registration also provides certain evidentiary advantages. If the author chose to make the optional registration of his claim to the renewal term during the final year of the original term, then the resulting certificate of renewal registration constitutes *prima facie* evidence of the validity of the facts stated in the certificate.[33]

8.3.4 Unpublished Works Created Before 1978

As noted previously, under the 1909 Act an unpublished work was not protected under the federal copyright law at all. Rather, it was protected under state common law copyright. Such state protection effectively endured for an unlimited term, provided the author did not publish the work.

---

31. *See supra* § 8.1.2.
32. 17 U.S.C. § 304(a)(4)(A).

33. 17 U.S.C. § 304(a)(4)(B).

With the adoption of the 1976 Act, Congress decided to bring all such unpublished works under the scope of federal copyright. That meant that these pre-existing but unpublished works would now only be protected for a limited time. As a general matter, Congress granted these works the same basic terms as those applying to new works created after the effective date of the 1976 law.[34] In the typical case of a work created by an individual author, that meant that originally such works were granted the life-plus–50 years term, and after the adoption of the CTEA, that term was enlarged to life-plus–70. For example, assume Vice President Spiro Agnew wrote a novel in 1970 about a corrupt vice president of the United States, but never published the work, hoping to revise and improve it. Agnew died in 1996. Prior to January 1, 1978 (the effective date of the 1976 Act), Agnew's novel was protected by perpetual common law copyright. After that date the state law protection was pre-empted, and the novel was protected under federal law, with a finite term of protection. Specifically, the federal copyright in this novel will expire in the year 2066, 70 years after the death of the author.

For older works, however, this system posed a problem. Imagine a work written in 1812 by Elbridge Gerry, Vice President of the United States in the administration of James Madison, containing a justification for drawing congressional districts to favor incumbents. Assume that Gerry, who died in 1814, never published the work, fearing it would embarrass President Madison, and that none of his descendants have done so in the succeeding two centuries. Until January 1, 1978, Gerry's manuscript would have been protected by common law copyright. After that date, the state protection was displaced and it became subject to federal copyright law, including the then controlling life-plus–50 durational term. Here, however, application of the duration rule means that the term of copyright expired in 1864 (1814 + 50), more than a century before the current copyright act took effect. The result is that Gerry's manuscript would have been immediately injected in the public domain the minute the 1976 Act became effective!

This struck the Congress as both unfair and unwise, so they provided that in the case of previously unpublished works, "[i]n no case, however, shall the term of copyright in such a work expire before December 31, 2002; and if the work is published on or before December 31, 2002, the term of copyright shall not expire before December 31, 2047."[35] Thus, in the preceding hypothetical, if Gerry's heirs had not published the book between 1978 and the end of 2002, the copyright would have expired on December 31, 2002. If

---

34. 17 U.S.C. § 303.   **35.** *Id.*

they did publish the book during that 25–year window the copyright will endure until the end of 2047.

§ 8.4 Criticisms of the CTEA and the *Eldred* Decision

Copyright terms are very long. An individual who writes a novel, composes a song, or paints a canvass at age 30 and then lives to age 80 will secure a total of 120 years of protection under the current statute (that is the 50 years of her remaining life plus 70 years of post-mortem protection). No one alive at the time the work is created will live to see it fall into the public domain (absent some significant advances in the medical sciences). If the author has a newborn child at age 30 when she creates that work, and if each of her descendants also have a child when they turn 30, the original author's great-great grandchild—born 40 years after the author's death—will enjoy 30 years of royalties from the work, assuming it retains some commercial popularity! It is, frankly, absurd, to think that this potential financial reward to progeny in the distant future can operate in any meaningful way as an incentive to creativity.

It is not surprising, then, that when Congress considered the CTEA, many objected that the proposed elongation of the copyright term was unnecessary and unwise. Pointing out that the statute would largely inure to the benefit of corporate interests many sarcastically dubbed the bill the "Mickey Mouse Protection Act" because it extended the soon-to-expire copyright on one of the Disney Corporations most valuable copyrighted properties.[36] Congress apparently did not find these objections persuasive. It justified the elongation of the copyright term by the need to harmonize the duration of copyright in the United States with the law in the European Union, and pointed to increases in life expectancies and to the fact that people tended to postpone having children to later in life as further justifications for its actions. Cynics were, well, cynical.

Given the controversy, it was almost inevitable that the CTEA would be challenged in court. That challenge came in *Eldred v. Ashcroft*.[37] Plaintiffs in this case described themselves as individuals and businesses who used materials in the public domain in connection with their commercial activities. They alleged that the CTEA was unconstitutional for violating both the Patent and Copyright Clause of the Constitution, and for inconsistency with the First

---

36. *See e.g.*, Herbert Hovenkamp, *Innovation and the Domain of Competition Policy*, 60 ALA. L. REV. 103, 126 (2008); Lawrence Lessig, *Copyright's* *First Amendment*, 48 UCLA L. REV. 1057, 1065 (2001).

37. 537 U.S. 186, 123 S.Ct. 769, 154 L.Ed.2d 683 (2003).

Amendment. The case wound up in the Supreme Court where the justices, by a vote of 7–2 upheld the statute.

The plaintiffs first claimed that the CTEA violated the constitutional limitation that empowers Congress to grant copyright only for "limited Times." They did not argue that life-plus–70 was "unlimited" with regard to newly created works—that would have been an argument doomed to failure from the outset. Rather they insisted that the problem was with the elongation of the copyright term for works already in existence. They claimed that once a work was created and its term of protection fixed by the statutes then on the books, Congress could not constitutionally augment that term. The Court, however, concluded that "text, history and precedent" all demonstrated that Congress had acted permissibly.

Writing for the majority, Justice Ginsburg noted that virtually every prospective adjustment to the copyright term in U.S. history had been accompanied by a simultaneous elongation of the term for already existing materials. The Court was unwilling to find such a long-standing and unbroken practice unconstitutional.[38] The Court also found a rational basis for the legislation in Congress's desire to harmonize U.S. law with that of the European Union, and it credited the Congressional claims that a longer copyright term would "encourage copyright holders to invest in the restoration and public distribution of their works." It rejected the plaintiffs claims that the periodic extension of the copyright term constituted the grant of perpetual protection in piecemeal fashion. It concluded that through its consistent past practice, Congress had implicitly promised authors of existing works that they would be treated in parity with new authors if the copyright term were extended, that such a promise acted as part of the incentive for those authors, and that thus, Congress had made an entirely legitimate judgment about how best to advance the progress of science and the useful arts.

Turning to the First Amendment claims, the Court found no conflict between the CTEA and principles of free speech. It noted that the copyright statute actually promotes expression, which is consistent with First Amendment values. Moreover, it observed that various features of the copyright scheme—notably the idea-expression distinction and the fair use doctrine—constituted "built-in First Amendment accommodations" which prevented any transgression of that amendment despite the length of the copyright term. It concluded that "when, as in this case, Congress had not

38. Justice Stevens noted in his dissent that "the fact that Congress had repeatedly acted on a mistaken interpretation of the Constitution does not qualify our duty to invalidate an unconstitutional practice when it is finally challenged in an appropriate case ..."

altered the traditional contours of copyright protection, further First Amendment scrutiny is unnecessary."

Justice Breyer began a lengthy dissent by noting that "copyright statutes must serve public, not private ends." He noted that the CTEA imposed significant "expression-related" costs on the public, because of the significant additional royalties that copyright owners could extract during the longer term, and because the longer term would impose transaction costs on users who had to track down the owners of works that might be a century or more old. He contrasted this with what he saw as the minimal incentive benefits of the statute, concluding that "the incentive-related numbers are far too small for Congress to have concluded rationally, even with respect to new works, that the extension's economic-incentive effect could justify the serious expression-related harms . . ."

From a purely doctrinal point of view, you might think *Eldred* uninteresting. It upholds the CTEA. What more need be said? Indeed, you might think that you would be none the worse if we had not bothered to tell you about the opinion at all since it leaves the previously described statutory scheme unmolested. The case's lingering importance lies, however, in its suggestion that Congress is not entirely free to tinker with the structure of copyright law without bumping up against First Amendment concerns. The Court's reference to the "traditional contours" of copyright suggest that Congress might not find such a congenial judicial reception if, in future legislation, it tried to narrow the fair use doctrine, or extend the reach of copyright beyond expression to cover underlying ideas.[39] While those who consider the CTEA unwise may be frustrated that the Court did not find a way to strike it down, they might take some comfort in the fact that the opinion seems to mark out a boundary line that Congress cannot cross in the future.

§ 8.5 Termination of Transfers

As we have noted, the two-term duration system in place under the 1909 Act gave authors a "second bite at the apple." If an author had assigned away his initial copyright interest for a pittance shortly after the creation of the work and the work proved to be a blockbuster success, he could still reap a reward 28 years down the road, when the initial term expired and the renewal term began. Of course, the judicial declaration permitting the assignment of the renewal term interest in advance significantly eviscerated this protective feature of the law—most grantees were clever

---

39. *See, e.g.*, Marshall Leaffer, *Life after Eldred: The Supreme Court and the Future of Copyright*, 30 WM. MITCHELL L. REV. 1597, 1605 (2004) ("what Justice Ginsberg said about the interplay of copyright and the First Amendment indicates real constraints on the scope of copyright law.").

enough to ask for the renewal term, and most authors were in no permission to refuse. But philosophically, at least, the 1909 statute embodied the idea of a second chance that would allow authors to re-evaluate their options after the public had a chance to react to the work.

Despite the move to a unitary term of protection under the 1976 Act, Congress thought it wise to preserve some form of this second bite at the apple. It did so by including a mechanism in the statute that permits authors to cancel a previously executed assignment or license after a specified period of time.[40] Congress also recognized that, when it elongated the duration of copyright from 56 years to 75 years for pre-existing works, it conferred a 19–year "windfall" of copyright protection. Prior to the new law, most grantees would not have expected to enjoy rights in the work for those extra 19 years, and, presumably, the price they paid for the grant would not have included any compensation for them. Congress therefore decided that the original author should be able to recover back that 19–year bonus period. Of course, the adoption of the Bono Act, conferred yet another "windfall" of 20 more years protection, with the same considerations in play.

The result is three separate provisions in the current statute that each deal with "termination of transfers." These fairly unique provisions allow copyright owners the unilateral and unconditional right to cancel bargains they previously entered into, creating the statutory equivalent of what is known on the grade school playground as a "do over." Thus, even though the 1976 Act eliminated the renewal term in favor of a unitary copyright term, the policy of protecting authors from unremunerative transfers remains.

These three provisions have many features in common. Unfortunately, they also have some differences. The most sensible way to proceed, therefore, is to take them up one by one. We promise to do our best to avoid repetition where possible.

8.5.1 Termination of Pre–1978 Transfers Under Section 304(c)

Section 304(c) is designed to allow authors and their families to enjoy the financial rewards resulting from legislative extensions to the copyright term. Recall that the 1976 Act lengthened the renewal term of copyright by 19 years. As a result, the renewal term increased from 28 years to 47 years, for a total of 75 years of copyright protection. Of course, as we have repeatedly noted, the Sonny Bono Act further increased copyright terms by another 20 years, for a total of 95 years of protection. Congress decided that authors and their families should benefit from this elongation of

40. H.R. No. 94–1476, 94th Cong., 2d Sess. 124 (1976).

protection rather than their transferees, and so included a provision that would allow the "recapture" of these extra years of copyright protection.

A termination under section 304(c) is only possible regarding *a pre–1978 grant of a renewal term interest*. This is not an arbitrary rule but rather reflects the very rationale for the provision. A grant that did *not* include a renewal term interest is one where the author retained the entire renewal term for himself. Thus, there would be no need to terminate such a grant in order to permit the author to enjoy the 39 bonus years of protection—he never gave them away in the first place. A post–1978 grant of a renewal term interest[41] would have been made with full knowledge of the increased renewal term, and the compensation paid by the grantee would presumably reflect that fact. Moreover, as we shall see, this post–1978 grant can be terminated by another provision of the statute. So, to repeat the crucial point, a section 304(c) termination only applies to a pre–1978 grant of a renewal term interest.

As we saw earlier, under the 1909 statute, renewal term interests were contingent, and could ultimately vest in any member of a statutorily defined list. In other words, if the author died before the renewal term began, the renewal belonged to a surviving spouse and/or children; if there were no such parties, it belonged to the executor of the author's will for the benefit of the beneficiaries of the will; and so on. Any one of these parties might have conveyed the renewal term interest, either contingently during the initial term of protection, or after they had come to own it definitively once the renewal term began. Consequently, section 304(c) allows termination of a grant made by any person who owned a renewal term interest in the copyright. However, a very important limitations must be noted. Transfers involving works made for hire and dispositions by will may not be terminated under this provision.[42]

You might wonder what happens if the renewal interest in a particular copyright was owned by multiple parties and if more than one of them had joined in executing a grant. For instance, assume that Alice wrote a novel, and died before the renewal term began, leaving no surviving spouse, but four children. Assuming the necessary renewal was filed at the Copyright Office, those children became equal co-owners of the renewal copyright interest at the start of the renewal term. Assume that thereafter three of the four

---

41. Works *created* after 1978 have a unitary term of protection and thus no "renewal interest" at all. However, there can be a post–1978 transfer of the renewal term interest in a *pre–1978 work*. For instance, assume that author published a novel in 1960, and filed for renewal, as required, in 1988. Assume

that in 1990 he then assigned the balance of the renewal term to a publishing company. Although this assignment is of a "renewal interest," it would *not* be subject to termination under section 304(c) because it took place after 1978.

42. 17 U.S.C. § 304(c)

children then licensed a book publisher to reproduce and distribute copies of the novel. Who can terminate that grant to the publisher? Alternatively, image that three songwriters—Tom, Dick, and Harry—collaborated on a song, and that two of them, Tom and Dick, then licensed a recording company to make and distribute recordings of that song during the renewal period. The statute deals with these two situations slightly differently.

Where the grant was executed by persons *other than the author*, the grant my be terminated "by the surviving person or persons who executed it."[43] Thus, in the four children example in the preceding paragraph, if all three of the children who executed the grant were living at the time when termination is possible, all three would have to agree to the termination. If some had passed away, those still alive would have to agree.[44] Where the grant was *executed by multiple authors*, however, the grant can be terminated by any one author "to the extent of [that] particular author's share in the ownership of the renewal copyright."[45] Thus in the Tom, Dick, and Harry example above, Tom could terminate the grant without needing Dick's cooperation or collaboration.

Under this scheme, when a non-author who granted away his or her renewal term interest has died before termination is statutorily permissible, that grantor's heirs are out of luck. In the case of deceased authors, however, the statute is more generous. Specifically, a dead author's termination interest is owned as follows:

(A) If the author dies without children, leaving only a widow/widower, then the widow or widower owns the entire termination interest.

(B) If the author leaves surviving children, without a widow/widower, then the children take the entire interest *per stirpes*.

(C) If both a widow/widower and children survive, the widow(er) takes a 50 percent interest and the children take the other 50 percent *per stirpes*.

(D) If no widow/widower, children or grandchildren are living, then the author's executor, administrator, personal representative, or trustee owns the author's entire termination interest.[46]

If, under these rules, the termination interest is controlled by multiple parties, it can only be exercised by a majority vote.

---

43. 17 U.S.C. § 304(c)(1).

44. *See,* Nimmer, § 11.03[B] ("a single grantor may not terminate his or her portion of the grant (unless he or she is the sole survivor), and a non- unanimous majority may not terminate the grant.").

45. 17 U.S.C. § 304(c)(1).

46. 17 U.S.C. § 304(c)(2)

However, that majority must be calculated via the *per stirpes* rule, which provides that each "branch" of the family receives an equal share of the termination interest, regardless of the number of persons in that branch.

For those not familiar with the *per stirpes* concept, an example is in order. Let us assume that Andy assigns away both the initial term and the renewal term interest in his novel to a publishing company, and that this assignment eventually vests because Andy survived into the renewal term. However, let us make the additional melancholy assumption that before the date arrives for termination Andy has passed away. Our hypothetical Andy is survived by his wife, Wanda, two surviving children, Carol and Candice, and three grandchildren, Gary, Greg, and Gloria, born to Andy's son Carl, who pre-deceased him. These 6 individuals would collectively control Andy's right to terminate the grant in the portions described above.

Wanda would be an indispensable party to any termination, because she controls one-half of the termination interest. No combination of children and grandchildren acting together can get to a majority without her participation. But what if Carol and Candice, Gary and Greg all oppose termination, while Wanda and the remaining grandchild, Gloria, favor it. It might seem that we now have more than one-half in favor, but that would be incorrect. This is because under the *per stirpes* approach the three grandchildren exercise Carl's rights by majority vote. Since Gary and Greg are against terminating, it is as if Carl himself were living and opposed it himself. Hence there is a 50–50 stalemate and with the necessary majority absent Wanda and Gloria would unable to terminate.

We come now to the crucial question of timing. Section 304(c) provides that termination can occur at any time within the five-year period beginning at the end of 56 years from the date copyright was originally secured, or beginning on January 1, 1978, whichever is later. In most cases, copyright would have been secured when the work was published with notice, so the termination "window" runs from 56 years after publication through 61 years after publication. Termination is not, however, automatic or self-executing. Advance written notice must be sent to the grantee in order to effectuate the termination of transfer. The notice must be served on the grantee or its "successor in title,"[47] not less than two nor more than ten years before the effective date of the termination, and the notice must specify a specific termination date that falls within the termination window.[48] It must also comply

---

47. The regulations issued by the copyright office require the party serving the termination notice to undertake a reasonable investigation to identify the current owner of the rights being terminated. 37 C.F.R. § 201.10(d)(2).

48. 17 U.S.C. § 304(c)(4)(A).

with Copyright Office regulations and be recorded in the Copyright Office.[49]

Termination causes all rights to revert to those having the power to terminate. The former grantee may continue to use derivative works under the terms of the former grant, however, provided that they were prepared before termination. No new derivative works may be prepared after the effective termination date.[50] Since a grantee might hasten to prepare additional derivative works upon receipt of a termination notice, these rules may suggest that terminating parties would be wise to give the shortest possible notice permissible under the statute. After termination, the owners are tenants-in-common who can authorize further grants if signed by the same number and proportion as are required to terminate. Any such further grant is effective for all owners, even those who did not join in signing it.[51]

To avoid the situation that arose under the 1909 Act, where renewal interests could be assigned away in advance, section 304(c) explicitly declares that "termination of the grant may be effected notwithstanding any agreement to the contrary, including an agreement to make a will or to make any future grant."[52] Thus a grantee of renewal term rights cannot ask the grantor to include in the grant a provision promising not to terminate, and the right to terminate is essentially inalienable.

An example illustrates the workings of § 304. Suppose that author Boggins procured a valid copyright upon her novel, "The Habit," in 1945 by publishing it in that year. Boggins assigns both her initial copyright term, as well as her expectancy interest in the renewal term, to Colossal Movie Studio. Under the split-term regime of the 1909 Act, the renewal term would commence in 1973 (1945 + 28). Assuming that Boggins survived into the renewal term and that the necessary filing was made with the Copyright Office, the renewal term would vest in Colossal Movie Studio. Under the 1909 Act, the copyright would have expired in 2001 (1945 + 28 + 28). However, the 1976 Act extended the copyright term to 2020 (1945 + 28 + 47), with the Sonny Bono Act then delaying the expiration date to 2040 (1945 + 28 + 47 + 20).

Under § 304(c), Boggins may terminate the grant to Colossal at any date in the period from 2002 through 2007, which is a 5–year

---

49. 17 U.S.C. § 304(c)(4)(B). The relevant regulation is at 37 C.F.R. § 201.10.

50. 17 U.S.C. § 304(c)(6). In this regard, the statutory approach is contrary to the rule in *Stewart v. Abend*, 495 U.S. 207, 110 S.Ct. 1750, 109 L.Ed.2d 184 (1990), discussed earlier in the text, which held that one who pre-

pared a derivative work under license could not continue to exploit that work without the permission of the party holding the renewal term rights in the copyright of the underlying work.

51. 17 U.S.C. § 304(c)(6)(D).

52. 17 U.S.C. § 304(c)(5).

period starting 56 years after publication. This gives Colossal the full term it bargained for when it paid for an assignment of the original and renewal terms under the 1909 Act, since at the time it bought the copyright, it expected to have exclusive rights only for 56 years. To effectuate this termination, Boggins could have served a notice of her intent to terminate as early as 1992, 10 years in advance of the earliest termination date. She could also have served that notice as late as 2005, which is 2 years in advance of the latest possible termination.[53]

If Boggins was no longer living at the relevant times, her heirs could seek termination, provided a *per stirpes* majority of them agreed to do so. The result of the termination is that Boggins or her heirs would own the copyright for its remaining 39 years of extended protection under the 1976 Act, as amended by the Sonny Bono Act.[54] They could at that point, enter into new negotiations with Colossal and execute a new grant at a new price. Alternatively, they could assign or license the copyright in the work to others for some or all of the remaining 39 year period of exclusivity, or they could simply hold the rights and exploit them themselves.

8.5.2 Termination of Pre–1978 Transfers Under Section 304(d)

Imagine that you had authored a work in 1935, and then assigned both the original and renewal term interest in that work to a grantee for a royalty equal to 10 percent of sales. If you had written this work as a young man or woman, you might still be living 56 years later in 1991 when you would be entitled to terminate the grant under section 304(c). So you consult with your financial advisors and you are told that based on the expected economic conditions and predicted popularity of the work during the remaining 19 years of copyright, the 10 percent royalty is a good deal. Based on this analysis, you do nothing, and let your termination rights expire 5 years later in 1996, content to collect royalties under the original agreement until your copyright ends in 2010.

However one morning in 1998 you open the paper to discover that the term of copyright protection has just been extended for 20 additional years by the Sonny Bono Act. This means your copyright

---

53. If you are mathematically inclined you will note that the "notice window" will always be 13 years long (in the example above it was from 1992 to 2005). That is because you can give notice at any time during an 8–year period (a maximum of 10 years in advance, and minimum of 2 years in advance) and the notice can identify any date in the five-year termination window. Eight plus five makes 13.

54. To be precise, if the termination date selected was not the first possible date within the termination "window", than the post-termination period of ownership would be, correspondingly shorter.

will not expire until 2030. Incidentally, at this point you have learned that your grandchildren all want to attend very expensive colleges. Although you will not likely live through the end of the newly expanded copyright term, you would like to see if you can extract more money from the copyright for the benefit of your heirs. Are you stuck with the terms of the original 1935 grant, or can you recapture the 20 extra years of exclusivity conferred by the CTEA and then attempt to renegotiate a better deal with another grantee?

Good news. You are not stuck. The CTEA includes a provision—section 304(d)—that allows you to recapture the 20 bonus years added to the copyright term by that law, provided certain preconditions are met. It provides that

> In the case of any copyright ... subsisting in its renewal term on the effective date of the Sonny Bono Copyright Term Extension Act for which the termination right provided in subsection(c) has expired by such date, where the author or owner of the termination right has not previously exercised such termination right, the exclusive or nonexclusive grant of a transfer or license of the renewal copyright or any right under it, executed before January 1, 1978 ... other than by will is subject to termination ...[55]

This termination may be effected any time during the 5 year period that begins 75 years after copyright in the work was first secured. In all other respects—such as who may terminate, when notice must be served, and how derivative works are treated—the various rules of section 304(c) govern for section 304(d) terminations.

To appreciate when 304(d) can be invoked, let us look a bit more closely at the preconditions set out in the statutory language quoted above. The effective date of the Sonny Bono Act was October 27, 1998. The first condition under 304(d) is that the copyright must still be in its renewal term on that date. In our hypothetical case, that was true—the work was published in 1935, and under the pre-Bono version of the 1976 Act it was protected for a total of 75 years, all the way until 2010. Any work published in 1923 or later would meet this condition because prior to the CTEA the term of protection was 75 years and 1923 + 75 = 1998.[56]

Next, the termination right under 304(c) must have "expired" by the effective date of the Bono Act, namely October 27, 1998. The section 304(c) termination window runs from 56 years after publication until 61 years after publication, but notice must be given a

---

55. 17 U.S.C. § 304(d).

56. All copyrights expire on December 31st of the relevant year, 17 U.S.C.

§ 305. Thus a copyright due to expire in 1998 would still have been subsisting on October 27th of that year.

minimum of two years before the last possible termination date, which is 59 years after publication. In our hypo, that would have been 1994 (1935 + 59 = 1994). Consequently, this right would indeed have already expired by October 1998 when the Bono Act was signed. If you are mathematically adept, you will note that this means that a 304(d) termination is only possible for works published on or before October 26, 1939, because that date is just one day more than 59 years before the effective date of the Sonny Bono Act.[57]

Finally, the author must not have exercised his or her rights under section 304(c), which was the case in our hypothetical above. Thus in the hypo you or your statutorily designated successors would have a right to terminate the grant on a date of your choosing in the window from 2010 to 2015 provided that you gave advance notice no more than 10 but no less than 2 years in advance of the selected date. The result will be recapture of (all or most) of the 20 bonus years granted by the CTEA.

8.5.3   Case Law Under Sections 304(c) and 304(d)

It hardly needs saying that the scheme described above lays out a daunting path for copyright owners. As one district court observed, "the termination provisions contained in the Copyright Act of 1976 have aptly been characterized as formalistic and complex, such that authors, or their heirs, successfully terminating the grant to the copyright in their original work of authorship is a feat accomplished 'against all odds.' "[58]

This complexity is magnified because in many cases, the grants that are purportedly terminated do not involve a single individual work, but rather a group of works, often all chronicling the adventures of a hugely popular character who becomes increasingly defined in each successive story.[59] In these kinds of cases there can be dozens of derivative works, with resulting disputes over the original date of publication of various works and hence ambiguity about the calculation of the proper termination window and notice dates. There can also be dozens of licensees and sub-licensees,

---

57. *See,* 67 Fed. Reg. 69134, 69135 (Nov. 15, 2002) (Copyright Office analysis of amendments to regulations governing termination of transfers).

58. Siegel v. Warner Bros. Ent. Inc., 542 F.Supp.2d 1098 (C.D. Cal. 2008) (quoting Patry on Copyright). *See also,* William Patry, *The Failure of the American Copyright System: Protecting the Idle Rich,* 72 NOTRE DAME L. REV. 907 (1997)

59. For instance, termination controversies have arisen over the rights to

Tarzan, Superman, Captain America, Winnie the Pooh and Lassie. *See,* Burroughs v. Metro–Goldwyn–Mayer, Inc., 683 F.2d 610 (2d Cir. 1982); Siegel v. Warner Bros. Ent. Inc., 542 F.Supp.2d 1098 (C.D. Cal. 2008) (Superman); Marvel Characters v. Simon, 310 F.3d 280 (2d Cir. 2002) (Captain America); Milne ex rel. Coyne v. Stephen Slesinger, Inc., 430 F.3d 1036 (9th Cir. 2005) (Winnie the Pooh); Classic Media v. Mewborn, 532 F.3d 978 (9th Cir. 2008).

raising questions of who is entitled to notice and how diligent the author must be in tracking down the parties.

In other situations decades of acrimony between grantor and grantee may have led to a tortured litigation history with multiple amendments to the original grant or with settlement agreements that may purport to alter or reaffirm the original grant. The case law interpreting sections 304(c) and (d) consequently tends to be very fact specific.

Some cases illustrate the pitfalls posed by the notice requirement. For instance, in *Burroughs v. Metro–Goldwyn–Mayer, Inc.,*[60] the famous author Edgar Rice Burroughs had assigned his copyright interests in several of his famous Tarzan stories to a family owned-corporation called ERB, Inc. In turn, ERB, Inc. granted a nonexclusive license to film rights in certain *Tarzan* stories and characters to MGM. In 1977 the author's heirs served a notice of termination on ERB, Inc., but not MGM. That notice listed 9 of the 14 works covered by the original grant but due to a careless error, omitted 5 titles.[61]

When MGM sought to produce a new movie featuring Tarzan in 1981, the author's heirs brought suit, claiming that they had effectively terminated the *Tarzan* license. However, because the termination notice had failed to list the five licensed titles, the Second Circuit found that MGM still had the rights to use those works, and that those rights, in turn, were sufficient to allow it to exploit the Tarzan character.

In a concurring opinion, Judge Newman disagreed with his colleagues on the significance of the omission of the five titles. Under his analysis, if "the character Tarzan is sufficiently delineated to support a copyright ... there is no dispute that the delineation was complete upon the 1912 appearance of the first Tarzan title *Tarzan of the Apes*. Subsequent titles, including the omitted five, contained original exploits of Tarzan, but were not original with respect to the character itself." In his view, then, the failure to list the five titles would allow MGM to continue to use only those precise stories, but did not leave them with rights to the Tarzan character more generally.

Nonetheless, Judge Newman found the heirs' notice to be defective for a different reason—namely because it had not been served upon MGM. By giving notice only to the family-owned corporation which was the nominal grantee from Burroughs, the heirs were effectively serving notice upon themselves. Judge New-

---

60.   683 F.2d 610 (2d Cir. 1982).

61.   The omitted works were The Son of Tarzan; Tarzan, Lord of the Jungle; Tarzan, Guard of the Jungle; The Tarzan Twins; and our personal favorite, Tarzan and the Ant Men.

man concluded that the heirs should have served MGM, the realistic grantee under the circumstances.

Other cases have grappled with whether subsequent agreements between the parties eliminated the right to terminate the original grant. For instance, in *Milne ex rel. Coyne v. Stephen Slesinger, Inc.*,[62] the Ninth Circuit had to consider a purported termination of a grant concerning the copyright rights to the beloved and fabulously lucrative character Winnie the Pooh. Between 1924 and 1928 author A.A. Milne secured copyright in four works introducing Pooh Bear and his various friends to the world. In 1930 Milne granted Stephen Slesinger exclusive merchandising rights to these characters during both the initial and renewal term of the copyrights in return for percentage royalties.[63] Slesinger in turn conveyed these rights to a corporate entity called Stephen Slessinger, Inc. (SSI). Milne died in 1956.[64] In 1961 SSI assigned its rights over to the Disney company. In 1983, with the possibility of termination of the original Milne grant imminent[65] Disney approached Milne's son Christopher Robin,[66] and suggested that they negotiate a new agreement. As the court put it, "using the bargaining power conferred by his termination right [he] negotiated and signed on April 1, 1983 a more lucrative deal with SSI and Disney...."

In November of 2002 Milne's granddaughter Claire served a notice of termination under section 304(d) on SSI specifying an effective date of 2004.[67] SSI argued, however, that the 1930 grant could not be terminated because it was no longer in existence, having been supplanted by the 1983 agreement between Christopher and SSI. The court agreed with this claim, and thus found Claire's effort to terminate ineffective.

To avoid the effect of the 1983 agreement, Claire pointed to the provision of the statute that provides that termination of a grant may be effected "notwithstanding any agreement to the contrary." The court was unmoved, however, observing that

62. 430 F.3d 1036 (9th Cir. 2005)

63. Slesinger was a literary agent, comic strip syndicator, and pioneer of the licensing industry. If you are curious about him, some information is available at http://www.stephenslesinger.com/index.php?id=16.

64. Since the last of the copyrights involved in the case was secured in 1928, Milne lived long enough so that the grant of renewal rights vested in his grantee (1928 + 28 = 1956).

65. The earliest termination date for the earliest work would have been 1924 + 56 or 1980. The latest termination date for the latest work would have been 1928 + 61 or 1989.

66. Really.

67. The 304(d) termination window would be from 75 to 80 years after initial publication of the works in 1924, through 1928. That would be from 1999 through 2004 for the oldest work and from 2003 to 2008 for the newest. Claire's choice of 2004 conveniently fell within the 5–year window for all four works.

> The beneficiaries of the Pooh Properties Trust were able to obtain considerably more money as a result of the bargaining power wielded by the author's son Christopher, who was believed to own a statutory right to terminate the 1930 grant.... Although Christopher presumably could have served a termination notice, he elected instead to use his leverage to obtain a better deal for the Pooh Properties Trust. His daughter, Claire, was a beneficiary of this new arrangement and her current dissatisfaction provides no reason to discredit the validity of the 1983 agreement.... [68]

In arriving at this conclusion, the *Milne* court distinguished an earlier opinion of the Second Circuit in *Marvel Characters, Inc. v. Simon.*[69] That suit involved efforts by Joseph Simon, the creator of Captain America, to terminate a grant he had made of the copyright interest in that character to the predecessors of the current Marvel Comics. In the 1960s, as part of a settlement of some earlier litigation, Mr. Simon signed an agreement which characterized the copyright interests as works made for hire. When Simon attempted termination years later, Marvel pointed to that agreement and argued that termination was not available with regard to a work made for hire.

The Second Circuit refused to give effect to the characterization of the work contained in the settlement. It reasoned that this was precisely the kind of forbidden waiver of termination rights contemplated by the "no agreement to the contrary" clause in the statute. As that court explained, "if an agreement between an author and a publisher that a work was created for hire were outside the purpose of § 304(C)(5), the termination provision would be rendered a nullity; litigation savvy publisher would be able to utilize their superior bargaining position to compel authors to agree that a work was created for hire in order to get their works published."

The *Milne* court read the *Marvel* decision as one forbidding the *after-the-fact recharacterization* of a work. Finding that the 1983 agreement between Christopher Milne and SSI operated only prospectively, it concluded that the *Marvel* decision did not require it to treat the 1983 agreement as a forbidden "agreement to the contrary."[70]

Just a few years later, however, the Ninth Circuit confronted another situation involving a renegotiation of an underlying grant

---

68.   430 F.3d at 1044–45.

69.   310 F.3d 280 (2d Cir. 2002).

70.   *Accord*, Penguin Group (USA) Inc. v. Steinbeck, 537 F.3d 193 (2d Cir. 2008), *cert. denied*, ___ U.S. ___, 129 S.Ct. 2383, 173 L.Ed.2d 1326 (2009) (new 1994 grant terminated earlier grants from the 1930s involving several of John Steinbeck's novels, thus precluding statutory termination of those original grants).

followed by an effort at termination, and this time it found the renegotiated grant to be a forbidden "agreement to the contrary." In 1938 Eric Knight authored the story *Lassie Come Home* and published it *Saturday Evening Post* magazine. Two years later he expanded the story into a full-length novel. He died in 1943 long before the expiration of the initial term of copyright in these works, so when the initial term of copyright in the story and novel ended in 1966 and 1968 respectively, the renewal interests belonged to his widow and three daughters. They properly renewed.

Some years later, in 1976, one of those daughters, Winifred Mewborn, assigned all television and movie rights in the renewal term to a production company for the lump sum of $11,000. When the production company was finally able to obtain a similar assignment from her sisters, those assignments included ancillary rights, such as merchandising. So the production company returned to Winifred and persuaded her to execute a second assignment in March, 1978, once again conveying movie and television rights, but this time also including the ancillary rights. She was paid $3,000 for this second agreement.

In 1996, Winifred served a notice of termination under section 304(c), seeking to cancel her own 1976 grant, effective May 1, 1998. Over the next several years the parties exchanged what the court characterized as "bombastic," "acrimonious," and "vituperative" correspondence, culminating in a declaratory judgment suit filed by the production company's successor. In *Classic Media, Inc. v. Mewborn* the court ultimately decided in favor of Winifred, and distinguished its own prior decision in *Milne*.[71] The crucial difference, according to the *Mewborn* court, was that when Christopher Milne renegotiated his deal with Disney, he had a present right to terminate, and used his leverage to secure a more lucrative deal. Hence, the subsequent agreement in *Milne* did not subvert the termination rights or the Congressional purpose of insuring authors and their heirs a "second bite at the apple." By contrast, "unlike Milne, Mewborn had nothing in hand with which to bargain."

The result seems to be that in the Ninth Circuit, the renegotiation of a decades old grant at a time when termination is possible will effectively rescind the old grant and make it non-terminable at any point down the road. However, earlier renegotiations, before the grantor has the weapon of possible termination readily at hand, and where the author or heirs thus lack bargaining power, will not have such an effect.

71. Classic Media, Inc. v. Mewborn,
532 F.3d 978 (9th Cir. 2008).

8.5.4   Termination of Post–1978 Transfers Under Section 203

A copyright owner who negotiated a license or assignment after January 1, 1978 would—at least in theory—have been fully aware of the adjustments to the copyright term made by the new statute. There would be no need to give such a copyright owner a right to re-capture the "windfall" of the 19 extra years tacked on to the renewal term because he would have known about the elongated term at the time any deal was negotiated. There would still be the possibility, however, that such a copyright owner might enter into a contract immediately after creating the work before it was possible to determine its market value. If the work proved popular and the contract was for a long duration, a grantee who paid a pittance might enjoy decades of enormous profits, with the author deprived of any meaningful share. In other words, solicitude for the author might still justify giving him a "second bite at the apple" independent of any elongation of the copyright term.[72]

To deal with that situation, the 1976 Act contains yet another termination provision—section 203. This provision provides a right of termination for any "exclusive or nonexclusive grant of a transfer or license of copyright ... executed by the author on or after January 1, 1978, otherwise than by will."[73] As this language makes plain, the provision relates to *post–1978 grants* only, regardless of when the work was created or published. As it also makes plain, this provision only covers grants *by the author*. Thus, if an author assigns a copyright to his sister, and she shortly thereafter then assigns to a publisher, the sister would have no right to terminate her grant. She is stuck with her bargain. As with the termination right under sections 304(c) and (d), the section 203 termination right is not available for works made for hire, nor is it available for transfers by will.

A section 203 termination can occur during the five-year period starting at the end of 35 years from the date of the execution of the grant. Unlike the section 304 termination windows, which are measures *from the date copyright was first secured* (usually the date

---

72. One commentator has summarized this rationale a bit more skeptically as follows: "What justifies the Act's disregard for authors' initial grants over thirty-five years old? Legislative history and commentary answer that the termination rights aim to correct the sorts of bad bargains that struggling authors make in desperation and, after later success, come to regret. Termination rights reflect, in other words, a paternalistic view of authors. Authors need termination rights so they can second-guess

their choices, thus correcting the market's failure to foresee and fairly price the future value of long-term grants. The now-famous Stephen King, for instance, can thereby renegotiate a publishing contract he rashly accepted as a credulous and eager novice." Tom Bell, *Authors' Welfare: Copyright as a Statutory Mechanism for Redistributing Rights*, 69 BROOK. L. REV. 229, 252–53 (2003).

73. 17 U.S.C. § 203.

of publication), the section 203 window is measured *from the date of the grant*. The point here is to allow the grantee a predictable, and fairly long period in which to exploit the work under the original contract terms before the grant can be terminated and the deal can be renegotiated.

There is also a special provision in section 203 providing that where a grant includes a right of publication, the termination window will be either the five-year period beginning 35 years after publication, or 40 years after the grant was made, which ever is earlier.[74] This curious rule requires a bit of explanation. A publisher who is the grantee of copyright rights from an author is not likely to be able to get the work into print immediately after a grant is executed. The work might need to be edited, the physical production of copies might take time, there might be a marketing campaign before publication, and so on. Of course, the publisher does not begin to make any money until the work is actually published and available for sale. So, the statute seeks to guarantee the publisher a full 35-year period to exploit the work under the grant by not starting the "termination clock" until publication. On the other hand, if the publisher were to delay publication indefinitely, the author would never get the right to terminate. So if the publisher procrastinates more than five years in getting the book into print, the clock will start running regardless. That is the point of the alternative 40–years-from-the-grant proviso.

If a grant has been executed by two or more authors of a joint work, termination under section 203 requires the agreement of a majority of those who executed the original grant. For instance, assume that the 5 members of a band collaborated on a new song and that thereafter three of them—Jermaine, Tito, and Marlon— co-signed a "synch" license allowing a motion picture production company to use the song as part of a movie soundtrack.[75] At the appropriate time some decades later, any two of these three could terminate the grant. If only Tito wanted to terminate, however, he would be out of luck. This is contrary to the approach in section 304, where each co-author can terminate individually as to his own proportionate share of the copyright.[76]

In most other respects, section 203 operates similarly to section 304. There is the same advance notice requirement, with the same timing requirements. There are the same rules concerning control of the termination right where an author has died, including the same requirement of majority action under the *per stirpes* approach

---

74. 17 U.S.C. § 203(a)(3).

75. Recall that these three would have to account to the other two co-authors for a proportionate share of the profits received from this transaction. *See* § 5.3.2, *supra*.

76. *Supra,* at note 45.

when the deceased author has left multiple heirs. There is the same rule permitting the former grantee to continue to use derivative works prepared under the terms of the former grant, provided that they were prepared before termination and forbidding the preparation of any new derivative works after the effective termination date.[77]

Following a termination of transfer under section 203, all rights revert to the those having the power to terminate. Further grants may be made if signed by the same number and proportion of owners as are required for termination. This further grant is effective for all owners, even those who did not join in signing it.[78]

To take a relatively simple example, suppose that a Mr. Rander authored a novel entitled "King of the Rings" in 1979. In 1980, he licenses Magnificent Movie Studios (MMS) to prepare a movie version of the novel, to distribute that movie version theatrically, to reproduce and distribute that version on DVDs, and to make as many remakes of the movie as it may choose. The license recites that it is for "the full remaining term of the copyright in the underlying work." Rander would be able to terminate this license effective on any date from 2015 through 2020 (that is 35 to 40 years after the grant). He could serve notice to this effect as early as 2005 (10 years before the earliest termination date) or as late at 2018 (2 years before the latest termination date). If Rander had died before these date arrived, his widow and/or children could exercise his rights, provided a *per stirpes* majority of them concurred.

Because any movies made before the effective date of termination would be derivative works, MMS could continue to exhibit and distribute those under the terms of the original grant. Thus if that grant provided for royalties based on a percentage of revenues, MMS would still have to pay those to Rander. Rander would have no leverage to renegotiate that rate. However MMS would not be free to remake the movie. That right would be cut off by the termination and it would have to renegotiate with Rander or his heirs if it wanted to do that.

Section 203 has not yet spawned any litigation. The first terminations under this provision will cover grants made in the year 1978, and the earliest they could become effective would be 35 years thereafter in 2013. It will likely be in that year or shortly thereafter that we will see the first flurry of lawsuits. Some of that litigation is likely to involve the recording industry. While it has long been the custom for recording artists to execute contracts with record labels stipulating that the resulting sound recordings are

---

77. 17 U.S.C. § 203(b). **78.** 17 U.S.C. § 203(b)(3).

"works made for hire," that is far from clear.[79] If these works are *not* works made for hire, performers may attempt to argue that their contracts were actually terminable assignments. Given that some of the recordings in question remain both popular and lucrative, the question is likely to be litigated with some passion.[80]

§ 8.6　Copyright Restoration for Certain Foreign Works

One of the few straightforward rules regarding copyright duration is that once a work falls into the public domain it remains there. Alas, even this reliable rule has an exception.

The story here requires us to recall the American fascination with formalities as a condition for copyright protection. For instance, we have seen elsewhere in this volume that strict compliance with the notice requirement on publicly distributed copies of works was for most of our history a precondition of copyright protection.[81] As this chapter has revealed, prior to 1992 the requirement of an affirmative renewal application was also essential in order to enjoy the full term of copyright (thereafter renewal became automatic).

Not surprisingly, many foreign authors did not observe these formalities. We say "not surprisingly" because no such formalities were required in their home countries. The result was that some of the works of some foreign authors, though still protected in their home countries and in most of the rest of the world, had fallen into the public domain in the United States. In 1989 the United States finally adhered to the Berne Convention, the leading international treaty regarding copyright issues. Article 18 of Berne requires new signatories to protect the copyrights of all works from other Berne member states that have not yet entered the public domain in their countries of origin.[82] Nonetheless, the United States ignored the problem and other nations, eager to see us participate in Berne, bit their tongue.

However three years later, in 1992, when the United States entered into the North American Free Trade Agreement, or NAFTA, our continental trading partners requested that we deal with this issue. The issue was particularly salient to Mexico because

---

79. Recording artists are not usually employees of the record labels, and sound recordings are not listed in the statute as one of the nine types of independently commissioned works which can be made into a work made for hire by contract. For a full discussion, *see* § 5.2.2, *supra*.

80. For a general discussion, *see*, Daniel Gould, *Time's Up: Copyright Ter-*

mination, Work-for-Hire and the Recording Industry, 31 COLUM. J.L. & ARTS 91 (2007).

81. *See* § 4.2, *supra*.

82. The full text of the Berne Convention can be found at: http://www.cornell.edu/treaties/berne/overview.html.

there was a large film industry in that country and many Mexican films had fallen into the public domain in the United States due to failure to observe formalities.[83]

Congress responded the following year by adding a new section 104A to the copyright statute, providing for restoration of copyright in certain motion pictures.[84] Just one year later, the major trading nations of the world concluded negotiations on what was to become the World Trade Organization Agreement. As a result, in the statute known as the Uruguay Round Agreements Act (URAA),[85] the United States amended section 104A to make it applicable to all foreign works that had lost copyright due to non-compliance with formalities. The result is the unprecedented resurrection of copyright in works previously in the public domain.

The scheme created by section 104A has been characterized as "highly technical, convoluted, oftentimes difficult to decipher and fraught with potential unintended consequences."[86] We will endeavor to sketch the basics with a broad brush. A public domain work must fulfill four requirements in order for its copyright to be restored. First, the copyright must have been forfeited for one of three statutorily specified reasons, namely: (1) formalities such as notice or registration had not been observed, (2) the work was a sound recording published before February 15, 1972, or (3) the United States and the nation of the work's origin did not enjoy copyright relations.[87] If the work is in the public domain for any other reasons section 104A will not restore copyright.

Second, the work must not be in the public domain in its nation of origin due to the expiration of the term of protection.[88] Third, at least one of the authors of the work had to have been a national or domiciliary of a so-called "eligible country."[89] An eligible country must either be a World Trade Organization (WTO)

---

83. *See generally* CARL J. MORA, MEXICAN CINEMA: REFLECTIONS OF A SOCIETY, 1896–1988 (1989).

84. *See*, § 334 Pub. L. 103–182, 107 Stat. 2115 (Dec. 8, 1993). Some commentators argue that section 104A significantly exceeds the requirements of the Berne Conventions. *See, e.g.*, Peter Jaszi, *Goodbye to All That—A Reluctant (and Perhaps Premature) Adieu to a Constitutionally–Grounded Discourse of Public Interest in Copyright Law*, 29 VAND. J. TRANSNAT'L L. 595, 607 (1996) ("Section 104A of the Copyright Act not only fulfills the mandate of Article 18 but goes well beyond it.").

85. Pub. L. No. 103–465, 108 Stat. 4809 (1994).

86. William Gable, *Restoration of Copyrights: Dueling Trolls and Other Oddities Under Section 104A of the Copyright Act*, 29 COLUM. J. L. & ARTS 181, 187 (2005).

87. 17 U.S.C. § 104A(h)(6)(c). An example of a work in the third category would be material published in China before it became a member of the WTO. Because the United States did not have any copyright treaty with China such a work would have been injected into the U.S. public domain upon publication. Copyright in such a work is restored by section 104A. *See* NIMMER, § 9A.04[A][1][b][ii].

88. 17 U.S.C. § 104A(h)(6)(B).

89. 17 U.S.C. § 104A(h)(6)(d).

member, Berne Convention signatory, or the subject of a Presidential proclamation.[90] Importantly, although the United States is a WTO member and Berne signatory, it is expressly excluded from the list of eligible countries. As a result of this definition, domestic parties whose works were injected into the public domain by publication without notice, or failure to renew, cannot rely upon § 104A for restoration of their copyrights. Fourth, if the work was published, it must have been published in an eligible country and not published in the United States within 30 days following such publication.[91]

For eligible works, restoration is automatic, effective on January 1, 1996.[92] On that date, all covered works leap from the public domain back into the shelter of copyright protection. The restored copyright subsists for the duration of the statutory term as if the work had never entered the public domain.[93] Ownership of the restored copyright vests initially in the author or other proprietor as determined by the law of the source country of the work.[94] Copyrights in restored works provide their proprietors with the same rights as other sorts of copyrights.

A moment's reflection suggests that the removal of works from the public domain could seriously prejudice parties who had built their business on the premise that a particular work or group of works was freely available. Such parties might have significant inventories of copies or phonorecords of restored works, perhaps produced at great expense, that it would now be illegal to sell to the public. Such parties might have entered into contracts to perform restored works, and have expended money to reserve a theater and pay actors and directors, only to confront the dilemma that the performance would now be an infringement. Such parties might have produced derivative works, such as a movie based on a novel, or a recording based on a song, which they could no longer legally exploit once copyright in the underlying work was restored.

Much of the complexity of section 104A is due to the Congressional effort to protect the interest of persons in this situation, who are referred to in the statute as "reliance parties." A reliance party is one who engaged in acts which would have been infringing before the source country of the work became an "eligible country," and continued to do so thereafter.[95] The definition also includes any

90. 17 U.S.C. § 104A(h)(3).

91. 17 U.S.C. § 104A(h)(6)(d).

92. For nations that were not members of either the WTO or Berne on this date, the relevant date is whenever they adhere to one of those two agreements.

93. 17 U.S.C. § 104A(a)(1).

94. 17 U.S.C. § 104A(b).

95. 17 U.S.C. § 104a(h)(4). Countries that were members of the Berne Convention when the URAA was adopted became eligible countries on the date the URAA was signed, namely on December 8, 1994, even though the effective date of copyright restoration was

party who either made or acquired one or more copies or phonorecords of a work before that same date.

In order to enforce a restored copyright against a reliance party, the owner of copyright in a restored work must serve a notice of intent to do so. The statute permits this notice to either be served directly on the reliance party, or to be filed with the Copyright Office. In the latter case, however, the notice had to be filed within 24 months after the date of restoration—which for most holders of restored copyrights means that such a notice would have had to have been filed by December 31, 1997.[96] After receiving notice, a reliance party is allowed a twelve-month grace period in which to sell off copies of the restored work, or to continue to perform, distribute, or display the restored work, without liability to the copyright owner. If the reliance party had created any derivative works prior to restoration, the statute allows the reliance party to continue to exploit such works upon payment of "reasonable compensation" to the holder of the restored copyright.[97]

Interpretation of the definition of a "reliance party" became crucial in *Troll Co. v. Uneeda Doll Co.*,[98] which involved a dispute over the copyright to "troll dolls," characterized by the court as "those ugly but somehow endearing plastic dolls with oversized heads, big grins, pot bellies, and frizzy hair." The dolls were created by a woodcarver from Denmark in the 1950s and fell into the public domain when copies lacking proper copyright notice were sold in the United States. Uneeda, the defendant company in the case, had sold troll dolls in the United States periodically starting in the mid–1960s. In 2005, the plaintiff served a notice of intent to enforce a restored copyright on Uneeda, and then commenced suit for copyright infringement. Uneeda claimed that the suit was premature because it was a reliance party entitled to a twelve-month period in which to sell off its inventory.

It was clear that Uneeda had sold troll dolls before Denmark became an "eligible country." The problem was that it had suspended sales for almost a decade, only resuming them after the crucial date. The question was thus whether section 104A required an uninterrupted course of conduct by a purported reliance party, or whether "periodic renewal of cyclical exploitation" was enough to achieve reliance party status. The court concluded that both

not until January 1, 1996. Thus, in most cases, to be a reliance party one must have engaged in the defined activities prior to late 1994. *See*, Patry § 24:39; Nimmer, § 9A.04[C][1][b][ii].

96. 17 U.S.C. § 104A(d)(2). The statute requires that these notices must be published in the Federal Register. 17 U.S.C. § 104A(e)(1)(B).

97. 17 U.S.C. § 104A(d)(3). If the parties cannot agree on reasonable compensation for the use of a derivative work, the statute says the matter should be determined by an action in federal district court.

98. 483 F.3d 150 (2d Cir. 2007).

policy and legislative history required that the defendant must engage in a continuous course of conduct in order to be deemed a reliance party. It reasoned that a

> party that has invested time and resources into *ongoing exploitation* of a work in reliance on the work's public domain status would incur substantial harm from the sudden inability to engage in that business; the URAA therefore requires owners of restored copyrights to notify such parties of their intent to enforce and gives those parties a year after notification to sell off their inventories. By contrast, a party that has voluntarily ceased exploitation for a non-trivial period of time, here, nine or ten years—even where such exploitation was episodic due to the cyclical nature of consumers' interest in the product— has a less substantial interest in being able to resume that exploitation after restoration.[99]

Perhaps the most fundamental question raised by section 104A is whether Congress has the Constitutional authority to remove works from the public domain. That question was put before the Tenth Circuit in *Golan v. Gonzales*.[100] There, a group of orchestra conductors, educators, performers, and others challenged the copyright restoration provisions of the URAA as inconsistent with both the Copyright Clause and the First Amendment of the Constitution.[101] The court rejected the claim based on the copyright clause, but concluded that there were significant questions about the statute's compatibility with free speech principles requiring a remand. Thereafter, the district court concluded that the statute violated the First Amendment only to be reversed by the Tenth Circuit.[102]

Regarding the copyright clause, the plaintiffs claimed that if Congress were allowed to remove works from the public domain, it would have a blank check to evade the "limited times" language in the relevant Constitutional grant of authority. While acknowledging the theoretical merit of the claim, the court did not find the concern persuasive in light of the actual history of section 104A. As

---

99. 483 F.3d at 159 [emphasis supplied].

100. 501 F.3d 1179 (10th Cir. 2007).

101. The plaintiffs in *Golan* also challenged the Sonny Bono Act in this suit, claiming that its life-plus-70 term violated the "limited times" language of the Copyright Clause of the Constitution because it was "effectively perpetual"— a claim the plaintiffs in *Eldred* had chosen not to make. The court rebuffed this argument commenting "though plaintiffs may be correct that the *Eldred* Court did not technically address this term, the rationale underlying *Eldred* compels us to conclude that the CTEA-imposed timespan passes constitutional muster." 501 F.3d at 1185. *See also* Kahle v. Gonzales, 487 F.3d 697 (9th Cir.2007).

102. Golan v. Holder, 611 F.Supp.2d 1165 (D.Colo. 2009) rev'd, ___ F.3d ___, 2010 WL 2473217 (10th Cir. 2010).

it put it, "it would be troubling if Congress adopted a consistent practice of restoring works in the public domain in an effort to confer perpetual monopolies. But this argument is similar to one the *Eldred* plaintiffs raised, and, like the *Eldred* Court, we are mindful that 'a regime of perpetual copyrights is clearly not the situation before us.'" Echoing the rational basis analysis of *Eldred*, the *Golan* court found the Congressional justification for section 104A adequate, concluding "we do not believe that the decision to comply with the Berne Convention, which secures copyright protections for American works abroad, is so irrational or so unrelated to the aims of the Copyright Clause that it exceeds the reach of congressional power."

Turning to the First Amendment, the court began its analysis with the observation in *Eldred* that copyright legislation requires First Amendment scrutiny when it alters "the traditional contours of copyright protection." It characterized the idea that works in the public domain should remain there as a "bedrock principle" of copyright law noting that "until [the URAA] every statutory scheme preserved the same sequence. A work progressed from (1) creation; (2) to copyright; (3) to the public domain. Under [the URAA] the copyright sequence no longer necessarily ends with the public domain: indeed, it may begin there. Thus, by copyrighting works in the public domain, the URAA has altered the ordinary copyright sequence." It also noted that Congressional practice for most of U.S. history had been to avoid removing works from the public domain. Consequently, it concluded that section 104A altered a "traditional contour" of copyright.

It then concluded that this alteration implicated the plaintiffs' First Amendment interests. When the works were in the public domain, plaintiffs had an unrestrained right to use them. Insofar as they did so for artistic purposes, the court noted that they were exercising a right near the core of the Constitutional protection. By restoring copyright to the works in question, the URAA rendered their use more expensive—in some cases prohibitively so—and thus burdened the plaintiff's First Amendment rights. The *Golan* court also found that copyright laws "built-in free speech safeguards"— namely the idea/expression principle and the fair use doctrine— were inadequate to protect the plaintiff's free speech interests, and that the URAA did not incorporate any other safeguards for free expression. It thus determined that a remand was in order to allow the trial court to conduct a full First Amendment analysis.

On remand, Judge Babcock characterized the statute as a "content neutral" regulation of speech, which could only be upheld if it was "narrowly tailored to serve a significant governmental interest.''[103] The government proffered three statutory objectives that it claimed constituted the governmental interests sufficient to sustain the URAA: (1) it was necessary to comply with U.S. treaty obligations under Berne; (2) it helps protect the copyright interests of U.S. authors in foreign countries; and (3) in rectifies historic inequities which had unfairly penalized foreign authors. Regarding the first justification, the district judge determined that Congress could have complied with Berne without significant interference with First Amendment rights by incorporating additional exceptions into the statutory scheme. In other words, Congress could have defined "reliance parties" more broadly to include those with free speech interests as well as commercial interests, and it could have done more to protect them. Judge Babcock found the government's evidence on the other two justifications inadequate. As a result, he granted summary judgment for the plaintiffs.

To the great relief of Congress, the Executive Branch, and many U.S. trading partners, the Tenth Circuit reversed on appeal.[104] The Court of Appeals parted company with Judge Babcock on the issue of whether the URAA was narrowly tailored to advance the government's interest in protecting the works of U.S. authors overseas. In so doing the Tenth Circuit recognized that the URAA addressed the recognized problem of substantial exploitation of U.S. works overseas without consent or compensation. The Tenth Circuit observed that if the URAA had provided stronger protection to U.S. reliance parties, other jurisdictions may have acted similarly, thereby providing fewer rights for U.S. authors overseas. And even if other jurisdictions, particularly the United Kingdom, arguably provided greater protection for reliance parties, the availability of a less-speech-restrictive alternative did not necessarily invalidate the statute. With a nod towards the deference that courts accord to decisions of Congress and the Executive Branch in foreign affairs, the Tenth Circuit concluded the URAA did not burden substantially more speech than necessary to secure protection for U.S. works in foreign countries. Although the copyright restoration provisions of the URAA may potentially be subject to constitutional challenges in the other judicial circuits, the thorough consideration of these issues in the *Golan* litigation should provide confidence they will survive such opposition in the future.

103.   611 F.Supp.2d at 1170.

104.   609   F.3d   1076   (10th   Cir. 2010).

Chapter 9

COPYRIGHT INFRINGEMENT

Table of Sections

Once one is familiar with the types of works protected by copyright, and the various rights granted copyright owners by the statute, the concept of infringement seems simple enough. Because all of the statutory rights are "exclusive," infringement occurs when anyone other than the copyright owner engages in any of the itemized rights without the copyright owner's permission. Thus it is infringement to copy, adapt, distribute, perform, or display a protected work, or to violate rights of attribution or integrity in a work of visual art, unless the acts in question are expressly exempted from infringement liability by a specific provision in the statute. This principle is codified in section 501(a) of the current copyright act: "Anyone who violates any of the exclusive rights of the copyright owner as provided by section 106 or of the author as provided in section 106A(a), . . . is an infringer of the copyright or the rights of the author, as the case may be."[1] Furthermore, one need not be the owner of the entire copyright interest to bring an infringement suit. The owner of any exclusive right under a copyright may sue for infringement of that particular right.[2]

Despite the straightforward nature of the idea of copyright infringement, complexity in infringement analysis arises for several reasons. First, as noted much earlier in this text, truly independent creation of a work does not constitute infringement even if the result of defendant's efforts is something very similar to plaintiff's work, because such independent creation does not violate any of the copyright owner's exclusive rights.[3] There are other, equally innocent reasons why defendant's work might appear similar to plaintiff's. For instance, they both may have copied from the same public domain source. Thus, merely because the defendant's work resembles the plaintiff's does not by itself mean that the defendant is an infringer. Much of the law of infringement is about distinguishing between cases of permissible resemblance, and cases where the resemblance occurs because the defendant impermissibly copied the plaintiff's work.

Second, infringement does not require verbatim copying. As we shall see, many forms of non-verbatim copying are also actionable. As Judge Learned Hand said in one of his most celebrated copyright decisions, "it is of course essential to any protection of literary property, whether at common-law or under the statute, that the right cannot be limited literally to the text, else a plagiarist would escape by immaterial variation."[4] In other words, changing a few words or notes or colors here or there will not insulate a defendant from liability. Indeed, a defendant can be liable even if there is no literal resemblance at all between his work and the

---

1. 17 U.S.C. § 501(a).

2. 17 U.S.C. § 501(b). This is a function of the divisibility of copyright under the 1976 Act. Thus, an exclusive licensee of a play who was granted the rights to perform that play in Kansas City during the month of April could sue any other party who attempted to per-

form that play in that city in that month.

3. *See supra* Chapter 2.

4. Nichols v. Universal Pictures Corp., 45 F.2d 119, 121 (2d Cir.1930), *cert. denied*, 282 U.S. 902, 51 S.Ct. 216, 75 L.Ed. 795 (1931).

plaintiff's if he has taken the protected non-literal pattern of the work. On the other hand, not all non-literal elements of a work are protected. The basic plot of a novel, the basic tune of a song, or the basic structure of a computer program may be an unprotectable idea.[5] Thus here again, the law of infringement has had to develop various line-drawing principles designed to sort out permissible from impermissible conduct.

§ 9.1 The Elements of Copyright Infringement

There are a surprisingly large number of formulas for infringement floating around in the case law, no doubt due to the difficulties of line drawing alluded to above. Different courts use different terms to express the same concepts, and the concepts are combined or broken up in different ways depending on the nature and complexity of the case. Boiled down, however, all of these different tests and all of the different vocabulary are driving at the same basic concepts. In order to prevail, an infringement plaintiff must prove, first, that the defendant actually did copy plaintiff's work, and second, that this copying was impermissible because it constitutes "improper appropriation."[6] The first issue, copying, is essentially factual in nature. The second, improper appropriation, is a legal conclusion. These concepts are explored in detail in the subsections that follow.

9.1.1 Proof of Copying

Many copyright infringement claims involve alleged violations of the reproduction right—the right to make copies. Even alleged violations of the adaptation and performance rights involve the making of copies as a step in the infringing activities. Consequently, the first thing an infringement plaintiff must do is prove that the defendant actually copied his work. Without such proof, it is possible that any similarity between the two works might be due to coincidence.

Plaintiff's obligation to prove copying does not require the plaintiff to prove that the defendant had an impermissible intent. A defendant will be liable for infringement even if that infringement was innocent. For instance, if a defendant copies portions of plaintiff's work under the mistaken belief that it has fallen into the public domain, that defendant is nonetheless an infringer, despite his good faith. This doctrine has recently become significant in the

---

5. *See supra* Chapter 2.

6. Plaintiff must also prove ownership of a valid copyright in the work. Feist Publications, Inc. v. Rural Tel. Serv. Co., 499 U.S. 340, 111 S.Ct. 1282,

113 L.Ed.2d 358 (1991). The issues that bear on ownership—such as originality, compliance with formalities, etc.—have been covered in previous chapters of this book.

computer industry. In *Playboy Enterprises, Inc. v. Frena*,[7] the operator of a computer bulletin board was held liable for infringement when a subscriber placed copyrighted pictures from *Playboy* magazine on the bulletin board without his knowledge. The court observed that "it does not matter that [the defendant] may have been unaware of the copyright infringement."[8]

Courts have even held that the defendant will still be considered an infringer even if the defendant's copying is merely subconscious. A classic illustration of that situation is the case of *Bright Tunes Music Corp. v. Harrisongs Music, Ltd.*[9] The plaintiff in that case held the copyright on the song *He's So Fine*. The late George Harrison composed a song entitled *My Sweet Lord* which was alleged to infringe *He's So Fine*. The court concluded that Harrison did not deliberately copy plaintiff's work, but still held him liable as an infringer because it found that he subconsciously had plaintiff's tune in mind when he created his own. The principle was established long before George Harrison got sued. As Learned Hand said in his 1936 decision in *Sheldon v. Metro–Goldwyn Pictures Corp.*, "unconscious plagiarism is actionable quite as much as deliberate."[10]

So how, then, does a plaintiff prove copying? If plaintiff can offer the eyewitness testimony of an observer who saw the defendant engage in copying, the plaintiff will, of course, prevail on this point. As you might guess, however, such testimony is not often available. Plagiarists rarely work with an audience present. Not surprisingly, therefore, infringement plaintiffs usually prove copying through circumstantial evidence.

The usual circumstantial showing has two prongs. The plaintiff must first show that the defendant had access to his copyrighted work. If the defendant never saw or heard plaintiff's work, any similarities between the two could not, by definition, be due to copying. Second, the plaintiff must show some resemblance between the two works. Mere access does not prove copying unless the two works are somewhat alike. It is sometimes said that these

7. 839 F.Supp. 1552 (M.D.Fla. 1993).

8. *Id.* at 1559. For an interesting discussion of the implications of this rule, *see* Ned Snow, *Copytraps*, 84 IND. L.J. 285 (2009). Professor Snow concludes: "The Copyright Act's strict liability regime fails to contemplate a virtual existence. The current regime assumes that copyright distribution occurs by physical procurement rather than by online copying. It assumes that innocent infringement is excep-

tional and isolated rather than frequent and widespread. It assumes that identifying infringers is costly rather than efficient. The copy nature of the Internet thus contradicts the assumptions of copyright's strict liability regime. The Internet renders the strict liability regime obsolete."

9. 420 F.Supp. 177 (S.D.N.Y.1976), *aff'd sub nom*, ABKCO Music, Inc. v. Harrisongs Music, Ltd., 722 F.2d 988 (2d Cir.1983).

10. 81 F.2d 49, 54 (2d Cir.1936).

two prongs are inversely related to each other. On this view, if there is a high degree of resemblance between the works, then even weak evidence of access will suffice to show that the defendant copied from the plaintiff, particularly if the works are lengthy or complex. Conversely, if access is undisputed, even moderate resemblance might suffice to establish copying. A complete absence of evidence on one of the two prongs, however, should logically preclude a finding of copying, and many courts have said just that.[11]

9.1.1.1 Access

Access can be proved by direct evidence, if such evidence is available. Testimony that the defendant has a copy of plaintiff's book in his office, or a CD recording of plaintiff's song at his home, would be nearly conclusive on the point. Where such direct evidence is lacking, the plaintiff will usually offer a more circumstantial case. Note how the inferential links multiply—we prove access circumstantially and then that access, coupled with a resemblance between the two works is itself circumstantial evidence of copying.

If plaintiff's work has proved popular and has been widely disseminated, that fact by itself may be sufficient to establish access. For example, in the *Bright Tunes* case discussed above, the plaintiff's song *He's So Fine* had been number one on the Billboard pop music charts in the United States for five weeks and had achieved a comparable degree of success in England. This was sufficient to raise an inference that Harrison had access to the song, particularly given his own involvement in the music industry and the likelihood that he paid attention to what other musicians were doing. On this logic, it is likely that courts would find that virtually everyone except a hermit has access to a best-selling novel or a blockbuster motion picture.

For less famous or unpublished works, it is usually necessary to offer some evidence that defendant at least had an opportunity to see the plaintiff's work.[12] This concept was likely strained to its outer limits in *Three Boys Music Corp. v. Bolton*,[13] where the Isley Brothers asserted that Bolton's 1991 hit "Love Is a Wonderful Thing" infringed the copyright of their 1966 song of the same name. No evidence of record suggested that Bolton had direct access to the Isley Brothers recording. The Ninth Circuit nonetheless upheld a jury verdict of infringement based upon testimony that Bolton grew up listening to groups such as the Isley Brothers; that the Isley Brothers' song was widely disseminated on radio and

---

11. In Arnstein v. Porter, 154 F.2d 464, 468 (2d Cir.1946), Learned Hand noted that "of course, if there are no similarities, no amount of evidence of access will suffice to prove copying."

12. *See, e.g.*, Robert R. Jones Assocs. v. Nino Homes, 858 F.2d 274, 277 (6th Cir. 1988).

13. 212 F.3d 477 (9th Cir. 2000).

television stations; that Bolton admitted he was a huge fan of the Isley Brothers; and that Bolton contemplated the possibility that he was subconsciously drawing on another work when he recorded his song. The Court of Appeals seemed sympathetic to Bolton's observation that he was only 13 years old in 1966 and acknowledged the "weaknesses" of a "twenty-five-years-after-the-fact-subconscious copying claim." Yet it found that substantial evidence supported the jury's verdict and upheld an award of $5.4 million in favor of the Isley Brothers.

Proof of this sort is also often relied upon in cases where plaintiff has submitted work to one unit of a large organization. For instance, an author might submit a novel or screenplay to a large movie production company in the hope that they will like it enough to want to license the rights to produce a movie. Shortly thereafter, the crestfallen author receives a postcard from a low level employee declaring that the company is not interested. A year later, the company then releases a movie with a plot closely resembling the one in plaintiff's work. If the person who drafted the screenplay for the company's movie was a company employee, the court might infer access in this situation unless the company could prove that it kept plaintiff's submission segregated and its company screenwriter did not look at it. This is sometimes called the "corporate receipt doctrine."

Not every instance of "corporate receipt" will suffice to trigger an inference of access. For instance, in *Jones v. Blige*,[14] music producers Leonard Jones and James White asserted that Mary J. Blige's hit song "Family Affair" infringed on their own work "Party Ain't Crunk." Jones and White asked an aspiring rap artist, Tim Acker (aka "Benevolence"), to record "Party Ain't Crunk." White then submitted the recording on CD to Blige's publisher, Universal Music Group, Inc. A Universal producer, McKaie, received the CD, decided not to pursue the work further, and returned it. Blige subsequently wrote the lyrics to "Family Affair" along with her brother and a team of writers, and then recorded her vocals over music created by Andrew Young (aka "Dr. Dre"). When the producers heard "Family Affair" on the radio, they believed that it infringed their own song "Party Ain't Crunk" and filed charges of copyright infringement.

Although Jones and White attempted to rely upon the corporate receipt doctrine to demonstrate that the defendants had access to "Party Ain't Crunk," the Sixth Circuit was unsympathetic. The Court of Appeals explained that such a "bare corporate receipt" did not provide sufficient proof of access under the facts of this case. No evidence suggested that Blige, Dr. Dre, or the other artists who

14. 558 F.3d 485 (6th Cir. 2009).

contributed to "Family Affair" even knew McKaie, who worked in a different division of Universal. This "attenuated corporate connection" meant that an assumption of access would constitute an "implausible leap." *Jones v. Blige* suggests that courts possess some sympathy towards copyright owners who must establish a chain of access to a work within a corporation. But that sympathy is not unbounded: plaintiffs who rely upon the corporate receipt doctrine must at the very minimum demonstrate a reasonable possibility that their work made its way to the creators of the accused infringement.

Yet another way to show access is to attempt to prove that there are "striking similarities" between plaintiff's and defendant's works. The logic here is that the works resemble each other so closely that the only possible explanation is that defendant must have had access to plaintiff's work. The similarities must be "so striking and of such nature as to preclude the possibility of coincidence, accident or independent creation."[15] Obviously, the more complex the work, the more powerful the inference. If plaintiff has written a computer program with 100,000 lines of code, and if defendant's work is a virtually identical program, the inference of access and copying is very strong. On the other hand, if plaintiff's work is a minimalist abstract painting consisting of only a few spare geometric shapes, the fact that defendant's work is strikingly similar might not be as persuasive. Courts will allow expert testimony on the issue of striking similarity, which can help the plaintiff rule out the possibility of independent creation.

A pair of decisions from the Seventh Circuit illustrate these principles. In the first, *Selle v. Gibb,*[16] Ronald Selle asserted that the Bee Gees hit "How Deep Is Your Love" infringed the copyright of his song "Let It End." Prior to the composition of "How Deep Is Your Love," Selle had played "Let It End" two or three times in the Chicago area. He also sent a tape and lead sheet of the music to eleven music recording and publishing companies; eight of those companies returned the music to Selle, while three failed to respond. Although Selle admitted that he had no direct proof that the Bee Gees had heard "Let It End," he argued that "How Deep Is Your Love" was so strikingly similar that access could be inferred.

The Seventh Circuit disagreed and dismissed Selle's claim. The Court of Appeals relied upon the detailed evidence provided by the Bee Gees and their staff regarding the creation of "How Deep Is Your Love." It also observed that alleged substantial similarity should involve a "sufficiently unique or complex context" to suggest a common origin of the protected work and the accused

---

15. Scott v. WKJG, Inc., 376 F.2d 467, 469 (7th Cir.1967).

16. 741 F.2d 896 (7th Cir. 1984).

infringement. Popular music, which tends towards short songs that repeat a basic theme, does not always provide this context, and Selle had failed to provide expert testimony to the contrary. Because assuming that the Bee Gees had access to "Let It End" would be no more than speculation, the Seventh Circuit brought an end to the litigation.

The plaintiff met with more success in *Ty, Inc. v. GMA Accessories, Inc.*[17] Ty was the manufacturer of the once fabulously popular "Beanie Babies" line of stuffed animals. Ty contended that the copyright-protected designs of two of the Beanie Babies, Squealer and Daisy, were infringed by GMA's "Preston the Pig" and "Louie the Cow." Focusing on the two pig stuffed animals, Judge Posner concluded that GMA's Preston was strikingly similar to the protected Beanie Baby Squealer. In particular, the two pigs had the same length, a nearly identical snout, a ribbon around their necks, and three toes (in contrast to the cloven hooves of real pigs). Judge Posner distinguished *Selle v. Gibb* because in that case it was possible that songs might have been strikingly similar not because one was copied from the other, but rather because both were based upon similar material in the public domain. By contrast, GMA had not identified any pig in the public domain, real or fanciful, that Preston resembled. Further, GMA could have readily located and purchased one of Ty's Squealer dolls. As a result, the Seventh Circuit affirmed the award of a preliminary injunction in favor of Ty.

9.1.1.2   Resemblance

It should be obvious that access alone does not prove that defendant copied from plaintiff. For instance, both of your current authors have a copy of the *Lord of the Rings* novels by J.R.R. Tolkien in our homes, but anyone who is familiar with those books and has read portions of this Hornbook can readily see, from the absence of elves and wizards if nothing else, that we did not copy this book from Tolkien's works (which may also explain why no one has contacted us about movie rights thus far). Consequently, in order to establish copying, the plaintiff must show that there are at least some resemblances between his work and the one created by defendant.

Before developing this notion any further some discussion of terminology might be helpful. Many cases and law review articles use the term "similarity" rather than resemblance for this second prong of the copying inquiry. That usage has led to confusion because, as we shall see, "similarity" is also used as a term of art in the "improper appropriation" phase of infringement analysis. In an

17.   132 F.3d 1167 (7th Cir. 1997).

effort to dissipate some of that confusion, the late copyright scholar Alan Latman coined the term "probative similarity for the issue now under discussion."[18] The adjective "probative" reminds us that the similarity in question at this stage of the analysis is *probative of the issue of copying.* While Professor Latman's phrase adds precision, it is a bit cumbersome. The adjective is sometime forgotten, leaving us back with the initial confusion. To simplify the following discussion we recommend the use of the term "resemblance" instead, though we note that this is our own coinage and the term is not in general use by courts.

Once plaintiff has proved access, any resemblance of consequence will be enough to show copying. Even if the resemblance relates to unprotected elements of a work, such as public domain material, facts, or ideas, the resemblance is evidence that defendant copied from plaintiff. Of course, if the plaintiff relied on a showing of "striking similarity" to prove access, no further proof of resemblance is necessary since by definition there will be a strong resemblance between the two works. The showing of "striking similarity" by itself becomes evidence of copying, merging the two subsidiary inquiries of access and resemblance into a single evidentiary point.

One form of resemblance that has figured prominently in the case law of infringement is the existence of common errors in both defendant's and plaintiff's works. Plaintiff's copyrighted work may contain various factual or artistic errors. Some of these may have crept into plaintiff's work inadvertently, while others might have been intentionally inserted as a trap to detect infringers. For instance, cartographers will sometimes insert fictional towns in their copyrighted maps and directory publishers will sometimes include fictional listings. If a defendant who produces a map or a directory dealing with the same subject matter had access to plaintiff's work, and defendant's work contains the same errors, this will be significant proof of copying. Indeed, one court has observed that "courts have regarded the existence of common errors in two similar works as the strongest evidence of piracy."[19]

In *Feist Publications Inc. v. Rural Telephone Service Co.,*[20] the plaintiff claimed copyright protection in a telephone directory. There was no question that defendant had access to plaintiff's directory as it had been widely distributed in the service area in question. Defendant's work also resembled plaintiff's in that there were more than 1300 entries that were identical in the two volumes

---

18. Alan Latman, *"Probative Similarity" as Proof of Copying: Toward Dispelling Some Myths in Copyright Infringement,* 90 COLUM. L. REV. 1187 (1990).

19. Eckes v. Card Prices Update, 736 F.2d 859, 863 (2d Cir.1984).

20. 499 U.S. 340, 111 S.Ct. 1282, 113 L.Ed.2d 358 (1991).

but, of course, that might be explained by the possibility that the defendant engaged in independent research to compile its listings. Plaintiff was especially aided in showing copying by the fact that defendant's work included four fictitious entries contained in plaintiff's directory. That could only be explained if defendant copied plaintiff's work. Note that plaintiff ultimately lost in *Feist* despite its proof of copying because that copying was not considered to be an improper appropriation, an issue that is addressed in the next section.

9.1.2   Proof of Improper Appropriation

Even though defendant copied from plaintiff's work, defendant might not be an infringer. The copied material might not be protected matter. For instance, it might constitute the unprotected idea at the heart of a work, or it might comprise public domain materials. Thus, plaintiff must do more than show copying to prevail in an infringement suit. Plaintiff must also show that the copying was illicit.

Here again, careful analysis requires dividing the issue into subparts. To demonstrate improper appropriation plaintiff must show first that the copied material was protected expression, and second that an ordinary observer would find the copied protected expression in defendant's work to be substantially similar to plaintiff's work.

9.1.2.1   Copied Material Must Be Protected Expression

Defendant is only an infringer if he has copied protected material from plaintiff's work. In cases involving literal copying, this issue is usually pretty simple. If the copied material meets the tests of originality and the copyright on the material has not yet expired, the material is protected and plaintiff has succeeded on this element of the case. This is true even if defendant copied only bits and pieces of plaintiff's work and scattered the copied material throughout the infringing work—a situation Professor Nimmer has labeled "fragmented literal similarity."[21]

The more controversial cases arise when the alleged copying involves non-literal elements of plaintiff's work—a situation Nimmer calls "comprehensive non-literal similarity."[22] If defendant has copied the general plot of a novel or the overall structure of a computer program, that copying may be either lawful or unlawful depending on whether the plot or structure is considered protecta-

21. NIMMER, § 13.03[A][2].
22. NIMMER, § 13.03[A][1].

ble expression or an unprotectable idea. As Judge Learned Hand noted in one of the most famous passages in all of copyright law:

> Upon any work, and especially upon a play, a great number of patterns of increasing generality will fit equally well, as more and more of the incident is left out. The last may perhaps be no more than the most general statement of what the play is about, and at times might consist only of its title; but there is a point in this series of abstractions where they are no longer protected, since otherwise the playwright could prevent the use of his "ideas" to which, apart from their expression, his property is never extended.[23]

While this "abstractions" test is eloquently put, it does not offer any particularly helpful bright line for decisions. The question of whether the copied elements fall on the idea or the expression side of the line, or "series of abstractions," is always subjective and decided on a case-by-case basis. Judge Hand said as much in a subsequent decision, *Peter Pan Fabrics, Inc. v. Martin Weiner Corp.*,[24] conceding that "no principle can be stated as to when an imitator has gone beyond the 'idea' and has borrowed its 'expression.' Decisions must therefore inevitably be *ad hoc*."

Some examples from the case law show how courts have attempted to apply this notion to concrete fact patterns. In *Beal v. Paramount Pictures Corp.*[25] the plaintiff alleged that the copyright in her adventure novel *The Arab Heart* had been infringed by defendant's movie *Coming to America*, starring Eddie Murphy. Both works involved stories of "young crown princes from wealthy royal families coming to America where they meet the women they will marry. Both feature a strong ruler who (with varying degrees of intensity) initially prefers that the prince enter into an arranged marriage." There were, however, numerous differences between the plot details in the works. After analyzing the plot, mood, characterization, pace, setting, and sequence of events in both works, the court concluded that "although there are a few broad similarities between the works, they involve ideas and other general themes that are not susceptible to copyright protection." In other words, it found that the only copied elements of plaintiff's work were in the realm of the unprotectable, and that therefore the defendant was not an infringer.

In *Sheldon v. Metro–Goldwyn Pictures Corp.*[26] plaintiff alleged that defendant's motion picture, entitled *Letty Lynton*, infringed

---

23. Nichols v. Universal Pictures Corp., 45 F.2d 119, 121 (2d Cir.1930), *cert. denied*, 282 U.S. 902, 51 S.Ct. 216, 75 L.Ed. 795 (1931).

24. 274 F.2d 487, 489 (2d Cir.1960).

25. 20 F.3d 454 (11th Cir.1994), *cert. denied*, 513 U.S. 1062, 115 S.Ct. 675, 130 L.Ed.2d 607 (1994).

26. 81 F.2d 49 (2d Cir.1936).

the copyright in his play, entitled *Dishonored Lady*. Both works were based on a celebrated criminal trial in nineteenth century Scotland. As Learned Hand explained, that real-world episode began when a young woman named Madeleine Smith had an affair with a man named L'Angelier and then "poured out her feelings in letters of the utmost ardor and indiscretion, and at times of a candor beyond the standards then, and even yet permissible for well-nurtured young women." Ms. Smith eventually broke off this relationship in favor of another man, but L'Angelier threatened to show the rather explicit love letters to her father. Shortly thereafter, L'Angelier died of arsenic poisoning and Smith was accused of the murder. At her trial there was evidence that Smith had purchased arsenic, but she offered evidence of an alibi for the time of the alleged murder and was acquitted by the jury.

Plaintiff's play took only the basic outline of this situation—"the acquittal of a wanton young woman, who to extricate herself from an amour that stood in the way of a respectable marriage, poisoned her lover"—and substituted new details for the story, moving the action to New York City and making the lover an Argentinian dancer who is poisoned with strychnine. Defendant's movie was based on a book, which in turn was also based on the real Madeleine Smith case. Many of the details in the movie resembled those in plaintiff's play, however. For instance, the lover in the movie was also South American and he was also poisoned with strychnine. After a detailed review of the similarities of characters and incidents, Judge Hand concluded that the defendant's work had indeed crossed the line and taken not just ideas, but protected expression.

In attempting to determine if defendant has copied protected material, some courts begin by trying to eliminate all unprotected components of plaintiff's work. This technique has been called the "subtractive" approach to infringement analysis.[27] For instance, in a case involving alleged infringement of a computer program, *Computer Associates International, Inc. v. Altai, Inc.*,[28] the Second Circuit indicated that it would "sift out all non-protectable material" in order to arrive at the "kernel, or possible kernels, of creative expression." The approach has also been used in literary copyright cases. In *Alexander v. Haley*,[29] the court reached its conclusion that the book *Roots* did not infringe plaintiff's novel dealing with slavery by first subtracting out unprotected material from plaintiff's work, such as the many historical facts included in that work. Once that

---

27. *See* Craig Joyce, Marshall Leaffer, Peter Jaszi, & Tyler Ochoa, Copyright Law 647–48 (8th ed. 2010).

28. 982 F.2d 693, 706 (2d Cir.1992). This case has been followed by a number

of other federal circuits. For further discussion of this case, *see infra* § 9.4.

29. 460 F.Supp. 40 (S.D.N.Y.1978).

process was completed, the court found it obvious that the defendant had not taken any protected material from the plaintiff.

The subtractive approach ensures that a defendant will not be faulted for copying elements of a work that he was legally entitled to copy. Carelessly applied, however, it may not provide plaintiffs with adequate protection. This is because the *organization and arrangement* of otherwise unprotected material can be sufficiently original to warrant protection under copyright law. For instance, many compilations, such as trade directories or almanacs, contain individual nuggets of factual information which are not themselves copyrightable. If the compiler exercises originality in selecting or arranging the data, however, there is little doubt that the compilation as a whole is protectable. An overzealous use of the subtractive approach might lead a court to subtract out each entry in the compilation in order to find the protectable "kernel." Such an approach would leave no protected material at all! This would obviously run counter to the intent of the copyright statute and deny plaintiff protection that he plainly deserves. Thus, like all legal tests, the subtractive approach must be used cautiously and with an eye towards its underlying purpose.

To avoid the pitfalls of the subtractive approach, other courts have insisted that the works involved in copyright infringement litigation be compared in their entirety. This approach is sometimes labeled either the "totality" or "total concept and feel" approach. The Ninth Circuit opinion in *Sid & Marty Krofft Television Productions, Inc. v. McDonald's Corp.*,[30] illustrates this approach in action. The Kroffts had developed a children's TV program called H.R. Pufnstuf. It featured a variety of fanciful costumed characters who lived in a place called Living Island, which "was inhabited by moving trees and talking books." The mayor of the Island was a cummerbund-wearing dragon with a big head and a wide mouth.

McDonald's, the defendant in the case, wanted to develop an advertising campaign targeted at children. When it was unable to license the Pufnstuf characters, it developed its own fantasy land called McDonaldland. It, too, involved an "imaginary world inhabited by anthropomorphic plants and animals and other fanciful creatures." The mayor of McDonaldland, Mayor McCheese, had a big head (which was, not surprisingly, a cheeseburger) and a wide mouth. The court refused to break up or "dissect" plaintiff's work to separate protected from unprotected components, noting that "it is the combination of many different elements which may command copyright protection because of its particular subjective quality." The court found that because the "total concept and feel" of the two works was the same, the defendant had indeed taken protected

30. 562 F.2d 1157 (9th Cir.1977).

material and (because the works were substantially similar) was thus liable for infringement.

Courts have been particularly apt to resort to the total concept and feel approach in cases involving works that appeal to the eye, such as audiovisual works or art and sculpture. Thus, it has recently been invoked in cases involving a "diamond shaped spinning trophy,"[31] a cartoon squirrel/rat hybrid,[32] and the carved ornamental woodwork on items of furniture.[33] The total concept and feel approach is not limited to such cases however. Thus, the Second Circuit used the test in a case alleging that the novel *The DaVinci Code* infringed an earlier work called *Daughter of God*,[34] a trial court in that circuit invoked it in a case where the author of a novel concerning the fictional trial of Judas Iscariot claimed that a play based on the same concept was infringing,[35] and another trial court used it in a case involving "two cookbooks designed to help parents trick their children into eating healthy food."[36]

The totality test avoids undervaluing plaintiff's originality in the selection and arrangement of materials in his or her work. It does, however, run the risk of overextending copyright protection. For instance, plaintiff might prepare a volume containing the complete works of William Shakespeare with critical commentary in a number of footnotes scattered throughout the volume. Defendant might prepare his own annotated volume of the works of Shakespeare after consulting plaintiff's book. Obviously, the two volumes will have a similar "feel"—they will both be filled with Elizabethan poetry and a scholarly explication of that poetry closely juxtaposed to it. Moreover, they will have in common the full text of all the plays. Equally obvious, however, is that plaintiff ought to have no claim of copyright in the text of the plays.

Under a subtractive approach, we would ignore the words of Shakespeare—which are, of course, in the public domain—and compare only the remaining material. Under a totality approach, however, there is a danger that defendant might be found to be an infringer because of the overall similarity of the two books, despite the fact that the similarity relates primarily to materials that the defendant had a lawful right to copy. As one commentator put it,

31. Crown Awards, Inc. v. Discount Trophy & Co., Crown Awards, Inc. v. Discount Trophy & Co., Inc. 326 Fed. Appx. 575 (2d Cir. 2009).

32. Silberstein v. John Does 1–10, 242 Fed.Appx. 720 (2d Cir. 2007).

33. Amini Innovation Corp. v. Anthony California, Inc. Amini Innovation Corp. v. Anthony California, Inc. 439 F.3d 1365 (Fed. Cir. 2006).

34. Brown v. Perdue, 2005 WL 1863673 (S.D.N.Y. 2005), *aff'd*, 177 Fed. Appx. 121 (2d Cir. 2006) ("No reasonable jury could conclude that the total concept and feel of The Da Vinci Code is substantially similar to that of Daughter of God.").

35. Porto v. Guirgis, 659 F.Supp.2d 597 (S.D.N.Y 2009).

36. LaPine v. Seinfeld, 2009 WL 2902584 (S.D.N.Y. 2009).

"The full implication of 'total concept and feel' copyright protection becomes apparent when one considers just how abstract and subjective the 'total concept and feel' of a work can be. . . . *Krofft* strongly suggests that the very mood a work creates constitutes its protectable expression. If copyright claims can in fact be maintained at such a high level of abstraction, practically any similarity could conceivably support a finding of infringement."[37] Just as with the subtractive approach, therefore, one must use a totality analysis cautiously, with larger principles in mind, in order to ensure that an illogical conclusion is not reached.

9.1.2.2 Substantial Similarity

The final step on plaintiff's road to victory in infringement litigation is to prove that an ordinary observer would view the protected material copied by the defendant to be "substantially similar" to plaintiff's work. As the Seventh Circuit put it, in this phase of the analysis the court must ask "whether the accused work is so similar to the plaintiff's work that an ordinary reasonable person would conclude that the defendant unlawfully appropriated the plaintiff's protectable expression by taking material of substance and value."[38] This test is subjective. We are trying to determine whether the degree of copying of protected material rises to a level of significance warranting legal prohibition. Indeed, some courts and academic writers refer to this step in the analysis as the "audience" test to remind us that the inquiry concerns the reactions of those to whom the work is directed.

The substantial similarity or "audience" test can readily be understood in light of the economic goals of copyright law. If the defendant's work is substantially similar to plaintiff's, users of defendant's work will have no need or desire to subsequently purchase plaintiff's. The fact that the two are substantially similar makes them substitutes for each other, and that means that plaintiff will lose sales unless the defendant's activities are enjoined. As Justice Story put it more than 150 years ago, "[i]f so much is taken that the value of the original is sensibly diminished, or the labors of the original author are substantially to an injurious extent appropriated by another, that is sufficient in point of law to constitute a piracy. . . ."[39] Since the hope of economic reward in the form of sales is what supposedly induced the plaintiff to author his work in the first place, we must forbid defendant's production of substan-

---

37. Alfred C. Yen, *A First Amendment Perspective on the Idea/Expression Dichotomy and Copyright in a Work's "Total Concept and Feel"*, 38 EMORY L.J. 393, 410–11 (1989).

38. Atari, Inc. v. North American Philips Consumer Electronics Corp., 672 F.2d 607, 614 (7th Cir.1982).

39. Folsom v. Marsh, 9 F.Cas. 342 No. 4901 (C.C.D.Mass.1841).

tially similar work, or else incentives for creative activity will be destroyed.

While the ultimate determination of substantial similarity is a subjective question for the jury, there are some principles to guide the decision. For instance, it is irrelevant, in assessing substantial similarity, how much new material a defendant may have added to the portions copied from the plaintiff's work. If a defendant copies one chapter from plaintiff's lengthy book and then adds dozens of new chapters to accompany the copied material that will not, in any way, immunize him from liability. This makes good intuitive sense. If you rob my car and store it in a garage with 50 automobiles you have purchased with your own money, that does not make you any less a car thief than if you had stored my car in an empty garage.

Whether the material copied by defendant must constitute a significant portion of *plaintiff*'s work is somewhat less clear. Professor Nimmer in his treatise says "[t]he question in each case is whether the similarity relates to matter that constitutes a substantial portion of plaintiff's work. . . . The quantitative relation of the similar material to the total material contained in plaintiff's work is certainly of importance. However even if the similar material is quantitatively small, if it is qualitatively important, the trier of fact may properly find substantial similarity. . . . If, however, the similarity is only as to nonessential matters, then a finding of no substantial similarity should result."[40] A number of cases support this view. For instance, one case characterized the copying of only 30 characters from a computer program consisting of 50 pages of source code as *de minimis*.[41] There are, of course, cases finding infringement where a defendant has copied only a few lines or notes from plaintiff's work, but those can often be explained on the basis that the copied portion was the "heart" of the work and was thus qualitatively significant, even though quantitatively minimal.

On the other hand, Professor Goldstein takes issue with the Nimmer view in his treatise. He says "liability should be unaffected by the proportion the elements taken bear to plaintiff's work as a whole. . . . If the plaintiff had written only the portion appropriated, and if this portion were sufficiently expressive to qualify for copyright, there would be no doubt of plaintiff's success in an infringement action, for defendant in this situation would have copied plaintiff's entire work. It is perverse to excuse a defendant for having taken the very same portion just because plaintiff has published it in conjunction with other expression."[42]

40. Nimmer, § 13.03[A][2].

41. Vault Corp. v. Quaid Software Ltd., 847 F.2d 255, 267 (5th Cir.1988).

42. Paul Goldstein, Copyright (3d ed. 2005) § 7.3.1 at 7:28–29.

The disagreement between these two noted copyright scholars may not make much of a practical difference. Even if quantitatively small and qualitatively insignificant copying from plaintiff's work is deemed infringing, as Professor Goldstein argues it should be, in many cases it will have little effect on the market for plaintiff's work. That means that it may likely be excused under the fair use defense, as we shall see in the following chapter. Indeed, the disagreement between these two noted treatise writers can be recast as one concerning the assignment of the burden of proof. Under Professor Goldstein's view, since any copying of protected matter, no matter how *de minimis*, is treated as infringing, the defendant will bear the burden of invoking and proving the fair use defense. On the other hand, if *de minimis* copying is held to be non-infringing, as Professor Nimmer suggests, then the plaintiff will have the obligation of proving that the copying is more than *de minimis* and has crossed the line of substantiality.

Given the economic justification for copyright law generally and for the substantial similarity test in particular, it would seem that Professor Nimmer has the better of the argument. A work that bears only a *de minimis* similarity to plaintiff's work is unlikely to be much of a substitute for it, and is thus unlikely to undermine incentives very much. For instance, there is little chance I will forego buying John Grisham's latest novel because another book by another author, which I have already read, contains three sentences lifted verbatim from Grisham.

Of course, Professor Goldstein could quite properly argue that the question is not whether the works as a whole are substitutes, but whether the pirated portion is a substitute for the corresponding bit of original expression. It is true, at least as an abstract matter, that I would not pay to read Grisham's three sentences if I have already read them in another book. While Professor Goldstein's point has theoretical merit, consumers don't purchase disembodied pieces of copyrighted works, but rather the work as a whole. There is usually no market for three sentence prose bits. Indeed, the first author's decision to group various bits of expression together into a single work usually reflects a view that it is the full combination of those pieces that will have artistic and commercial appeal. Thus, if defendant has copied only a *de minimis* portion of the plaintiff's work, there seems little reason to afford plaintiff a judicial remedy.

Another important aspect of the substantial similarity or "audience" test is its focus on the "ordinary observer." The essence of the ordinary observer test was summarized, like so many copyright doctrines, in an opinion by Judge Learned Hand. In one of his last decisions on the bench, Hand wrote that works should be deemed substantially similar if "the ordinary observer, unless he set out to detect the disparities, would be disposed to overlook them, and regard their aesthetic appeal as the same."[43] However, courts have sometimes been troubled by the need to use an ordinary observer as the standard of comparison, especially when the works are complex and not directed at the general public. The fear is that for certain specialized works, a hypothetical reasonable person might be inclined to either overestimate or underestimate the degree of similarity.

In *Dawson v. Hinshaw Music, Inc.*,[44] the court confronted allegations of infringement involving two similar arrangements of a traditional spiritual entitled *Ezekiel Saw De Wheel*. The court noted that the reason substantial similarity was usually analyzed from the perspective of an ordinary observer was that most works are intended for an audience composed of just such observers. It went on to observe that "if the intended audience is more narrow in that it possesses specialized expertise, relevant to the purchasing decision, that lay people would lack, the court's inquiry should focus on whether a member of the intended audience would find the two works to be substantially similar."[45] The court concluded that the proper focus in the case before it should be on church choir directors. The court did caution, however, that departures from an ordinary observer standard should only be undertaken when the intended audience for a work possesses specialized expertise. As we shall see, this view has proven particularly influential in cases involving alleged infringement of computer software.

Professor Nimmer argues in his treatise that the "audience" test should be discarded.[46] The treatise suggests that the test has been applied inconsistently, is ill-suited for use in connection with technologically complicated works, and may be inconsistent with the language in the Supreme Court's opinion in *Feist*. Much of Professor Nimmer's criticism seems directed at cases that, under the rhetoric of an audience test, fail to carefully analyze the issue of *copying*. These criticized cases merely ask whether the overall impression of the two works would lead casual observers to a spontaneous impression of copying. As the Nimmer treatise notes, "the Copyright Act is intended to protect writers from the theft of the fruits of their labor, not to protect against the general public's 'spontaneous and immediate' *impression* that the fruits have been stolen."[47]

---

43. Peter Pan Fabrics, Inc. v. Martin Weiner Corp., 274 F.2d 487, 489 (2d Cir.1960).

44. 905 F.2d 731 (4th Cir.1990), *cert. denied*, 498 U.S. 981, 111 S.Ct. 511, 112 L.Ed.2d 523 (1990).

45. 905 F.2d at 736.

46. NIMMER, § 13.03[E][1][b].

47. *Id.* at 13–94.

The problem that prompts Professor Nimmer's criticism is a consequence of the sloppy and inconsistent use of vocabulary that plagues copyright infringement analysis. If the phrase "audience test" leads courts to simply turn both plaintiff's and defendant's works over to the jury and ask them if their spontaneous and immediate reaction is one of copying, then Nimmer is surely right that the test is misguided. On the other hand if the phrase "audience test" is properly limited to the final stage of a four–step infringement analysis, as detailed in the foregoing sections, most of Nimmer's concerns would vanish. Fortunately, few recent decisions seem to be using the "audience" test in the fashion criticized by Professor Nimmer. Instead, most of these newer cases ask about audience reaction only after unprotected elements of the work have been filtered out.

At least one recent opinion departs from the usual copyright infringement requirement that the accused work be substantially similar to the protected work. *Bridgeport Music, Inc. v. Dimension Films*[48] involved the unauthorized sampling of sound recordings. Given the popularity of sampling among recording artists, the opinion has significant implications for the record industry.

Bridgeport Music owned the copyright in the Funkadelic sound recording "Get Off Your Ass and Jam." While recording the song "100 Miles and Runnin'," the band N.W.A. copied a two-second sample from Funkadelic's recording, lowered the pitch, and "looped" (repeated) the sample five times in its song. The district court concluded that no reasonable juror, including one familiar with the works of Funkadelic, would recognize the source of the sample without having been told of its source. The district court therefore dismissed Bridgeport Music's infringement claim on the grounds that N.W.A.'s copying had been *de minimus*.

On appeal, the Sixth Circuit reversed the district court and held that any unlicensed digital sampling constituted copyright infringement. The court of appeals observed that the Copyright Act granted the copyright proprietor of a sound recording the exclusive right to "prepare a derivative work in which the actual sounds fixed in the sound recording are rearranged, remixed, or otherwise altered in sequence or quality," but stipulated that protection did "not extend to the making or duplication of another sound recording that consists *entirely* of an independent fixation of other sounds, even though such sounds imitate or simulate those in the copyrighted sound recording."[49] The Sixth Circuit reasoned that this statutory language—and in particular the term "entirely"— precluded the use of a substantial similarity standard, and summa-

---

48. 401 F.3d 647 (6th Cir. 2004).   **49.** 17 U.S.C. § 117(b) (emphasis added).

rized its holding with the pithy aphorism—"Get a license or do not sample."

The upshot of the *Bridgeport Music* ruling is that—at least in the Sixth Circuit—sampling of any portion of a protected sound recording, regardless of length, constitutes infringement absent the permission of the copyright owner. *Bridgeport Music* effectively prevents accused sound recording samplers from relying upon the *de minimis* doctrine in the Sixth Circuit. Notably, *Bridgeport Music* does not preclude the availability of other defenses, such as fair use, even within the context of sampling.

In our opinion, the core holding of *Bridgeport Music* is mistaken. The provision the court relies upon is actually meant as a *limitation* on the rights of sound recording copyright owners. It is more than curious to invoke that provision to expand their rights so that they can prevail even when a defendant has taken a trivial portion of their work and used it in a way that would be unrecognizable to a listener. As the Nimmer treatise observes with its characteristic panache, "By validating entire sound-alike recordings, the quoted sentence [of the statute] contains no implication that partial sound duplications are to be treated any differently from what is required by the traditional standards of copyright law—which, for decades prior to adoption of the 1976 Act and unceasingly in the decades since, has included the requirement of substantial similarity."[50]

Moreover, *Bridgeport Music* effectively elevates the scope of protection awarded to sound recordings in comparison with other copyrighted works. Given that sound recordings are generally awarded more limited statutory rights than other types of works,[51] this is more than a bit ironic. Furthermore the opinion seems to extend copyright protection to material that lacks originality since it forbids the taking of even a single beat of a drum or pluck of a guitar. The opinion has been criticized in the academic literature,[52] and for what it is worth, we cast our votes with the critics.

§ 9.2 Other Ways of Framing the Infringement Analysis

The foregoing discussion sets out a formal infringement analysis that normally requires four steps. Plaintiff must prove (1) access and (2) resemblance (or probative similarity, which is the same thing) in order to show copying, and then must show that the

---

50. NIMMER, § 13.03[A][2][b].

51. *See supra* § 3.7.

52. *See, e.g.,* Matthew R. Brodin, *Bridgeport Music, Inc. v. Dimension Films: The Death of the Substantial* *Similarity Test in Digital Sampling Copyright Infringement Claims—The Sixth Circuit's Flawed Attempt at a Bright-line Rule,* 6 MINN. J.L. SCI. & TECH. 825 (2005).

copying was (3) of protected material which (4) an ordinary observer would find substantially similar to plaintiff's work.

Many courts and commentators compress this analysis, however, into two steps. It is often said that proof of infringement requires only a showing of (1) access and (2) substantial similarity. Where, in this foreshortened analytic outline, have the other elements gone? When this type of formula is used, the missing elements are usually either non-controversial, or implicit in the court's analysis without being stated outright. Thus, courts may dispense with any need to analyze "resemblance" as part of a separate "copying" analysis because they feel such resemblance is inherent in proof of substantial similarity. They may not explicitly discuss "protected expression" as a separate element of the "improper appropriation" analysis but they may often ask if the works have "substantially similar expression." Professor Leaffer illustrates this compression of concepts in the following passage:

> not every taking or use of another's copyrighted work amounts to substantial similarity. A third party may freely copy the ideas embodied in a work but cannot copy the author's expression beyond what the law allows. And even if some of the expression is copied, there must be a substantial, material taking to constitute infringement. Thus, to say that the works are substantially similar is to say that the defendant has copied a substantial and material amount of plaintiff's protected expression.[53]

The Supreme Court seems to have compressed the formal four-step analysis even further. Writing in *Feist*, the Court defined infringement as "copying of constituent elements of the work that are original."[54] This bit of black letter law makes no reference at all to substantial similarity or the ordinary observer, nor is there any reference to protected material, or even to access. It is probable, however, that the Court was merely using a form of shorthand and that all four of the traditional elements lurk within this concise phrase.

Copying, of course, can be proved by showing both access and resemblance. The Court in *Feist* had no need to subdivide the copying inquiry and discuss those points, however, because copying was not significantly disputed in the case. The reference to elements of a work that are "original" clearly is synonymous with the "protected expression" prong of the four-part test. While the quoted phrase makes no explicit reference to substantial similarity, that

53. Marshall Leaffer, Understanding Copyright Law 424 (5th ed. 2010).

54. *Feist Publications, Inc. v. Rural Telephone Service Co.*, 499 U.S. 340,

361, 111 S.Ct. 1282, 113 L.Ed.2d 358 (1991).

may be because the crucial issue in the case was whether the plaintiff's work possessed sufficient originality to be protected in the first place. Given the Court's conclusion that it did not, there was no reason to worry about how similar plaintiff's and defendant's works might be. Moreover, by using the word "copying," the Court may have meant copying of protected material in an amount that would strike an ordinary observer as more than *de mininis*—the usual test for infringement—but not have spelled the point out because it was unnecessary to the decision in the case before it. This is how some lower courts have interpreted *Feist* in the years since it was decided.[55] Absent further indication from the Supreme Court that it has something special in mind, there is nothing in its phrasing to suggest a substantive—as opposed to a rhetorical—departure from the traditional mode of infringement analysis.

In the Tower of Babel that is infringement analysis, there is still more terminological confusion because of a whole new vocabulary introduced by the Ninth Circuit in a line of decisions beginning with *Sid & Marty Krofft Television Productions, Inc. v. McDonald's Corp.*[56] As indicated in section 9.1.2.1 above, that case involved allegations that certain McDonaldland TV commercials infringed plaintiff's copyrighted H.R. Pufnstuf program. In the opinion, the court stated that the first step in infringement analysis was to determine whether the two works have substantially similar ideas, and that the second step was to determine if they use substantially similar expression to express those ideas. This approach can only be described as curious. The fact that two works have similar ideas may indicate that one is copied from the other, although even that may be dubious if the ideas are pedestrian or well-known in the genre. However, similarity of ideas is not at all relevant to a finding of unlawful appropriation, since by definition, defendant is legally entitled to copy plaintiff's ideas.

Krofft then went on to label these two tests. It called the inquiry into identity of ideas an "extrinsic" test, because it was supposedly objective in nature and, the court said, expert testimony and analytic dissection would be appropriate in applying this test. It called the inquiry into identity of expression an "intrinsic" test, because it related to the subjective reactions of the audience for the work, and it declared that this test should be conducted based on

---

55. *See, e.g.,* Lipton v. Nature Co., 71 F.3d 464, 470–71 (2d Cir.1995) ("a successful copyright action requires proof that the defendant copied protected elements of the plaintiff's work ... copying may be inferred where a plaintiff establishes that the defendant had access to the copyrighted work and that substantial similarities exist as to protectible material in the two works."); Warren Publishing, Inc. v. Microdos Data Corp., 115 F.3d 1509, 1516 n. 19 (11th Cir.1997), *cert. denied,* 522 U.S. 963, 118 S.Ct. 397, 139 L.Ed.2d 311 (1997).

56. 562 F.2d 1157 (9th Cir.1977).

the total concept and feel of the work without breaking it up into constituent elements.

Much ink has been spilled by commentators either speculating on just what the *Krofft* court meant, or in criticism of its approach. Subsequent Ninth Circuit cases have continued to use the "extrinsic" and "intrinsic" language, but have slowly reshaped the meanings of those words, so that whatever they may have meant originally, they are now practically identical to the concepts of "protected expression" analysis and "substantial similarity" analysis used by most other courts. To the extent that the words extrinsic and intrinsic have become nothing more than alternative ways of saying objective and subjective respectively, they add little to infringement discussions except the potential for confusion.

What emerges from a careful study of judicial language and actual judicial practices is the realization that there is no significant substantive difference implied when some courts and writers analyze copyright infringement in four steps, and some do it in only two or even one. Nor does there appear to be much difference between tests worded in the conventional language and those that are phrased in terms of "intrinsic" and "extrinsic" analysis. Decisions about whether one work infringes another are often excruciatingly difficult. The blizzard of tests, sub-tests, terminological innovations, and clarifications reflects nothing more than judicial striving to bring some clarity and predictability to the endeavor. While we can applaud the goals that prompt these efforts, we can only grin and bear it when we encounter the confusing vocabulary.

§ 9.3 Infringement Analysis in Computer Related Cases

Verbatim copying of computer code is now clearly understood to be impermissible.[57] On the other hand, one of the more contentious areas of copyright law in recent years has been the degree to which third parties may copy *non-literal* elements of computer software without incurring infringement liability. These non-literal elements might include the organizational structure of the program as a whole, or the "user-interface"—the menus, key commands, and other features that govern how the user interacts with the program. The protectability of these elements of computer programs was considered in the chapter on the subject matter of copyright, in section 2.2.2. It is useful to look at the problem again, however, because the same case law also illuminates how infringement analysis is conducted in computer software cases.

57. *See supra* § 3.1.3.

One of the first courts to confront the question of non-literal infringement of software was *Whelan Associates, Inc. v. Jaslow Dental Laboratory, Inc.*[58] Both parties in that case had written programs that were designed to be used in managing a dental office. The defendant's program did not incorporate verbatim any of the actual computer code from the plaintiff's work. Nonetheless, there were considerable similarities in the two works. The decision in *Whelan* was notable for at least two reasons. First, although "substantial similarity" analysis in most infringement cases is decided based on the subjective reactions of ordinary observers, *Whelan* departed from the conventional approach and chose instead to rely heavily on the testimony of experts, observing that there were a "growing number of courts which do not apply the ordinary observer test in copyright cases involving exceptionally difficult materials like computer programs." You may recall that this was the approach embraced by the court in *Dawson*, discussed in section 9.1.2.2 above.

Even more controversially, in trying to identify the protectable non-literal elements of a computer program, the *Whelan* court concluded that "copyright protection of computer programs may extend beyond the programs' literal code to their structure, sequence and organization." The court seemed to suggest that each program had only one, single, unprotectable idea, and that all other non-literal aspects of the program were protectable expression.

It is, of course, routine to note that copyright protection can extend to non-literal aspects of a copyrighted work. The *Whelan* approach raised eyebrows, however, because, given the unique attributes of computer software, many felt that it extended protection to matters that were not properly within the scope of copyright. For instance, the sequence of sub-routines in a computer program might be dictated by the function the program must perform. It might be impossible for another programmer to write a competing program without following the same sequence. The same might be true for the "structure" or "organization" of the program. In this sense computer programs may differ markedly from novels, plays, or movies. Affording a plaintiff protection over structure, sequence, or organization of a computer program might then expand the plaintiff's monopoly from expression into ideas, methods, and processes. Not surprisingly, *Whelan* was criticized by both academic writers and other courts.[59] Its approach struck many as

---

58. 797 F.2d 1222 (3d Cir.1986).

59. *See, e.g.*, Plains Cotton Cooperative Ass'n v. Goodpasture Computer Service, Inc., 807 F.2d 1256 (5th Cir. 1987), *cert. denied*, 484 U.S. 821, 108 S.Ct. 80, 98 L.Ed.2d 42 (1987) (declining to "embrace *Whelan*"). "The crucial flaw in [Whelan's] reasoning is that it assumes that only one 'idea,' in copyright law terms, underlies any computer program, and that once a separable idea can be identified, everything else must

excessively pro-plaintiff and likely to chill software development and competition in the software industry.

Throughout the balance of the 1980s various courts attempted to refine the analysis for copyright infringement in the computer software context. In 1992 the Second Circuit decided *Computer Associates Int'l, Inc. v. Altai, Inc.*,[60] a case that has supplanted *Whelan* as the leading authority on determination of infringement in the computer software context, and which has proven influential with other circuits around the country.

Computer Associates had authored a job scheduling program for mainframe computers called CA–Scheduler. A sub-program of CA–Scheduler, called Adapter, converted the computer languages of various programs into languages compatible with the mainframe's operating system. In 1982 the defendant, Altai, began marketing its own scheduling program, called Zeke. In the following year, to make Zeke compatible with a wider variety of operating systems, Altai hired a former Computer Associates employee to prepare a sub-program called Oscar. The original version of Oscar clearly infringed plaintiff's Adapter sub-program because the former employee had retained copies of the actual computer code for Adapter and incorporated chunks of that code verbatim into Oscar. When that fact was discovered, the Oscar program was rewritten by Altai programmers who had no access to the Adapter code. The question in the case was whether the re-written or second generation version of the Oscar program infringed Adapter. Although there was no literal similarity between the two, there were a number of structural and organizational similarities.

To resolve the question, the *Altai* court developed an approach which is usually labeled the "abstraction-filtration-comparison test." It is profitable to look at the court's language setting out the test:

> In ascertaining substantial similarity under this approach, a court would first break down the alleged infringed program into its constituent structural parts. Then, by examining each of these parts for such things as incorporated ideas, expression that is necessarily incidental to those ideas, and elements that are taken from the public domain,

be expression." NIMMER § 13.03[F] (2002). *See also* Steven R. Englund, *Note, Idea, Process, or Protected Expression?: Determining the Scope of Copyright Protection of the Structure of Computer Programs*, 88 MICH. L. REV. 866, 881 (1990); Peter S. Menell, *An Analysis of the Scope of Copyright Protection for Application Programs*, 41 STAN. L. REV. 1045, 1074, 1082 (1989); Mark T.

Kretschmer, *Note, Copyright Protection for Software Architecture: Just Say No!*, 1988 COLUM. BUS L. REV. 823, 837–39 (1988); Peter G. Spivack, *Comment, Does Form Follow Function? The Idea/Expression Dichotomy in Copyright Protection of Computer Software*, 35 U.C.L.A. L. REV. 723, 747–55 (1988).

60. 982 F.2d 693 (2d Cir.1992).

a court would be able to sift out all non-protectable material. Left with a kernel, or possible kernels, of creative expression after following this process of elimination, the court's last step would be to compare this material with the structure of an allegedly infringing program. The result of this comparison will determine whether the protectable elements of the programs at issue are substantially similar so as to warrant a finding of infringement.

This, of course, is the basic subtractive version of the "improper appropriation" analysis, re-worded to apply more closely to computer program cases. The abstraction and filtration steps in the *Altai* approach mirror the usual effort to identify and separate protected material common to both plaintiff's and defendant's works. The comparison step in *Altai* is analogous to the substantial similarity analysis that is used more generally in infringement cases.

The abstraction/filtration process helps courts identify aspects of a program that might be dictated by external factors, such as the need to make the program compatible with a given operating system or a given piece of hardware, or standards prevalent in the industry that will be using the software product. Once identified, these elements or aspects will be filtered out. A defendant will not be considered an infringer if these are the only aspects of the program which are copied.

Like *Whelan, Altai* endorses the use of expert witnesses in the final "comparison" phase of its analysis. Although experts are not usually used in the substantial similarity phase of infringement litigation because of the traditional focus on the "ordinary observer," computer software poses unique problems that make an ordinary observer test awkward. Users of computer programs usually do not even see the programs themselves, but only the output on a computer screen. Neither of us have any idea what the code for our word processing programs looks like, nor could we discern whether the literal code or the non-literal structure of two competing word processors (such as Microsoft Word and WordPerfect) were substantially similar. Computer users might perceive two programs to be similar if they performed the same functions, even though their expressive elements could be quite different. For example, two spreadsheets might look roughly similar on the screen and manipulate data the same way, but the expressive elements of the programs might be completely different. The use of experts in software infringement cases thus seems both sensible and virtually inevitable.

The widespread use of computers has also created a rather different infringement problem, this one involving the Internet.

Operators of various Internet sites or companies that allow subscribers to create personal web pages on their computers often permit users to post material onto their sites by uploading it. Other users can then access the material by logging on to the internet through the facilities of an internet service provider (or ISP) and view that material, or if they choose, they may download copies of the material onto their own computers. Not surprisingly, some of the material that winds up at sites such as these is often copyrighted text or images which have been posted without the permission of the copyright owners. While there is little doubt that the subscriber doing the posting is an infringer, pursuing a lawsuit against that individual is not likely to provide much useful relief—for every one poster who is enjoined, there will be 50 more who continue to infringe. Consequently, copyright owners have increasingly focused their legal attention on the ISPs.

At first blush, the plaintiffs would seem to have a strong case against the ISP. After the subscriber posts the copyrighted material both of those Internet participants will necessarily have copies of it on the hard drives of their computers at least for temporary periods and often for much longer. Moreover, even if they are not aware of the copyright status of the material in question, copyright infringement does not require knowledge or intent for liability. Thus these entities would appear to be at considerable risk for copyright infringement liability.

This is substantially the view taken in the first case to consider the issue, *Playboy Enterprises, Inc. v. Frena.*[61] Mr. Frena was the operator of a Bulletin Board System ("BBS") called Techs Warehouse.[62] The material on that BBS included 170 copyrighted photographs from Playboy magazine, which had apparently been placed there by subscribers. Frena alleged that he did not know about the subscriber activities and that he removed the material from his BBS as soon as he was notified of Playboy's complaint. The court nonetheless found Frena liable for direct infringement. The court reasoned that Frena had violated both the distribution and display rights of the copyright owner. The opinion did not, however, address whether the activities in question should also be considered violations of the reproduction right.

Two years later, in *Religious Technology Center v. Netcom On–Line Communication Services, Inc.,*[63] another court was confronted

---

61. 839 F.Supp. 1552 (M.D. Fla. 1993).

62. Our more senior readers will recall that a BBS was a precursor to a contemporary Internet forum. Users employed dial-up modems to connect to remote computer systems in order to read news, exchange messages, and download software and other material, typically at painfully slow rates of speed. The rise of the Internet in the 1990s led to the decline of the BBS.

63. 907 F.Supp. 1361 (N.D.Cal. 1995).

with substantially similar facts. In that case, a man named Dennis Erlich was engaged in a dispute with the Church of Scientology. As part of that controversy, he posted on an Internet newsgroup called "alt.relgion.scientology" lengthy excerpts from various copyrighted works belonging to the Scientology movement. To be more precise, he did this by posting the material on a BBS operated by a Mr. Klemesrud, who in turn put the material on the Internet by using the facilities of Netcom, a large ISP. After failing to convince Erlich to desist, the copyright owner sued him as well as Klemesrud and Netcom for infringement.

The court exonerated both the BBS and the ISP. While noting that knowledge and intent are not elements of infringement, the court concluded that one cannot be liable unless he has undertaken the allegedly infringing acts volitionally. In other words, the defendant must at least do the copying, even if he does not know that the material is protected. It found that element missing in a situation where the BBS and ISP are passive and the copies of the offending materials are being placed on its computers by subscribers.[64] It used the same reasoning to distinguish *Frena* with regard to the distribution and display rights, observing that "only the subscriber should be liable for causing the distribution of plaintiffs' work, as the contributing actions of the BBS provider are automatic and indiscriminate."[65] The *Netcom* court did clearly indicate, however, that ISPs and BBS operators could be held liable under theories of contributory infringement or vicarious liability, subjects that are taken up in the immediately following section of this chapter.

Legal uncertainties resulting from these and other decisions prompted Congress to act. Title II of the Digital Millennium Copyright Act (DMCA) added a new § 512 to the Copyright Act.[66] Congress enacted this provision at the behest of ISPs such as America Online (AOL), Comcast, and EarthLink, who argued that copyright infringement concerns would stifle their industry and limit productive activity on the Internet. Congress intended to insulate ISPs from financial liability for infringing acts that occur on their computer systems, provided that certain procedures are followed. Generally speaking, these "safe harbors" apply to "service providers" which offer (1) transitory digital network communications, (2) system caching, (3) storing information at the request

---

64. "Although copyright is a strict liability statute, there should still be some elements of volition or causation which is lacking where a defendant's system is merely used to create a copy by a third party." 907 F.Supp. at 1370.

65. *Id.* at 1372. *Netcom* was followed in two later cases from the same

district, Sega Enterprises, Ltd. v. MAPHIA, 948 F.Supp. 923 (N.D.Cal.1996) and Sega Enterprises, Ltd. v. Sabella, 1996 WL 780560 (N.D.Cal.1996).

66. Pub. L. No. 105–304, 112 Stat. 2860 (1998).

of users, and (4) providing information location tools such as hypertext links.

To qualify for any of the § 512 safe harbors, an ISP must adopt, implement, and notify customers of a policy that allows the ISP to terminate an account holder who repeatedly infringes. In addition, the ISP must not interfere with "standard technical measures" used by copyright owners to protect their works.[67] Eligibility for a particular safe harbor then depends on compliance with additional requirements specific to that safe harbor.[68]

The most significant of the safe harbors is provided in § 512(c), which immunizes from financial liability ISPs that store copyright-protected materials on their servers. This protection applies to ISPs that: (1) do not know or have reason to know of infringing material;[69] (2) do not benefit financially from infringing activity, in the event the ISP has the right and ability to control such activity;[70] and (3) designate on their web site, and identify to the Copyright Office, an agent capable receiving notifications from copyright holders that the ISP is hosting infringing materials.[71] In addition, if the ISP learns that the material is infringing, it must act expeditiously to remove or disable access to the material.[72]

Section 512(c) also requires ISPs that wish to qualify for the safe harbor to comply with an elaborate protocol known as the "notice-and-take-down" procedure. Under this mechanism, a copyright holder that feels that someone has posted infringing materials on a site operated by an ISP may serve a written, good faith notice of infringement on that ISP.[73] An ISP that qualifies under the previously noted criteria is then immunized from liability if the ISP complies with a specified procedure for removing the identified material from its computers.[74] The ISP must also take reasonable steps to notify the account holder that it has removed or disabled access to the allegedly infringing material.

The account holder may then submit a written, signed counter-notification to the ISP stipulating both that the material at issue was removed or disabled due to mistake or misidentification, and that the account holder subjects himself to the personal jurisdiction of a federal district court. Upon receipt of a counter-notification, the ISP must then inform the copyright holder that the material will be replaced or reinstated. The ISP must then replace or reinstate the material unless the copyright holder brings suit against the account holder. The DMCA also allows copyright hold-

---

67.   17 U.S.C. § 512(i).

68.   17 U.S.C. § 512(n).

69.   17 U.S.C. § 512(c)(1)(A). In *Viacom Int'l Inc. v. YouTube, Inc.*, __ F.Supp. 2d, 2010 WL 2532404 (S.D.N.Y. June 23, 2010), the court held that such knowledge must be of "specific and identifiable infringements of particular individual items. Mere knowledge of prevalence of such activity is not enough."

70.   17 U.S.C. § 512(c)(1)(B).

71.   17 U.S.C. § 512(c)(2).

72.   17 U.S.C. § 512(c)(1)(A).

73.   17 U.S.C. § 512(c)(3).

74.   17 U.S.C. § 512(g).

ers to obtain from a federal district court, in specified circumstances, a subpoena against the ISP requesting the name of an account holder who is allegedly infringing.[75]

A hypothetical illustrates the complex notice-and-taken-down procedure. Suppose that music fan Louis Acorn places a video of the hit song "Joker Face" on the Internet hosting site UToob.com. Lady Gojo, the owner of copyright in "Joker Face," subsequently learns of Acorn's copy. Lady Gojo may then send a letter to UToob's designated agent asserting that Acorn's copy of "Joker Face" constitutes a copyright infringement. In order to qualify for the safe harbor, UToob must expeditiously remove, or disable access to, Acorn's copy of "Joker Face" from its servers.

UToob must then notify Acorn that it has removed the "Joker Face" video from his web site. Acorn then has the option to send a counter-notice to UToob. Acorn's notice must include a statement that he has a good faith belief that "Joker Face" was mistakenly removed. Acorn must also consent to the jurisdiction of the appropriate U.S. district court. If Acorn chooses to file a counter-notice, UToob must notify Lady Gojo. If Lady Gojo does not commence copyright infringement litigation within 10-14 business days following receipt of the counter-notice, then UToob must restore "Joker Face" to Acorn's website.

When it crafted the notice-and-take-down provisions, Congress was concerned that they might be subject to abuse. For example, an individual could serve a take-down notice asking an ISP to remove an embarrassing photo or other uploaded document even though it is not the owner of copyright. Section 512(f) therefore provides that an individual "who knowingly materially misrepresents . . . (1) that material or activity is infringing, or (2) that material or activity was removed or disabled by mistake or misidentification" is liable for damages to those injured by this misrepresentation. In plain English this means that an ISP customer whose non-infringing work is the subject of an improper takedown notice may seek recourse against the party who filed the unfounded request.

Perhaps the most notorious episode that has yet arisen under § 512(f) involved Stephanie Lenz's video "Let's Go Crazy #1." Lenz videotaped a 29-second clip of her 13-month-old son dancing in her kitchen to the Prince song "Let's Go Crazy." The song was audible—but barely, given the poor quality of the recording—for about 20 seconds of her video. Lenz then posted the video on YouTube.com, a popular Internet hosting site. Universal Music Corporation, the owner of the copyright in "Let's Go Crazy," sent

---

75. 17 U.S.C. § 512(h).

YouTube a DMCA takedown notice. YouTube removed the video the following day. Lenz responded with a counter-notice, stating that "Let's Go Crazy #1" was wrongfully removed and demanding that it be reposted. YouTube reposted the video about six weeks later.[76]

When Lenz subsequently filed suit against Universal, Universal filed a motion to dismiss her claim of misrepresentation under § 512(f). Lenz argued that the DMCA requires the copyright owner to consider the fair use doctrine—which this text takes up in further detail in Chapter 10—in formulating a "good faith belief" under § 512(c)(3)(A)(v) that "use of the material in the manner complained of is not authorized by the copyright owner, its agent, or the law." The court ruled in favor of Lenz, concluding that in order to form a good faith belief, a copyright holder must consider whether a particular use of copyrighted material qualifies as a fair use. The court considered this holding consistent with the DMCA's established requirement that a content owner "make an initial review of the potentially infringing material prior to sending a takedown notice."[77] At the time this book goes to press, the litigation between Lenz and Universal continues, even as the "Let's Go Crazy #1" video has been viewed over one million times.

Section 512 provides three additional safe harbors for ISPs. One exempts a compliant ISP from damages for conveying transitory digital network communications of copyrighted material, such as an e-mail with an infringing attachment. Under § 512(a), an ISP is insulated from monetary liability for copyright infringement if it satisfies several additional conditions. In particular, someone other than the ISP must have initiated the transmission and selected its recipients; the transmission must be accomplished through an automated process where the ISP does not select the transmission's recipients or modify its contents; and the ISP must not retain a copy for a longer period than is necessary to complete the transmission.

The safe harbor of § 512(b) pertains to "caching," a term that describes the temporary storage of material to improve the performance of a computer system. For example, an ISP might temporarily store material on a website that its users are accessing frequently, only to face a charge that it is making an unauthorized copy of copyright-protected material. Under § 512(b) ISPs are insulated from monetary liability for copyright infringement if persons other than the ISP made the material available online and requested its contents; the ISP does not modify its contents; and

---

76. *See* Lenz v. Universal Music Corp., 572 F. Supp. 2d 1150 (N.D. Cal. 2008).

77. *Id.* at 1154–55.

the caching is carried out through an automated technical process. The ISP must also comply with any "conditions" imposed by the copyright owner, including password protection and time periods for updating the cached copy. In addition, the ISP must comply with the notice-and-take-down procedure that applies under § 512(c).

The final safe harbor that applies to ISPs pertains to "information location tools" such as hyperlinks. Obviously, this safe harbor provides considerable comfort to Internet search engines such as Google or Yahoo, since the results they return in response to a given request may often send users to sites where infringing material could be located. Section 512(d) exempts ISPs from liability if they provide a link to an on-line location that contains infringing material. The requirements that pertain to the § 512(c) safe harbor involving ISP knowledge, lack of fiscal benefit, and the "notice-and-take-down" procedure, apply here as well.

Although § 512 exempts compliant ISPs from monetary liability, it affords more limited protection against injunctive relief. Section 512(j) allows courts to enjoin ISPs from providing access to infringing material upon consideration of the potential burdens to the ISP and the potential harm to the copyright owner.

Section 512(h) also allows a copyright owner to obtain an ex parte order requiring an ISP to identify an alleged infringer. The copyright owner need not commence an infringement suit in order to obtain the order. Rather, it need only file with the court (1) a copy of its notice-and-takedown notification "described in subsection (c)(3)(A)"; (2) a proposed subpoena that will be issued to the service provider; and (3) a sworn declaration that this information is being obtained solely to pursue rights protected "under this title."[78] Although this automatic order appears to provide a potent mechanism for identifying copyright infringers, in practice the courts have interpreted this provision narrowly. In *Recording Industry Association of America, Inc. v. Verizon Internet Services*,[79] the D.C. Circuit held that the specific reference within § 512(h) to § 512(c)(3)(A) limited the scope of the order to activities that fall within § 512(c)—namely, the storage of copyright-protected materials on their servers. Other activities that fall within the other safe harbors of § 512—and in particular an ISP's role as a transmitter of materials under § 512(a)—were held not to be subject to the subpoena. This limited reading of § 512(h) has severely limited the usefulness of this provision to content providers who wish to police peer-to-peer file sharing over the Internet.

78. 17 U.S.C. § 512(h)(2).
79. 351 F.3d 1229 (Fed. Cir. 2003).

The § 512 safe harbors are very complex, but bear in mind that they are entirely voluntary. An ISP that does not follow these procedures may continue to assert other defenses, such as the fair use privilege, should a copyright owner bring a charge of infringement against it.[80]

§ 9.4   Indirect Forms of Infringement

As hotels, bar owners, and television stations have occasionally discovered to their chagrin, one need not do the actual copying or performing to be held liable for copyright infringement. While the copyright statute itself does not impose liability on anyone other than direct infringers, courts have nonetheless long held that, where appropriate, others can be held liable as well. The principal theories which will lead to the imposition of liability on those only indirectly involved in the infringing conduct are vicarious liability and contributory infringement. In both cases, however, bear in mind that there can be no "secondary liability" unless there is an act of "primary" infringment. You might wonder why copyright owners bother with secondary parties—why they don't just sue the primary infringers. In many cases, however, the primary infringers are hard to find, too numerous, or outside the jurisdiction of the court. Secondary liability thus enables the copyright owner to secure effective relief by taking action against a party whose conduct is instrumental to the violation.

9.4.1   Vicarious Infringement

As one trial court put it, "The purpose of imposing vicarious liability is to punish one who unfairly reaps the benefits of another's infringing behavior."[81] Consequently, vicarious liability for copyright infringement will be imposed on a party who has both (1) the right and ability to supervise a direct infringer plus (2) a financial interest in the infringement.[82] This type of liability can be imposed even in the absence of any knowledge that the infringement is taking place. Moreover, while vicarious copyright liability developed out of the doctrine of respondeat superior, which holds an employer liable for the torts of an employee, it is clear that one

---

80.   17 U.S.C. § 512(*l*).

81.   Artists Music, Inc. v. Reed Publishing, Inc., 31 U.S.P.Q.2d 1623, 1626 (S.D.N.Y.1994).

82.   Shapiro, Bernstein & Co. v. H.L. Green Co., 316 F.2d 304, 307 (2d Cir.1963) ("When the right and ability to supervise coalesce with an obvious and direct financial interest in the ex-

ploitation of copyright materials—even in the absence of actual knowledge that the copyright monopoly is being impaired—the purposes of copyright law may be best effectuated by the imposition of liability upon the beneficiary of that exploitation."); Polygram Int'l Pub. Inc. v. Nevada/TIG, Inc., 855 F.Supp. 1314, 1324 (D.Mass.1994).

can be vicariously liable for copyright infringement based on acts of an independent contractor.[83]

Thus theater owners where infringing performances of dramatic or audiovisual works take place can be held as vicarious infringers, as can hotel and restaurant owners, when infringing musical performances occur on their property. In situations like these, the property owner has some degree of control over the activities of the musicians or actors and stands to benefit from ticket sales, drink sales, or rentals, as the case may be. At least in the music business, premises owners can also easily protect themselves from vicarious liability by obtaining blanket licenses from the major performing rights societies such as ASCAP or BMI.[84]

To satisfy the financial benefit test the benefit realized must in some way relate directly to the infringing activities of the primary infringer. The mere fact that the direct infringer pays rent for the premises where the infringement is conducted will usually not be sufficient. If the infringing activities serve as a magnet, however, attracting patrons to the premises, and if the defendant shares in the income generated by patrons because of commissions, ticket sales, or incidental revenues, there is adequate financial interest to establish vicarious liability.

For instance in *Fonovisa, Inc. v. Cherry Auction, Inc.*,[85] the defendant operated a flea market, or "swap meet," at which third-party vendors could rent booths to sell a variety of items to the public. Customers had to pay an admission fee to gain access to the premises. Cherry Auction also charged for parking and sold refreshments to the patrons of its flea market. Some of the vendors at the flea market were engaged in the routine sale of counterfeit musical recordings that infringed plaintiff's copyrights.[86] Plaintiff sued Cherry Auction, in part on a vicarious liability theory. The Ninth Circuit found that "the defendants reap substantial financial benefits from admission fees, concession stand sales and parking fees, all of which flow directly from customers who want to buy the counterfeit recordings at bargain basement prices." That was enough to satisfy the financial benefit requirement because, as the *Fonovisa* court put it, the nub of the matter is whether the infringing activities "enhance the attractiveness of the venue to potential customers."

83. Gershwin Publishing Corp. v. Columbia Artists Management, Inc., 443 F.2d 1159, 1162 (2d Cir.1971).

84. See § 6.4.3, *supra*.

85. 76 F.3d 259, 263 (9th Cir.1996).

86. Note that there might not have been any evidence that the primary infringer—the vendor of the phonorecords—had actually manufactured the infringing items. Such proof is not required, however, because the mere sale of the infringing recordings violated the copyright owners' distribution rights.

The control element of the vicarious liability test requires actual, as opposed to mere theoretical or legal, control. In most cases finding vicarious liability, the defendant had a clear right of supervision over the primary infringing party. In *Fonovisa* for instance, the court noted that the defendant swap meet operator "had the right to terminate vendors for any reasons whatsoever and through that right had the ability to control the activities of vendors on the premises."[87] By way of contrast, an ordinary landlord, who turns over possession of premises for a specified term of months or years in return for a flat rental, is unlikely to be found to have the control necessary to trigger vicarious liability even if a tenant uses the property as a location to manufacture counterfeit tapes or CDs.

There are other situations where parties may be held vicariously liable. Courts have imposed liability on sponsors of radio or television programs, if they have the requisite power to supervise and control the program content.[88] A national organization with supervision and control over a local organization was held liable when the latter organized an infringing concert.[89] Parent corporations can be held liable for the acts of their subsidiaries if they have "a direct financial interest in the infringing activity, and ... the right and ability to supervise the subsidiary, which is evidenced by some continuing connection between the two in regard to the infringing activity."[90]

9.4.2 Contributory Infringement

Contributory infringement is found when the defendant "with knowledge of the infringing activity, induces, causes or materially contributes to the infringing conduct of another...."[91] Unlike vicarious liability, where knowledge is irrelevant, knowledge of the behavior of the primary infringer is a key aspect of contributory liability. The easiest cases of contributory infringement involve parties who actively encourage or induce the direct or primary infringer to engage in the disputed conduct. For instance, a publisher that suggests the inclusion of a lengthy copyrighted passage in an author's book would plainly be subject to liability as a contributory infringer. Even without encouragement the requisite knowledge and material contribution might also be present when a computer bulletin board operator or Internet service provider re-

---

87. 76 F.3d at 262.

88. *See e.g.*, Davis v. E.I. DuPont de Nemours & Co., 240 F.Supp. 612 (S.D.N.Y.1965).

89. Gershwin Publishing Corp. v. Columbia Artists Management, Inc., 443 F.2d 1159 (2d Cir.1971).

90. Banff Ltd. v. Limited, Inc., 869 F.Supp. 1103, 1110 (S.D.N.Y.1994).

91. Gershwin Publish Corp. v. Columbia Artists Management, Inc., 443 F.2d 1159, 1162 (2d Cir.1971).

fuses to remove infringing materials posted by subscribers after receiving complaints from the copyright owner.[92]

The requirement of "material contribution" to the infringement can also be made out by showing the defendant supplied the primary infringer with some item necessary to engage in the infringing activity. Under this principle, it is contributory infringement to lend copyrighted material such as books or tapes to another party with knowledge that the other party is planning to make illegal copies of that material. Similarly, the legislative history notes that "a person who lawfully acquires an authorized copy of a motion picture would be an infringer if he or she engages in the business of renting it to others for purposes of an unauthorized public performance."[93]

In *Columbia Pictures Industries, Inc. v. Aveco, Inc.*,[94] the Third Circuit said that providing the site and facilities for infringing activity is also sufficient to constitute contributory infringement. In that case, defendant operated a videocassette rental store which also provided on-premises viewing rooms for customers. The court found that the playing of the cassettes in the viewing rooms by the customers was a public performance in violation of the copyright owner's exclusive performance right. It went on to hold that the store operator could be liable as a contributory infringer in connection with this activity.

The Supreme Court addressed issues of contributory infringement in *Sony Corp. v. Universal City Studios, Inc.*[95] The plaintiffs in that well-known case alleged that home videotaping of copyrighted television programs constituted infringement. Recognizing that it would be impossible to enforce their copyrights against millions of individuals engaged in home taping they also added claims against Sony, a VCR manufacturer. Plaintiff's theory was that Sony had supplied the machines to consumers with knowledge that they would be used for infringing purposes, thus making Sony a contributory infringer.

The Supreme Court rejected that idea. First, and most famously, it found that much of the copying activity of the VCR users was not itself infringing, because it was protected by the fair use doctrine. That ruling will be considered in detail in the immediately following chapter but for present purposes we reiterate a point

---

92. *See, e.g.* Religious Technology Center v. Netcom On–Line Communication Services, 907 F.Supp. 1361, 1374 (N.D.Cal.1995).

93. H.R.Rep. No. 1476, 94th Cong., 2d Sess. 61, reprinted in 1976 U.S.Code Cong. & Ad.News at 5674; see S.Rep. No. 473, 94th Cong., 1st Sess. 57 (1975).

94. Columbia Pictures Industries, Inc. v. Aveco, Inc., 800 F.2d 59 (3d Cir. 1986).

95. 464 U.S. 417, 104 S.Ct. 774, 78 L.Ed.2d 574 (1984).

made at the start of this material—namely that absent any primary infringement there cannot be any contributory infringement.

Secondly, the Supreme Court found that the sale of VCRs was not contributorily infringing even though some consumers might use the machine to engage in illicit behaviors because the VCR was "capable of commercially significant noninfringing uses." In other words, there are many functions for VCRs other than impermissibly taping copyrighted material. They can be used to watch lawfully rented videotapes in private settings. They can be used to both watch and duplicate homemade videos of the family vacation or of grandma kissing the baby. They can be used to tape non-copyrighted materials that might be broadcast, such as old movies on which the copyrights might have lapsed because of non-renewal. With such a wide range of legal uses for the machines it becomes impossible to say that the VCR manufacturer has knowledge that any particular machine will be used to violate the law. The contributory infringement analysis in *Sony* means that those who sell devices such as photocopiers and even printing presses cannot be held secondarily liable for the activities of those who buy the devices unless there is some additional proof that the vendor knows the device will be used for infringing purposes.

On the other hand, if a party sells a device which is solely or primarily useful only for conducting infringing acts, that party will be a contributory infringer. A good example is *A & M Records v. Abdallah*.[96] There, defendant was selling "time loaded" audio-cassettes to individuals who used them as blanks to make piratical recordings. A time loaded cassette has only sufficient tape to match a time requirement imposed by a purchaser, rather than an even 30, 60, or 90 minutes of tape. Time loaded cassettes prevent running out of tape at the end of a recording, and avoid waste and silence at the end of one side of the recording before the other side begins to play. Not only did defendant sell such tapes to customers with knowledge of the purpose for which they would be used, he even occasionally timed copyrighted sound recordings for his customers so as to inform them of the length of tape to order. The court found defendant liable for contributory infringement, observing "*Sony* requires that the product being sold have a 'substantial' noninfringing use, and although time-loaded cassettes can be used for legitimate purposes, these purposes are insubstantial given the number of Mr. Abdallah's customers that were using them for counterfeiting purposes."

96. 948 F.Supp. 1449 (C.D.Cal. 1996).

9.4.3 Peer-to-Peer File Sharing

One of the most dramatic technological developments over the past decade has been the rise of file sharing through peer-to-peer ("P2P") networks. By 2010, P2P file sharing was the largest contributor to network traffic on the Internet. Consumers most commonly use P2P networks to download music encoded in MP3 or other digital audio encoding formats using high speed, broadband Internet connections. But this technology may be used to transfer any digitally stored information, including documents, electronic books, computer programs, television shows, and films.[97]

P2P technology presents opportunities for sharing information that are truly revolutionary. Yet songwriters, music publishers, software houses, movie studios, and other content providers have justifiable fears that file sharing through P2P networks may result in massive unauthorized downloading of their protected works of authorship. Launching copyright infringement suits against every individual who has downloaded copyright-protected material would be impracticable, though goodness knows, the recording industry has been trying to do just that.[98] Copyright owners have therefore charged the distributors of P2P software with vicarious and contributory infringement. The application of traditional tort doctrines to groundbreaking Internet-based technologies has not always been a seamless exercise. It has also challenged courts to develop principles that can allow legitimate uses of P2P technology to flourish, but at the same time check the unprecedented volume of copyright infringement that these networks can promote.

Prior to Supreme Court intervention, two decisions from the Courts of Appeals seemed to point in different directions regarding third party liability for P2P file sharing. In the first of these, *A & M Records, Inc. v. Napster, Inc.*,[99] the Ninth Circuit considered claims by record companies and music publishers that the distributors of the notorious file-sharing service Napster had committed contributory copyright infringement. Napster allowed individuals to download its MusicShare software from its website. The free file-sharing software allowed users to make MP3 music files, located on the hard drive of their personal computers, available for download by other Napster users. The MusicShare software also allowed a Napster user to perform a search of a centralized file index to find MP3 files located on the PCs of other users, and then to download those files. Most of the files shared on the Napster system were subject to copyright, yet Napster did not prevent the sharing of such copyrighted works.

---

97. *See* Seth Robert Belzley, *Grokster and Efficiency in Music*, 10 Va. J. L. & Tech. 10 (2005).

98. *See* William Henslee, *Money for Nothing and Music for Free? Why the RIAA Should Continue to Sue Illegal File–Sharers*, 9 J. Marshall Rev. Intell. Prop. L. 1 (2009).

99. 239 F.3d 1004 (9th Cir. 2001).

Members of the music industry brought suit against Napster for copyright infringement. Napster did not contest that its users directly infringed, and as we will discuss elsewhere in this text, the Ninth Circuit rejected Napster's assertion that the fair use defense excused the activities of the end-users.[100] The issue before the court, then, was whether Napster was secondarily liable for the direct infringement under either contributory or vicarious infringement theories.

With respect to contributory infringement, the Ninth Circuit reasoned that Napster knew its users were direct copyright infringers and materially contributed to their infringement through its centralized servers and searching index. The Court of Appeals also rejected Napster's citation of the *Sony* decision, along with its efforts to identify legitimate, noninfringing file sharing, such as the exchange of public domain music. According to the Ninth Circuit, "Napster's actual, specific knowledge of direct infringement renders *Sony's* holding of limited assistance to Napster."[101] The Ninth Circuit also held that Napster was liable for vicarious infringement. The Ninth Circuit explained that Napster derived significant advertising revenue that was based upon the number of users of its system, giving it a direct financial stake in the infringing activity. The Court of Appeals further reasoned that Napster could have blocked infringing users but failed to do so. The lesson seems to be that where a distributor of a product has actual knowledge of specific infringing acts by the users of that product, and also has the capacity to stop them, the continued distribution of the product will trigger secondary liability.

The second notable file-sharing decision, *In re Aimster Copyright Litigation*,[102] hailed from the Seventh Circuit. Individuals had used the Aimster system to exchange music and other files over the AOL Instant Messaging System, known as "AIM," as well as the Internet. The district court awarded a preliminary injunction in favor of various music copyright owners, and on appeal the Seventh Circuit affirmed. Judge Posner agreed that the copyright proprietors were likely to succeed on their contributory infringement claim. In doing so, however, he made explicit his view "that the Ninth Circuit erred in [*Napster*] in suggesting that actual knowledge of specific infringing uses is a sufficient condition for deeming a facilitator a contributory infringer."[103] Judge Posner instead viewed the *Sony* case as compelling an inquiry into whether users are actually making non-infringing uses of the system, and also a cost-benefit analysis of the efforts required to police infringing uses. As Aimster introduced no evidence of the non-infringing uses of its

---

100. *See infra* § 10.5.1.

101. 239 F.3d at 1020.

102. 334 F.3d 643 (7th Cir. 2003).

103. *Id.* at 649.

system, and further failed to show that it would have been dispro-
portionately costly to eliminate or reduce substantially the infringing uses, neither part of this standard had been met.

The difference in views between the Seventh and Ninth Circuits set the stage for Supreme Court intervention, which ultimately occurred in the *Metro–Goldwyn–Mayer Studios, Inc. v. Grokster,
Ltd.*[104] This time the content providers squared off against two
other P2P networks, Grokster and StreamCast. In contrast to
Napster, these services did not maintain a centralized index of files.
Rather, each user maintained a list of files that he or she was
willing to share. The Ninth Circuit seized upon the decentralized
architecture of the accused services to distinguish this case from
Fonovisa v. Cherry Auction and *Napster* itself: "The nature of the
relationship between Grokster and StreamCast and their users is
significantly different from the nature of the relationship between a
swap meet operator and its participants, or prior versions of Napster and its users, since Grokster and StreamCast are more truly
decentralized, peer-to-peer file-sharing networks."[105] The Ninth Circuit concluded that Grokster and StreamCast lacked the ability to
prevent specific infringements and thus could not face liability.

On review, the Supreme Court reversed. The High Court held
that the Ninth Circuit had misapplied the earlier *Sony* decision,
concluding that *Sony* does not provide the governing rule of law
when an accused infringer "actively induces" copyright infringement. Stated differently, if a defendant intends users to employ a
device in order to infringe copyright and tacitly exhorts them to do
so, then the defendant is liable for infringement as a matter of
fundamental tort principles—even if that device is capable of substantial non-infringing uses. Viewed in this manner, *Sony* offered
principles for assessing liability when there was no evidence that
the defendant's purpose was to promote copyright infringement.
When the defendant did harbor such an intent, however, *Sony* did
not preclude infringement liability.

The Court concluded that three aspects of the Grokster and
StreamCast services indicated an intent to induce infringement.
First, both services attempted to meet a known demand for copyright infringement—the market consisting of former Napster users.
Second, the two services made no effort to block infringing uses
through filtering tools or other mechanisms. Finally, the defendants' revenues were based upon advertising, a business model that
was in turn founded upon a high rate of copyright infringement. In
combination, these factors convinced the Court that the defendants
had an unmistakable intention to foster infringement. Satisfied

104.   545 U.S. 913, 125 S.Ct. 2764,   **105.**   380 F.3d 1154, 1165 (9th Cir.
162 L.Ed.2d 781 (2005).   2004).

that users of Grokster and StreamCast had committed acts of direct infringement on a "gigantic scale," the Court concluded that these two P2P systems were liable for inducement.

To synthesize all this case law, it seems that the distributor of a product (including software) can be secondary liable for infringement in any of three situations. First, if it distributes a product that has no, or virtually no, non-infringing uses, that will be enough for liability (think time-loaded cassette tapes). Second, even if the product does have substantial non-infringing uses, it can also be liable if it knows of specific infringements, and has the ability to stop them (think *Napster*)–Judge Posner would add that this ability to stop them must be at a reasonable cost. Third and finally, even if the product has substantial non-infringing uses, and even if its "architecture" does not give the distributor knowledge of specific infringements, the distributor can still be secondarily liable if it induces, encourages, or "exhorts" infringement (think *Grokster).* Moreover, that inducement need not be explicit—it can be inferred from aspects of the distributor's business model, and from the products design.

The *Grokster* decision frustrated some observers and worried others. Those who were frustrated had hoped that the opinion would either clarify or modify the *Sony* rule by specifying the level of non-infringing uses that should be considered "substantial," and thus qualify as non-infringing. Those who find the opinion worrisome focus on the ambiguous guidelines the Court articulated to determine when a distributor has "induced" infringement. Grokster was found to have induced infringement based on the way it conducted its business and designed its system, but it is unclear what other methods of doing business or other system designs might also be considered to impermissibly "induce." Professor Boyle makes the point effectively with a powerful analogy:

> [I]f one were launching the iPod today, it is not clear how it would fare under *Grokster's* standard. . . . There is Apple's "tainted" advertising campaign, urging users to "Rip, Mix and Burn." Does this not suggest complicity or even intent? There is the fact that the iPod does not restrict itself solely to proprietary formats protected by digital rights management. It also allows uncontrolled MP3 files despite the fact that this format is "notoriously" used to transfer files against the wishes of the copyright owner. This, surely, is a "failure to police." And finally there is the fact that it would cost about $10,000 to fill an iPod with songs downloaded from iTunes. Clearly Apple must be aware that much of the music that fills iPods is illicitly copied. They are profiting from the fact to drive demand for the product just as Grokster was profiting from the

attractions of illicit traffic to drive people to use their service![106]

In the view of these critics, *Grokster* ultimately leaves high technology entrepreneurs with considerable uncertainty should they choose to distribute products that possess both infringing and non-infringing uses.[107] In the face of this uncertainty some products may never see the light of day. It is this potential suppression of technology and innovation that causes some thoughtful observers to take a dim view of *Grokster*.

Setting the legal niceties aside, the efforts of copyright enforcers to crack down on P2P networks may ultimately prove extremely difficult, and in the end perhaps entirely futile. Ironically, the intellectual property laws have in this case unquestionably inspired considerable technological advancement—ones designed specifically to allow users to evade charges of copyright infringement with minimal effort and minimal risk of detection! Current technologies include "darknets"—covert portions of the Internet not easily accessed by outsiders, where insiders swap files with virtual impunity; encryption techniques that conceal the identity of protected works of authorship; and stealth technologies, such as purchasing foreign Internet Protocol (IP) addresses that allow individuals to download files "anonymously." The result is that content providers have been increasingly challenged to use other mechanisms, such as their own anti-copying technologies, in order to sustain their own business models.

§ 9.5   Jurisdiction and Procedure

Under 28 U.S.C. § 1338(a), federal courts have subject matter jurisdiction over "any civil action arising under any Act of Congress relating to ... copyrights ..."[108] This statute goes on to provide that this "jurisdiction shall be exclusive of the courts of the states." In other words, claims arising under the copyright laws can only be filed in federal court. While this provision seems simple enough, litigants and courts have had difficulty determining just when a case "arises under" copyright law.

Where the plaintiff makes a straightforward allegation of infringement, there is little question that the claim arises under the statute. Given the limitations of language and the ingenuity of

---

106. JAMES BOYLE, THE PUBLIC DOMAIN 79 (2008).

107. *See generally* Jane C. Ginsburg, *Separating the Sony Sheep from the Grokster Goats: Reckoning the Future Business Plans of Copyright–Dependent Technology Entrepreneurs*, 50 ARIZ. L. REV. 577 (2008), who observes "even

businesses not initially built on infringement, but in which infringement comes to play an increasingly profitable part, may find themselves liable unless they take good faith measures to forestall infringements."

108. 28 U.S.C. § 1338(a).

lawyers, however, ambiguous cases can arise. For instance a copyright owner and a licensee may disagree over whether their license permits exploitation of the work in a new medium, such as videotapes or in interactive computer applications. That dispute is, in one sense, a dispute over contract interpretation, a traditional subject of state law. On the other hand, it implicates the policies of the Copyright Act, and in that sense could be said to "arise" under that Act.

In a well-known passage, the Second Circuit attempted to clarify the issue, observing that "an action 'arises under' the Copyright Act if and only if the complaint is for a remedy expressly granted by the Act, ... or asserts a claim requiring construction of the Act ... or at the very least and perhaps more doubtfully, presents a case where a distinctive policy of the Act requires that federal principles control the disposition of the claim. The general interest that copyrights, like all other forms of property, should be enjoyed by their true owner is not enough to meet this last test."[109] The Ninth Circuit, quoting bits of language from a number of different courts, has said that courts should focus on "the 'primary and controlling purpose' of the suit, the 'principle issue,' the 'fundamental controversy,' and the 'gist' or 'essence' of the plaintiff's claim,"[110] to determine if it arises under the copyright statute.

Under this approach exclusive federal jurisdiction has been held appropriate in cases concerning whether a work should be treated as a work made for hire,[111] and in disputes over payments owned under the compulsory licensing provisions of the 1976 Act.[112] Another example of this logic at work is the Second Circuit's decision in *Merchant v. Levy*.[113] Plaintiffs in that case had been members of a singing group called "The Teenagers" and claimed that they had written the original version of a song called *Fools* in 1955. However, when the copyright in that song was registered with the Copyright Office in 1956, the documents listed two other individuals as the authors. By the late 1980s, having received no royalties, plaintiffs filed suit for a declaration that they were co-owners of the copyright and for an accounting of royalties. Although the defendants argued that there was no basis for federal subject matter jurisdiction, the court rejected those contentions. It noted that unlike a case where an ownership dispute might arise

---

109. T.B. Harms Co. v. Eliscu, 339 F.2d 823, 828 (2d Cir.1964), *cert. denied*, 381 U.S. 915, 85 S.Ct. 1534, 14 L.Ed.2d 435 (1965).

110. Topolos v. Caldewey, 698 F.2d 991, 993 (9th Cir.1983).

111. Royalty Control Corp. v. Sanco, Inc., 175 U.S.P.Q. 641, 643 (N.D.Cal. 1972).

112. T.B. Harms Co. v. Eliscu, 339 F.2d 823, 828 (2d Cir.1964), *cert. denied*, 381 U.S. 915, 85 S.Ct. 1534, 14 L.Ed.2d 435 (1965).

113. 92 F.3d 51 (2d Cir.1996), *cert. denied*, 519 U.S. 1108, 117 S.Ct. 943, 136 L.Ed.2d 833 (1997).

under a contract, the dispute before it concerned the interpretation of the joint authorship concept under the copyright statute itself. This seems logical because Congress presumably wanted the federal courts, and the federal courts alone, to make pronouncements on ambiguous provisions of the copyright laws, and cases such as these require just such pronouncements.

By way of contrast, a suit alleging non-payment of royalties under a copyright licensing agreement does not "arise under" the copyright laws,[114] and must be litigated in state court—unless, of course, there is diversity of citizenship—because the legal issues involved are unlikely to involve consideration of weighty matters of copyright policy. Cases of this type are really nothing more than contract disputes where the subject matter of the contract happens coincidentally to be a copyright. There is little risk that a state court decision on the matter will result in confusion over the meaning of important aspects of the copyright statute.

In those cases where a plaintiff alleges both a claim arising under the copyright laws and additional claims based on state law, the federal courts may have power to decide those additional claims under the doctrine of supplemental jurisdiction. 28 U.S.C. § 1338(b) provides that "the district courts shall have original jurisdiction of any civil action asserting a claim of unfair competition when joined with a substantial and related claim under the copyright, patent, plant variety protection or trade-mark laws." This provision gives the federal courts supplemental jurisdiction, but only over state claims that involve "unfair competition" and only when those claims are "related" to a federal intellectual property claim that is "substantial." While the language of this section might suggest that federal jurisdiction is mandatory when the various statutory tests are satisfied, the Federal Circuit has held that trial courts should still use discretion in determining whether or not to assume jurisdiction over an unfair competition claim.[115]

In administering this supplemental jurisdiction provision the courts have interpreted the concept of "unfair competition" broadly to include such matters as trade secret theft, conversion of intellectual property, and various forms of passing off and common law trademark infringement.[116] If plaintiff's non-federal claims are not

---

114. Bevan v. Columbia Broadcasting System, Inc., 329 F.Supp. 601 (S.D.N.Y.1971).

115. Verdegaal Bros. v. Union Oil Co., 750 F.2d 947, 950 (Fed Cir.1984).

116. Mars Inc. v. Kabushiki–Kaisha Nippon Conlux, 24 F.3d 1368, 1372–73 (Fed.Cir.1994) ("The common law concept of 'unfair competition' has not been confined to any rigid definition and encompasses a variety of types of commercial or business conduct considered 'contrary to good conscience,' including acts of trademark and trade dress infringement, false advertising, dilution, and trade secret theft . . .").

unfair competition claims, plaintiff can still ask the federal court to take jurisdiction over them under the general doctrine of supplemental jurisdiction, provided those non-federal claims "are so related to claims in the action within such original jurisdiction that they form part of the same case or controversy . . ."[117] In the decided cases, the most difficult issue under section 1338(b) has proven to be whether the state law claim is genuinely "related" to the federal intellectual property claim. While there has been some disagreement among the courts, the emerging consensus seems to require that both the copyright claim and the non-federal claim arise from a common nucleus of operative fact in order for them to be considered related.[118] This standard will, of course, be familiar to aficionados of civil procedure as the general standard for assertion of supplemental jurisdiction.

In its 2010 decision in *Reed Elsevier, Inc. v. Muchnick*,[119] the Supreme Court resolved the rather technical question of whether the registration requirement of § 411 was jurisdictional in nature. That litigation centered around a proposed settlement that aimed to resolve copyright infringement litigation between free-lance authors, on one side, and various magazines, newspapers, and other publishers, on the other. The authors complained that the publishers had copied their articles into a number of electronic databases without their permission—and, of course, without additional compensation. The Supreme Court sided with the authors in its 2001 decision in *New York Times Co. v. Tasini*.[120]

Years of negotiation followed the issuance of the *Tasini* opinion. After agreeing to an $18 million settlement, the parties returned to the courts, requesting that the District Court certify a class for settlement and approve the agreement. But the Second Circuit concluded that the federal courts lacked subject matter jurisdiction because the authors had not registered the great majority of the articles with the Copyright Office. As you will recall from an earlier discussion in this text, § 411(a) of the Copyright Act stipulates that registration is a predicate to bringing an action for infringement of a U.S. work.[121] Viewing the registration requirement as jurisdictional in character, the Second Circuit ruled that the federal courts lacked authority to approve the settlement.

Disagreeing with the Second Circuit, the Supreme Court reversed and remanded. The Court observed that 28 U.S.C. § 1338(a), the statute granting federal courts subject matter juris-

---

117. That doctrine is codified in 28 U.S.C. § 1367.

118. See, e.g., J.M. Huber Corp. v. Positive Action Tool Of Ohio Co., Inc., 879 F.Supp. 705, 710 (S.D.Tex.1995); Kupferberg, Goldberg & Niemark, L.L.C. v. Father and Son Pizza, Ltd., 1997 WL 158332, *2 (N.D.Ill.1997).

119. ___ U.S. ___, 130 S.Ct. 1237, 176 L.Ed.2d 17 (2010).

120. 533 U.S. 483, 121 S.Ct. 2381, 150 L.Ed.2d 500 (2001).

121. See supra § 5.4.

diction, did not speak to registration. Nor did § 411(a) of the Copyright Act clearly state the registration requirement was jurisdictional. The Court further observed that the Copyright Act expressly allowed courts to adjudicate claims involving unregistered works where U.S. works are not involved, where the infringement claims involves rights of attribution and integrity under § 106A, and where the Copyright Office refused to register a work. It would be an unusual result, the Court reasoned, to accord jurisdictional significance to a requirement ridden with exceptions. As a result of *Reed Elsevier, Inc. v. Muchnick*, registration remains a pre-condition for proprietors of U.S works to bring a copyright infringement suit. But this holding may expedite judicial ability to promote settlement of disputes that at least in part involve unregistered works.

Most other jurisdictional and procedural aspects of copyright litigation are identical to those governing all civil suits in federal courts. Thus, general principles of personal jurisdiction and venue apply. Not surprisingly, pleading and discovery practice are controlled by the Federal Rules of Civil Procedure. The details of these schemes are, mercifully, beyond the scope of this book.

§ 9.6   Remedies

The copyright statute provides a broad range of remedies to the successful plaintiff. Not all remedies are available in every case, however. Moreover a fairly substantial set of rules has grown up around the various remedies. Obviously, from the point of view of a client considering copyright litigation, the availability of an adequate remedy is a crucial question which counsel should thoroughly consider before going forward with a suit.

9.6.1   Injunctions

Copyright plaintiffs may seek two types of injunctions—preliminary and permanent.[122] In determining whether an injunction should be granted, courts in copyright cases are guided by the same principles that generally govern the grant of equitable remedies and injunctive relief in other branches of the law.

Courts grant preliminary injunctions early in the prosecution of a lawsuit to prevent further conduct by the defendant harmful to the plaintiff. A preliminary injunction remains in force until the lawsuit can be fully adjudicated and a final judgment can be rendered. To obtain a preliminary injunction, a plaintiff must show that he will likely prevail on the merits of the case; that he will sustain irreparable harm unless the injunction is granted; and that

122.   17 U.S.C. § 502.

the balance of hardships tips in his favor.[123] The precise formula used by courts in determining if a preliminary injunction is appropriate varies from circuit to circuit. A strong showing on one of these elements will often balance out a weak showing on another. Indeed, some courts will presume irreparable harm if the plaintiff can make out a strong showing of infringement.[124] The defendant is entitled to notice and a hearing before a preliminary injunction will issue.

If the plaintiff feels that the delay associated with the notice and hearing required for a preliminary injunction will itself cause irreparable harm, the plaintiff can ask for a temporary restraining order (TRO) in an ex parte application to the court.[125] While the copyright statute itself makes no reference to TROs, the legislative history of section 502 shows that Congress contemplated such relief where appropriate.[126] The procedures for granting TROs are set out in Rule 65 of the Federal Rules of Civil Procedure. A TRO will usually remain in effect for only a brief period of time—usually until the court can schedule a hearing on the propriety of a preliminary injunction.

At the close of the case, the court may grant a permanent injunction in plaintiff's favor if plaintiff has proven infringement. Such an injunction will forbid further acts of infringement and can be enforced by contempt sanctions. In *eBay Inc. v. MercExchange, L.L.C.*,[127] the Supreme Court explained that in order for a prevailing plaintiff to obtain a permanent injunction, it must demonstrate (1) that it has suffered an irreparable injury; (2) that legal remedies, such as damages, are inadequate to compensate for that injury; (3) that the balance of hardships indicates that equitable relief is warranted; and (4) the public interest would not be disserved by a permanent injunction. Although *eBay* was a patent case, the Court explicitly stated that these principles applied in copyright disputes as well.

In practice, prevailing copyright holders ordinarily obtain injunctions largely on the theory that infringement is a continuing harm and that the magnitude of the harm will often be difficult to evaluate in monetary terms. A plaintiff need not show that the infringement was willful in order to obtain an injunction.[128] But as

---

123. See, e.g., Hasbro Bradley, Inc. v. Sparkle Toys, Inc., 780 F.2d 189, 192 (2d Cir.1985); Apple Computer, Inc. v. Formula Intl. Inc., 725 F.2d 521, 523 (9th Cir.1984).

124. See, e.g., Video Trip Corp. v. Lightning Video, Inc., 866 F.2d 50, 51–52 (2d Cir.1989) ("existence of irreparable injury is presumed upon a showing of a prima facie case of copyright infringement.").

125. *See* Fed. R. Civ. P. 65(b).

126. H.R.Rep. No. 1476, 94th Cong., 2d Sess. 160, reprinted in 1976 U.S.Code Cong. & Ad.News at 5674.

127. 547 U.S. 388, 126 S.Ct. 1837, 164 L.Ed.2d 641 (2006).

128. Williams Elec., Inc. v. Artic Intl., Inc., 685 F.2d 870, 878 (3d Cir. 1982).

indicated by *eBay*, issuance of a permanent injunction is not automatic. A court may refuse to issue one if it feels that future infringement is unlikely or if other considerations make it unnecessary. The Supreme Court has also suggested that in some cases, such as a parody found to be beyond the scope of the fair use defense,[129] an injunction might not be appropriate because the defendant's work may have creative elements and there may be a strong public interest in its continued availability.[130] In such a case plaintiff will be limited to a monetary recovery.

9.6.2 Monetary Recoveries

The current copyright statute refers to three types of monetary recovery that may be available to a successful copyright infringement plaintiff—actual damages, defendant's profits, and statutory damages. Under section 504(b) of the statute a plaintiff may recover "the actual damages suffered by him or her as a result of the infringement," plus "any profits of the infringer that are attributable to the infringement and ... not taken into account in computing the actual damages." Alternatively, plaintiff may "recover, instead of actual damages and profits, an award of statutory damages for all infringements involved in the action...."[131] The choice of which remedy to pursue lies in the hands of the plaintiff, who may elect either the actual damages/profits measure or the statutory damages measure at any time before final judgement in the case.

The legislative history accompanying the 1976 Act explained why plaintiffs are entitled to *both* their own damages as well as defendant's profits if they chose the first option described above. The two types of awards serve different purposes. "Damages are awarded to compensate the copyright owner for losses from the infringement, and profits are awarded to prevent the infringer from unfairly benefitting from a wrongful act."[132] Of course the two items must be calculated in a way that avoids duplicative recovery. If a defendant has sold infringing copies of a work in direct competition with the plaintiff, plaintiff's damages and defendant's profits may simply be two sides of the same coin. For instance, much of the revenue earned by a defendant who sells bootleg videotapes is revenue that plaintiff would have earned if there had been no infringement. In such a case, awarding the plaintiff its own lost profits as a measure of actual damages and then adding the

---

129. *See infra* § 10.6.

130. Campbell v. Acuff–Rose Music, Inc., 510 U.S. 569, 578 n. 10, 114 S.Ct. 1164, 127 L.Ed.2d 500 (1994) ("the goals of the copyright law ... are not always best served by automatically granting injunctive relief when parodists are found to have gone beyond the bounds of fair use").

131. 17 U.S.C. § 504(c).

132. H.R.Rep. No. 1476, 94th Cong., 2d Sess.1 61, reprinted in 1976 U.S.Code Cong. & Ad.News at 5674.

profits earned by the defendant might be a form of double counting. For all intents and purposes, this plaintiff will have to choose between a recovery based either on its own lost sales or one based on defendant's profits.[133]

9.6.2.1 Actual Damages

A copyright owner's actual damages usually consist of either his own lost profits on sales, or lost royalties. Lost profits on sales is most relevant in cases where the defendant has sold infringing copies of a work in direct competition with the plaintiff or has otherwise competed with the plaintiff in his primary market. Lost royalties are a more logical and typical measure when the defendant has made unauthorized derivative works of a type that do not directly compete with plaintiff or has engaged in unauthorized public performances. For example, if the plaintiff is the owner of the copyright in a novel and the defendant made and sold unauthorized copies of the novel, plaintiff's damages would be based on the lost profit on sales measure, since consumers who purchased from the defendant would, in all likelihood, have bought from plaintiff if no infringing copies were available. On the other hand, if the defendant prepares a screenplay based on plaintiff's novel and produces a movie from the screenplay, a lost royalty measure would be more appropriate because plaintiff could have marketed the movie rights to someone else for a reasonable royalty but for the infringing acts of the defendant.

Obviously, there will be much that is uncertain in either measure of actual damages. Where an infringer sells at lower prices or different profit margins than the plaintiff it may be a complex matter to extrapolate from defendant's sales to determine the profits that plaintiff would have made but for those sales. Where the infringer is exploiting a new and different market, there may be no reliable indication of what a reasonable royalty rate might have been. Courts will do the best they can with the evidence offered by the parties, and it is often said that any doubts concerning the amount of damages will be resolved against the defendant.[134] The plaintiff is also entitled to any incidental items of damage over and above the lost profits on sales or the lost royalties if he is able to prove them.

---

133. On the other hand, if defendant has low production costs, its profit per copy sold may be greater than plaintiff's profit. In such a case plaintiff is entitled to its own lost profits as a damage remedy plus the difference between its lost profits and defendant's actual profits. *See* NIMMER, Copyright § 14.02[A].

134. *See, e.g.,* Brewer v. Hustler Magazine, 749 F.2d 527, 529 (9th Cir. 1984); Northwest Airlines v. American Airlines, Inc., 870 F.Supp. 1504, 1513 (D.Minn.1994).

9.6.2.2 Profits

Where the defendant has made and sold multiple copies of plaintiff's copyrighted work or publicly performed the work for a paying audience it is likely that he realized a profit by doing so, and plaintiff may recover that profit as part of the relief in a successful copyright action. The objective of such an award is to deprive the defendant of illicit financial benefit traceable to his infringing conduct. When pursuing an award of defendant's profits, plaintiff need only offer evidence of defendant's gross revenues associated with the infringing activity. It is then up to the defendant to prove "his or her deductible expense and the elements of profit attributable to factors other than the copyrighted work."[135]

The award will include not only the direct profits earned from sales of infringing items or of tickets to infringing performances, but also indirect profits. *Frank Music Corp. v. Metro–Goldwyn–Mayer, Inc.*,[136] is illustrative. There, plaintiffs owned the copyright to various songs from the musical Kismet. The defendant used portions of five of those songs in a musical called *Hallelujah Hollywood,* staged in the showroom of its lavish Las Vegas hotel and casino. In determining defendant's profits, the Ninth Circuit included a portion of MGM's earnings on hotel and gambling operations attributable to the increased traffic generated by the infringing performance in the showroom.

Deductible expenses include the defendant's costs of producing infringing copies or phonorecords, or of mounting the infringing performance or display, as the case may be, as well as associated overhead costs. They do not include the value of any unsold inventory of infringing materials in defendant's possession at the time of suit, since by definition, defendant has earned no profits in connection with unsold items.

The determination of profits becomes more complex when the defendant has added additional creative material to the portions copied from the plaintiff. Thus, in the *Frank Music* case, MGM coupled the infringing material from Kismet with many other songs and variety acts. The infringing material comprised only 6 minutes of a show that lasted an hour and a half. While MGM was held to be an infringer, not all of its profits were traceable to the use of the copyrighted work. In such a case, courts will attempt to apportion the profits. There is no precise formula used in making such apportionments. The current copyright statute places the burden on the defendant to prove "the elements of profit attributable to factors other than the copyrighted work."[137]

---

135. 17 U.S.C. § 504(b).

136. 772 F.2d 505, 517 (9th Cir. 1985).

137. *Id.* This rule is consistent with that adopted by the Supreme Court un-

der the 1909 Act in Sheldon v. Metro–Goldwyn Pictures Corp., 309 U.S. 390,

9.6.2.3   Statutory Damages

For certain types of infringement, an award of actual damages plus defendant's profits might not be very satisfactory. The defendant might not have any profits, as would be the case where a defendant posts a copyrighted story on a web page on the internet and thousands of readers then download the story for free. Similarly, the plaintiff might have difficulty proving actual damages, perhaps because the story was only one of many appearing in a magazine, making it hard to show lost sales due to defendant's infringing conduct. Consequently the statute provides an alternative of "statutory damages"—a form of liquidated or "in lieu" monetary compensation which the plaintiff can pursue at its own option. There is one precondition, however. In order to seek statutory damages, the plaintiff must have registered the work prior to the date of the infringing conduct, or, in the case of a published work, within three months thereafter.[138]

The court can fix the amount of the statutory damage award at any amount not less than $750 or more than $30,000. If the plaintiff has proved that the infringement was committed willfully, the court can enhance the amount of the statutory damage award to a sum of not more than $150,000. On the other hand, if the defendant can prove that he "was not aware and had no reason to believe that his or her acts constituted an infringement of copyright" the court can reduce the award to a sum of not less than $200. Statutory damages are not available against nonprofit educational institutions, libraries, or public broadcasting entities or their employees if they had reasonable grounds to believe that the challenged activities constituted fair use under section 107 of the statute. Thus a teacher who distributes copies of a work to his students, on the reasonable but mistaken assumption that fair use applies, cannot be held liable for statutory damages. Such a teacher would remain liable for actual damages if the copyright owner could, in fact, document them.

Section 504(c) provides that a statutory damage award is available "for all infringements involved in the action, with respect to any one work, for which any one infringer is liable...." The legislative history elaborates that "a single infringer of a single work is liable for a single amount ... no matter how many acts of infringement are involved in the action and regardless of whether the acts were separate, isolated or occurred in a related series."[139]

396, 60 S.Ct. 681, 84 L.Ed. 825 (1940) ("only that part of the profits found to be attributable to the use of the copyrighted material as distinguished from what the infringer himself has supplied" are recoverable).

138.   17 U.S.C. § 412. *See supra* § 4.3.

139.   H.R.Rep. No. 1476, 94th Cong., 2d Sess.162, reprinted in 1976 U.S.Code Cong. & Ad.News at 5674. *See also* Walt Disney Co. v. Powell, 897 F.2d

This means that only one award of statutory damages will be made for each of the plaintiff's works that has been infringed, no matter how many acts of infringement the defendant may have committed. Even if the defendant made tens of thousands of copies of plaintiff's copyrighted videogame or copyrighted movie, or infringed multiple rights of the plaintiff by copying and then performing the work, there can only be a single award.

Of course, if there has been massive copying of a single work, a court is likely to find that the infringement was willful, and also likely to make an award at or near the high end of the permissible range, namely $150,000. Moreover, in such cases, plaintiff may have strong evidence concerning defendant's profits and choose to pursue that remedy instead of asking for statutory damages.

Note, however, that plaintiffs are entitled to multiple awards of statutory damages if the defendant has infringed multiple works. In *Playboy Enterprises, Inc. v. Webbworld, Inc.*,[140] the plaintiff sued the operator of an adult-oriented web site for posting copyrighted pictures from Playboy magazine without permission. The trial judge granted summary judgment for Playboy concerning 62 different photographs. The judge set the appropriate level of statutory damages at $5,000, but because there were 62 different works involved, multiplied the award times 62 and entered judgment against defendant for $310,000.

Section 504(c)(1) stipulates that for purposes of the statutory damages determination, "all the parts of a compilation or derivative work constitute one work." The question of whether each infringed episode of a television series comprises "one work" for purposes of this section, or whether the entire series taken as whole is "one work", has been frequently litigated. For example, in *Columbia Pictures Television v. Krypton Broadcasting*,[141] three television stations broadcast episodes of "Who's the Boss," "T.J. Hooker," and other series without the permission of the copyright holder. Predictably, the defendant broadcasters asserted that the entirety of each series constituted "one work" within the meaning of § 504(c). In support of this contention, the broadcasters observed that the copyright owner licensed the works as a series, and argued that the series should be seen as a "compilation."

565 (D.C.Cir.1990). For a criticism of this doctrine and an argument in favor of multiple awards of statutory damage for multiple infringements of a single work, see Peter Thea, *Note: Statutory Damages for the Multiple Infringement of a Copyrighted Work: A Doctrine Whose Time Has Come, Again*, 6 CARDO-ZO ARTS & ENT. L. J. 463 (1988).

140. 968 F.Supp. 1171 (N.D.Tex. 1997).

141. 106 F.3d 284 (9th Cir. 1997). Although the Supreme Court subsequently reversed and remanded for a jury trial, the Court did not disturb the Ninth's Circuit interpretation of the phrase "with respect to any one work" in § 504(c).

As have other courts, the Ninth Circuit instead sided with the copyright proprietor, reasoning that each individual episode constituted "one work" eligible for its own individual award of statutory damages. The Court of Appeals reasoned that each episode was individually written, produced, and registered with the Copyright Office; that the episodes could be repeated and broadcast in varying orders over the course of years at the option of the broadcaster; and that viewers could watch as many episodes as they wished. As a result, each episode was not assembled into a collective whole, but rather could "live its own copyright life" and be subject to an individual award of statutory damages.

The Supreme Court has held that the Seventh Amendment of the U.S. Constitution provides a right to a jury determination of the amount of statutory damages.[142] In the event neither party requests a jury, trial judges consider a variety of factors when fixing the amount of a statutory damage award. They sometimes try to estimate what actual damages and defendant's profits might have been and use that figure as a basis. The nature of the infringement will also influence the court in setting the amount of a statutory judgement award. If defendant's behavior seems flagrant the court may opt for a higher award to act as a deterrent.[143] Where the plaintiff is unlikely to have been economically harmed by the defendant's activities, and if the defendant did not profit from his infringement, many courts have chosen to award only the minimum statutory amount.

Statutory damages have proven to be highly significant in suits against parties accused of downloading copyrighted music. Almost by definition, such parties have made copies of multiple works—often of hundreds of works. Usually, however, they have only made one copy of each work. In any event, even a modest per-work statutory damage award can add up to a daunting sum, and if the jury sets a high figure for each work, the amounts involved can become astronomical. Thus, in one case that attracted a great deal of media attention, a jury found a Minnesota woman liable for statutory damages of $80,000 per song for each of 24 songs, for a total award of 1.92 million dollars! In post-trial proceedings, however, the judge in that case reduced the award to $2250 per song, or a "mere" $54,000 total.[144] In another case, a Boston University stu-

---

142. See Feltner v. Columbia Pictures Television, Inc., 523 U.S. 340, 118 S.Ct. 1279, 140 L.Ed.2d 438 (1998).

143. "Among the factors a court may consider in setting statutory damage amounts are: the expenses saved and profits reaped by the infringer, the deterrent effect of the award on defen-

dant and on third parties, and the infringer's state of mind in committing the infringement." Playboy Enterprises v. Webbworld, Inc., 968 F.Supp. 1171 (N.D.Tex.1997).

144. Capitol Records Inc. v. Thomas–Rasset, 680 F.Supp.2d 1045 (D.Minn. 2010).

dent was held liable for statutory damages totaling $675,000 for downloading 30 songs.[145]

These examples suggest that the current statutory damages provision does not make sense in the digital context where copyright owners are asserting claims against end users rather than against unlicensed competitors who are mass producing copies and selling them in direct competition with the copyright owner. In our view, the statutory damage provision was meant to approximate actual damages in a case where proof of actual damages would be difficult or impossible. It makes sense to allow a plaintiff to recover $80,000 in statutory damages against a commercial pirate who made and sold 40,000 illicit copies of a (single) book or (single) movie on a DVD, because such an award approximates actual damages of $2 per copy—a plausible estimate of the harm of each lost sale. In the file sharing cases the approximate actual damages are likely no more than $1.29 per work, as that is the price of a legal download on iTunes. After all, if a conventional retailer civilly sued a defendant for shoplifting 24 CDs from a record store, the maximum compensatory damages recoverable would be the price of those CDs. Even if statutory damages are meant to include a punitive damages component, the Supreme Court has suggested that punitive damages in excess of 3 or 4 times actual injury may violate due process.[146] An award of $150 against the student who impermissibly downloads 30 songs represents full compensation for the wrongfully appropriated property, plus a considerable penalty for $40 worth of stolen music. An award of $675,000 shocks the conscience.

9.6.3 Costs and Attorneys' Fees

Section 505 of the Copyright Act grants the court power to award both costs and attorney's fees to the prevailing party. Such awards are entirely within the discretion of the court. Under the provisions of section 412, however, an award of attorney's fees is not available if the plaintiff did not obtain copyright registration prior to the acts of infringement alleged in the suit or within the statutorily provided grace period thereafter.[147]

Historically, the courts used a different standard depending on whether they were making attorney's fees awards to plaintiffs or

---

145. Jonathan Saltzman, *Student must Pay $675k for Songs*, Boston Globe, August 1, 2009, http://www.boston.com/news/local/massachusetts/articles/2009/08/01/bu_student_fined_675000_for_illegal_music_downloads/.

146. *See, e.g.*, BMW of North America, Inc. v. Gore, 517 U.S. 559, 116 S.Ct.

1589, 134 L.Ed.2d 809 (1996); State Farm Mut. Auto. Ins. Co. v. Campbell, 538 U.S. 408, 425, 123 S.Ct. 1513, 155 L.Ed.2d 585 (2003) ("in practice, few awards exceeding a single-digit ratio between punitive and compensatory damages, to a significant degree, will satisfy due process.").

147. *See supra* § 4.3.

defendants. Courts often granted prevailing plaintiffs fees routinely, without requiring a showing that the infringement was particularly egregious or willful. On the other hand, these same courts were considerably more reluctant to make such awards to victorious defendants, doing so only when there was an indication that plaintiff sued frivolously or in bad faith.[148]

In *Fogerty v. Fantasy Inc.*,[149] the Supreme Court held that such disparate treatment was inconsistent with both the statutory language and congressional intent. It also rejected a suggestion by the defendant in the case to interpret the statute to make fee awards to the winner automatic in every case. Consequently, the Court mandated that attorney's fees be awarded in an "evenhanded" manner that fell within the discretion of the trial judge.

The Supreme Court opinion in *Fogerty* provided little guidance for lower courts as to the factors that should govern fee awards, conceding that there "is no precise rule or formula for making these determinations." One of the pre-*Fogerty* decisions applying the "evenhanded" approach, *Lieb v. Topstone Industries, Inc.*,[150] suggested that relevant factors in deciding whether to award attorney fees were frivolousness, motivation, objective reasonableness, the need to compensate the prevailing party, and deterrence. Having determined that fees should be awarded, the court may not award a sum greater than what the client was charged, but it may award less than that amount. Factors that may be considered in determining the amount that is reasonable under the circumstances include the relative complexity of the litigation, the relative financial strength of the parties, the amount of damages awarded, and the presence of bad faith.[151]

Since *Fogerty*, other courts have had the opportunity to expand upon these "*Lieb* factors." In *Assessment Technologies v. Wiredata, Inc.*, Judge Posner stated unequivocally that the "two most important considerations in determining whether to award attorneys' fees in a copyright case are the strength of the prevailing party's case and the amount of damages or other relief the party obtained."[152] Under this view, when the case is a close one and the award of damages generous, the case for an award of attorney fees is not compelling. But when the claim was frivolous and the prevailing party obtained no relief at all, then the need for an attorney fee award is more urgent.

148. For a general discussion, see Robert S. La Plante, *Awarding Attorney's Fees in Copyright Infringement Cases: The Sensible Use of a Dual Standard*, 51 ALB. L. REV. 239 (1987).

149. 510 U.S. 517, 114 S.Ct. 1023, 127 L.Ed.2d 455 (1994).

150. 788 F.2d 151 (3d Cir. 1986).

151. *Id.* at 156.

152. 361 F.3d 434, 436 (7th Cir. 2004).

This interpretation of the "evenhanded" approach provides a sound method for promoting socially desirable levels of copyright enforcement. The prospect of being ordered to pay the defendant's attorney fees may reduce the filing of frivolous lawsuits, but the concern is that it may provide too much deterrence and discourage good-faith, but uncertain claims. For example, prior to *Fogerty*, less financially secure plaintiffs might have been guaranteed fees at the conclusion of a successful suit. Although these individuals now cannot be sure that such fees will be awarded if they prevail, they are less likely to face circumstances where they recover a piddling sum on the merits but are saddled with a six-figure bill from their lawyers.

9.6.4 Impounding and Destruction of Infringing Articles

Section 503(a) of the copyright statute empowers the court to order the "impounding," or seizure, of all copies and phonorecords made or used in violation of the copyright owner's rights. The "plates molds, matrices, masters, tapes, film negatives, or other articles by means of which such copies or phonorecords may be reproduced" may also be seized. This provision authorizes the seizure not only of piratical copies held by defendant, but also of items such as printing presses, computers, VCRs, or CD burners in defendant's possession, if they were used in the manufacture of the infringing copies.

The statute provides that the remedy of impoundment may be had "at any time while an action" for copyright infringement is pending. This permits a plaintiff to seek the seizure of infringing articles as a form of preliminary relief to prevent continued violations in the period before the case can be resolved and to insure that infringing materials will be on hand for eventual destruction if plaintiff should win the case. Procedural matters relating to impoundment are governed by a special set of rules promulgated by the Supreme Court and known as the Copyright Rules of Practice.[153] Those rules require that a plaintiff requesting impoundment must post a bond in a sum equal to at least twice the value of the items to be impounded.[154]

Interestingly, the Copyright Rules seem to contemplate that the seizure can be carried out without any advance notice to the defendant, although they do provide that a post-seizure hearing on the impoundment can be granted in the discretion of the court. The Rules also do not require the plaintiff to make a showing of likely success as a condition of an impoundment order. At least one court has suggested that the procedure outlined in the Copyright Rules is

153. These rules can be found immediately following 17 U.S.C. § 501.

154. Copyright Rules of Practice, Rules 3, 4.

inconsistent with section 503 of the copyright statute. In *WPOW v. MRLJ Enters.*,[155] the court reasoned that section 503 makes the impoundment remedy discretionary with the court and concluded that discretion could not logically be exercised without a pre-seizure hearing and notice to the defendant in all but the most unusual circumstances.

Some courts have gone even further and opined that the procedures in the Copyright Rules may be unconstitutional because of conflict with the defendant's due process rights. As the court in *Paramount Pictures Corp. v. Doe*[156] explained, "the procedure for impoundment under the Copyright Rules ... is constitutionally infirm in multiple respects.... The applicability of the rules is not limited to situations where the defendant likely could conceal or destroy the infringing materials. The rules do not require the plaintiff to demonstrate the merits of the underlying infringement claim and likewise do not even require that the application be made by one with personal knowledge of the pertinent facts."

To avoid these constitutional problems, many courts require copyright plaintiffs seeking impoundment to comply with the provisions of Rule 65 of the Federal Rules of Civil Procedure, which deals with preliminary injunctions and temporary restraining orders. As the *Paramount* court went on to explain, "in addition to requiring plaintiffs to post bond, courts require a showing of the merits of plaintiffs' underlying infringement action and the particular circumstances justifying proceeding ex parte; and they fashion orders of seizure which require the plaintiff and defendant to appear at a post-seizure hearing, thus providing the defendant a prompt opportunity to challenge the propriety of the seizure."[157] In courts following this approach, a plaintiff might still be able to secure pre-trial impoundment on an ex parte application, but only after demonstrating both the urgency of the situation and its own likelihood of success on the merits.

Under the immediately following subsection of the statute, 503(b), the court may order "the destruction or other reasonable disposition of all copies or phonorecords found to have been made or used in violation of the copyright owner's exclusive rights" as part of a final judgment in an infringement case. While the court is empowered to order destruction, it need not do so, and it may instead order the items to be turned over to the plaintiff. This would permit the plaintiff to sell them and realize the profit instead

---

155. 584 F.Supp. 132 (D.D.C.1984).

156. 821 F.Supp. 82, 88 (E.D.N.Y. 1993). See generally Paul S. Owens, *Impoundment Procedures Under the Copyright Act: The Constitutional Infirmities*, 14 Hofstra L. Rev. 211 (1985).

157. 821 F.Supp. at 88, citing district court opinions from Kansas, New York, and the District of Columbia.

of simply wasting the resources associated with production of the items.

9.6.5 Criminal Sanctions

As anyone who has ever rented a videotape DVD knows from the accompanying FBI warning, under certain circumstances copyright infringement is a crime. Section 506(a) of the Copyright Act provides that "any person who infringes a copyright willfully and for purposes of commercial advantage or private financial gain," can be punished criminally. The nature of the punishment is set out in § 2319 of Title 18 of the U.S. Code. If defendant reproduces or distributes 10 or more copies or phonorecords of one or more works within a 180–day period and those works have a retail value of more than $2,500, the conduct is classified as a felony and the defendant can be imprisoned for a period of up to five years and fined up to $250,000 for a first offense and imprisoned for up to 10 years and fined up to $250,000 for a second or subsequent offense. In all other cases of criminal conviction for copyright infringement, the conduct is a misdemeanor carrying a maximum term of imprisonment of one year and a maximum potential fine of $25,000.[158] Under section 506(b) of the Copyright Act, upon conviction, all infringing copies or phonorecords and all devices used in the manufacture of such items shall be ordered forfeited to the court and shall be destroyed. This forfeiture and destruction is mandatory in criminal cases.

The more serious, felony-level punishments for infringement were originally limited to offenses involving sound recordings and audiovisual works, but Congress amended those provisions in 1992 so that they now apply to all types of work covered by the copyright statute. The legislative history of the 1992 amendments reflects a particular concern with large-scale software piracy. While the penalties are certainly severe, as a practical matter they have not proved very effective tools against copyright piracy. Even when a defendant is arrested in a warehouse filled with counterfeit videotapes or CDs, the government rarely has direct proof that defendant made the infringing copies. While they may have proof that the defendant sold some of the copies, the government must prove beyond a reasonable doubt that the defendant did not know that the copies had not been subject to a valid first sale by the copyright owner or a licensee.[159] This has proven to be a high hurdle for prosecutors.

---

158. The terms of imprisonment for criminal copyright infringement are set out in section 2319 of Title 18. To determine the fines for those same offenses, that provision cross-references to section 3571.

159. United States v. Atherton, 561 F.2d 747 (9th Cir.1977).

As the statutory text indicates, infringement is only criminal if done "willfully." On its face, the term "willful" could mean either that the defendant merely intended to make or distribute copies; or instead that he did so with the more specific intent to violate a known legal duty or prohibition. The courts have adopted the latter position. As a result, the defendant must know the work in question is protected by copyright, and must also know that his acts constitute copyright infringement. This standard is not objective, but rather is based upon the beliefs of the individual criminal defendant.

For example, in *United States v. Moran*,[160] the rather unlikely defendant was a full-time Omaha, Nebraska, police officer who moonlighted as the proprietor of a "mom-and-pop" movie rental business. Pursuant to this latter endeavor, Moran purchased legitimate copies of several motion pictures that were under copyright, including such classics as "Crocodile Dundee II," "Hell–Bound: Hellraiser II," and "Mystic Pizza." Moran then made a copy of each of the tapes he purchased. Moran testified that by doing so, he was simply "insuring" tapes that might be vandalized by his customers, and that it was his practice not to rent both the original and duplicate tapes at the same time. Moran explained that he had formulated his belief about "insuring" after talking to colleagues in the business, although perhaps mindful of his full-time job, he did not specifically identify his sources.

Under these facts, the court found that the defendant had not acted willfully and was therefore not guilty of criminal conduct. The court observed that Moran often purchased multiple copies of the same movie, but made only one copy of each authorized version purchased. Further, Moran's practice of "insuring" was not conducted in such a way to maximize profits, which presumably would have been his purpose if he had acted willfully. The court also characterized Moran as "obviously not sophisticated"—normally not the sort of compliment one might hope to receive, but one that weighed in his favor here. That Moran was a "street cop" and had cooperated with law enforcement authorities were also to his benefit.

The holding in *Moran* and other cases also tends to make criminal copyright violations more difficult to prosecute. Of course, in cases of non-literal copying, it is unlikely that the defendant can be found criminally liable because he can always argue that he believed he was permissibly copying unprotected ideas rather than protected expression. However, where the copying is large-scale verbatim duplication of computer programs or DVDs and the cir-

160. 757 F.Supp. 1046 (D. Neb. 1991).

cumstances are less favorable to the defendant than they were to Officer Moran, the willfulness issue is quite apparent.

The statute also requires that the copying be done for the purposes of "commercial advantage or private financial gain." The reference to private financial gain suggests that even isolated copying of protected works such as computer programs, sound recordings, or movies, done by private users at home, in order to save the cost of a retail copy of the work might be considered a criminal violation, albeit a misdemeanor. However, some of the legislative history surrounding the 1992 amendments to the criminal provision imply that this might not be the case. For instance, Senator Hatch, the sponsor of the 1992 legislation, observed in floor debate that "the copying must be undertaken to make money, and even incidental financial benefits that might accrue as a result of the copying should not contravene the law where the achievement of those benefits [was] not the motivation behind the copying."[161]

Of course, this statement is itself ambiguous. When a home user copies software borrowed from a friend, she does not engage in the activity to "make money" but she surely realizes an "incidental financial benefit" because she now need not pay for a copy of the program. Moreover, one might argue that her "motivation" in making that copy was to receive that precise "incidental financial benefit." On the other hand, it is possible her primary motive was actually convenience, not the financial benefit. Fortunately, as a practical matter the issue is probably unimportant because no rational prosecutor is likely to devote resources to prosecuting private users engaged in incidental copying. Indeed, such copying is usually not discoverable by any means short of wholesale violation of the Fourth Amendment—although technological innovation may soon make it much easier to detect private copying, especially where computers are involved.

The relatively modest efforts devoted to enforcement of the criminal provisions of the copyright laws are apparent from a study of annual reports issued by the U.S. Department of Justice. They reveal that in 2007 a total of 40 individuals were prosecuted. In 2008 the number was 81.[162]

Additional subsections of section 506 deal with the fraudulent use of copyright notices, the fraudulent removal of copyright notices, and false representations made to the Copyright Office in connection with applications for copyright registration. Violation of an author's moral rights under the Visual Artists Rights Act, codified in section 106A of the copyright statute, will subject the

161. 138 Cong. Rec. S17959 (Oct.8, 1992).

162. http://www.uscourts.gov/ judbus2008/appendices/D02DSep08.pdf at page 231.

offender to civil liability but are specifically exempted from criminal sanction.

§ 9.7 Defenses Other Than Fair Use

Once a plaintiff has made out a prima facie case of copyright infringement the defendant may attempt to interpose an affirmative defense. The most important and perhaps most frequently invoked defense is "fair use," codified in section 107 of the current statute. Because of the significance of that defense and the many issues it raises, we shall defer further consideration of it until the following chapter. The sections that follow take up several other defenses common in copyright litigation.

9.7.1 Copyright Misuse

Parties seeking equitable relief, such as injunctions, have long been subject to a defense known as "unclean hands." Under this principle, a court will not come to the aid of a plaintiff who has himself committed wrongful acts to the prejudice of the defendant. This general principle is the source of the more specific defense known as "copyright misuse." Generally stated, if an alleged infringer can show that the plaintiff-copyright-owner committed some form of misconduct either in obtaining or enforcing the copyright, the court can make a finding of copyright misuse and deny all relief to the copyright owner. Despite the doctrine's roots in the law of equity, a finding of misuse will result in denial not just of injunctive relief, but of monetary relief as well.[163]

Courts were slow to embrace the idea of copyright misuse. While the Supreme Court articulated a concept of *patent* misuse in 1942 in the *Morton Salt* decision,[164] copyright cases in the decades that followed often explicitly declined to entertain the argument of copyright misuse.[165] Only recently have defendants been able to prevail on claims of misuse. One of the first such cases sustaining the defense was the Fourth Circuit's 1990 decision in *Lasercomb America, Inc. v. Reynolds.*[166] Lasercomb owned the copyright in an industrial software program used in box and carton production. Lasercomb licensed various firms to use the software. One of the licensees made copies of the software not permitted by the license and Lasercomb sued for infringement. At trial, the defendant

---

163. F.E.L. Publications Ltd. v. Catholic Bishop, 506 F.Supp. 1127, 1137 (N.D.Ill.1981), rev'd on other grounds, 214 USPQ 409 (7th Cir.1982).

164. Morton Salt Co. v. G.S. Suppiger, 314 U.S. 488, 62 S.Ct. 402, 86 L.Ed. 363 (1942).

165. See e.g., Harms, Inc. v. Sansom House Enterprises, Inc., 162 F.Supp. 129, 135 (E.D.Pa.1958), *aff'd on other grounds sub nom.* Leo Feist, Inc. v. Lew Tendler Tavern, Inc., 267 F.2d 494 (3d Cir.1959); Orth–O–Vision, Inc. v. Home Box Office, 474 F.Supp. 672, 686 (S.D.N.Y.1979).

166. 911 F.2d 970 (4th Cir.1990).

pointed out that Lasercomb's license included a provision forbidding licensees from investigating or developing any competing software products for a period of 99 years. The court found this provision inconsistent with the policies underlying the copyright laws and harmful to the public interest because it tended to inhibit competition and to forbid the free copying of ideas, a central tenet of copyright law. It thus refused to enforce the copyright and denied Lasercomb relief despite the clear evidence of infringement.

The 1997 decision of the Ninth Circuit in *Practice Management Information Corp. v. American Medical Association* also held that a copyright had been misused.[167] There, the AMA licensed a government agency to use a copyrighted system of medical procedure codes in connection with the Medicaid program. Under the license the relevant government agency agreed not to adopt any other competing set of codes. A competitor of the AMA sought a declaratory judgment that it could freely copy the AMA codes. The court held that the restrictive provision in the license agreement constituted misuse of the copyright, and consequently held the copyright to be unenforceable.

The principal type of misconduct that will lead to a finding of misuse is anti-competitive conduct of the sort forbidden by the spirit, if not the letter of the antitrust laws, as illustrated by *Lasercomb* and *PMI*. However, the mere invocation of an antitrust claim will not exonerate the defendant. There must be proof that the antitrust violations or anti-competitive conduct in question are so significant that the policy of enforcing the antitrust laws outweighs the equally important policy of preventing copyright infringement.

Though some courts would limit the misuse concept to acts that are outright antitrust violations,[168] other types of behaviors have been held to trigger the doctrine. For instance, if a copyright plaintiff has previously made intentional misrepresentations to the Copyright Office concerning the status of the work, courts may decline to enforce the copyright.[169] Similarly, where the copyright owner has made spurious threats of infringement litigation[170] or has dealt unfairly with the defendant in prior face-to-face transactions,[171] courts have been willing to deny enforcement of the copy-

---

167. 121 F.3d 516 (9th Cir.1997).

168. Saturday Evening Post Company v. Rumbleseat Press, Inc., 816 F.2d 1191 (7th Cir.1987).

169. Masquerade Novelty, Inc. v. Unique Industries, Inc., 912 F.2d 663, 667 (3d Cir.1990); Russ Berrie & Co. v. Jerry Elsner Co., 482 F.Supp. 980, 988 (S.D.N.Y.1980).

170. *Cf.* Vogue Ring Creations, Inc. v. Hardman, 410 F.Supp. 609, 616 (D.R.I.1976). Sham litigation has been held to be a violation of the antitrust laws under certain circumstances, *California Motor Transport Co. v. Trucking Unlimited*, 404 U.S. 508, 510–11, 92 S.Ct. 609, 30 L.Ed.2d 642 (1972).

171. T.B. Harms & Francis, Day & Hunter v. Stern, 231 F. 645 (2d Cir. 1916).

right. In all these situations, however, there is a reluctance to exculpate the defendant unless the plaintiff's misconduct is fairly egregious.

Courts have also pointed out that "a copyright holder who [has] misused a copyright [is] not forever barred from bringing a suit for infringement. Instead, the copyright holder 'is free to bring a suit for infringement once it has purged itself of the misuse.' . . . [I]n order for a court to find that there has been a purge of copyright misuse, the copyright holder must show that 'the improper practice has been abandoned and that the consequences of the misuse of the [copyright] have been dissipated.' "[172]

9.7.2 Statute of Limitations, Laches, and Estoppel

Copyright claims may be stymied by a trio of defenses that all relate to delay, passage of time, or the reliance interests of defendants. The first of these, the statute of limitations, is a statutory bright line rule dictating when a suit must be brought, while laches and estoppel are more *ad hoc* and equitable in nature. All three are based on the notion that copyright owners who fail to pursue their rights promptly may not deserve the assistance of a court, and that defendants may have developed a reliance interest in the status quo.

Under section 507(b) of the copyright act "no civil action shall be maintained . . . unless it is commenced within three years after the claim accrued." The statute of limitations for criminal prosecutions is identical. Where infringing activity involves a series of acts committed over a period of time, the limitations period runs from the last act of infringement.[173] In such a situation, most courts limit recoverable damages to those attributable to the three–year period preceding the filing of the complaint,[174] though there is contrary authority granting plaintiff monetary remedies for all infringements, even those more than three years old.[175]

If the copyright owner can show that he was unaware of the infringing activities, that may operate to "toll" or suspend the statute of limitations. Courts are most inclined to toll the limitations period where the defendant deliberately concealed his infringing activity. The equities in this situation, labeled "fraudulent concealment," strongly favor the plaintiff. To show fraudulent

---

172. Altmayer–Pizzorno v. L–Soft Intern., Inc. 302 Fed.Appx. 148, 156 (4th Cir. 2008), quoting Morton Salt Co., 314 U.S. 488, 62 S.Ct. 402, 86 L.Ed. 363 (1942).

173. Taylor v. Meirick, 712 F.2d 1112, 1117 (7th Cir.1983) (defendant sold copyrighted maps from 1976 through 1979; plaintiff's suit filed in 1980 held not time-barred).

174. See, e.g., Roley v. New World Pictures Ltd., 19 F.3d 479 (9th Cir. 1994).

175. Taylor v. Meirick, 712 F.2d 1112, 1119 (7th Cir.1983).

concealment, plaintiff must show that "the defendant used fraudulent means to keep the plaintiff unaware of his cause of action, and also that the plaintiff was, in fact, ignorant of the existence of his cause of action."[176] Even without evidence of affirmative concealment, some courts will toll the statute until a plaintiff exercising reasonable diligence could have learned of his cause of action, although other courts disagree and decline to toll in these circumstances.[177]

The defense of laches is conceptually related to the statute of limitations, but distinct from it in the details of its application. A defendant may invoke laches as a defense if the copyright owner has unnecessarily delayed in bringing suit and defendant both relied on that delay and was prejudiced by it. The most conspicuous difference between the laches defense and the statute of limitations defense is the absence of a specific bright line time period for laches.

For laches the determination of whether plaintiff's delay was excessive is made on a case by case basis. "Factors relevant to the issue include the death or unavailability of important witnesses, the dulling of memories through the passage of time, the loss of relevant records, and continuing investments and outlays by the alleged infringer in connection with the operation of its business."[178] Thus, in *Slifka v. Citation Fabrics Corp.*[179] the plaintiff sent the defendant a telegram in September, 1970, accusing defendant of infringement in connection with a fabric design. The plaintiff took no further action until February, 1971, when it filed its complaint for copyright infringement. In the interim, the defendant had produced 150,000 additional yards of the fabric with the disputed design. The court found that because of plaintiff's failure to pursue the matter more consistently and aggressively, his action was barred by laches. Generally, if the work is one with a short commercial life, such as a computer program or a pop song, less delay by plaintiff will be tolerated than in more leisurely industries such as book publishing or live theater.

The general rule is that the successful assertion of laches bars retrospective damages but not prospective relief. As the Fifth Circuit explained, "[t]he effect of laches is merely to withhold damages for infringement which occurred prior to the filing of the

---

176. Wood v. Santa Barbara Chamber of Commerce, Inc., 705 F.2d 1515, 1521 (9th Cir.1983), *cert. denied*, 465 U.S. 1081, 104 S.Ct. 1446, 79 L.Ed.2d 765 (1984).

177. Compare Taylor v. Meirick, 712 F.2d 1112, 1117 (7th Cir.1983) (tolling) with Wood v. Santa Barbara Chamber of Commerce, Inc., 705 F.2d 1515

(9th Cir.1983), *cert. denied*, 465 U.S. 1081, 104 S.Ct. 1446, 79 L.Ed.2d 765 (1984) (no tolling).

178. Eisenman Chemical Co. v. NL Industries, 595 F.Supp. 141, 147 (D.Nev. 1984).

179. 329 F.Supp. 1392 (S.D.N.Y. 1971).

suit."[180] The Ninth Circuit follows a minority view by allowing one exception to this principle. In that court laches may bar a claim for prospective injunctive relief where "the feared future infringements are identical to the alleged past infringements" and are "subject to the same prejudice that bars retrospective relief."[181]

The courts have also split on whether laches is available as a defense to bar claims of copyright infringement that were brought within the three-year statute of limitations. A number of the Circuit Courts of Appeals have concluded that laches can never bar claims that arose within the three-year statutory limit. Representative of this line of cases is the decision of the Fourth Circuit in *Lyons Partnership, L.P. v. Morris Costumes, Inc.*[182] There the plaintiff sued to enjoin the defendant from renting or selling copies of its "Duffy the Dragon" costume, which was claimed to be a knock-off of the unforgettable Barney, the purple dinosaur of public television fame. The plaintiffs became aware of the accused costume rentals in April 1993 but did not file suit until May 2, 1997.

Both the plaintiff and the accused costume company recognized that rentals and sales that occurred within three years of the date the plaintiff filed its complaint were not defeated by the Copyright Act's statute of limitations. But the defendant asserted that these claims should be barred under the doctrine of laches. The Fourth Circuit flatly disagreed, stating that "separation of powers principles dictate that an equitable timeliness rule adopted by courts cannot bar claims that are brought within the legislatively prescribed statute of limitations."[183]

Other courts have reached different conclusions on this issue. For example, the Eleventh Circuit explicitly disagreed with *Lyons Partnership*, holding that "there is a strong presumption that a plaintiff's suit is timely if filed before limitations has run," but nonetheless allowing laches to be recognized in "extraordinary circumstances."[184] In contrast with the concern for separation of powers articulated by the Fourth Circuit, the Eleventh Circuit stressed that the laches doctrine arose from equity—a set of principles that resists bright-line rules.

180. Studiengesellschaft Kohle mbH v. Eastman Kodak Co., 616 F.2d 1315, 1325 (5th Cir.1980).

181. Danjaq L.L.C. v. Sony Corp., 263 F.3d 942, 959 (9th Cir. 2001).

182. 243 F.3d 789 (4th Cir. 2001).

183. *Id.* at 797.

184. Peter Letterese and Associates, Inc. v. World Institute of Scientology Enterprises, Int'l, 533 F.3d 1287, 1320 (11th Cir. 2008). *See also,* Jackson v. Axton, 25 F.3d 884, 888 (9th Cir. 1994), *overruled on other grounds by* Fogerty v. Fantasy, Inc., 510 U.S. 517, 114 S.Ct. 1023, 127 L.Ed.2d 455 (1994) ("Though both laches and statutes of limitations may give defendants repose, laches, unlike a statute of limitations, is premised on a showing of prejudice. Thus, as Appellees note, laches may apply whether or not any statutory limitations period runs.").

Our sense is that the Eleventh Circuit has the better of the argument. In adopting a three-year statute of limitations, we doubt Congress meant to guarantee that all claims could be brought within the three-year window regardless of circumstances. Rather, it is more likely that Congress meant to conclusively bar all claims filed beyond that time on the theory that after three years evidence would be stale and the defendant would have detrimentally relied on plaintiff's inaction. Where a defendant can show those same problems with evidence and reliance inside the three-year period, it seems appropriate to us to bar the claim.[185]

The third defense in this trilogy is estoppel. Estoppel does not focus on passage of time like laches and statute of limitations claims, but rather on the fact that plaintiff has led defendant to believe that his conduct is unobjectionable, and now ought not be allowed to predicate a lawsuit on that very conduct. In order to make out the defense "(1) the party to be estopped must know the facts; (2) he must intend that his conduct shall be acted on or must so act that the party asserting the estoppel has a right to believe it is so intended; (3) the latter must be ignorant of the true facts; and (4) he must rely on the former's conduct to his injury."[186] Thus, if a screenwriter proposed to prepare a screenplay based loosely on a novel, and explains his concept to the copyright owner in the novel, and if that copyright owner indicates that in his opinion such a screenplay would be non-infringing, and if the screenwriter goes forward and thereafter the novelist sues for infringement, he or she is likely to be estopped from asserting his claim.

9.7.3 Abandonment

The copyright owner of a work is free to dedicate that work to the public domain. Such an owner is said to have abandoned his copyright. Not surprisingly, infringement defendants will occasionally attempt to argue abandonment as a way to avoid liability. Courts find abandonment if the owner has performed "some overt act indicative of an intent to surrender rights in the copyrighted work and to allow the public to copy it."[187] The copyright owner can explicitly abandon his rights by placing a legend on the work indicating that others may freely copy it.

185. For an opposing view, *see,* Ryan Christopher Locke, *Resetting the Doomsday Clock: Is it Constitutional for Laches to Bar Copyright Infringement Claims Within the Statute of Limitations?*, 6 BUFF. INTELL. PROP. L.J. 133 (2009).

186. Hampton v. Paramount Pictures Corp., 279 F.2d 100, 104 (9th Cir.

1960), *cert. denied*, 364 U.S. 882, 81 S.Ct. 170, 5 L.Ed.2d 103 (1960).

187. Rohauer v. Killiam Shows, Inc., 379 F.Supp. 723, 730 (S.D.N.Y. 1974), *rev'd on other ground*, 551 F.2d 484 (2d Cir. 1977), *cert. denied*, 431 U.S. 949, 97 S.Ct. 2666, 53 L.Ed.2d 266 (1977).

Abandonment can also be found circumstantially based on the conduct of the copyright owner. For example, one court found copyright to have been abandoned when the copyright owner, a TV station, destroyed its only copy of broadcast videotapes by erasing or taping over them.[188] Other examples of overt acts that have lead to a finding of abandonment include widespread dissemination of copies of the work without a copyright notice during the period when such notice was legally required, and knowing failure of the copyright owner to take action against widespread infringement.

9.7.4 Innocent Intent

Intent is not an element of a copyright infringement cause of action.[189] The defendant can be held liable even if the copying was done innocently and in good faith. Thus, innocent intent is not a defense to copyright infringement. The fact that the defendant acted with an innocent intent can, however, affect the remedies that will be afforded.

A number of factors might cause a court to label defendant's behavior "innocent." Prior to 1989, when copyright notice became optional, the defendant might have copied from a copy lacking notice in the good faith belief that the material was unprotected. Even today the lack of notice may mislead some users not conversant with the subtleties of copyright law. In other situations, common in the music industry, the plaintiff may have reproduced the copyrighted material through subconscious memory of plaintiff's work. In still other cases, a defendant may have honestly believed that he was copying only the unprotected ideas contained within a work and not any of its protected expression only to be subsequently told by a judge that he guessed wrong.

The current statute deals most explicitly with good faith related to lack of notice. Under section 405(b) "any person who innocently infringes a copyright, in reliance upon an authorized copy or phonorecord from which the copyright notice has been omitted and which was publicly distributed by authority of the copyright owner before [March 1, 1989], incurs no liability for actual or statutory damages ... for any infringing acts committed before receiving actual notice that registration for the work has been made ... if such person proves that he or she was misled by the omission of notice." The statute goes on to make it clear, however, that such an innocent infringer can be enjoined from future acts of infringement, can be required to pay over any profits attributable to the infringe-

---

188. Pacific & S. Co. v. Duncan, 572 F.Supp. 1186 (N.D.Ga.1983), *aff'd*, 744 F.2d 1490 (11th Cir.1984), *cert. denied*, 471 U.S. 1004, 105 S.Ct. 1867, 85 L.Ed.2d 161 (1985).

189. *See, e.g.*, Fitzgerald Publishing Co. v. Baylor Publishing Co., 807 F.2d 1110, 1113 (2d Cir.1986) ("intent or knowledge is not an element of infringement").

ment, or can be required to pay a reasonable license fee to the copyright owner in order to continue his activities.

There was no comparable provision in the 1909 Copyright Act, because under that the statute, the public distribution of copies without notice would have injected the work into the public domain, thus completely exonerating the defendant from any infringement liability. Since 1989 copyright notice has been optional. Thus the fact that a defendant copied from a noticeless copy of a recent work should not be automatically treated as evidence that the defendant was acting in good faith, absent further circumstances.

Other forms of good faith can be taken into account by the court in assessing damages. For instance the provision on statutory damages specifically provides for a lowering of the minimum damage award in cases where "the infringer was not aware and had no reason to believe that his or her acts constituted an infringement." In the post–1989 era, however, a copyright owner can foreclose the assertion of innocence in mitigation of damages by the simple device of including a copyright notice on publicly distributed copies of the work. Under section 401(d) "if a notice of copyright … appears on the published copy or copies to which a defendant in a copyright infringement suit had access, then no weight shall be given to such a defendant's interposition of a defense based on innocent infringement in mitigation of actual or statutory damages…."[190]

9.7.5 Sovereign Immunity

The federal government has no immunity with respect to alleged copyright infringement. Claims against the United States must, however, be filed in the U.S. Court of Federal Claims.[191] In 1990, Congress sought to clarify the exposure of state governments to copyright infringement liability by adopting the Copyright Remedy Clarification Act of 1990.[192] Section 511 of the Copyright Act now stipulates that "[a]ny State, any instrumentality of a State, and any officer or employee of a State … shall be subject to the provisions of this title in the same manner and to the same extent as any nongovernmental entity."[193] Section 511 specifically provides that states will not be immune from suit by virtue of the U.S. Constitution's Eleventh Amendment—a provision that forbids states from being sued by private individuals in federal court—or any other doctrine of sovereign immunity. This legislation overturned the weight of prior authority, which had often held states to be immune

---

190. 17 U.S.C. § 401(d). A parallel provision, 17 U.S.C. § 402(d), covers phonorecords.

191. 28 U.S.C. § 1498.

192. Pub. L. No. 101–553, 104 Stat. 2749 (1990).

193. 17 U.S.C. § 511(a).

from infringement liability, much to the frustration of copyright holders.

Events subsequent to the 1990 legislation have rendered the continued vitality of § 511 extremely suspect, to say the least. In 1999, the U.S. Supreme Court decided *Florida Prepaid Postsecondary Expense Board v. College Savings Bank*,[194] concerning an analogous provision in the patent statute, as well as *College Savings Bank v. Florida Prepaid Postsecondary Expense Board*,[195] addressing a similar provision in the trademark statute. In these decisions the Court held that Congress had not validly abrogated state immunity to charges of trademark and patent infringement in the federal courts. The virtually inescapable conclusion from these opinions is that the 1990 copyright legislation is similarly invalid.

It is important to note that, as extended to the copyright law, the two *Florida Prepaid* decisions do not render state governments free from any legal obligations under the federal copyright statutes. These decisions do appear to bar copyright holders from calling state governments before the federal courts, the most effective tribunal for exercising their rights.[196] Copyright holders could, at least in theory, assert applicable common law claims within a state court. A variety of legislative proposals have been forwarded to address the liability of state governments for copyright infringement, but as yet none has been enacted.[197]

---

194. 527 U.S. 627, 119 S.Ct. 2199, 144 L.Ed.2d 575 (1999).

195. 527 U.S. 666, 119 S.Ct. 2219, 144 L.Ed.2d 605 (1999).

196. *See* Peter Bray, *After* College Savings Board v. Florida Prepaid, *Are States Subject to Suit for Copyright In-*

fringement?, 36 Houston L. Rev. 1531 (1999).

197. *See, e.g. Legislation/State Immunity: Draft Leahy/Hatch Amendment Stiffens IP Protection/Immunity Waiver Trade-off*, 64 Copyright J. 32 (May 10, 2002).

Chapter 10

THE FAIR USE DEFENSE

Table of Sections

§ 10.1 History and Rationale of Fair Use

A perfectly airtight system of copyright would probably be intolerable. Many individuals need or desire to use copyrighted works in ways that do not seriously threaten the interests of the copyright owner, but that do tend to promote the social goals of advancement and dissemination of knowledge and learning. One readily thinks of the book reviewer who wishes to quote a portion of a volume being reviewed, or the teacher who wishes to distribute copies of a current news story to her students. Others may merely use copyrighted works in an incidental and casual way, such as the TV or movie producer who prepares a program showing a copyrighted poster in the background of a scene[1] or the DVR owner who records a copyrighted broadcast for viewing at a more convenient

---

1. Sandoval v. New Line Cinema Corp., 973 F.Supp. 409 (S.D.N.Y.1997), *aff'd*, 147 F.3d 215 (2d Cir.1998). In Ringgold v. Black Entertainment TV, Inc., 126 F.3d 70 (2d Cir.1997), however, the user of a copyrighted poster on the set of a TV sitcom where all or part of the poster was visible for 26 seconds was held not entitled to summary judgment on the fair use question.

time. Each of these users might find it impractical to seek permission from the copyright owner because of the expense and nuisance involved. If, as a consequence, such individuals decided to forgo the use of the copyrighted material, our society would be worse off with no corresponding benefit in the form of enhanced incentives to copyright owners.

The fair use defense is the copyright doctrine that provides flexibility in the system. The Supreme Court has noted that it is a "guarantee of breathing space at the heart of copyright,"[2] and the Second Circuit has observed that the fair use doctrine prevents "rigid application of the copyright statute when, on occasion, it would stifle the very creativity which that law is designed to foster."[3] It exempts from liability certain modest uses of copyrighted work when those uses will not undermine the economic interests of the copyright owner. It is unequivocally the most important defense in copyright law, both in terms of how often it is asserted by defendants and in terms of its importance to basic copyright policies.

The fair use doctrine can be traced back to a mid-nineteenth century decision of Justice Story, sitting as a district judge, in *Folsom v. Marsh*.[4] Both parties in that case were biographers of George Washington. Plaintiff had the exclusive rights to publish Washington's papers[5] and did so in the form of a 12-volume work. The defendant prepared a 2-volume pseudo-autobiography, "in which Washington is made mainly to tell the story of his own life, by inserting therein his letters and his messages, and other written documents." Defendant's book contained 388 pages of material copied verbatim from plaintiff's work. Justice Story found this to be infringing, but recognized that sometimes there could be "justifiable use of the original materials such as the law recognizes as no infringement of the copyright of the plaintiff." He went on to indicate that in determining if a defendant's use of plaintiff's materials was "justifiable" we should "look to the nature and objects of the selections made, the quantity and value of the materials used, and the degree in which the use may prejudice the

2. Campbell v. Acuff–Rose Music, Inc., 510 U.S. 569, 579, 114 S.Ct. 1164, 127 L.Ed.2d 500 (1994).

3. Iowa State University Research Foundation, Inc. v. American Broadcasting Co., 621 F.2d 57 (2d Cir.1980). Almost 200 years ago the British jurist Lord Ellenborough made the same point when he said "while I shall think myself bound to secure every man in the enjoyment of his copyright, one must not put

manacles upon science." Cary v. Kearsley, 170 Eng. Rep. 679, 681 (K.B.1802).

4. 9 F.Cas. 342 (C.C.D.Mass.1841).

5. President Washington apparently left his papers to his nephew, Bushrod Washington, a justice of the Supreme Court, who in turn conveyed the interest in these papers to Chief Justice John Marshall and Jared Sparks. Folsom, the plaintiff, was the publisher of Sparks' 12–volume work.

sale, or diminish the profits, or supersede the objects, of the original work."

For the next 135 years, courts relied upon this judicial language as the basis for a common law fair use doctrine. When Congress revised the copyright laws in 1976 it chose to codify the idea of fair use in section 107. The legislative language substantially mirrors the ideas first articulated by Justice Story in *Folsom*. The section provides:

> Notwithstanding the provisions of sections 106 and 106A, the fair use of a copyrighted work, including such use by reproduction in copies or phonorecords or by any other means specified by that section, for purposes such as criticism, comment, news reporting, teaching (including multiple copies for classroom use), scholarship, or research, is not an infringement of copyright. In determining whether the use made of a work in any particular case is a fair use the factors to be considered shall include—
>
> (1) the purpose and character of the use, including whether such use is of a commercial nature or is for nonprofit education purposes;
>
> (2) the nature of the copyrighted work;
>
> (3) the amount and substantiality of the portion used in relation to the copyrighted work as a whole; and
>
> (4) the effect of the use upon the potential market for or value of the copyrighted work.
>
> The fact that a work is unpublished shall not itself bar a finding of fair use if such a finding is made upon consideration of all the above factors.

There is broad consensus among the courts that the fair use doctrine is a true affirmative defense, meaning that the defendant bears the burden of proof,[6] although some courts have suggested that after a preliminary showing on some of the fair use elements, the burden will shift back to plaintiff to rebut the claim of fair use. Courts also describe the fair use inquiry as a "mixed question of law and fact."[7]

Some scholars have attempted to justify the fair use defense on economic grounds. This argument focuses particularly on the problem of "transaction costs." Economic theory assumes that, since

---

6. *See, e.g.*, American Geophysical Union v. Texaco, Inc., 60 F.3d 913, 918 (2d Cir.1994), *cert. dismissed*, 516 U.S. 1005, 116 S.Ct. 592, 133 L.Ed.2d 486 (1995).

7. *See, e.g.*, Harper & Row Publishers v. Nation Enterprises, 471 U.S. 539, 560, 105 S.Ct. 2218, 85 L.Ed.2d 588 (1985).

copyright owners want to maximize their revenues, they will license others to use their works when the amount they can obtain for the license exceeds the amount they could earn from other uses of the work that will be precluded if they grant the license. For example, the copyright owner of a novel knows that once he grants movie rights to one party, very few others will want to purchase the same type of rights for the same work. For all practical purposes, any movie producer will want exclusive rights, and thus the grant of a license to movie producer "alpha" will preclude licensing to "beta." In this simple situation, the copyright owner will license the movie to the highest bidder.

On the other side of the transaction, a prospective licensee will pay a price that reflects his valuation of the copyrighted material. If the copyright owner demands a million dollars for movie rights to his novel, and the producer feels that he cannot pay that much and still make a profit, he will not enter into the license. As a result, licensing will occur when it is to the mutual benefit of both parties, and as the economists see it, society will benefit as well, because the work will be put to its most greatly valued use.

In some cases, however, the parties may never reach this ideal bargain because of "transaction costs." For instance, assume a teacher wishes to duplicate and distribute a magazine article to his class of 25 students. Assume further that the copyright owner of the article would be willing to license that use for a minimum of one dollar a copy. Perhaps the owner feels that $25 is the amount by which demand for the original magazine will be depressed when 25 copies of the article are distributed free in class. Assume still further that the teacher would be willing to pay a maximum of $25 for the privilege of distributing the work. Perhaps this is the value of the license to the teacher because he thinks that by using the article he will be considered a good teacher and get a $25 raise next year, or perhaps he is planning to charge the students and knows that the most they would be willing to pay is $1 per copy. In theory the two ought to be able to strike a deal and such a deal would result in an increase in efficiency and an enhancement of social welfare.

However, in order to obtain a copyright license the teacher may need to spend 30 minutes of his time on the phone procuring the license, which we can value at $5 for the sake of argument, and $5 more on the price of the long distance phone call (this teacher has a very unusual calling plan on his cell phone). Consequently, the cost to the teacher for the license would actually be the $25 license fee plus $10 additional, making a total of $35—more than the maximum he is willing to pay. If the teacher were to ask the magazine to license the use for $15, so that his total cost would drop back to his maximum of $25, the magazine would refuse, because $15 will not compensate it for lost magazine sales, which is to say it is below its minimum license price. In this situation, no license will be granted or even sought and the use will not take place. Yet the use "should" take place, under economic thinking, because but for the transaction costs, both parties would be better off. The situation is sometimes labelled a case of "market failure."

Moreover, in this situation, a further benefit would be realized if the teacher were allowed to use the copyrighted materials because, in addition to the private benefits realized by the students and the teacher, the public at large presumably realizes benefits when the use of the article results in a better educated citizenry. Factoring public benefits into the equation means that even if the transaction costs were at or near zero, desirable copyright bargains might not take place. To appreciate the point it might help to change the numbers. Assume that the copyright owner would demand $30 for the license to use the article, while the teacher is still only willing to pay $25. Assume that we can value the public benefit in improved education that flows from the use of this article at $10. In this situation, the total benefits from the use are $35, which can be obtained for a cost of only $30. Again, an economist would reason that use "should" take place because it is efficient and will enhance total social welfare. Unfortunately, however, the teacher has no way to collect the $10 from the public, and will not pay more than $25 himself. Consequently once again no transaction will take place.

In the economic view of things, the fair use doctrine is responsive to these problems. By permitting the teacher to use the work for free, the teacher (and his students) are benefitted, along with the public to a degree that outweighs the costs to the copyright owner. Thus some scholars have argued that the fair use doctrine should only be available when transaction costs are high and market failure is likely[8] or when public benefits associated with a given use are significant and cannot be captured in the form of private payments.

Other writers have attempted to justify the fair use concept on moral or philosophical grounds.[9] Still others have argued that the fair use doctrine helps implement privacy concerns.[10] These authors

---

8. *See, e.g.*, Wendy Gordon, *Fair Use As Market Failure: A Structural and Economic Analysis of the Betamax Case and Its Predecessors*, 82 COLUM. L. REV. 1600 (1982) ("fair use should be awarded . . . to the defendant when: 1) market failure is present; 2) transfer of the use to the defendant is socially desirable; and 3) and award of fair use would not cause substantial injury to the incentives of the plaintiff copyright owner.");

William M. Landes & Richard Posner, *An Economic Analysis of Copyright Law*, 18 J. LEGAL STUD. 325 (1989).

9. *See e.g.*, William W. Fisher III, *Reconstructing the Fair Use Doctrine*, 101 HARV. L. REV. 1659 (1988).

10. Stephen B. Thau, *Copyright, Privacy, and Fair Use*, 24 HOFSTRA L. REV. 179 (1995).

have recognized that in recent years, copyright owners have been able to employ new technologies to reduce transaction costs. It now may take only a few seconds and a free Internet connection to pay to use copyrighted materials. If fair use is only available in cases where transaction costs are high, these technological developments would mean that the fair use doctrine will be constantly shrinking without any consideration of the larger public interests the doctrine is designed to serve.

Courts, however, do not often delve into the justification for the fair use doctrine. Not surprisingly, most simply accept it as a given because of its presence in the statutory text. The vast majority of fair use opinions have concerned themselves with elaborating on the itemized statutory factors, applying those factors to the facts of the case and occasionally attempting to lay out rules for how those factors should be balanced. The decisions are highly fact specific and generalizations are hard to come by.

§ 10.2 The Fair Use Factors

Fair use has often been described as an "equitable rule of reason,"[11] an area where judges are expected to balance equities and develop the law incrementally, in response to the facts of each case. The legislative history of the provision states explicitly that "the courts must be free to adapt the doctrine to particular situations on a case-by-case basis."[12] The rules of fair use are so open-ended that one judge even complained the "doctrine is entirely equitable and is so flexible as virtually to defy definition"[13] and one appellate panel has called it "the most troublesome in the whole law of copyright."[14] While the Supreme Court has decided three fair use cases to date, those cases did not lay down any clear approach to guide fair use decision making, and there is much in the cases that, at least on the surface, is seemingly contradictory.

In attempting to make sense of this amorphous area, the logical place to begin is with the statutory text. The first portion of section 107 is a preamble that lists several illustrative types of fair use. It then goes on to list four factors that courts are to consider in determining if a use is a fair use. The statute itself does not indicate how the factors are to be weighed.

---

11. Sony Corp. of America v. Universal City Studios, Inc., 464 U.S. 417, 448, 104 S.Ct. 774, 78 L.Ed.2d 574 (1984); H.R. Rep. No. 1476, 94th Cong. 2d Sess. 65 (1976), reprinted in 1976 U.S. Code Cong. & Admin. News 5659, 5679.

12. H.R. Rep. No. 1476, 94th Cong. 2d Sess. 66 (1976), reprinted in 1976 U.S. Code Cong. & Admin. News 5659, 5680.

13. Time, Inc. v. Bernard Geis Associates, 293 F.Supp. 130 (S.D.N.Y.1968) (Wyatt, J.).

14. Dellar v. Samuel Goldwyn, Inc., 104 F.2d 661, 662 (2d Cir.1939) (per curiam).

Fortunately, at least two things seem readily apparent from the statutory list of factors. Section 107 specifies that the analysis "shall include" the itemized criteria. First, the word "include" indicates that other factors may also be considered where the court deems appropriate. Courts have occasionally pointed to factors other than the itemized four. Thus, some courts have considered the bad faith of a defendant as reason to deny the fair use defense,[15] and others have pointed to industry custom as a factor militating in defendant's favor.[16] There are also cases that attempt to weigh the public interest in defendant's activities as a component of the fair use calculus[17] or that consider the privacy implications of defendant's conduct in analyzing the defense.[18] However, it is relatively uncommon for courts to go beyond the statutory list.

Second, the word "shall" indicates that all four of the listed factors must be addressed. This means that fair use opinions tend to have a predictable structure with four separate sections, each one devoted to a member of the statutory quartet. We will conform to this custom and consider the nuances of these four statutory criteria in the following subsections.

10.2.1 Purpose and Character of the Use

The first fair use factor focuses on the "purpose and character" of the use the defendant is making of the material. This seems to continue the theme of the preamble to section 107, which itemizes several types of uses that the statutory drafters considered illustrative of fair use. The six itemized uses in the preamble are (1) criticism; (2) comment; (3) news reporting; (4) teaching; (5) scholarship; and (6) research. This is neither an exhaustive list, nor is it a list of safe harbors. Because the list is preceded by the words "such as" it seems clear that Congress did not mean to limit the availability of the defense to only these six types of use.[19] The Eleventh

15. Roy Export Co. Establishment v. Columbia Broadcasting System, Inc., 503 F.Supp. 1137 (S.D.N.Y.1980), aff'd, 672 F.2d 1095 (2d Cir.1982), cert. denied, 459 U.S. 826, 103 S.Ct. 60, 74 L.Ed.2d 63 (1982); Time Inc. v. Bernard Geis Associates, 293 F.Supp. 130, 146 (S.D.N.Y.1968).

16. See, e.g., Triangle Publications, Inc. v. Knight–Ridder Newspapers, Inc., 626 F.2d 1171 (5th Cir.1980); Williams & Wilkins Co. v. United States, 203 Ct. Cl. 74, 487 F.2d 1345, 1353–56 (Ct.Cl. 1973), aff'd by an equally divided court, 420 U.S. 376, 95 S.Ct. 1344, 43 L.Ed.2d 264 (1975).

17. Time, Inc. v. Bernard Geis Assocs., 293 F.Supp. 130 (S.D.N.Y.1968)

(noting the "public interest in having the fullest information available on the murder of President Kennedy" in finding magazine's publication of frames of copyrighted movie to be protected by fair use defense).

18. New Era Publications Int'l v. Henry Holt and Co., Inc., 695 F.Supp. 1493, 1505 (S.D.N.Y.1988), aff'd 873 F.2d 576 (2d Cir.1989) ("in making a fair use analysis balancing the nature of the protected work with the fair use purpose sought to be served, privacy interests may be an appropriate consideration").

19. Harper & Row Publishers, Inc. v. Nation Enterprises, 471 U.S. 539, 562, 105 S.Ct. 2218, 85 L.Ed.2d 588 (1985).

Circuit has even held it to be reversible error for a court to decline to engage in fair use analysis simply because the defendant's activities are not on the itemized list.[20]

On the other hand, just because a defendant purports to be engaged in one of the itemized activities does not mean that such a defendant will prevail on a claim of fair use. A teacher should not expect to escape liability under the rubric of "fair use" if he makes two dozen photocopies of a 500 page textbook and distributes one each to every member of his class. An illustration of this principle in action can be found in *Los Angeles News Service v. KCAL–TV Channel 9*.[21]

In 1991 Rodney King, who is African–American, was arrested for drunk driving after a high speed chase. A bystander videotaped the arrest, which showed several officers beating King. The officers were subsequently tried for using excessive force, but they were acquitted. The acquittals sparked outrage in Los Angeles and led to riots, during which a truck driver named Reginald Denny was beaten by an angry mob. The Denny beating was also captured on video, this time by a news helicopter hovering above the scene belonging to the eventual plaintiff, Los Angeles News Service (LANS). When a rival news outlet, KCAL, broadcast 30 seconds of the four minute video without obtaining a license from the plaintiff, LANS sued for infringement.

At trial, KCAL attempted a fair use defense, pointing out that it was engaged in news reporting, one of the uses mentioned in the preamble to section 107. The district held that the fair use defense applied and granted summary judgment to the defendant. On appeal, however, the Ninth Circuit reversed, finding that defendant's status as a news reporting entity could be outweighed by other considerations in the case so as to make the fair use defense unavailable.

Another decision, *Nunez v. Caribbean International News Corp.*,[22] placed more weight on the inclusion of "news reporting" in the preamble of section 107. There, a professional photographer named Sixto Nunez photographed Miss Puerto Rico Universe, Joyce Giraud, for Giraud's modeling portfolio. Giraud appeared semi-nude or nude in some of the photographs. In accordance with industry practice, Nunez circulated the photographs to the Puerto Rico modeling community to help boost Giraud's modeling career, but instead the photographs sparked controversy regarding Gi-

---

20. Pacific & Southern Co. v. Duncan, 744 F.2d 1490 (11th Cir.1984).

21. 108 F.3d 1119 (9th Cir.1997), *cert. denied*, 522 U.S. 823, 118 S.Ct. 81, 139 L.Ed.2d 39 (1997).

22. 235 F.3d 18 (1st Cir. 2000).

raud's suitability to hold the coveted Miss Puerto Rico Universe title. As the scandal spread, El Vocero newspaper covered the story, featuring Nunez's photographs on the front page. Nunez sued the newspaper for copyright infringement because the paper reproduced the photographs without seeking Nunez's permission first.

When the newspaper responded by asserting a fair use defense, the First Circuit focused the majority of its analysis on the purpose and character of the use. While the court recognized that the newspaper utilized the photographs to "entice" and "titillate" readers, it felt that this commercial use amounted to more than mere copying. The pictures served to explain the news story surrounding the fitness of Giraud to retain her title as Miss Puerto Rico Universe. While recognizing that newsworthiness alone is not sufficient to establish fair use, the court emphasized the transformation from the photographs' original use as creative modeling shots to their informative, news-conveying function in El Vocero. Based on this transformation in purpose, the court decided that the first factor either favored fair use or was neutral.

Though the First Circuit emphasized that there was no blanket "newsworthiness" fair use privilege that would allow newspapers to use copyrighted images whenever the photographs conveyed a story, the court did, in fact, put much weight on this element. While the court showed concern that newspapers could manufacture news stories in order to abuse copyright protection, it simultaneously hung its hat on the "transformative" nature of the new work when framed in a news article. The decisive weight the court gave to newsworthiness on these facts may have been related to timing: if the reproduction of a copyrighted photograph in an article precedes and/or creates the story, then that reproduction may not be fair use. However, if the news coverage of the copyrighted image follows an already-breaking story, then the use is more likely to be fair.

In any event, many writers have speculated about what the six itemized uses in the preamble have in common. If an underlying theme could be identified, it might be useful in structuring the inquiry under the first fair use factor. Professor Goldstein has noted that all of the itemized uses in the preamble "characteristically involve situations in which the social, political and cultural benefits of the use will outweigh any consequent losses to the copyright proprietor, and in which the time and expense of negotiations ... will often foreclose a negotiated transaction."[23] Professor Leaffer points out that all of the listed uses are "productive uses,"

---

23. PAUL GOLDSTEIN, COPYRIGHT § 10.2.1 at 10:19–10:20 (1996).

namely those "that build on the work of others, by adding ... socially valuable creative elements."[24]

The "productive use" idea, sometimes also called "transformative use," seems based on the notion that a defendant who claims the benefit of the fair use defense ought to have contributed in some way to the overall social inventory of literary or artistic products. If the defendant merely engaged in a "reproductive use" by copying plaintiff's work verbatim without adding anything, the argument is that there would be little social benefit to defendant's activities, and thus little reason to excuse the use.

The Supreme Court has vacillated on the importance of "productive" or "transformative" use in the fair use calculus. In *Sony Corp. of America v. Universal City Studios, Inc.*,[25] the Court had to determine whether home videotaping of copyrighted television programming was infringing or protected under the fair use doctrine. In a 5–4 decision, the Court found the practice to be fair use. Home videotaping, of course, is not a productive or transformative use. The home taper does not add material to the tape, manipulate the contents in any way, or create a derivative work. It is a classic "reproductive" use which, on the foregoing logic, ought to be disfavored under the fair use analysis. The *Sony* Court opined, however, that the fair use inquiry is not "rigidly circumscribed" by a productive use requirement, and that while "the distinction between 'productive' and 'unproductive' uses may be helpful in calibrating the balance ... it cannot be wholly determinative."[26] To fortify the point, the Court cited a number of nonproductive uses that it felt could qualify for the fair use defense, such as "a teacher who copies for the sake of broadening his personal understanding of his specialty ... a legislator who copies for the sake of broadening her understanding of what her constituents are watching ... a constituent who copies a news program to help make a decision on how to vote ... in a hospital setting, using a VTR to enable a patient to see programs he would otherwise miss ... contributing to the psychological well-being of the patient."[27]

Ten years later, the Supreme Court decided *Campbell v. Acuff–Rose Music, Inc.*[28] The plaintiff in that case owned the copyright to the popular tune *Oh Pretty Woman*. Defendants, the rap group 2 Live Crew, without securing the permission of the plaintiff, prepared an alleged parody version of the song, entitled *Pretty Woman*. Defendant's version, unlike the original, was a rap song, and had substantially different words from the plaintiff's "sweet, not to say

24. MARSHALL LEAFFER, UNDERSTANDING COPYRIGHT LAW (5th ed. 2010).

25. 464 U.S. 417, 448, 104 S.Ct. 774, 78 L.Ed.2d 574 (1984).

26. *Id.* at 456, n. 40.

27. *Id.*

28. 510 U.S. 569, 114 S.Ct. 1164, 127 L.Ed.2d 500 (1994).

syrupy"[29] original, but plainly used much of the original's melody and some of the original's words. When they were sued for infringement, Mr. Campbell and his Crew claimed the protection of the fair use defense for their parody. The issues specific to parody are considered below in section 10.6. For present purposes it is enough to note that the Supreme Court concluded that the fair use defense was valid on these facts and exonerated the defendants.

In contrast to the practice of home taping that had been at issue in *Sony*, the activities of 2 Live Crew were clearly "transformative." Unlike the passive or purely reproductive conduct of the home video taper, 2 Live Crew added substantially new words to the original tune of plaintiff's work and changed the format from ballad to rap. The *Campbell* Court placed significant reliance on these facts. While it noted that "transformative use is not absolutely necessary for a finding of fair use," it pointed out that "the goal of copyright ... is generally furthered by the creation of transformative works.... [T]he more transformative the new work, the less will be the significance of other factors...."[30] Thus, while the first fair use factor is not "rigidly circumscribed" by a productive use requirement and such a requirement is "not absolutely necessary," *Campbell* suggests that it will be a significant variable in the fair use equation.

In accord with the *Campbell* decision, the Second Circuit correlated a work's transformative status with the applicability of the fair use doctrine in *Castle Rock Entertainment, Inc. v. Carol Publishing Group, Inc.*[31] The defendants had authored and published a trivia quiz book called *The SAT*, which tested the reader's knowledge of events and characters depicted in the then-popular sitcom *Seinfeld*. The book contained 643 questions and answers divided into five levels of difficulty. The SAT derived every question and correct answer from a fictional moment in the *Seinfeld* episodes, drawing from 84 of the 86 *Seinfeld* episodes that had been broadcast as of publication. Forty-one questions and/or answers contained dialogue from *Seinfeld*. The name "Seinfeld" and pictures of the principal actors graced the cover and several pages of the book. In the Second Circuit's opinion rejecting the fair use argument, the court, somewhat obviously, noted that "the book simply poses trivia questions" and that "... [a]ny transformative purpose possessed by *The SAT* is slight to non-existent."

In a colorful assessment of the facts, the Second Circuit dismissed defendants' claim that the trivia book fulfilled the transformative purpose of critiquing and decoding Seinfeld's "mystique" in

29. Leibovitz v. Paramount Pictures Corp., 948 F.Supp. 1214, 1219 (S.D.N.Y.1996).

30. 510 U.S. at 579.

31. 955 F.Supp. 260 (S.D.N.Y. 1997), *aff'd*, 150 F.3d 132 (2d Cir. 1998).

an original manner. Though conceding that creating levels of difficulty was "somewhat more original than arranging a telephone book in alphabetical order," the court embraced Castle Rock's claim that "had defendants been half as creative in creating *The SAT* as were their lawyers in crafting these arguments about transformation, defendants might have a colorable fair use claim." The court found the first statutory factor to weigh against fair use because *The SAT* drew directly from the episodes with little alteration. In its view the quiz book's regurgitation of *Seinfeld* episodes failed to serve a transformative purpose, such as education, criticism, commentary, parody, or research. Instead, the book merely repackaged *Seinfeld* scenes to entertain the show's viewers. The court depended heavily on the absence of a transformative status in denying Carol Publishing Group's fair use claim.

The "purpose and character of the use" inquiry is not, however, limited to an exploration of the transformative/reproductive dichotomy. The statute itself instructs us to consider "whether such use is of a commercial nature or is for nonprofit education purposes." Consequently, courts have devoted considerable attention to a second dichotomy—the one between commercial and noncommercial uses—as well. The Court in *Sony* placed heavy emphasis on this aspect of the first fair use factor, relying on the non-commercial nature of home taping as one of the chief reasons for excusing it under the fair use doctrine. By way of contrast, the *Sony* Court suggested that the making of copies for a commercial purpose "would presumptively be unfair." Of course this statement must be considered in light of the purely reproductive, non-transformative type of copying at issue in *Sony*.

Refusing to extend the fair use defense to commercial reproductive copying seems entirely logical. Verbatim copying of a plaintiff's works, combined with commercial motives poses the greatest risk of usurping plaintiff's market and depriving him of an economic reward. That, in turn, poses the threat of undermining incentives for creativity. Moreover, the lack of transformative activity by the defendants tends to reduce the likely social benefit flowing from the activity. With the costs high and the benefits low, there is little reason to label the use "fair." It should therefore be a rare case when a commercial and non-transformative use is excused under the fair use doctrine, though even here, one can imagine appropriate cases. For instance, the reproduction for commercial sale of an obscure, decades-old, and out-of-print academic book after a diligent but unsuccessful effort to locate the copyright owner might be the kind of activity that ought to be immunized from liability even though it is neither transformative nor non-commercial.

In the years after *Sony* was decided, many lower courts suggested that there was a virtual per se rule against granting the fair use defense to any commercial user, regardless of the other facts and circumstances. Such an interpretation, however, virtually reads the fair use concept right out of the statute. Many uses that seem intuitively within the scope of the fair use concept are nonetheless conducted for profit. News reporting is done primarily by profit-making commercial ventures like magazines, television stations, and newspapers. Criticism is often published in similar, commercially oriented publications. Much teaching takes place in commercial trade and vocational schools and much research is conducted at profit-making corporations. As one trial judge put it, "publishers of educational textbooks are as profit-motivated as publishers of scandal-mongering tabloid newspapers. And a serious scholar should not be despised and denied the law's protection because he hopes to earn a living through his scholarship. The protection of the statute should not turn on sackcloth and missionary zeal."[32] A blanket rule that denies the fair use defense as soon as a commercial purpose for defendant's conduct is unearthed therefore seems counterintuitive and unworkable.

This concern was addressed and put to rest in the *Campbell* decision. *Campbell* recognized that "if . . . commerciality carried presumptive force against a finding of fairness, the presumption would swallow nearly all of the illustrative uses listed in the preamble paragraph of § 107, including news reporting, comment, criticism, teaching, scholarship, and research, since these activities 'are generally conducted for profit in this country.' "[33] Indeed, the defendants' parody in that case was commercial in nature. The Supreme Court nonetheless found them to be fair users, exempt from liability. The *Campbell* Court emphasized that *Sony's* discussion of commercial motives was not meant to raise a "hard evidentiary presumption. . . . *Sony* stands for the proposition that the 'fact that publication was commercial as opposed to nonprofit is a separate factor that tends to weigh against a finding of fair use.' . . . But that is all, and the fact that even the force of that tendency will vary with the context is a further reason against elevating commerciality to hard presumptive significance."

Of course, just as *Sony's* views on reproductive use must be considered in the context of the facts before it, so must *Campbell's* views on commercial motives. The *Campbell* Court confronted a transformative use, and one where, because of the parody nature of defendant's activities, it was extremely unlikely that plaintiff would grant permission to use the work at any price. In such a context it

---

32. Salinger v. Random House, Inc., 650 F.Supp. 413, 425 (S.D.N.Y.1986), *rev'd*, 811 F.2d 90 (2d Cir.1987), *cert. denied*, 484 U.S. 890, 108 S.Ct. 213, 98 L.Ed.2d 177 (1987).

33. 510 U.S. at 584. The words in single quotes are from Justice Brennan's dissent in Harper & Row v. The Nation, 471 U.S. 539, 105 S.Ct. 2218, 85 L.Ed.2d 588 (1985).

is not entirely surprising that the Court did not find the commercial character of defendant's activities controlling.

There is a further problem with both dichotomies considered under the first fair use element. That is the problem of characterization. It is often not at all obvious whether a use should be labeled transformative versus reproductive. The same doubts can arise along the commercial/noncommercial axis. A good illustration of the problem is *Princeton University Press v. Michigan Document Services*.[34] Plaintiffs owned copyrights in a variety of educational and scholarly books. Professors at the University of Michigan selected excerpts from various of these works for inclusion in "coursepacks," and requested a commercial copyshop to mass produce those coursepacks for sale to students. The defendant was one such copyshop, and it produced coursepacks without securing permissions or paying license fees to the plaintiffs. When the plaintiffs sued for copyright infringement, the defendant raised the fair use defense.

Were the activities of the copyshop transformative or reproductive? One could make a case for either categorization. The excepts were copied verbatim, making the use look merely reproductive, but the combination of various works into an anthology format has creative elements that make the activity look arguably transformative. After all, anthologies are a form of compilation which the copyright laws recognize as a species of original authorship. The Sixth Circuit observed that "the inquiry into the transformative aspect of the use assesses the likely benefit to society from the use—the more the original work has been transformed, the more likely it is that a distinct and valuable new product has been created." In other words the question of "transformation" is not a matter of yea or nay, but rather one of degree.

In the *Princeton* case, the benefit to society was not inconsiderable since the defendant's activities enhanced education, but the degree of transformation of the work was not overwhelming. The problem was particularly vexing in the context of that case because the preamble of section 107 speaks of "multiple copies for classroom use" when alluding to teaching as an illustration of fair use. The court ultimately resolved this aspect of the first factor against defendants, stating "if you make verbatim copies of 95 pages of a 316–page book, you have not transformed the 95 pages very much—even if you juxtapose them to excerpts from other works and package everything conveniently. This kind of mechanical 'transformation' bears little resemblance to the creative metamor-

---

34. 99 F.3d 1381 (6th Cir.1996) (en banc), *cert. denied*, 520 U.S. 1156, 117   S.Ct. 1336, 137 L.Ed.2d 495 (1997).

phosis accomplished by the parodists in the *Campbell* case."[35] Of course, juxtaposition is a classic form of creative authorship and the court's decision to summarily label it a "mechanical" transformation is frustratingly conclusory.

The same ambiguity surrounds the commercial versus non-commercial categorization of the activities in *Princeton University Press*. The defendant copy shop was a profit-making business. That clearly weighs in favor of calling the activities at issue in the case "commercial." Because of the efficiency of its operation, however, it was able to sell the coursepacks for a lower price than if the professor had made the copies at the university and sold them to the students at cost. Moreover, the ultimate use of the material was by students in the purely non-commercial atmosphere of liberal arts courses at the university. In this sense, the ultimate use of the material was "noncommercial." Once again, the court resolved this issue against the defendants, noting that the actual defendant being sued was a for-profit copyshop, and observing that "if the fairness of making copies depends on what the ultimate consumer does with the copies, it is hard to see how the manufacture of pirated editions of any copyrighted work of scholarship could ever be an unfair use."[36]

The facts of *Princeton University Press* illustrate the difficulty of fair use analysis generally and especially of the characterizations required to apply the first fair use factor. The majority[37] may have been persuaded to call the use here commercial and non-transformative because of its concern about the effect the use would have on plaintiff's market for its educational and scholarly books. That concern may be legitimate, but it constitutes a form of double counting, as the effect on the market is supposed to be explicitly considered in the fourth fair use factor.

Another issue that has appeared repeatedly when courts have analyzed the first fair use factor is the relevance of the fact that the defendant requested a license from the plaintiff that was refused. Some courts have reasoned that defendant's request reveals an awareness that the proposed use exceeds the bounds of the permissible. This argument seems to have been put to rest by the Supreme Court in *Campbell*, which stated explicitly that "being denied permission to use a work does not weigh against a finding of fair use."[38] Of course that case involved a parody, and parodists are almost never granted permission. Nonetheless, the statement seems sound as a general rule. No one wants to be sued, even if they are

---

35. *Id.* at 1389.

36. *Id.* at 1386, n.2

37. The case was decided by an 8–5 vote of the en banc court, with three of the five dissenters preparing separate opinions.

38. 510 U.S. at 586, n.18.

quite confident they can prevail on a fair use defense. It may be cheaper and less time consuming to secure a license, if plaintiff can be persuaded to grant one at an acceptable price. If permission is denied and defendant nonetheless goes forward, it would be ironic indeed to penalize him "for this modest show of consideration."[39]

A decision hailing from the Second Circuit, *Warner Brothers Entertainment Inc. v. RDR Books*,[40] provides a nuanced analysis of the different aspects of the first fair use factor. In that case the defendant sought to publish an encyclopedia, titled *The Lexicon: An Unauthorized Guide to Harry Potter Fiction and Related Materials*, that provided an "A-to-Z guide to the creatures, objects, events, and places that exist in the world of *Harry Potter*." The District Court readily concluded that the entries of the Lexicon, which drew heavily from the seven Harry Potter novels and companion books by J.K. Rowling, were infringements. The court further concluded that the Lexicon was not a fair use of the *Harry Potter* series. In doing so, the court reasoned that "the purpose and character of the use" weighed in favor of the plaintiffs to a limited extent.

The court initially determined that the purpose of the Lexicon was transformative—the encyclopedia intended to provide its readers with a reference guide to the intricate world of the *Harry Potter* series, while J.K. Rowling wrote with the purpose of telling an entertaining and thought-provoking story. These circumstances were in contrast to those of the *Castle Rock Entertainment* case discussed immediately above. In *Castle Rock*, both the accused trivia book and *Seinfeld* television series on which it was based had the same purpose, namely to amuse and entertain. The *Warner Brothers v. RDR Books* court expressed concern, however, that the execution of the Lexicon fell short of this transformative purpose. In many instances the Lexicon simply copied passages from one of the *Harry Potter* books with few or no citations to the particular book from which the material was taken. These practices diminished the Lexicon's usefulness as a reference work. Although the court found that the author of the Lexicon, a die-hard *Harry Potter* fan, had acted in good faith, it further observed that the Lexicon was intended to be a commercial, for-profit work. On balance, then, the court held that the first fair use factor weighed "only slightly" in favor of the plaintiffs.

10.2.2 Nature of the Work

The second factor instructs us to consider the nature of the copyrighted work. This implies that some works are entitled to a broader scope of protection than others, and that has been the

---

39. Fisher v. Dees, 794 F.2d 432, 437 (9th Cir.1986).

40. 575 F.Supp.2d 513 (S.D.N.Y. 2008).

consistent view of the courts. The general rule affords the greatest degree of protection to highly creative works, and the least to works that are factual or practical in nature. The scope of fair use is, of course, reciprocal to the degree of protection. This means that defendants are most likely to succeed on a fair use claim with respect to a factual work, and least likely to succeed where the work is creative. As the Supreme Court recently put it, "[t]his factor calls for recognition that some works are closer to the core of intended copyright protection than others, with the consequence that fair use is more difficult to establish when the former works are copied."[41]

At least one justification for this approach is the general rule that copyright only extends to the original aspects of a work. Works that are primarily factual, like almanacs, statistical tables, and the like, contain less original authorship than works of fiction like a novel or stage play. Secondly, the need to reproduce material of a factual nature is often greater than the need to reproduce works of fiction. Consequently, it is appropriate to permit a somewhat broader scope of fair use for works of the former type. Similarly, defendants may be afforded greater latitude to copy from works of an academic or scholarly nature both because it is customary in the academic community to rely heavily on prior academic work and because academic writers may have a strong need to quote extensively from prior work.

Another aspect of the "nature" of plaintiff's work that may bear on fair use analysis is how readily available the work is to the general public. There is language in the legislative history of the 1976 Act indicating that fair use should be more liberally applied where copies of the work being copied are difficult or impossible to obtain. As the Committee Report observed "if the work is 'out of print' and unavailable for purchase through normal channels, the user may have more justification for reproducing it than in the ordinary case, but the existence of organizations licensed to provide photocopies of out-of-print works at reasonable cost is a factor to be considered."[42]

Still another aspect of this second factor that has received both judicial and legislative attention is whether plaintiff's work is published or unpublished. Almost by definition, the author of an unpublished work has not yet received any economic reward from the marketing of his work. He may anticipate reaping that reward in the future upon publication of the work and may have chosen to

41. Campbell v. Acuff–Rose Music, Inc., 510 U.S. 569, 586, 114 S.Ct. 1164, 127 L.Ed.2d 500 (1994). *See also* Harper & Row v. The Nation, 471 U.S. 539, 563, 105 S.Ct. 2218, 85 L.Ed.2d 588 (1985) ("The law generally recognizes a greater need to disseminate factual works than works of fiction or fantasy.").

42. S.Rep. No. 94–473, 94th Cong., 1st Sess. 64 (1965).

delay so that he can improve the work or wait for a moment when its market value will be at its peak. If another party were to publish the work without permission, that might seriously undermine or totally destroy the author's ability to secure any market reward at all. The effect on incentives for creativity could be considerable. Using a cost-benefit mind set, a defendant should have to make a very strong showing of social benefit in order to overcome the presumed harm to incentives when reproducing unpublished works.

The Supreme Court addressed precisely this point in *Harper & Row, Publishers, Inc. v. Nation Enterprises*.[43] The case involved the memoirs of former President Gerald Ford, prepared after he left office. The most intriguing portions of Ford's book were the sections recounting Ford's decision to pardon his predecessor in office, Richard Nixon, who had resigned under the cloud of the Watergate scandal. Ford had licensed Harper & Row to publish these memoirs, and they, in turn, granted *Time* magazine an exclusive license to publish excerpts of the book one week before the full book was to be shipped to bookstores. A few weeks before the scheduled publication date, a pirated copy of the manuscript was delivered to a political magazine called *The Nation*. The editors of that publication hastily prepared a story about the book, and arranged to have the manuscript returned to Harper & Row before its absence could be discovered. The *Nation* story quoted only 300 words verbatim from Ford's 200,000–word book. However, one consequence of the *Nation's* actions was that *Time* cancelled its arrangement with Harper & Row, pursuant to its contract. Harper & Row then sued *The Nation* for copyright infringement, and the defendant raised the fair use defense.

The Supreme Court found in favor of Harper & Row and rejected the fair use defense, despite the relatively small amount of material used and the fact that the defendant was purportedly engaged in news reporting. In reaching this result, it put heavy weight on the fact that, at the time of defendant's activities, the plaintiff's work had not yet been published. The Court concluded that "the author's right to control the first public appearance of his expression weighs against such use of the work before its release. The right of first publication encompasses not only the choice whether to publish at all, but also the choices of when, where, and in what form first to publish a work."[44] Quoting from the legislative history of the 1976 Act, the Court stressed that "the unpublished nature of a work is 'a key, though not necessarily determinative, factor' tending to negate a defense of fair use."[45]

---

43.   471 U.S. 539, 105 S.Ct. 2218, 85 L.Ed.2d 588 (1985).

44.   471 U.S. at 564.

45.   *Id.* at 554.

In the years following the *Harper & Row* decision, however, the lower courts—especially the Second Circuit—tended to afford near conclusive weight to the unpublished status of the work as a basis for denying the fair use defense, despite the "not necessarily determinative" caveat in the Supreme Court's opinion.[46] A *per se* rule that quoting from unpublished works could never be justified as fair use, however, might significantly hinder the work of historians and biographers who often need to quote from unpublished letters, diaries, and manuscripts of historical or literary figures. One can also imagine the need of news outlets to quote unpublished materials, such as corporate memos, in reporting on instances of public or private corruption. To respond to the growing concern about the direction of the case law, Congress amended the fair use provision of the copyright statute in 1992 to add a new final sentence, reading "the fact that a work is unpublished shall not itself bar a finding of fair use if such finding is made upon consideration of all the above factors."[47] The legislative history of this amendment makes it plain that Congress wanted to ensure that scholars could safely make use of reasonable portions of unpublished materials without being exposed to liability. On the other hand, it is equally clear that the unpublished status of a work will continue to be a significant factor weighing against application of the fair use defense in many situations.

10.2.3 Amount and Substantiality of the Portion Used

The third fair use factor embodies the logical intuition that the more of a work a defendant takes, the more likely the use is to undermine the plaintiff's markets. Consequently, extensive takings are less likely to be adjudged fair than more terse borrowings. Courts have often considered the third fair use factor to be closely bound up with the first, which instructs courts to look to the nature and character of the use. As the *Campbell* Court noted "the extent of permissible copying varies with the purpose and character of the use." In the case of parody, fairly extensive copying may be essential to permit the public to recognize the original that the parody is poking fun at. Far less would ordinarily be required for the purposes of a movie review on the evening news.

Moreover, in applying the third factor courts focus not merely on the quantity of material taken, but also on the significance of that material to plaintiff's work as a whole. The inquiry is thus

---

46. *See e.g.*, Salinger v. Random House, Inc., 811 F.2d 90 (2d Cir.1987), *cert. denied*, 484 U.S. 890, 108 S.Ct. 213, 98 L.Ed.2d 177 (1987) (no fair use defense available for use of the unpublished letters of author J.D. Salinger in a biography). To the opposite effect, however, is Wright v. Warner Books, 953 F.2d 731 (2d Cir.1991), permitting limited quotations from unpublished letters and journals in a biography.

47. Act of October 24, 1992, Pub. L.No. 102–492, 106 Stat. 3145.

both quantitative and qualitative. An excellent illustration of this is the Supreme Court's decision in *Harper & Row* discussed in the preceding section. In that case, *The Nation* reproduced only 300 words out of the 200,000 in President Ford's book. The Court nonetheless found that this taking was "substantial" and militated against a finding of fair use, because the portion taken constituted the very heart of the work, and its appearance in The Nation would quite likely undermine plaintiff's market.

Resolution of the third factors places courts in the sometimes uncomfortable position of having to assess how much copying of another's work is reasonably necessary given the "purposes and character" of the accused infringer's use. The recent decision in *Warner Brothers Entertainment Inc. v. RDR Books* illustrates this difficulty.[48] As discussed previously in this chapter, that case involved an unauthorized encyclopedia that catalogued information arising from the *Harry Potter* series of books. There, the court recognized that to fulfill its purpose as reference work, the Lexicon would necessarily have to make considerable use of the original J.K. Rowling novels. It was also mindful that the characters occupying the *Harry Potter* universe had colorful, lively names—the "Dementors" and "Mundungus Fletcher" come to mind—and that the Lexicon should be allowed to use those invented names in order to serve as a reference. However, the court ultimately concluded that the Lexicon's extensive borrowing of J.K. Rowling's original expression had exceeded that informational purpose. Too often had the author of the Lexicon simply copied a passage from one of the original novels instead of drafting a more succinct description that involved less copyrighted material. Because the Lexicon borrowed more original expression than was reasonably needed to create a reference guide, the third fair use factor weighed against it.

The general principle that animates this factor is that defendants should limit themselves to taking the smallest quantity of plaintiff's work consistent with their own purposes. That will minimize the harm to the copyright owner while still securing the benefits the fair use doctrine was meant to further. If a teacher wants to illustrate the writing style of a contemporary author in a creative writing course, the excerpt should be long enough to provide an adequate illustration, but no longer. If a movie critic wants to show a clip to illustrate his claim that the dialogue of the movie is infantile and unbelievable, the clip should be limited to the length necessary to make the point. When the taking exceeds such limits, it begins to harm the plaintiff without enhancing the social benefit that comes from the defendants activities.

48.   575 F.Supp.2d 513 (S.D.N.Y. 2008).

10.2.4   Effect on the Market

The fourth fair use factor directs courts to consider the effect of defendant's use on the potential market for plaintiff's work. The Supreme Court has declared that this factor is "undoubtedly the single most important element of fair use,"[49] and this theme has been echoed repeatedly by the lower courts. This is only logical. If defendant's conduct causes significant numbers of people to refrain from paying for access to the plaintiff's work, that could destroy the very incentives that are at the heart of the copyright system. Such a use should rarely be labeled "fair." In applying this factor, a court is supposed to consider not only the market effects of this particular defendant's conduct, but the market implications if the defendant's conduct were to become widely engaged in by others.[50] Moreover, the focus is not merely on the current markets for plaintiff's work, but must consider the consequences in potential markets that the plaintiff-copyright owner may not yet have exploited.

Consideration of potential markets is logically part of the market assessment required by the fair use doctrine because the copyright statute assigns to the copyright owner the exclusive right to make derivative works. The fact that a defendant acts more promptly than the plaintiff in exploiting a particular derivative market should not, by itself, deprive that plaintiff of the statutory adaptation right. To put the point more concretely, it would be odd indeed if a defendant could make a movie based on a copyrighted novel without the permission of the copyright owner, and then invoke the fair use defense on the grounds that the movie will not cut into the sales of the novel, but may even boost them! While that may be true, the activities of such a defendant surely interfere with the copyright owner's rights to profit from derivative works in the form of motion pictures. The inapplicability of fair use to cases such as these is even more apparent when we remember that copyright owners often delay in producing derivative works for strategic reasons, hoping to bring the derivative work to the market at what they consider to be the optimum moment. Thus, the fact that the copyright owner has not yet licensed movie rights is not necessarily evidence of any lack of interest in doing so in the future.

On the other hand, as many litigants, courts, and commentators have noted, this fourth factor, with its focus on potential markets, can degenerate into entirely circular reasoning. In a sense, every use affects a "potential" market for the work. For instance, copyright owners might wish to charge book reviewers a fee for

---

49. Harper & Row v. The Nation, 471 U.S. 539, 566, 105 S.Ct. 2218, 85 L.Ed.2d 588 (1985).

50. To negate fair use one need only show that if the challenged use "should become widespread, it would adversely affect the potential market for the copyrighted work." Sony v. Universal City Studios, 464 U.S. 417, 451, 104 S.Ct. 774, 78 L.Ed.2d 574 (1984).

using brief quotations from published books in their book reviews. When the shocked reviewers protest that such use should be protected under the fair use doctrine, the copyright owners could point to the fourth factor and claim that the uncompensated use of quotes adversely affects the "potential" market for "quotation royalties" that they hope to establish, and that it should therefore be held outside the scope of fair use. To put the proposition the other way around, the application of the fair use defense to this practice forecloses any such quotation royalty revenues, and the practice of quoting without getting permission thus has an effect on the "potential market" of licensing such quotes.[51]

This circularity problem is rendered even more complex because the advance of technology makes it possible for copyright owners to develop methods for charging for uses that until recently were impossible to monitor and economically exploit. Twenty years ago it might have been unthinkable to imagine a workable licensing system that could be used to charge for the use of brief quotations in newspaper reviews of newly published books. The advent of virtually instantaneous electronic communication via e-mail, secure methods of on-line payment of fees, comprehensive computer data bases, and the availability of the text of many major newspapers on-line might combine to make such a system much more plausible today.

In 1994, a panel of the Second Circuit in *American Geophysical Union v. Texaco Inc.*[52] suggested, over a dissent, that such changes in the ability of copyright owners to collect fees are a significant factor in denying the fair use defense.[53] This seems particularly curious. The fair use defense would mean very little if it only covered those uses that plaintiffs have not yet figured out how to charge for. We want reviewers, teachers, reporters, parodists, and scholars to have at least some degree of free access to copyrighted works not merely as a concession to the practical limits of the copyright owners' abilities to force them to pay. There is a broad consensus that most of these uses promote the common good. Demanding that copyright owners allow such uses without complaint or demand for payment could also be considered a *quid pro quo* for the more general protections afforded by the copyright

---

51. *See, e.g.*, Williams & Wilkins Co. v. United States, 203 Ct.Cl. 74, 487 F.2d 1345 (1973), *aff'd by an equally divided Court*, 420 U.S. 376, 95 S.Ct. 1344, 43 L.Ed.2d 264 (1975) ("It is wrong to measure the detriment to plaintiff by loss of presumed royalty income—a standard which necessarily assumed that plaintiff had a right to issue licenses. That would be true, of course, only if it were first decided that the defendant's practices did not constitute 'fair use.' In determining whether the company has been sufficiently hurt to cause these practices to become 'unfair' one cannot assume at the start the merit of plaintiff's position. . . .").

52. 60 F.3d 913 (2d Cir.1994).

53. *Id.* at 929–30.

statute against wholesale copying. Regardless of technical feasibility it is almost unseemly to demand payment for uses of this nature.

To escape from this circularly, the Supreme Court has noted that "the market for potential derivative uses includes only those that creators of original works would in general develop or license others to develop."[54] Similarly, the *American Geophysical* court suggested that inquiry under the fourth factor should be limited to "traditional, reasonable, or likely to be developed markets...."[55] For example, it is traditional for movies to be made from novels. If a defendant makes an unauthorized movie version of plaintiff's copyrighted book, that activity will plainly affect a *traditional* potential market, even though the plaintiff may not yet have taken any steps to sell the movie rights to the novel. On the other hand, copyright owners have never attempted to charge reviewers who seek only to quote brief passages from books. Even if a copyright owner claimed an intention to do so in the future, that would not be a traditional market for the work.

Of course, one need not be a Holmes or Brandeis to realize that the "traditional, reasonable, or likely to be developed" formula is itself vague and that there is no clear way to discern when a given market is traditional or reasonable. For instance, until recently it would not have been traditional to license a novel for use as the basis of a video game, but that is surely more a function of the novelty of video games than of any lack of interest in such a market by authors.

Professor Nimmer has suggested that the solution lies in what he calls a functional approach.[56] Under this test, "if regardless of medium, the defendant's work, although containing substantially similar material, performs a different function than that of the plaintiff's, the defense of fair use may be invoked."[57] As an illustration of the principle, Nimmer cites a number of cases where the reproduction of song lyrics in magazines was held to be fair use. Nimmer explains the results by noting that "the functions differed in that plaintiff's sheet music was intended to be used for singing or musical performances, while defendant's article was a literary presentation that incidentally included the disputed lyrics. Persons interested in obtaining plaintiff's music for musical purposes would not find that need fulfilled through the purchase of defendant's magazine article." He makes a similar point with respect to the different functions fulfilled by books and book reviews that quote from those books. While Nimmer's functional test has only been

---

54. Campbell v. Acuff–Rose Music, Inc., 510 U.S. 569, 592, 114 S.Ct. 1164, 127 L.Ed.2d 500 (1994).

55. American Geophysical Union v. Texaco Inc., 60 F.3d 913, 930 (2d Cir. 1994), *cert. dismissed*, 516 U.S. 1005, 116 S.Ct. 592, 133 L.Ed.2d 486 (1995).

56. Nimmer, § 13.03[B] (2002).

57. *Id.*

invoked by name in a relatively few cases, it does seem a helpful way to determine which potential markets are properly considered under the fourth fair use factor.

Of course the difficulties that surround application of the "effect on the market" factor vary with the type of situation confronting a court. It is possible to identify three categories of cases. In the first, the defendant's use is directly competitive with the plaintiff's work. Here, the effect on the market can usually be measured in a straightforward way, typically dependant on the amount of the work used and whether the use is commercial in nature. Where the defendant has instead used some or all of plaintiff's work to make a derivative work, the next question should be whether the derivative work in question is a customary or regularly exploited type of derivative for the category of underlying work in question, regardless of whether this particular plaintiff has yet chosen to pursue the market. Examples would include the market for movie versions of novels, and the market for posters depicting one-of-a-kind pictorial and graphic works. In cases such as these, the effect on a potential market can again be assessed based on the quantity of the work used and whether the use is commercial in nature.

It is the final category of cases that poses the real difficulty of circularity. Those are cases where the defendant's derivative work is in a market not customarily or regularly exploited, and one which this particular plaintiff cannot prove he had concrete plans to enter in the foreseeable future. In cases of this sort the fair use dispute is really about whether the plaintiff should be guaranteed the exclusive right to exploit that market in question despite the fact that the market opportunity was not generally recognized or appreciated until the defendant came along.

It seems best to attempt to resolve this difficult case by referring back to the basic trade-offs that animate the fair use defense and copyright law generally. The question in these cases should be recast as whether the defendant's use is likely to undermine incentives to a degree more significant than the social benefits realized from the use in question. If the plaintiff's work has already been highly successful, allowing the defendant who first unearthed the heretofore unexploited derivative use to go forward unmolested is unlikely to undermine either the incentives of this particular plaintiff or those of others similarly situated. Moreover, the suggested approach acts as an incentive to others, encouraging them to invent new ways to use and disseminate works.

For instance, re-consider *Castle Rock Entertainment v. Carol Publishing Group.*[58] You will recall that in that case, defendant

---

58. 955 F.Supp. 260 (S.D.N.Y. 1997), *aff'd*, 150 F.3d 132 (2d Cir.1998).

prepared a quiz book based on plaintiff's *Seinfeld* sitcom. In spite of proof that the *Seinfeld* sitcom's audience grew after *The SAT's* publication, the Second Circuit did not feel that a possible positive effect of defendant's work on the market for the original work established fair use. It thought it more consequential that *"The SAT* substitutes for a derivative market that a television program copyright owner such as Castle Rock 'would in general develop or license others to develop.' Because *The SAT* borrows exclusively from Seinfeld and not from any other television or entertainment programs, *The SAT* is likely to fill a market niche that Castle Rock would in general develop."[59]

The Second Circuit maintained that denying artists their monopoly over derivative versions of their original works because the artists chose not to "saturate" those potential markets runs counter to the Copyright Act's purpose of advancing the arts. *The SAT* usurped the plaintiff's potential derivative market for quiz books because the quiz book added nothing beyond what the *Seinfeld* sitcom had created. Though Castle Rock had no concrete interest in publishing a *Seinfeld* quiz book, the court concluded that the decision to create a derivative work belonged to Castle Rock and not Carol Publishing. Consequently, the "harm to potential market" factor weighed against defendant's claim of fair use.

The *Castle Rock* court did not address the conventionality of a derivative quiz book market and did not attempt to explicitly assess the likelihood that Castle Rock would have entered that market. The opinion may nonetheless have balanced the tendency of the defendant's use to undermine the incentives of the plaintiff against the social benefits flowing from that use, as mentioned previously. One could argue that the desire to create the next *Seinfeld* is surely enough to motivate screenplay writers even if they know, up front, that they will be denied revenue from the hypothetical quiz book market down the road if the show is a blockbuster hit. On the other hand, one must ask if any social benefit at all is realized from a *Seinfeld* quiz book. The court indeed noted that the quiz book provided no transformative use and only repackaged the *Seinfeld* show. Viewing some sort of transformative use (i.e. commentary, critique, parody, etc.) as necessary to establish that the use was socially beneficial, *Castle Rock* ruled that the absence of transformation on these facts made even the smallest infringement on the plaintiff's incentives unacceptable regardless of whether a derivative quiz book market for TV shows was customary or rare.

In another decision from the Second Circuit, *New Era Publications International v. Carol Publishing Group*,[60] the court came out

---

59. 150 F.3d at 145, quoting *Campbell*, 510 U.S. at 592.

60. 904 F.2d 152 (2d Cir. 1990).

the other way and found that the fourth fair use factor favored the accused infringer. There author Jonathan Caven–Atack, a former member of the Church of Scientology, wrote a book regarding his investigation of that religion and its founder, L. Ron Hubbard. Having been jaded by his experiences with the Church of Scientology, the author wrote a critical biography quoting many passages from Hubbard's own works to portray Hubbard as a "vindictive and profoundly disturbed" person whose religion was a "dangerous cult." Carol agreed to publish Caven–Atack's book but New Era, the exclusive licensee of Hubbard's works, sued for copyright infringement, claiming that the book copied "substantial portions" of Hubbard's works.

New Era Publishing argued that it intended to publish its own biography of Hubbard containing excerpts from Hubbard's works. New Era contended that Carol's publication would harm the market for the eventual New Era biography and claimed that this harm to their "potential market" should defeat the fair use defense. The Second Circuit disagreed and instead reasoned that potential customers would not be deterred from purchasing a favorable biography because of a preceding unfavorable biography quoting from Hubbard's works. The court stressed that diminished sales of Hubbard's works caused by convincing criticism of his ideology is not the kind of "effect on the market" that counts against fair use. The Second Circuit concluded that "the critique and the copyrighted work serve fundamentally different functions" and thus the critical biography would not harm the market for the copyrighted work or derivative works within the meaning of factor four. Finding that the other fair use factors also weighed in favor of Carol Publishing, the court held that the critical biography constituted fair use of Hubbard's works.

§ 10.3   Fair Use and Photocopying

The problem of photocopying was very much in the minds of the authors of the 1976 Act. Effective and inexpensive photocopiers had become widely available in the years leading up to the adoption of the new statute and copyright owners lobbied hard for provisions that would ensure their markets would not be destroyed by the use of this new technology. One context where this problem was particularly important was education, given the almost irresistible tendency for teachers to photocopy and distribute materials to their students. The text of section 107 alludes to that problem by including, in the preamble, the phrase "multiple copies for classroom use" in the list of illustrative fair uses. Moreover, even though such uses are reproductive rather than transformative, suggesting that they might be disfavored under the first fair use factor, the Supreme Court in *Campbell* noted that "[t]he obvious statutory exception to this focus on transformative uses is the straight reproduction of multiple copies for classroom distribution."[61]

Congress did not intend, however, to give carte blanche permission for educational copying. That would make it impossible for the authors and publishers of textbooks to earn any profits for their work, destroying incentives and ultimately impoverishing education. The question was where to draw the lines between permissible and impermissible educational copying. Rather than dealing with the problem directly in the statutory text, the Congress left representatives of copyright owners and the educational community to their own devices to develop a solution. The result was a document entitled *Agreement on Guidelines for Classroom Copying in Not-for-Profit Educational Institutions*. The document was incorporated in the report of the Judiciary Committee of the House of Representatives on the bill that ultimately became the Copyright Act of 1976.[62] It deals only with copying from printed sources such as books and periodicals, and does not address at all the copying of musical or audiovisual works for educational purposes. Those matters are dealt with in separate guideline documents.[63]

The Classroom Copying Guidelines are meant to provide a safe harbor. Staying within the limits specified by the Guidelines should ensure that a teacher cannot be held liable for infringement by virtue of her classroom copying, although technically the Guidelines are not binding on courts, and even copying within their limits could theoretically be held infringing by an unusually zealous court. Conversely, copying more than the amounts specified, or under conditions different than those specified can still qualify as fair use, based on the traditional analysis of the fair use factors, because the guidelines represent only minimum standards of fair use.[64] Recall, also, that employees of non-profit educational institutions cannot be held liable for statutory damages if they had reasonable grounds to believe that their copying was fair use.[65]

The first section of the Guidelines covers copying by teachers for their own use—such as when a teacher photocopies a newspaper

---

61. *Id.* at 579, n.11

62. H.R. Rep. No. 94–1476, 94th Cong., 2d Sess. 68–70 (1976). Interestingly, both the American Association of University Professors and the Association of American Law Schools (the professional organization of law professors) did not agree to these guidelines because they were, in its view, "too restrictive with respect to classroom situations at the university and graduate level." *Id.* at 72.

63. The music guidelines appear at H.R. Rep. No. 94–1476, 94th Cong., 2d Sess. 70–74 (1976) and Guidelines for Off–Air Taping of Copyrighted Works for Educational Use appear at H.R. Rep. No. 97–495, 97th Cong., 2d Sess. (1982).

64. Marcus v. Rowley, 695 F.2d 1171, 1178 (9th Cir.1983).

65. *See* discussion at § 9.6.2.3, *supra* and 17 U.S.C. § 504(c)(2).

article for later review in connection with the preparation of a lesson plan. The second section addresses the making of multiple copies for classroom use. In order to come within the guidelines, the teacher must meet tests of (1) brevity, (2) spontaneity, and (3) cumulative effect. The Guidelines also require each copy distributed to students to bear a notice of copyright, an early precursor of the provisions of the Digital Millennium Copyright Act requiring the preservation of so-called "copyright management information" on digitally distributed works.[66]

The brevity test is satisfied when the teacher stays within certain bright line quantitative limits set out in the Guidelines, such as "an excerpt from any prose work of not more than 1,000 words or 10% of the work, whichever is less." The spontaneity test requires that "the copying is at the instance and inspiration of the individual teacher and ... the inspiration and decision to use the work and moment of its use for maximum teaching effectiveness are so close in time that it would be unreasonable to expect a timely reply to a request for permission." Under this test, if, during the summer, a teacher comes across copyrighted material that might be useful in an upcoming class to be taught the following fall, he could not safely rely on the Guidelines since there would be ample time to secure permission before the start of school in September. Also, a teacher who has used a given excerpt once without permission could not use it in subsequent semesters under the Guidelines since, by definition, there would be sufficient time to obtain permission. As Professor Nimmer has wryly observed, the brevity requirements "would seem to place a premium on lack of advance preparation of course materials."[67]

With the advent of e-mail and the Internet, where permission to use copyrighted material can potentially be obtained within a matter of minutes, the spontaneity requirements of the classroom guidelines, read literally, might deny the fair use privilege to virtually all twenty-first century classroom copying. This is obviously a development that none of the parties who negotiated the Guidelines contemplated, and it suggests that their continued vitality should be a matter of some skepticism. The third test, relating to cumulative effects, limits the number of excerpts that may be copied from the same author the number of times the same teacher can make classroom copies during each term, and requires that the copies be for only one course in the school.

Anyone who has been even moderately awake in a classroom will appreciate that many teachers engage in photocopying that exceeds the scope of the Guidelines. Excerpts are often much longer

---

66. *See supra* § 7.3.

67. Nimmer, § 13.05[E][3][d] (2002).

than permitted, and they are often used over and over again each semester without any effort to secure permission. As the decision in *Marcus v. Rowley* indicates, such practices may result in holdings of copyright infringement.[68] There, a continuing education instructor copied eleven of thirty-five pages from the plaintiff's cake decorating booklet in her own readings packet. She assigned that packet during multiple school years without acknowledging the plaintiff for her work or paying her a licensing fee. The Ninth Circuit concluded the instructor violated the Guidelines: The extent of copying exceeded the brevity requirement, the instructor possessed sufficient time to request permission to use the protected work, and the plaintiff's copyright had not been acknowledged. The Court of Appeals further concluded that the instructor could not rely on the general fair use defense either, as both the protected and accused works were designed for instructional purposes and a substantial portion of the protected work had been copied.

That decisions like *Marcus v. Rowley* have not inspired greater instructor compliance with the Guidelines may be explained in a number of ways. Many teachers may not be aware of the Guidelines. Others may feel that there is little likelihood their activities will come to the attention of the copyright owners, and that any harm suffered by those owners would be virtually zero. Still others might believe that although their activities exceed the Guidelines, they are nonetheless fair use under the general approach of section 107.

It would seem that the case for fair use outside the Guidelines would be stronger for materials that are not designed primarily for a classroom audience, and weaker for those that are. Thus, if a teacher copies a lengthy magazine article from *Newsweek* or *Time* about the exploration of Mars and uses it every semester over a period of three years, the activity probably violates the Guideline tests of brevity and spontaneity. However, the character and purpose of the teacher's use is noncommercial and specifically referenced in the preamble to section 107; the nature of plaintiff's work is at least partially factual in nature; and the effect on the potential market is not likely to be significant (though to be sure, there is obviously an effect on the potential derivative market for post-publication reprint licensing revenues).

On the other hand if the teacher copies and distributes 30 pages of an astronomy text instead, the market effect will likely be much greater because there will be less likelihood that students will be required to buy the book and case for fair use should be correspondingly less.[69] Along these lines, as we noted earlier in this

---

68.   695 F.2d 1171 (9th Cir.1983).

69.   Thus in Wihtol v. Crow, 309 F.2d 777 (8th Cir.1962), decided under

chapter, judicial opinions have concluded that the photocopying by outside copyshops of significant excerpts from multiple academic works so as to create new anthologies (also known as "course-packs") was not protected by fair use and thus infringing.[70]

Another aspect of the photocopying conundrum involves libraries and the degree to which they may make photocopies both for their own purposes or for the use of library patrons. Rather than leave the question of library copying to the relatively vague provisions of the fair use doctrine, Congress addressed it specifically in section 108, which spells out rather precisely the scope of permissible library copying. Because the contours of section 108 do not involve fair use, but rather involve a direct limitation of the reproduction rights of copyright owners, we have discussed the mechanics of that section earlier, in Chapter 6 of this book. Bear in mind, however, that if a given library engages in photocopying beyond the scope of section 108, it remains free to attempt to justify that copying under the more general provisions of section 107 as fair use.

A final context in which the fair use status of photocopying activities should be considered is copying, particularly of copyrighted journal articles, by corporate research departments, hospitals, law firms, and other intellectually oriented institutions. When such an enterprise subscribes to only a few copies of a journal and then makes copies of those journals, or selected articles appearing in them, for wider circulation to members of its staff, the copyright owners lose sales to effectively their only real audience for the work. In *Williams & Wilkins Co. v. United States*[71] a publisher of medical journals sued the U.S. government for photocopying taking place at the National Institutes of Health (NIH). The NIH subscribed to only one or two copies of each journal and then routinely made copies of journal articles for researchers who requested them. The total extent of copying was several million pages per year. The Court of Claims found the activity to be fair use, suggesting that a contrary result might be harmful to medical research and indicating that the problem was one which "calls fundamentally for legislative solution." A dissenting judge described the opinion as "the Dred Scott decision of copyright law" and while the Supreme

---

the 1909 Act and prior to the promulgation of the Classroom Copying Guidelines, the defendant teacher made 48 copies of the entirety of a song and distributed them to the school choir. The court found that the activity was not fair use and held the teacher liable for infringement.

70. Basic Books v. Kinko's Graphics Corp., 758 F.Supp. 1522 (S.D.N.Y.1991);

Princeton University Press v. Michigan Document Services, 99 F.3d 1381 (6th Cir.1996) (en banc), *cert. denied*, 520 U.S. 1156, 117 S.Ct. 1336, 137 L.Ed.2d 495.

71. 203 Ct.Cl. 74, 487 F.2d 1345 (1973), aff'd by an equally divided court, 420 U.S. 376, 95 S.Ct. 1344, 43 L.Ed.2d 264 (1975).

Court agreed to review the case, it deadlocked on a 4–4 vote, Justice Blackmun not participating, leaving the lower court opinion standing. The *Williams & Wilkins* opinion has been sharply criticized by Professor Nimmer and others for failing to adequately safeguard copyright owners against the threats to their economic interests posed by photocopying technology.

By way of contrast we have the more recent case of *American Geophysical Union v. Texaco Inc.*[72] There, the Second Circuit found that a similar practice of systematic copying of journal articles by the research department of Texaco, a for-profit business, did not constitute fair use. The *American Geophysical* court was heavily influenced by the fact that in the years since the decision in *Williams & Wilkins* a system of convenient licensing had been developed. That system, administered by an entity called the Copyright Clearance Center (CCC), provides a centralized location to which fees can be paid avoiding the transaction costs associated with contacting the copyright owners of hundreds of different journal articles. Based on a statistical model, the CCC offers users the option of paying a flat annual licensing fee for the privilege of "all you can eat" copying from works registered with the CCC.

In the court's view the availability of this system made all the difference. As the *American Geophysical* court observed "it is not unsound to conclude that the right to seek payment for a particular use tends to become legally cognizable under the fourth fair use factor when the means for paying for such a use is made easier. This notion is not inherently troubling: it is sensible that a particular unauthorized use should be considered 'more fair' when there is no ready market or means to pay for the use, while such an unauthorized use should be considered 'less fair' when there is a ready market or means to pay for the use."[73]

On the other hand, just because copyright owners figure out a way to charge for a particular type of use and can persuade or intimidate some significant portion of users to go along with the system, that should not automatically conclude the fair use inquiry merely on the grounds of lost revenue. If the CCC developed a system of charging for brief excerpts in book reviews, under which entities like *The New York Times* could pay a flat fee each year for the privilege of quoting from as many books as they liked in such reviews, there would still be strong public policy reasons to allow such quotation free of charge under the fair use defense. It is inconsistent with the free exchange of ideas that copyright law is supposed to promote to require that those who wish to comment on

72. 60 F.3d 913 (2d Cir.1994), *cert. dismissed*, 516 U.S. 1005, 116 S.Ct. 592, 133 L.Ed.2d 486 (1995).

73. 60 F.3d at 930–31.

the works of others should have to pay those others tribute in order to do so.

§ 10.4   Fair Use and Home Taping

The recent proliferation of devices such as recordable DVD players, MP3 players, broad-band Internet connections, and older technologies like dual-deck cassette tape recorders and home video players has made home copying of copyrighted material virtually effortless. These technologies have opened up a veritable Pandora's box of problems in the application of the fair use doctrine. The march of technology has repeatedly forced the courts and Congress to confront the question of just how much private copying should be acceptable under the fair use doctrine.

The facet of the problem involving home videotaping of copyrighted material broadcast for free home viewing via television was resolved by the Supreme Court in *Sony Corp. of America v. Universal City Studios*,[74] which was discussed above in the connection with the first fair use factor. Universal, the plaintiff in that case, was the owner of copyrights on certain programs broadcast on TV. It sued Sony on a theory of contributory infringement. It alleged that Sony's sale of videocassette recorders was done with the knowledge that home viewers were using the machines to make copies of copyrighted works in violation of its reproduction rights.[75] Of course, in order for Sony to be liable under this theory, the activities of the home viewers had to be infringing. Sony argued that home taping could not be infringing because it was protected under the fair use defense. The Court sided with Sony, though the result was on a close 5–4 vote with a strong dissent by Justice Blackmun.

The majority concluded that home taping was primarily for "time shifting" purposes, meaning that people did it so that they could watch their favorite programs at hours other than the times that they were broadcast.[76] The court felt that the non-commercial nature of the activity minimized the market effect, and that the plaintiff had failed to make a sufficient evidentiary showing of harm from the activity.

One might wonder what sort of remedy might have been imposed if the case had come out the other way. After all, individual suits against millions of home tapers to secure injunctions that

74. 464 U.S. 417, 104 S.Ct. 774, 78 L.Ed.2d 574 (1984).

75. *See supra* § 9.4.

76. For the youthful reader this may seem odd, but back in the day, television programs were not available on demand over the Internet, which had not been invented yet, nor were they constantly being replayed on 600 cable channels, which also did not exist. If you missed the show, you missed it, unless you taped it.

would themselves be virtually impossible to enforce would not be a very practical solution, which was why the plaintiffs did not sue individual end users in the first place. More plausible would have been an injunction forbidding Sony and other VCR manufacturers from making machines with taping capacity. This would have solved the problem, but at the cost of repressing a valuable new technology.

Alternatively, the court might have imposed a royalty on each VCR sold—or for that matter on each blank cassette tape sold—with the money going into a fund to be distributed amongst the affected copyright holders. This resembles the situation in a number of European countries.[77] While this solution has a rough equitable appeal, it calls for a series of complex determinations better suited for legislative than judicial resolution. The majority opinion of Justice Stevens recognizes this point, observing that "it may well be that Congress will take a fresh look at this new technology, just as it so often has examined other innovations in the past. But it is not our job to apply laws that have not yet been written."

Congress declined the invitation to address home videotaping, so *Sony* remains the last word, making it clear that noncommercial home videotaping, at least for "time shifting" purposes, is protected as fair use. The case, however, did not have any occasion to deal with the issue of home *audio* taping, a related and highly significant issue. To understate matters somewhat, it is not unheard of for music fans to borrow a CD from a friend or family member and make a cassette or "burn a CD" for themselves, or to buy a CD and make a second copy on a portable device such as an MP3 player, or, in older days, even to simply record music as it is broadcast over the radio. Some people have even been known to download music over the Internet! (We will have a bit more to say about that a little later in this chapter). All these practices raise issues similar to those considered in *Sony*. Unlike the videotaping problem, however, audiotaping has been addressed primarily by Congress, rather than the courts.

Prior to 1972, sound recordings were not protected by copyright in the United States. Thus anyone could copy them without violating the rights of the party who prepared the sound recording. Under this state of the law, record piracy flourished. While duplication of sound recordings did implicate the copyright interests of the holder of copyright in the underlying musical composition, those rights were subject to a compulsory license.[78] Consequently, it was perfectly legal under federal law to make unauthorized duplicates

77. *See* Don E. Tomlinson & Timothy Nielander, *Red Apples and Green Persimmons: A Comparative Analysis of Audio Home–Recording Royalty Laws in* *the United States and Abroad,* 20 MISS. COLL. L. REV. 5 (1999).

78. *See supra* § 6.1.2.

of hit albums, provided only that the compulsory license fees were paid for use of the musical composition.[79]

To rectify the situation, Congress amended the Copyright Act in 1971 to bring sound recordings within the scope of its protection.[80] The issue of home taping was not a primary concern of this legislation, but the legislative history did address the problem, noting "it is not the intention ... to restrain the home recording, from broadcast or from tapes or records, of recorded performances, where home recording is for the private use and with no purpose of reproducing or otherwise capitalizing commercially on it."[81] Of course, only a few years later Congress adopted the 1976 Act, which thoroughly overhauled all of copyright law. Neither the text of the 1976 Act nor its legislative history made any specific reference to the problem of home audiotaping, leading to uncertainty over the continued vitality of the quoted passage from the legislative history of the 1971 statute.

Of course, when Congress expressed its views on home audiotaping in 1971, home audiotaping was a relatively minor problem. Audio cassettes and convenient cassette decks were only about 7 or 8 years old, and the sound quality of a homemade tape was nowhere near comparable to that available on commercially produced records. With the march of technology, that situation changed. By the early 1990s the advent of digital recording technology made it possible for homemade tapes to essentially duplicate the quality of commercial CDs. By the late 1990s burnable CDs provided near perfect audio copies.

The recording industry recognized that this posed a serious threat to its financial interests. Once someone bought a CD and lent it to a friend to be digitally copied, that digital copy could be lent to still other friends and so on and so on, ad infinitum. A single CD sale could displace dozens of additional sales down the road. To stave off this situation, the recording industry once again appealed to Congress, and it responded with a new piece of legislation called the Audio Home Recording Act (AHRA).[82]

We have discussed the AHRA earlier in the chapter on the specialized rights of copyright owners, specifically at section 7.5 of this volume. To save you the bother of flipping back, we will recap some of the high points here. The AHRA has two principal features.

---

79. Several states passed laws forbidding this practice. The Supreme Court held in Goldstein v. California, 412 U.S. 546, 93 S.Ct. 2303 (1973) that California's version of such a statute was not preempted by the federal copyright laws.

80. Pub. L. No. 92–140, 85 Stat. 391 (1971) (codified as amended at 17 U.S.C. § 102(7) and other scattered sections).

81. H.R. Rep. No. 487, 92d Cong., 1st Sess. at 7.

82. Pub. L. 102–563, 106 Stat. 4244.

First, it requires manufacturers of "digital audio recording devices" to equip them with a "serial copy management system" or SCMS. SCMS prevents making a copy of a copy. Thus home users would be physically able to make a high quality digital copy of an original store-bought digital audio tape, including one borrowed from a friend, but would be unable to copy a copy of that tape previously made by a friend. This prevents the problem of each privately made copy becoming a master for still further copying down the line. Second, AHRA imposed a royalty fee on the sale of digital audio devices and on blank digital audio tapes, with the proceeds to be divided among relevant copyright owners and performers.

In addition, the statute deals specifically with the issue of home audio-taping by providing that: "No action may be brought under this title alleging infringement of copyright based on the manufacture, importation or distribution of a digital audio recording device, a digital audio recording medium, an analog recording device, or an analog recording medium, or based on the noncommercial use by a consumer of such device or medium for making digital musical recordings or analog musical recordings."[83] The provision thus specifically immunizes home taping, whether accomplished with digital equipment or with older devices such as an ordinary cassette tape deck or even the more archaic reel-to-reel tape. The legislative history makes this point plain, stating: "In the case of home taping, the exemption protects all noncommercial copying by consumers of digital and analog musical recordings. Manufacturers, importers, and distributors of digital and analog recording devices and media have a complete exemption from copyright infringement claims based on the manufacture, importation, or distribution of such devices and media."[84]

As we noted earlier, the AHRA is a narrowly worded statute that has not aged well. All of the parties involved in the drafting of the AHRA focused upon digital audio taping—a technology that was quickly superseded by subsequent industrial advances. A principal problem is that AHRA applies only to recording devices that are primarily marketed or designed to copy music.[85] Most home taping of music in the twenty-first century, however, is done on home computers connected to the Internet. Because home computers perform a great number of tasks in addition to copying recordings, they do not fall within the definition of "digital audio recording devices" in AHRA. This means that the most significant contemporary copyright disputes—those involving file swapping and music downloading—are simply unaddressed by this legislation.

83. 17 U.S.C. § 1008.

84. H.R. Rep. No. 102–873(I), at 18 (1992).

85. 17 U.S.C. § 1001(3).

§ 10.5   Fair Use and Computer Software

Just as the widespread use and exploitation of computers has caused problems for copyright law in other areas, it has lead to some troublesome questions under the fair use doctrine as well. One of these concerns is the problem of "reverse engineering" of software. Often, in order to develop a software program that can successfully compete with an existing product, a firm must be able to review the specific program code of the existing product. The developer may have the perfectly legitimate goal of learning about the unprotectable ideas that make the program work with no intention of ultimately copying the code that constitutes the protected expression in that program. This, however, poses a problem.

Publicly distributed versions of computer programs are usually in forms that are not humanly readable. First, they are on media such as floppy disks or CDs, and second, they are usually distributed in the form of binary object code—a series of ones and zeros—that are nearly incomprehensible to all but the most extreme computer nerds. A competitor could, of course, run the program through a computer, which can be instructed to convert the program back to a source code form that is comprehensible to human beings (a process known as decompilation) and to display the results on the computer screen. The problem is that courts have repeatedly held that loading a program into memory constitutes making a copy of that program, and the decompilation may even constitute the preparation of a derivative work because it is a translation of sorts. Thus, anyone seeking to study a software program to gain access to its underlying ideas would be in violation of the copyright owner's reproduction and adaptation rights unless decompilation and loading into memory are held to be within the fair use defense.

When the Ninth Circuit was confronted with just this problem in *Sega Enterprises Ltd. v. Accolade, Inc.*,[86] it held the fair use defense to be applicable. Sega, as you are no doubt aware, manufactured the Genesis game system, which included a console and game cartridges. Accolade wanted to make its own game cartridges that would run on the Sega console, but this required the software in the Accolade games to be compatible with the Sega system. To do that "Accolade ... 'reverse engineered' Sega's video game programs in order to discover the requirements for compatibility with the Genesis console. As part of the reverse engineering process ... Accolade purchased a Genesis console and three Sega game cartridges, wired a decompiler into the console circuitry, and generated printouts of the resulting source code. Accolade engineers studied and annotated the printouts in order to identify areas of commonal-

---

86.   977 F.2d 1510 (9th Cir.1992).

ity among the three game programs. They then loaded the disassembled code back into a computer, and experimented to discover the interface specifications for the Genesis console by modifying the programs and studying the results."[87]

The *Accolade* court conducted a conventional fair use analysis, considering each of the four statutory factors. On the first factor, the character of defendant's use, it noted that while Accolade's ultimate purposes were commercial, the immediate purpose of its reverse engineering activity was for study, and no other method for studying Sega programs was available. The court also seemed swayed by the transformative nature of Accolade's activities, noting that it served to increase the number of games available for use with the Sega console.

Regarding factor two, the nature of the copyrighted work, the court characterized a computer program as a utilitarian work, with many features dictated by functional rather than aesthetic considerations. It noted that unlike other works, where the underlying ideas that animate the work are readily accessible to the human eye, the ideas of a computer program are only accessible after decompilation, and found that this too cut in favor of fair use.

Turning to the third factor, the court recognized that Accolade had copied the entirety of Sega's program when it made its decompiled transcripts, but gave that fact little weight because in the ultimate Accolade product, only minimal amounts of plaintiff's work were used. Finally, as to the effect on the market, the court found that while Accolade's games might compete with Sega's in the generic sense, they would not "usurp" the market for any particular game. As the Ninth Circuit put it, "there is no basis for assuming that Accolade's 'Ishido' has significantly affected the market for Sega's 'Altered Beast,' since a consumer might easily purchase both."

The Ninth Circuit extended the reasoning of *Accolade* in its subsequent opinion in *Sony Computer Entertainment, Inc. v. Connectix Corp.*[88] Sony manufactured the PlayStation, a video game console that accepted gaming software stored on compact discs (CDs). In addition to its computer hardware, the PlayStation console incorporated software called "Sony BIOS."[89] Connectix sold software titled the "Virtual Game Station" that allowed consumers to load PlayStation games on their personal computers. In order to develop the Virtual Game Station, Connectix reverse engineered the Sony BIOS. Sony responded by asserting charges of copyright infringement.

---

87. 977 F.2d at 1515.

88. 203 F.3d 596 (9th Cir. 2000).

89. BIOS is an acronym for "Basic Input/Output Software."

The Ninth Circuit ultimately rejected Sony's claims under the doctrine of fair use. The reasoning of *Connectix* proceeded along the lines of *Accolade*, but the Ninth Circuit addressed two additional arguments worthy of note here. First, Connectix's engineers copied the Sony BIOS on frequent occasions throughout the process of developing and debugging the Virtual Game Station. Although the Ninth Circuit accepted Sony's assertion that Connectix could have used less efficient techniques to develop the Virtual Game Station— namely, reverse engineering the entire Sony BIOS first before developing the Virtual Game Station—it did not think that this possibility undermined the ability of Connectix to assert fair use. Once an accused infringer established the need for reverse engineering, the Ninth Circuit concluded, the number of times the chosen method was used was not pertinent to the fair use analysis. To hold otherwise might promote inefficiency and require courts to supervise the engineering efforts of software firms in too great a detail, the Ninth Circuit explained.

Second, Sony had asserted—and the district court had agreed— that the Virtual Game Station could not be viewed as transformative because "a computer screen and a television screen are interchangeable." The Court of Appeals saw the matter differently, holding that Connectix had provided a wholly new product that afforded opportunities for game play on a new hardware platform. The conclusion that the Virtual Game Station was "modestly transformative" also drove the Ninth Circuit's analysis of the final fair use factor, the effect of Connectix's use on the potential market for the PlayStation. Because the Virtual Game Station was transformative, the Court of Appeals viewed it as a "legitimate competitor" in the market for Sony game platform market. In the words of the Ninth Circuit, "some economic loss by Sony as a result of this competition [did] not compel a finding of no fair use. Sony understandably seeks control over the market for devices that play games Sony produces or licenses. The copyright law, however, does not confer such a monopoly...."[90]

The opinions in *Accolade* and *Connectix* seem a sensible accommodation to the realities of computer technology. Without reverse engineering competition in software would undoubtedly be stifled. Reverse engineering, in turn, cannot be accomplished without making at least one copy of the work. It seems entirely appropriate to characterize copying for reverse engineering purposes as a fair use to promote competition, and to ensure that computer programmers have the same access to a fund of common ideas as novelists, poets, architects, and choreographers.

90. 203 F.3d at 607.

10.5.1   Fair Use and File Swapping

The fair use privilege took central stage in one of the most notorious and vigorously contested copyright showdowns in recent years, *A & M Records v. Napster*.[91] The well-known *Napster* litigation involved a "peer-to-peer" system that allow users to swap computer files storing audio recordings. These files were encoded in a digital format known as "MP3."[92] The Napster system allowed Internet users to make MP3 files stored on their computer hard drives available to others for download. The Napster software continuously updated links to millions of MP3 files and also facilitated the ready identification, copying, and distribution of those files through what amounted to a massive and easily searched index of music files. Because the Napster software was easy to use and attracted so many users, participants could readily access and copy millions of digitally encoded sound recordings.

Members of the music industry brought suit against Napster, claiming that by offering software that allowed users to exchange pirated music, Napster was liable for contributory and vicarious infringement of copyright. Among Napster's defenses was the fair use privilege. Napster urged that its software, like the VCR at issue in *Sony Corp. of America v. Universal City Studios, Inc.*,[93] was capable of substantial non-infringing uses. Napster cited as examples of such non-infringing uses the exchange of both public domain songs as well as authorized samples of protected works. Napster also explained that its users often downloaded songs they already had purchased on audio CD, thereby "space shifting" (from storage on a CD to storage on a computer hard drive) in an effort to create a compelling analogy to the successful "time shifting" argument in *Sony v. Universal*. According to Napster, space shifting was a legitimate use under the fair use principles established in the *Sony v. Universal* case.

The district court rejected Napster's fair use argument, and on appeal the Court of Appeals for the Ninth Circuit affirmed.[94] In applying the first of the four fair use factors, the purpose and character of the use, the Ninth Circuit concluded that the use was not "transformative" and was sufficiently commercial to weigh in favor of infringement. It said the use could not be considered personal in a situation where host users were distributing their music files to anonymous requesters, rather than friends, and that

---

91. 239 F.3d 1004 (9th Cir.2001).

92. MP3 is a shortened version of the abbreviation "MPEG–1 Audio Layer 3." MPEG is the acronym for the Moving Pictures Experts Group, an industry organization that develops protocols for data compression. The vast majority of the audio files floating around the Internet are in the MP3 compressed format.

93. 464 U.S. 417, 448, 104 S.Ct. 774, 78 L.Ed.2d 574 (1984).

94. A & M Records, Inc. v. Napster, Inc., 239 F.3d 1004 (9th Cir.2001).

Napster users were receiving for free something they would ordinarily have to buy.

Turning to the second fair use factor, the nature of the plaintiffs' works, the court noted that musical compositions and recordings were clearly creative in nature. This holding cut against a conclusion of fair use. As to the third fair use factor, the portion of the copyrighted work used, the court reasoned that Napster users ordinarily copied the entire work. This conclusion also suggested that the fair use privilege did not apply.

The Ninth Circuit agreed with plaintiffs that the fourth fair use factor, the effect of Napster upon the market for the copyrighted works, also weighed against a finding of fair use. The Ninth Circuit upheld the district court's findings that Napster would have a deleterious effect upon the present and future digital download market. The court sustained the finding that Napster led to reduced purchases of CDs by college students and raised barriers to entry into the market for the digital downloading of music.

The court then turned its attention to two particular sorts of uses, sampling and "space-shifting," that Napster claimed were wrongly excluded as fair uses. Napster first claimed that some of its users downloaded MP3 files in order to sample the music before making a purchase. The Court of Appeals rejected the contention that sampling constituted a fair use, however. According to the Ninth Circuit, the more music Napster users sampled, the less likely they were to purchase audio CDs. Napster was also judged to have adverse effects on the nascent digital download market.

The Ninth Circuit also held that the *Sony v. Universal* case did not excuse users from "space-shifting" by downloading MP3 files they already own on audio CD. The court reasoned that the majority of the users of the VCRs at issue in *Sony v. Universal* merely enjoyed the broadcasts at home. VCRs ordinarily did not expose the copyrighted material to individuals outside the home of the device's user. In contrast, the Napster software potentially made music available to millions of other users.

The court therefore had little trouble concluding that the file-sharing activities of Napster users were unlikely to fall within the fair use privilege. The award of an injunction effectively put an end to Napster, which later declared bankruptcy and shut down its site.[95]

---

95. Napster's trademarks were purchased by a firm that reincarnated the site as a legitimate on-line music service which charges for subscriptions and downloads. Napster is now owned by Best Buy. For the full story of the rise and fall of Napster, *see*, JOSEPH MENN, ALL THE RAVE: THE RISE AND FALL OF SHAWN FANNING'S NAPSTER (2003).

The Napster litigation was only the first battle in the war between the music industry and file-sharing software developers. The ink on the *Napster* decision was barely dry before new file-sharing products such as Grokster, KaZaa, and Morpheus Music City appeared on the scene. A chief distinction between Napster and these second generation software programs was that the newer systems do not employ a central server with a directory of all the files on users' computers, permitting the developers to argue that even if the file-swapping of end-users did not constitute fair use, they had no way to either monitor it or stop it. We have explored the courts reactions to these products and these arguments in the preceding chapter dealing with infringement, so we will not repeat ourselves here. The key point to emphasize, as we leave the subject, is that *private file sharing of music and movie files over the Internet is not fair use.* Any other result would essentially eviscerate copyright for those industries and destroy most of the incentives to make new recordings and movies for future enjoyment.

10.5.2   Fair Use and Internet Search Engines

With the expansion of copyrighted information available on the Internet and the development of search engines to sift through this material, the courts have struggled to define the scope of the fair use privilege in this new context. In *Kelly v. Arriba Soft Co.,*[96] professional photographer Leslie Kelly posted his copyrighted images of the American West on his web site and licensed his images for use on third-party web sites. Arriba operated an image search engine that worked much like a standard search engine, but produced small, "thumbnail" image results rather than text. Arriba amassed a large image database by creating a computer program that "crawled" the Internet and visited web sites, downloading full-sized copies of images onto Arriba's server. The program then generated small, low-resolution thumbnail images for the database and deleted the full-sized copy from the Arriba server.

Arriba's crawler visited Kelly's web site as well as several third-party sites containing Kelly's licensed images and copied over thirty-five of Kelly's copyrighted images to the Arriba database. Having never given Arriba permission to copy his images to the database, Kelly sued for copyright infringement. Arriba argued that the use of Kelly's thumbnail images in its database qualified as fair use. The Ninth Circuit turned to the four fair use factors to evaluate the situation.

Under the first factor, the court assessed the commercial purpose and the transformative nature of Kelly's images in Arriba's database. The court recognized that Arriba neither used Kelly's

96.   336 F.3d 811 (9th Cir. 2003).

images to promote its web site nor did Arriba profit by selling Kelly's images. This lack of exploitation caused the commercial nature to weigh only slightly against a fair use finding. The court then deemed Arriba's creation and use of Kelly's thumbnail images transformative. Although Arriba merely replicated Kelly's images into smaller, lower-quality versions of the original images, the Ninth Circuit focused on the new *function* of these images. While Kelly's images served a strictly aesthetic purpose, Arriba utilized the thumbnail images in a larger search engine as a tool to "help index and improve access to images on the Internet and their related web sites." Given that enlarging the images resulted in a significant loss of clarity, the court found it highly unlikely that a user of Arriba's search engine would use the thumbnails for an aesthetic purpose.

The court distinguished Arriba's copying of Kelly's images onto its database from the copying of music onto MP3 databases in cases like *Napster* based on the difference in functions between the original and copied versions. Napster allowed for the conversion of audio recordings into MP3 format as part of a searchable database, but both the original and new version served the same entertainment function. Conversely, Arriba's conversion of Kelly's images into thumbnails only slightly transformed the image itself, but new version functioned as an Internet search tool rather than a piece of artwork. Arriba's crawler program produced an image that did not supersede the purpose of Kelly's images; it transformed the art into a tool to improve access to information on the Internet.

The Ninth Circuit then turned to the nature of the copyrighted work and the substantiality of the portion used. The court balanced the fact that creative works, like photographs, are the core materials that copyright law is meant to protect with the published status of Kelly's images. Because Kelly's images appeared on the Internet prior to Arriba's use of the images in its database, this factor weighed only slightly against fair use. In addition, the fact that Arriba copied Kelly's images as a whole did not weigh against Arriba because the court reasoned that users needed to view the entire image in order to recognize the image.

Finally, the court analyzed the effect on the potential market and the value of the copyrighted work. Kelly's images had several potential markets. Kelly could use the photographs to attract Internet users to his web site, where he could sell advertising space, books, or travel packages to the American West. Another market that Kelly had exploited involved the licensing of his images to other web sites or to stock photo databases for sale of Kelly's images to customers. The court found that Arriba's use of thumbnail images did not harm the market for or value of Kelly's images. By displaying Kelly's thumbnail images on Arriba's results page, users would be guided to Kelly's web site rather than away from it. In order to see or download the full-size image, the user would still be required to visit Kelly's site because the thumbnail images would lose clarity when enlarged. In addition, Arriba did not license its thumbnails to other parties, leaving Kelly's licensing market intact. As a result, the fourth factor favored a fair use argument. When tallying the factors, the court ultimately concluded that Arriba's use of Kelly's thumbnail images in its search engine constituted fair use.

The Ninth Circuit confirmed its analysis in *Arriba* in its subsequent decision in *Perfect 10, Inc. v. Amazon.com, Inc.*[97] Perfect 10 published images of nude models that were accessible, via subscription, on an Internet website. The accused infringer, Google, operated a search engine that automatically accesses numerous web sites and indexes them on a database. When a user makes a search request on the Google website, Google software reviews its database and sends relevant websites to the user's computer. In the course of these operations, Google automatically scanned the images on Perfect 10's website and displayed thumbnail versions of them in response to search queries. The district court concluded that Google violated Perfect 10's display rights but, in contrast to *Kelly*, held that the fair use privilege did not apply. In so doing, the district court distinguished Google from the Arriba search engine on two grounds: (1) Google received financial benefits from the display of Perfect 10's images through its own advertising program; and (2) a growing market existed for the display of thumbnail images of nude models on cellular telephones.[98]

Following an appeal, the Ninth Circuit reversed the district court's holding. The Court of Appeals emphasized the transformative nature of an Internet search engine. "Although an image may have been created originally to serve an entertainment, aesthetic, or informative function, a search engine transforms the image into a pointer directing a user to a source of information." The Ninth Circuit further observed that no evidence of record suggested that even a single Google user had downloaded a thumbnail image onto his cellular telephone. It also found the particular advertising program that Google employed not to be commercially significant. With the remainder of its analysis proceeding along the lines of *Arriba*, the Ninth Circuit concluded that Google's use of Perfect 10's images was fair.

In its decisions in *Arriba* and *Perfect 10*, the Ninth Circuit seemed to imply that if the owner of copyrighted material puts his

---

97.   508 F.3d 1146 (9th Cir. 2007).

98.   416 F.Supp.2d 828 (C.D. Cal. 2006). Quite a convenience for the busy porn afficianado on the go.

work on the Internet, he opens himself up to others viewing and using his images as part of this network of information. One must consider what might have occurred if the court had ruled in favor of Kelly. The wealth of knowledge that is the Internet may have become an unnavigable mess. If search engines could not directly provide copyrighted image results, would they be able to provide links to copyrighted images? How would they describe or identify them? Would search engines be unable to provide copyrighted text results? In addition, one must ask who would be "protected" by the banishment of copyrighted material from search engine databases. In such a world, user "hits" to web sites containing copyrighted material would likely decline significantly, for the sole reason that Internet users would be unable to locate them.

In its *Perfect 10* decision, the Ninth Circuit made a point of noting "the importance of analyzing fair use flexibly in light of new circumstances."[99] The Google Books Library Project demonstrates just how dramatically different our current circumstances are from those of just a few years ago. In 2004, Google announced a "modest" goal: to copy tens of millions of books onto an electronic database and allow users to search for them online. Google partnered with several major research libraries, invested millions of dollars, and commenced what will likely become several decades of scanning. The Library Project is intended to make the world's knowledge readily searchable through an easy to use, accessible database. Rather than allowing the wholesale viewing of all the books in its database, the Google Book search engine issues its results in the form of "snippets." Snippets consist of small, relevant excerpts from various books containing the user's search term. While viewers can access the full text of public domain books containing the search term, only snippets of copyrighted works are viewable. Google then provides links to locations where users can purchase or borrow the relevant books.

The Library Project met with outrage from many copyright holders. In response, Google established an "opt out" procedure through which copyright holders could request that their books be excluded from the database. The dissatisfaction of many rights holders with this proposal was evidence by a September 20, 2005, class action copyright infringement lawsuit by the Authors Guild and several individual authors. Because Google is scanning the full text of books into its database, its activities are unequivocally infringing. Google's supporters nonetheless believe that the Library Project is protected by the fair use defense, in large part based upon the analysis in *Arriba* and *Perfect 10*.

99. 508 F.3d at 1166.

In a nutshell, although the Library Project is commercial in nature, Google could assert it is highly transformative. While the purpose of the copied book might have been entertainment or education, Google's database provides users with information, much like a traditional card catalogue. No copyright holder should fear that his potential purchasers are curling up by the fire with a laptop to read some snippets containing the phrase "high speed chase" instead of his latest thriller. As to the third fair use factor, "the amount and substantiality of the portion used in relation to the copyrighted work as a whole," Google can rely upon the reasoning in the two Ninth Circuit opinions. Just as it is necessary to copy entire images to create a search database and thumbnail results, so too must Google copy entire books to create the Google Book search database and the snippet results. Google can nonetheless plausibly assert that the heart of the work is reserved to the copyright holder. Whereas the search engines in *Arriba* and *Perfect 10* displayed a lower-quality image, Google's results show only a little piece of the copyrighted books, offering the searcher a snippet just large enough to ascertain the relevancy of the sources.

Finally, under a market harm assessment, Google can claim that it may actually enlarge the market for searchable books. The Library Project may increase the public's exposure to books that it may never have learned about otherwise, especially for out-of-print books and unknown authors. The search results Google supplies come with links that users can follow to purchase the books. Overall, electronic snippets are not likely to serve as a market substitute for reading an entire book. Derivative markets for such snippets are probably not consequential because publishers would be unlikely to license such small pieces of books.

The copyright holders may avail themselves of several counter-arguments. Under the second fair use factor, the "nature of the work," they could point out that few rights holders had previously made their books available online, unlike the copyright owners of the pictures at issue in *Arriba* or *Perfect 10*. In addition, Google scans both fiction and non-fiction books. As well, the plaintiffs could simply assert *Arriba* and *Perfect 10* were wrongly decided. As these two decisions originated in the Ninth Circuit, they are not controlling authority in the Second Circuit, where the Google litigation is based. The plaintiffs could further emphasize that the Library Project involves an unprecedented amount of copying of analog works. As a result, although Google seems to be in a position to mount robust arguments in favor of its fair use position, the outcome is by no means certain.

These competing positions may never be the subject of formal judicial resolution. The parties reached an initial settlement on October 28, 2008, that has since been amended. As of the time this book goes to press, the settlement continues to await judicial approval—a necessity because the litigation was fashioned as a class action. In its current form, the settlement would establish a Book Rights Registry to distribute payments from Google to copyright owners. Google will make an initial payment of at least $45 million to the Registry for books already scanned and would provide additional payments in the future. As of now, the settlement establishes various categories for books that dictate their treatment on Google Books. In particular, for certain books, Google would be able to display the entire work rather than merely a snippet. The final wording of the settlement agreement—and indeed, whether a settlement may be achieved at all—remain to be seen.[100]

Unsurprisingly, Google has received both praise and criticism for granting unprecedented access to information—including works of authorship under another's copyright. While the potential benefit to researchers and the public is enormous, concerns have been expressed about investing this degree of control over access to knowledge in the hands of a single commercial entity. Some observers believe that judicial assessment of the fair use arguments presents a superior alternative to settlement and have criticized Google for "abandoning" its fair use position. Although the outcome of this litigation remains to be seen, it is apparent that the world of books is on the cusp of entering the digital era, and that copyright's fair use doctrine will play a significant role in that transition.

§ 10.6   Fair Use and Parody

Parody has been defined as a "literary or artistic work that imitates the characteristic style of an author or a work for comic effect or ridicule."[101] In other words it might be a spoof of a poem to show how pretentious the author's word choice has been, or a caricature of a painting that mocks the political or aesthetic agenda of the painter. Courts have struggled for decades with the place of parody under the fair use doctrine. At least two aspects of parody have made it especially troubling. First, a parodist must necessarily borrow considerable amounts from the work being mocked. Without such extensive borrowing, the target of the parody will be obscure and the humor will be lost. Of course extensive borrowing has usually resulted in a denial of the fair use defense. Second, because parody is critical of the original work, the author of the underlying work is highly unlikely to grant permission to the

100. *See* Jonathan Band, *The Long and Winding Road to the Google Books Settlement*, 9 J. MARSHALL REV. INTELL. PROP. L. 227 (2010).

101. Campbell, 510 U.S. at 580.

parodist, and is likely to litigate with vigor when the parody appears on the market.

Prior to the Supreme Court's decision in *Campbell v. Acuff–Rose Music, Inc.*[102] the lower courts decided a number of parody cases but few consistent themes emerged from those decisions. Some courts manifested considerable hostility to parody. For instance the Ninth Circuit found that an underground comic book mocking Mickey Mouse by depicting him as a sexually promiscuous drug smuggler did not qualify for the fair use defense.[103] Other courts, however, were more charitable, as when the Second Circuit found that a television parody of the New York advertising jingle "I Love New York" on the *Saturday Night Live* television show, using the lyrics "I Love Sodom," was fair use.[104]

Campbell was the Supreme Court's first opportunity to clarify the fair use status of parody.[105] At the outset, Justice Souter's opinion makes it clear that parody can qualify for the fair use defense. It is not automatically beyond the pale. On the other hand, just like other forms of comment and criticism, parody is not automatically immunized from infringement liability. The Court explicitly rejected defendant's argument that any parodic use should be considered presumptively fair. Rather, courts must still consider all of the statutory factors and resolve "close questions of judgement" to determine if the fair use defense is appropriate under the facts of the case. The opinion is especially illuminating because each of those factors takes on slightly different characteristics when applied in a parody case.

Under the first fair use factor, the nature and character of the use, parodies pose something of a paradox. On the one hand, they are almost always "transformative" because the parody is a new and different work which builds upon, but alters the original. This normally cuts in favor of the defense. On the other hand, parodies are usually "commercial." In *Campbell* the defendant 2 Live Crew included its parody song on a publicly marketed CD, inserting it between the tracks *Me So Horny* and *My Seven Bizzos*, presumably with the goal of making money. A commercial purpose of this sort typically cuts against fair use. As noted in section 10.2.1 above, the

---

102. 510 U.S. 569, 114 S.Ct. 1164, 127 L.Ed.2d 500 (1994).

103. Walt Disney Productions v. Air Pirates, 581 F.2d 751 (9th Cir.1978), *cert. denied*, 439 U.S. 1132, 99 S.Ct. 1054, 59 L.Ed.2d 94 (1979).

104. Elsmere Music, Inc. v. National Broadcasting Co., 623 F.2d 252 (2d Cir.1980).

105. In the 1950's, the Supreme Court granted certiorari on a parody

case involving a television skit by the comedian Jack Benny spoofing the movie *Gaslight*. However, only eight justices participated in the decision of the case, and the Court found itself equally divided, four to four. It issued no opinion. See Benny v. Loew's Inc., 239 F.2d 532 (9th Cir.1956), *aff'd by an equally divided court sub nom.* Columbia Broadcasting System, Inc. v. Loew's Inc., 356 U.S. 43, 78 S.Ct. 667, 2 L.Ed.2d 583 (1958).

Campbell Court took pains to stress that there is no hard and fast presumption against fair use for commercial works. The opinion seems to suggest that particularly in cases of parody, the more transformative the defendant's work, the less significant will be its commercial nature.

In order to benefit from this somewhat more generous pro-defendant analysis, however, the defendant's work must truly be a parody. A true parody targets and criticizes the original work, not society at large. If one wanted to borrow the words or music of *Oh Pretty Woman* to write a song critical of Hillary Clinton, such a work would not be a parody, because the target of the criticism is not the original musical composition or composer but something external to the work. One can satirize Secretary Clinton by writing new lyrics to virtually any song under the sun. There is no particular reason to borrow *Oh Pretty Woman*.[106] Of course, if one's goal is to criticize *Oh Pretty Woman* itself, the need to use the melody or some of the lyrics of the original work is much more compelling. Moreover, it is in cases of true parody that the original author is least likely to grant a license and thus where the availability of the fair use defense is most important if such works are ever to see the light of day.

Applying this standard to the case before it, the *Campbell* Court held that the 2 Live Crew Song "reasonably could be perceived as commenting on the original or criticizing it to some degree." It found that the words of defendant's song could "be taken as a comment on the naivete of the original of an earlier day, as a rejection of its sentiment that ignores the ugliness of street life and the debasement that it signifies." This is perhaps a generous interpretation of a song whose words included "Big hairy woman you need to shave that stuff/ Big hairy woman, you know I bet it's tough/ Big hairy woman all that hair ain't legit/ Cause you look like Cousin It/ Big hairy woman." Nonetheless, it illustrates the central fact that in order to receive the more favorable consideration under the fair use defense reflected in *Campbell* the work must be a true parody that targets the original.

The importance of this threshold inquiry into whether the work is a true parody is illustrated by two cases decided shortly after the *Campbell* decision. In *Dr. Seuss Enterprises. v. Penguin Books U.S.A., Inc.*,[107] defendant authored a short illustrated book entitled *The Cat NOT In The Hat*. The book recounted the events

---

106. "If . . . the commentary has no critical bearing on the substance or style of the original composition, which the alleged infringer merely uses to get attention or to avoid the drudgery in working up something fresh, the claim to fairness in borrowing from another's work diminishes accordingly (if it does not vanish), and other factors, like the extent of its commerciality loom larger." *Campbell*, 510 U.S. at 580.

107. 109 F.3d 1394 (9th Cir.1997).

of the celebrated O.J. Simpson murder trial in the poetry style of Dr. Seuss, the famous author of children's books, and contained illustrations paralleling those that appear in various Seuss books but consisting of such things as a caricature of Mr. Simpson holding a bloody glove. The court refused to analyze defendant's work under the more generous fair use standards set out in *Campbell* because it concluded that the book was not a genuine parody. In its view, the book did not target the works of Dr. Seuss, but was primarily a satire on the various events surrounding the Simpson affair. Viewing the work as a non-parody, the court found its commercial status to weigh heavily against fair use, and ultimately held the work to be infringing.

By way of contrast is *Leibovitz v. Paramount Pictures.*[108] Annie Leibovitz, the celebrated portrait photographer, had taken several pictures of the actress Demi Moore when Moore was eight months pregnant. One of those photographs, of Moore nude but concealing her private parts with her hands, appeared on the cover of Vanity Fair magazine and, not surprisingly, stirred considerable public comment. About two years later, Paramount, as part of its publicity for the movie *Naked Gun 33 1/3*, prepared an advertisement that superimposed the smirking, guilty face of actor Leslie Nielson—the star of the movie—over the body of a very pregnant woman posed identically to Ms. Moore in the Leibovitz photo. This hybrid photo ran over the caption "Due in March," a reference to the upcoming movie's release date but, of course, also a pun suggesting that Mr. Nielson would give birth in that month.

The court found Paramount's work to be a true parody: "The Nielsen ad clearly takes satiric aim directly at the Moore photograph. From the outset, it was intended to make a mockery of an image that had become 'a cultural icon.' ... In fact, without reference to the Moore photograph, the Nielsen ad simply is not very funny. Like all parodies, it relies for its comic effect on the contrast between the original—a serious portrayal of a beautiful woman taking great pride in the majesty of her pregnant body— and the new work—a ridiculous image of a smirking, foolish-looking pregnant man." Having found the work to be a genuine parody, the court went on to exonerate the defendant under the fair use defense despite the commercial purpose of defendant's use of the material.

Turning to the second fair use factor, the "nature of the copyrighted work," *Campbell* reveals that it will usually be of minimal importance in parody cases. Most parodies target creative or fictional works. There are very few parodies of almanacs or statistical tables. While the fact that plaintiff's work is fictional and

108. 948 F.Supp. 1214 (S.D.N.Y. 1996).

creative usually cuts against the fair use defense this is not so in parody cases. As Justice Souter explained, the fact that plaintiff's work was creative "is not ... ever likely to help much in separating the fair use sheep from the infringing goats in a parody case, since parodies almost invariably copy publicly known, expressive works." The rationale for the diminished importance of this factor seems persuasive. Normally, we allow a broader scope of fair use for factual works because of the need of subsequent authors to use those facts. We are more reluctant to allow borrowing where the work is fictional and expressive because the need to borrow is less pressing. A parodist, however, must borrow from the fictional or expressive works he targets just as surely as a historian must borrow the facts of prior books in his field of research.

The third factor, the "amount and substantiality of the portion used in relation to the copyrighted work as a whole" also takes on a slightly different complexion in parody cases. This is because, as *Campbell* notes, "parody's humor, or in any event its comment, necessarily springs from recognizable allusion to its object through distorted imitation." In other words, the parodist must borrow sufficiently from the underlying work that the public can identify what is being parodied. This often will require not only borrowing a relatively large quantity of material from the original, but may also often require using those portions that are qualitatively most significant—what is sometimes called the "heart" of the work. A music parodist may use the most recognizable few bars of the song being ridiculed, just as a comic spoof of a movie will likely target the most famous or memorable scene. In light of these considerations courts usually permit a parodist to take at least sufficient material so as to be able to "conjure up" the original. The parodist may be entitled to take even more if it builds upon the original and contributes something new for humorous effect or commentary.[109]

Unfortunately, *Campbell* did not attempt to lay down any further guidelines about the scope of permissible borrowing in parody cases. In fact, the Court did not even resolve the issue in the case before it, but remanded for further findings on whether 2 Live Crew's repetitive use of the bass riff in the original song was excessive. Much of the concern about the extent of material taken by the parodist revolves around the scope and nature of the effect of the parody on the market for the original, the fourth factor in fair use analysis.

The Eleventh Circuit grappled with the interplay of the third and fourth factors in *SunTrust Bank v. Houghton Mifflin Co.*[110] As

---

109. Tin Pan Apple v. Miller Brewing Co., Inc., 737 F.Supp. 826, 830 (S.D.N.Y.1990).

110. 268 F.3d 1257 (11th Cir. 2001).

the copyright owner of the famed novel, *Gone With the Wind*, Suntrust Bank sought to enjoin defendant from publishing her novel, *The Wind Done Gone*. *The Wind Done Gone* featured the same characters, settings, and plot as the original novel, lifting entire sections in "wholesale fashion." The first half of defendant's book copied the storyline of *Gone With the Wind*, but the new work distinguished itself from the original by telling the story from the perspective of a black slave. *The Wind Done Gone* inverted the attributes of the black and white characters in the original work to create a "specific criticism" of the depiction of slavery in *Gone With the Wind*. The Eleventh Circuit found this alteration transformative in character and deemed the novel a parody.

The court then turned to the question of how much of the original, copyrighted material a parody may use to criticize the original without infringing on the copyright. Looking back to *Campbell*, the court noted that using more than the bare minimum amount of copyrighted material required to conjure up the original work for critique did not automatically denote infringement. Rather, the court analyzed the third factor by asking to what extent the extraneous material in the parody negatively affected the potential market of the original copyright by causing the parody to act as a market substitute for the original. While Suntrust provided ample support for the value of *Gone With the Wind*—its worldwide sales were second only to the Bible—plaintiff proffered little evidence that *The Wind Done Gone* would substantially harm *Gone With the Wind*'s potential or original market. Consequently, the Eleventh Circuit held that in conjunction with a lack of any significant effect on market value, using a substantial portion of the original work in a parody still entitled the defendant to a fair use defense.

It is at the level of the final factor that the parodist finds his greatest protection. This may seem ironic. After all, parody will, quite often, depress the market for the original work. Those who come into contact with the parody first may conclude that the original work is banal, pretentious, or otherwise not worth their time and money. This effect, however, is not the market effect that the statute forbids. As *Campbell* notes, "when a lethal parody, like a scathing theater review, kills demand for the original, it does not produce a harm cognizable under the Copyright Act."

The only market harm that is cognizable under fair use analysis is the tendency of defendant's work to substitute for plaintiff's work, or various derivative works that plaintiff might subsequently put on the market. A movie based on a novel will both substitute for the novel in the eyes of some patrons, who now dispense with reading the book because they've seen the movie, and will also make it difficult if not impossible for the copyright owner to prepare an authorized movie version of the book. Parody, as Justice

Souter points out in his opinion, rarely has this market substitution effect, because "the parody and the original usually serve different market functions." For instance, a not inconsiderable number of parodies might be considered vulgar or far too sexually explicit by fans of the original work. Consumers who want to enjoy the original version of *Oh Pretty Woman* will not find the 2 Live Crew version to be much of a proxy. Reading *The Wind Done Gone* will not sate the reader's appetite for the antebellum niceties of *Gone With the Wind.*

One might think that there is a market effect flowing from unauthorized parody distinct from the critical disparagement associated with that genre. If parody is protected under the fair use doctrine the owner of the copyright in the original will not be able to obtain any revenue by licensing parodies. That particular derivative market will be foreclosed because no rational parodist will pay to prepare a work the law says that he may prepare for free. However, the *Campbell* court also refused to recognize this type of lost revenue as a remediable harm under copyright law. "The market for potential derivative uses includes only those that creators of original works would in general develop or license others to develop. Yet the unlikelihood that creators of imaginative works will license critical reviews or lampoons of their own productions removes such uses from the very notion of a potential licensing market." The *Campbell* Court distinguished the derivative market for parodies from the derivative market for a legitimate rap version of *Oh Pretty Woman* and instructed the court of appeals to limit its consideration only to the question of whether the 2 Live Crew version might hurt this latter market on remand.

While *Campbell* did much to clarify the nature of the fair use inquiry in parody cases, the future resolution of such cases will hardly be automatic. Questions of characterization and balancing still abound. Courts must determine whether the defendant's work targets the plaintiff's original or merely uses that original to ridicule society at large. They must determine if the defendant took only as much as was necessary to make an effective parody, but no more. They must sort out the effect the parody may have on legitimate derivative markets from its tendency to depress sales of the original by virtue of its critical message. Where these factors point in opposing directions, courts must attempt a balance.

It would seem to be the lesson of *Campbell* that in close cases this balance should be resolved in favor of the parodist. Parodists typically target works that are already famous and well known in popular culture—*Oh Pretty Woman, The Cat in the Hat,* Leibovitz's picture of Demi Moore, and *Gone With the Wind.* These works will already have earned their authors considerable reward. Future authors will hardly hesitate to create new works by reasoning "my work may become fabulously famous, earn me a great deal of money, then become subject to a parody, which will somewhat reduce my ultimate return, so never mind!" Given that parody tends to target only successful works, and tends not to pose any real threat of usurping the market for the original, courts ought to treat parodies generously in the post-*Campbell* world.

§ 10.7 Fair Use and the First Amendment

At first blush one might assume that the copyright laws and the First Amendment guarantee of free speech work at cross-purposes. After all, copyright legally proscribes the use of a wide variety of expression, where those expressions are deemed to be the legal property of another. If we produce a movie, the plot details of which closely resemble an earlier cinematic classic such as *Legally Blonde* or *Indiana Jones and the Kingdom of the Crystal Skull*, there is a good chance that we will be enjoined from distributing it. If we want to write a political essay criticizing the president's handling of foreign affairs using substantially the same words as a previous columnist, again, there is a good chance we will be enjoined.

Nonetheless, historically there has been a broad consensus, among both courts and commentators, that enforcement of copyright laws does not conflict with the First Amendment. This is because, as the Supreme Court pointed out in its decision in *Eldred v. Ashcroft*,[111] First Amendment values are already built in to the structure of the copyright act.

Two aspects of copyright doctrine in particular are usually cited as eliminating any risk of interference with free speech concerns. The first of these is the idea/expression distinction, discussed in some depth earlier in this volume. Since copyright only protects the expression of an author—his or her words, notes, lines, or images—others are free to use the underlying ideas of the work. It is not a violation of the copyright in *Legally Blonde* for us to make a movie about a blonde sorority member who goes to law school, or even a movie about a blonde woman law student who defies expectations and achieves great academic success despite the initial hostility of her classmates. The idea/expression dichotomy guarantees that any imposition on our ability to express ourselves will be relatively minimal, and thus there should be few First Amendment implications from enforcement of the copyright law prohibition against copying protected expression.

The second copyright doctrine that accommodates free speech and copyright is, of course, the fair use defense. Under the fair use

---

111. 537 U.S. 186, 123 S.Ct. 769, 154 L.Ed.2d 683 (2003). The case is dis-   cussed in depth in Chapter 8 of this work.

doctrine, activities that would otherwise be infringing because they appropriate an impermissible amount of the expression of a copyrighted work can be excused if they advance a socially beneficial purpose. Given the flexibility of fair use, courts can invoke the doctrine whenever there is any danger that copyright enforcement might be inconsistent with free speech principles. Interestingly, the Supreme Court has even cautioned that the fair use defense not be stretched too far in a desire to promote First Amendment values. Because "freedom of thought and expression 'includes both the right to speak freely and the right to refrain from speaking at all,' "[112] carte blanche permission to copy another's expression may actually interfere with the rights of the original author.

In addition to flexibility afforded by the idea/expression and fair use doctrines, courts often point out that rather than stifling expression, copyright actually furthers First Amendment values because of its tendency to encourage the creation of expressive works. As the Fifth Circuit has put it, "the judgment of the Constitution is that free expression is enriched by protecting the creations of authors from exploitation by others, and the Copyright Act is the congressional implementation of that judgment."[113] If the First Amendment is seen not merely as a guarantee to each individual to say whatever he pleases but as a provision designed to advance the goal of robust debate in society, it seems plain that the protections of copyright and the incentives they create for authors fit hand and glove with the First Amendment.

In recent years, however, as Congress and the courts have responded to new digital technologies by giving copyright owners more and more rights and by narrowing the scope of the fair use defense, several academic writers have asserted that explicit First Amendment limitations upon copyright should be established.[114] In a world with shrinking fair use prerogatives the courts will have to begin to grapple with more and more claims predicated directly on constitutional grounds.

§ 10.8 Fair Use and International Standards

The United States is far from the only jurisdiction that establishes certain limitations upon the exclusive rights awarded to copyright proprietors. However, the flexible and open-ended fair use defense has counterparts in only a few other nations. Section

---

112. Harper & Row Publishers, Inc. v. Nation Enter., 471 U.S. 539, 559, 105 S.Ct. 2218, 85 L.Ed.2d 588 (1985) (quoting Wooley v. Maynard, 430 U.S. 705, 714, 97 S.Ct. 1428, 51 L.Ed.2d 752 (1977)).

113. Dallas Cowboys Cheerleaders, Inc. v. Scoreboard Posters, Inc., 600 F.2d 1184 (5th Cir.1979).

114. *See* Neil Weinstock Netanel, *Locating Copyright Within the First Amendment Skein*, 54 STAN. L. REV. 1 (2001).

107 of the U.S. Copyright Act should be contrasted with the far more specific user privileges found in the author's rights statutes in many jurisdictions that follow the civil law tradition. For example, the legislation of many civil law nations establishes detailed, enumerated exceptions with regard to the use of a work for education, news reporting, quotation, research, and private noncommercial purposes.[115] Perhaps more tellingly, even other common-law countries tend to provide for more cabined user privileges than the U.S. fair use doctrine. For example, the "fair dealing" principle followed in Canada and the United Kingdom is widely acknowledged to be a more restrained concept than its U.S. analogue.[116] In functional terms, the U.S. fair use privilege exhibits a degree of versatility and breadth that comparable doctrines in most other jurisdictions do not.

The distinction between the law of the United States and the great majority of its trading partners may prove to be of more than scholarly interest. As we discusses in greater detail in Chapter 12, U.S. membership in the World Trade Organization (WTO) compels its compliance with the Agreement on Trade–Related Aspects of Intellectual Property Rights, known conventionally as the TRIPS Agreement.[117] The TRIPS Agreement in part sets forth minimum standards of intellectual property protection. With respect to copyright, the TRIPS Agreement requires WTO members to comply with the substantive obligations of an earlier international agreement, the Berne Convention. These obligations include rights of reproduction, adaptation, translation, and public performance.[118]

The TRIPS Agreement further allows for WTO member states to enact certain "limitations or exceptions" to these exclusive rights. Yet the permissible extent of derogation is arguably far less expansive than the U.S. fair privilege. In particular, Article 13 of the TRIPS Agreement stipulates that:

> Members shall confine limitations or exceptions to exclusive rights to certain special cases which do not conflict with a normal exploitation of the work and do not unreasonably prejudice the legitimate interests of the author.[119]

115. *See* Holger Postel, *The Fair Use Doctrine in the U.S. American Copyright Act and Similar Regulations in the German Law*, 5 CHI.-KENT J. INTELL. PROP. 142 (2006).

116. *See* Barry Sookman & Dan Glover, *Why Canada Should Not Adopt Fair Use: A Joint Submission to the Copyright Consultations*, 22 I.P.J. 29 (Dec. 2009).

117. Agreement on Trade–Related Aspects of Intellectual Property Rights, Apr. 15, 1994, Marrekesh Agreement Establishing the World Trade Organization, 33 I.L.M. 1197.

118. Berne Convention, Articles 8, 9, 11, 12.

119. The text of Article 13 of TRIPS is based upon Article 9(2) of the Berne Convention.

At least a colorable argument can be made that the U.S. fair privilege fails to comply with Article 13 of the TRIPS Agreement. In particular, the fair use may not be seen as sufficiently "certain." As the House Report accompanying the 1976 Act observes, fair use is a doctrine with "no real definition." Section 107 merely sets forth "a set of criteria, which though in no case definitive or determinative, provides some gauge for balancing the equities."[120] As well, fair use is not limited to "special cases," as it potentially applies to any use of any work of authorship.[121]

Although the shortcomings of the U.S. fair use privilege with respect to the TRIPS Agreement have led to considerable scholarly commentary, they have not yet resulted in a challenge before the WTO. Should such a challenge occur, the United States—for many years a proponent of heightened levels of copyright enforcement around the world—might not find itself in an enviable position. Still, other commentators have asserted that Article 13 of the TRIPS Agreement and the fair use doctrine share common goals and that fair use jurisprudence is more predictable than is commonly supposed.[122] As a result, although fair use qualifies as one of the core principles of U.S. copyright, its status under the emerging international law of copyright is less certain.

120. H.R. Rep. No. 94–1476 at 65 (1976).

121. *See* Ruth Okediji, *Toward an International Fair Use Doctrine*, 39 Co-LUM. J. TRANSNAT'L L. 75 (2000).

122. *See* Pamela Samuelson, *Unbundling Fair Uses*, 77 FORDHAM L. REV. 2537 (2009).

Chapter 11

STATE REMEDIES ANALOGOUS TO COPYRIGHT AND FEDERAL PREEMPTION

Table of Sections

§ 11.1 Compensation for the Use of Ideas

It is a basic premise of copyright law that ideas themselves, as distinguished from the way in which they may be expressed, are not subject to legal protection. We are all free to copy the ideas of others without paying for them and without fear of any legal liability. This is true for both commercial and literary ideas. If someone opens a restaurant with all the servers on roller skates and it proves to be a big smash hit, you too can open a restaurant with all the servers on roller skates. If someone hits on the idea of equipping hotel rooms with business equipment like fax machines and copiers, you too may put fax machines and copiers in the rooms of your hotel. If someone writes a novel about a secret society devoted to toppling the Catholic Church, you can write your own novel on the same theme. Absent a patent, ideas are generally common property and in many respects the copying of ideas is the lifeblood of competition.[1] If the rule were otherwise the first hotel with in-room fax machine would have a monopoly on that amenity.

There are, however situations where you may incur an obligation to pay for the use of someone else's ideas. If someone approaches you with the representation that they have an idea that will enhance your business, and you *agree* to pay them *to induce them to disclose* that idea, it seems morally appropriate to hold you to your bargain and the law will often do just that. Even if you don't explicitly promise to pay for the idea, the circumstances may indicate that you intended for payment to take place, or that your use of the idea without compensation would amount to unjust enrichment.

Whether payment is required in such a situation is a matter of state law. That of course requires us to note two cautions before getting into details. First, the precise rules concerning who must pay for an idea and what types of ideas are protectable vary from state to state. Second, these rules are subject to possible federal preemption if they conflict with the principles embodied in federal laws such as the copyright act. We will be considering federal preemption in some detail later in this chapter.[2]

While disputes over the obligation to pay for ideas can arise in a wide variety of contexts, certain fact patterns recur. Among the more common situations are cases involving individuals who submit plot ideas for entertainment programs, such as television shows or movies, to producers or entertainment companies. In these cases, although the ideas are nominally rejected, the producer soon comes out with a program bearing a strong similarity to the plaintiff's idea. Another common scenario involves persons who submit unsolicited marketing or product improvement ideas to consumer goods companies. Again, the idea is nominally rejected, but a few months later, the manufacturer might begin selling a product or using an advertising campaign resembling the one suggested by the plaintiff.

---

1. "The general rule of law is that the noblest of human productions—knowledge, truth ascertained, conceptions and ideas—become, after voluntary communication to others, free as the air to common use." International News Service v. Associated Press, 248 U.S. 215, 39 S.Ct. 68, 63 L.Ed. 211 (1918) (Brandeis, J. dissenting). *See also* Desny v. Wilder, 46 Cal.2d 715, 731, 299 P.2d 257 (1956).

2. *See infra* §§ 11.4, 11.5.

In some of these cases the plaintiff-idea-submitter may have signed a form contract, often with language absolving the recipient of any duty to pay for the idea at all

Note that in virtually all cases of this sort, the parties have had some direct contact with each other, either in person or through the mails. In other words, the plaintiff does not claim a general property right in the idea that would entitle him to compensation from a complete stranger. The idea submission cases do not rest upon a claim against the whole world, but rather focus on a course of dealings between the person who generated the idea and the one person he shared it with.

Over the years courts have used many different theories to justify requiring payment for an idea. Some decisions rely on contract theories, predicating the duty to compensate on either an express or implied agreement to pay. Some older decisions purport to rest on a theft of property or misappropriation notion. Still others purport to find a relationship of trust and confidence between the idea submitter and the idea recipient, and justify a duty to pay based on a breach of this relationship.[3] The elements that a plaintiff must prove vary with the theory invoked. Unfortunately plaintiffs often assert multiple claims in the same case and not all courts are equally adept at articulating the basis for their decisions. Some garble the elements or use terminology loosely. The result is that the idea-submission cases often appear either formulaic, tedious or incoherent—and sometimes all three at once! Fortunately for twenty-first century lawyers and law students, the bulk of the contemporary cases are usually resolved on contract theories.[4]

Generally speaking, a plaintiff must establish three key facts in cases of this sort. First he must show that the idea in question was "novel." Second there must be some indication that the idea as proffered to the defendant was "definite and concrete." Finally plaintiff must prove that he disclosed the idea in circumstances in which compensation is appropriate.[5] The first two of these elements relate to the nature of the idea itself, while the last of them focuses on the nature of the relationship between the parties and their course of dealing. Stated negatively, these elements mean that the law will not mandate payment for well-known or trite ideas, vague or nebulous concepts, or ideas lacking in commercial value. It also

3. This is essentially a tort claim in the nature of constructive fraud.

4. For a full explanation of the history of the various theories and how they differ, see Nimmer, Chapter 19D.

5. Hamilton National Bank v. Belt, 210 F.2d 706 (D.C. Cir. 1953). *See generally*, Arthur Miller, *Common Law Protection for Products of the Mind: An "Idea" Whose Time Has Come*, 119 HARV. L. REV. 705, 719 (2006) ("for nearly a century now, concreteness and novelty have insinuated themselves as threshold requirements for an idea claim.").

means that there will be no obligation to pay for the idea unless there was an advance agreement to do so, or at least circumstances where denying the plaintiff payment would be unjust. Even if all these elements are met, the defendant can escape liability by showing that he independently developed the idea and therefore did not "take" it from the plaintiff.

11.1.1 The Novelty Requirement

It is commonly said that only novel ideas will be protected under state law. Unfortunately, the various idea submission cases have attached different meanings to the simple term "novel." In cases where the plaintiff claims relief based upon an express contract most courts interpret the requirement to mean that the plaintiff must show only that the idea was new to that particular defendant, even if others in the same industry were already familiar with the idea.[6] On the other hand, where no express contract exists, some courts have set the bar higher and demanded proof that the idea was not within the public domain at the time it was disclosed in order to fulfill the novelty requirement. This more demanding standard of "general novelty" as opposed to mere "novelty-to-the-buyer" resembles the patent law's novelty requirement.[7]

The decision of the Court of Appeals for the Second Circuit in *Nadel v. Play–By–Play Toys & Novelties, Inc.*,[8] explores this distinction. Nadel was an independent inventor who developed a new table-top monkey toy that incorporated a mechanism that allowed it to spin when set on a flat surface. Nadel alleged that pursuant to toy industry custom treating the submission of an idea as confidential, he demonstrated his toy to a representative of Play–By–Play. According to Nadel, Play–By–Play later marketed a Tazmanian Devil toy ("Tornado Taz") that utilized his disclosed idea.

Nadel subsequently brought suit against Play–By–Play for use of his idea. The district court granted summary judgment in favor of Play–By–Play. On appeal, the Second Circuit reversed. The Second Circuit ruled that under New York law, there was no requirement of "general" novelty in all cases involving the disclosure of ideas. As it explained, "the longstanding requirement that an idea have originality or general novelty in order to support a *misappropriation* claim does not apply to contract claims.... For

---

6. *See, e.g.* Johnson v. Benjamin Moore & Co., 347 N.J.Super. 71, 788 A.2d 906, 919 (App.Div.2002); Nadel v. Play-by-Play Toys & Novelties, Inc., 208 F.3d 368, 375 (2d Cir. 2000) (applying New York Law); Apfel v. Prudential–Bache Securities, Inc., 81 N.Y.2d 470, 600 N.Y.S.2d 433, 616 N.E.2d 1095 (1993).

7. 35 U.S.C. § 102.

8. 208 F.3d 368 (2d Cir. 2000). The opinion was written by then Circuit Judge, now Justice Sotomayor.

contract-based claims in submission-of-idea cases, a showing of novelty to the buyer will supply sufficient consideration to support a contract."[9] In other words, in New York, a plaintiff relying on a *misappropriation* theory must show that the submitted idea presented an inventive concept outside the public domain—something new to the industry at large. In contrast, for *contract-based* claims, the requirement that an idea have novelty mandates only that the plaintiff prove the idea was novel vis-a-vis that particular defendant.

The Second Circuit justified this distinction by reasoning that "a misappropriation claim can only arise from the taking of an idea that is original or novel in absolute terms, because the law of property does not protect against the misappropriation or theft of that which is free and available to all. . . . 'Since . . . non-novel ideas are not protectible as property, they cannot be stolen.'."[10] Reflecting on this a moment, it effectively means that the "misappropriation of property" theory in an idea-submission case is only plausible where the plaintiff's idea is, for all intents and purposes, a secret, because only then would there be general novelty. Thus, claims of misappropriation of "property" in an idea are close cousins of cases alleging theft of trade secrets.[11] For contract-based claims, however, the *Nadel* court felt the "novelty to the buyer" standard was more appropriate, because a particular buyer might be unaware of a previously known idea and be willing to enter into a contract to acquire and exploit it in order to save time in scouring the public domain in order to find it.[12]

The court further specified that, as a matter of law, some ideas are so commonplace that the defendant is deemed to have knowledge of the idea. In such cases, neither a property-based nor a contract-based claim for uncompensated use of an idea would succeed. A wonderful example of this principle in action is *Soule v. Bon Ami Co.*[13] In that case, the plaintiff approached the defendant company and told them that he had an idea which would increase their profits, and offered to disclose it for one half of any profit increase realized. Plaintiff then disclosed his idea, which was that

---

9.   208 F.3d at 376, interpreting Apfel v. Prudential–Bache Securities, Inc, 81 N.Y.2d 470, 600 N.Y.S.2d 433, 616 N.E.2d 1095 (1993). The *Nadel* court used the terms "general novelty" and "originality" interchangeably. This is unfortunate, at least to students of copyright law, because originality in the copyright sense does not require "general novelty" at all.

10.   208 F.3d at 378. citing Murray v. National Broadcasting Co., Inc., 844 F.2d 988 (2d Cir. 1988).

11.   For an illuminating—dare we say brilliant—discussion of trade secrets, *see generally*, ROGER SCHECHTER & JOHN THOMAS, PRINCIPLES OF PATENT LAW § 13.1 (2004).

12.   208 F.3d at 377.

13.   201 App. Div. 794, 195 N.Y.S. 574 (1922), *aff'd*, 235 N.Y. 609, 139 N.E. 754 (1923).

Bon Ami should raise its prices and this would result in an increase in profits. Shortly thereafter Bon Ami raised its prices. Plaintiff sued to recover, but the court denied relief. Of plaintiff's idea, the court observed "this was not new, it was not original and I am at a loss to understand how it could be deemed valuable. . . . No person can by contract monopolize an idea that is common and general to the whole world."

The *Nadel* case also usefully provided some criteria that can be used to assess the novelty of an idea. Factors cited by the court included:

> the idea's specificity or generality (is it a generic concept or one of specific application?), its commonality (how many people know of this idea?), its uniqueness (how different is this idea from generally known ideas?), and its commercial availability (how widespread is the idea's use in the industry?). *Cf. Murray,* 844 F.2d at 993 ("In assessing whether an idea is in the public domain, the central issue is the uniqueness of the creation."); *AEB & Assocs.,* 853 F.Supp. at 734 ("[N]ovelty cannot be found where the idea consists of nothing more than a variation on a basic theme."); *Educational Sales Programs,* 317 N.Y.S.2d at 844 (noting that an idea "must show[ ] genuine novelty and invention, and not a merely clever or useful adaptation of existing knowledge" in order to be considered original or novel). Thus, for example, a once original or novel idea may become so widely disseminated over the course of time that it enters the body of common knowledge. When this occurs, the idea ceases to be novel or original.[14]

An earlier case arising under New York law sheds some further light on how courts approach determinations of novelty. In *Downey v. General Foods,*[15] Downey approached General Foods, the makers of Jell-O® brand flavored gelatin, and told them he had an idea that would increase their sales. The idea was that they should advertise the product as Mr. Wiggle. Downey had apparently discovered that his own children went into paroxysms of delight when he applied this appellation to their gelatinous desserts and so assumed that the other children of America would be similarly mesmerized. Par for the course, General Foods turned Mr. Downey away but soon thereafter embarked on an ad campaign emphasizing its product's ability to wiggle. The court rejected Downey's claim because it found his idea lacked novelty. It noted that the idea was merely the use of a word descriptive of "the most obvious characteristic of Jell-O with the prefix 'Mr.' added . . ." In other words it was

14.   31 N.Y.2d 56, 334 N.Y.S.2d 874, 286 N.E.2d 257 (1972).

15.   208 F.3d at 378.

obvious and banal. Moreover there was evidence that General Foods had alluded to Jell–O's wiggalicious properties in some of its own earlier advertising, and that Pillsbury, a competitor, was calling its rival product "Jiggly." Downey's idea was thus neither novel-to-the-buyer nor did it have general novelty in the field.

Other ideas found to lack sufficient novelty in the cases include the notion that a women's golf magazine should be targeted to women aged 25 to 40 with above-average incomes;[16] the idea that depicting an infant in a high chair eating and enjoying yogurt would be a good way to advertise yogurt;[17] an idea for leasing and managing rental real estate that involved placing rental coordinators in satellite offices;[18] and an idea for a cross-marketing venture between the National Basketball Association and the Mattel toy company.[19] As one court tersely summarized, "[n]ovelty is the opposite of shopworn, hackneyed, and commonplace."[20]

11.1.2   The Idea Must Be Concrete

The requirement of concreteness is not often the subject of much controversy in idea cases. The courts that have addressed this requirement seem to contemplate that the idea in question must be ready to use, which is to say capable of commercial application without further intellectual development. Alternatively, one could say that the idea must be reasonably specific. In one case involving an idea for a new radio program, the court observed that "concreteness may lie between the boundaries of mere generality on the one hand and, on the other, a full script containing the words to be uttered and delineating the action to be portrayed."[21] The requirement no doubt reflects a judicial concern that if the idea is too nebulous it will be impossible to adjudicate whether the defendant actually used something obtained from plaintiff. Moreover, the more vague and general the idea, the more likely it is that the idea is commonly known and in the public domain.

In cases predicted on an express contract theory, there is some authority that idea need not be concrete.[22] These cases seem to be

---

16. Educational Sales Programs, Inc. v. Dreyfus Corp., 65 Misc.2d 412, 317 N.Y.S.2d 840 (1970) (argument that idea was novel characterized as "ludicrous" by the court).

17. Bram v. Dannon Milk Products, Inc., 33 A.D.2d 1010, 307 N.Y.S.2d 571 (1st Dept. 1970).

18. Wilson v. Barton & Ludwig, Inc., 163 Ga.App. 721, 296 S.E.2d 74 (1982).

19. Khreativity Unlimited. v. Mattel, Inc., 101 F.Supp.2d 177 (S.D.N.Y.),

aff'd, 242 F.3d 366 (2000), *cert. denied*, 534 U.S. 822, 122 S.Ct. 57, 151 L.Ed.2d 25 (2001).

20. Chandler v. Roach, 156 Cal. App.2d 435, 439, 319 P.2d 776, 779 (1957).

21. Hamilton National Bank v. Belt, 210 F.2d 706 (D.C. Cir. 1953).

22. "[W]hether or not the idea is original or concrete, recovery may be permitted if there was an express promise to pay for its use." Vantage Point, Inc. v. Parker Bros., 529 F.Supp. 1204,

based on the notion that legally competent parties are free to shape their bargain however they see fit, and if the defendant promises to pay for a vague, nebulous, or abstract idea, there is no reason not to hold him to that promise. Even in cases based on other theories, the Nimmer treatise argues that this requirement is a bit of an anomaly, because when an idea is so concrete that it is ready for immediate use, it often ceases to be merely an idea, and may become copyrightable expression.[23]

11.1.3 Circumstances Evidencing an Obligation to Pay

The easiest case for requiring a defendant to pay for an idea obtained from the plaintiff is when the defendant has agreed to do so in advance in a written contract. While the typical contract will normally make payment contingent on defendant's actual use of the idea, the parties can agree that plaintiff will be paid whether or not defendant chooses to implement the idea in question. Some courts have felt that such contracts should be unenforceable when the idea is not novel, on the theory that because such an idea has no value, there is no consideration for defendant's promise to pay.[24] As indicated in the discussion of novelty earlier in this chapter, however, the vast majority of courts hold that an express agreement to pay for the idea is binding whether or not the idea is novel. If theoretical purity is required, the consideration in such a case can be found in the plaintiff's efforts incurred in disclosing the idea. Defendants in idea appropriation cases are, after all, usually sophisticated businesses. They are fully capable of conditioning payment on the novelty of the idea to be disclosed if that is their wish. If the contract is silent on that point, then it seems appropriate to require payment regardless of novelty.

Sometimes the contract to pay for the idea will be oral rather than written in nature. The validity of such agreements requires consideration of the Statute of Frauds. Such statutes, which require that certain types of contracts be put in writing, vary from state to state. The typical contract for disclosure and use of an idea should not run afoul of the various prohibitions of the Statute of Frauds, but generalizations can be risky in this murky corner of the contract law landscape, so each state's approach to this issue may be different.

1216 (E.D.N.Y. 1981), *aff'd without op. sub. nom.* Vantage Point, Inc. v. Milton Bradley, 697 F.2d 301 (2d Cir.1982).

23. NIMMER, § 19D.06[A] ("courts that strictly adhere to the rule that only concrete ideas may be protected arguably do not protect ideas at all.").

24. *See e.g.,* Masline v. New York, New Haven and Hartford, R.R., 95 Conn. 702, 112 A. 639 (1921) (Oral contract for disclosure of plaintiff's idea that defendant railroad should sell advertising space in its stations and cars to make more money held unenforceable because of lack of consideration).

Even when the parties have not explicitly agreed orally or in writing for payment for the use of the idea, the surrounding facts and circumstances of the idea disclosure may lead a court to imply the existence of a contract and a duty to pay. This is basic contract law. When you visit the barber and get a haircut, unless your barber is eccentric you are not asked to sign a contract promising to pay for the services, nor do you orally declare "I promise to pay you twenty dollars on completion of the haircut." Your obligation is implied from your conduct and the general custom of such transactions. The same logic applies in the idea submission context. Of course, like all contracts, an implied-in-fact contract requires mutual assent. The idea-submitter cannot blurt out the idea and then claim that the other party impliedly agreed to pay for it just because that other party was in earshot.[25] Generally an agreement will be implied if the idea-submitter conditions his disclosure of the idea on the condition that he will be paid if it is used, and the recipient knows that condition and voluntarily accepts disclosure with such knowledge.[26] Where the idea has been solicited, courts are also inclined to find an implied promise to pay. Such factors as the specific conduct of the parties, industry custom, and the course of dealing are all relevant to determining whether a contract should be implied in fact.[27]

11.1.4 The Defense of Independent Development

To protect themselves from liability, many companies have implemented a practice of segregating unsolicited ideas. In other words, they keep letters and suggestion forms received through the mail from the public in a designated place where product development or marketing personnel cannot have access to them. If the company thereafter comes up with the same idea as one previously submitted by a stranger, by definition, it did not appropriate the idea from that stranger. Because such a defendant can document independent development of the idea, it is immunized from liability for idea appropriation, even if the idea submitted by the outsider is genuinely novel, concrete and useful.

This situation is well illustrated by *Downey v. General Foods*,[28] the wiggling Jell–O case alluded to earlier in this chapter. In that case, Downey had received an "Idea Submittal Form," from General Foods, which he used to submit his proposal. The form was received by an General Foods employee whose job it was to file

---

25. Similarly, a stranger cannot run up to you in the street, begin cutting your hair, and then demand that you pay for the service.

26. *See, e.g.,* Desny v. Wilder, 46 Cal.2d 715, 299 P.2d 257 (1956); Mann v. Columbia Pictures, 128 Cal.App.3d 628, 180 Cal.Rptr. 522 (1982).

27. *Nadel*, 208 F.3d at 377.

28. 31 N.Y.2d 56, 334 N.Y.Supp.2d 874, 286 N.E.2d 257 (1972).

these forms away in a locked cabinet. Nice work if you can get it, we suppose. In any event, there was evidence in the case that no other General Foods employee ever saw the form sent in by Mr. Downey. Coincidentally, some time later, General Foods began using Downey's proposed wiggling theme in its advertising for Jell–O gelatin.

As we have noted, the Second Circuit denied Downey's claim. You will recall that it found that his idea was not novel, based on evidence presented by General Foods that it had used variants on the theme some years prior to receiving Downey's proposal.[29] In an alternative holding, however, the court also noted that the General Foods protocol for handling the idea made it highly unlikely that it had derived the notion from Downey. Because the evidence indicated that they must necessarily have hit upon the wiggling concept by themselves, they incurred no liability. Of course, while the practice of quarantining ideas that come in unbidden from the general public can prevent liability for idea theft, it can also deprive the company of the benefit of new ideas and fresh perspectives.

§ 11.2   The Misappropriation Doctrine

The cases discussed in the previous section involved parties who produced a creative intangible—an idea—and then disclosed it to a single identifiable party in confidence and with the expectation, or at least hope, of receiving compensation. This is not the only situation where parties have sought legal protection for non-copyrightable intangibles. Many firms regularly engage in the business of producing creative intangible products, such as information, data, or entertainment, and selling these intangibles not merely to a single individual, but rather to the public at large. Occasionally others, often competitors, will attempt to reproduce this intangible product and sell it themselves, without the permission of the creator. They are often able to undersell the original creator because they incurred no cost in developing the intangible, merely a cost in reproducing it. One might consider their conduct dubious on both economic and moral grounds.

Over 90 years ago, a creator in just this position turned to the courts for relief, arguing that a competitor had "misappropriated" a valuable asset and should be prevented from continuing to do so under the law of unfair competition. The dispute ultimately reached the U.S. Supreme Court, where the cause of action for misappropriation was first articulated in the case of *INS v. Associated Press*.[30] Even when decided the case was controversial, howev-

---

29. For instance, in a culturally insensitive magazine ad published before the receipt of Downey's suggestion, General Foods advised parents to make a "wigglewam" of Jell–O for their tribe.

30. 248 U.S. 215, 39 S.Ct. 68, 63 L.Ed. 211 (1918).

er, and the misappropriation doctrine has remained the subject of criticism down to the present day. While some courts have followed *INS* and even expanded the scope of the misappropriation doctrine, many others have expressed skepticism or outright hostility to misappropriation claims. The current status of the claim has been cast into even further doubt by the provisions and commentary of the Restatement of Unfair Competition.[31] The story necessarily begins, however, with a look at the details of the *INS* case.

11.2.1   The *INS* Decision

The two parties in the famous *INS* case—the Associated Press and the International News Service—were both news wire services. That means each was a membership organization composed of various newspapers around the country. Each member newspaper promised to share its local stories with other members of the organization by placing them "on the wire." In addition, each member paid dues to the respective organizations. In return, the organization hired correspondents who reported on national and international stories. Those reports were also placed "on the wire." In this way, an AP member paper in Albany, New York, or Amarillo, Texas, could get news of a major flood in Sacramento, California (placed on the wire by AP's Sacramento member), as well as news about an assassination in Europe (placed on the wire by an AP correspondent).

During World War I the International News Service had published several war-related reports critical of the British government and the manner in which it was prosecuting the war. As a result the British government barred INS from using British cables to transmit news back across the Atlantic. Without the use of those cables, INS was essentially unable to report on the events in Europe, in which the American reading public was keenly interested. Left with no direct source of war news, INS hit upon a scheme. It instructed its employees to purchase copies of AP member newspapers in East Coast cities as soon as those papers hit the streets. INS employees would then rewrite the stories in their own words and put them on the INS wire. This enabled INS members in cities further west to publish those stories at the same time as, or sometimes even before the competing AP paper in the same town, because of the time difference between the east and west coasts. The INS papers did not indicate that the stories had been obtained from AP or, for that matter, make any reference to AP whatsoever. Suffice it to say that AP was not pleased.

AP filed suit in federal court against INS for common law unfair competition. The basis of federal jurisdiction was diversity of

---

31. Restatement (Third) of Unfair Competition (1995).

citizenship. Since the case was decided long before the decision in *Erie R.R. v. Tompkins*,[32] the substantive basis for the decision was general federal common law. The case was ultimately decided by the U.S. Supreme Court with dissents from both Justice Holmes and Justice Brandeis.

As a preliminary matter, it is useful to note that INS's conduct did not violate the copyright laws because it did not copy the expression contained within the AP stories, only the ideas and facts that they revealed.[33] The case also did not present the usual situation posed by unfair competition allegations. The usual unfair competition claim involves a defendant who passes off his own goods as those of the plaintiff who has a better or stronger reputation. For the INS case to fit this mold, INS would have had to develop the stories by itself, but then publish them under the AP brand name (something it might have done if its own name and those of its reporters lacked credibility). In the actual case, just the opposite was involved. INS used not AP's name, but AP's product, and sold that product under its own name. Thus the case did not fit easily into any pre-existing legal category and the Supreme Court was sailing on uncharted legal waters when it attempted to resolve the dispute.[34]

Justice Pitney, writing for the majority, found for AP, holding that INS's conduct constituted an actionable variety of unfair competition. He reasoned that AP had a form of property interest in its news reporting, at least while the stories were fresh, and that INS had effectively stolen this intangible property when it "pirated the news stories." Conceding that the news could not be property vis-a-vis the public, he stressed that between competitors it was "stock in trade, to be gathered at the cost of enterprise, organization, skill, labor, and money and to be distributed and sold to those who will pay money for it, as for any other merchandise."[35] In a phrase that has become a pithy summary of the reasoning of the case, he said that INS was "endeavoring to reap where it has not

32. 304 U.S. 64, 58 S.Ct. 817, 82 L.Ed. 1188 (1938).

33. *See supra* § 2.3. It is also possible that the relevant newspapers did not bear proper copyright notices, which would have injected even the expression contained in the stories into the public domain.

34. In trademark disputes, this type of conduct is called "reverse passing off." The Supreme Court ultimately took up the question of whether reverse passing off of intellectual work product could violate the federal trademark statute in Dastar Corp. v. Twentieth Century Fox Film Corp., 539 U.S. 23, 123 S.Ct. 2041, 156 L.Ed.2d 18 (2003). It held that these facts did not give rise to a claim for "false designation of origin" under the federal trademark statute because the "origin" of goods referred only their physical origin, not to by that statutory language meant their creative or intellectual origin.

35. 248 U.S. at 236.

sown, and ... is appropriating to itself the harvest of those who have sown."[36]

The majority in the INS case seems to have been most concerned with the effect a contrary result might have had on incentives. If INS could freely use AP stories as the basis of its own reportage without permission or payment, INS would not need to hire any of its own reporters (even after the limits on its European activities were lifted). Without the expense of reporters, INS would have lower costs than AP and could charge its members lower dues. That, in turn, might lead to an exodus of members from AP to INS, making it impossible for AP to continue to afford to pay reporters to gather the news. In this view, INS was a typical free rider and its conduct, left unregulated, had the potential to kill the goose that lays the golden eggs.

Justice Brandeis, in dissent, saw things rather differently. His chief concern was with the preservation of vigorous competition. He rejected the idea that the facts and information contained in news stories could be vested with the attributes of property and made the subject of a new tort of misappropriation, pointing out in his usual forceful language that "the general rule of law is, that the noblest of human productions—knowledge, truths ascertained, conceptions and ideas—became, after voluntary communication to others, free as the air to common use."[37] He went on to observe that "the rule for which the plaintiff contends would effect an important extension of property rights and a corresponding curtailment of the free use of knowledge and of ideas." In the end, Brandeis felt that if a remedy was to be afforded on facts of this sort, it would have to come from the legislature, not the Court.

Justice Holmes agreed with Brandeis that there could be no property interests in the "hot news items" that were at the core of the case. As he put it, "when an uncopyrighted combination of words is published there is no general right to forbid other people repeating them—in other words there is no property in the combination or in the thoughts or facts that the words express." The sole legally cognizable harm he could identify in the conduct of the INS was its failure to give credit to the AP in its stories. Thus, he would have resolved the case by entering a narrow injunction requiring INS to divulge that it had obtained the news from AP, but he would not have enjoined their ongoing practice of using AP materials as the basis for their own stories.

Distilling a black letter holding from *INS* is no mean feat, and the case has provoked considerable academic commentary.[38] Of

---

36. 248 U.S. at 239.

37. 248 U.S. at 250.

38. Among the many articles considering the case and the misappropriation doctrine generally are Richard A.

course the opinion can be read to resolve only the situation directly before the court. On this view, the case would mean nothing more than that the informational content of "hot news" is a protected intangible that cannot be appropriated by a competitor to the detriment of the party who first developed the information. Read this way, the rule of *INS* would govern only a narrow class of cases, but might still retain some considerable commercial importance given new digital realities. For instance, in *Associated Press v. All Headline News Corp.*,[39] the defendant AHN scoured various web sites for news stories, rewrote them, and posted them under its own name on its own site. When AP sued them, AHN moved to dismiss, but a federal district court applying New York law, denied the motion, stating flatly that "a cause of action for misappropriation of hot news remains viable under New York law...."

Of course the opinion would be of only limited importance if read in such a stingy fashion. A slightly more expansive reading would construe *INS* to apply in any case where the plaintiff generates time-sensitive material not covered by copyright law which is taken and used by the defendant before the plaintiff can fully exploit it. In other words, one might construe the misappropriation doctrine as similar to the right of first publication.

At its most general level, *INS* seems to stand for the proposition that the common law will protect any intangible economic asset not already covered by copyright, at least where the asset is "stock in trade" which is intended for sale to the public and where the defendant who misappropriates it is a direct competitor. Several courts have read the case at this higher level of generality and, in the process, tried to distill its essence into a list of elements.

For instance, one Texas court summarized those elements as "(i) the creation of plaintiff's product through extensive time, labor, skill and money, (ii) the defendant's use of that product in competition with the plaintiff, thereby gaining a special advantage in that competition (i.e., a 'free ride') because defendant is burdened with little or none of the expense incurred by the plaintiff, and (iii) commercial damage to the plaintiff."[40] The Wisconsin Supreme Court used a very similar formula, itemizing the elements as "(1) time, labor and money expended in the creation of the thing appropriated; (2) competition; and (3) commercial damage to the

Epstein, *International News Service v. Associated Press: Custom and Law as Sources of Property Rights in News*, 78 VA. L. REV. 85 (1992); Leo J. Raskind, *The Misappropriation Doctrine as a Competitive Norm of Intellectual Property Law*, 75 MINN. L. REV. 875 (1991); and Douglas G. Baird, *Common Law Intellec-*

tual Property and the Legacy of International News Service v. Associated Press, 50 U. CHI. L. REV. 411 (1983).

39. 608 F.Supp.2d 454 (S.D.N.Y. 2009).

40. United States Sporting Products, Inc. v. Johnny Stewart Game Calls, Inc., 865 S.W.2d 214, 218 (1993).

plaintiff.''[41] Read this way, the doctrine seeks to advance the same incentive preserving philosophy as the copyright laws themselves, but perhaps at the risk of interfering with robust competition and the free dissemination of ideas or information. This is all a bit abstract however. In the years following the *INS* decision, lower courts from many jurisdictions were confronted with cases requiring application of the misappropriation concept to a wide variety of fact patterns. It is to their decisions in those cases that we now turn.

11.2.2   From *INS* to the Restatement of Unfair Competition

Although *INS* was a decision of the highest court in the land, its peculiar posture gave the case only limited precedential effect. As a pre-*Erie* non-statutory decision, the Court was expounding on general federal common law, a body of law governing only cases filed in federal court and predicated on diversity of citizenship. After *Erie*, general federal common law ceased to govern even in that category of cases, and the federal courts were required to resort to state law doctrines to resolve cases founded on diversity jurisdiction. Given that *INS* was not binding on the states, it is hardly surprising to discover that some states chose to follow it while others either repudiated it or never had the opportunity to address the issue one way or the other.

The misappropriation doctrine had perhaps its most enthusiastic reception in the courts of New York. In a series of decisions in that state plaintiffs were able to secure legal protection for non-copyrightable intangibles as varied as live opera performances,[42] the live radio broadcast of the World Series,[43] and the appearance of buildings at a world's fair.[44] Other states adopting the *INS* doctrine

---

41. Mercury Record Productions, Inc. v. Economic Consultants, Inc., 64 Wis.2d 163, 218 N.W.2d 705 (1974). The Second Circuit devised an even longer list of elements, interpreting the claim more narrowly, to require that ''(i) the plaintiff generates or collects information at some cost or expense; (ii) the value of the information is highly time-sensitive; (iii) the defendant's use of the information constitutes free-riding on the plaintiff's costly efforts to generate or collect it; (iv) the defendant's use of the information is in direct competition with a product or service offered by the plaintiff; (v) the ability of other parties to free-ride on the efforts of the plaintiff would so reduce the incentive to produce the product or service that its existence or quality could be substantially threatened.'' National Basketball Association

v. Motorola, Inc., 105 F.3d 841, 852 (2d Cir.1997) (citations omitted).

42. Metropolitan Opera Ass'n v. Wagner–Nichols Recorder Corp., 199 Misc. 786, 101 N.Y.S.2d 483 (1950), *aff'd* 279 A.D. 632, 107 N.Y.S.2d 795 (1951).

43. Mutual Broadcasting Sys., Inc. v. Muzak Corp., 177 Misc. 489, 30 N.Y.S.2d 419 (1941). Compare the Texas case of Loeb v. Turner, 257 S.W.2d 800 (Tex. Civ. App. 1953) where defendant's use of plaintiffs radio broadcast of certain car races as the basis for its own roughly simultaneous broadcast of a "recreation" of the races was held not to be misappropriation.

44. New York World's Fair 1964–1965 Corp. v. Colourpicture Publishers, Inc., 21 A.D. 896, 251 N.Y.S.2d 885 (1964).

in the decades shortly after its decision included Missouri,[45] Pennsylvania,[46] and Texas.[47]

Note, however, that the actual outcomes in many of these cases have been rendered moot by the subsequent passage of the 1976 Copyright Act and the numerous amendments to that act which have expanded the scope of copyright protection. For instance many of the intangibles at the core of those cases are now protected by copyright, such as architecture and live broadcasts that are simultaneously being recorded. Even un-fixed musical performances are now protected under federal law by an anti-bootlegging statute, and are also the subject of a recent international agreement. This suggests that the results in these cases from the middle decades of the twentieth century may reflect judicial efforts to use the misappropriation doctrine to fill gaps in a still primitive copyright regime, where moral and equitable considerations seemed to require some form of remedy for the plaintiffs.

Moreover, not all judges were as receptive to the misappropriation concept as the state judges in New York. One of the most skeptical was Learned Hand, who, in his role as a judge on the U.S. Court of Appeals for the Second Circuit, was charged with applying New York law in common law diversity cases. He set out his concerns most fully in *Cheney Brothers v. Doris Silk Corp.*[48] Both parties in the case manufactured silks. Every season the plaintiff would, at great effort, develop new designs, only some of which would achieve any measure of popularity and economic success. These designs were not protected by either patent or copyright. The defendant copied one of plaintiff's patterns and the plaintiff filed suit under the misappropriation theory.

Judge Hand rejected the claim. He was greatly troubled by the potential for conflict between the federal intellectual property statutes and a broad open-ended version of misappropriation law. He was inclined to limit the *INS* case to its own particular facts because "[t]he difficulties of understanding it otherwise are insuperable. We are to suppose that the court meant to create a sort of common-law patent or copyright for reasons of justice. Either would flagrantly conflict with the scheme which Congress has for

---

45. National Tel. Directory Co. v. Dawson Mfg. Co., 214 Mo.App. 683, 263 S.W. 483 (1924).

46. Waring v. WDAS Broadcasting Station, Inc., 327 Pa. 433, 194 A. 631 (1937).

47. *Gilmore v. Sammons*, 269 S.W. 861 (Tex. Civ. App. 1925). According to one commentator, a total of 14 states have adopted the misappropriation doctrine at one time or another. *See* Edmund J. Sease, *Misappropriation is Seventy–Five Years Old: Should We Bury It or Revive It?*, 70 No. Dak. L. Rev. 781, 801 (1994) (listing Alaska, California, Colorado, Delaware, Illinois, Maryland, Missouri, New Jersey, New York, North Carolina, Pennsylvania, South Carolina, Texas, and Wisconsin).

48. 35 F.2d 279 (2d Cir. 1929), *cert. denied*, 281 U.S. 728, 50 S.Ct. 245, 74 L.Ed. 1145 (1930).

more than a century devised to cover the subject-matter."[49] A number of other opinions from the Second Circuit during the 1940s and 1950s followed Judge Hand's approach and read the *INS* case narrowly, even when purportedly applying New York law.[50]

Much of this disagreement, and the state of the pre–1978 misappropriation case law generally, is no longer of much importance. On the one hand, with the modernization and expansion of the scope of copyright coverage, plaintiffs no longer need to invoke misappropriation in nearly so many cases, and state courts no longer have the incentive to expand the cause of action to do justice in what they may previously have seen as troublesome cases. Victimized plaintiffs can now simply sue for copyright infringement. On the other hand, the expansion of copyright has also expanded the range of state law causes of action that are preempted by federal law. While preemption is considered in depth at the end of this chapter, it is important to note at this point that many of the older state misappropriation cases would not be decided the same way today because the state claim would be held preempted, due to conflict with the letter or spirit of one of the federal intellectual property statutes. Similarly, many of the post–1978 cases alleging claims of misappropriation are devoted to analysis of the pre-emption issue, rather than a discussion of the merits of the misappropriation claim itself.

In the last few decades, another curious twist has crept into the misappropriate case law. In *INS* and in many of the New York state cases that followed in its wake, the intangible asset created by the plaintiff was one which was created over and over again, and sold anew to the public with each subsequent re-creation. For instance, the AP prepared new news stories daily, just as a baseball league plays new games daily and an opera company stages new performances daily. The public would not pay for old news, nor does it want to see the same baseball game or opera over and over. In this sense, Justice Pitney used a very apt phrase when, in *INS* he characterized the intangible there at issue as "stock in trade." To enlarge on this metaphor, these assets are almost a form of intangible inventory, and the misappropriation plaintiff claims that his "intangible goods" are being stolen, depriving him of the ability to make a profit.

By contrast, some of the more recent cases have involved an intangible asset that can best be characterized as a formula. These formulas are not re-created periodically, but rather developed only

49. 35 F.2d at 280.

50. See e.g., R.C.A. Mfg. Co., Inc. v. Whiteman, 114 F.2d 86 (2d Cir.), *cert. denied*, 311 U.S. 712, 61 S.Ct. 394, 85 L.Ed. 463 (1940); National Comics Publications, Inc. v. Fawcett Publications, Inc., 191 F.2d 594 (2d Cir. 1951); G. Ricordi & Co. v. Haendler, 194 F.2d 914 (2d Cir. 1952).

once, usually early in the plaintiff's business activities, nor are they sold to the public in any real sense—rather they provide an underlying basis or foundation for its ongoing business activities. They also lack any element of time-sensitivity, the very attribute that makes "hot news" hot.

For instance, in both *Standard & Poor's Corp. v. Commodity Exchange, Inc.*[51] and *Board of Trade of the City of Chicago v. Dow Jones & Co.*[52] the intangible in question was a securities index. Such indices, including the well known Standard and Poors 500 and Dow Jones Industrial Index involved in the cases, are arrived at by an algebraic manipulation of the prices of several securities that the index-creator chooses to include in the index. Once created, the index can then provide a record of market performance that is comparable from day to day and year to year. In both of these cases, after the plaintiffs had created an index, and after that index had achieved credibility in the financial markets, defendants wanted to use that index as the basis for the sale of futures contracts. Both courts enjoined the use of the index, invoking the misappropriation doctrine to do so.

United States Golf Assoc. v. St. Andrews Systems[53] also involved a formula, but came to a contrary result. The USGA, as the governing body for amateur golf in the United States, had developed the methodology for calculating a golf handicap. This is a number that adjusts golfing scores so that players of differing abilities can compete against each other. Perhaps more importantly, it makes it feasible for bad players to gamble on the outcome of a golf match without feeling that they are always going to lose the bet. Like a stock index a handicap formula requires a relatively simple algebraic manipulation of data, in this case the scores achieved by a given golfer over the past several rounds he has played. In the early 1980s St. Andrews Systems began marketing a handheld computer which would enable golfers to calculate and update their handicaps automatically. The computer was programmed with USGA's formula. USGA sued St. Andrew's, alleging misappropriation, in a diversity suit filed in federal court.

The Third Circuit, applying New Jersey law, concluded that no misappropriation claim was set out, but it did not ground that result on the nature of the intangible (i.e., that it was a formula rather than stock in trade). Rather, it denied relief because the parties were not in direct competition, and it assumed that direct competition was a necessary element of the tort under the law of New Jersey. Presumably, the court would have granted relief if the

---

51. 683 F.2d 704 (2d Cir. 1982).

52. 98 Ill.2d 109, 74 Ill.Dec. 582, 456 N.E.2d 84 (1983).

53. 749 F.2d 1028 (3d Cir. 1984).

defendant had been a competing golf association that had adopted the USGA's handicap formula and began using it as its own.

After its loss in the Third Circuit, the USGA revised its handicap formula, and continued to bring state misappropriation claims against unauthorized users of that formula in different jurisdictions. Its batting average (if you will excuse the mixed sports metaphor) in these subsequent cases was pretty good. It prevailed in five out of five.[54] As the intermediate appellate court in California put it, under that state's law, "the essential elements of a misappropriation claim simply do not include any . . . requirement of proof of direct competition between the plaintiff and defendant."[55] That same court noted that "protection of the USGA handicapping 'business' is necessary to protect the basic incentive for the production of the idea or information involved . . ."

Whatever one makes of the misappropriation doctrine generally, its extension to the "formula" cases seems curious. The defendants in these cases are typically not using plaintiff's formula to save effort or engage in direct free-riding. Nor are they are swooping in and taking an intangible while it is "hot." Rather, they use the intellectual work-product of the plaintiff because it has become, in effect, an industry standard. There is nothing inherently superior about the USGA formula for calculating handicaps, but given that organization's dominance in the golfing world, its formula has become the common way for golfers to measure their performance against each other. Similarly, there are many ways to design a stock index, but the Dow has become, by its long usage if nothing else, a major yardstick by which stock market performance is measured.

Anyone, whether a newspaper, a computer vendor, or even a direct competitor, could not really enter the market or any collateral markets without access to these types of formula. Also, almost by definition, when a formula has achieved "industry standard" status, it has already earned its developer a significant reward. Thus, even if the balancing act between preservation of incentives and promotion of competition is difficult in the usual misappropriation case, the formula cases seem easy. Despite the assertion of the

---

54. Only the California case is published. That case is United States Golf Ass'n v. Arroyo Software Corp., 69 Cal. App.4th 607, 81 Cal.Rptr.2d 708 (1st Dist. 1999). The other four decisions are United States Golf Association v. Data–Max, Inc. (Ill. Cir. Ct., July 21, 1989) No. 89–CH–04995; United States Golf Association v. International Golfers Club, Inc. (Tenn. Ch. Ct., Aug. 1, 1994) No. 103076–2; International Golfers Club, Inc. v. United States Golf Association (U.S.Dist. Ct., D.N.J., July 22, 1994) No. 93–3246 (applying Tennessee law); and Parsons Technology, Inc. v. United States Golf Association (U.S. Dist. Ct., N.D.Iowa, Mar. 6, 1995) No. C93–318.

55. United States Golf Ass'n v. Arroyo Software Corp., 69 Cal.App.4th 607, 81 Cal.Rptr.2d 708 (1st Dist. 1999).

California decision quoted in the preceding paragraph, it seems to us that third party use of them poses little risk of undermining incentives, and fosters greater competition. In our view, therefore, the conduct ought to be held permissible.

Whether the misappropriation doctrine is construed to protect only intangibles that are "stock-in-trade" or whether it is considered broad enough to protect formulas as well, it does not grant the plaintiff absolute control over all profitable explortation of the material in question. That is the lesson of *Dow Jones & Co. v. International Securities Exchange.*[56] In that case, the creators of the Dow Jones Industrial Average and the Standard & Poors 500 Index had each licensed other parties to create what is known as an "exchange traded fund" or ETF based on its respective formula. An ETF is roughly similar to a mutual fund—it consists of a market basket of securities which are bundled together and shares of which can be traded on a stock exchange just like a stock. The ETF for the Dow is called DIAMONDS while the corresponding fund for the Standard and Poors is called the Standard and Poors Depository Receipt or SPDR (pronounced "spider"). In 2005, the defendant—a stock exchange—announced that it was planning to offer options trading in DIAMONDS and SPDRs. The plaintiff claimed misappropriation, but on these facts the Second Circuit found that the doctrine did not apply.

The court assumed—without deciding—that the plaintiffs did have protectable interests in both their indices and in the ETFs that were designed to track those indices. However it held that those interests did not allow it to exercise control over all further transactions in those EFT shares. As the court put it,

> by authorizing the creation of ETF's using their proprietary formulas, and the sale of the ETF shares to the public, the plaintiffs have relinquished any right to control resale and public trading of those shares, notwithstanding the fact that plaintiff's intellectual property may be embedded in the shares.... [A]n option to purchase or sell ETF shares is ... nothing more than a means of conditional trading in ETF shares ... We see no reason why the plaintiff's authorization of public sale of the ETF shares ... does not necessarily permit option trading in these shares....

International Securities thus endorses something resembling the first sale exhaustion principle for misappropriation claims. That doctrine, as you may recall from earlier chapters, declares that the first transfer of an object embodying protected intellectual property rights terminates or "exhausts" the IP rights in that object. In

---

56.   451 F.3d 295 (2d Cir. 2006).

other words, once you buy a copy of a copyrighted novel, you may resell that copy or otherwise dispose of it as you wish. The *International Securities* case seems to be saying that once you exploit an intangible covered by the misappropriation doctrine by incorporating it into a tradable product, you cannot control further transactions in that product. This accords with our intuition about the *INS* case itself. If the defendants in that case had purchased several copies of newspapers containing AP stories and opened a facility where members of the public could, on the payment of a penny, enter and read those copies for a maximum of 15 minutes, it is hard to imagine that any member of the Supreme Court would have found that actionable.

11.2.3   The Restatement and Misappropriation

Although both the first and second Restatement of Torts addressed some matters of unfair competition law, such as trade secrets, neither considered the status of the misappropriation doctrine at all.[57] In the early 1990s the American Law Institute began the preparation of new restatement dealing directly and exclusively with the law regulating competitive practices. The result of this effort was the publication, in 1995, of the Restatement (Third) of Unfair Competition, so named because of its roots in the two earlier Torts Restatements.

Section 38 of that Restatement provides:

> One who causes harm to the commercial relations of another by appropriating the other's intangible trade values is subject to liability to the other for such harm only if:
>
> > (a) the actor is subject to liability for an appropriation of the other's trade secret under the rules sated in §§ 39–45; or
> >
> > (b) the actor is subject to liability for an appropriation of the commercial value of the other's identity under the rules states in §§ 46–49; or
> >
> > (c) the appropriation is actionable by the other under federal or state statutes or international agreements, or is actionable as a breach of contract, or as an infringement of common law copyright as preserved under federal copyright law.

This provision declares that there can be no common law remedies for theft of intangible assets other than trade secret law and the right of publicity. Under this approach, the misappropria-

---

57. Competitive injury and theft of intellectual property have always been considered a branch of the law of Torts.

tion doctrine of *INS* no longer exists. If a defendant uses someone else's information or formula or other intangible but is not guilty of transgressing a federal intellectual property statute such as the copyright laws, and if his conduct does not logically fit within the categories of trade secret theft or the right of publicity, the Restatement authors take the view that the conduct is a permissible form of competition. If there is any doubt about that interpretation from the text of the Restatement, the accompanying commentary makes the point explicit. That commentary points out:

> Although courts have occasionally invoked the *INS* decision on an ad hoc basis ... they have not articulated coherent principles for its application. It is clear that no general rule of law prohibits the appropriation of a competitor's ideas, innovations, or other intangible assets once they become publicly known. In addition, the federal patent and copyright statutes now preempt a considerable portion of the domain in which the common law tort might otherwise apply. The better approach, and the one most likely to achieve an appropriate balance between the competing interests, does not recognize a residual common law tort of misappropriation.[58]

In the decade and a half since the promulgation of this new Restatement, there have been relatively few cases one way or the other dealing explicitly with the misappropriation doctrine—a few dozen in the federal courts and approximately ten coming from state courts. Several of these turn out, on closer examination, to involve fairly traditional theft of trade secret claims, in which the court uses the rhetoric of "misappropriation" and cites *INS*, but does not really apply that theory in the fashion we have been discussing in this chapter.[59] Of those opinions that are "classic" misappropriation fact patterns, only a minority cite the Restatement, often only in passing. Thus it is still too early to know if the Restatement's rejection of the generic misappropriation claim will carry the day and the claim will become extinct. Our intuition is that the claim will survive, but only as a very limited conceptual pigeonhole for cases that do not fit neatly into any other doctrinal category, but where equitable considerations seem to require some kind of remedy for a plaintiff in order to preserve incentives for creativity.

---

58. RESTATEMENT (THIRD) UNFAIR COMPETITION § 38, comment b (1995).

59. *See, e.g.,* Louis Capital Markets, L.P. v. REFCO Group Ltd., LLC, 9 Misc.3d 283, 801 N.Y.S.2d 490 (Sup. Ct. 2005); Rosenberg, Minc & Armstrong v. Mallilo & Grossman, 8 Misc.3d 394, 798 N.Y.S.2d 322 (Sup. Ct. 2005); KCH Services, Inc. v. Vanaire, Inc., 2007 WL 2571671 (W.D.Ky. 2007); and DVD Copy Control Ass'n, Inc. v. Bunner, 31 Cal.4th 864, 75 P.3d 1, 4 Cal.Rptr.3d 69 (2003).

This is probably for the best. Because of the amorphous nature of the elements of misappropriation, courts are often asked to apply it to squelch pro-competitive activities or to shrink the public domain. For instance, plaintiffs in older cases sought to use it to prevent the copying of books or comic strips[60] on which the copyright had expired, and to restrain the use of words that did not otherwise qualify for trademark protection because they lacked sufficient distinctiveness.[61] While claims like these should fail on grounds of federal preemption, that issue is not always raised by defendants or properly analyzed by courts. A narrowly construed misappropriation doctrine is likely to avoid some of this sort of mischief and preserve robust competition and a rich public domain, while leaving the rare deserving plaintiff with the possibility of a remedy.

§ 11.3   The Right of Publicity

Americans are mesmerized by celebrity and the exploitation of celebrity cachet is a big business. Products such as clothing or athletic gear adorned with the picture or name of a well-known and charismatic athlete or entertainer can sell for a significant premium over generic versions of the same item. Even objects that have no value other than as icons of the celebrity, such as dolls, posters, or masks, can command a lucrative market. Not surprisingly celebrities have attempted to capture the economic benefit associated with this market for themselves. For ease of discussion, we can call the intangible asset that is the basis of this market "persona."

By its very nature, persona is not fixed in a tangible medium of expression (although manifestations of persona can be fixed, such as when an athlete places his name on a line of shirts or when an actor appears in a movie.) Consequently federal copyright law does not protect "persona" nor could it, as persona is presumably not within the constitutional definition of a "writing." Over the last half century however, the state courts have fashioned a theory to provide protection to persona. This resulting legal right is usually called the "right of publicity."[62]

The right of publicity is sometimes said to have its roots in the misappropriation doctrine, and sometimes in the law of privacy.

60. National Comics Publications, Inc. v. Fawcett Publications, Inc., 191 F.2d 594 (2d Cir. 1951).

61. See Flexitized, Inc. v. National Flexitized Corp., 335 F.2d 774 (2d Cir. 1964), cert. denied, 380 U.S. 913, 85 S.Ct. 899, 13 L.Ed.2d 799 (1965).

62. The first case to use this label was Haelan Laboratories Inc. v. Topps Chewing Gum, Inc., 202 F.2d 866, 868 (2d Cir.), cert. denied, 346 U.S. 816, 74 S.Ct. 26, 98 L.Ed. 343 (1953). In the following year the theory was embellished in what has become an oft-cited law review article, see, Melville B. Nimmer, The Right of Publicity, 19 LAW & CONTEMP. PROBS., 203 (1954).

The outgrowth and relationship of the right of publicity to the misappropriation concept seems clear. The economic value of one's persona can easily be thought of as an intangible asset developed by the expenditure of effort on the part of the person in question, just as the hot news in the *INS* case was an asset belonging to the Associated Press and developed by it after considerable effort. Just like the news, persona is also often stock in trade—at least when the affected individual is a celebrity—because much of what celebrities do is to sell to the public various opportunities to bask in their reflected glow. When others attempt to capitalize on the value of a celebrity's persona without having paid for it, they are "reaping where they have not sown", just as the INS did when it misappropriated news stories from the Associated Press.

The connections between the right of publicity and the law of privacy are a bit more complicated. Although initially thought of as a single concept in the law, Dean Prosser persuasively argued in a now celebrated law review article[63] that the word "privacy" as used in the case law was actually an umbrella term that included four essentially different causes of action. Three of these are not particularly relevant to the present discussion—namely (1) the tort of "intrusion," which protects us from invasions of our physical privacy such as wiretapping; (2) the tort of "disclosure," which forbids the revelation of private matter that would prove embarrassing or disturbing, such as the unauthorized release of medical records; and (3) the tort of "false light," which addresses the circulation of material that would place the plaintiff in an inaccurate context, such as adding the name of an individual to a political petition despite his disagreement with its contents.

It is in the fourth branch of the law of privacy that some courts found a basis for the right of publicity. That branch—which Prosser denominated "appropriation"—forbids the use of the name or likeness of another person for a commercial advantage. Note, however, that as a privacy claim, the interest that this cause of action seeks to vindicate is not economic. Rather it is the sense of personal violation that one might feel if, upon venturing out to the supermarket, one unexpectedly saw one's face staring back from a jar of peanut butter or an end-of-aisle poster welcoming shoppers to the store. In other words, Prosser's fourth privacy tort involves *conduct* essentially equivalent to the modern right of publicity, but it seeks to rectify a *different type of injury.*[64]

In some older right of publicity cases, courts spilled considerable ink debating whether the property misappropriation or privacy

---

63. William L. Prosser, *Privacy*, 48 Cal. L. Rev. 383 (1960).

64. For a discussion of the privacy roots of the publicity doctrine see *Hirsch*

v. S.C. Johnson & Son, Inc., 90 Wis.2d 379, 280 N.W.2d 129 (1979).

theory provided the sounder justification for a right of publicity. The choice of theory, in turn, often influenced the resolution of certain finer points of doctrine. Fortunately, in more recent years, the courts have largely moved away from this theoretical discourse and settled on a fairly uniform list of elements that a plaintiff must prove in a right of publicity action. As the authors of the Restatement of Unfair Competition summarize,

> [c]ourts in a number of jurisdictions came to distinguish claims for injury to personal feelings caused by an unauthorized use of the plaintiff's identity from claims seeking redress for an appropriation of the commercial value of the identity. The latter claim was sometimes denominated a "right of publicity" to distinguish it from the protection available to personal interest under the "right of privacy." ... The distinction between the publicity and privacy actions, however, relates primarily to the nature of the harm suffered by the plaintiff; similar substantive rules govern the determination of liability.[65]

According to the Restatement a person has a claim for violation of his or her right of publicity if a defendant appropriates the commercial value of plaintiff's identity by using the plaintiff's name, likeness, or "other indicia of identity" without consent and for purposes of trade.[66] "Purposes of trade" are defined as use for advertising the sale of goods or services, or use on merchandise or in connection with services. The Restatement authors note, however that use for the purposes of trade "does not ordinarily include the use of a person's identity in news reporting, commentary, entertainment, works of fiction or nonfiction, or in advertising that is incidental to such use."[67] Thus one need not secure permission or pay a royalty to feature a photograph of a sports star in the sports pages of the local newspaper or on the cover of an issue of *Sports Illustrated* magazine, or to prepare an unauthorized biography of a Hollywood star using the star's name as the title of the book.

The Restatement's policy justifications for the right of publicity draw on both the privacy and misappropriation themes. The relevant comment cites five rationales: (1) protection of "an individual's interest in personal dignity and autonomy"; (2) "secur[ing] for plaintiffs the commercial value of their fame"; (3) "prevent[ing] the unjust enrichment of others seeking to appropriate" the commercial value of plaintiffs' fame for themselves; (4) "preventing harm-

---

65. See RESTATEMENT (THIRD) UNFAIR COMPETITION § 46 (1995), comment b.

66. *Id.*

67. See RESTATEMENT (THIRD) UNFAIR COMPETITION § 47 (1995). Of course, those who use another's name or likeness in a newsworthy context remain subject to liability for defamation or invasion of privacy if they commit the elements of those independent torts.

ful or excessive commercial use that may dilute the value of [a person's] identity"; and (5) "afford[ing] protection against false suggestions of endorsement or sponsorship."[68]

The second and fourth of these justifications are explicitly economic—they refer to a plaintiff's ability to make money from his identity by guaranteeing him an exclusive right to exploit his persona and by preventing overexposure that may make that persona less valuable. The fifth justification is essentially a trademark law rational, and protects economic interests indirectly—if a third party were free to imply sponsorship of shoddy or distasteful goods that could harm the plaintiff's reputation and diminish its value for future exploitation. The third principle cited—prevention of unjust enrichment—is also indirectly economic in nature, seeking to prevent others from "reaping where they have not sown," but it also has moral overtones In any event, these four justifications resemble those which underlie the misappropriation doctrine. The first justification offered by the Restatement—preservation of dignity—is more obviously rooted in the law of privacy.

Two final points are worthy of note. In some states the right of publicity has been codified and is now a matter of statute.[69] Obviously, when litigating in one of these states the specific language of such statutes takes precedence over the general statement of elements in the preceding paragraph. While these statutes can create some degree of clarity about the scope of the right of publicity, they do not always supercede the common law cause of action—about 8 states have held that their law recognizes both a statutory and common law claim, often with different elements.[70] Second, bear in mind that in approximately 20 (mostly smaller) states there is no authority at all on whether the right of publicity is recognized. While it is likely that these jurisdictions would follow the lead of their larger siblings and recognize the right if pressed to do so one cannot be sure. Some have advocated a federal right of publicity to create national uniformity on the subject and to minimize forum shopping,[71] but thus far Congress has shown little appetite to take up the issue.

---

68. RESTATEMENT (THIRD) OF UNFAIR COMPETITION § 46, Cmt. c (1995). These policy justifications have been endorsed by courts. *See, e.g.,* C.B.C. Distribution and Marketing, Inc. v. Major League Baseball, 443 F.Supp.2d 1077, 1089–90 (E.D.Mo. 2006), *aff'd,* 505 F.3d 818 (8th Cir. 2007), *cert. denied,* ___ U.S. ___, 128 S.Ct. 2872, 171 L.Ed.2d 831 (2008). *Cf.* Cardtoons, L.C. v. Major League Baseball Players Ass'n, 95 F.3d 959 (10th Cir. 1996) (containing a lengthy discussion of the policy bases for the right of publicity).

69. *See, e.g.,* California Civil Code § 3334.1; Virginia Code § 8.01–40. Almost 20 states have adopted statutes of this type.

70. States that have both a statutory and common law right of publicity include California, Florida, Illinois, Kentucky, Ohio, Texas, Utah, and Wisconsin.

71. *See, e.g.,* Sean D. Whaley, *"I'm a Highway Star": An Outline for a Federal Right of Publicity,* 31 HASTINGS COMM. & ENT. L.J. 257 (2009); Eric J.

11.3.1   Aspects of Persona Protected by the Right of Publicity

There is general agreement that the right of publicity forbids the unauthorized use of the name or likeness of another individual for commercial purposes without that person's consent. Thus one cannot sell trading cards bearing a picture of basketball star LeBron James without his permission nor could one sell posters depicting actress Jennifer Anniston without hers. Similarly, one could not sell baseball bats marked with the name of New York Yankees star Derek Jeter, or use a photograph of Justin Timberlake in a magazine advertisement for toothpaste.

Courts have not, however, limited the right of publicity to cases where the defendant uses an actual picture or the precise legal name of the plaintiff. They have also forbidden the use of look-alikes, nicknames, and phrases that are evocative of the plaintiff's identity. In this spirit, one court invoked the doctrine to provide relief against a video rental store that used a celebrity look-alike resembling Woody Allen in one of its commercials.[72] Another court found a violation of Mohammed Ali's right of publicity when an adult oriented magazine published a drawing of a nude African–American boxer labeled THE GREATEST, which had become Ali's widely known nickname.[73] Still another granted relief to comedian and late night talk show host Johnny Carson when a purveyor of portable toilets used the phrase HERE'S JOHNNY for its products, since that phrase was used to introduce Carson when he was the host of the *Tonight* show and thus evoked his personality to lend a whimsical cachet to the porta-potties.[74]

Several jurisdictions have expanded the attributes of persona covered by the right of publicity even further. For instance, by both statute and common law, California's right of publicity also protects voice. In *Midler v. Ford*[75] the Ford Motor Company wanted to hire the performer Bette Midler to sing the song *Do You Want To Dance* as background music for an upcoming commercial. Ms. Midler declined to participate, so Ford hired another singer who had previously worked with Midler and could do a convincing imitation of her voice. They recorded this other individual singing the song in question and used it in the commercial. The upshot was, of course, a suit by Midler, alleging violation of her rights under California law.

Goodman, *A National Identity Crisis: the Need for a Federal Right of Publicity Statute*, 9 DePaul-LCA J. Art. & Ent. L. 227 (1999).

72. Allen v. National Video, Inc., 610 F.Supp. 612 (S.D.N.Y. 1985).

73. Ali v. Playgirl, Inc., 447 F.Supp. 723, 728 (S.D.N.Y. 1978).

74. Carson v. Here's Johnny Portable Toilets, Inc., 698 F.2d 831, 837 (6th Cir. 1983) (applying Michigan law).

75. 849 F.2d 460 (9th Cir. 1988).

The court held that Midler could not state a claim under the California statute because it only protects the voice of the plaintiff, and Ford did not use Midler's actual voice but rather the voice of a sound alike. Interestingly however, it did find that Ford had violated Midler's common law publicity rights, because the common law right in California was not limited to a specific list of attributes of persona and could reach any evocation of identity.[76] The court concluded that a vocal imitation was part of Midler's identity or persona by asking itself a series of rhetorical questions: "Why did the defendants ask Midler to sing if her voice was not of value to them? Why did they studiously acquire the services of a sound-alike and instruct her to imitate Midler if Midler's voice was not of value to them? What they sought was an attribute of Midler's identity.... The human voice is one of the most palpable ways identity is manifested.... To impersonate her voice is to pirate her identity." The court cautioned that not every vocal imitation in an advertisement would amount to a violation of the right of publicity, but suggested no line to distinguish the permissible from impermissible uses.

Whether or not you agree that the right of publicity should encompass the plaintiff's actual voice and/or vocal imitations, the *Midler* opinion is puzzling for a somewhat different reason. As developed much earlier in this volume,[77] the copyright statute limits the reproduction rights of parties who hold copyrights in sound recordings. More specifically, it declares that it is only copyright infringement to recapture the actual sounds of a copyrighted sound recording, and that it is thus permissible to make an imitative or "sound alike recording" (assuming that the person who prepares that recording has obtained permission to use the underlying song or invoked a compulsory license allowing him to do so). An imitative recording necessarily involves using a sound-alike of the voice of the original recording artist. If the *Midler* case is right, therefore, the California common law right of publicity specifically forbids conduct that the copyright statute explicitly permits.

As we discuss in the final section of this chapter dealing with federal pre-emption of state claims, it is possible that Congress was indifferent to state prohibition of imitative recordings and was willing to leave it to the various states to decide whether they would allow or forbid it. On the other hand, Congress may have affirmatively felt that it was a necessary part of the calibration of rights in the music industry to allow imitative recordings. If this latter speculation about the congressional intent is correct, the

---

76. In this regard, see, e.g., Comedy III Productions, Inc. v. Gary Saderup, Inc., 25 Cal.4th 387, 395, 106 Cal. Rptr.2d 126, 21 P.3d 797 (2001); Abdul-Jabbar v. General Motors Corp., 85 F.3d 407 (9th Cir. 1966).

77. *See* § 6.1.2.4 *supra.*

version of the right of publicity embraced by *Midler* ought to be preempted under the Supremacy Clause. Yet the *Midler* court dismissed the issue in a single sentence, declaring "Midler does not seek damages for Ford's use of *Do You Want To Dance*, and thus her claim is not preempted by federal copyright law." The Nimmer treatise faults the opinion—justifiably in our view—for failing "to address the key issue."[78]

Returning to the question of what other aspects of persona are protected, a few cases have found a right of publicity violation when a defendant used a depiction of some physical object closely associated with the plaintiff. In *Motschenbacher v. R.J. Reynolds Tobacco Co.*,[79] plaintiff Motschenbacher was a famous race car driver. The defendant prepared a television commercial that included a picture of his highly recognizable car. It was not possible to make out the features of the driver himself in the ad. Nonetheless, the Ninth Circuit found a violation of California's common law right of publicity because the "markings were not only peculiar to the plaintiff's cars but they caused some persons to think the car in question was plaintiff's and to infer that the person driving the car was the plaintiff."

Note that in *Motschenbacher*, as in *Midler*, the defendant's evocation of the plaintiff was not being directly sold to the public. The defendant in *Motschenbacher* was a tobacco company and it was not trying to sell car racing paraphernalia or talismanic objects that allowed consumers to show their loyalty to Mr. Motschenbacher. Rather, the photo of the car was being used to bolster the credibility of an advertisement. Consumers were left to conclude that Motschenbacher supported Reynolds' products just as they were likely to surmise that Midler supported Ford's. In other words, the defendants were implying a message of celebrity endorsement which was entirely inaccurate. False representations of this sort in advertising are actionable under section 43(a) of the federal trademark statute, commonly known as the Lanham Act.

That the essence of the wrongs in these cases was primarily the false claim of endorsement rather that the "theft" of "intangible persona" can be illustrated by a variation on the facts of *Midler*. If the defendants had decided to have the sound-alike singer appear in front of the camera during the commercial, rather than using the voice over, it would still be using a vocal imitation of Ms. Midler. In

78. Nimmer § 1.01 at fn 599. *See also* KNB Enterprises v. Matthews, 78 Cal.App.4th 362, 371 n.10, 92 Cal. Rptr.2d 713, 720 n.10 (2d Dist. 2000). Bear in mind that holding Ms. Midler's publicity claim to be pre-empted would not have left her without a remedy given the specific facts involved. She still could have argued that the use of the sound-alike recording as background music suggested, falsely, that she endorsed Ford's products. This is a form of unfair competition specifically forbidden by the Lanham Act.

79. 498 F.2d 821 (9th Cir. 1974).

such a case, however, consumers could see for themselves that it was someone other than Midler in the ad, and would be much less likely to infer any endorsement by her of the Ford products. If that had been the situation, we think it unlikely that a court would afford relief for the "theft" of the sound of Midler's voice, even though it had been used without her permission.

While the Restatement cites the implication of a false endorsement as a justification for the right of publicity, your present authors are skeptical that the right of publicity needs to be expanded to reach such cases. If the plaintiff is concerned about false endorsement, he or she should be obligated to show that consumer do, in fact, infer sponsorship, otherwise the right of publicity becomes nothing more than a shortcut around the requirements of the trademark statute. We would prefer a more limited publicity claim that only applies when a defendant takes the saleable intangible of the plaintiff's persona, and sells it as his own. That was not the situation in either *Motschenbacher* or *Midler*.

If voice and physical accessories can evoke persona, what about mere context. That issue arose in the well-known *White v. Samsung Electronics America, Inc.*[80] In the late 1980s Samsung developed a series of advertisements designed to emphasize the longevity of its products. Each ad depicted a Samsung product in the early twenty-first century along with some fictional and humorous counter-intuitive information. One ad, for instance, depicted a raw steak alongside text reading "revealed to be health food, 2010 A.D."[81] The ad that was the subject of the litigation "depicted a robot, dressed in a wig, gown, and jewelry ... consciously selected to resemble [Vanna] White's hair and dress." The robot was posed next to a game board which is instantly recognizable as the Wheel of Fortune game show set, in a stance for which White is famous. The caption of the ad read: "Longest-running game show, 2012 A.D." Of course Samsung had not obtained permission from Vanna White before running these ads, and when she learned of them, she sued. The court found in Ms. White's favor, holding that the defendants had "appropriated her identity" and rejected Samsung's argument that the advertisement should escape liability as a parody.

Judge Alarcon dissented from the panel decision. He observed that "the majority's position seems to allow any famous person or entity to bring suit based on any commercial advertisement that depicts a character or role performed by the plaintiff. Under the majority's view of the law, Gene Autry could have brought an

---

80. 971 F.2d 1395 (9th Cir. 1992), *cert. denied*, 508 U.S. 951, 113 S.Ct. 2443, 124 L.Ed.2d 660 (1993).

81. The cited year having arrived, we decided to research the proposition.

You can find a summary of the "Health Benefits of Beef" here: http://www.beef. org/udocs/Beef% 20Bytes% 20Health.pdf.

action for damages against all other singing cowboys. Clint Eastwood would be able to sue anyone who plays a tall, soft-spoken cowboy, unless, of course, Jimmy Stewart had not previously enjoined Clint Eastwood. Johnny Weismuller would have been able to sue each actor who played the role of Tarzan. Sylvester Stallone could sue actors who play blue-collar boxers. . . . ''

Although Samsung petitioned for rehearing en banc, its request was denied. Judge Kozinski, however, filed a blistering dissent from the denial of rehearing,[82] arguing passionately about the dangers of an overbroad interpretation of the right of publicity. He wrote "consider how sweeping this new right is. What is it about the ad that makes people think of White? It's not the robot's wig, clothes or jewelry; there must be ten million blond women (many of them quasi-famous) who wear dresses and jewelry like White's. It's that the robot is posed near the 'Wheel of Fortune' game board. Remove the game board from the ad, and no one would think of Vanna White. But once you include the game board, anybody standing beside it—a brunette woman, a man wearing women's clothes, a monkey in a wig and gown—would evoke White's image, precisely the way the robot did. It's the 'Wheel of Fortune' set, not the robot's face or dress or jewelry that evokes White's image. The panel is giving White an exclusive right not in what she looks like or who she is, but in what she does for a living.''

As in *Midler* and *Motschenbacher*, the defendants clearly did evoke an association with the plaintiff. Unlike those cases, however, it is unlikely that the consuming public assumed that there was any endorsement. The humorous or parody nature of the ad likely dispelled any such notions for all but the most clueless observers. Thus, using the right of publicity as an alternative route to squelch an unauthorized implicit endorsement was hardly necessary in this case. On the other hand, there was no attempt here by the defendant to sell an item whose value was enhanced by its association with Vanna White. There was no picture of White on the actual Samsung VCRs which would make them more coveted to owners, nor was Samsung planning to sell videotapes of its own advertisement to Vanna fans. Vanna's incentives to continue her "work" as a letter-turner were unlikely to have been undermined by Samsung's conduct and the ability to market "serious" versions of her persona to endorse products or as memorabila would not likely have been diluted by Samsung's whimsical advertisement.

82. White v. Samsung Electronics America, Inc., 989 F.2d 1512 (9th Cir. 1993).

11.3.2   Plaintiffs Eligible to Assert the Right of Publicity

There is no question that public figures, such as well-known actors, athletes, and musicians, may claim the right of publicity, and most of the cases involve plaintiffs of this sort, although in some, their fame might be characterized as rather modest. The courts have split, however, on whether non-celebrities may claim the right of publicity as well.[83] The majority of courts, supported by the Restatement, hold that the right of publicity potentially extends to everyone.[84] Under this view, the extent of the plaintiff's fame determines only the amount of damages, not the existence of a cause of action in tort.[85] In contrast, the minority position is that the right of publicity is enjoyed only by those who can prove that their identities enjoy a significant commercial value.[86]

The merits of these competing views have been subject to some debate. Some commentators believe that extending the right of publicity beyond a "celebrity right" provokes litigation and places overly expansive restrictions upon commercial speech. On the other hand, determining whether a particular individual enjoys "public figure" status has been likened to "trying to nail a jellyfish to the wall."[87] Because non-celebrity plaintiffs can be expected to turn to the right of publicity only rarely, given the limited damages available even in jurisdictions following the majority view, this issue may be somewhat more of theoretical than practical importance. There also seems no reason to deny relief to an "average Joe" (or even a "Joe the Plumber") whose image is taken and used on a billboard because he had "just the right look" an advertising agency was seeking. In the age of Facebook we are all celebrities to some degree and the risk that someone might make an unauthorized commercial use of one's image is greater than ever.

Within the realm of the famous, one might question whether the right of publicity should be granted to politicians, the clergy, military heroes, and other noble persons for whom economic reward is not the usual motivation for engaging in the activities that made them famous. There are very few case squarely confronting this issue. In one, the estate of Rev. Martin Luther King Jr. sued a party who was selling busts of Dr. King.[88] The court granted relief,

---

83. See Alicia M. Hunt, *Everyone Wants to Be a Star: Extensive Publicity Rights for Noncelebrities Unduly Restrict Commercial Speech*, 95 Nw. L. Rev. 1605 (2001).

84. See RESTATEMENT (THIRD) UNFAIR COMPETITION § 46, comment d (1995).

85. See Canessa v. J.I. Kislak, 97 N.J.Super. 327, 235 A.2d 62, 75 (Ct. Law Div. 1967) (stating that the degree of celebrity is "relevant only to the question of damages.").

86. See, e.g., Cox v. Hatch, 761 P.2d 556, 557 (Utah 1988).

87. Rosanova v. Playboy Enters., Inc., 411 F.Supp. 440, 443 (S.D. Ga. 1976).

88. Martin Luther King, Jr., Ctr. for Social Change, Inc. v. American Heritage Prod., Inc., 250 Ga. 135, 296 S.E.2d 697 (1982) (responding to certified questions from the U.S. Court of Appeals for the Eleventh Circuit) ("That we should single out for protection after

holding that it was not necessary under Georgia law for Dr. King to have exploited his fame to make money during his lifetime. Beyond that, the opinion does not squarely address the question of the relevance, if any, that King was not the same type of celebrity as Woody Allen or Bette Midler.

If the right of publicity is a property-based theory designed to preserve incentive for creativity, the result in the *King* case seems hard to justify. Dr. King did not devote his career to racial reconciliation and civil rights because he thought he could then make lots of money selling memorabilia. It is not likely that we would have fewer candidates for public office or fewer altruists or heroes if we did not hold out the carrot of eventual financial reward—and perhaps the ones that we would not have are the ones that we would not want. On the other hand there is something unseemly about allowing a third party to "cash in" on King's fame instead of allowing the economic rewards to be captured by his family and put to uses that they deem consistent with his memory. That unseemliness was much in evidence in the period surrounding the Obama inauguration when there was an explosion in materials bearing the President's name and likeness, including some in questionable taste.[89]

A final class of potential publicity plaintiffs might consist of the infamous. Those who commit heinous deeds often achieve considerable notoriety. It is not beyond the realm of imagination to think that an entrepreneur might attempt to use the name or image of an assassin, terrorist, dictator, or criminal on products sold for a profit. Indeed, every October brings us at least a few Halloween masks of this sort. Should such persons or their heirs be given a legal right to prevent others from using their persona? In other words, should the family of Saddam Hussein be able to prevent the sale of masks bearing his likeness? Certainly the property and incentive justifications become perverse when applied to cases such as this. There is no social benefit in encouraging people to engage in evil so that they can subsequently capitalize on their infamy. Moreover, even the privacy rationales seem dubious in cases of this sort—the types of people we are discussing can be said to have forfeited any right to have their delicate sensibilities left unmolest-

death those entertainers and athletes who exploit their personae during life, and deny protection after death to those who enjoy public acclamation but did not exploit themselves during life, puts a premium on exploitation. Having found that there are valid reasons for recognizing the right of publicity during life, we find no reason to protect after death

only those who took commercial advantage of their fame.").

89. We refer here to a line of thong underwear bearing the Obama campaign logo, pictures of the president-elect, and the Obama slogan "Yes You Can." *See,* http://clothing.cafepress.com/president-barack-obama_undergarments (visited March 22, 2009).

ed. Although the problem is intriguing, we are not aware of any publicity cases brought by infamous plaintiffs thus far.[90]

In any event, rather than carving out categories of ineligible plaintiffs, perhaps the best approach—as it often is in the law—would be for courts to evaluate publicity claims in light of the purposes of the cause of action. If the defendant's conduct would not destroy plaintiff's incentives to engage in worthwhile and socially approved pursuits by denying him economic reward, and if that conduct would not offend plaintiff's sense of dignity in cases where it is deserving of protection, there is no reason to grant the plaintiff relief. Both free competition and free expression can be served in such cases by leaving the defendant unmolested and the plaintiff uncompensated.

11.3.3   The Right of Publicity and the First Amendment

No construction of a state right of publicity can preclude the use of the name or image of a politician or other public figure for the purposes of core political commentary. Most states avoid any constitutional conflict by characterizing most such uses as newsworthy and not for purposes of trade. That means that they do not violate the right of publicity as a matter of state law. If a state law violation is made out in such a situation, however, the constitutional right of free speech will trump the state claim. No state law can forbid the use of negative images of politicians in editorial cartoons or critical references to them in op-ed columns.

Indeed, in cases where the defendant is selling expressive products with a critical message, the First Amendment argument will likely succeed even when the plaintiff is a "commercial" rather than "political" celebrity. Thus in *Cardtoons, L.C. v. Major League Baseball Players Ass'n*,[91] the aptly named Cardtoons had prepared a series of baseball trading cards parodying several major league players. The cards featured caricatures and some sarcastic text mocking the players for, among other things, their greed. The players, though their association, threatened to sue for violation of their rights of publicity, so Cardtoons sought a declaratory judgment that their conduct was permissible. The court engaged in a balancing test and sided with Cardtoons, finding that its First Amendment interests outweighed the player's state law rights. Note that the result would have likely been different if the defen-

---

90. About 40 states have adopted so-called "Son of Sam" laws that prevent individuals from profiting from criminal acts, by for instance, writing a book about them. *See, e.g.*, Kan. Stat. Ann. § 74–7319; Nev. Rev. Stat. Ann. § 217.265; 42 Pa.C.S. § 8312. Under these statutes, proceeds that would have been payable to the criminal are diverted to the benefit of victims. One could imagine a court citing such statutes as evidence of a public policy that would preclude a right of publicity claim by a criminal.

91. 95 F.3d 959, 970 (10th Cir. 1996).

dant used a negative caricature of a baseball player in a advertisement for a product such as razor blades or toner cartridges. Where the very item being offered for sale is expressive however—a book, magazine, film, poster, bumper sticker or, as in this case a trading card—the First Amendment considerations loom larger and outweigh the plaintiff's interest in protecting his persona. Barry Bonds is no more entitled to insulate himself from criticism that Barack Obama.

The courts in California have refined the balancing test by borrowing from the fair use doctrine in copyright law. Specifically, they focus on whether the defendant's use of attributes of the plaintiff's person is "transformative." As the highest court of that state put it:

> When artistic expression takes the form of a literal depiction or imitation of a celebrity for commercial gain, directly trespassing on the right of publicity without adding significant expression beyond that trespass, the state law interest in protecting the fruits of artistic labor outweighs the expressive interests of the imitative artist. On the other hand, when a work contains significant transformative elements, it is not only especially worthy of First Amendment protection, but it is also less likely to interfere with the economic interest protected by the right of publicity.[92]

Thus the depiction in a comic book of rock musicians Johnny and Edgar Winter as half-man, half-worm albinos who were born from the rape of their mother by a supernatural worm creature that had escaped from a hole in the ground, was deemed constitutionally protected because it was transformative.[93] On the other hand, the sale of t-shirts bearing silk-screened images of the Three Stooges drawn by an artist with over 25 years experience was considered insufficiently transformative and thus not protected.[94] One could imagine, however, cases where the California approach might lead to difficulty. For instance what if you wanted to sell T-shirts bearing a photograph of a baseball player accused of using steroids with the legend "Just Say No" printed underneath. This seems to be fair comment on a matter of public importance. The use of the slogan creates a double entendre, evoking a celebrated

92. Comedy III Productions, Inc. v. Gary Saderup, Inc., 25 Cal.4th 387, 405, 21 P.3d 797, 808, 106 Cal.Rptr.2d 126, 140 (2001).

93. Winter v. DC Comics, 30 Cal.4th 881, 134 Cal.Rptr.2d 634, 69 P.3d 473 (2003).

94. Comedy III Productions, Inc. v. Gary Saderup, Inc., 25 Cal.4th 387, 21 P.3d 797, 106 Cal.Rptr.2d 126 (2001).

anti-drug slogan while also suggesting criticism of the depicted ball player.

Because the image remains unaltered in this hypothetical it is unclear if the California rule would treat this hypothetical T-shirt as "transformative." The same opinion that announced the "transformative" test noted that "the transformative elements or creative contributions that require First Amendment protection are not confined to parody and can take many forms, from factual reporting to fictionalized portrayal from heavy-handed lampooning to subtle social criticism." It may be that a California court would find our mythical T-shirt to be "subtle social criticism" and thus protected. That seems a sound result, but it makes the "transformative" test so expansive as to simply reduce it to asking whether the defendant has engaged in protected speech—which is where we started the inquiry.

In rare cases the First Amendment may apply not because of the content of the defendant's message but because of the forum in which he disseminates it. Consider, for instance, *New York Magazine v. Metropolitan Transportation Authority.*[95] The controversy leading to that case started in the mid–1990s, when New York magazine decided to run an advertisements on the exterior of city buses that poked fun at then newly elected Mayor Rudy Giuliani. The advertisement featured the magazine's logo and text reading: "Possibly the only good thing in New York Rudy hasn't taken credit for." The mayor's office complained to the Transit Authority (the MTA), which removed the advertising under one of its regulations which banned advertising violative of New York's right of publicity. The magazine then sought an injunction requiring the MTA to restore the advertisements.

The Second Circuit held for the magazine on First Amendment grounds. It found that the advertising space on the outside of buses was a "designated public forum" because the MTA had historically allowed political advertising on its buses. As it result, it found the MTA's actions to be an impermissible content-based prior restraint of protected commercial speech. The court did not, however, rule out the possibility that Mayor Giuliani could recover damages for this use of his name,[96] and the dissenting judge characterized the advertisement as "plainly" violating New York's right of publicity statute.[97] Note that the defendant here was engaged in conventional advertising—its primary goal was to sell magazines not to editorialize about Giuliani. Had it attempted to place the same advertisement on a privately owned billboard whose owner refused it be-

---

95. 136 F.3d 123 (1998).

96. As near as we can discover the mayor never did sue.

97. 136 F.3d at 132.

cause of fear of legal liability, it would have had no recourse. It was allowed to put the ad on the buses only because the buses were government owned and operated, and their First Amendment defense would have been dubious if Giuliani had chosen to sue.

The Supreme Court has opined only once on the interaction of the right of publicity and the First Amendment, but unfortunately the facts of the case make its opinion of limited utility. Hugo Zacchini, the eventual plaintiff in the case was a "human cannonball." He made his living traveling to county fairs and being shot out of a large gun into a net. In the late summer of 1972 he was scheduled to perform at the Geauga County Fair in Burton Ohio. A freelance reporter for a local television station filmed the act, and the station telecast the entire 15–second performance on its 11:00 PM newscast with what the Court characterized as "favorable commentary." Zacchini sued under Ohio state law for a violation of his right of publicity, and the station defended by invoking the First Amendment. Apparently the human cannonball gig pays well, because Zacchini had the resources to fight all the way to the Supreme Court, where he prevailed.[98]

The key factor in the Court's decision was that the TV station had taken Zacchini's entire act. As Justice White, writing for the 5–4 majority noted, "the effect of a public broadcast of the performance is similar to preventing petitioner from charging an admission fee ... Moreover, the broadcast of petitioner's entire performance, unlike the unauthorized use of name for purposes of trade or the incidental use of a name or picture by the press, goes to the heart of petitioner's ability to earn a living as an entertainer...." Presumably the station could have escaped liability if it had shown only a few seconds of the act, or limited itself to an interview with Mr. Zacchini. On the facts presented, however, the majority reasoned that Zacchini's interests in his livelihood outweighed the station's First Amendment interests.[99]

The outcome in *Zacchini* provides minimal guidance for lower courts seeking to reconcile the right of publicity and the First Amendment. Cases where a defendant appropriates the plaintiff's "entire act" are likely to be as rare as, well, human cannonballs. In the more than 30 years since the case was decided there have been no others squarely governed by it. It does stand for the proposition that even media outlets do not have a blanket immunity against publicity claims—they cannot merely incant the word "news" and

98. Zacchini v. Scripps–Howard Broadcasting Co., 433 U.S. 562, 97 S.Ct. 2849, 53 L.Ed.2d 965 (1977).

99. The television station also argued that its broadcast actually helped Mr. Zacchini by promoting his act and encouraging people to see it in person. The Court noted that if this was true, Zacchini would be unable to prove damages and thus would recover nothing.

escape liability. Beyond that however, we must wait patiently for the Supreme Court to shed further light on the issue.

11.3.4 Duration of Publicity Rights

The states disagree about whether the right of publicity survives the death of the plaintiff and inures to the benefit of his or her heirs. This is one of those issues that often turns on whether a given state grounds its right of publicity in misappropriation theory or privacy theory. Because privacy rights have long been considered personal, courts that view publicity law as a branch of privacy have sometimes held that no right of publicity claim can be asserted once the plaintiff has died. Thus New York and a few other jurisdictions terminate the right of publicity with the death of the individual.[100]

The majority of states, however treat publicity as a property right and thus provide for a descendible right of publicity if a survivor or transferee exists,[101] although there is a considerable diversity of rules governing the duration of the right. The Virginia statute calls for a right of publicity extending 20 years beyond the death of the personality,[102] for example, while Indiana and Oklahoma legislation call for a duration of 100 years after death;[103] most of the other state statutes provide a term somewhere in between these extremes. Some language in the opinions reflects a desire to conform the period of protection to the general duration of copyright, which would mean a 70 year period of protection. The general rule is that the existence of a *post mortem* right of publicity is determined by the law of the domicile of the estate.[104]

§ 11.4   Express Federal Preemption of State Claims by the Federal Copyright Act

In our federal system, federal law takes precedence over state law. To be more precise, state statutes and common law doctrines are void if they would conflict outright with federal statutes or undermine their basic purposes. The three state remedies discussed in this chapter all nibble around the edges of copyright law and copyright policy and might, in some cases, work at cross-purposes with the federal scheme. For instance, in the idea-submission context, requiring those who receive ideas from outsiders to pay for them might conflict with the general rule of copyright law that there is no protection for ideas.[105] When states forbid the use of data or information generated by others under the rubric of the

---

100.   See Pirone v. MacMillan, Inc., 894 F.2d 579, 585–86 (2d Cir. 1990).

101.   *See, e.g.,* California Civil Code § 3334.1.

102.   Virginia Code § 8.01–40.

103.   Indiana § 32–36–1–8; Oklahoma Title 12, § 1448(G).

104.   See Cairns v. Franklin Mint Co., 24 F.Supp.2d 1013 (C.D. Cal. 1998).

105.   *Id.*

misappropriation doctrine, there is the potential of conflict with the copyright rule that denies protection to facts and historical data.[106] Protection of a celebrity's persona under the heading of the right of publicity might deny a copyright owner the right to use material that incorporates the voice or image of another person despite a seeming federal right to make copies of that material. As a result, each of the three regimes we have examined earlier in this chapter, along with other doctrines of state law, may raise issues of federal preemption.

Before getting into matters of legal doctrine, just a brief orientation note. A preemption argument will only arise with regard to a claim predicated on a state-law theory. Claims under other federal statutes, such as the federal trademark or patent laws cannot be "preempted" by the copyright statute, though a court may have to reconcile inconsistencies between those different federal statutes. Second, it will almost always be the defendant who raises the issue of preemption, because by doing so, the defendant hopes to defeat plaintiff's reliance on the state law theory. You might think that this just gets defendant from the frying pan to the fire because the very argument that shows preemption may tend to show a reciprocal violation of federal copyright law. However in many cases the federal copyright claim may not be available for a variety of procedural reasons (such as res judicata or statutes of limitations) or may not be viable on the merits. So when will a defendant be successful in claiming pre-emption?

The Copyright Act of 1909 was silent on this question. Moreover, as we have explored in some depth in an earlier chapter, copyright law at that time was essentially a "dual" system with state protection for unpublished works and federal protection arising after publication. Consequently courts had to engage in a fair amount of guesswork about just what Congress intended concerning preemption of state law. With the passage of the Copyright Act of 1976, Congress decided to make its preemptive intent explicit. It did that in § 301 of the new law.[107] That provision calls for the preemption of state law claims that provide rights "equivalent to any of the exclusive rights within the general scope of copyright as specified by section 106 in works of authorship that are fixed in a

---

106. *See supra* § 3.3.

107. You may recall that we encountered this provision earlier. It is the section of the statute that abolished the so-called "common law" copyright that had existed from the late eighteenth century up until 1978. The decision to abolish common law copyright is, of course, an explicit pre-emption of a pre-existing state remedy for authors and

thus a logical part of the scheme set out section 301. Section 301(a) has been termed "the most fundamental change in the copyright system 'since its inception.' " David E. Shipley, *Publicity Never Dies; It Just Fades Away: The Right of Publicity and Federal Preemption*, 66 CORNELL L.REV. 673, 701 (1981) (quoting U.S. Copyright Office, General Guide to the Copyright Act of 1976 2:1 (1977)).

tangible medium of expression and come within the subject matter of copyright as specified by sections 102 and 103. . . ." As restated by the Court of Appeals for the Second Circuit, § 301 preempts a state law claim if:

> (i) the state law claim seeks to vindicate "legal or equitable rights that are equivalent" to one of the bundle of exclusive rights already protected by copyright law under 17 U.S.C. § 106—styled the "general scope requirement"; and (ii) the particular work to which the state law claim is being applied falls within the type of works protected by the Copyright Act under Sections 102 and 103—styled the "subject matter requirement."[108]

The "general scope requirement" compels an inquiry into whether the state law provides a right that may be violated by an act which, in and of itself, would infringe one of the § 106 exclusive rights—namely the rights of reproduction, adaptation, distribution, public display, or public performance.[109] In applying this prong of the preemption test, courts often employ what has been termed the "extra element" test.[110] This test asks whether violation of the state law requires proof of some additional facts over and above showing that defendant engaged in mere acts of reproduction or performance. If so, then the state law is judged qualitatively different from a charge of copyright infringement and therefore withstands federal preemption. If not, the state law is pre-empted.

The second prong of the federal preemption analysis, the "subject matter requirement," determines whether the state law protects a work of authorship within the subject matter of copyright as provided in sections 102 and 103. Thus, to be preempted the state law must relate to an original work of authorship fixed in a tangible medium of expression. The subject matter of copyright also includes those things that Congress specifically itemized as *unprotected* by § 102(b), such as ideas, methods of operation, and discoveries. The subject matter "of copyright" in other words, is not things "that are protected by copyright" but rather "all the

---

108. National Basketball Ass'n v. Motorola, Inc., 105 F.3d 841, 848 (2d Cir. 1997).

109. *See supra* Chapter 6.

110. See Worth v. Universal Pictures, Inc., 5 F.Supp.2d 816, 821 (C.D. Cal. 1997). This test has been criticized as circular. As one commentator put it, "The problem with this test is that it does not provide any real guidance to the courts. There is always some difference between the state law and the Copyright Act, so a court that wants to avoid preemption can always find some difference, however small, that is the 'extra element' needed to avoid preemption. The net result is that courts seem to first decide independently whether or not they think preemption should apply, and then label the result accordingly. . . . Thus, to be preempted the 'extra element' test has proved circular in practice, and the cases are ad hoc, inconsistent, or wrong." Schuyler Moore, *Straightening Out Copyright Preemption*, 9 UCLA Ent. L. Rev. 201, 204 (2002).

things addressed in the copyright statute." Thus because ideas are indeed addressed in the copyright statute (by the provision that commands that they be left free for all to use) they are part of the subject matter of copyright. That means that a hypothetical state law that purported to simply forbid the copying of an generally known idea in the public domain could not stand—it would be preempted.

A slightly more involved example can further illustrate the workings of § 301. Suppose that the state of West Carolina enacted the Marcel Marceau Act, a statute that prohibits the public performance of pantomimes without the permission of the author, if those pantomimes had been appropriately fixed in a tangible medium of expression. This legislation fulfills the general scope requirement for preemption because the public performance right applies to pantomimes under § 106(4) and the state statute is triggered by a defendant's performance—plaintiff need not prove any extra elements. The subject matter requirement is also met because pantomimes are copyrightable subject matter under § 102(4). As a result, § 301 applies and this hypothetical legislation is preempted. This makes perfect sense when you consider that the state statute might have collateral provisions that differ from federal copyright law. For instance, it might provide for a term of protection of 200 years for the protected pantomimes, or it might provide for damages equal to 20 percent of the net worth of the defendant. Such provisions would confound the balance of rights and remedies that Congress tried to devise to cover the very situation at issue. That is why Congress wanted such a statute to be displaced.

Note, by way of contrast that if the state statute protected *unfixed* pantomimes against appropriation against video camera-wielding pirates, there would be no preemption. This follows because unfixed pantomimes are not within the subject matter of the copyright laws. It also makes sense. Since Congress did not choose to address works in this category (i.e., unfixed), it must have had no strong feelings about whether or how they should be protected. The state statute would therefore not undermine any congressional objectives.

11.4.1 Preemption of Idea Submission and Other Contract Based Claims

Let us apply these general principles to the various causes of action discussed earlier in this chapter. Most "idea submission" cases present a relatively easy preemption analysis under section 301. Because plaintiffs in these cases must prove an agreement to pay for the idea—either express or implied—there is an "extra element" that is not normally required of a copyright plaintiff. To put the same point another way, a state law demanding that you will be held to your promise to pay does not provide rights "equivalent" to copyright, which forbids reproduction of protected material by the whole world.

This extra element analysis was also used in *ProCD, Inc. v. Zeidenberg*,[111] which was not an idea-submission case but did involve a plaintiff invoking a state contract law theory against a defendant who had copied its data. In that case, ProCD had distributed a national directory of telephone listings on compact discs. The discs included a "shrinkwrap license"—a form contract intended to bind the purchaser when she opens the software packaging.[112] The plaintiff's shrinkwrap license limited consumer access to the directory for personal use only. Zeidenberg purchased the discs and, in defiance of the shrinkwrap license terms, uploaded the telephone directory and made it available over the Internet for commercial purposes. ProCD sued him on a number of theories, including breach of contract. Zeidenberg responded by arguing that the state law contract claim should be preempted under § 301.[113] Zeidenberg's argument was that the data on the disks constituted a compilation, which is within the subject matter of copyright, and that he had merely copied and distributed that compilation, which are rights granted to a copyright owner. Thus, he said, the states could not regulate his behavior and ProCD's sole recourse would have to be under the copyright statute.

On appeal, the Seventh Circuit disagreed with Zeidenberg and held that § 301 did not preempt the contact claim. Judge Easterbrook reasoned that the exclusive rights conferred on copyright owners by the Copyright Act apply against all other persons, even strangers to the copyright proprietor. To be judged equivalent to copyright, the state law rights under consideration must also be ubiquitous—a right against the whole world. Contract claims did not fulfill this standard because they generally affect only the parties that have assented to the agreement. Effectively, there is a "plus factor" in a contract claim—the need for the plaintiff to prove an agreement—which is not necessary in a copyright suit. Although the Seventh Circuit stated that it did not intend to state a categorical rule that all state claims identified as "contract" would survive preemption, it is difficult to imagine a contract claim that could not pass Judge Easterbrook's test.

111. 86 F.3d 1447 (7th Cir. 1996).

112. The more contemporary version of the shrinkwrap license is the so-called "clickwrap" license—the terms and conditions which appear before you can download software to your computer and which, at least based on intuition and anecdote, no one reads. *See e.g.,* Nathan J. Davis, Note, *Presumed Assent: The Judicial Acceptance of Clickwrap*, 22 BERKELEY TECH. L.J. 577 (2007).

113. Recall that the typical phone directory will not have sufficient creativity to merit copyright protection. Thus, if the defendant could have defeated the state law contract claim in this case, it likely would have escaped liability for copyright infringement.

However, the Nimmer treatise notes that "the rule safeguarding contract causes of action against copyright pre-emption is less than categorical."[114] For instance, in *Endemol Entertainment B.V. v. Twentieth Television Inc.*[115] Endemol had developed a television show produced in Europe under the title "Forgive Me." With the intention of licensing rights to the show in the United States, Endemol presented a producer named Jonathan Goodson with the "Forgive Me" show concept. The parties understood that this disclosure was made in confidence and that Endemol would be compensated for any use of the disclosed ideas. Goodson and his co-defendants later developed a U.S. show titled "Forgive and Forget" that, according to Endemol, improperly appropriated the substance of "Forgive Me." Endemol brought suit, in part claiming that the defendants had breached an implied-in-fact contract to pay for the idea. The defendants moved to dismiss this claim on preemption grounds.

The trial court agreed with the defendants and held that § 301 preempted Endemol's implied-in-fact contract claim and rejected Endemol's claim that contracts differed from copyright because contract rights were generally not enforceable against strangers to the transaction. The court instead reasoned that the claim asserted "no violation of rights separate from those copyright law was designed to protect" and would create "no additional rights other than promising not to benefit from the copyrighted work."[116] The *ProCD* decision was distinguished on the grounds that the contract at issue there included additional promises that provided an "extra element" beyond the rights afforded by the Copyright Act.[117]

As these two opinions suggest, the "general scope" or "extra element" inquiry is highly manipulable. Although § 301 calls upon the courts to determine whether a state law provides rights "equivalent to any of the exclusive rights within the general scope of copyright," the statute does not define the term "equivalent." The result has been a great deal of confusion and varying judicial interpretations.[118] Moreover judicial focus upon the "extra element"

---

114. NIMMER, § 1.01[B][1][a].

115. 48 U.S.P.Q.2d 1524 (C.D. Cal. 1998).

116. *Id.* at 1528.

117. *Id.* Another federal district court has noted that "[a]lthough courts have generally held that the Copyright Act does not preempt actions for breach of contract . . ., the majority of courts addressing the issue have found that the Act preempts implied-in-fact contracts." Fisher v. Viacom Int'l Inc., 115 F. Supp.

2d 535, 541 (D.Md. 2000) (citing numerous cases).

118. For a particularly curious interpretation *see* Stewart Title of California, Inc. v. Fidelity National Title Co., 279 Fed. Appx. 473 (9th Cir. 2008). Plaintiff sued defendant for using some of its insurance forms without permission. It asserted both a federal copyright claim and misappropriation claim under California law. The court held that the misappropriation claim was not preempted reasoning that it "includes an 'extra element' because it encompass-

standard has arguably encouraged courts to concentrate upon the technicalities of a particular state law, rather than its policies and effects, and may merely invite the states to incorporate a trivial additional requirement into an intrusive cause of action to avoid preemption. In our view, copyright law would benefit if courts focused their attention upon whether a challenged state law poses an obstacle to the policy aspirations of the Copyright Act, an inquiry which is, after all, the central question raised by traditional preemption analysis under the Constitution's Supremacy Clause.

Bear in mind that if a plaintiff in an idea-submission fact pattern basis his claim on a "quasi-contract" or "conversion" theory, rather than relying on a supposed express or implied agreement to pay, there is no "extra element" under any interpretative approach. Granting the plaintiff recovery on such a theory confers a general "property right" in the underlying idea and forbids all unauthorized use of the idea even if there was no agreement to pay. This is, of course, identical to the rights provided by the reproduction right under copyright law. Consequently, state law claims for idea appropriation on a pure theft of property theory should be pre-empted.[119]

11.4.2 Preemption of the Misappropriation Cause of Action

What, then, happens to state law misappropriation claims? The misappropriation tort is clearly a property based theory that purports to create rights against the whole world. When the Associated Press sued INS for pirating its news they were not claiming a breach of any prior agreement. They merely complained of the defendant's unauthorized reproduction of their intangible intellectual property. Such a claim does not implicate any "extra element" over and above what a copyright plaintiff shows when he sues for violation of the reproduction right. Put another way, the misappropriation tort gives a plaintiff an exclusive right to reproduce his valuable intangible, no more and no less, which sounds identical to the right conferred by copyright law.

Thus, if a misappropriation claim in a particular case is to escape preemption, it will have to be under the second prong of the section 301 test concerning the "subject matter of copyright"

---

es protection against improper *use*, thereby making the rights protected qualitatively different from those afforded in the Copyright Act." (emphasis in original). Thus, even if the forms lacked sufficient originality to sustain a federal copyright, this court was willing to allow plaintiff to enjoin the defendant's use under state law! This seems precisely

the kind of result the preemption doctrine and Supremacy Clause seek to prevent.

119. Professor Nimmer refers to claims of this sort as "contract-based torts" and concluded that "pre-emption in this context would . . . appear to be justified." NIMMER, § 1.01[B][1][a][ii].

rather than under the "general scope" prong which was crucial in the idea submission cases. As we noted above, however, copyrightable subject matter has expanded considerably since the time of the *INS* case. The question that leaves us with is whether there is any nugget of subject matter left that it is outside the realm of copyright and thus properly protectible by a non-preempted state misappropriation cause of action.

The legislative history of the 1976 Act reveals that Congress specifically considered this question. Indeed, at one point, the relevant bill included conclusory language specifically declaring misappropriation claims were not preempted, but that language was eventually stricken during debate in the House of Representatives, and most who have studied the history have found congressional intent on this question murky at best.[120] The Second Circuit's opinion in *National Basketball Ass'n v. Motorola, Inc.*[121] illustrates how the courts have dealt with some of the resulting ambiguity.

Back in technologically primitive 1996, Motorola developed a paging device called Sports Trax which it sold to the public for $200. It arranged with a company called STATS to supply statistical information about NBA basketball games while they were in progress. The information, which included the score, which team had possession of the ball, time remaining in the game, and the like, was updated every two minutes. The NBA sued Motorola on a variety of claims, one of which was a state law misappropriation cause of action. It claimed that the information about the games while in progress was analogous to a form of "hot news" in which it had a property interest. The NBA consequently accused Motorola of "pirating" that intangible property, just as the Associated Press had accused INS of piracy decades earlier. The NBA responded with the argument that any such claim was pre-empted by the federal copyright statute.

The Second Circuit recognized the distinction between the *broadcast* of a sporting event and the underlying game itself—a distinction which the district court had found crucial. It noted that the former was within the subject matter of copyright because of the creative authorship exercised by cameramen, sound engineers, and directors, but that the latter was not a copyrighted work because "[s]ports events are not 'authored' in any common sense of the word.... Unlike movies, plays, television programs, or operas, athletic events are competitive and have no underlying script." The court also pointed out that while the "facts" contained in a sports broadcast (such as the score) are not *protected by copyright*, they are still part of the "subject matter of copyright" because the

---

120. *See   generally*   Nimmer § 1.01[B][1][f].

121.   105 F.3d 841 (2d Cir. 1997).

copyright statute specifically addresses facts and ideas and commands that they be left free for all to copy.[122] Finally it concluded that "although game broadcasts are copyrightable while the underlying games are not, the Copyright Act should not be read to distinguish between the two when analyzing the preemption of a misappropriation claim based on copying or taking from the copyrightable work. It held, in other words, that states could not, via the misappropriation tort, prevent the dissemination of facts revealed by or contained in a copyrighted work (the game broadcast) by claiming to protect the intellectual effort necessary to stage the underlying event.

The *National Basketball* court did conclude, however, that a narrow "hot news" misappropriation claim did survive preemption. According to the court:

> The surviving "hot-news" *INS*-like claim is limited to cases where: (i) a plaintiff generates or gathers information at a cost; (ii) the information is time-sensitive; (iii) a defendant's use of the information constitutes free riding on the plaintiff's efforts; (iv) the defendant is in direct competition with a product or service offered by the plaintiffs; and (v) the ability of other parties to free-ride on the efforts of the plaintiff or others would so reduce the incentive to produce the product or service that its existence or quality would be substantially threatened.[123]

This analysis concedes that the factual information misappropriated in a hot news case is within the subject matter of copyright and returns us back to the "general scope" prong of preemption that we considered earlier in this section. It finds the "extra element" to be present only where the plaintiff can show "(i) the time-sensitive value of factual information, (ii) the free-riding by a defendant, and (iii) the threat to the very existence of the product or service provided by the plaintiff." It found that the activities of the defendants in the case at bar did not meet that test. Concisely put, there was little risk that the NBA would stop staging basketball games if Motorola was allowed to disseminate data about scores.

The *National Basketball* opinion is complicated and highly sophisticated. It holds the misappropriation tort not preempted in the rare case where the defendant's conduct is not merely theft, but also incentive-destroying and free riding. This fits the "extra element" paradigm because an author suing for copyright infringement need not show that if the defendant is left unrestrained the

---

122. The court put it this way: "Copyrightable material often contains uncopyrightable elements within it, but Section 301 preemption bars state law misappropriation claims with respect to uncopyrightable as well as copyrightable elements." Id. at 849.

123. *Id.* at 845.

original author will no longer be willing to engage in authorship. It also gives effect to the statements in the legislative history that some form of misappropriation survived the adoption of the 1976 statute. On the other hand it uses preemption to narrow the range of misappropriation claims to make sure that the tort cannot be used to thwart the Congressional purpose of leaving facts and ideas freely copyable. If states choose to retain a misappropriation claim[124] this seems a prudent balance of the competing policy considerations.

11.4.3 Preemption of the Right of Publicity

The final theory considered in this chapter, namely claims based on the right of publicity, have also frequently resulted in preemption claims. The general view seems to be that these claims should escape preemption in a fair number of cases because they seek to protect subject matter—a "persona" or "identity"—that is not addressed by the copyright statute. Nonetheless, many copyrighted works contain images of specific identifiable individuals, and the copyright owner may wish to exploit the work by performing it or displaying it. When the individual depicted files a state law claim for violation of right of publicity and the defendant responds by pointing to his copyright in the movie, photograph, or other work, the stage is set for more complex preemption haggling.

A pair of Seventh Circuit decisions reflects some of the confusion that these claims have engendered. *Baltimore Orioles v. Major League Baseball Players Ass'n*[125] involved a dispute between the major league baseball clubs and the players over the broadcast rights to the players' performances during major league baseball games. The players claimed that their state law right of publicity prevented the teams from telecasting the game without their permission. Effectively they wanted the teams to share a chunk of the revenue earned from selling broadcast rights to the networks. The clubs sought a declaratory judgment that any such publicity rights were pre-empted by the copyright statute. The district court found that the clubs owned a copyright in the telecasts as works made for hire and that the clubs' copyright in the telecasts preempted the players' rights of publicity in their performances.[126] The Seventh Circuit affirmed.

It first considered whether the intangible the players sought to protect was within the subject matter of copyright. It defined that intangible as their "performances" and it concluded that "[t]he Players' performances are embodied in a copy, viz, the videotape of

---

124. See discussion *supra* at § 11.2 indicating that the future of the claim *as a matter of state law* is not free from doubt.

125. 805 F.2d 663 (7th Cir. 1986).

126. *Id.* at 667.

the telecast, from which the performances can be perceived, reproduced, and otherwise communicated indefinitely. Hence, their performances are fixed in tangible form, and any property rights in the performances that are equivalent to any of the rights encompassed in a copyright are preempted.... [O]nce a performance is reduced to tangible form, there is no distinction between the performance and the recording of the performance for the purpose of preemption under § 301(a)."

Turning next to the question of whether the state right of publicity covered a right "equivalent" to any of those in the copyright statute, the court found that the invocation of the right of publicity here was directed at forbidding broadcasts of baseball games. Noting that a broadcast is a form of "performance" under the copyright laws, it had no trouble finding that the publicity claim and copyright claim involving the same material were equivalent. It thus held the players' state law claim to be preempted.

Almost 20 years later, the same court decided *Toney v. L'Oreal USA, Inc.*[127] There, a model named June Toney authorized the use of her photograph on packages of a hair relaxing product, and in related print advertisements for that product, for a limited period of time. When the defendants continued using the relevant photos after the specified time period, Ms. Toney filed a right of publicity claim under the relevant Illinois state statute. The defendant argued that this claim was preempted under the copyright statute. Initially the panel found preemption, but on rehearing they vacated their original opinion, reversed themselves, and held that Toney's claim was not preempted.[128]

The opinion is relatively brief. The court noted that the subject matter of a right of publicity claim "is not a particular picture or photograph of plaintiff. Rather, what is protected by the right of publicity is the very identity or persona of the plaintiff as a human being."[129] It thus held that state law here did not deal with material within the subject matter of copyright. As it summarized, "[t]here is no 'work of authorship' at issue in Toney's right of publicity claim. A person's likeness—her persona—is not authored and it is not fixed. The fact that an image of the person might be fixed in a copyrightable photograph does not change this." The court also found that the right of publicity claim was not equivalent to a copyright claim, because the plaintiff had to prove the "commercial value" of the persona in order to recover under the Illinois state statute. In the court's words, "the purpose of the [Illinois Right of

---

127. 406 F.3d 905 (7th Cir. 2005).

128. Interestingly, Ms. Toney was represented by counsel during the original appeal, but proceeded pro se in her victorious argument on rehearing.

129. 406 F.3d at 908, quoting J. THOMAS McCARTHY, 2 RTS. OF PUBLICITY & PRIVACY § 11:52 (2d ed.2004).

Publicity statute] is to allow a person to control the commercial value of his or her identity." Unlike copyright law, 'commercial purpose' is an element required by the [state law]."[130] This dictated the finding of no pre-emption.[131]

It then turned its attention to the seemingly conflicting opinion in *Baltimore Orioles*. It declared that the earlier decision "has been widely criticized by our sister circuits and by several commentators" but provided no citations to support that assertion. Fearing that the older opinion could be read as entirely preempting the right of the publicity, the *Toney* court took the opportunity to "clarify" the *Baltimore Orioles* holding, doing so with the following language:

> *Baltimore Orioles* holds that state laws that intrude on the domain of copyright are preempted even if the particular expression is neither copyrighted nor copyrightable. Such a result is essential in order to preserve the extent of the public domain established by copyright law. Therefore, states may not create rights in material that was published more than 75 years ago, even though that material is not subject to federal copyright. Also, states may not create copyright-like protections in materials that are not original enough for federal protection, such as a telephone book with listings in alphabetical order. *Baltimore Orioles* itself makes clear that "[a] player's right of publicity in his name or likeness would not be preempted if a company, without the consent of the player, used the player's name to advertise its product." Therefore, the bottom line is that Toney's claim under the Illinois right of publicity statute is not preempted by federal copyright law.[132]

It is difficult to know what to make of this terse analysis. The *Toney* court seemed to feel the use of Toney's image after the contractually agreed upon period *for advertising purposes* was the crucial factor distinguishing the two cases. Unfortunately the court does not reveal why an advertising motive on the part of defendant

---

130. For a critique of the view that "commercial purpose" is an "extra element" that makes publicity claims different from copyright claims, *see* Joseph P. Bauer, *Addressing the Incoherency of the Preemption Provision of the Copyright Act of 1976*, 10 VAND. J. ENT. & TECH. L. 1, 75–76 (2007).

131. *See also* Facenda v. N.F.L. Films, Inc., 542 F.3d 1007 (3d Cir. 2008). In that case, the defendant used clips of the identifiable voice of a well-known sportscaster in a 30–minute tele-

vision program touting its licensed football oriented videogame. When the heirs of the sportscaster filed suit under the Pennsylvania right of publicity statute, the NFL argued express pre-emption based on the copyright act. Although the court did not cite *Toney* it followed its analysis, holding that the "commercial purpose" requirement of state law was an "extra element" and that a voice was not copyrightable subject matter because it was not fixed.

132. *Id.* at 911 (citations omitted).

precludes preemption, while claims based on the use of a plaintiff's image *for entertainment purposes* should be preempted. Perhaps the *Toney* court simply did not want to explicitly overrule the *Orioles* decision, but one is left baffled about where the wavering line of preemption is supposed to be drawn.

The real difficulty in this pair of cases is that an intangible asset outside the scope of copyright—a "persona"—became incorporated within a copyright work (either the tape of the baseball game or the photograph of Ms. Toney). This sets up a conflict between state law, which grants control over persona to the depicted individual and federal copyright law, which allows the copyright owner to exploit his copyrighted work. Viewed strictly as a matter of *express* preemption under section 301 of the copyright act, we might try to mechanically deal with the cases by saying that because persona is outside the scope of copyright, none of these claims should be preempted. That would, however, be quite odd. It would mean, for instance, that the producer of a movie would not be free to exhibit the motion picture after having spent months and millions to film it because to do so might violate the rights of publicity of the various actors in the film! The answer to this conundrum lies in a second type of preemption, which we take up in the section that follows.

§ 11.5   Implied Federal Preemption of State Claims by Federal Copyright Law

Even if a federal statute does not explicitly address the subject of preemption of state law, state law can still be preempted by necessary implication. There are two species of implied preemption. First, a state law will be set aside if the federal statute reflects a congressional intent to "occupy the field." However, the courts have not attributed such an intent to the federal copyright statute.[133] Secondly, a state law can be impliedly preempted if it is incompatible with the federal statute and its purposes. This doctrine is often referred to as "conflict preemption," a fairly straightforward name for the idea that if the state and federal laws work at cross-purposes, the state law must give way. The usual test is to determine if the state law "stands as an obstacle to the accomplishment and execution of the full purposes and objectives of Congress."[134]

One can imagine many scenarios in which state law might conflict with the purposes of copyright. Specifically, a state statute might so hamper a copyright owner's ability to use a copyrighted

---

133. *See* Goldstein v. California, 412 U.S. 546, 93 S.Ct. 2303, 37 L.Ed.2d 163 (1973).

134. Hines v. Davidowitz, 312 U.S. 52, 67, 61 S.Ct. 399, 404, 85 L.Ed. 581 (1941). *See also* NIMMER § 1.01[B][3][a].

work as to render the copyright worthless. Alternatively, a state law might so hamper the public's ability to use material in the public domain, that the federal policies protecting the public domain would be subverted. In both of this situations the state law should be impliedly preempted regardless of whether the express preemption test of section 301 can be met. The two right of publicity cases discussed in the immediately preceding subsection raise the first of these risks. The baseball players and the model who brought state claims in those cases were effectively seeking to prevent the holder of a federal copyright from exploiting the copyrighted work.

The Third Circuit recently analyzed this very conundrum in *Facenda v. N.F.L. Films, Inc.*[135] The plaintiffs in that case were the heirs of renowned sportscaster John Facenda, described by the court as a "Philadelphia broadcasting legend." Facenda had provided commentary for many NFL games over the years. Those broadcasts were, of course, taped, and the NFL owned the copyrights to them. In 2005 NFL Films produced a 22–minute program called *The Making of Madden NFL '06.* Ostensibly a documentary about the preparation of the video game referenced in its title, the court found it to be essentially nothing more than an infomercial. In any event, NFL Films included a total of 13 seconds of Facenda's prior taped commentary in the program, leading his estate to sue for violation of his right of publicity under Pennsylvania law.

Predictably, the NFL argued that the state claims were expressly preempted by the copyright statute. The Third Circuit, however, found neither test of section 301 to be satisfied. On the "general scope" prong, the Court of Appeals concluded that Pennsylvania law required proof of an extra element beyond mere reproduction—namely that the plaintiff's voice had "commercial value." On the "subject matter of copyright" prong, the court followed the approach in *Toney* and held that a "voice" was outside the scope of copyright because it was neither fixed, nor was it the "writing of an author." Consequently the NFL moved on to its next argument and asserted "conflict preemption."

To analyze this contention, the court adopted a two-part framework proposed by David Nimmer (of copyright treatise fame) for dealing with potential incompatibility between copyright and the right of publicity. Under the Nimmer approach, the first step is to "look to how the copyrighted work featuring the plaintiff's identity is used."[136] Where the defendant's use is "expressive" Nimmer—and the Third Circuit—find the federal interests particularly significant, and thus weigh that fact in favor of preemption of a state

---

135. 542 F.3d 1007 (3d Cir. 2008).   **136.** *Id.* at 1029.

claim. Thus the author of an unauthorized biography of a celebrity ought not to be exposed to liability for violation of the right of publicity because a biography is expressive and thus any right of publicity claim will be preempted. On the other hand, where the defendant's use is "for the purposes of trade," such as in an advertisement, the federal interests weigh less heavily. In such cases the states' desire to protect plaintiffs from having their identity appropriated looms larger and preemption should be less likely.

The second Nimmer–*Facenda* factor considers the purpose of the use the plaintiff consented to when he or she agreed to participate or collaborate in the creation of a copyrighted work. If the plaintiff agrees to act in a movie, plaintiff's subsequent complaints under state law about the reproduction, distribution, and performance of that movie should be preempted. On the other hand, if still images from that same movie were used to adorn packages of breakfast cereal, and such uses were not contemplated in the actor's contract with the movie production company, that would cut against preemption. The actor would have a good chance of success in a right of publicity claim.

Applying this two-pronged framework to the facts before it, the *Facenda* court did not find any conflict-preemption. It held that the *Making of Madden* program was primarily for purposes of trade because it was designed to promote sales of the video game. It also found that when Mr. Facenda agreed to participate in making copyrighted football broadcasts his purpose did not include the use of his identity to market collateral products.[137] The net effect was that the Facenda estate was entitled to summary judgment on the right of publicity claim.

The *Facenda* test will not reduce the copyright-publicity interface to a simple paint-by-numbers exercise even if it is adopted by other courts. Determining the line between expressive work and work "for purposes of trade" can be tricky. Much advertising is highly creative, and the principle of artistic non-discrimination in copyright law which we encountered very early in this volume may suggest that the federal interest in promoting creative authorship in television commercials or billboards is greater than Nimmer and the Third Circuit have allowed. Discerning the plaintiff's purpose in allowing his image to be used is also likely to be vexing in at least

---

137. The *Facenda* court strongly implies that under this two-pronged approach the *Toney* court reached the wrong result, quoting Nimmer's analysis to that effect at some length. This follows because, although the use of Ms. Toney's photograph was clearly for advertising and not for art, Toney's purpose in posing for the photograph was precisely to allow it to be used as packaging and advertising. As Nimmer puts it, the defendants in that case "did exactly what she agreed to."

some cases. Not all contracts are carefully drawn, as any review of a first-year contracts casebook will reveal. Perhaps knowledgeable players in the copyright industries will react to all this by routinely securing waivers of state publicity claims in all contracts to avoid any risk of exposure under state law. If so, the delicate dance in *Facenda* to preserve the state cause of action will prove to be a pyrrhic victory for publicity plaintiffs.

Finally, bear in mind that this discussion of conflict preemption only deals with the intersection of copyright and publicity law. The *Facenda* analysis is not likely to be relevant in other situations. For instance, a state statute that forbids the reverse engineering of computer programs conflicts with the purposes of copyright law in significant ways and would be preempted,[138] but you won't get to that conclusion with the two-part test above.

138. *See*, Vault Corp. v. Quaid Software Ltd., 847 F.2d 255 (5th Cir. 1988) ("The provision in Louisiana's License Act, which permits a software producer to prohibit the adaptation of its licensed computer program by decompilation or disassembly, conflicts with the rights of computer program owners under § 117 and clearly 'touches upon an area' of federal copyright law. For this reason, . . . we hold that at least this provision of Louisiana's License Act is preempted by federal law.").

Chapter 12

COPYRIGHT IN THE INTERNATIONAL PERSPECTIVE

Table of Sections

The international dimension of copyright has never been so important. Movies, music, software, and other works authored by U.S. citizens enjoy popularity around the world. In the era of the Internet, these works may be copied and distributed globally in a matter of moments. Yet, although copyrighted works observe few boundaries, copyright law itself remains strictly territorial. Each nation's copyright laws extend only as far as its own borders.

Although no true global copyright system exists, the copyright regimes of the United States and its trading partners are linked through a handful of international agreements. These agreements do not create a universal copyright law, in that they do not provide for a single source of rights effective worldwide. Yet they allow authors to claim a national copyright almost anywhere in the world. This Chapter discusses the most significant of the agreements that, together, comprise the international copyright system.

§ 12.1   Foreign Authors

Foreign authors may obtain protection under U.S. copyright law through a number of avenues. If a work of authorship has not yet been published, then U.S. law is quite clear. Under § 104(a), all unpublished works are subject to U.S. copyright protection "without regard to the nationality or domicile of the author." So long as an unpublished foreign work has not yet fallen into the public domain—for example, through the expiration of the statutory term of copyright—it enjoys copyright just as other works do.

On the other hand, if a work has been published, it must fall into at least one of four potentially overlapping categories set out in § 104(b) in order to enjoy U.S. copyright. First, at least one of its authors must qualify as (1) a citizen or domiciliary of the United States, (2) a country with which the United States has copyright relations under an international agreement, or (3) be a stateless person.[1] Alternatively, a published work will be protected under U.S. law if it was first published in the United States or in a foreign nation that, on the date of first publication, is a signatory to a copyright treaty of which the United States is also a member.[2] The third possible way for a work to secure domestic copyright protection is if it was published by the United Nations or one of its specialized agencies, or by the Organization of American States.[3] Finally, a published work will also be given U.S. rights if it falls within the scope of a Presidential proclamation affording U.S. copyright protection to works originating in a particular foreign country. Such a proclamation must be based upon the President's finding that that country extends protection to U.S. works on substantially the same basis that it provides to its own works.[4] Interested readers are invited to consult Copyright Office Circular 38a for a detailed list of U.S. copyright relations with other nations.[5]

Let us apply these rules to some concrete cases. Study of the relevant treaties reveals that France and the United States have copyright relations; by way of contrast Ethiopia is not a party of any of the key international agreements concerning copyright. Assume first that Pierre, a French citizen living temporarily in Ethiopia, publishes a book of poems in Ethiopia. Is this book of poems protected under U.S. copyright law? The answer is yes, under the first listed possibility in section 104, because Pierre is a citizen of a country (France) with which the United States has copyright relations. The same result would follow if John, a U.S. citizen, had published in Ethiopia.

Now assume that Biruk, an Ethiopian citizen temporarily living in Paris, publishes a book of poems in France. Is this work protected under U.S. law? Again, the answer is affirmative, this time by virtue of the second prong of section 104, because the work

---

1. 17 U.S.C. § 104(b)(1).

2. 17 U.S.C. § 104(b)(2), (3), (4).

3. 17 U.S.C. § 104(b)(5).

4. 17 U.S.C. § 104(b)(6).

5. Circular 38a is available at http://www.copyright.gov/circs/circ38a.pdf.

was first published in a country (France) that is a signatory to a treaty that the United States has also signed. Note that if Biruk subsequently republished that same book of poems in Ethiopia, their copyright status under the U.S. law will not change, because the focus is only on the country of *first* publication. Finally, what if Biruk returns home to Ethiopia and publishes a second book of poetry? This work will *not* be protected under U.S. law. Neither the test that focuses on the nationality of the author, nor the test that focuses on the place of first publication has been satisfied. On the other hand if Biruk had co-authored that second book with Pierre and published it in Ethiopia, it would be protected because one of the two authors met the nationality test.

It turns out that the vast majority of the nations of the world are signatories to at least one copyright treaty that the United States has also signed. The few exceptions include Afghanistan, Eritrea, Ethiopia, Iran, Iraq, San Marino, and Turkmenistan. All admirable places in their own way, we suppose, but not a particularly long or consequential list in the grand scheme of things. This means that the vast majority of published works around the world will qualify for U.S. protection, either because of where they were published or because of the nationality of their author.

§ 12.2   The Berne Convention

As the previous discussion reveals, whether or not a foreign author enjoys U.S. copyright may depend on whether a particular foreign state has joined a pertinent international agreement pertaining to copyright. This state of affairs suggests the usefulness of a review of the relevant treaties. The best starting point is the International Union for the Protection of Literary and Artistic Works, known more simply as the Berne Convention. The Berne Convention, formed in 1886 and subsequently revised on seven occasions, remains the premier multilaterial copyright agreement. The latest of these provisions, concluded in Paris in 1971, forms the current Berne Convention test.[6]

The Berne Convention was not fashioned as a model copyright code. Berne is instead based upon the principle of "national treatment."[7] National treatment requires that Berne signatory states accord to foreign works eligible under Berne the same protection granted to their own nationals. It is essentially a simple principle of non-discrimination. In addition, it specifies minimum standards of protection that Berne signatories agree to offer domestically. As

6. Convention Concerning the Creation of an International Union for the Protection of Literary and Artistic Works (Sept. 9, 1886, revised in 1896, 1908, 1928, 1948, 1967, 1971).

7. Peter Berger, *The Berne Convention: Its History and Its Key Role in the Future*, 3 J. L. & TECH. 1, 16–17 (1988).

these standards provide the floor, not the ceiling of required copyright protection, member states may choose to provide more robust copyright laws than mandated by Berne and, historically, many have done so.

Among the core substantive provisions of the Berne Convention, Article 2, mandates a capacious scope of copyright protection. Copyright extends to "every production in the literary, scientific and artistic domain, whatever may be the mode or form of expression."[8] Article 2 offers an illustrative list of works eligible for copyright, including writings, choreographic works, works of drawing, architecture, photographic works, and applied art.[9]

The Berne Convention further specifies the individuals eligible for protection in Article 3. Berne requires that protection be afforded to works, whether published or not, of an author who is a national or habitual resident of a Berne signatory state. In addition, authors who are not nationals or residents of a Berne signatory state may obtain protection if their works are either (1) first published in a Berne signatory state or (2) published simultaneously in a Berne signatory state and a state that has not acceded to the Berne Convention.[10] This provision is implemented in U.S. law by aspects of section 104 of the copyright statute, which we discussed in the immediately preceding section. Under Berne, a work is considered to have been simultaneously published in a Berne signatory state so long as the work was published there within 30 days of the first publication in a non-member state.[11]

Article 5(2) of the Berne Convention requires that, for works outside their country of origin, copyright protection be afforded without formalities. The term "formalities" includes several traditional features of U.S. copyright law, including Copyright Office registration and the placement of notice on copies of the work. Article 5(2) abolishes these requirements for works outside of their country of origin. Although formalities can be imposed by a given country on its own domestic authors, signatories of the treaty agree that when a work originates from a Berne signatory state, that work must be protected automatically in all other Berne countries.

The Berne Convention also requires that member states afford authors certain economic and moral rights. Among the economic rights are the reproduction, adaptation, translation, and public performance rights.[12] Article 6*bis* additionally recognizes two moral rights—those of attribution and integrity. Berne also recognizes

---

8. Berne Convention, Article 2(1).

9. Berne Convention, Article 2(1).

10. Berne Convention, Article 3(1).

11. Berne Convention, Article 3(4).

12. Berne Convention, Articles 8, 9, 11, 12.

certain limitations on these rights, including a right to make quotations and to use protected works for teaching purposes.[13]

The minimum copyright term under Berne is the life of the author plus 50 years or, in the case of anonymous or pseduonymous works, 50 years from the date of publication. Article 7 of the Berne Convention specifies that signatories may grant terms in excess of this minimum.[14] In cases where Berne Convention signatories offer different terms of protection, "the term shall not exceed the term fixed in the country of the origin of the work."[15] This "rule of the shorter term" forms a significant exception to the usual national treatment principle central to the Berne Convention.

For example, suppose that the imaginary country of Xambia provides for a copyright term of the life of the author plus 50 years. In a second fictitious state, Zyria, the term of protection is the life of the author plus 75 years. Assume further that both nations are Berne Convention signatories, and that neither the Xambian nor Zyrian copyright statute speaks to the rule of the shorter term. An author publishes a book in Xambia on June 1, 1970, and dies on March 1, 1980. As a consequence of the rule of the shorter term, copyright in that work will expire in both Xambia and Zyria on January 1, 2031, based upon the Xambian copyright terms. That's because March 1, 1980, plus 50 years is March 1, 2030, and the end of copyright term is deemed to be January 1st of the following year.

Congress had this principle very much in mind when it extended the copyright term by twenty years in the 1998 Sonny Bono Act. Although some other Berne signatory states offered a term of protection of life plus seventy years to their own nationals, these jurisdictions would have accorded U.S. works the shorter term of life plus fifty years, because that was the term under the 1976 Act as originally enacted. The proposition that U.S. authors would be disadvantaged in "Berne plus" jurisdictions was among the arguments offered for passing the Bono Act.

The default rule for international agreements is that, absent an explicit statement to the contrary, they apply only prospectively. The Berne Convention expressly indicates that its provisions have retroactive effect, however. Article 18(1) explains that "[t]his Convention shall apply to all works which, at the moment of its coming into force, have not yet fallen into the public domain in the country of origin through the expiry of the term of protection." The practical effect of this Rule of Retroactivity is that a country that newly joins the Berne Convention must not only protect works from Berne member states written after the date of accession, but

---

13. Berne Convention, Articles 10, 10*bis*.

14. Berne Convention, Article 7(6).

15. Berne Convention, Article 7(8).

also all existing works from each Berne member state that remain under copyright protection in their country of origin. Of course, all the other Berne member states must protect works originating from the new member state that remain under copyright there as well.

An example illustrates the Rule of Retroactivity. Suppose that the fictitious state of Albion is a member state of Berne as of 2010, while another such jurisdiction, Bavern, is not. Albion and Bavern have had no formal copyright relations previously, and as a result works from one state were considered part of the public domain in the other. Suppose further, then, that Bavern becomes a signatory to the Berne Convention as January 1, 2011. As of that date, Bavern must recognize copyright in all works of authorship (1) where the country of origin is Albion and (2) that remain under copyright in Albion. For its part, Albion must recognize copyright in all works of authorship (1) where the country of origin is Bavern and (2) that remain under copyright in Bavern. These copyrights must be recognized even though these works were previously considered to lie within the public domain within one state, and could be freely exploited there.

This rule of retroactive protection conflicts with the usual norm of intellectual property law that works that are no longer subject to proprietary rights irretrievably fall into the public domain and may be freely used by others. A rationale for this norm is that individuals who have begun to exploit what they believe to be a public domain work may face hardships if the work once more is subject to copyright. Out of recognition of this potentially harsh result, Article 18(3) of Berne provides that "the respective countries shall determine, each in so far as it is concerned, the conditions of application of this principle." This provision provides Berne member states with some flexibility in how they will implement the Rule of Retroactivity, particularly with respect to individuals who have exploited works where copyright protection had not been available.

§ 12.3 U.S. Accession to Berne

The United States did not accede to the Berne Convention until March 1, 1989, more than a century after Berne's formation.[16] Among the factors motivating this delay was the distinct U.S. copyright tradition. Features such as notice, registration, deposit, and a set term based upon the date of publication simply did not comport with Berne Convention requirements. Domestic publish-

---

16. *See* William Belanger, *U.S. Compliance with the Berne Convention,* 3 GEO. MASON INDEPENDENT L. REV. 373 (1995).

ers, who took economic advantage of these distinctions, further encouraged the United States to go its own way.

Although the United States long remained aloof from the Berne Union, it did rely upon other agreements to protect its copyright interests abroad. The very first multilateral copyright treaty signed by the United States was the Buenos Aires Convention in 1911, which provided protection in 16 other nations of the Western Hemisphere. The most interesting feature of that treaty was that it required the use of the words "All Rights Reserved" as part of the copyright notice in order to guarantee that protection would be afforded by all member states. All members of the Buenos Aires Convention are now bound by the TRIPS Agreement and must dispense with formalities as a condition for copyright protection. Use of "All Rights Reserved" is now completely unnecessary, but the phrase lingers on due to some kind of odd legal inertia or, more likely, paranoia, by book publishers.

Through the first half of the twentieth century, the United States entered into a number of additional bilateral agreements calling for mutual recognition of copyrights. In 1955, the United States encouraged the formation of the Universal Copyright Convention ("UCC").[17] The UCC was effectively a more tolerant version of the Berne Convention. Formalities were assessed more leniently, and the compulsory copyright term was shorter, resulting in compatibility with U.S. copyright law. With the subsequent U.S. accession to the Berne Convention, as well as the rise of the TRIPS Agreement, the UCC has become nearly irrelevant to the world copyright order.

The 1976 Act moved the United States in the direction of compliance with the Berne Convention. For example, the 1976 Act eliminated a copyright term based upon the date of publication, instead moving to the term required by the Berne Convention, the life of the author plus 50 years. There was much work to be done, however, before the United States could join Berne. As originally enacted, the 1976 Act maintained formalities such as notice, deposit, and registration, and it did not recognize moral rights.

As U.S. popular culture and information goods became increasingly valuable export commodities, the value of U.S. membership in the Berne Union became apparent. At last moved to accede to Berne, Congress in 1988 enacted the Berne Convention Implementation Act ("BCIA").[18] Congress adopted a minimalist approach with the BCIA. Only changes deemed absolutely necessary to ensure Berne compliance were introduced into U.S. law. The most

---

17. Universal Copyright Convention, Sept. 8 1952, 216 U.N.T.S. 132, revised July 24, 1971, 943 U.N.T.S. 178.

18. Pub. L. No. 100–568, 102 Stat. 2853.

significant of these changes, discussed earlier in this book, in Chapter 3, concerned statutory formalities. Once an obligatory feature of U.S. copyright law, the formalities of notice, deposit, and registration have been reduced to recommended but virtually voluntary options in most cases.

The BCIA also declares the Berne Convention to be executory, rather than self-executing, under U.S. law.[19] As a result, the Berne Convention is effective in the United States only to the extent that Congress passes domestic legislation implementing its obligations. It is not possible in the United States, as is the case in some other countries, for private parties to claim legal rights directly under the Berne Convention. The U.S. Copyright Act further explains that "[a]ny rights in a work eligible for protection under this title . . . shall not be expanded or reduced by virtue of . . . the Berne Convention. . . ."[20] One consequence of this provision is that the rule of the shorter term does not apply in the United States.[21]

Upon further consideration of the BCIA's minimalist approach, Congress later judged some of its changes to be overly modest. Additional implementing legislation was deemed prudent. The Visual Artist's Rights Act of 1990 (VARA),[22] which establishes the rights of attribution and integrity for certain visual artwork, furthered U.S. compliance with the moral rights standards of Article 6*bis* of Berne. VARA is discussed further in this text at § 7.1.2. As well, the "useful article" doctrine, had rendered the availability of copyright protection for architectural works uncertain. In view of the Berne Article 2 requirement that architectural works should enjoy copyright, Congress amended § 102(a) of the Copyright Act to recognize expressly copyright in architectural works.[23]

Recall that Article 18 of the Berne Convention establishes a Rule of Retroactivity that requires new signatories to Berne to protect all existing works from other Berne member states that remains subject to copyright in their country of origin. When it enacted the BCIA, Congress chose not to afford copyright protection to any foreign work that had fallen into the public domain in the United States. Congress revisited the issue in 1994, however prompted, in part, by some new IP obligations contained in the North American Free Trade Agreement, or NAFTA. As a result it enacted § 104A, a complex provision that grants "restored" copyrights to works that were in the public domain in the United States

---

19. *Id.* at § 2(1).

20. 17 U.S.C. § 104A(c).

21. 17 U.S.C. § 302(a).

22. Pub. L. No. 101–650, 104 Stat. 5089, 5128–33 (1990).

23. Pub. L. No. 101–650, §§ 704, 705 (1990).

due to, among other reasons, noncompliance with notice, renewal, or other formalities imposed by U.S. copyright law at the time.[24]

§ 12.4   The TRIPS Agreement

Although the venerable Berne Convention remains the world's preeminant copyright treaty, it suffers from two notable defects. First, consensus must be achieved among its signatory states for revision to occur.[25] As Berne's numerous signatory states possess widely varying copyright interests, unanimity has become virtually impossible to achieve. Consequently the Berne Convention no longer serves as a viable platform for copyright reform.

Second, the obligations of the Berne Convention cannot be practically enforced. The Berne Convention stipulates that compliance disputes are to be adjudicated before the International Court of Justice. As this tribunal effectively lacks the authority to enforce its judgments, no such suit has ever been brought.[26] Each signatory's sense of honor, along with diplomatic efforts from other member states, are effectively the only compliance measures that exist under Berne.

A recognition of these failings, along with a growing perception of the strong connection between intellectual property and international trade, resulted in the shift of copyright treaty-making efforts into new fora. In 1993, the United States joined with Canada and Mexico in the North American Free Trade Agreement (NAFTA). NAFTA includes a number of provisions harmonizing its signatories' intellectual property laws, including copyright.

Shortly after acceding to NAFTA, the United States became a member of the newly formed World Trade Organization (WTO). Negotiations leading to the WTO resulted in an Agreement on Trade–Related Aspects of Intellectual Property Rights, the so-called TRIPS Agreement.[27] The TRIPS Agreement is the most advanced multinational agreement on intellectual property yet completed. Because every WTO member has agreed to comply with the TRIPS Agreement, its core provisions merit review here.

The TRIPS Agreement expounds both national treatment and "most favored nation" principles.[28] As with Berne, the national

---

24. A full discussion of § 104A can be found in § 8.6 of this volume.

25. Berne Convention, Art. 27(3).

26. Ralph Oman, *The United States and the Berne Union: An Extended Courtship*, 3 J. L. & Tech. 71, 115 (1988).

27. Agreement on Trade–Related Aspects of Intellectual Property Rights, Apr. 15, 1994, Marrekesh Agreement Establishing the World Trade Organization

[hereinafter the WTO Agreement], Annex 1C, in Results of the Uruguay Round of Multilateral Trade Negotiations 1 (1994) [hereinafter Uruguay Round Results] 365 (1994), 33 I.L.M. 1197.

28. TRIPS Agreement, Art. 3 (national treatment) and Art. 4 (most favored nation).

treatment principle provides that each WTO member must accord to nationals of another member treatment no less favorable than it accords to its own nationals. Under the "most favored nation" provisions, with limited exceptions, any privilege granted to nationals of one WTO member state must be afforded to nationals of all WTO member states.

The TRIPS Agreement also sets forth minimum standards of intellectual property protection. With respect to copyright, the TRIPS Agreement incorporates Berne's substantive obligations. All WTO members must comply with Articles 1 through 21 of the Berne Convention, with the exception of Article 6*bis* (pertaining to moral rights).[29] The TRIPS Agreement additionally requires WTO member states to protect computer programs as literary works, as well as data compilations that, by virtue of their selection or arrangement, constitute "intellectual creations."[30] The TRIPS Agreement also calls for rental rights for computer programs and cinematographic works.[31]

Article 13 of the TRIPS Agreement allows for WTO members to provide "limitations and exceptions" to the minimum exclusion rights it stipulates. To comply with the TRIPS Agreement, an exception must meet three requirements. First, the exception must be confined to "certain special cases" that must be narrow in both a quantitative and qualitative sense, and also pursue an exceptional or distinctive objective. Second, the exception must not "conflict with a normal exploitation of the work" in that it does not enter into economic competition with the ways that copyright holders normally extract economic value from their works. Finally, the exception must "not unreasonably prejudice the legitimate interests of the right holder" such that it causes an unreasonable loss of income to the copyright owner.[32]

Perhaps the most significant aspect of the TRIPS Agreement is that its obligations are more readily enforced than those of predecessor agreements. Disagreements between WTO member states over TRIPS Agreement compliance are subject to the WTO Dispute Settlement Understanding.[33] These provisions call for initial consultations between WTO member states in order to resolve a dispute. If the consultations fail, one of the parties may request the Dispute Settlement Body to establish a panel. This process leads to briefings, meetings before the panel, and ultimately a final panel report. The right to appeal the case to an Appellate Body is automatic.

29. TRIPS Agreement, Art. 9(1).

30. TRIPS Agreement, Art. 10(2).

31. TRIPS Agreement, Art. 11.

32. The WTO panel decision articulating these standards, *United States—*

Section 110(5) of the U.S. Copyright Act, WT/DS160/R, was discussed previously in this treatise at section 6.4.2.3.

33. TRIPS Agreement, Art. 64.

Failure to abide by WTO Dispute Settlement Body rulings may result in compensation to the injured party. The injured party may suspend concessions or other obligations under the TRIPS Agreement, or possibly another WTO agreement, at a level equivalent to the damages suffered.

§ 12.5 Additional International Copyright Agreements

The Rome Convention. The International Convention for the Protection of Performers, Producers of Phonograms and Broadcasting Organizations was signed in Rome in 1961.[34] By focusing upon performers, record producers, and broadcasters, the Rome Convention is said to concern "neighboring rights"—rights akin to copyright but concerning nontraditional subject matter. Rome Convention signatories agree to provide minimum protection standards by restricting the broadcasting of live performances, the recording of unfixed performances, and in certain circumstances, the reproduction of a fixation of the performance. The United States, which does not confer public performance rights in sound recordings, has not joined the Rome Convention.

The Geneva Phonograms Convention. The Convention for the Protection of Producers of Phonograms Against Unauthorized Duplication of Their Phonograms was formed in Geneva in 1971.[35] Signatories agree to protect nationals of other member states against the unauthorized manufacture, importation and distribution of copies of sound recordings. In other words, signatory states agree to outlaw record piracy. The United States became a party to the Geneva Phonogram Convention in 1974.

Brussels Satellite Convention. The Convention Relating to the Distribution of Programme–Carrying Signals Transmitted by Satellite was formed in Brussels in 1974.[36] Signatories to the Brussels Convention pledge to take adequate measures to prevent the misappropriation of satellite signals. The United States became a party to the Brussels Satellite Convention in 1985.

The WIPO Treaties. Two treaties were completed under the auspices of the World Intellectual Property Organization (WIPO) in 1996. The WIPO Copyright Treaty includes a number of different

---

34. International Convention for the Protection of Performers, Producers of Phonograms and Broadcasting Organizations, art. 15(2), 496 U.N.T.S. 43 (Oct. 26, 1961).

35. Convention for the Protection of Producers of Phonograms Against Unauthorized Duplication of Their Pho-

nograms, Oct. 29, 1971, 25 U.S.T. 309, 866 U.N.T.S. 67.

36. Convention Relating to the Distribution of Programme–Carrying Signals Transmitted by Satellite, May 21, 1974, 13 I.L.M. 1444.

provisions that build upon the Berne Convention.[37] Article 2 of the WIPO Copyright Treaty calls for the protection of computer programs as literary works, while Article 5 provides for the copyright protection of data compilations that, by virtue of their selection or arrangement, constitute "intellectual creations." Signatories to the WIPO Copyright Treaty also agree to confer distribution and rental rights to computer works, movies, and works embodied in phonograms. The WIPO Copyright Treaty further obliged signatories to provide legal protection for technological protection measures and rights management information. The Digital Millennium Copyright Act of 1998, discussed earlier in this text, implemented these latter obligations domestically.

The second WIPO treaty, the WIPO Performances and Phonograms Treaty, calls for the grant of additional rights beyond those mandated by the Geneva Phonograms Convention.[38] This treaty confirms that the reproduction right accorded to phonogram producers extends to "any manner or form," including digital media. The treaty also builds upon the TRIPS Agreement by articulating a right to prevent the fixation, reproduction, broadcasting, and communication to the public of live performances. The United States became a signatory to both WIPO treaties in 1998.

§ 12.6 Copyright Enforcement Across Borders

12.6.1 U.S. Law and Extraterritorial Infringing Acts

Accession to the Berne Convention reinforced a principal tenet in U.S. law, the concept of territoriality. Copyright has traditionally been granted by the government of a single nation, and has effect only within that territory. Under the doctrine of territoriality, authors of creative works must obtain and enforce their rights in each jurisdiction where copyright is desired.

The Ninth Circuit considered the principle of territoriality at some length in *Subafilms, Ltd. v. MGM–Pathe Communications Co.*[39] Subafilms and a band named The Beatles had partnered with Hearst Corporation to produce the animated motion picture "Yellow Submarine." Hearst in turn contracted with United Artists Corporation (UA) to distribute and finance the film, which it did, releasing the film in 1968 in theaters and then on television. When the technologically advanced home video market took hold in the 1980s, UA's successor company, MGM, authorized "Yellow Submarine" for videocassette distribution.

---

37. World Intellectual Property Organization Copyright Treaty, adopted Dec. 20, 1996, art. 11, 36 I.L.M. 65, 71.

38. World Intellectual Property Organization, Performances and Phono-grams Treaty, adopted Dec. 20, 1996, art. 18, 36 I.L.M. 76, 86.

39. 24 F.3d 1088 (9th Cir. 1994) (*en banc*).

Subafilms and Hearst objected to the videocassette distribution and brought a suit for copyright infringement and breach of contract. The original agreements had of course not anticipated the development of the videocassette market. Although some of the videocassettes were sold in the United States, other were distributed abroad. However, initial authorization to distribute all of the videocassettes occurred in the United States. The *en banc* panel of the Ninth Circuit assessed whether a claim for infringement could be brought under U.S. copyright law for that portion of the infringing conduct that took place abroad, but was authorized within the United States.

The Ninth Circuit determined that the authorization of an extraterritorial act of infringement, without more, was not actionable under U.S. copyright law. The court concluded that the phrase "to authorize" in the Copyright Act was meant to codify the doctrine of contributory infringement, rather than establish a new form of liability for illegal authorization.[40] Subafilms argued that United States copyright laws extend to extraterritorial acts of infringement when the acts "result in adverse effects within the United States." In response, the Ninth Circuit refused to "overturn over eighty years of consistent jurisprudence on the extraterritorial reach of the copyright laws without further guidance from Congress." The court maintained that Congress has always legislated under the presumption of territoriality unless it clearly expressed otherwise. A contrary holding would create international discord, the court reasoned, creating clashes between the United States and other nations.

The holding in *Subafilms* has been criticized for fragmenting multinational copyright litigation and working hardships upon copyright holders within the global economy.[41] Territoriality remains the essential axiom of the international copyright order, however, and for the time being there seems little chance that it will be modified. It should also be appreciated that in *Subafilms*, the accused infringement was the authorization within the United States of acts that took place overseas. Should cognizable acts of infringement actually occur in the United States, however, then the U.S. copyright law will indeed apply.

12.6.2 U.S. Courts and Foreign Copyright Law

The Ninth Circuit's ruling in *Subafilms* was in part based upon the notion that U.S. courts should not apply U.S. copyright law with respect to foreign activities. This ruling suggests another possibility: To what extent could a U.S. court apply *foreign* copy-

---

40. 17 U.S.C. § 106 (2006).

41. *Curb v. MCA Records, Inc.*, 898 F.Supp. 586 (M.D. Tenn. 1995).

right law with respect to foreign activities? As a general matter, U.S. courts ordinarily do not hear claims of copyright infringement based upon the laws of another nation, leaving them to the courts of those states that established the rights. As a matter of subject matter jurisdiction, however, such cases may potentially be brought before U.S. courts. For example, the federal courts may hear a claim of foreign copyright infringement if the standards of diversity jurisdiction are met—namely, where the parties are from different states or foreign countries, and the amount in controversy exceeds $75,000.[42]

One instance of a U.S. court confronting claims of foreign copyright infringement was *London Film Productions Ltd. v. Intercontinental Communications, Inc.*[43] London Films, a British corporation, sued New York-based Intercontinental in the U.S. District Court for the Southern District of New York. London Films asserted that Intercontinental had marketed several motion pictures in Chile, Costa Rica, Equador, Panama, Peru, and Venezuela that were protected by its copyright. The district court possessed personal jurisdiction over Intercontinental and subject matter jurisdiction over the dispute based upon diversity jurisdiction. Intercontinental nonetheless filed a motion to dismiss. Intercontinental argued that the district court should abstain from exercising jurisdiction due to the absence of a charge of U.S. copyright infringement, because the litigation would require the court to comprehend unfamiliar foreign statutes, and because a ruling of a U.S. court with respect to the status of a foreign copyright would violate the "act of state" doctrine.

The district court rejected each of these assertions. Judge Carter reasoned that U.S. courts possessed an interest in ensuring that U.S. firms, such as Intercontinental, complied with the laws of other nations. Denying this interest might render foreign jurisdictions unwilling to hear a complaint against their own citizens for violations of U.S. law. The court also concluded that hearing the case would not require it to judge the acts of a foreign sovereign within its own territory, contrary to the act of state doctrine. Because the relevant jurisdictions were signatories of the Berne Convention, copyright had arisen in each of them without the necessity of government intervention. Finally, although the court agreed that the lawsuit might require it to interpret foreign law, it reasoned that Intercontinental was not subject to personal jurisdiction elsewhere. With no other available forum for London Films to assert its claims, the court denied Intercontinental's motion to dismiss.

42.　8 U.S.C. § 1332(a).　　　　　**43.**　580 F.Supp. 47 (S.D.N.Y. 1984).

Cases such as *London Films* remain relatively rare occurrences. Adjudication of copyright disputes most commonly occurs within the jurisdiction that recognizes those proprietary rights and where the infringing acts occurred. Yet as information technologies allow for virtually instantaneous distribution of the identical work in many jurisdictions, consolidated multinational copyright enforcement efforts may become more common in days yet to come.

12.6.3 Choice of Law

As we have seen, U.S. courts potentially may resolve claims of foreign copyright infringement based upon foreign copyright law, although litigants have asked them to do so infrequently. Domestic application of foreign copyright law is not limited to this context, however. U.S. courts may possibly be called upon to adjudicate issues arising under foreign copyright law within a domestic infringement suit. The reason is that under established choice of law principles, the law of another nation may bear a more significant relationship to an issue in the case—in particular, ownership of copyright—than that of the United States. The leading decision of the Second Circuit in *Itar–Tass Russian News Agency v. Russian Kurier*[44] is representative, offering a detailed analysis of the application of choice of law principles to copyright.

In that case, newspaper publisher Kurier admitted to having copied approximately five hundred articles that had first appeared in the Russian press. When the Russian publishers and newspaper sued Kurier in the United States for infringement, the question of choice of law took center stage. The court divided its choice of law analysis into two parts, the determination of ownership and the assessment of infringement. On the ownership question, the Second Circuit looked to the choice of law rules generally applicable to property, stating that the interests of the parties in the property are determined by the law of the state with which the property and parties share the most significant relationship. Because Russian nationals had written and published the articles in Russia, it concluded that Russian law should determine the ownership of the articles. On the other hand, it felt the infringement question was in the nature of a tort claim. Noting that Kurier's potentially infringing acts occurred in the United States, the Court of Appeals concluded that, under the choice of law principle known as *lex loci delicti* ("the place of the infringing act"), U.S. law should govern the issue of infringement.

With the choice of law issues resolved, the court addressed the dispute at hand. For a U.S. infringement suit to be permissible, the copyright owner must enjoy an "exclusive right" to the work under 17 U.S.C. § 501(b). Under Russian law, the court found that

44.   153 F.3d 82 (2d Cir. 1998).

newspapers are exempt from obtaining "exclusive rights" to their articles, which are retained instead by the individual authors. Newspaper publishers only retain compilation rights to the arrangement and presentation of the articles. The Court of Appeals held that if Kurier only copied individual articles, then only the authors had "exclusive rights" to sue for infringement under U.S. copyright law. If Kurier had instead copied sections of the newspapers or elements of their compilations—headlines, photographs, etc.—then the newspaper publishers could sue for injunctive relief and damages for infringement of their compilation rights. The Second Circuit also held that as a news agency distributing articles to newspapers, the Russian News Agency did not fall under the newspaper exemption, and so could sue for damages and injunctive relief for the use of its articles as well. U.S. law would of course apply to these claims and the determination of the damages.

As the court in *Itar–Tass* resolved the choice of law issue, it wrestled with the binding principle of national treatment. Under that concept, foreign authors are to be accorded the same intellectual property protection given to U.S. authors. Yet a choice of law analysis that results in the application of foreign law may lead to a different result than would U.S. copyright principles. The Second Circuit was content to reach a rather debatable understanding of national treatment that only embraced the issue of infringement. The holding in *Itar–Tass* has nonetheless proven significant, and the number of reported copyright decisions applying foreign law to questions of copyright ownership has grown in its wake.

Table of Cases

H

I

J

Index

References are to Pages

BERNE CONVENTION—Cont'd
Digital Millennium Copyright Act enactment, 279
Executory vs self-executing effect, 547
Fair use defense, 485
Federal legislation implementing, 8, 118, 123
Formal requirements, 8
Implementation Act, 545
Moral rights, 267
Notice, 116
Organization, 542
Overview, 14
Retroactive application, 545
Scope of protection, 543
Term of protection
Generally, 544
Foreign works, 355
TRIPS Agreement compared, 548
Uruguay Round Agreements Act, 356
Visual Artist's Rights Act, 547

BERNE CONVENTION IMPLEMENTATION ACT
Generally, 545
Enactment, 528, 545
Formal requirements of US law, 8
Notices, 123
Retroactivity, 118

BLANK FORMS
Copyrightability, 43, 98

BLUEPRINTS AND PLANS
Architectural works, 83

BMI
See Performing Rights Societies, this index

BOOTLEG RECORDINGS
Fixation issue, 41

BROADCASTING
See also Television and Radio, this index
Audio Home Recording Act, this index
Brussels Satellite Convention, 550
Digital Performance Right in Sound Recordings Act, this index
Educational television and radio programs use of sound recordings, 202
Fairness in Music Licensing Act, 251
Home-style exception, public performance right, 249
Live events, fixation, 39
Payola, 239
Performing Rights Societies, this index
Public broadcasters, compulsory licenses, 247
Public performance right
Generally, 238, 241, 243
Home-style exception, 249

BROADCASTING—Cont'd
Satellite Home View Extension and Reauthorization Act of 2004, 260
Satellite Home Viewer Improvement Act, 260
Secondary transmissions, 257
Synch licenses, 204
Vicarious infringement liability of sponsors, 396

BRUSSELS SATELLITE CONVENTION
International copyright, 550

BUFFERING
Fixation issue, 38
Reproduction issue, 190

BUILDING CODES
Copyrightability, 96

BUILDINGS
Architectural works and resulting buildings distinguished, 83

BURDEN OF PROOF
Copyrightability, 47
Infringement
Generally, 47, 364
Damages, 411

CABLE TELEVISION
See also Television and Radio, this index
Secondary transmissions, 258

CELEBRITIES
See Right of Publicity, this index

CELESTIAL JUKEBOX
See Digital Performance Right in Sound Recordings Act, this index

CELL PHONES
Firmware, DMCA anti-circumvention provision exceptions, 293

CHARTS
See Pictorial, Graphic, and Sculptural Works, this index

CHOREOGRAPHIC WORKS
See Pantomimes and Choreographic Works, this index

CIRCUMVENTION OF COPY PROTECTION
See Digital Millennium Copyright Act, this index

CIVIL LAW REGIMES
Author's rights, 485

CLASSROOMS
See also Educational Activities, this index